ADAM SMITH AS STUDENT & PROFESSOR

William R. Scott

William R. Scott (1868-1940) occupied the Adam Smith Chair of Political Economy at the University of Glasgow, and devoted a great deal of his time to research on the life and work of Adam Smith.

The present volume, *Adam Smith as Student and Professor* (1937), the result of this painstaking research, is second only to John Rae's *Life of Adam Smith* in the light it throws on Adam Smith's life and thought.

It is profusely illustrated with pictures of Adam Smith and the places associated with him, facsimiles of documents, and examples of Adam Smith's own handwriting.

There is an early draft of part of *The Wealth of Nations,* and quite a few Adam Smith letters, previously unpublished or hard to locate.

"Prof. Scott does not aspire to rewrite John Rae's *Life of Adam Smith,* but limits himself to the aim of compiling a collection of material and documents which will bring a stage nearer an eventual definitive *Life;* though, as a personal record, Rae's book is so excellent and further personal details are so scarce, that it is

(Continued on back flap)

REPRINTS OF ECONOMIC CLASSICS

ADAM SMITH
AS STUDENT AND PROFESSOR

STATUE OF ADAM SMITH BY GASSER OF VIENNA (*circ.* 1867)
(Hunterian Library of the University of Glasgow—the gift of the Adam Smith Club of Glasgow.)

ADAM SMITH
AS STUDENT AND PROFESSOR

With Unpublished Documents, including Parts of the "Edinburgh Lectures", a Draft of *The Wealth of Nations*, Extracts from the Muniments of the University of Glasgow and Correspondence

BY
WILLIAM ROBERT SCOTT
D.PHIL., LITT.D., HON. LL.D. (ST. ANDREWS AND DUBLIN)
ADAM SMITH PROFESSOR OF POLITICAL ECONOMY IN THE UNIVERSITY OF GLASGOW
AND FELLOW OF THE BRITISH ACADEMY

[THE ADAM SMITH LIBRARY]

REPRINTS OF ECONOMIC CLASSICS

AUGUSTUS M. KELLEY · PUBLISHER
NEW YORK · 1965

ORIGINAL EDITION 1937

LIBRARY OF CONGRESS CATALOGUE CARD NUMBER
65-26379

PRINTED IN THE UNITED STATES OF AMERICA
by NEW CITY PRINTING COMPANY
UNION CITY, NEW JERSEY 07087

To
My Colleagues in
The Court and Senate of
The University of Glasgow
On the Two Hundredth Anniversary
Of Adam Smith's Matriculation There

MDCCXXXVII—MDCCCCXXXVII

PREFACE

For a considerable period it has appeared to me that the early history of Political Economy would be clearer if more were known of the life and the surroundings of Adam Smith. While it is true that some of the problems with which this quest began still await solution, on the other hand by a series of fortunate events so much has come to light that it appeared inadvisable to postpone publication of the chief results which have emerged.

The method of presentation involved considerable difficulties. That which has been adopted may require some explanation, more especially since it will, at the same time, provide a general outline of the treatment of the material. It might have been moulded on some of the books which occupy the attention of the Crime Club. For here, also, there were many clues to be followed. Some were altogether misleading, others promised well at first, and then petered out : while a few, after seeming to fail, in the end gave unexpected and even valuable results. Although such mechanism of investigation might have a personal interest, it would be unreasonable to expect anyone to waste time in disentangling all the involved details. Dr. James Bonar, who was good enough not only to place his unrivalled knowledge of Adam Smith and the relevant literature of the eighteenth century at my disposal, but also to read and improve the manuscript of Part I and the proofs of Parts II and III, suggested the writing of a complete life of Adam Smith. This has already been done, very excellently, by John Rae. On reflection it appeared that the time was not yet ripe for such an undertaking—and that for several reasons. Besides new information which is quite decisive, there is also much that requires a considerable amount of interpretation. Indeed, it would be difficult to find another case where the events to be recorded suffer so much from involution, so that it is often necessary to work backwards, rather than in the natural order. This is fatal to an easy, flowing narrative. When at some future date the meaning and the sequence of events as here detailed has been either established or else disproved, it should be a comparatively simple matter to tell a plain, straightforward tale. Moreover, considering how many books have appeared since Rae wrote, each of which contributes its mite of detail to the general picture, it is to be expected that during the next generation more of the same type will be issued. It is to be anticipated that a systematic enquiry in France would yield some new particulars relating to Adam Smith during the time he spent there ; indeed our knowledge of this period of his life would be immensely increased if (in spite of the disclaimer of Dugald Stewart) a diary, which it is reported that he kept while he was abroad, could be traced. According to the account of an Edinburgh bookseller, the original manuscript was in his possession a number of years ago, but he has no particulars of the person to whom he sold it. Also it is to be expected that further letters written by, or to, Adam Smith will be discovered. With these considerations in view, the manner in which the new material has been dealt with is in one respect the exact opposite of that adopted by Rae. His narrative shows immense skill in concealing gaps : whereas in the present work these are rather emphasised in the hope of stimulating scholars of the future to fill them up.

The life of Adam Smith, as presented by Rae, is a highly artistic picture of the author of *The Wealth of Nations*. It may be asking too much, but one cannot suppress an urgent desire to know more of Adam Smith—the man—so as to explain to oneself how he came to be able to accomplish the work which he did. Rae's account of his early life is as complete as the materials then available permitted, yet one cannot escape the impression that the personality of Adam Smith is absorbed in the background, so that there is, in reality, no adequate explanation of the essential qualities of heart and mind, as these gradually developed, in order to give birth in due season to his epoch-making book. Thus it seemed wise to confine the following pages, in the main, to the earlier part of Adam Smith's career as an attempt towards the elucidation of this problem. At the same time particulars of a later date came to light which could not be withheld—as for instance the circumstances (as described on p. 274) when he was intercepted and robbed by a highwayman. These later events can easily be filled into Rae's account at the proper places. Also, the papers of the Scottish Customs during the period Adam Smith was a Commissioner, both at the Record Office and H.M. General Register House, Edinburgh, are now available for consultation. These are being examined by Mr. Henry Higgs, C.B., and it is to be hoped that they will yield something of considerable interest to be recorded by his accomplished pen.

Increasing knowledge of Adam Smith shows that the secret of his genius is to be found in that part of his life before he became celebrated, which may be conveniently dated as the period before he went to France, and it is these years which are the chief concern of the subsequent pages.

Part I is a general narrative terminating at the beginning of the year 1764, in which, for reasons already stated, it seemed unnecessary to do more than mention, and that for the sake of connection, episodes which have been treated adequately by Rae.

Part II comprises various documents which, with a very few exceptions (as far as is known) are published for the first time. They include a number of letters, a considerable proportion of which come from the Papers of the Revd. Dr. David Douglas Bannerman, a descendant of David Douglas, Lord Reston, who was Adam Smith's heir. To these are to be added some others (which belonged to the late Miss M. A. Bannerman), and which were discovered in a secret receptacle in

PREFACE

the bureau which is illustrated in Plate XI. In the printing of these and other letters the practice of the eighteenth century of placing the date, sometimes at the beginning and sometimes at the end, is inconvenient to the reader, and I have taken the liberty of moving it to the beginning in those cases where it is appended in the original.

Part III is an annotated print of the manuscript of an early draft—probably the first draft—of *The Wealth of Nations*, as a separate work. In view of its importance, the somewhat numerous notes, in which even small corrections or modifications of the manuscript have been described, may be found of interest.

Part IV presents a series of facsimiles of handwriting, both that of Adam Smith himself and of most of his amanuenses. It includes reproductions of such portions of the Edinburgh lectures as are economic and which by a fortunate chance have been recovered. For reasons which are stated in the Introduction to this Part, the character of script, both of Adam Smith and his amanuenses, is of interest in relation to his style, the construction of his books and, in some cases, it is helpful in assigning a date for certain of his writings where this is doubtful.

It gives me much pleasure to record my deep indebtedness to the public bodies and private persons who have allowed me to print or reproduce documents or other memorials of Adam Smith, namely, the Public Record Office, London ; H.M. General Register House, Edinburgh ; the National Library, Edinburgh ; the State Historical Museum, Moscow ; the Bodleian Library and the Master and Fellows of Balliol College, Oxford ; the University of Glasgow ; the University of Edinburgh ; the Goldsmiths' Library, University of London ; Harvard College Library ; the Imperial University of Tokio ; Aberdeen City Council ; Kirkcaldy Burgh Council ; the Mitchell Library, Glasgow ; Boston Public Library ; New York Public Library ; the Pierpont Morgan Library, New York ; the Pennsylvania Historical Society ; the late Duke of Buccleuch and his Grace the present Duke ; the Marchioness of Lansdowne ; Sir W. F. Stuart-Menteth, Bart. ; Sir Edmund Findlay, Bart. ; Mrs. H. Bannerman and Dr. J. P. Bannerman ; Miss J. E. S. Black ; Miss Cunningham and Mr. J. D. Cunningham ; the late Professor Foxwell ; Professor J. H. Hollander ; Mr. J. Y. Lockhart (Kirkcaldy) ; Professor Seligman ; and Mr. and Miss Tullis of Strathenry.

Then, too, from the nature of the circumstances the enquiry branched out in very many directions. In several of these I had no special competence ; and the patience of those who were experts in these subjects and who most willingly placed their knowledge at my disposal, has proved very remarkable. An attempt has been made in the text or the notes to indicate the chief contribution of each. This, however, is impossible in two types of cases, namely those relating to searches for documents which have not yielded satisfactory results. Then, also, there were many libraries and museums in which the members of the staff gave me most valuable aid in those troublesome investigations which, in the initial stages,

PREFACE

cannot be formulated with precision. Thus my thanks are due to all the following: the Earl of Buchan; the Earl of Carnarvon; Sir Francis Grant, the Lord Lyon; the Right Hon. Sir Archibald Sinclair, Bart.; Sir James Douglas, Bart.; Sir John Stirling Maxwell, Bart.; Sir W. A. Craigie; Miss Haldane, O.M.; Professor Abbot; Professor Alekseev; Mr. Henry Alexander (a former Lord Provost of Aberdeen); Mr. J. B. Alexander (Town Clerk Depute, Kirkcaldy); Professor Atkinson; Mr. W. Mornington Barker (Provincial Bank of Ireland); Messrs. Bell, Bannerman and Findlay, W.S.; Mdlle de Beaulieu; Mr. J. D. Boswell; Dr. J. M. Bulloch; Mr. H. J. Butchart, D.S.O. (Aberdeen); Mr. Donald Cameron (Union Bank of Scotland); Mr. Douglas Clephane; Mr. R. J. Davidson (Sheriff Clerk, Office, Cupar); Dr. Hans Degen (Copenhagen); Mr. Alexander Dougal, W.S. (Edinburgh); Mr. G. S. Frazer (Town Clerk, Aberdeen); Mr. Douglas A. Foulis (Edinburgh); Miss Marjorie Ferguson; Professor Edwin F. Gay (California); Mr. E. N. Geijer (of the College of Arms); Mr. S. Glassford and Mr. W. Forbes Gray (both of Edinburgh); Mrs. F. V. Hadden (Cheltenham); Dr. Henry Hamilton; Mr. T. F. Harley (Asst. Secy., University of Edinburgh); Mr. Edward Heawood; Mr. Henry Higgs, C.B.; Professor Hillhouse; Mr. Norman L. Hird; Professor T. H. Hughes; Mr. R. A. Humphreys; Mr. William Hutton (Town Clerk, Kirkcaldy); Dr. Carl Iversen (Copenhagen); Professor D. T. Jack; Messrs. Jameson, Maclae and Baird, writers; Professors Kamo and Kawai (both of Tokyo); Mr. J. M. Keynes, C.B.; Mr. S. C. Leman; Messrs. T. and W. Liddle and Martin, W.S.; Mr. D. M. Low; Mr. George G. M'Donald; the late Mr. A. T. M'Robert (Editor, *Scottish Notes and Queries*); the late Professor Martin, Ch.L.H.; Mr. R. W. Martin, W.S.; Mrs. T. Moore (Yeovil); Professor Namier; Professor Axel Neilsen (Copenhagen); Dr. Onions; Mr. J. Ormiston (Factor, Buccleuch Estates); Colonel St. Clair Oswald of Dunnikier; Mr. Andrew R. Page (Chamberlain of Argyll); Revd. W. H. Drummond Page (Leslie, Fife); Dr. L. L. Price; Mr. W. Rankine (Rosneath); Mr. A. B. Rodger (who kindly made a special examination of the Balliol documents for me); Mr. J. H. Romanes, W.S.; Messrs. Russell and Dunlop, W.S. (Edinburgh); Mr. T. M. Sadlier (of Office of Arms, Dublin); Major Keith Scott of Orchard; Mr. L. A. Scrogie (Town Clerk Depute, Aberdeen); Mr. Kenneth Sisam (Oxford Dictionary); Dr. Baird Smith, C.B.E.; Mr. W. Mitchell Smith (Aberdeen); Dr. D. Stenhouse (formerly Town Clerk, Glasgow); Mr. T. J. Stenning (Warden of Wadham); Professor Tenabe (Tokyo); Mr. George Eyre-Todd; Dr. B. Homer Vanderblue (New York); Revd. Dr. H. T. J. Waring and Mr. C. Boog Watson (both of Edinburgh); Miss M. G. Watt (Llandrindod Wells); and the late Professor Westergaard. At libraries, museums and galleries I am specially indebted to the following—at the British Museum to Sir George Hill and Mr. V. Scholderer; at the Library of the India Office (Record Department) to Mr. W. T. Ottewill; at the Library of the Custom House, London, to Mr. J. H. Newman; at H.M.

PREFACE

General Register House, Edinburgh, to Mr. W. Angus, Mr. Henry Paton and Mr. Henry Donnelly; at the National Library, Edinburgh, to Dr. Meikle and Mr. Dobie; at the National Portrait Gallery to Mr. H. M. Hake; at the Scottish National Portrait Gallery to Mr. Stanley Cursitor and Mr. A. E. Haswell Miller; at the University of Glasgow—for University documents to Mr. J. C. Ballantyne, Clerk of Faculties—for the University Library to Dr. W. R. Cunningham (who helped in the reading of some difficult documents and in many other ways), and Mr. Wilson Steel; at Balliol College Library to Mr. J. B. Mynors; at Aberdeen University Library to Dr. Douglas Simpson; at Edinburgh University Library to Mr. F. C. Nicholson and Mr. L. W. Sharp; at the Library of the Royal Technical College, Glasgow, to Mr. W. G. Burrell; at New College Library, Edinburgh, to Revd. Dr. A. Mitchell Hunter; at the Library, Queen's University, Belfast, to Mr. K. Povey; at the Institute of Historical Research to Mr. Guy Parsloe; at the Library of the Royal College of Physicians and Surgeons, Edinburgh, to Mr. T. H. Graham; at the Royal Society, Edinburgh, to Mr. G. A. Stewart; at Baillie's Institution Library, Glasgow, to Mr. James R. Anderson; at the Mitchell Library, Glasgow, to Mr. S. A. Pitt; at the Signet Library, Edinburgh, to Mr. J. Minto; at the City of Birmingham Library to Mr. H. M. Cashmore; at the Library of the Royal Geographical Society to Mr. G. R. Crone; at the United Services Club to Paymaster Captain R. R. Hoare; at the Churches and Universities (Scotland) Widows' Fund to Mr. Thomas B. Martin; at the Church of Ireland Library, Dublin, to Miss Geraldine Fitzgerald; at the Presbyterian Historical Society Library, Belfast, to Miss J. L. M. Stewart; at the Baker Library, Harvard, to Dr. A. H. Cole (who aided greatly in tracing letters of Adam Smith in American libraries); at Yale University Library to Mr. Andrew Keogh; at New York Public Library to Mr. K. D. Metcalf.

The late Mr. S. Douglas Jackson was good enough to undertake the heavy task of preparing the Index. The Carnegie Trust for the Universities of Scotland has generously defrayed the cost of expert assistance on certain enquiries. The University of Glasgow has given me the fullest access to all its documents, providing for the transcriptions of a number of them and undertaking the publication of this volume.

W. R. S.

CORRIGENDA

p. x, *for* " G. S. Frazer " *read* " G. S. Fraser ".
p. x, *for* " L. A. Scrogie " *read* " N. A. Scorgie ".
p. xi, *for* " J. B. Mynors " *read* " R. A. B. Mynors ".
p. 38, note [6], *for* " p. 262 " *read* " p. 263 ".
p. 57, ll. 1 and 2, *for* sentence beginning " In 1748 " *read* " In 1747 there had been issued by the former a new edition of the *Essai Phisique sur l'Oeconomie Animale* ".
p. 63, l. 13, *for* " De Brosses' " *read* " De Brosse's ".
p. 90, l. 17, *for* " Sterling " *read* " Stirling ".
p. 264, note [4], *for* " Neckar " *read* " Necker ".
p. 274, l. 14, *for* " afeared " *read* " assured ".
p. 274, l. 15, *delete* " of ".
p. 396, note [8], l. 1, *for* " Atterbury " *read* " Adderbury ".

CONTENTS

	PAGE
PREFACE - - - - - - - - - - - -	vii

PART I

THE LIFE OF ADAM SMITH, 1723–1763

CHAP.

I. EDINBURGH AT THE BEGINNING OF THE EIGHTEENTH CENTURY

Great political tension between the Revolution and the Union : the Scottish Ministry of 1705 included, as one of the Secretaries of State, Hugh, Earl of Loudoun, whose private secretary was Adam Smith (father of the economist) : Adam Smith descended from the Smiths of Rothiebirsben and Inveramsay in Aberdeenshire : many of this family possessed marked administrative ability : varied duties of a private secretary of the period : his appointment as Clerk of the Court Martial in 1707 and Comptroller of Customs at Kirkcaldy in 1714 -   3

II. COURTS MARTIAL AND CUSTOMS

Between 1707 and 1723 the Clerk of the Court Martial in Scotland acted as a deputy-Judge Advocate : attempt of the Judge Advocate-General to impose a deputy on Scotland : Adam Smith's protest : the effect of the Rebellion of 1715 on this controversy : duties of the office : possible echoes of these in the writings of his son Adam : the first marriage of Adam Smith, senior ; birth of a son, Hugh, in 1709 : appointment of Adam Smith as Comptroller of Customs at Kirkcaldy in 1714 : duties of the office : purchasing power of his official salaries and fees : death of his wife, 1716-18 : his second marriage to Margaret Douglas of Strathenry in 1720 : the associations of her family with Mary, Queen of Scots : death of Adam Smith, W.S., in January 1723 -   -   -   13

III. THE BOYHOOD OF ADAM SMITH (1723–1737)

Adam Smith, son of the late Comptroller of Customs, was born at Kirkcaldy in the spring of 1723 and baptised 5th June of that year : in spite of the early death of his father he was moderately provided for : another version of the tale of his being stolen by gypsies : particulars of the tinkler-gypsies of the period : possible effect of this incident on his work : some traits of character which became more strongly marked in his maturity : the delicacy of his health, when young : industry and agriculture in the vicinity of Kirkcaldy—shipping, collieries, salt pans, the naileries at Pathhead or Dunnikier, and the management of a Fifeshire estate of moderate size -   -   -   -   -   -   20

IV. ADAM SMITH AS A STUDENT AT GLASGOW AND BALLIOL (1737–1746)

The reasons for Adam Smith being sent to Glasgow University in 1737 : the City and the University at this time : distinguished Professors : some traces of his life as an undergraduate : solution of the problem whether he graduated or not : in 1740 awarded a Snell Exhibition, tenable at Balliol College, Oxford : state of Balliol at this time : friends he made there : his expenses : though he did not return to Kirkcaldy for six years, all his holidays were not spent at Oxford : his further study of the Classics : the question when and where he acquired his taste for modern literature : after six years at Oxford he felt unable to fulfil the condition of his Exhibition in the acceptance of Orders of the Church of England : the reason he was able to refuse and at the same time retain the Exhibition : his leaving Balliol, four years before the termination of the Exhibition, may have been related to consequences of the Rebellion of 1745 : grounds for thinking that his early disgust at Oxford may have been modified later - 28

V. THE CIRCUMSTANCES AND THE SUBJECT-MATTER OF ADAM SMITH'S PUBLIC LECTURES AT EDINBURGH (1748–1751)

After two years' search Adam Smith found a use for his talents in courses of public lectures : the organisation of these by James Oswald, Robert Craigie and Henry Home of Kames : not held at, nor authorised by, the University : popularity of lectures in Edinburgh at this period : reasons for concluding that Adam Smith's lectures were under the auspices of an existing Society, probably the Philosophical Society : the first course on literary criticism, the last on Jurisprudence : summary of the first course : the second may have been a continuation of it or perhaps Philosophical : the problem of the important third course on Jurisprudence : how the topics discussed can be recreated and verified : the discovery of the MS. of parts of the lectures : the treatment of economic questions midway between Hutcheson and the *Glasgow Lectures* : the posthumous Essays " on the Imitative Arts " and " English and Italian Verses " are considerably later than this period : some side-lights on Adam Smith's personal affairs from 1746 to 1751—the statement that he tried to write English verse and failed is shown to be unsupported by evidence : resignation of the Snell in 1749 : heir to his half-brother in 1750 : he forms a taste for the clubs for discussion of the period : investigation of the contradictory accounts, namely that he did not join in the debates and that he delivered long monologues : his friends : did he fall in love while at Edinburgh? - - 47

VI. ADAM SMITH'S SETTLEMENT IN GLASGOW (1751–1764)

Appointed Professor of Logic in 1751 : exchanged to the Chair of Moral Philosophy in 1752 : income from the Chair and its relation to current prices : the Professors' houses : changes in the staff since he left in 1740 : the Moral Philosophy class-room and hours of lectures : the amount of time required by these duties : Adam Smith as lecturer and public speaker—the explanation of varying accounts : through historical causes the business of the University was considerable : how this was organised : the very large share of Adam Smith in this work shows the want of foundation for statements that he was deficient in business ability and acumen : the University records reveal how greatly his colleagues relied on him in practical affairs : more, perhaps, than administrative efficiency he had personal qualities which won the respect and regard of the staff : his complete disinterestedness : the peculiarities of his absence of mind : the power of recall : great as was his concentration, his

CONTENTS

CHAP.

retentiveness was yet more : the city was his laboratory : changes in it between 1740 and 1750 : control of life and manners by the ministers : condemnation of the theatre : robbery : the immense trade in tobacco : a rising standard of comfort : lively interest in the principles of commerce : Andrew Cochrane's Political Economy Club : publication and sale of Economic books : clubs to which Adam Smith belonged at this period : time spent in attending them : amount of his leisure during the Session - - - - - - - 66

VII. THE CONSTITUTIONAL QUESTION IN THE UNIVERSITY OF GLASGOW FROM 1761

The issues involved were fundamental in the administration and finance of Scottish Universities in the eighteenth century : they were shaped by the personalities of the chief actors and depend to a considerable extent on their characters : Adam Smith's colleagues : the characters of three of these were important, namely Leechman, Moor and Anderson ; of these Moor is the enigma : as to the government of the University, prior to 1755, there had been three meetings, *i.e.* those presided over by the Principal, the Dean and the Rector : from 1755 the Principal's meeting was abandoned, with the result of concentrating business in that of the Rector : when Leechman was appointed Principal in 1761 his policy was not only to restore, but to extend the powers of the Principal's meeting : Adam Smith, as Dean of Faculty, presided at a Rector's meeting in 1761, the legality of which was disputed : his efforts towards conciliation : in 1762 he was appointed convener of a committee to report on the respective powers of the Rector and the Principal : this report obtained a very large measure of support : it just missed securing complete unanimity : the strange reasons for this : after Adam Smith left Glasgow the situation deteriorated, quarrels were frequent, and the matters in dispute became the subject of an important action in the Court of Session in 1771.

Adam Smith had given special attention to the finances of the University and had urged the adoption of a better system of accounting : after his departure Anderson took up this question : it was debated with much acrimony, leading to another action, which resulted in the " Shaw Park Decree " of 1775 : this date suggests that Adam Smith was most fortunate in the time of his resignation : if he had remained, the pressure of business and the time spent on these disputes would have made it difficult, if not impossible, for *The Wealth of Nations* to have appeared when it did or in its present form : further particulars of Adam Smith's appointment as tutor of the Duke of Buccleuch : his support of T. Young as his successor : reactions of this on his relations with Reid - - - - - - - - - - 84

VIII. ADAM SMITH AMONG HIS FRIENDS

Dugald Stewart's account of " the extravagant and fanciful opinions " expressed by Adam Smith in his social hours : suggestions that some of these may have been great thoughts, such as the " golden dream " of a federated Empire : Stewart and A. Carlyle both state that Adam Smith failed in forming an estimate of character : if this is true, it reflects seriously on the "impartial spectator" of the *Theory of Moral Sentiments* : several reasons for distrusting the statements of both : if Stewart had not said it, he would have been in danger of trouble in his University and Carlyle in the General Assembly : on the contrary, Adam Smith's estimate of character showed remarkably sound judgement : relations with the brothers Foulis : the Academy of Arts, which was indirectly related to an undiscovered bust of Adam Smith : it is mentioned by Rae but should be dated at least fifteen years later than it is placed by him : the problem whether it was based on the Tassie medallion or was earlier : the Muir-Romanes portrait : was it contemporaneous or posthumous ? " the maid of Fife " and Adam Smith's second disappointment in love—French ladies pay court to him - - - 98

IX. ADAM SMITH'S STUDIES (1751–1763)

Adam Smith's discovery of *laissez faire* had been made by 1749, if not before : his approach to it was through Grotius, Puffendorf, Cumberland, Gershom Carmichael and Hutcheson : there were three stages in his intellectual progress at Glasgow, each comprising about four years :

(a) 1751-1755. In the Edinburgh Lectures his theory was verified by an inductive enquiry based on a historical analysis : to this he now began to add another, which was contemporary, showing in the case of Scotland, and particularly the West, how, on restraint being withdrawn, commerce flourished : the continuance of his studies in jurisprudence : was there an "Oswald Document" ? the lecture of 1755 : the problems it raises : there were two charges of plagiarism, not one, and these were separated by between fifteen and twenty years : personal relations, as affected by the second charge, explain Stewart's treatment, which would otherwise be most perplexing : discussion as to whether the later charge of plagiarism against Ferguson and Robertson was justified : speculations as to the fate of the lecture of 1755 :

(b) 1755-1759. These years were devoted mainly to the writing of the *Theory of Moral Sentiments* : the beginnings were in the MS. of the Edinburgh Lectures : these required to be extended and transformed from isolated discourses into a connected argument : the *Theory* has important biographical aspects in so far as it provides a revelation of Adam Smith's own mental processes : the success of the *Theory* : the meeting with Dr. Johnson : here also two similar incidents, dated about 1761 and 1777, have been telescoped together : the provocation given by Adam Smith : the continuance of his work on Jurisprudence.

(c) 1759-1763. After the publication of the *Theory*, Adam Smith began to revise the Edinburgh Lectures on Jurisprudence, incorporating the additional material he had collected over a period of more than ten years : the *Glasgow Lectures* represent the form reached by 1762-1763 : the circumstances under which the economic portion came to be treated separately, probably in the summer or autumn of 1763 : his friends were expecting publication soon after 1764 : there is no decisive evidence that, prior to the visit to France, Adam Smith was influenced by the Physiocrats ; but, at the same time, he was affected by French influence, so that, in this respect, both he and the Physiocrats, drew general inspiration from a common source   111

CONTENTS

PART II

DOCUMENTS

(A few documents which are known to have been printed previously are marked *. These were usually issued privately, and are very rare. Several (which were published) are included as necessary to explain others which follow them.)

	PAGE
A. OFFICIAL AND LEGAL PAPERS	
I. Commission in favour of Adam Smith, W.S., as Clerk of the Court Martial of Scotland, 18th April, 1707	129
II. Will of Adam Smith, W.S., 13th November, 1722	129
III. Retour of Adam Smith, younger, as heir of Adam Smith, W.S., 9th September, 1724	133
IV. Proceedings in a Decreet Arbitral, 22nd March, 1739, to 10th January, 1740. Clearing of Accounts between Hercules Smith, representing the late Hercules Smith, Collector of Customs at Kirkcaldy, and Adam Smith, a minor, by his curator, Adam Smith, representing the late Adam Smith, W.S., Comptroller	133
V. Gen. Retornatus Adami Smith fratri. Adam Smith, heir to his half-brother, Hugh, 1750	135
VI. Sale of Property in the City of Aberdeen, by Adam Smith, 1757	135
B. ADAM SMITH AS A STUDENT, 1737–1749	
I.*Matriculation at the University of Glasgow, 14th November, 1737	136
II. Minute of Adam Smith's appointment as a Snell Exhibitioner, 4th March, 1740	136
III. Letter of Resignation of the Snell Exhibition, addressed to Dr. Leigh, Master of Balliol, 4th February, 1749	137
IV. Minute of his resignation of this Exhibition in the Records of the University of Glasgow, 28th April, 1749	137
C. APPOINTMENT TO PROFESSORSHIPS AT THE UNIVERSITY OF GLASGOW	
I. Professor of Logic	137
II. Professor of Moral Philosophy	139
D. ADAM SMITH AND THE ADMINISTRATION OF THE PROPERTY OF THE UNIVERSITY	
I. The back courts of the Professors' houses next the garden	140
II. The Dangerous State of the Principal's House	141
III. Report on Dr. Lindesay's House	144

CONTENTS

		PAGE
IV.	Report on four Houses (Nos. 3 to 6) in the Professors' Court	144
V.	Repairs to the Principal's House and to three Houses in the Professors' Court	144
VI.	Repairs to the House lately occupied by William Ruat	144
VII.	Transfer of the Principal's House to William Leechman	145
VIII.	Repairs to the Anatomy Room	145
IX.	Encroachments on the College Lands and Nuisances	145
X.	Alteration of Bridges on Molendinar to lessen flooding	145
XI.	Stopping a Road over the College Lands	146
XII.	Apparatus and Accommodation for the Natural Philosophy Class	146
XIII.	Repairs to the Mathematical Class Rooms and a new Chemical Laboratory	147
XIV.	Curator of the College Rooms	148
XV.	The Fencing Academy	149

E. Questions of Law and Finance, arising out of Administration of the University Property

I.	Proceedings at a typical Faculty Meeting	150
II.	Fixing the Payment by College Vassals	151
III.	A Question of Law concerning a feu in Virginia St.	152
IV.	A Question of the Charge of certain Salaries in the College Accounts	152
V.	Accounts of the Sub-Deanery as between the present and the late Factor	152
VI.	The Mortification of the Duchess of Hamilton	153
VII.	A feu-duty of 12d Scots	155
VIII.	Clearing the Accounts of the Revenue	
	(*a*) the Archbishopric before the Barons of the Exchequer	155
	(*b*) Ordinary Revenue before the Treasury	156
IX.	The University repays a loan to the Ship Bank	158
X.	Loan by the University to distressed Russian Students	158
XI.	Examination of the Old Valuation of the Lands of Yoker	159
XII.	The System of keeping the University Accounts	159
XIII.	Examination of the State of the Dundonald Mortification	160

F. Some Transactions relating to the Snell Exhibitions — 161

G. The University and the City

I.	Students and Petty Customs	163
II.	Protest against the Erection of a Playhouse in the City	163

CONTENTS

H. Ceremonial Addresses and a Presentation
    I. To King George III — 166
    II. To the King of Sicily — 168

I. The University Library
    I. Its Resources in the time of Adam Smith — 168
    II. Minutes — 173
    III. " Dr. Smith's Quaestor Accounts from 26th June, 1758, to 26th June, 1760 " — 178

J. Adam Smith as Dean of Faculty — 184

K. Transactions relating to Professors
    I. The Translation of John Anderson from the Chair of Oriental Languages to that of Natural Philosophy — 188
    II. The Case of William Ruat — 190
    III. The Case of James Moor, Professor of Greek — 195

L. Adam Smith, Vice-Rector
    I. Adam Smith, Præses — 199
    II. The Legality of Adam Smith's Procedure questioned — 200
    III. Confirmed by the Rector — 201
    IV. The Respective Powers of Rector and Principal — 202
    V. Adam Smith's Report on the Powers of Rector and Principal — 202
    VI. Adam Smith confirmed as Præses and later as Vice-Rector — 216
    VII. Further Discussions on the Powers of Rector and Principal — 217

M. Adam Smith's Resignation — 220

N. Extracts from Documents produced by the Parties in the action of Declarator in the Court of Session, 1766–1771, relating to the Report on the Jurisdiction of the Rector, 1762, and other Issues raised in that Period
    I.*Pursuer's Information — 222
    II.*Defender's Reply — 224
    III.*Further Memorial from Pursuer — 224
    Table showing a List of Rectors, Deans of Faculty, Principals and Professors at the University of Glasgow, 1751–1776 - *to face p.* 224
    IV.*Decision in the Process of Declarator — 225
    V. (a) *Sederunt at the first of the Meetings of the Ordinary Visitors at Shaw Park, 1775 — 225
        (b) *Decree of the Ordinary Visitors at Shaw Park, 1775 — 226
        (c) *Decision on the Reclaiming Petition against the Decree passed at Shaw Park, 1776 — 228

CONTENTS

O. "Adamus Smith, Rector Magnificus", 1787–1788   PAGE
    I. Elected by the Four Nations, 1787 - - - - - - 228
    II. *Acceptance of Election - - - - - - - 229
    III. Installation and Appointment of a Vice-Rector - - - 230
    IV. Reappointed, 1788 - - - - - - - - 231

P. Adam Smith's Correspondence
    I. Adam Smith to William Smith, 24th August, 1740 - - - 232
    II. Adam Smith to his Mother, 23rd October, 1741 - - - 232
    III. Adam Smith to his Mother, 12th May, [? 1742] - - - 233
    IV. Alexander Wedderburn to Adam Smith, 20th March, [? 1754] - 233
    V. Adam Smith, Collector of Customs at Alloa to Adam Smith, Professor at Glasgow, 27th August, 1754 - - - - - 235
    VI. Adam Smith to William Johnstone, 19th August, 1758 - - 236
    VII. Adam Ferguson to ——, 17th April, 1759 - - - - 236
    VIII. Andrew Millar to Adam Smith, 26th April, 1759 - - 238
    IX. William Robertson to Adam Smith, 14th June, [? 1759] - - 238
    X. Gilbert Elliot of Minto to Adam Smith, 14th November, 1758 - 239
    XI. Adam Smith to Lord Fitzmaurice, 21st February, 1759 - - 240
    XII. Adam Smith to Lord Shelburne, 10th March, 1759 - - 242
    XIII. Adam Smith to Lord Shelburne, 4th April, 1759 - - 243
    XIV. Lord Shelburne to Adam Smith, 26th April, 1759 - - 245
    XV. Adam Smith to Lord Shelburne, 23rd July, 1759 - - 248
    XVI. Adam Smith to Lord Shelburne, 31st August, 1759 - - 249
    XVII. Adam Smith to Lord Shelburne, 29th October, 1759 - - 250
    XVIII. Adam Smith to Lord Shelburne, 3rd December, 1759 - - 251
    XIX. Adam Smith to Lord Shelburne, 15th July, 1760 - - 253
    XX. Adam Smith to William Strahan, 30th December, 1760 - 254
    XXI. William Cullen to Adam Smith, 24th June, 1761 - - 255
    XXII. Adam Ferguson to Adam Smith, 5th November, 1761 - 255
    XXIII. Joseph Black to Adam Smith, 23rd January, 1764 - - 256
    XXIV. John Millar to Adam Smith, 2nd February, 1764 - - 257
    XXV. John Glassford to Adam Smith, 5th November, 1764 - - 258
    XXVI.*Adam Smith as Commissioner for taking Evidence at Toulouse in the Douglas Cause, 4th October, 1765 - - - 259
    XXVII. Depositions sent by Madame Denis of Ferney, to Adam Smith, dated 11th October, 1765 - - - - - - 260
    XXVIII. "Etat des Habit, Linge et Effet apartenant a Monsieur Smith" [? 1765–1766] - - - - - - - - 261

CONTENTS xxi

		PAGE
XXIX.	Adam Smith to David Hume, [? August, 1765[	262
XXX.	Adam Smith to David Hume, [? September or October, 1765]	263
XXXI.	Adam Smith to David Hume, 13th March, 1766	264
XXXII.	Adam Smith to [? Andrew Millar], 30th August, 1767	265
XXXIII.	Adam Smith to [Lord Hailes], 23rd May, 1769	265
XXXIV.	Adam Smith to John Davidson, 11th March, 1771	267
XXXV.	Adam Smith to John Davidson, [? Autumn, 1771]	267
XXXVI.	John Roebuck to Adam Smith, 1st November, 1775	268
XXXVII.	Alexander Wedderburn to Adam Smith, 6th June, 1776	269
XXXVIII.*	Adam Smith to David Hume, 16th June, 1776	271
XXXIX.	Adam Ferguson to Adam Smith, 12th April, 1777	273
XL.	Alexander Wedderburn to Adam Smith, 30th October, 1777	274
XLI.	Sir Grey Cooper to Adam Smith, 7th November, 1777	275
XLII.	Adam Smith to Mr. Spottiswood, 21st January, 1778	275
XLIII.	Adam Smith to William Strahan, 5th February, 1778	276
XLIV.	[? John Macpherson] to Adam Smith, 28th November, 1778	276
XLV.	Duc de la Rochefoucauld to Adam Smith, 6th August, 1779	278
XLVI.	Adam Smith to Peter Anker, [? October, 1780]	280
XLVII.	Adam Smith to Andreas Holt [? October, 1780]	281
XLVIII.	Henry Mackenzie to Mr. Carmichael, 1781	284
XLIX.	Henry Mackenzie to Adam Smith, 7th June, 1782	284
L.	John Logan to Henry Mackenzie, 6th June, 1782	285
LI.	T. Cadell to Adam Smith, 12th October, 1782	286
LII.	Adam Smith to William Strahan, 22nd May, 1783	286
LIII.	George Dempster to Adam Smith, 18th December, 1783	287
LIV.	Adam Smith to John Davidson, 25th February, 1783	288
LV.	Adam Smith to —— [? after 1783]	288
LVI.	Adam Smith to William Strahan, 10th June, 1784	290
LVII.	Adam Smith to [? T. Cadell], 10th August, 1784	291
LVIII.	Adam Smith to [? T. Cadell], 16th November, 1784	292
LIX.	Adam Smith to Revd. Dr. James Monteath, 22nd February, 1785	292
LX.	Lord Porchester to Adam Smith, 24th August, 1785	293
LXI.	Adam Smith to George Chalmers, 10th November, 1785	294
LXII.	Adam Smith to George Chalmers, 3rd December, 1785	296
LXIII.	Adam Smith to [? William Strahan], 13th February, 1786	296
LXIV.	Adam Smith to [? Sir John Sinclair of Ulbster], 11th April, 1786	297

CONTENTS

		PAGE
LXV.	Adam Smith to the Abbé Morellet, May 1786	298
LXVI.	Adam Smith to Thomas Cadell, 7th May, 1786	299
LXVII.	Adam Smith to John Bruce, 3rd October, 1786	299
LXVIII.	Adam Smith to [Lieutenant-Colonel Alexander Ross], 13th December, 1786	300
LXIX.	Adam Smith to Joseph Black, 9th May, 1787	301
LXX.	Henry Dundas to Adam Smith, 21st March, 1787	302
LXXI.	Adam Smith to Henry Dundas, 18th July, 1787	303
LXXII.	John Logan to Adam Smith, 20th August, 1787	304
LXXIII.	Adam Smith to ——, 11th October, 1788	305
LXXIV.	Adam Smith to Revd. Dr. James Monteath, 16th September, 1788	306
LXXV.	Adam Smith to Revd. Dr. James Stewart Monteath, 2nd February, 1789	306
LXXVI.	Revd. James Stuart Menteath to Adam Smith, 20th April, 1789	308
LXXVII.	Adam Smith to Revd. Dr. James Stewart Monteath, 9th May, 1789	309
LXXVIII.	Adam Smith to Thomas Cadell, 31st March, 1789	309
LXXIX.	Adam Smith to David Douglas, 21st January, 1790	310
LXXX.	The Duke of Buccleuch to Adam Smith, 24th February, 1790	311
LXXXI.	John Millar to David Douglas, 10th August, 1790	311
LXXXII.	Lord Loughborough to [? David Douglas], 14th August, 1790	313
LXXXIII.	Thomas Cadell to Henry Mackenzie, 21st December, 1792	314

PART III

AN EARLY DRAFT OF PART OF *THE WEALTH OF NATIONS* (*c.* 1763)

INTRODUCTION - - - - - - - - - - - 317

THE MANUSCRIPT

    Chap. 2.   Of the nature and Causes of public opulence - - - - 322

    Chap. 3d.   Of the Rule of Exchanging or of the Circumstances which regulate the prices of Commodities - - - - - - - - 345

    Chap. 4th.   Of money, its nature, origin and history, considered, first, as the measure of value, and secondly as the instrument of Commerce - 346

    Chap. 5th.   Concerning the Causes of the slow progress of opulence - - 351

CONTENTS xxiii

PART IV

FACSIMILES OF THE HANDWRITING OF ADAM SMITH, OF SOME OF HIS RELATIVES AND OF HIS AMANUENSES

	PAGE
Introduction	359
Signature of William Smith, his Cousin, a Regent at Aberdeen	362
Signature of Hercules Smith, his Cousin, Collector of Customs at Kirkcaldy	362
Signature of Adam Smith, W.S., his father	362
Signature of Margaret Douglas, his mother	362
Signatures of Adam Smith, when a schoolboy, 1733	363
Signature of Adam Smith on Matriculation at Glasgow, 14th November, 1737	364
His writing in a book he used at Glasgow	365
A letter to his mother from Balliol	366
Resignation of the Snell Exhibition, 4th February, 1749	366
Signatures to the Professor's Oath, as Dean of Faculty, as Vice-Rector and as Rector, 1751–1790	367
Title Page, Aristotle, *Ethics*, 1610, from the old Moral Philosophy Class Library with inscriptions by another Adam Smith (*circ.* 1762–1763)	368
Adam Smith's Table of Contents in a volume of " Tucker's Tracts "	369
Adam Smith's Table of Contents in a volume entitled " Political Pamphlets "	369
Adam Smith's Table of Contents in a volume entitled " Political Tracts "	370
The earliest form of the Essay on the Affinity between English and Italian Verses (*circ.* 1777–1784)	371
Adam Smith to Thomas Cadell, 15th March, 1788	374
Adam Smith to Henry Dundas, 25th March, 1789	377
Part of one of the Lectures Adam Smith gave at Edinburgh, 1749–1751, in the hand of his first amanuensis.—Division of Labour—" the Philosopher and the Porter "	379
Part of another of the Edinburgh Lectures in the hand of the same amanuensis. " Land and Water Carriage "	383
Specimens of the Manuscript of an early draft of *The Wealth of Nations*, in the hand of the second amanuensis, with corrections in Adam Smith's own hand	386
Title Page of the Glasgow Lectures	388
A page of the Text of the Glasgow Lectures	389
Title Page of the " Catalgue of Books belonging to Adam Smith, Esqr., 1781 "	390
A Page of this Catalogue	391
Three types of the Description of Professors in the Matriculation Album of the University of Glasgow	392

CONTENTS

APPENDICES

	PAGE
I. The Smiths of Rothiebirsben, Inveramsay and Seton, Aberdeenshire	395
II. Proprietors of Properties at the Castlegate, Aberdeen	408
III. Scottish Posts at the End of the Seventeenth Century in relation to Alexander Smith, Postmaster-General for Scotland	409
IV. The Strathenry-Forrester-Douglas Family of Strathenry, Fife	411
V. The Houses occupied by Adam Smith in the Professors' Court of the Old College, Glasgow	415
VI. Adam Smith's Difficulties in the Incorporation of New Material in his Manuscripts	422
VII. Adam Smith and his Russian Admirers in the Eighteenth Century by Professor Michael P. Alekseev, Leningrad	424
Index	433

PLATES

Statue of Adam Smith by Gasser (*circ.* 1867)	*Frontispiece*
I. Strathenry Castle	*to face p.* 24
II. Kirkcaldy Burgh School	,, 26
III. View of Glasgow from the North-East in 1762	,, 30
IV. The College or University of Glasgow (*circ.* 1693)	,, 32
V. The Black Stone Chair	,, 34
VI. Exhibition of the Glasgow Academy in the College on the King's Birthday, 1762	,, 104
VII. Balliol College (*circ.* 1707)	,, 136
VIII. (*a*) Glasgow College, Outer Court	,, 144
(*b*) Glasgow College, Professors' Court	,, 144
IX. The Fore Hall of the College	,, 150
X. Adam Smith's House in Kirkcaldy	,, 264
XI. Adam Smith's Bureau	,, 266
XII. Adam Smith's Chair, Reading Desk, Candlesticks and Snuff Box	,, 272
XIII. Examples of Parrot Ornament in Scottish Bookbinding	,, 290
XIV. Tassie's Medallion of Adam Smith " in the antique manner "	,, 304
XV. Watermark on paper used by Adam Smith while he was at Glasgow	,, 322
XVI. Head of Adam Smith on the Ayrshire Half-penny and on the Penny of Scotland, 1797	,, 348
Plan of the College Glasgow, showing Professors' Court with Houses occupied by Adam Smith	,, 421

PART I

THE LIFE OF ADAM SMITH, 1723-1763

CHAPTER I

EDINBURGH AT THE BEGINNING OF THE EIGHTEENTH CENTURY

A Toast ! A Toast—To the most noble and right honourable John Campbell, Baron of Bristol ![1]

This health was drunk with enthusiasm by a company at Whitehall in November, 1705. It is the last that one of them remembered before—as he said himself —he became " incapable ". The party consisted of some of the younger Campbells, their friends and political associates who were in attendance on John, second Duke of Argyle, and other Scottish high officials. Argyle had succeeded his father in the dukedom in 1703. Already, having at the age of twenty-seven won fame as a soldier, his appointment as Lord High Commissioner to the Scottish Parliament had been announced not long before. The glories of the clan had been celebrated and the duke had been toasted under each of his titles, an anticipated English one being reserved till the end of a long list. Amongst those who joined in the celebration was Colin Campbell. The name was common in the clan, but it is probable that this " Colin " was Chamberlain of Argyle, a position corresponding to the chief land-agent or steward of a great English estate. Another was Captain Peter Campbell and a third John Philip,[2] who was private secretary to James, first Earl of Seafield, the Scottish Lord High Chancellor. There was another private secretary, Adam Smith, whose chief was Hugh Campbell, Earl of Loudoun, one of the Secretaries of State.

An uproarious celebration of this type, so characteristic of the period, is

---

[1] Marlborough had recommended Argyle for an English peerage. In May 1705 he raised the matter himself in a letter to Godolphin on the grounds of the enmity which he had incurred as Commissioner and as compensation for the great sums of money he had to lay out in virtue of his office. Later he emphasized the importance of being able to take part in the debates of the House of Lords when the question of the Union was under consideration (*Intimate Society Letters*, ed. by the Duke of Argyle, 1910, i, p. 20). Needless to say—as might be expected under the circumstances—the title of the toast involves much confusion. In 1703 Sir John Hervey had been created Baron of Bristol. A fortnight after the incident recorded above, Argyle was created Earl of Greenwich and Baron of Chatham.

[2] John Philip to John Stewart, Under-keeper of the Great Seal, 19th November, 1705, in W. Fraser, *The Earls of Cromartie*, i, p. 295. It was Seafield who is reported to have said, towards the end of the final sitting of the last Scottish Parliament, " Now there is the end of an auld sang."

deserving of notice since it is the first record of a man who was destined, nearly twenty years later, to be the father of Adam Smith, the economist.

The times and this particular occasion were of special interest and excitement. From the Revolution to the Rebellion of 1715 Scotland was in a state of great political agitation and Edinburgh was the centre of the storm. The circumstances are well known, but they may be referred to briefly, as a background for such indications of the administrative personalities and problems as can be collected, these latter being necessary for the purposes of the present narrative.

The union of the Crowns of England and Scotland in 1603 was considered to have been disadvantageous to Scotland, chiefly, perhaps, in isolating the country from the European nations, while the cessation of Border warfare and few opportunities for service in the armies of the Continent had left many of the most adventurous and enterprising young men without opportunities to push their fortunes. It has been said that " throughout the entire century Scotland was a withered and severed branch, and her people knew it ".[1] The disabilities from the Scottish point of view were threefold, ecclesiastical, political and commercial. Towards the end of the century the last became most severely felt. England's trade had developed and, under the colonial system, Scotland was excluded from it. In the last twenty years of the century a comprehensive scheme was conceived which aimed at accomplishing in that period what England had required more than ten times as long to achieve. The first stage was the establishment of industries—a policy which in a poor country was hampered by scarcity of capital and the lack of technical skill. In so far as the plan succeeded—and it did achieve a modest measure of progress—a market for exports was essential. This in turn resulted in the foundation of the company trading to Africa and the Indies, better known as the Darien Company—the grandeur of the conception being inversely related to the execution of it.[2] When the collapse came the distress which resulted was felt everywhere. Noblemen, landed proprietors, corporations, even universities (Glasgow resolved to subscribe for £1000 of the capital), merchants and professional men took up stock to a larger extent than they could afford to pay for, when the calls became due.[3] The reduction in normal spending power extended the suffering throughout the community. At the beginning of the eighteenth century the poverty of the country was extreme. The Exchequer suffered, and the salaries of Government servants and pensioners were in arrear. In 1704 the Duke of Argyle wrote to Lord Godolphin that the failure of the

---

[1] P. Hume Brown in *The Union of 1707*, 1907, p. 4.
[2] W. R. Scott, ed., *A Scottish Cloth Manufactory*, 1681-1703, pp. xxxiii-lv.
[3] W. R. Scott, *Joint Stock Companies to 1720*, ii, pp. 217-19.

Treasury to aid the Scottish Revenue by a grant of £12,000 to meet deficiencies of the salary list had cost the Government party twenty votes in Parliament.[1] Very many members were compelled to take advantage of their immunity from arrest for debt during the period the House was sitting, spending the rest of the year in the Liberties of Holyrood House. Money was extraordinarily scarce, the country was undergoing severe deflation and prices were remarkably low.

The feeling was universal that the failure of the scheme for a Scottish colonial empire had been most unfairly wrecked by the jealousy of the English East India Company, and this transferred the growing quarrel from the economic to the political plane. The Scottish Parliament was becoming restive. On the death of William III. it was dissolved, having sat for fourteen years. The new Parliament which met on 6th May, 1703, amidst the shifting ambitions of political parties, was definitely opposed to anything that was known, or suspected, to be the policy of the English ministry. Godolphin regarded the settlement of the succession as the most urgent question of domestic politics. Queensberry, the Commissioner, found the temper of the House exceedingly difficult. It was carried against him that, before any other business (including supply), the House should proceed to consider measures which, on the decease of the Queen, should secure the religion, liberty and trade of the country. A clause, in what came to be known as the Act of Security, was designed to have the effect that the successor to the Scottish Crown should not be the same person who succeeded to the English Throne, unless, during the current session, measures were settled and enacted " which would secure the religion, liberty and trade of the nation from the English or any foreign influence ". Parliament became increasingly aroused. Debates were stormy and then disorderly, and the session was prorogued on 16th September. These proceedings were highly unsatisfactory from the standpoint of the Court, and the position of Queensberry was weakened. It became impossible when the Jacobite plot, associated with his name, was discovered. The next session opened on 6th July, 1704, with the Marquis of Tweeddale as Commissioner and several changes amongst the Ministers. At length the Royal Assent was given to the Act of Security, and this measure caused great disquiet in England, where an Aliens Act was passed early in 1705 under which if Commissioners were not appointed by both countries to treat for a union, Scotsmen not resident in England, Ireland or the Colonies should be declared aliens, the export of horses, arms

---

[1] Duke of Argyle, ed., *Intimate Society Letters*, i, p. 26. A year later £20,000 was lent under royal warrant to the Scottish government to meet the Commissioner's expenses and arrears of salaries and pensions. This transaction resulted in the charges of bribery for the passing of the Act of Union made by Lockhart and others—J. H. Burton, *History of Scotland*, viii, pp. 178-9 ; W. L. Mathieson, *Scotland and the Union*, 1905, pp. 144-5.

and ammunition to Scotland prohibited, as also the import to England of cattle, coals and linen from Scotland. War was freely talked of. An apparently accidental occurrence inflamed passion in Scotland and induced considerable anger in England. This was the execution in Edinburgh of Captain Green and two of the members of the crew of the *Worcester*, which had been seized on a charge of piracy.[1] The Ministers had failed to act with decision and they were replaced. The Duke of Argyle became Commissioner, Queensberry Privy Seal, Murray of Philiphaugh Lord Register, the Earl of Glasgow Treasurer Depute; the Earl of Seafield was once more Chancellor, having the remarkable record of holding office, whatever party was in power, almost continuously since 1695. Owing to the necessity of one at least of the Ministry being in London frequently there were two Secretaries of State. One was the Marquis of Annandale—a man of impatient and overbearing temper, of whom it was said that he was included " as the Indians worship the devil, out of fear ".[2] It was not long before Argyle found him intolerable, and he was succeeded by the unfortunate Earl of Mar. The other Secretary was Hugh, Earl of Loudoun, a much younger man, who at an early age had shown himself politically minded. At the time of the Revolution he was a student at Glasgow, and he was the leader of a band of undergraduates who, on 30th November, 1688, burned effigies of the Pope and the Archbishops of St. Andrews and Glasgow.[3] He took his seat in Parliament in 1696 and was sworn in as a member of the Privy Council in 1697. His advancement was rapid. In 1698 he was appointed an Extraordinary Lord of Session on the strong recommendation of Archibald, the first Duke of Argyle, who supported him as " a mettled young fellow and a noted Presbyterian ".[4] By 1704 he was a Commissioner of the Treasury and the next year he was appointed by the Council one of the Assessors at the trial of Captain Green.[5]

A new session of Parliament opened on 28th June, 1705. For a month opinion fluctuated, but by 24th August an Act for a Treaty of Union received a first reading. In the country there was much hostility to the measure and there were frequent riots in Edinburgh and in other cities. The difficulty as to the appointment of Commissioners for Scotland was overcome when a resolution was carried to leave the naming of them to the Queen. The way was now open for the Conference, which opened at Westminster on 16th April, 1706. Articles of

---

[1] A. Lang, *Historical Mysteries*, 1904, pp. 193-213.
[2] W. L. Mathieson, *Scotland and the Union*, 1905, p. 105.
[3] G. Eyre-Todd, *History of Glasgow*, 1934, iii, p. 1.
[4] Brunton and Haig, *Senators of the College of Justice*, 1832, p. 468.
[5] *Hist. MSS. Com., Hamilton Papers, Supplementary Report*, 1932, p. 165.

Union having been agreed, the final session of the Scots Parliament was opened on 3rd October, 1706. Argyle had ceased to be Commissioner and Anne was most reluctant to accept Queensberry as his successor. She wrote, " Though he is none of my choice, I own it goes mightily against me. It grates my soul to take a man into my service who has not only betrayed me but tricked me several times, one that has been obnoxious to his own countrymen these many years and one I can never be convinced can be of any use."[1] Yet Queensberry did prove his usefulness, from the point of view of the Court, in piloting the Act of Union through the Scottish Parliament; and the completed Treaty of Union was ratified on 16th January, 1707, and became operative on 1st of May.

In view of these circumstances the Scottish capital passed from one crisis to another—the strain and excitement increasing during the last three years before the Union. To those who were charged with the responsibilities of office and of administration the ever-present danger of Jacobite plots and intrigues was an added anxiety. While there is fairly complete information on the working of the Treasury, the Exchequer, the Customs, Excise, the Navy and the Army in England, data for such of these offices as existed in Scotland are less complete, while very little indeed is known of the administration of other ministries. The office of the Secretaries of State in Scotland was of particular importance at this period and it is unfortunate that the details of its administration under Annandale and Loudoun and Loudoun and Mar are scanty. Loudoun was appointed on 5th June, 1705, and his correspondence, a service of information and his interviews had all to be arranged. The method adopted at the time was that a personal or private secretary also took charge of the official business. These men were usually young. They were exceedingly carefully chosen after very full enquiry, and they were regarded, having rendered good service, as being the natural recipients of such promotion as was available or could be created for them. Thus six secretaries of one of the Ministers obtained comparatively important legal and administrative positions. When Loudoun was appointed, his private secretary was Adam Smith,[2] who descended from a family of Aberdeenshire lairds at one

---

[1] B. C. Brown, ed., *Letters and Instructions of Queen Anne*, 1935, p. 160.

[2] Adam Smith was born in 1679 (Appendix I). He studied at King's University, Aberdeen, under a cousin, William Black, then sub-principal (Univ. Glas. Libry., Bannerman MSS., Wm. Smith to Adam Smith, 8th July, 1713). He went to Edinburgh, and it may be inferred from these papers including a sheet of theses for the graduation of 1698, that he studied there also, possibly Law. After finishing his course, he made a voyage to Bordeaux in October of the same year. The ship was delayed eleven days in the Downs by contrary winds. By an error of navigation it was wrecked on the west coast of France, and Adam Smith reached Bordeaux by land twenty days after his departure from Leith (MSS. as above, " Jurnall "). The " Inventar of the books " (Bannerman Papers), which was drawn up for his executry, shows that, though the number was not large, he was a man of considerable culture. The works, the titles of which are given, may be

time identified with Rothiebirsben and later with Inveramsay. As so often happened at this period, the senior, or at least the more wealthy branch, was strongly Jacobite,[1] while the younger sons were even more forceful on the other side. Indeed it might be said that the Revolution made this family of Smiths, for it showed that many of them possessed very marked administrative ability, and for almost a century they are to be found in important positions. It appears that they had powerful influence; but while this might secure an initial appointment, it would not account for frequent promotions, often to the head of a branch of their particular service. Thus Adam Smith had a brother, considerably his senior, who began his career as a writer or solicitor in Edinburgh, became General Collector of Taxation in Scotland and was Postmaster General for Scotland[2] when he died in the winter of 1701-2, before he was forty. Another, William Smith, a nephew of Alexander and Adam, succeeded the latter as secretary to the Earl of Loudoun, then became steward and later secretary to John, second Duke of Argyle (who was the most powerful person in Scotland in the early part of the eighteenth century), being appointed later one of the secretaries of the Office of Ordnance and a Yeoman of the King's Wine Cellar. Others of the family were in responsible positions in the Customs and Excise, as for instance a brother of William Smith named Adam, who was Collector at Kirkcaldy, and became Inspector of Customs at the out-ports of Scotland. Evidently they were people of varied gifts, for some of them were Professors in the Aberdeen Universities, while several of the women were famed for their beauty, and their fate—tragic or happy—was celebrated in verse.[3]

Loudoun had the most complete confidence in his secretary, Adam Smith. In fact, he trusted him so far as to have a charter under the Great Seal issued to him, dated 28th April, 1707, for the lands of Shankstown and Glasnock in

---

classified as follows: Divinity and Devotional, 31; History and Biography (English and Continental) and English Literature, 14; Classics (chiefly Latin), 9; Law, 9; French, 5; Science, 4; Miscellaneous, 8. An interesting entry is "A Discourse about Trade." A few (but very few) of the titles appear in the Catalogue of Adam Smith's Library of 1781.

[1] William Smith, a Regent of Marischal College—who was connected with Adam Smith, W.S.—presented the Address of that College to the Pretender at Fetteresso on 29th December, 1715—A. and H. Tayler, *1715, The Story of the Rising*, 1936, p. 131. He had been deeply involved in the preparation and the conduct of the Rebellion. After the failure of the rising he succeeded in obtaining a protection from the Lord Advocate admitting him to bail. Adam Cockburn, Lord Justice Clerk, having received information of his many criminal acts and examined him, decided " to commit him judgeing the crimes in the information not baillable "—A. and H. Tayler, *Jacobites of Aberdeenshire*, 1934, p. 184. Eventually Smith was liberated; but was dismissed from his position as Regent.

[2] See Appendix III for the state of the Scottish Post Office at this time.

[3] These and other points of interest about this family are detailed in Appendix I.

Ayrshire, which appear to have been in reality his own property.¹ All the reports from the factor and other officials of the estate came through him. When he was in London, letters were received at least once a week and the gist of these submitted to Loudoun for approval. Much of his time must have been spent on finance. It was the practice to draw on the factor of the estate for the expenses of the London house; and, in bad seasons, it was difficult, and sometimes impossible, to meet the bills when they came due. Rents were still paid partly in kind, and meal accumulated which was unsaleable except at a serious loss. In 1711 Irish meal was sold at ½ merk Scots per peck which, according to the Ayrshire measure, would represent approximately 2s. 3d. sterling for two Imperial bushels, if heaped, or for one Imperial bushel, if " straik ".² In many cases rents could not be collected and the best that the factor could promise was that, when the Earl and his secretary came to Loudoun in the summer of 1712, they would " want neither meal nor malt as he could not get a peck sold ". The same year a " diligence " or process was threatened, so it is little wonder that, in a moment of exasperation at the drafts from London, the factor wrote " the arrears of rent dismay me mightily and make me to wish many a tyme I had broken my legs when I crossed Clyde ".

Further, being of a friendly disposition, Adam Smith carried out a great many commissions for friends upon most varied matters. For one he endeavoured to obtain a payment on account of a debt due by the Marquis of Annandale, for another to negotiate the sale of a cup belonging to the Earl of Findlater if £3 could be obtained for it. His friend, Robert Arbuthnot, one of the auditors of the Scottish Exchequer, asked him to purchase ivory and fine woods for a cabinet-maker whom he patronised, then to find a wig-maker who had on hands a peruke rejected by " sparks and beaux ", which might be secured for between 40s. and 50s. The Countess of Stair was a lady who believed in the superiority of the male judgement even in unexpected circumstances. She proposed to make " a mantie gown and a pilliecoat " for her granddaughter. The material, which was to be calico, must be chosen by James Hog, an official of the Court of Exchequer in Edinburgh and Adam Smith, who was in London for the winter, it was to be cut out by Lilias Smith in Edinburgh, and made up by a seamstress in Bath. The good lady had many perplexities before she completed this jigsaw puzzle.³

---

[1] P.R.O. : S.P. Scotland, Warrant Book, 22, p. 427 ; General Register of Sasines, Edinburgh, vol. 95, ff. 22, 32-8.

[2] R. W. Cochran-Patrick, *Mediaeval Scotland*, 1892, p. 167.

[3] These particulars are collected from the correspondence of Adam Smith, W.S., which has been found amongst the papers of the late Rev. D. D. Bannerman, D.D., now in the Library, University of Glasgow.

Such small and diversified duties were the merest interludes in the tense political drama. The private secretary was required to be in attendance on his chief during the Parliamentary session in Edinburgh, also when other duties arose, as for instance the trial of Captain Green. He accompanied him to London and effected the necessary *liaison* with the English Government offices, as required. Also, it was part of his duties to arrange the programme when his chief went on tour with the large suite which was usual in those days. It may be that what Mrs. Margaret Smith—the second wife—repeated concerning these progresses was one of the sources whence came the scathing references in *The Wealth of Nations* to the luxury of the great in this respect. For instance, on 28th March, 1707, the City of Glasgow admitted as burgesses, *gratis*, eleven of the Earl of Loudoun's party, the list of which is headed by the name of his secretary. This was far surpassed when the Duke of Argyle passed through Glasgow on 6th January, 1716, for the final operation in the crushing of the Rebellion, on which occasion thirty-five persons were admitted to the freedom.[1] If this was the time when Robert Simson, the celebrated mathematician (to whom reference will be made later in a very different connection) waited on the Duke, it affords an instance of the manner in which grave historical issues are sometimes lightened by the whimsicalities of individuals. Simson combined absentmindedness in relation to ordinary events, when his mind was intensely concentrated, with a childlike curiosity about trivialities when he was at leisure. There was a delay in his being received, the Duke being greatly engaged, and Simson began to converse with a young man " who was well looking, though plainly dressed ". He tried by every device, short of a direct question, to ascertain who the stranger might be. The other divined the simple artifice of the scholar and frustrated his enquiries. Simson, who could restrain his thirst for information no longer, made an excuse to leave the room so as to discover who his companion was. The latter caught his hand as he was moving towards the door, exclaiming, " Honest Robin, I know your errand very well. You wish to discover who I am. My name is Loudoun, at your service." [2]

An important part of Adam Smith's duties was to shape the drafts of Loudoun's official correspondence, and it is probable that the documents in the Scottish Warrant books, signed by Loudoun, were drawn up by him. Later, when Loudoun was Keeper of the Great Seal, many of these were in Latin. There is one draft which is of very great historical interest. This is an undated paper

---

[1] J. R. Anderson, ed., *Burgesses of Glasgow* (1573-1750), Scottish Records Soc., pp. 272, 316. Simson was admitted the same day, his name preceding that of the Duke of Argyle on the burgess roll.

[2] J. Ramsay, *Scotland and Scotsmen*, i, p. 278.

which describes a Jacobite plot in which Baillie was implicated and which occurred while Queensberry was Commissioner. It is not improbable that it may have been connected with the plot which goes by his name. If so, the year would be 1703. Amongst the papers of Adam Smith there are four pages representing the beginning of a narrative of the case. This is evidently the original draft, for at various stages in it, where the letters in cipher are referred to, it is said " here insert the letter ". This document consists of four pages ending in the middle of the events of 23rd December, [1703 ?].[1] Other papers relate to the ordinary routine business of the period. A number are concerned with matters of patronage, and there are several proxies for the election of Scottish representative Peers in the first Parliament after the Union.

It was one of the miscellaneous qualifications of a secretary in the years before the Union that he required to be something of a swordsman. Adam Smith was concerned with the preparation of the Scottish case during the Union debates. He became very friendly with John Clerk of Penicuik, the diarist, one of the Scottish Commissioners, and with the Hon. William Dalrymple, afterwards Earl of Stair, a Commissioner of the Equivalent.[2] It is to be expected that he met Defoe when the latter visited Scotland at this time. The statesmen who were known to be in favour of the Union were most unpopular in Edinburgh and were attacked by the mob on more than one occasion. Their officials were much more subject to violence, and several of them had narrow escapes. Nor was Edinburgh the only place where swords might be drawn. Loudoun's first colleague, as secretary, was Annandale. Argyle, then Commissioner, caused his dismissal, being unable to tolerate a manner often of extreme insolence. This had a sequel. Annandale was reported to be intriguing against the Union. He, with some friends and supporters, chanced to meet Argyle and Loudoun with their gentlemen in the vicinity of Whitehall. Argyle is said by an eyewitness to have given Annandale " very base names to his face ", adding, in a marked manner, that he was going to the fields to walk. He went accompanied by Loudoun. Annandale followed with Major Douglas, " but did not what he ought to have done ".[3]

When the Union had come into operation, the administrative problems really began. There was a whole series of these in the assimilation of the practice of the Scottish offices to that established in England. The resulting patronage created difficulties in several directions. There were new offices to be filled ; but, if there was to be administrative union, a proportion of officials trained in

[1] Glas. Univ. Libry., Bannerman MSS.   [2] See below the Will of Adam Smith, p. 131.
[3] Sir W. Fraser, *Earls of Cromartie*, i, p. 292.

English methods would be needed in Scotland. At the same time it was desirable, in view of the public feeling, to keep these as few as possible.[1] There were aspirants for posts, and those in office who considered they had earned promotion. Then as Seafield became active on behalf of his friends it was feared by those holding appointments that they might be superseded.[2]

Adam Smith was affected by these changes, though not quite in the way described. The office of Clerk of the Court Martial in Scotland was much sought after, as is shown by the efforts made in 1698 to secure the influence of Carstares for a candidate.[3] A part-time post, it was extremely well paid. Adam Smith may have acted temporarily for the last occupant, since amongst his papers there are documents dated two years before his appointment—the Commission being dated 18th April, 1707. In the previous month he had been admitted a Writer of the Signet,[4] a branch of the legal profession which is peculiar to Scotland, combining many of the duties of solicitors with those of conveyancing counsel in England and also the management of large landed estates.[5] He was able to continue as Secretary to Loudoun, who was now Keeper of the Great Seal. There is a statement in existence specifying the grants and charters which passed the Great Seal of Scotland and the fees paid (which amounted to £2813 13s. 4d. Scots) from 18th May, 1708, to 29th August, 1712, and which was drawn up by James Craig and Adam Smith.[6] Dugald Stewart states that he practised as a Solicitor in Edinburgh,[7] but it is difficult to understand how this would be possible, owing to his being in London during most of the winter. Loudoun was deprived of his office as Keeper of the Great Seal in 1713, but it was not for this reason that (as Rae suggests[8]) Adam Smith ceased to be his secretary. He continued till January or February 1714, being succeeded by his nephew, William Smith. The reason for his resignation was that he had been appointed, through the influence of Loudoun and Sir William Wyndham, Comptroller of Customs at Kirkcaldy, from 12th February, 1714.[9]

---

[1] It appears that considerable promotion was required to induce suitable men to move to Edinburgh. In the Scottish State Papers there are numerous complaints of the changed social conditions and the high cost of living—very inadequately compensated for by the low price of whisky.

[2] S.P.D., Scotland, Series II, lv.

[3] J. McCormick, ed., *Carstares State Papers*, 1774, p. 453.

[4] *Hist. Writers of H.M. Signet*, Edin., 1890, p. 187.

[5] R. B. Haldane, *Life of Adam Smith*, 1887, p. 15.

[6] Bannerman Papers, Univ. Libry. Glasg.

[7] D. Stewart, *Memoir of Adam Smith*, 1811, p. 1.

[8] Rae, *Life of Adam Smith*, p. 1.

[9] Letter from Adam Smith to Earl of Loudoun, 13th February, 1714 (Glas. Univ. Libry., Bannerman MSS.).

CHAPTER II

COURTS MARTIAL AND CUSTOMS

For about seven years after the Union Adam Smith, W.S., lived in Edinburgh, in a house in the " Old Provost's Close ", dividing his time between the various avocations already mentioned. His duties as a private secretary have already been described; those of the Clerk of Court Martial and Councils of War in Scotland, which continued till the end of his life, next call for notice—all the more since Rae was misled by the only authority that was available to him, and his statement requires modification. He relied on the *Essay on Military Law and the Practice of Courts Martial* by A. Fraser Tytler, who had been a Deputy Judge Advocate in Scotland and was later elevated to the Bench as Lord Woodhouselee in 1802. In his time, and for many years before, the two offices of Judge Advocate and Clerk were combined, and Rae believed that was so with Adam Smith, W.S.[1] More detailed information makes it quite clear that this was not so. The Commission of Adam Smith was as Clerk,[2] his will gives him this description and not that of Judge Advocate,[3] nor could he have received the latter title between the date of his will and that of his death, for when his son signed a deed in 1757 for the sale of property in Aberdeen, in which the title is recapitulated, that description remained unchanged.[4] Nor was he the first to fill this position, for his commission states that he succeeded John Dalrymple, a member of a very eminent legal family.

The origin of the office goes back to the first regular Mutiny Act of 1689, which was caused by the dissatisfaction in the Army at the favour shown by William III. to his Dutch troops, the immediate occasion being the mutiny of a Scottish regiment which was under orders for the front to replace one recruited in Holland.[5] At the Union the relation of the Scottish Clerk of the Court Martial to the Judge Advocate General was not determined. He, in fact, acted both as Clerk and as Deputy Judge Advocate. In England a Deputy Judge Advocate was always appointed. At a later date in Scotland the title of Deputy Judge Advocate was added to that of Clerk. At this early period departmental friction

---

[1] Rae, *Life of Adam Smith*, p. 1.   [2] See below, p. 129.   [3] See below, p. 130.

[4] This deed is at the Town House, Aberdeen (see below, p. 135). There is a copy amongst the Bannerman Papers (Univ. Libry. Glasg.).

[5] A. F. Tytler, *Essay on Military Law*, 1812, p. 103.

resulted. When warrants were issued for the holding of General Courts Martial at Edinburgh on 27th May, 1709, and 2nd April, 1710, the Judge Advocate General intervened and endeavoured to appoint a deputy. He applied to the Treasury on 3rd January, 1711, for authority to appoint a deputy for Scotland at the usual allowance of 10s. per day.[1] Adam Smith had very powerful friends, and he considered framing a petition to the Queen in protest against such an invasion of her commission to him.[2] He was well able to conserve his rights, and on 16th June, 1714, the warrant for holding Courts Martial was addressed to him.[3] The outbreak of the Rebellion had an effect on this controversy. The Duke of Argyle was commander-in-chief of the forces in North Britain, and, in virtue of this appointment, issued summons for Courts Martial,[4] which had the effect of cutting out the attempted interference from London. Adam Smith spent a considerable time on the duties of his office during 1716 at the Camp at Stirling.[5] From this period he seems to have had no further trouble. Meanwhile, he had been strengthening his position in other ways. He suffered from a policy of retrenchment in losing an increase in his pay which was reduced to the original 7s. 6d. a day, and that was in arrear. He was successful in securing his appointment on the staff of the Scottish Command and in having his pay secured on the establishment of guards and garrisons.[6] He also embarked on an enquiry as to the powers and emoluments of Deputy Judge Advocates in Flanders in order to obtain similar advancement.[7] The point which had arisen was that his commission applied only to the General Court Martial, in addition to which there were regimental Courts, and he was endeavouring to secure employment in these also.

The duties of this office consisted in supervising the procedure, such as reading the charges, ensuring the prisoner's right to challenge any member of the Court, directing the attention of the Court to any legal point which arose and, as sanctioned by custom, assisting the prisoner in his defence. Also the Clerk took down the whole evidence in writing, and in his report he was entitled to advert to any legal question to which due weight had not been given in the verdict of the Court.[8]

---

[1] P.R.O.—W.O., 30/88.
[2] Letter from J. Aitkine, 7th July, 1713 (Bannerman MSS., Univ. Libry. Glasg.).
[3] P.R.O.—W.O., 30/21.
[4] Warrant, 14th February, 1716 (Bannerman MSS., Univ. Libry. Glasg.).
[5] Letter from Wm. Smith, 24th December, 1715, and Adam Smith's expense-account (Bannerman MSS., Univ. Libry. Glasg.).
[6] Letter from Wm. Smith, 11th February, 1716 (Bannerman MSS., Univ. Libry. Glasg.).
[7] Letter from Wm. Smith, 24th December, 1715 (Bannerman MSS., Univ. Libry. Glasg.).
[8] A. F. Tytler, *Essay on Military Law*, 1822, pp. 255, 263.

HIS FATHER'S OFFICES

None of the reports of Adam Smith can be traced either at the Record Office or at the General Register House. Since they covered the period of the Rebellion, they might be expected to be of interest. Amongst the Bannerman papers there is the abstract of evidence in a trial on 28th January, 1709, held in the Canongate Tolbooth at Edinburgh, where the death penalty was exacted.

This aspect of the career of Adam Smith, W.S., is of special interest, since traces of it are to be found in the work of his son, Adam Smith, the economist, whose mother would, no doubt, have related to him some of the more important incidents in the life of his father. Prominence is given in the manuscript of one of the Edinburgh Lectures and also in the revision of it in *The Theory of Moral Sentiments* to the execution of a sentry who had been found asleep at his post.[1] It is easy to imagine that there had been cases of this kind in the official life of the Clerk of the Court Martial and that he had discussed these with his wife in great mental distress. These, being related to his son by the mother, impressed him sufficiently to cause him to use them as illustrations in his writings.

The Courts Martial before the Rebellion were held, usually, or always, in Edinburgh, which was convenient to Adam Smith as long as he continued to reside there. He had married, about the time the Act of Union was passed, Lilias or Lily, the eldest daughter of Sir George Drummond of Milnab, who had been Provost of Edinburgh as far back as 1683.[2] He is to be distinguished from another and more celebrated Provost of the same name who held the office six times. One son, who was called Hugh, was born of this marriage. He was baptised in Edinburgh on 2nd September, 1709.[3]

After more than six years of married life the husband wrote to the wife from London in the following terms:

Ap: 11, 1713.

My Dearest Lillie,

I have yours of the 4th. and am glad that Hew's ear runs, it will doe him good, I hope. You wryte nothing of yourself, which makes me hope that you are well, my Dearest Lillie, I heartily wish it may be so.

You wroat me formerly, my Dearest Lillie, that you had £200 goods and debts which I am very glad off—but perhaps, My Dear Lillie you doe not charge yourself with what is owing to Mr. Luen and to Mr. Garbrand, viz. to Mr.

---

[1] It occurs in one of the MSS. described in Chap. V in relation to the discussion of punishment in the general interest of society and again in *The Theory of Moral Sentiments*, 1759, p. 54.

[2] *Book of Old Edinburgh Club*, iv, pp. 3, 5-11, 20. *Memoirs of Sir J. Clerk*, 1892, p. 54.

[3] J. Bonar, *Library of Adam Smith*, 1932, pp. 207-8. It is evident the marriage contract, dated 13th November, 1710, was a post-nuptial one. Some further particulars of Sir G. Drummond of Milnab will be found in Appendix I.

Luen about £20 and to Mr. Garbrand about £7, but, be that as it will, I think, my Dearest Lillie, its very well you have so much, therefor, my Dear, doe not be uneasie, for I think you have managed extraordinarily. I wish I could manage as well. My Dearest Lillie if you'll but take care of your health you cannot disoblige me, for, I'm sure, I have nothing els to quarrell you for but want of care of yourself, for I'm affraid you are too saving of what's necessary for you, which, my Dearest Lillie, will not please me, therefore I beg of you, my Dear, not to grudge yourself whatever may be necessary for you. My Dearest Lillie I beg of you to tell me ingenuously, how you are, for I will not be easie till I know.

My Dearest Lillie, I have been all day in the City and am a little weary, but, blessed be God, am otherwise very well. My Dearest Lillie God bless and preserve you.

Dearest Lillie farewell.[1]

Early in 1714 the positions of Collector and Comptroller in the Customs at Kirkcaldy were about to become vacant, and Adam Smith's cousin Hercules Smith, who had been Collector at Montrose, was appointed to the same office at Kirkcaldy, while Adam Smith himself became Comptroller.[2] The Collector was the chief official at his port. He had to collect the duties and to account for the monies received. The Comptroller (as the name implies) was to act as a check on the Collector, and he was required to present an independent account. Since his duties were less onerous, though highly responsible, his salary was lower, being about two-thirds that of the Collector.[3] Both united in the endeavour to detect and prevent smuggling, which was rife. This " free trade " was encouraged by some of the lairds, and the record of the period is one of violence. At Prestonpans in 1699 the officers were assailed by a multitude of men and women " who did bruise and bleed them to ane admirable height ".[4] At Montrose in 1735 the Collector was unable to convey seizures without a military guard.[5] The same year at Nairn there was an affray on the beach when a young laird (who was taking part with the smugglers) was killed. The next year an attack on an excise officer resulted in the Porteous Riots in Edinburgh.[6] In order to compensate the officials for the risk they incurred in making seizures and to encourage diligence, it was

---

[1] In possession of W. R. Scott. The references to Lily Smith's financial state are interesting at a period so long prior to the Married Women's Property Act.
[2] Salary List of the Customs at Kirkcaldy, Gen. Reg. Ho., Edin.
[3] H. Hall, *History of the Customs Revenue*, 1885, ii, p. 50.
[4] R. Chambers, *Domestic Annals of Scotland*, 1861, iii, p. 215.
[5] W. D. Chester, *Chronicles of the Customs Dept.*, 1885, pp. 93-4.
[6] R. Chambers, *Domestic Annals of Scotland*, 1861, iii, pp. 589, 594-5.

HIS FATHER'S OFFICES

one of the many perquisites of Collectors and Comptrollers to receive 1s. each in the £ of the value of uncustomed goods they detected. This appears from the will of a relative by marriage of the Smiths, George Middleton, who was Comptroller at Aberdeen.[1] There were very many other fees and perquisites. This system continued into the nineteenth century when, in 1831, officials of the Customs, known as cocket writers, whose salaries were £60 a year, made an income of at least £1000.[2] About the middle of the eighteenth century there was another Adam Smith of this family who was Collector of Customs at Alloa and who was in receipt of £30 a year salary and the same amount as Collector of Salt Duty,[3] but who stated that his actual receipt from his offices was above £200 a year.[4] Yet another Adam Smith bears testimony on the subject—this time the author of *The Wealth of Nations*—when, in the course of his duties in 1782, he had occasion to report on a proposal for lowering the fees charged; and, as an argument against any drastic proposal, he urged that " the income of many officers may be so far reduced as to make it difficult for them to subsist in the society which, in reason, ought to belong to them ".[5] It was these earnings from fees which explain why it was worth Adam Smith's while to move from Edinburgh to Kirkcaldy and why he used such influence as he could command to secure the Collectorship there. Kirkcaldy stood fourth among the Scottish ports in 1691-4 in respect to the collection of customs.[6] This would affect the amount of fees received by the Collector and Comptroller. Even if his income only exceeded his nominal salary in the same proportion as that of the Collector at Alloa—and it is not improbable the excess was greater—this office would bring him in about £133 a year. As Clerk of the Court Martial his pay came to £137 5s. per annum.[7] While he had something to spend on a clerk, there were his allowances and also some extras, so that his total earnings from his offices under the Government cannot have been less than £275 a year. In Scottish currency this would be over £3000 Scots, and that is a better measure of the purchasing power of money at this time. Prices, especially in the country, were remarkably low. Hence the £ Scots was rather a large unit and the Scottish merk (*i.e.* two-thirds of a £) was commonly

---

[1] Aberdeen Testaments at Gen. Reg. House, Edin., dated 1st March, 1773.

[2] W. D. Chester, *Chronicles of the Customs Department*, London, 1885, p. 17.

[3] MS. List of Officers of the Customs and Salt Duty, 1752, Gen. Reg. House, Edin.

[4] See his letter, printed below, p. 235.

[5] P.R.O.—T.I./570. Quoted from a copy of the original, very kindly lent to me by Mr. Henry Higgs, C.B.

[6] Customs and Excise—Miscellaneous Accounts and Papers, 1691-1707, at Gen. Reg. House, Edin.

[7] Pay account, 1712-17 (Bannerman MSS., Univ. Libry. Glasg.).

used, indeed very generally for prices of estates and for marriage portions. From another point of view the position may be illustrated by a comparison with the earnings of holders of important offices. Judges, with the exception of the President of the Court of Session, the Lord Justice General and Lord Justice Clerk, received £300 sterling a year, the Solicitor of the Exchequer £200, each of the auditors of the Exchequer £150 each. Clearly, for the times, Adam Smith had attained to a large income, especially when it is considered that he was only thirty-five. In addition, his will reveals that he had quite considerable private means.[1]

Adam Smith had settled in comfort at Kirkcaldy, and had many friends amongst the Fifeshire lairds, such as James Oswald of Dunnikier, who had been Provost of Kirkcaldy, M.P. for the burgh from 1702-7 (when he voted against the Union in every division at which he was present), and from 1710-15 represented the new group of burghs in the United Parliament. Another was John Douglas of Strathenry, to whom further reference will be made in a moment. This fair prospect was clouded by the death of his wife, Lilias, between the end of 1716 and the middle of 1718.[2] In 1720 he married Margaret, a daughter of Robert Douglas, M.P., and sister of the John Douglas who has just been alluded to. As has been mentioned, the Smiths were connected with one romantic episode in Scottish history. The Douglases of Strathenry were linked with another—the imprisonment of Mary Queen of Scots at Loch Leven (which is about five miles from Strathenry) and her escape. Robert Douglas of Strathenry was a great-grandson of Sir William Douglas of Lochleven (afterwards Earl of Morton) who was the custodian of the Queen at his castle on an island of the loch. It was a great-great-grand-uncle, George, who planned the escape.[3] In this family, also, there was a tradition of good looks, the daughters of Sir William Douglas being called " the seven pearls of Loch Leven ". To anyone who cares to follow the history of the family further back, as described elsewhere,[4] it will be found that they were previously Forresters and, still earlier, " Strathenry of Strathenry "—the meaning of the name being " the King's strath ".

[1] See below, pp. 129-33, where the will is summarised. In the Bannerman Papers there is a " Statement of Adam Smith's Affairs, 1722 ". This gives his income in sterling in that year from interest in bonds, and this amounted to £137 19s. 5½d. Some addition should be made to this sum, as, for instance, the rent of his house in Aberdeen, which was £90 Scots or £7 10s. sterling. Also he was investing his savings and the income from such investments came in the next year.

[2] These dates are based on his having written to her at the earlier date when she was in Edinburgh nursing her mother, Lady Drummond, who was ill. The later one is fixed by his making a will, from which it appears he was then a widower (Bannerman MSS., Univ. Libry. Glasg.).

[3] This George is not to be confused with another George—" little Douglas "—the page who stole the keys—C. Mackie, *Castles, Palaces and Prisons of Queen Mary*, 1753, p. 362.

[4] Particulars will be found below in Appendix IV.

The second marriage did not last long, for Adam Smith died on or about 25th January, 1723,[1] and the tale will continue with the responsibilities of his widow, who survived him by more than sixty years.

[1] Customs Salary List, Kirkcaldy, for above date, Gen. Reg. House, Edin. The register of burials of the Parish Church of Kirkcaldy at this period is not extant. When the present church was built a number of old tombstones were removed, so that if the monument to Adam Smith, senior, survived to that time it may have disappeared then.

CHAPTER III

THE BOYHOOD OF ADAM SMITH

After January 1723 there is a complete change in the setting of this story. Instead of a rising young official, moving amongst great events, there is a young wife suddenly bereaved. Instead of executions by order of a Court Martial, there is the prospect of a child to engage the attention of, and in part to console, the widow. During the period of waiting, the character of Margaret Smith may be considered. From her portrait, which is in the possession of the Cunningham family,[1] it is easy to imagine that she had the beauty of her branch of the Douglases. Contemporary accounts agree that she was deeply religious. Her judgement in the affairs of life which came under her attention was sound and at the same time charitable. There could have been few better mothers for a fatherless boy.

We do not know the date of the birth of her son, who was named Adam after his father. It is clear that, unless there was a much longer interval than is usual between the birth and baptism, the former event was separated from the death of the father by fully three months. The date of the baptism was 5th June, 1723.[2] It is certain that the birth took place in Kirkcaldy, but not in the house which Adam Smith occupied with his mother after his return from France and which is illustrated in Plate X,[3] but in another house in the High Street. These facts may account for some conflict in tradition as to which were the houses in which Adam Smith lived, of which there were two. The difference is established by the report of John Callander (who had come on a visit to Kirkcaldy either from Edinburgh or Craigforth, and stayed with Adam Smith); he said that Smith " had shown him the house in which he first drew breath ".[4]

The child was delicate, and the mother had a hard task in rearing him. She had also a part in conjunction with the trustees in the education of her stepson

---

[1] There is a photogravure of this painting at p. xxii of Dr. Bonar's *Library of Adam Smith*, second edition, 1932.

[2] The certificate of baptism is printed in *ibid*. p. 208.

[3] This house was pulled down in 1834, not 1844, as is stated on a plaque placed on the wall of the bank which was erected on the site. Much of the garden at the back remains exactly as it was in Adam Smith's time.

[4] Edinburgh University MSS., La II, 451/2.

HIS BOYHOOD

Hugh, who in 1724 was at a boarding school in Perth kept by John Martin. Later in that year he was ill, as is shown by a correspondence between two of his curators, William Walker and James Oswald. The former speaks of his being in " a very dangerous condition ",[1] and he was under the care of Dr. Clerk, who had been a friend of his father and who was the most distinguished physician in Edinburgh of his time.[2] It may be guessed that Hugh Smith had very imperfect health. There is no further information concerning him until his half-brother became his heir in 1750. Since in these proceedings there is no mention of his having an occupation, it may perhaps be inferred that weak health prevented him from taking an active part in life. His master testified that " he profited right well at his books ". It may possibly be conjectured that he suffered from some form of pulmonary complaint, since William Walker was of opinion that " Kirkcaldy was not a fitt place for one of his distemper being so much exposed to the sea aire, but rather inclyne he should be sent to the country ".

Before Adam Smith was two years old he was declared nearest heir of provision, that is, of his share of the moveable property, of his father. To the practice of the present day this appears strange, but reference to the authorities quoted below will show that this was strictly in accordance with the law of the period.[3] Though the salary of Adam Smith, W.S., and, more important, his fees and commissions had come to an end, as will be seen,[4] he had considerable private means. Under Scots law Adam Smith, the son, and his mother were well provided for, though this might not be the impression derived from the reading of the will of Adam Smith, W.S.[5] Under Scots law of the time, Hugh inherited the property at Aberdeen as heir ; this, however, formed only a small proportion of the value of the total. Of the remainder, the widow was entitled to one-third and the two children to another third divided equally, while the will affected the remaining third,[6] which was devised to the elder son, Hugh. There are two modifications which may have operated in different directions. There was a marriage contract dated 17th November, 1720, and under it (which is safeguarded in the will) the position of the widow and her child may have been secured beyond the respective legal rights of each. On the other hand, it will appear from the will of Adam Smith, W.S., that the greater part of his estate consisted of bonds (or mortgages) on landed property bearing interest, and these, subject to certain exceptions, were

---

[1] Letters of John Martin and William Smith—Bannerman MSS., Univ. Libry. Glas. The duties of tutors and curators in Scots Law at this period are detailed in *The Tutor's Guide, relating to Pupils and Minors and their Tutors and Curators*, Edin. 1714.

[2] See below, p. 131 note [5].   [3] See below, p. 133.
[4] See above, p. 18 note [1], and below, p. 131.   [5] See below, p. 130.
[6] Stair, *Institutions of the Law of Scotland*, viii, § 52 ; *cf.* Adam Smith, *Glasgow Lectures*, p. 87.

not included in the computation of the estate of which the widow was entitled to one-third; but against this, the position of Margaret Smith was subject to the provisions of her marriage contract, which is not available.[1] It is rather significant that Adam Smith himself draws attention to this provision of Scots law. Considering the very great purchasing power of money at the period, it is plain that there were ample funds to educate him well and also to give him a start in life, if as is possible, but not certain, only a modest one. No time was lost in protecting the interests of the two children, for, on 21st February, 1723, two of the tutors and curators (or trustees) appeared through their lawyer, at the Burgh Court of Kirkcaldy, in order to have their appointment of James Oswald of Dunnikier, as factor or agent, registered in the books of that Court.[2] He did not survive to execute this duty for a long period. His descendants have no record of the date of his death, but it is known that his eldest son, also named James, who had a distinguished political career, lost his father in childhood.[3] Since he was born in 1715 it is evident the father cannot have lived long after 1723. In the thirties another Adam Smith, a nephew of the testator [4] and who was Collector of Customs at Kirkcaldy and later Inspector of Customs at the Outports, was acting on behalf of Adam Smith.[5]

Margaret Smith was in the habit of visiting her brother at Strathenry and her sisters, who were married to Fife lairds, one being the wife of David Skene of Pitlour. It was through one of these expeditions, when Adam Smith was about three years old, that the incident (which everyone who has read his life remembers) occurred. Dugald Stewart gives his authority as George Drysdale. He was a son of John Drysdale, who was the minister of Kirkcaldy and who died four years after Adam Smith, W.S. His sons and the boy, Adam, were educated together, and they remained friends through life. Adam Smith was particularly intimate with one of them, John Drysdale, Minister of the Tron Kirk, who was Moderator of the General Assembly in 1773. It is an interesting fact that the Tullis family, which purchased Strathenry from the Douglases, is descended, on the female side, from John Drysdale of Kirkcaldy and that they have fuller details and, in one part of the tale, a variation which is of interest and may be of some importance.

---

[1] Stair, *Institutions of the Law of Scotland*, viii, § 47. If Adam Smith is correctly reported in the *Glasgow Lectures* he states (p. 87) that bonds " go to the children ", which may have been so in his own case.

[2] " Factory " of above date by John Douglas and Archibald Arnot in favour of James Oswald, kindly extracted for me by Mr. William Hutton, Town Clerk, Kirkcaldy.

[3] *Memorials of the Rt. Hon. James Oswald*, Edin., 1825, p. xvi.

[4] Executry Account of William Smith for Mrs. Margaret Smith, 1735, Bannerman MSS., Univ. Glasg. Libry.   [5] See below, p. 133.

HIS BOYHOOD

To form a picture of what happened it is necessary to refer to some points connected with the place. The two views of Strathenry Castle (Plate I) give a fair idea of the old home of the family. In 1726 it was either unoccupied or used as the residence of a younger member of the family. On lower ground, a little over 100 yds. in a straight line, there is the mansion house which was built by Margaret Smith's father. The ground between the two buildings is planted with old trees, and there are two avenues, one of which is approximately 250 paces from the front door of Strathenry House to the Castle. Taking the shorter avenue, known as the " back avenue " at a distance of 70 paces from the Castle, there is a large rectangular stone, now standing about two feet above the ground. At present it is completely concealed by a very old yew. According to the tradition it was from this place that the child was carried by the tinklers or gypsies and not from the door of the house.[1] Considering the circumstances on the spot one feels the essential rightness of this account. If in 1726 the yew was comparatively young, the child had his little sylvan house and his table.

The tinklers were a lower type than the gypsies proper,[2] and they were two of several classes of the vagabonds of the period which constituted a most serious social problem. Andrew Fletcher of Saltoun, writing in 1698, said : " There are at this day in Scotland . . . two hundred thousand people begging from door to door. . . . And though the number of them be perhaps double of what it was formerly, by reason of this present great distress, yet in all times there have been about one hundred thousand of these vagabonds, who have lived without any regard or subjection either to the laws of the land, or even those of God and nature ; fathers incestuously accompanying with their own daughters, the son with the mother, and the brother with the sister. . . . Many murders have been discovered among them ; and they are not only a most unspeakable oppression to poor tenants (who, if they give not bread or some kind of provision to perhaps forty such villains in one day, are sure to be insulted by them), but they rob many poor people who live in houses distant from any neighbourhood." [3] Nor was the threat of Meg Merrilies in *Guy Mannering*, " we'll see if the red cock will craw not in his bonnie barn yard ae morning before day dawning ", an idle one, since in 1714 a country house at Greenhead in Roxburgh was fired by the band of Patrick Faa or Faw.[4]

---

[1] Mr. Douglas Clephane—the representative of the Douglases of Strathenry—confirms this form of the tradition.

[2] Andrew McCormick, *Tinkler-Gypsies*, Dumfries, 1907, p. 314.

[3] Andrew Fletcher, *Political Works*, Lond., 1732, pp. 144-5.

[4] William Chambers, *Exploits and Anecdotes of Scottish Gypsies*, Edin., 1886, p. 14.

While the lawless character of the roving bands is vividly attested by the judicial records of the time, it is not at first sight apparent why they should kidnap children, since they had the reputation of being remarkably fertile, and such a theft would seem to be merely adding to a number of useless followers which was already too large.[1] Possibly the reason of the kidnapping may have been for the value of the child's clothes, though in the country at this period, except on festive occasions, members of landed families were very plainly dressed. How little gypsies cared about the subsequent fate of the boy is shown by that of Peter Douglas, aged eleven, whose head was dashed against a tree by a tinkler whom he had seen stealing potatoes. This was as late as 1784.[2] To a less degree such instances may have been of the nature of reprisals against the legislation which subjected anyone, proved to be a gypsy, to transportation. The change from toleration, and even favour, to banishment is said to be founded on an incident in the life of James V. He sometimes came to know some of his people by assuming the disguise of a gaberlunzie-man or beggar. Not far from Wemyss, which is about eight miles from Strathenry, he was seized by gypsies and was compelled to carry their baggage on his back for several miles.[3]

When Adam Smith was caught by a tinkler woman at his stone and his cries stifled in her plaid or shawl, it would be easy for her to escape with her burden through the trees. The phrase " he was soon missed " is liable to mislead, if the reader infers that in a short time the boy was recovered. It may have been from George Drysdale that Stewart obtained the account of the gypsies being overtaken in Leslie wood. This seems improbable. It was distant only two miles from Strathenry and was watched by the servants of the Countess of Rothes. On the whole it was an unlikely place either for an encampment or a temporary harbourage. At that period gypsies were more numerous and daring than would be expected were it not for definite evidence as to the facts. They formed bands of considerable size. At Keith in 1700 it required sixty " stout fellows " to effect the arrest of the leader and some of his followers who were charged with " stealing sheep, oxen and horses, breaking into houses and taking away goods, robbing men of their purses and oppressing many poor people ". It was an added offence that they spent whole nights in dancing and debauchery, and they spoke a peculiar

---

[1] Walter Simson, *History of the Gypsies*, 1865, p. 258, in whose account, however, there is no sufficient distinction made between births and surviving children.

[2] Andrew McCormick, *Tinkler-Gypsies*, 1907, pp. 135, 139.

[3] Alexander Simson, *History of the Gypsies*, 1865, pp. 104, 105. The sequence of events is subject to some doubt; *cf.* D. MacRitchie, *Scottish Gypsies under the Stewarts*, Edin., 1894, p. 36; *Gypsy Lore Soc. Journal*, i, pp. 244, 245.

PLATE I. 1. STRATHENRY CASTLE
(From an old etching in A. H. Miller's *Fife, Pictorial and Historical*, 1895, ii, p. 80.)

2. AS AT THE PRESENT TIME
(From a photograph supplied by Mr. Tullis, the proprietor. The extension at the back is an addition.)

language.[1] There was a gypsy encampment at a place near Kirkcaldy called " John Marshall's Loan ". From this a well-marked pathway, known as the " Gypsy Way ", ran in a northerly direction and passed over the hill near Strathenry. It shows the permanence of the customs of this strange people that " the Way " is still in use. It is an open question whether the gypsy who carried off Adam Smith escaped by this path, as the tradition in the district asserts, or whether, instead of going south by it, she broke in an easterly direction towards Leslie wood, as Dugald Stewart was informed by George Drysdale. In that case it would be easy for a person carrying a child to escape from the vicinity of the houses. The Gypsy Way is in view for about two hundred yards from the bartizan of the Castle. In any case some time elapsed before Margaret Smith's brother could be summoned and he in turn could gather help, since the gypsies were frequently in moderate numbers. For these reasons according to some traditions the child was an appreciable time in the custody of his captors. It is this part of the episode which is of real importance. While the actual abduction would, almost certainly, disappear from the memory of Adam Smith as new impressions and experiences were superimposed upon it, there can be little doubt that the shock and, more especially, the constraint would remain deeply impressed on his sub-conscious mind, and this would engender an attitude which would be antipathetic to any enforced compliance and receptive to everything that was in the direction of freedom. It is, as the vision of a poet saw some such situation, that

> thought,
> Some buried feeling's ghost, a spirit pale,
> Sprang up.[2]

It is not intended to suggest that the origin of the doctrine of Free Trade is to be found in this episode. It must be recognised that the nurture of genius is one of the most intricate and subtle happenings and there are rarely sufficient data to explain it satisfactorily. Nevertheless, this is all the more reason to accept with gratitude such hints as it is possible to glean. The event described has its own place in making Adam Smith receptive of any light that came to him in later years both from his reading and his reflection.

In the very scanty records of these early years there are two strong hints of the man that Adam Smith was to be. He was noted, even then, for a disposition

---

[1] R. Chambers, *Domestic Annals of Scotland*, 1861, iii, pp. 233-7. The leader of this band is said to have been a natural son of a gentleman by a gypsy mother and went by the name of Macpherson. He went gaily to his execution, playing a death march which he had composed. This was the subject of an ode by Burns.

[2] Coventry Patmore, *Tamerton Church Tower and other Poems*.

which was, to an uncommon degree, friendly and generous.[1] These qualities were manifested all through his life and they broadened as the circle of those who came under their influence widened. As will be seen, on many occasions he had the gift of thinking the best of the persons with whom he came in contact, even when to most it would be difficult if not impossible. While it was true that he was generous with money, this was not as great a virtue as it is with most, for his wants in relation to his means were comparatively modest. But to see the real merit of men who must have often been irritating in the extreme was a quality of a very much higher order. Also, his habit of absence of mind and of speaking to himself—in reality letting his thought, quite naturally and unconsciously, find outward expression—is an early sign of his intense powers of concentration.

If one endeavours to get behind the very condensed account of Dugald Stewart, it may be guessed that his health gave his mother anxiety not only in childhood but while he was a boy. He may, for this reason, have been somewhat late in going to school. When he was sent to that at Kirkcaldy, the headmaster of which was probably connected with Mrs. Smith, since it is likely that one of her sisters was married to Henry Miller of Pourin, a brother or a cousin of the schoolmaster, he made rapid progress, the extent and accuracy of his memory being noted. The school buildings still exist, but they have been converted into a store, which is continued on one of the two playgrounds. It appears from a reconstruction of the internal arrangements that there were two class-rooms, each capable of containing classes of about thirty boys (Plate II). Rae gives an excellent and picturesque account of the years, extending from about 1731 or 1732 to 1737,[2] which Adam Smith spent there.

Kirkcaldy with its neighbourhood was not an unfavourable district in which the young Adam Smith could gather impressions. Though its population was small—it is said to have been about 1500 at this time—it had an extensive commerce, and the shipping berthed close to the houses. Thus it differed from an inland town of the same size in having contact with the outer world. We may be sure that Adam Smith loved the sea, for when he returned to his native place he chose a house with a garden opening on to the beach, and a part of the cliff is still shown, which is known as " Adam Smith's Seat ", where he was wont to sit looking over the Firth. Also there were specimens of the industries of the period. These included the collieries and salt-pans near, and a nailery, though his knowledge of the last industry would be developed most from the village at

---

[1] D. Stewart, *Biographical Memoirs of Adam Smith*, 1811, p. 6.
[2] Rae, *Life of Adam Smith*, pp. 5-7.

PLATE II. KIRKCALDY BURGH SCHOOL
(Where Adam Smith was educated, erected by the Town Council in 1725, closed, as a school, in 1843, now used as a store.)

HIS BOYHOOD

Dunnikier which at that time specialised in nail-making. This estate belonged to his great friend, James Oswald, who was still a minor, and there can be little doubt that the boys often went there, since it was within easy walking distance of Kirkcaldy. There were two of these villages adjoining each other, the one called Pathhead (which belonged to the Oswalds) and the other Sinclairtown, which was on the Dysart Estate. The nailers in the former carried on their daily work under the shadow of Ravenscraig Castle. Scrap iron was brought cheaply from the Continent and coal was almost at their doors. In Adam Smith's time the nail-makers had almost a monopoly of the trade with Edinburgh, Glasgow and the North of Scotland. They had their own customs. One of these, which is on record, is that of the funeral of a member of the craft. The sexton rang a hand-bell through the streets of the town, which was the warning for everyone to be ready for the nailers' box which was presented for offerings at the next warning bell. The men who followed the coffin marched in nightcaps and leather aprons.[1] Then, again, the visits which he made with his mother, or later alone to relatives, who were Fifeshire lairds, would familiarise him with agriculture. Indeed, *The Wealth of Nations* contains several little vignettes based on these early impressions which were amplified by later visits. The life was a very simple one. Such a property would consist of farms let to tenants and another portion which, as a rule, was farmed by the laird and his family. It is from a comparison of these medium-sized properties with the great estates, which he visited later, that he records a more favourable opinion of the former.[2]

[1] A. S. Cunningham, *Dysart, Past and Present, Pathhead, Sinclairtown and Gallatown*, Leven, 1912, pp. 86-7 ; see also below, p. 333 note [2].

[2] *Glasgow Lectures*, p. 229 ; *Wealth of Nations* (ed. Cannan), i, p. 363.

CHAPTER IV

ADAM SMITH AS A STUDENT AT GLASGOW AND BALLIOL

Adam Smith was late in going to the University. In the first half of the eighteenth century it was usual for youths to be entered at eleven or twelve years of age.[1] He was fourteen when he matriculated at Glasgow in November 1737.

It has been taken for granted that the reason which led his guardians to select Glasgow was the institution of the valuable Snell Exhibitions, which at that time were worth £40 a year, tenable at Balliol College, Oxford. In view of the high purchasing power of money at the period, this was a very valuable scholarship, being four or five times as great as most others of the time. There is, however, another consideration to be taken into account. The boy was most precious to his mother. He was far from strong, and it is certain that no academic prospects would induce her to sanction arrangements for him unless she was sure he would be well looked after. St. Andrews was near. There were still some of his father's friends at Edinburgh, and there were relatives at Aberdeen or near it. It turns out that he had connections at Glasgow also. There is reference to an aunt Jane, at a later date.[2] If, as may well have been the case, this lady was living in Glasgow in 1737, it would relieve the mind of Margaret Smith; and, the care of the boy being secure, the possibilities of a Snell Exhibition in the future may have been the determining factor in favour of Glasgow.

At this time a student's board and lodging were provided in several ways, and the cost varied according to the particular type selected. In the College there were chambers which were let to undergraduates, the usual rate being £1 sterling a year. In the previous century there had been a " common table " for meals, but this had been discontinued. Another method was for the student to live in lodgings. Thirty years after Adam Smith's time (when prices in Glasgow were considerably higher), the rent was as low as 1s. a week.[3] For those who had to be very economical it was usual to bring with them a supply of food, of which

---

[1] John Gibson, *History of Glasgow*, 1777, p. 193. Owing to the system of matriculation at the period, it has been thought by some that Adam Smith attended the University earlier than 1737. Elsewhere (see below, p. 33) reasons, which seem to be conclusive, are given for believing that 1737-38 was his first session. He came to Glasgow early in October for the beginning of lectures which commenced about the 10th of the month.

[2] See below, p. 235.   [3] J. Gibson, *History of Glasgow*, 1777, p. 195.

oatmeal or pease-meal formed the greater part, and it will be found later that Adam Smith, as a Professor, was involved in negotiations relating to special arrangements by which such supplies of meal for students were admitted into the city free of the local duties, to which they would otherwise have been liable.[1] On this basis it was possible to obtain a University education at an expenditure in cash of as little as about £5 sterling a year. The demand for rooms in College was declining owing to the desire of parents that such young students should live with a family, either known to them or recommended. Many of the Professors took charge of undergraduates in this way, boarding them in their houses and supervising their studies. Several of the early Snell Exhibitioners were selected from this group. For older students arrangements could be made for their living in boarding-houses which were often run by someone with a University connection —as for instance Mrs. Lindesay, the widow of a Professor, the rate for full board varying from 4s. to 10s. per week. The figures given by Adam Smith himself more than twenty years later are only a little higher, namely, £5 to £8 a quarter ; and, in the house of a Professor £10 per quarter. The expenses of the sons of a baronet and of a rich nobleman are estimated in the one case and detailed in the other also by him.[2] It is curious that no tradition has been preserved of how Adam Smith was established at Glasgow. In view of what has been said, it seems probable that he lived with the family of a relative or else that relative may have arranged for him to live with some Professor whose wife she knew would take good care of him. In the latter case his education would not be nearly so cheap as the earlier figures quoted. The fee for each University class was paid separately. Adam Smith was earnest and would take as many as he could find time for. It may be estimated that, during the three years he was at Glasgow, he attended eight. The cost of these would average rather less than £3 10s. a year.[3] The remainder of his outlay would be his living expenses, according to the method by which these were arranged. There are particulars of the average cost of the University session two years before Adam Smith matriculated. These relate to Robert Findlay, who was later Professor of Divinity and who is remembered on very diverse grounds. His course of lectures extended over no less than seventeen sessions, so that it would have been possible for a student to have heard the beginning of it, to have married and his son would have been ready for the end. Findlay wrote against Voltaire and he had a controversy with Dr. Alexander Geddes concerning the Clementine Octateuch, an early MS. of the Septuagint which was acquired for the Glasgow University Library during the period while

[1] See below, p. 163.   [2] See below, pp. 240-248.
[3] The " public " (or ordinary) classes cost £1 10s. 0d. ; the " private " (or advanced) classes, £1.

Adam Smith was a Professor.[1] Findlay's expenses for board were £25 Scots a quarter. With his fees and other charges his total outlay for the Arts session would not have exceeded £10 sterling.[2] Nearly a century after Adam Smith's time, when prices had risen greatly, the average outlay for the academic year was stated by Principal Macfarlane to have been about £20 for the poorer class of students.[3] This was higher than the average rate at St. Andrews from 1819-27. The itemised accounts of Duncan Dewar for these years show that he paid all his expenses, travelling, fees, lodgings, food, clothes, books, writing materials, luxuries and amusements at a trifle over £14 per session.[4] Food was very cheap, costing less than 6d. a day. On the other hand, he spent so large a proportion on books—11 per cent. of his outlay—that he deserves to have a statue erected in his honour by publishers, having devoted a percentage of his resources to book-buying which far exceeds the highest estimate of which they dream as an ideal. To a Glasgow student, who availed himself of the class libraries, so large an expenditure, under this head, would not be necessary. It is small wonder that Adam Smith found the fees and expenses at Balliol " were extraordinary and most extravagant ".[5]

It may seem something of a paradox to say that the attempt to recapture the impression made on the mind of Adam Smith by his coming to Glasgow will be easier for one who has never seen the modern city. It is better to think of Oxford or Cambridge in the nineteenth century, or of St. Andrews or of Heidelberg. Even so there was a difference. Like these the University was a distinct corporate entity with its privileges and powers distinct from those of the town. Like St. Andrews it stood almost in the shelter of a cathedral, though one which was unruined. The difference was in a quickening commercial life, which was rising, insistent and full of vigour, but, as yet, with no clear vision of where it was tending. It must have been a great change from Kirkcaldy to a city with a population which was ten times as great. Nearly every traveller who visited Glasgow in the seventeenth and the early part of the eighteenth century was impressed with the advantages of the situation, the beautiful views, the clearness of the air, the wide streets and the fine buildings. The University—or as it was generally called, " the College "—was outside the town. The nearest important

[1] H. M. B. Reid, *Divinity Professors in Univ. Glasg.*, 1923, pp. 271-84.

[2] J. Strang, *Glasgow and its Clubs*, 1857, pp. 303-4 (note). Strang evidently had a report of two different sessions, one of which is that quoted in the text. In the other—the last—his bill for board was £1 1s. sterling a month.

[3] *University Commission of 1826* (*Glasgow*), ii, p. 167.

[4] Sir P. R. Scott Lang, ed., *Duncan Dewar*, Glasgow, 1926, pp. 2-45, 108.

[5] See below, p. 232.

PLATE III. THE OLD COLLEGE FROM THE NORTH-EAST IN 1762.

The spectator stands on a hill, from which the ground slopes down to the Molendinar Burn. From it there is an ascent on which was the Great Garden of the College. Its tower is in the middle of the line of spires. The observatory is the building on the left with a low tower or dome.

(From an impression, picked by Foulis as being the best, and now at the Mitchell Library, Glasgow.)

buildings were the houses in the Drygate, several of which were the residences of local magnates, such as that of the Duke of Montrose. The sole survivor of these homes of the period is "Provand's Lordship", near the Cathedral.[1] The general appearance of the College and its surroundings can be gathered from Plates III and IV. In looking at these it has to be remembered that the second view—that of Captain Slezer which appeared in his *Theatrum Scotiæ*, first issued in 1693 with 67 other prints—was probably prepared earlier, since he had also engraved plates for two other somewhat similar volumes.[2] Thus there were several changes by the time Adam Smith became a student. The chief of these were the building of the Lion and Unicorn stair in the Outer Court (Plate VIIIa), the Professors' Court (Plate VIIIb) and the Library which was still in process of construction, though the needs of students for books were fairly well served by the Class Libraries and by the old University Library.

Napoleon is credited with the saying that in war the *morale* is to the material as ten to one. If this is so in an army, the proportion must be many times greater in an institution such as a university. When Adam Smith came to Glasgow there were intellectual influences there which proved exceedingly stimulating, not only to him but also to the youth of Scotland. Francis Hutcheson, who was just midway in his tenure of the Chair of Moral Philosophy when Adam Smith was his student, was undoubtedly a very great and a most stimulating teacher. Almost every one of his contemporaries, even when they did not agree with him, acknowledged his influence on the minds and character of the young. It is evident that there was something in his personality that had both power and appeal, which was incommunicable to the printed words of his writings. It was this which made him—as Adam Smith said many years afterwards—" the never-to-be-forgotten "—rather than the examples which are mentioned of his contribution to the academic life of his time (such as the introduction of lectures in English, in place of the prevailing Latin " dictates "), and his having been prominent in the revival of a zeal for Classical learning in Scotland. According to one of his students, to hear him on Cicero's philosophical writings " was a rich literary feast, for he was a more complete master of the Roman Classics and History than anyone at Glasgow ".[3] Alexander Dunlop, the Professor of Greek, participated

---

[1] T. Lugton, *Old Ludgings of Glasgow*, 1901, pp. 26-47.

[2] *Calendar Laing MSS.*, University of Edinburgh, ii (1925), p. 6.

[3] Dr. Wodrow of Stevenston in Lord Buchan's Correspondence (Glas. Univ. Libry.), ii, ff. 77, 137 ; *cf.* D. Murray, *Old College of Glasgow*, 1927, pp. 144, 515 ; W. R. Scott, *Francis Hutcheson*, 1900, pp. 61-77. It is perhaps a small point ; but, in its own way, characteristic that in 1733 Hutcheson presented to the Greek Class Library Froben's 1547 edition of Aristophanes, as is attested by an inscription of A. Dunlop. This volume is now in the University Library.

energetically with Hutcheson in this development. It was currently reported that these two managed all the affairs of the University [1]—certainly Dunlop was one of the Professors who projected and carried out the building of the Professors' Court.[2] There was also Robert Simson, who has a place in the history of Mathematics by his restoration of Greek Geometry.[3] He acted for many years as Clerk of the Senatus. Outside these activities, he was by nature a " clubable " man, and was a regular attendant at the meetings of all those which met for purposes of discussion on literary subjects.[4] John Loudon, first Regent, and later Professor of Logic, was distinguished as a student and seems to have been a good teacher, but he was indisposed to publish anything. Another of the Professors of this period was notable, but in a very different manner. This was John Simson, the Professor of Divinity. He had been before the General Assembly on a charge of heresy and was interdicted both from the discharge of ministerial functions and from teaching.[5] The University, however, refused to carry out the verdict of the Assembly to its logical conclusion and continued him in his Chair; indeed it was rumoured that, if Simson were deposed, a layman would be appointed as his successor.[6]

It was amongst such scenes and under these scholars that Adam Smith began his life as " bejan "[7] or first-year student. The opening of the session 1737-8 proceeded according to traditional form, which was put in writing at a later date. " On the 10th of October every year the Principal, the Professors of Physics, Ethics, Logic, Greek and Latin meet in the Faculty room at a quarter before eleven o'clock before noon, salute and shake hands. At eleven o'clock the little bell rings for each of the five gown classes, and each of the said Professors goes to his classroom, and names a censor, the hours of teaching and the books to be read. At quarter past 11 o'clock, the great bell rings, the Principal, the said Professors and the students go to the Common Hall, where the students are placed in their seats, a prayer is said *in English*, the general censor and the orator are appointed, the class censors are renamed, the Common Hall hours are published, together with such laws as the younger students are most apt to transgress; and, after prayer, all are dismissed. From the Common Hall the Principal and

[1] A. Carlyle, *Autobiography*, 1860, p. 71.
[2] See below, Appendix V.
[3] Lord Brougham, *English Men of Letters*, 1845, i, pp. 489-95.
[4] John Strang, *Glasgow and its Clubs*, 1857, pp. 2, 19; R. Duncan, *Literary History of Glasgow*, Glasgow, 1831 (Maitland Club), pp. 13, 120-1, 131-2.
[5] H. M. B. Reid, *Divinity Professors of Univ. of Glasg.*, Glasgow, 1923, pp. 207-34.
[6] Lord Buchan's Correspondence (Univ. Glasg. Libry.), ii, f. 161.
[7] I.e., *bijaune, bec jaune* or " yellow-neb "—D. Murray, *Old College*, 1927, p. 21.

PLATE IV. THE COLLEGE OR UNIVERSITY OF GLASGOW, *circ.* 1693

(From the original print by Slezer, reproduced from an impression at the Mitchell Library, Glasgow.)

AS A STUDENT

the said Professors return to the Faculty Room where there is the *Poculum Caritatis*, et *Resurgat in gloria, Alma Mater*—Q.F.F.Q.S." [1]

The curriculum for an arts degree extended over three years, but required five or six years if a student had not a moderate knowledge of Latin and Greek. For one who came well prepared it was necessary to pass the prescribed examinations in these subjects and to show that he was able to profit by the class of Logic which was that in which Adam Smith entered. At the end of his first year he became acquainted with the celebrated Black Stone Chair. This was a slab of black marble which goes back to the very early days of the University and the symbolism of which is unknown. About the time of Queen Anne, the original mounting having become greatly decayed, a new and very elaborate one was made, as may be gathered from the photograph of the chair in Plate V.[2] At the end of the session the student to be examined was conducted to it with a certain amount of ceremony by the bedellus, who turned over the sand-glass at the top. As long as the sand ran, the candidate was questioned by the Professor of the class he had attended, as to his knowledge of the work, and also by the Professor of the further class which he hoped to enter in the next session. Adam Smith began in Logic; the next class might be either Moral Philosophy or Natural Philosophy at his own choice. Having shown that he knew sufficient Logic, if he was proceeding to Moral Philosophy, he was examined in Greek; if proceeding to Natural Philosophy, in Mathematics.

There are a few traces of Adam Smith as an undergraduate at Glasgow, some of them of considerable interest. Being well advanced in Latin, it is probable he did not attend the public class, which was for beginners, but he may have taken the private or advanced class. Greek he certainly attended, for there is a copy of the *Encheiridion* of Epictetus, published at London and Cambridge in 1670, in the University Library at Glasgow, which has, besides the book-plate, his signature written on the fly-leaf in the same round schoolboy hand with which he signed the matriculation roll (see Plate, p. 364). It is evident the binding at the back (it is now in old half vellum) had become broken, and he again wrote his name in the inner part of a page, so that it is almost concealed in the newer

---

[1] From a printed notice, dated 1802, amongst miscellaneous notices in the office of the Clerk of Faculties. The words " in English " after the reference to the opening prayer have been added by hand. At the present time the opening prayer at Graduations is in Latin. The following is the explanation of the terms used : " the gown classes " (or those of the " togati " because it was at these that gowns were compulsory) were those for the M.A. degree, the censor took the attendances, the hours of the Common Hall related to meetings for discipline. The non-gown classes opened later in the year.

[2] All the inscriptions and many interesting particulars are given by the late Dr. David Murray in *The Old College*, 1927, pp. 88-91.

binding. What is worthy of note is that the " *Tabula* " of Cebes, which (as usual) is annexed to the *Encheiridion*, has in the margin a number of marks in old red pencil resembling stars. Now the *Tabula* was one of the text-books which was used by Dunlop in the Greek class,[1] and Dr. Cunningham, the University Librarian, has satisfied himself that the red stars are Adam Smith's marks of the passages which were prescribed for a day's reading in class. In addition two words of the text have been stroked out where, apparently, Dunlop had proposed an emendation which Adam Smith had not caught. A College friend, Dr. Archibald Maclaine, Minister of the Scottish Church at the Hague,[2] told Dugald Stewart that Adam Smith's favourite pursuits at the University were Mathematics and Natural Philosophy, and Dugald Stewart himself remembered his father, who was Professor of Mathematics at Edinburgh, discussing a particular problem which had been proposed to Adam Smith by Simson when their acquaintance began.[3] The interest in Physics is borne out by several of the posthumous *Essays*. At the same time this report contains a certain want of perspective. It is no doubt due to Maclaine coming in contact with Adam Smith when both were in the Natural Philosophy class, at which period it would be likely that he was concentrating on that subject. This is quite different from saying that Physics was the chief interest all through his course. Indeed, the terms in which he spoke of Hutcheson show the impression which had been made on him by the teacher, and there is also evidence that the subject had a very special interest for him. Grotius was a tradition in the Moral Philosophy Class,[4] and in its library there were a number of duplicate copies of his chief works. Amongst these there is one, on the end-paper of which the signature of Adam Smith is to be found. This is a fact of no little significance, for it shows that before he was seventeen he had some acquaintance with the conception of Natural Law. Another connection between Adam Smith and the Moral Philosophy Class, which was long thought might exist, has been proved by a discovery made by Mr. J. M. Keynes to rest on a false identification. In 1740—the last year Adam Smith was at Glasgow—Hume wrote to Hutcheson saying that his bookseller had sent " Mr. Smith " a copy of his *Treatise of Human Nature* and wishing to know what Mr. Smith " had done with the abstract ". Mr. Keynes has evidence to prove that the Christian name of the

[1] D. Murray, *R. and A. Foulis*, Glasgow, 1913, p. 17.

[2] W. I. Addison, *Matriculation Albums*, 1913, p. 22. Maclaine was an example of how a man may be fated to play many parts and have strange contacts. His brother was James Maclaine, " the gentleman highwayman " ; Archibald was tutor to the Prince of Orange and translated Mosheim's *Ecclesiastical History*.

[3] D. Stewart, *Memoir of Adam Smith*, 1811, p. 6.

[4] D. Murray, *The Old College*, 1927, p. 508.

PLATE V. THE BLACK STONE CHAIR
(From a photograph taken in the Old College.)

person mentioned was not Adam.[1] It is strange that as one point of contact is lost, the possibility of another appears. There has been found amongst the papers of Adam Smith an essay which may be one that he wrote when he was a student in Hutcheson's class. It certainly belongs to that period, as is plain from internal evidence. It is named an "Enquiry into the Laws which govern the Conduct of Individuals in Society".[2] It consists of 36 pages folio, and had apparently been submitted as a class essay, since there are occasional marks of correction.[3] It is clear that it was written under the strong influence of Hutcheson, as is shown by its beginning with an exposition of the moral sense. There is no trace of the ethical theory, which Adam Smith developed later; indeed, even if he is the author, this could not be expected when he had not yet reached the age of seventeen. What, to some extent, suggests Adam Smith is the space and attention which are given to the practical effects of theory rather than to the theory itself, such as rewards and punishments and the laws of nature in regard to society. The reason for some hesitation in accepting the attribution of it to Adam Smith which the circumstances of its discovery would seem to make inevitable, is that there is a doubt about the handwriting. It seems much too good to be his, and it differs from any that we have remaining except, to some extent, the letter which he wrote on 24th August, 1740, to his tutor and curator, William Smith.[4] The manuscript of that letter shows that, on a special occasion, he could write much more neatly and in what is in fact a different style. Again, the essay might be of Adam Smith's composition, but he may have employed an amanuensis to make a fair copy of what he himself had written. It has been said elsewhere that, in addition to Adam Smith's being a beau in his books, he was a positive dandy in his writing-paper.[5] When he could get it, he always used the best, which was a thick handmade Dutch paper, supplied to the British Government Offices and marked with the royal arms or some form of official badge associated with Britain. It appears that while this type of paper might have been made primarily for official use, it could be purchased by the public, while, alternatively,

---

[1] Mr. Keynes is preparing an account of the circumstances mentioned above.

[2] Bannerman MSS., Univ. Glasg. Libry.

[3] One mark possibly by Hutcheson on this Essay is of some interest. On the last page but one the writer, in discussing the final causes of rewards and punishments, says that "all civil claims and all controversies about things must be adjusted by the standard of right and wrong; for, where parties differ about *meum* et *tuum*, the plaintiff's opinion of the claim cannot be the rule, and as little the defendant's". Hutcheson had underlined the word "standard", possibly objecting to it or else thinking that the essayist should have shown how the moral sense provides such a standard. May it have been that Adam Smith had a dim idea, even at this time, that a moral sense, while it might suffice for a species of aesthetic appreciation of virtue, was insufficient for the decisions necessary in the practical affairs of life?

[4] See below, p. 232. [5] *Economic Journal*, Sept. 1935, p. 436.

he had so many relatives in the Government service that he could have obtained supplies from or through them. The letters he wrote from Oxford very shortly afterwards are on paper of a similar character. The watermark of that on which this essay is written consists of the ribbon of the garter containing the motto with a crown above and a bell suspended below. Inside the ribbon are the arms of George II., namely, 1st England and Scotland impaled, 2nd France, 3rd Ireland, 4th those of his dominions in Germany, namely, Brunswick, Luneberg and Saxony with an escutcheon charged with the crown of Charlemagne.

Outside the classroom there were all the other influences of the University. Here there is a complete lack of data. It may be that somewhere, quite unrecognised, there is a diary which gives some record of the life of students at Glasgow when Adam Smith was there and perhaps records some of his relations with his fellows. At this time the number of students was between 400 and 500. Alexander Carlyle, who was, later, minister of Inveresk and was libelled before his Presbytery for being present in a theatre at a performance of *Douglas*, was attending classes from 1743. From his description one wonders if Adam Smith took part in any of the discussions of the numerous College Clubs or, what is more likely from his disposition, attended the debates but did not speak? Did he join any of those who were invited to parties for dancing? Was he introduced to the inimitable Miss Mally Campbell, the daughter of the Principal, the most beautiful girl in the College set, " more sensible and more useful to a young man of parts than all the professors put together "?[1] And, more particularly, who were the undergraduates with whom he did not get on well, and who were his chief friends? Failing some new source of information, we are confronted with a permanent mark of interrogation on all these important points.

Returning to the academic side of Adam Smith's life at Glasgow, he completed his course for the M.A. degree with great distinction and graduated. Information which has come to light since the time of John Rae renders it necessary to correct the statement that Adam Smith did not complete the course required for a degree.[2] This statement is based on a misconception which was current in the University offices at the time Rae wrote, and has been amended in the account of the curriculum which has been given above. Since Adam Smith's name is not to be found in the roll of graduates, it might be inferred that he fulfilled the conditions but was not actually capped for the degree. Other official documents of the period, several of which are given elsewhere,[3] show that he actually had the degree. And this reveals a somewhat curious fact relating to the name of " Adam Smith," namely,

[1] A. Carlyle, *Autobiography*, 1860, p. 72.   [2] J. Rae, *Life*, p. 9.
[3] See below, pp. 137, 392.

that the University documents in more than one case fail to record it.[1] There was an Adam Smith, who matriculated under Loudon, in 1709,[2] but no further mention of him occurs ; it is quite possible he did not graduate. Next comes the subject of the present account, whose matriculation is entered, but not his graduation. Still more strange is the case of a third Adam Smith whose name appears on what was known as the stent roll of the graduating class of 1762-3 as having paid on or before 13th January, 1762, the amount levied on him for the celebration of his graduation and that of his companions.[3] He may have been a son of the Collector of Customs at Alloa,[4] and nothing short of sudden death would prevent anyone connected with Aberdeen from obtaining something for which he had paid in advance. Yet his name is not to be found either in the matriculation or the graduation rolls.

Towards the end of the session of 1739-40, two of the Snell Exhibitions to Balliol College became vacant. Adam Smith was elected to one of them and Charles Suttie, the third son of Sir James Suttie, Baronet, of Balgone, to the other, being the twenty-third and the twenty-fourth of the Exhibitioners whose names are known from the first, who was nominated in 1699. He left home towards the end of June of the same year (1740) riding on horseback to Oxford, where he matriculated on 7th of July.[5] He brought with him the absence of mind which has been mentioned previously, for he often told his friends, when a joint of roast beef was on the table, that the first occasion when he dined at Balliol he was abstracted and paid no attention to the meat before him, whereupon one of the servitors aroused him from his reflections, telling him to fall to, for he had never seen such a piece of beef in Scotland.[6]

If the plates of the old College, Glasgow, and Balliol be compared (Plates IV and VII), it will be observed that there was a general similarity in the two buildings. There the resemblance ended. When Adam Smith entered with eleven other freshmen there were about 100 undergraduates. Instead of several brilliant teachers at Glasgow those at Balliol were of no special distinction. They included Mr. Drake (Dean), Mr. Porter (Junior Dean), Dr. Sanford (Bursar), Mr. Hunsdon (Junior Bursar), Mr. Laud (Notary), all of whom were in orders. The Praelectors

---

[1] The City Records are also defective, for they fail to note the freedom granted to Adam Smith on 3rd May, 1762.

[2] *Munimenta Alme Universitatis Glasguensis*, 1854, iii, p. 192.

[3] Amongst papers of the Clerk of Faculties at Glasgow University.

[4] See p. 258 note [5]. Adam Smith, the Collector, was born at Aberdeen in 1711. He had a son, William, who was made an honorary burgess of Aberdeen in 1763.

[5] J. E. T. Rogers' edition of *Wealth of Nations*, 1869, i, p. vii.

[6] MSS. Edin. Univ. Libry., La II, 451/2 : cf. J. Rae, *Life of Adam Smith*, p. 18.

were Godwyn (Hebrew), Drake (Greek), Culme (Rhetoric and Poetry), Porter (Logic and Metaphysics).[1] They might be called teachers by courtesy, for, as Adam Smith himself tells, lectures were extremely few.[2] It was an age of dissipation, and, for the time, the love of learning was languishing. Besides there were bitter quarrels between the Colleges. Hearn, writing in 1726, said, " there are such differences now in the University of Oxford (hardly one college but where all the members are busied in law business and quarrels not at all relating to the promoting of learning) that good letters decay every day ".[3] The University was Jacobite at heart, and some of the heads of Colleges were said to be involved in the intrigues of this party. Of the same tendency was the High Borlace Club, and it was noted that when Dr. Leigh, the Master of Balliol, attended its meeting at the King's Head tavern, he was the first clergyman who had done so. Not much weight is to be given to the satire of the *terræ filius* who in 1733 said that the worthy head (Leigh) and men of Balliol—" I mean Belial—had yet to make their character and that of their house; the shape of their seats at the high table was indeed unexceptionable, and must have been excogitated with deep thought —but many of the men ate raw turnips, and the Dons used to punish some delinquents by sending them to the sacrament, and others by heavily fining them ".[4]

It was in such surroundings that Adam Smith had to settle down—surroundings in which Scotsmen were far from welcome. Their place at Balliol was not unlike that of the students who came from Ireland to Glasgow, described by Reid as " wild Irish teagues ", who were forced to sit on the back benches in the Divinity classrooms.[5] The unpopularity of Scotsmen in England, of which Hume complained at a later date,[6] was already most marked at Balliol, and the Snell Exhibitioners were in large measure cut off from the life of the College. For this reason most of the friends Adam Smith made at Oxford were members of this group. Amongst these were John Douglas, who was not a relation of Adam Smith's mother's family, having been descended from the Douglases of Tillyquilly in the Mearns. He went to Balliol first, with a Warner scholarship in 1738, and returned there as a Snell Exhibitioner in 1745. He exposed Lauder's allegation of plagiarism by Milton and the pretended conversion of Bower, prepared Clarendon's diary and letters for publication and also the Journal of Captain Cook's Voyages. He

---

[1] Records of Balliol College, very kindly extracted by Mr. A. B. Rodger.
[2] See below, p. 232.
[3] Quoted by C. Wordsworth, *Social Life at the English Universities in the Eighteenth Century*, Cambridge, 1874, p. 57.
[4] *Ibid.*, p. 305.   [5] W. R. Scott, *Francis Hutcheson*, 1900, p. 69.
[6] See below, p. 262; J. Y. T. Greig, *Letters of David Hume*, 1932, i, p. 378.

AS A STUDENT

belonged to Johnson's circle and is frequently mentioned by Boswell. In 1787 he was made Bishop of Carlisle, and in 1791 he was translated to the see of Salisbury.[1] Another friend was a Smith, named John, who was born at Maybole, Ayrshire, some four years earlier than Adam Smith, but who was nominated for a Snell Exhibition later. John Smith studied both Mathematics and Medicine. For a time he was well known in Oxford as a doctor. In 1766 he was appointed Savilian Professor of Geometry.[2] He sent his greetings to Adam Smith through a Glasgow student who was at St. Mary's Hall in 1762 and gave explanations to the Master and Fellows of Balliol on matters relating to the Snell Exhibitioners.[3] A third was James Stuart Menteith, with whom Adam Smith maintained an affectionate correspondence up till the end of his life.[4] Menteith was Rector of Barrowby in Lincolnshire until he inherited the property of Closeburn in Dumfriesshire. In 1762 two other Oxford friends sent greetings to Adam Smith through his former student, the Hon. Thomas Fitzmaurice, then at Oxford. These were Dr. King and Dr. Riall.[5] The first may have been the Rev. James King who obtained his D.D. in 1740. There is no Dr. Riall amongst Oxford graduates of the eighteenth century. It may be conjectured that he was a relative of Samuel Riall who matriculated at Glasgow in 1756 and entered at St. Mary's Hall, Oxford, in 1761.

College chambers of the period were not luxurious. There is an illustration in the *Oxford Sausage* of 1764 which shows an undergraduate seated " in a bare room with one little round table, one chair, an empty grate and (above the chimneypiece, which is quite unadorned) something which may stand either for a map of England or a much fractured oblong mirror ".[6] During the first year (the only one for which particulars are now available) his battells varied from 7s. 6d. to 10s. 8d. a week. This compares with 3s. to 19s. for other undergraduates of the College at the same time. As far as can be made out, his total battell bill for the year was £21 7s. 6d., to which was to be added his fees for tuition, as well as his miscellaneous expenses. At this time the Snell was worth £40 a year. On 2nd November, 1742, he was nominated for the exhibition, founded by Bishop Warner and named after him for purposes similar to those of the Snell, by the Archbishop of Canterbury and the Bishop of Rochester, so that someone of influence had recognised Adam Smith's merits. This exhibition was worth

---

[1] M. F. Conolly, *Eminent Men of Fife*, Cupar-Fife, 1864, pp. 147-50.

[2] W. I. Addison, *Snell Exhibitioners*, 1901, p. 45.

[3] See below, pp. 161-3.   [4] See below, pp. 292-309.

[5] Bannerman MSS., Univ. Glasg. Libry. T. Fitzmaurice to Adam Smith, 26th February, 1762.

[6] C. Wordsworth, *Social Life at the English Universities in the Eighteenth Century*, p. 57.

about £8 5s. a year, payable 1s. 3d. per week for commons during residence, and the surplus in cash from time to time.[1] Although Adam Smith complained of his expenses, considering that he had remittances from his tutors and curators[2] it is plain that he was living fairly well, making no attempt to vie with the extravagant, nor stinting himself like those who had to be extremely economical.

The cost of a journey from Oxford to Kirkcaldy may have been the reason, as Rae suggests,[3] that Adam Smith remained for six years at Oxford without returning to his home. This does not mean that he resided at Balliol during the whole of this period without any break. The letter, printed below,[4] shows that he visited Adderbury to stay with his cousin, William Smith, who at this time was Secretary to the Duke of Argyle. The letters written to his mother from Oxford indicate that from Kirkcaldy she exercised a careful watch on his health, which still was far from being robust. It is a matter of regret that these letters which were lent to Lord Brougham by Professor Cunningham (a descendant of a daughter of Lord Reston, the heir of Adam Smith) cannot now be found. They might have given some light on this important formative period of Adam Smith's life. He continued his study of the Classics, and it is from the Oxford period that he derived a knowledge and appreciation of Greek and Latin literature for which there had not been time during his three years at Glasgow. This is shown by the way he spent blank half-hours at the Custom House in Edinburgh, when he and another Commissioner were accustomed to quote from memory long passages of the classics.[5] There is no indication of the influence which directed his attention to modern literature. It may be conjectured that this began at Oxford rather than at Glasgow, but whence that influence came is unknown. It is just possible that it may have been due to one of his contemporaries. It appears from a letter written to Smith by Sir Gilbert Elliot that it was customary for the children of his friends and acquaintances to be taught to speak and read French.[6] One of this class may have been at Balliol and have followed up his teaching in this direction by a reading of the literature, communicating his appreciation of it to Adam Smith.

The Oxford of his time gave little if any help towards what was to be his life-work. In addition to what is known of the teaching of the period this appears in a rather remarkable manner. Edward Bentham, Fellow of Oriel, had published in 1745 *An Introduction to Moral Philosophy*. The next year—that in which Adam

---

[1] Records of Balliol College, very kindly extracted by Mr. A. B. Rodger.
[2] See below, p. 232.   [3] J. Rae, *Life*, p. 19.   [4] See below, p. 232.
[5] *Cf.* also other instances mentioned by Rae, *Life*, p. 23.
[6] See below, p. 240.

Smith went down—a member of the University had this tract interleaved in a fair-sized quarto. The book passed through several hands until after 1755 when one of them included quotations from Hutcheson's *System* which had then appeared. Each possessor added manuscript notes, so that the volume contains a symposium of the teaching of the subject over a period of at least ten years. Both the printed text and the manuscript notes repeat the Ethics of Cicero with a marked didactic tendency. The modern authors added in manuscript are Hutcheson and Warburton. Bentham, after defining " Politicks and Oeconomics ", adds that " their obligation might be deduced from the nature of man and his circumstances in these relations of life and therefore in a compleat system of Ethics they ought to be treated of distinctly. However, at the present I shall confine myself to the general plan upon which observations concerning this subject have commonly been methodised."[1] In view of this disclaimer it is to be expected that references to economic conditions would be few or non-existent. Industry is described as " the habit of application to some course of useful business and employment.... For the advantages of life are not merely offered to our acceptance, but to our acquisition : and the powers of body and mind requisite for that purpose are found to be of little use, unless improved by continual exercise."[2] " Money," it is said, " is the great instrument of commerce in civil societies. In order to enable ourselves therefore to come in for our reasonable share of civil happiness and to provide for our families and to exercise any rational act of generosity, it is requisite we learn both the value and the use of money ; that we extend our views forward, compute our income and regulate our expenses by it."[3] Though this passage is distinctly homiletic in character, it does convey some faint suggestion of value in use and in exchange, though not in the form in which Adam Smith ultimately developed it. While these quotations afforded little stimulus to the early genius of Adam Smith, it may be noted that Bentham shared the ideas of his time with regard to the Law of Nature, as for instance when he wrote " the apparent fitness of things, as manifested by the light of natural reason, is a presumptive proof, the best and only proof we have, that this or that course of action is agreeable to the Divine Will."[4] This, however, was less developed than what

---

[1] Pp. 2, 3.   [2] P. 53.   [3] P. 51.

[4] P. 27. The volume of notes is now at the University Library, Glasgow. It was found by the writer at the bookshop of Mr. James Glen in Glasgow. The latter had no recollection of where he procured the volume ; but, since most of his stock was acquired in Scotland, and chiefly in the West, it seems reasonable to infer that the book had been brought from Oxford by a Scottish student. With one exception, nothing can be learnt as to the different handwritings of the annotators, either at Oxford or at Glasgow. There appear to be seven of these ; and the notes were written not before 1746 and probably not later than a few years after 1755. Some contributions are of little interest. There is an inset page, written in a more formed hand than the remainder,

Adam Smith had learnt from the lectures and the writings of his teachers at Glasgow.

About the time that Adam Smith reached B.A. standing, which was on 5th May, 1744, he came to a serious decision which affected his whole life. The conditions of accepting a Snell Exhibition were that the exhibitioner gave a bond for £500 sterling—a very large sum at the time—that he should qualify himself for, and enter Orders of, the Church of England, but that he would not accept any preferment in England and Wales and that he should return to Scotland and " there be preferred or advanced as his or their capacities and parts shall deserve, but in noe case to come back into England, nor to goe into any other place but onely into the Kingdome of Scotland for his or their preferrment." [1] Adam Smith came to the conclusion that he would not, or could not, fulfil these conditions. Whether his religious conviction was unsettled by the reading of French authors or Hume is uncertain. According to one authority, but a relatively late one, his decision " was caused by the unceremonious manner in which he was treated by his superiors at Balliol when they discovered him reading one of the early lucubrations of Hume." [2] According to another account, the book, perhaps the *Treatise*, was confiscated and destroyed so that one at least of the copies, which escaped being " dead-born," suffered from infantile mortality. If Adam Smith had gone on with his studies for the Church, one wonders what would have been the result to him and to the world. His contemporary, Tucker, found that economic investigation was not incompatible with his duties as Dean of Gloucester. Adam

dealing with religion, which seems to be either notes of a Divinity lecture or for a sermon. Then there was a lazy youth who cut out passages from a text of Cicero's *De Officiis* and added the reference. Other notes by three different writers are in manuscript. That which was written last consisted of quotations from Hutcheson and Warburton's *Sermons*. It is not improbable that this person was a Scotsman. He may have been a Snell Exhibitioner. The tenure of these exhibitions was ten years, and the names of those on this foundation during the period of the notes were John Preston, James Stuart Menteth, Stewart Douglas, Andrew Wood, Adam Smith, Charles Suttie, Thomas Craufurd, John Stirling, John Smith, George Hamilton, John Douglas, —— Ramsay, Alexander Campbell, Charles James Sholto Douglas, Andrew Cheap, —— Bruce, George Wilsone, Alexander Campbell, Archibald Lamont and Norman Lamont. Finally, the inner cover has the signature " H. Hucheson " in a hand which appears to be different from that of the notes. There was a Hans Hutcheson, the son of Robert Hutcheson, a merchant in Newry, who matriculated at Glasgow in 1743. Though in the signature in the book of notes the letter " t " is omitted in the name, the writing agrees with the signature in the matriculation roll. No trace of an H. or Hans Hutcheson can be found at Oxford. What is curious is that the youth who matriculated at Glasgow was probably a relative (possibly a nephew) of Francis Hutcheson. The latter was brought up at Saintfield, Co. Down, and was the second son of a large family, the eldest of which was named Hans—W. R. Scott, *Francis Hutcheson*, pp. 5, 6.

[1] Will of John Snell, printed in W. I. Addison, *Snell Exhibitions*, Glasgow, 1901, pp. 199-200.

[2] J. Strang, *Glasgow and its Clubs*, 1857, p. 28. The first edition appeared in 1855. If Strang's tale is intended to refer to the *Treatise*, the fact that Adam Smith's Library contained in 1781 a copy of this book is rather against it.

Smith's lively sympathy with those whom life had treated hardly, as is shown very vividly in several passages in his early treatise on *Public Opulence*,[1] would have given scope for much good work while at the same time his balanced judgement would have restrained him from many of the errors which are the special danger of the sympathetic temperament. It is unlikely that he would have been a popular preacher, for his voice was rather harsh, and he had a difficulty in starting his discourse. It is to be feared that, as regards promotion, what one of his students at a later date, Henry Herbert, afterwards Lord Porchester and Earl of Carnarvon, wrote to him about Ogle, Dean of Winchester, that he would have been higher in the Church " but for his uncourtly disposition never having been able to resist showing his enthusiasm in any course coloured with publick liberty ",[2] would have applied to Adam Smith also. At a guess, if the business and administrative ability which he possessed had been recognised, he would have been an excellent Archdeacon. Whatever were the causes of his abandoning the intention of seeking Orders, there remained the question of the penalty for his failing to do so. This problem solved itself. Balliol and Glasgow were uneasy partners in the early history of these exhibitions. They were more often in the Courts than out of them. At this time there was a great Chancery suit proceeding, as such cases usually do, with all due deliberation. While the result was not reached until some fourteen years later, it is evident that there was a very clear anticipation that the obligation to take orders could not be enforced and that, therefore, there could be no penalty. This is shown by the fact that of ten exhibitioners before Adam Smith's time, six are known to have been ordained. Of the ten commencing with Adam Smith there was only one.[3]

The tenure of a Snell Exhibition was for ten years, to which an extension of one year might be added. Adam Smith left Balliol on or about 15th August, 1746,[4] and did not return. Several explanations are attributed to him. Besides that already mentioned, he told Callander of Craigforth that " he did not like Balliol and left in disgust ".[5] While the Mastership of Leigh resulted in a serious decline in the fortunes of the College—the numbers of undergraduates having fallen by 25 per cent. during the period Adam Smith was connected with it—when he had been there so long as six years would have appeared to one of his age, it seems he might well have remained till his exhibition terminated. Something

---

[1] See below, pp. 327, 341.   [2] See below, p. 294.

[3] W. I. Addison, *Snell Exhibitions*, 1901, pp. 37-48. The appendices of this book give a summary of the legal proceedings alluded to in the text.

[4] J. E. T. Rogers' edition *Wealth of Nations*, 1869, i, p. vii.

[5] Edin. Univ. MSS., La II, 451/2.

more than becoming weary with the place and the conditions is required to account for breaking away from such prospects, other than the Church, as Oxford might have offered him, and also the possible sacrifice of the remainder of his exhibition. It is believed that the explanation is to be found in some of the consequences of the Rebellion, which can well be imagined to have made his life in the College one of acute discomfort. Oxford at the time was thoroughly Jacobite, and, in this respect, Balliol was far from being the least prominent of the Colleges. When feeling is aroused, undergraduates can succeed in making the way of anyone unfortunate enough to be in a minority, exceedingly hard. Always Adam Smith spoke his mind freely, and in a College of seventy to eighty, his opinions in favour of the Revolution settlement were sure to have been known. If, as is not unlikely, his reading was made impossible and perhaps his books and papers injured, his position in the College would be difficult to maintain to any useful purpose. It is evident that Jacobite opinions had become dominant at Balliol; since, within a year from the time he had left, a party from the College had created a riot outside. Though there was evidence that those who were most prominent had disarmed two soldiers and had used many Jacobite expressions, not only did the authorities fail to take appropriate action, but those in fault were treated with general respect in Oxford.[1] If this interpretation of the situation is correct, it is easy to understand that Adam Smith, at first, would feel a certain amount of irritation at the want of toleration which deprived him of about a year and a half of the emoluments of his exhibition.[2] There are indications that, as time went on, he felt more warmly towards Balliol. The minutes, printed later,[3] show him in correspondence with the Master and Fellows about the affairs of the exhibitioners. There is another piece of evidence which tends in the same direction. This is a marginal note in a pamphlet in the Glasgow University Library. It is *A Proposal for publishing a poetical Translation, both in Latin and in English, of the Reverend Mr. Tutor Bentham's " Letter to a Young Gentleman of Oxford "*, London, 1748. It appears this tract belonged to some Snell Exhibitioner who filled up the names of those who were represented in print by initials and dashes. It was lent to Adam Smith, and he added another name in the margin. In the extract below the first addition is indicated by the letters within square brackets, and the second by italics:

" As to the odious parallel or comparison which it is pretended our author
" hath drawn in that place where he mentions Nero and Augustus,

[1] R. Blacow, *Letter to W. King, Principal of St. Mary Hall*, London, 1755, pp. 6, 21.
[2] His resignation addressed to the Master of Balliol was dated 4th February, 1749. See below, p. 137.
[3] See below, pp. 161-3.

AS A STUDENT

" though it hath been urged with much malice, yet it is a very trifling
" and frivolous objection. For I appeal to a gentleman of great worth
" and honour, my very good friend, Captain Fluellen, ' If it be well done,
" mark you now, to censure a man who speaks but in figures and com-
" parisons, especially if he speak in the way of argument, look you, and
" friendly communication. For expounding (to proceed in the honest
" Welshman's dialect) there is a little tutor in A[lban] H[all], there is also
" a little tutor in O[riel] C[ollege] : the little tutor in O— C— is called
" E[dwd] B—[m] : but it is out of my prains what is the name of the
" other little tutor ; * but it is all one, they are as like as my fingers to   * *Trott*
" my fingers, and there is parables and pratings and predications and
" politics and ambitions in both.' "[1]

This tract was bound with eight others, also relating to Oxford, not long after the last was issued, in 1771, which is shown by a part of Adam Smith's writing having been shaved by the binder, so that his note might be any time between 1748 and, say, 1775. Nothing is known of the person who collected the nine pamphlets. They form part of a large collection of tracts given in 1847 to the University by John Smith, who was the founder and secretary of the Maitland Club. They are earlier than those John Smith himself collected, and it appears probable that, since he was a bookseller, he purchased this volume when he acquired some library which was offered for sale. The volume has been rebound within the last forty years, so that, if the original cover contained any name or other indication of the original owner, this has now been lost.[2] Another consideration, pointing in the same direction, is that Adam Smith thought it worth while to preserve the volume *Parecbolæ, sive Excerpta e' Corpore Statutorum Universitatis Oxoniensis* which is entered in the Catalogue of his Library as it was in 1781.[3]

[1] " Shakes. ' *Henry V* '—pp. 12-13."

[2] In recent years all such indications, and even the old library labels, are transferred to the new binding. It is to be feared this was not so formerly.

[3] This MS. is now in the Collection of Adam Smith books at Tokyo Imperial University. The reference is to f. 73.

CHAPTER V

THE CIRCUMSTANCES AND THE SUBJECT-MATTER OF ADAM SMITH'S PUBLIC LECTURES AT EDINBURGH, 1748-1751

There is a certain amount of mystery about the circumstances and the subject-matter of the lectures which Adam Smith delivered at Edinburgh during the three years 1748 to 1751. When he returned from Oxford in August 1746,[1] he had to make his way in the world. His thoughts turned towards a tutorship of some young nobleman—this being at the time a recognised avenue to a University Professorship or to other positions suitable to a person with some considerable scholarship. In his own family there had been the case of the William Smith, a cousin of his father, already mentioned, who was governor to Charles, Lord Hay, afterwards twelfth Earl of Errol, and who had been a Regent at Marischal University, Aberdeen.[2] After the lapse of two years it had not been possible to secure the desired appointment; and, since Adam Smith was still reluctant to take Orders in the Church of England, it was necessary to find some other opening. His boyhood friend, James Oswald of Dunnikier, had become an advocate and, after being elected M.P. for Kirkcaldy Burghs from 1741 to 1747, was at this period representing Fifeshire. Then Adam Smith's mother was connected with Robert Craigie of Glendoick, who became President of the Court of Session in 1754, through his daughter, Cecilia, having married Colonel Robert Douglas of Strathenry.[3] Craigie's progress as an advocate had been slow; and, " in the earlier part of his life, he had for several years given private lectures in his chambers to students of law ".[4] Henry Home of Kames, afterwards elevated to the Bench as Lord Kames, was an intimate friend of James Oswald, and he was also one of the pioneers of the revival of letters in Edinburgh. His mind was acute and his interests were very wide. In addition to law, he wrote on moral philosophy, history, criticism and also agriculture.[5] His influence, however, was not so much

---

[1] J. E. T. Rogers, ed. *Wealth of Nations*, i, p. vii.
[2] See p. 132.   [3] See p. 396.
[4] Brunton and Haig, *Senators of the College of Justice*, p. 517; G. W. T. Omond, *Lord Advocates*, 1873, ii, p. 3.
[5] There is a rather amusing anecdote of his agricultural enquiries. He had an idea that the essence of manure could be concentrated. One day, when visiting a tenant, he saw an immense quantity of manure which was about to be spread on a field. Kames said to the tenant that by his

through his own writings as in arousing and stimulating others. He was conscious of the difficulty which, being self-educated, he had encountered in acquiring knowledge. Also the spirit of the time and place moved him towards a wider culture, both for intelligent people generally and especially for the members of his own profession. As to the first, classical learning was less cultivated than in the previous century; while, as yet, very slight attention was given to modern, and particularly European, literature.[1] As regards the legal profession, Tytler in his biography of Henry Home gives a species of manifesto which sets forth in detail the views of Kames on this subject. " The knowledge of the law of Scotland was, in those days (*i.e.* early in the eighteenth century), usually acquired by private study;[2] that is, by the perusal of Lord Stair's *Institutions*, the useful *Compend* under the same title by Sir George Mackenzie, the statute laws and the reports or decisions of the Court of Session; and the forms of judicial procedure were learned by the daily practice in the Supreme Court. . . . But while we allow the usefulness of those studies to a certain extent, it must be admitted that there are others no less important; and as the time of preparatory instruction for the profession of the law, as well as every other, is limited to a few years, it deserves seriously to be weighed, whether a considerable part of that time may not be more profitably employed in the acquisition of general knowledge; the elements of the sciences, as Physics or Natural History, the principles of Mechanics and Mathematics and in the elegant studies connected with the Belles Lettres and Criticism. It is to entertain a most narrow and illiberal view of the profession of a barrister, to account a knowledge of the laws, of cases and reports and of the forms of judicial proceedings, the sum of that learning which is necessary for the discharge of the duties or the attainment of eminence in his vocation. This profession, more than

process he could make the full of his *snuff box* go as far in producing a crop. " Gif ye do that ", said the doubting farmer of the old school, " I'll engage to carry hame the crop *in my pouch* "— John Kay, *Edinburgh Portraits*, Edin., 1842, i, p. 323. Kames himself published a treatise on the *Elements of Criticism* in 1762. The section on " Beauty of Language " probably owed much to Adam Smith, though Kames differed in preferring blank verse to rhyme (ed. 1824, p. 301).

[1] A. F. Tytler, *Henry Home of Kames*, Edin., 1807, i, pp. 8-11.

[2] In so far as Tytler's expression " usually acquired by private study " conveys the impression that no lectures were available, it is somewhat misleading, since there were three law Chairs at the University, established between 1707 and 1722. Judging by the *Discourse on the Rise and Progress of the Law of Scotland*, Edin., 1726, by one of the Professors, Alexander Bayne, Professor of Scots Law from 1722 to 1737—the course was not exacting. His *Discourse* numbered 37 pages small octavo size, the nature of which consisted of short notes supplementary to Stair's *Institutions*, dictated by the lecturer. He stated, " It will be your care, gentlemen, to take down these notes as accurately as you can; but I am not to expect that you are, during the first year, to examine the authorities to which I refer with any great measure of study " (p. 169—the reason the page number is higher than the total, given above, is that Ruddiman paged this tract continuously with the *Minor Practicks* of Thomas Hope of Craighall).

any other, requires an enlarged acquaintance not only with human nature in the knowledge of the passions and affections of the mind (a knowledge not to be gained but by the study of Philosophy) ; but it demands an extensive information of the various arts and sciences which constitute the occupations of mankind and of course give origin to a very great proportion of those legal questions which occupy the courts of justice. . . . In this light the pursuits of science and literature afford an unbounded field and endless variety of delightful occupation : and even in the latest hours of life [1] the reflection on the time thus spent and the anticipation of an honourable memorial in after ages are sources of consolation of which every ingenuous mind must fully feel the value. How melancholy was the reflection uttered on his deathbed by one of the ablest judges and lawyers of the last age, but whose whole mental stores were wholly limited to the ideas connected with his profession—' My life has been a chaos of nothing ' ".[2]

These three—James Oswald, Robert Craigie, with Kames as the moving spirit—outlined the project for a series of public lectures which would be different from any that were available at that time in Edinburgh. Such being the scheme, there is the difficulty how it was to be introduced to the public and made successful. As happened frequently in the endeavour to picture the life of Adam Smith, the situation has been artificially simplified by transporting known conditions of a later time to an earlier one. In this case Rae suggests that these lectures were probably given at the University.[3] While it is true that the success of Adam Smith's pioneering course followed by those of Robert Watson (later Principal of the University of St. Andrews) and of Hugh Blair, resulted in the foundation of the Professorship of Rhetoric and Belles Lettres in 1762,[4] an examination of the minutes of the Senatus, made by Mr. T. F. Harley, shows that there is no trace of Adam Smith having been appointed by the University to lecture nor of a room being granted for the purpose either to him or to any society for any such course of lectures. Accordingly, it is most unlikely that these lectures were authorised or patronised by the University.

It was a time when public lectures were extremely popular in Edinburgh. We find in 1748-9 Dr. Ebenezer MacFait was to begin his courses in Mathematics at his lodging on 8th November, Dr. Young announced his lectures on the Practice of Medicine also at his lodging, Dr. Demainbray on Experimental Philosophy " in the Lecture Room at Mrs. Baillie's lodging at the door of the land in the Flesh

---

[1] Kames proved the truth of this maxim. Within less than four days of his death a friend found him dictating to an amanuensis. On his expressing surprise, Kames replied, " Would you have me stay with my tongue in my cheek till death comes to fetch me ? "
[2] A. F. Tytler, *Life of Henry Home of Kames*, Edin., 1807, i, pp. 15-18.
[3] *Life of Adam Smith*, pp. 31-2.   [4] *Catalogue of Graduates of Univ. of Edin.*, p. xvii.

Market ", George Paterson advertised his readiness to teach Arithmetic, Algebra, Book-keeping, Geometry, Trigonometry, Geography, the use of the globes and Navigation, Dr. MacFait the System of Ancient and Modern Geometry and Dr. Plumer Chemistry.[1] It is rather remarkable that the Professors of the University also advertised in the Press, as for instance Matthew Stewart, Mathematics; the Professors of Medicine " the branches of that science "; Charles Mackay and John Erskine, Roman Antiquities, Scots Law and Universal History. John Stewart, Professor of Natural Philosophy, evidently had a streak of originality. He announced that on 10th November he " was just taking up his Colleges in the College of Edinburgh ", adding that " the ladies are always welcome to any experiment that can divert them " and in a later issue " the doors are always open to ladies ".[2] One wonders if Adam Smith would have considered the last " a certain degree of exactness " when he came to write a particular passage in *The Wealth of Nations* where he said, with regard to University teaching, " when the competition is free, the rivalship of competitors, who are all endeavouring to jostle one another out of employment, obliges every man to execute his work with a certain degree of exactness ".[3] It is not without some significance that there is a certain parallelism between the outside courses and those advertised by Professors. Whereas, where there were no private lectures, no University course in the subject is advertised. What is remarkable is that neither in 1748-9, nor in the succeeding two winters, is there any advertisement by Adam Smith or of any lectures including the subjects he dealt with. Accordingly, failing his own initiative or the influence of the University, one is forced to the conclusion that his lectures must have been organised by a body already in existence, which was able to secure a hall and communicate with its own members. Edinburgh at this period was a place of Clubs, some of which were of a literary character. Most, however, were informal, largely for social purposes, and meeting at the Coffee Houses or Inns.[4] Mr. W. Forbes Gray has made a special study of early Edinburgh Clubs and, in his opinion, the most probable one to have sponsored the lectures of Adam Smith was the Philosophical Society of Edinburgh, which

---

[1] *Caledonian Mercury*, 1748, 13th, 18th, 25th, 27th October, 29th November. Since the MS. Catalogue of Adam Smith's Library in 1781 (see below, Part II, § I) records no less than four copies of MacFait's *New System of Geography*, it is probable that he and Adam Smith became acquainted at this time.

[2] *Ibid.*, 1748, 4th, 10th, 13th, 17th, 21st, 25th October, 8th, 10th, 15th November. At that time the income of a Scottish University professor consisted of a small fixed salary, and the remainder was made up of the fees of students who attended his classes (see below, pp. 67-8).

[3] Ed. E. Cannan, ii, p. 249.

[4] This was so in the case of one celebrated Club—the Rankenian—founded in 1716 and which continued till after 1760.

was instituted in 1731 for the improvement of medical knowledge. In 1737, on the suggestion of Colin Maclaurin, the mathematician, its scope was extended to include science and literature,[1] and it is this body which seems to provide the conditions required.[2]

Assuming Adam Smith's lectures to have been organised, there remains the question of the subject-matter. New data, which will be discussed later, show that hitherto far too much has been taken for granted, and it now becomes possible to ascertain the topics dealt with and, to some extent, to assign these to distinct sessions. It has hitherto been assumed that the three courses were concerned with modern literature and literary criticism except perhaps the last. Tytler's language is somewhat ambiguous when it is analysed, namely, that Adam Smith " read a course of lectures on Rhetoric and the *Belles Lettres*. He delivered those lectures at Edinburgh in 1748 and the two following years." [3] While these are the lectures mentioned by other contemporaries, the sentence quoted does not necessarily mean that the three courses were all on this subject. In fact, there is the authority of an intimate friend of Adam Smith, John Callander of Craigforth, who describes a course on Civil Law which was given to students of Jurisprudence and the nature of which can be reconstructed.[4] It is not clear whether in this period he lectured on Metaphysics or Ethics. Thus while some of his lectures were " Philosophical " in the sense of the eighteenth century, they may not have been in that of the present day. Any decision turns on the period to which some of the posthumous *Essays on Philosophical Subjects* are assigned, namely, whether to the Edinburgh lectures or to Adam Smith's work as a Professor at Glasgow. Of these the fragment " on the External Senses " is most likely to have been written at Glasgow. Three others, namely, " The Principles which lead and direct Philosophical Enquiries " illustrated by the " History of Astronomy, of Ancient Physics and of Ancient Logic and Metaphysics " are not as uniform as the titles suggest. It is known definitely that the first—that on Astronomy—was written previous to the year 1758, in which year the return of a comet was predicted,[5] but how far before it is difficult to decide. It is not known

---

[1] Colin Maclaurin, *Account of Sir Isaac Newton's Philosophy* (ed. P. Murdoch), Lond. 1750, p. ix.

[2] The Select Society, which was started in 1754 and to which both Adam Smith and Kames belonged, changed its name in 1762 to " The Society for Promoting the Reading and Speaking of the English Language ".

[3] A. F. Tytler, *Henry Home of Kames*, Edin., 1807, i, p. 190.

[4] Edinburgh University MSS. La II, 451-2.

[5] A. Smith, *Essays on Philosophical Subjects*, 1795, p. 90. Stewart states that the " Essay on Physics " was one of Adam Smith's " earliest compositions ". It is not clear from the context whether this is intended as one of the earliest which have survived ; or earliest of all his writings —*Memoir*, p. 50.

at what date the scheme of work, which Adam Smith planned, was devised, though it can be guessed where these dissertations would have found their place in it. On the whole, the balance of probability is that they are more likely to belong to the first half of the later period rather than to the earlier one. It follows that the subjects of the Edinburgh lectures may be taken, at least provisionally, to have been two courses on Literature and Literary Criticism, followed by a final course on Jurisprudence. If one winter was assigned to lectures of a Philosophical nature, this would reduce the literary lectures to a single course. It is fairly clear from a number of indications that the lectures on Jurisprudence came last. That order is supported by the nature of Adam Smith's reading. He spent much time at Oxford on both ancient and modern literature. While he became acquainted with Grotius when he was an undergraduate at Glasgow,[1] extensive study would be required for this course, and according to Adam Smith himself the manuscript was written in 1749, probably in the summer;[2] and, as will appear, he continued his study of law in the earlier part of the time he spent at Glasgow.[3]

It is fortunate that a fairly complete account of the topics of the lectures on literature can be collected from various sources. When Adam Smith began his work at Glasgow, he had not only to teach the class of the Chair to which he had been elected, but at the same time to provide part of the lectures required for that of Moral Philosophy.[4] He utilised portions of the lectures he had given previously in Edinburgh. This fact is recorded by James Wodrow in a letter which he wrote to the Earl of Buchan, who will appear later in connection with Adam Smith, as Lord Cardross.[5] Wodrow had matriculated in 1740 and studied under Francis Hutcheson. He graduated in 1750, being Library Keeper till 1755 when he became minister of Dunlop and afterwards of Stevenston. The life of William Leechman, at this time Professor of Divinity and later Principal of the University of Glasgow, was written by him.[6] According to this account " Adam Smith delivered a set of admirable lectures on language (not as a grammarian but as a rhetorician) on the different kinds or characteristics of style suited to different subjects, simple, nervous, etc., the structure, the natural order, the proper arrangement of the different members of the sentence etc. He characterised the style and the genius of some of the best of the ancient writers and poets, but especially historians, Thucydides, Polybius etc. translating long passages of them, also the style of the best English classics, Lord Clarendon, Addison,

---

[1] See above, p. 34. [2] D. Stewart, *Memoir of Adam Smith*, Edin., 1811, p. 100.
[3] See below, p. 116. [4] See below, p. 140. [5] See below, p. 69.
[6] Prefixed to the edition of *Leechman's Sermons*, 2 vols., 1789.

Swift, Pope, etc; and, though his own didactic style in his last famous book (however suited to the subject)—the style of the former book was much superior [1]— was certainly not a model for good writing, yet his remarks and rules given in the lectures I speak of, were the result of a fine taste and sound judgement, well calculated to be exceedingly useful to young composers, so that I have often regretted that some part of them has never been published." [2] In addition to lectures in the University Adam Smith addressed a literary club which was composed of certain University Professors together with others interested in the subject. It is recorded that " he read papers to this society on Taste, Composition and the History of Philosophy which he had previously delivered while a lecturer on rhetoric in Edinburgh ".[3] The dissertation " On the Origin of Languages " would seem the natural preface to the analysis of prose style which Wodrow mentions, but there is the difficulty that it did not appear in the first edition of *The Theory of Moral Sentiments*, but was appended to the third edition which was issued in 1767. It is quite possible that this material dated back to the Edinburgh period, that when the first edition was published in 1759 Adam Smith hoped to complete his original comprehensive plan, but by 1767 after his absence in France, he began to realise how much time *The Wealth of Nations* would require, and he determined to publish the " Dissertation " without the other material to which it was probably a species of introduction. It is to be noted, however, that there are quotations from Rousseau in the " Dissertation " which would point to a date later than the Edinburgh period; unless, as was so often the case with Adam Smith, these had been inserted subsequently in a manuscript which had been written at an earlier date.

The foregoing data, together with reference to Blair's *Lectures*, the original composition of which had been aided by a loan of the manuscript of those delivered by Adam Smith and the report of his literary talks in *The Bee*,[4] enable some idea

---

[1] *Cf.* Hugh Blair, *Lectures on Rhetoric*, 1824, pp. 118, 128-31, 136, 144-50, 230, 454, 496-8, 516. It is curious how standards of criticism change. The following is a twentieth-century characterisation of the style of *The Theory of Moral Sentiments* : " I question whether a larger collection of pompous and empty platitudes was ever made by a great writer " (!)—J. H. Millar, *Literary History of Scotland*, 1903, p. 341.

[2] Univ. of Glasg. Libry. MSS., Murray Collection, Buchan Correspondence 1806-28, ii, p. 171. If it is true, as suggested below, that the dissertation on the Origin of Languages belonged to the Edinburgh period a portion was in fact published but not the part alluded to by Wodrow.

[3] R. Duncan, *Notes and Documents illustrative of the Literary History of Glasgow* (Maitland Club), 1831, p. 16. It will be seen from a letter written by John Millar and printed below (p. 312) that the first two parts of the " Essay on the Imitative Arts " were composed as lectures for this Society. The third part (which is on Dancing and remains unfinished) was promised but was not completed. It was begun after 1776 (see p. 283) but still wants the conclusion.

[4] James Anderson, *The Bee or Literary Intelligencer*, iii, pp. 1-8.

IN EDINBURGH, 1748-51

to be formed of the scope of this particular course. It was primarily a consideration of style and appreciation of it. The lectures may have begun by a study of the development of language (the " Dissertation "), they certainly proceeded to the analysis of expression commencing with prose and continuing to poetry. In the former the style of historians, orators and essayists was treated with illustrative extracts. In poetry his preference for rhyme over blank verse has obtained wide circulation through its bearing on a change in Johnson's attitude towards him, following a somewhat violent dispute.[1] He seems to have given great weight to the form of expression, approving of French and Italian verse. The eighteenth-century formalism appealed to him and he is quoted as saying " It is the duty of a poet to write like a gentleman. I dislike that homely style which some think fit to call the language of nature and simplicity and so forth." This, if a correct report, shows that there was at least an apparent discrepancy between Adam Smith, the critic, and Adam Smith, the economist.

Doubt has already been expressed whether a course of a Philosophical character was included in the Edinburgh series of lectures. Support for such a course appears to be derived from the definite statement, already quoted, that Adam Smith had lectured at Edinburgh on the History of Philosophy,[2] and this in turn seems almost a direct reference to the Essay on " The History of the Ancient Logic and Metaphysics ". Further, this essay is intended to be one of a series on " The Principles which direct Philosophical Enquiries " illustrated also by the History of Astronomy and Physics. Clearly, though not very marked in the existing fragments, Adam Smith had the question of method very strongly before him. It is significant that when he came to write on the *Encyclopédie* in the *Edinburgh Review* of July 1755 the two points on which he insists are this same question of method and the integration, not only of the sciences, but of these with the humanistic studies.[3] It is true that this interest in method may mean a return to a subject which he had worked at some six years before, or, alternatively, it may have been an inquiry which was now being commenced.

There remains the final course of the lectures of this series. For this up to the present time we have had only a few sentences preserved by Dugald Stewart and quoted from an important paper written by Adam Smith himself in 1755. These passages have been frequently reprinted but they are worth repeating, since some new data cast a fresh light upon them. " Man ", wrote Adam Smith in 1749, " is generally considered by statesmen and projectors as the materials of a

[1] See below, pp. 122-3.   [2] See above, p. 52.
[3] Second edition, Lond., 1818, pp. 126-7.

sort of political mechanics. Projectors disturb nature in the course of her operations in human affairs; and it requires no more than to let her alone and give her fair play in the pursuit of her ends that she may establish her own designs." And again, " little else is requisite to carry a state to the highest degree of opulence from the lowest barbarism, but peace, easy taxes and a tolerable administration of justice; all the rest being brought about by the natural course of things. All governments which thwart this natural course, which force things into another channel, or which endeavour to arrest the progress of society at a particular point are unnatural and to support themselves are obliged to be oppressive and tyrannical ".[1] This glimpse of a phase, which is of the greatest importance in the early development of Adam Smith, is extremely tantalising and has given rise to much speculation as to the setting in which these passages found their place. What led up to them and what conclusions were based upon them?

At least a partial answer is to be found in a contemporary account by John Callander of Craigforth who was an intimate friend of Adam Smith and who attended this final course of the Edinburgh lectures. He said that " Adam Smith taught Civil Law to students of Jurisprudence, such were the lectures which he here gave ".[2] This saying at first seems to introduce a fresh complexity. If, however, the passages quoted by Dugald Stewart be considered in relation to the concluding paragraph of *The Theory of Moral Sentiments* a connection will begin to appear. " It might have been expected that the reasonings of lawyers upon the different imperfections and improvements of the laws of different countries should have given occasion to an enquiry into what were the natural rules of justice, independent of all positive institution. It might have been expected that these reasonings should have led them to aim at establishing a system of what might properly be called natural jurisprudence, or a theory of the general principles which ought to run through, and be the foundation of, the laws of all nations. . . . Grotius seems to have been the first who attempted to give the world anything like a system of those principles which ought to run through and be the foundation of the laws of all nations; and his treatise on the laws of war and peace, with all its imperfections, is perhaps at this day the most complete work which has yet been given upon this subject." [3] While these words were written nearly four years later than those quoted by Dugald Stewart, the relationship of thought between them will be apparent, and this suggests that the final Edinburgh course was neither primarily philosophical nor economic but concerned with something of

---

[1] D. Stewart, *Memoir of Adam Smith*, Edin., 1811, p. 100.
[2] Edinburgh University Library MSS. La II, 451-2.
[3] Adam Smith, *Theory of Moral Sentiments*, 1759, pp. 549-50.

the nature of a Philosophy of Law or what at this period was called "Jurisprudence"—a term used in a wider sense than at present.

Callander enables the matter to be carried much further forward, though in a somewhat indirect manner. He continues the account, previously quoted, by adding that "Dr. Robertson had borrowed the first volume of his History of Charles V. from them (*i.e.* from these lectures) as every student could testify". Something will be said later about the question of plagiarism which is implied,[1] but what is relevant here is the clue this statement gives towards filling up the extremely vague particulars, hitherto available, of Adam Smith's teaching on this subject at Edinburgh. William Robertson, who had published a *History of Scotland during the Reigns of Queen Mary and James VI. till his Accession to the Crown of England* in 1759, and was appointed Principal of the University of Edinburgh in 1762, issued in 1769 *The History of the Reign of the Emperor Charles V. with a view of the Progress of Society in Europe from the subversion of the Roman Empire to the beginning of the Sixteenth Century*.[2] The first edition appeared in three volumes, the first of which consisted of " the view of the progress of society " during the period mentioned in the title. It is divided into three sections consisting of 192 pages, followed by lengthy illustrative notes. It is the first of these that was similar to the lectures given by Adam Smith,[3] which is concerned with " the progress of society with respect to government, laws and manners ". After an outline of the last years of the Roman Empire, the irruption of the barbarians is described and its effects discussed. Then Feudalism was established and its relationship to the legal system of Rome is examined in some detail with its effects on the sciences, the arts and religion. Next came the Crusades; and the benefits from them to property, commerce and manners were dealt with. This was followed by the rise of the towns, with a consequent increase of liberty. The progress of law, including the re-emergence of Roman Law, and the development of commerce towards the close of the period concluded this part of the survey.[4]

It is to be hoped that what no doubt seemed at first to be a highly incongruous amalgam of the Civil Law and a historical work has begun to take shape and to form itself into an original and interesting discourse. At the same time, the resemblance between Adam Smith's lectures and Robertson's work affords an indication of the nature of the former, not a complete picture. Callander reports that Adam Smith said Robertson " was able to form a good outline but he wanted industry to fill

[1] See below, pp. 116, 124.
[2] Dugald Stewart, " Memoir of William Robertson ", in *Biographical Memoirs*, Edin., 1811.
[3] The notes to this section are very extensive, so that Callander was perhaps justified in referring to the first volume as a whole.
[4] W. Robertson, *History of Charles V.*, Lond., 1769, i, pp. 1-82, 195-338.

up the plan ".[1] There was also another want—that of insight. There is nothing in Robertson's work to suggest the wider sweep of Adam Smith's generalisations, and especially the conception of natural law and a natural order. Then, too, his study of Roman law was more complete and detailed than that of Robertson. In this connection one's thoughts turn to the first part of the *Glasgow Lectures*, that entitled " Justice ". The resemblance to the last course of Edinburgh lectures is close but it should not be pushed too far, since reasons will be adduced later to indicate that Adam Smith renewed his legal studies after 1752.[2] In Robertson's " view of the state of society " the treatment of commerce is comparatively slight. It was much fuller in Adam Smith's lectures. One conclusion that can be stated with a fair degree of certainty is that Book III of *The Wealth of Nations* entitled " The different progress of Opulence in different nations " is traceable back through the early draft, printed below, and the *Glasgow Lectures* to this final course at Edinburgh. It accords with the whole treatment of society by Robertson and is confirmed by the quotation Adam Smith himself gave in 1755, which in effect contrasts the slow progress of opulence with what would happen if the natural course of things were allowed free play.

This account is confirmed from another and quite independent source. John Millar, who later became Adam Smith's colleague at Glasgow, attended his Moral Philosophy lectures as a post-graduate student. Millar himself said, in a note to his *Historical View of the English Government*, first published in 1803 : " I am happy to acknowledge the obligations I feel myself under to this illustrious Philosopher [Adam Smith], by having at an early period of life had the benefit of hearing his lectures on the History of Civil Society and of enjoying his unreserved conversation on the same subject. The great Montesquieu pointed out the road. He was the Lord Bacon in this branch of Philosophy. Dr. Smith is the Newton."[3] Millar is careful to deduce the progress of English institutions from the general European development ; and if his earlier work, *Observations on the Distinction of Ranks*, published in 1771, be included there is a striking similarity to the general treatment of Robertson. In addition to this historical enquiry there were analyses of contemporary conditions, such as the Division of Labour, so that it becomes clear that in these lectures Adam Smith had already laid the foundation of a great part of his economic work.[4]

There remain two observations still to be made. It is interesting to compare

---

[1] University of Edinburgh MSS., as above.

[2] See below, p. 124.   [3] Ed. 1803, ii, pp. 429-30.

[4] The fragments of these lectures, recently discovered (see below, pp. 379-85), provide several examples.

the respective starting points of Quesnay and Adam Smith. In 1748 there had been printed by the former the *Essai Physique sur l'Economie Animale*, in which there is mention of natural rights, a natural order and natural liberty, but as yet without any explicit economic reference.[1] Adam Smith, on the other hand, working from the more humanistic basis of law and government, had by 1749 at latest begun to apply the idea of natural liberty to commerce and industry and may have made some progress in this special investigation. These further data make it necessary to reconsider certain views of the present writer on the relation between Francis Hutcheson and Adam Smith. Soon after the publication of Professor Cannan's edition of the *Glasgow Lectures*, it was shown that the order of treatment both in the economic portion of the former and in *The Wealth of Nations* is the same as in Hutcheson's *System of Moral Philosophy*. It was suggested that Adam Smith may have used the *System* as the ground plan in preparing his own lectures.[2] Since this book did not appear till 1755, this would place the writing of the economic lectures later than now appears to be the case. If the economic matter in the final course at Edinburgh was arranged in the order of the *Glasgow Lectures*, Adam Smith cannot have worked from the *System* or the *Compend*, though the latter had appeared in Latin in 1742 and in English in 1747, but he may have used his notes of Hutcheson's lectures, and it will appear later that there is reason to think he did so.

So far an attempt has been made to make the best of the scanty evidence available. Then from two sources there came a flood of light which illumines the whole position. This was the finding amongst letters which belonged to Adam Smith one which gives an account of his studies after his return from France till he was settled as Commissioner of Customs (1767 to 1780) and which has a bearing on the earlier period. Also there are four documents, amounting to fifteen folio pages, most or all of which represent very early work.[3] They are written by an amanuensis, or perhaps by two amanuenses, different from the one who provided what has been called "an early draft of *The Wealth of Nations*" and which is printed below as Part III. The date of these four documents is of great importance. The many avocations of Adam Smith during the first eight years he was at Glasgow make it highly improbable, if not impossible, that they could have

---

[1] A. Oncken, *Œuvres de F. Quesnay*, 1888, pp. 754-8 ; W. R. Scott, " Adam Smith " (*Trans. Brit. Acad.*, x, p. 453).

[2] W. R. Scott, *Francis Hutcheson*, Camb., 1900, pp. 232-3, 235.

[3] Bannerman MSS., Univ. Libry. Glasg. It may be remarked that these papers were eventually traced after this chapter was written. The only alteration caused by their discovery was to exclude from the Edinburgh period the " Essay on the Imitative Arts " and to treat that on English and Italian verse as being of doubtful date. The evidence as to both will be given later.

been written then, and thus they may be assigned to the Edinburgh period. If so, the question at once arises how it has happened, in view of the very explicit statement of Dugald Stewart that, while the contents of the papers destroyed by Adam Smith's directions were unknown, they comprised all his unpublished papers except those reserved for the volume of posthumous essays, and Stewart believed they contained the manuscripts of " the lectures on rhetoric and jurisprudence delivered at Glasgow ". The manuscripts which have now been found were amongst letters kept by Adam Smith. There are four, three of which are one sheet of four pages, while the fourth is two sheets. It seems possible that they may have been removed from their proper places in sequence and sent to a correspondent in relation to some special point which had arisen. Being returned, they remained with the letters and thus escaped the destruction of the papers from which they had originally come. In one there is an allusion to " another discourse ", a second—that of 8 pp.—is complete,[1] the others in each case represent the final pages of a lecture. In this respect they differ from the manuscript draft of the *Wealth of Nations* (printed below in Part III), the chapters in which were long and a new chapter did not begin a fresh page, but followed the previous one, if there was room.

Arranging these fragments according to the outline of lectures of Jurisprudence, which has been constructed, the first was introductory to a group of lectures corresponding to the parts on Domestic Law and Private Law in the *Glasgow Lectures* and consists of three and three-quarter pages. There had been a very brief account of moral obligation, and the surviving manuscript begins with the statement that " duty, for its own sake and without any further view, is the natural and proper object of love and reward, and vice of hatred and punishment ". Here follow the sentences on the Atonement, which appeared in the first five editions of the *Theory of Moral Sentiments* with small alterations. At this point in the *Theory* a chapter ends, and in the next a different aspect of the subject is begun. Here the discussion continues with material rewards and punishments. The sentry found asleep at his post is discussed,[2] then the argument passes on to the institution of the civil magistrate. The authority of custom or statute law is traced back to the natural principles of justice, and the study of the rules which express it constitutes Natural Jurisprudence or the Theory of the General Principles of Law. Adam Smith indicates that he will give a particular

---

[1] The date of this paper is doubtful. It is discussed below, p. 266.

[2] See above, p. 15. This manuscript may be that which was found in a volume of Aristotle in 1831 (Rae, *Life*, p. 261) and described as that of a part of the *Theory of Moral Sentiments*. The beginning of it very closely resembles the corresponding part of the *Theory*. The remainder is quite different.

discourse upon that subject. The concluding part of this paper discusses the relation between Justice and Benevolence, and between the latter and resentment and punishment. No doubt the lectures went on (as indicated) to discuss how far these principles find expression in existing legal systems. According to Callander's account there must have been a considerable number of lectures given to " the progress of opulence ". It may be that is the place of the second paper, though it is difficult to see how it would have been suitable for a public audience. It consists of seven and three-quarter pages and is headed " Prices of corn, cattle etc. in Scotland from the earliest times to the death of James V ". The earliest date is 1243 and the latest 1561. This may have been a note for his own studies since the relative Latin passages are transcribed, or it may have been the copy of a paper on prices lent by Lord Hailes in 1769, or, again, of still later composition.[1] The two remaining documents are of such interest that they have been reproduced in full,[2] for here we have specimens of Adam Smith's earliest economic work. The first—that beginning with the philosopher and the porter—stands almost midway between Hutcheson and the *Glasgow Lectures*. It at once becomes apparent how Adam Smith, in following his teacher, was advancing beyond him. At the same time it is very significant that this document is an analysis of " the nature " of Division of Labour. There has yet to be worked out " its causes ". The words which have been deleted may cause some curiosity and speculation. In the reproduction a few may be decipherable. In the original manuscript sufficient patience has enabled almost all of them to be read. The general result is that all of them are stylistic. These are of three kinds. In dictating Adam Smith immediately thought of a word he preferred, and the first was scored out. Later he went over the manuscript with the amanuensis, and the latter wrote in variations in wording which had occurred to Adam Smith. Subsequently he revised it again and made a few changes himself.[3]

There remain two of the essays, published after the death of the author, which from their subject-matter might well date back to this early period. These are " the Nature of that Imitation which takes place in what are called the Imitative Arts " and " the Affinity between certain English and Italian Verses ", both of which treat of topics which would naturally find a place in the course or courses on literary criticism. As to the first—that on the Imitative Arts—there is Adam Smith's own statement that between the completion of *The Wealth of Nations* and his appointment as Commissioner of Customs, he was employing himself in working at this essay. Though there is no hint that it had been begun earlier,[4]

[1] See below, p. 265 note [4].
[2] See below, pp. 379-85.
[3] See below, p. 380.
[4] See below, p. 283.

what this statement means is that he had returned to the MS. which he had written at Glasgow and had begun the missing third part. Thus the only chance of recovering anything of the first two courses of lectures rests on the chance that the paper, in Adam Smith's writing, on " English and Italian verse " may go back to this period.[1] The dating of this manuscript presents considerable difficulty. There are its contents, the handwriting and the character of the paper on which it is written : as will be seen these point towards somewhat different conclusions. The whole treatment is so slight that it is obvious this manuscript represents Adam Smith's initial effort in dealing with the subject. So far, it might well fall within the Edinburgh period. At the same time, the other fragments, which have already been assigned to these lectures, are in the hand of an amanuensis, though there is just the possibility that in the first course he may not have employed an amanuensis, for Dugald Stewart's reference is confined to such work being done from 1749 to 1750.[2] The handwriting is indecisive. It seems fairly late, but when compared with the corrections on the other early fragments, it is by no means impossible both might have been about the same time. The paper and watermark are rather more helpful. Mention has already been made of Adam Smith's very marked preference for the best handmade paper, which in his time was made in Holland or in France. The only two letters written by his father show a similar preference. One of these, dated 1714, is on paper with the watermark A.R. surmounted by a crown, but without the wreath which seems to have been added in the succeeding reigns. The other, dated 27th November, 1716, has a watermark similar to that illustrated in Plate XV. The paper Adam Smith used, as a rule, bore this watermark, or the royal arms, or Britannia or a lion rampant—the royal monogram was on the other half of the sheet. Two of these—those with Britannia and the lion—are mentioned out of four by De Lalande as being the best then obtainable and were characterised as being " superfine ". Now the paper on which the note on English and Italian verses is written is an exception. This and a letter [3] are on a paper with a different watermark, which is believed to be the product of an early attempt to establish the manufacture of fine paper in England. On one half-sheet is the watermark mentioned above (Plate XV), and on the other half-sheet the name T. FRENCH. Therefore, if it is known when " T. French " began business, it would be possible to fix a lower limit for the composition of this draft essay. The letter on the same paper affords no help since

[1] Reproduced below, pp. 371-3.

[2] D. Stewart, *Memoir*, 1811, pp. 100-1. Adam Smith is there quoted as saying in 1755 that certain views were contained in the last course of lectures he gave at Edinburgh " which were written by the hand of a clerk who left my service six years ago ".

[3] See below, p. 288.

it is undated, but from internal evidence it cannot have been written before 1783. Unfortunately, while considerable attention has been given to early watermarks, those of the eighteenth century have not been examined with any great minuteness. Mr. Edward Heawood, who is the leading authority on the subject in Great Britain and to whom I am greatly indebted for much valuable information on the whole question, states that the first dated example of the appearance of " T French " as a watermark is in 1781, and that, as a matter of opinion, he cannot have been in business much before 1780. If this is correct, it follows that the manuscript, now under consideration, is comparatively late. It might belong to the vacant time between 1776 and 1778. Even that, on the available information as to the watermark, would be rather early and between 1780 and 1784 would be more probable. After 1784 Adam Smith's health was failing, and it is surprising that he had energy to improve on this draft to the extent shown by the published essay. In any case, whatever the date may be, it is most unlikely that it could be as early as the years Adam Smith spent at Edinburgh from 1748 to 1751.

One result of the foregoing enquiry is to show that this period was of very great importance in the origin of the study of Political Economy, for it was then that the central principle of Adam Smith's whole system was first outlined. Therefore any data relating to these three critical years, however slight and apparently irrelevant, may have considerable value. When so little is known, even scraps of information may afford a clue to something more.

Rae has dealt fully and satisfactorily with the collection of the poems of William Hamilton of Bangour by Adam Smith for the edition of Foulis in 1748.[1] The gloss that " he seems at this early period of his life to have had dreams of some day figuring as a poet himself ".[2] is exaggerated, if not wholly unfounded. The basis of this statement is to be found in the lines of Colton, referring to Adam Smith, in his poem on *Hypocrisy* :

> Yet when on Helicon he dar'd to draw
> His draft returned and unaccepted saw.

Colton can have had no special knowledge, for he was about ten years of age when Adam Smith died. He was a Fellow of King's College, Cambridge ; and, when *Hypocrisy* was printed in 1812, he had been presented to a College living at Prior's Portion, near Tiverton, Devon. Colton annotated his verses very liberally, and to those quoted there is appended a footnote—" Adam Smith, the great author of the *Wealth of Nations* could not draw *one farthing* on Mount Parnassus.

---

[1] Rae, *Life of Adam Smith*, pp. 38-9.   [2] *Ibid.*, pp. 34-5.

He often attempted to put together two lines in rhime ; but without success."[1] This, in turn, is a somewhat exaggerated version of one of the anecdotes of Adam Smith, written by a friend in Glasgow in 1791, namely, that " I could never find a single rhime in my life ".[2]

The traces of Adam Smith's personal life at this time are, almost necessarily, few. From the beginning his lectures were not only a literary but also a financial success. In 1758 when Hume was urging him to come to Edinburgh as Professor of Public Law and the Law of Nature and of Nations, the question of what the fees would be arose, and Hume reminded him that he made about £100 a year from one of the courses he had given from 1748 to 1751.[3] This enabled him to resign the Snell exhibition, which he did on 4th February, 1749.[4] In the next year his half-brother, Hugh, died unmarried, and, having made no disposition of his property, Adam Smith was served heir under the will of their father,[5] so that without being affluent, he was freed from any immediate pecuniary anxieties.

In coming to Edinburgh there would be several former friends of his father. Amongst these were the surviving tutors and curators, Colonel the Hon. William Dalrymple, now Earl of Dumfries, who later succeeded to the earldom of Stair, Sir John Clerk of Penicuik, and the cousin of the latter, who was the fashionable Edinburgh physician at the time.[6] Thus Adam Smith was certain of influential introductions. Accounts of his manner are contradictory. He is blamed by his contemporaries for absence of mind and for occasional prolixity. The former quality made him an excellent companion in a society which was bursting with ideas and anxious to express itself. Everything points to his having an affectionate and generous disposition. He was not only ready but eager to think the best of those he met, and it was at Edinburgh he acquired the taste for club life which remained one of his prominent characteristics. It is noteworthy how, when he moved to Glasgow, he made journeys to Edinburgh to attend meetings and to see his friends. At first one wonders how it happened that Adam Smith troubled to belong to and to give regular attendance at social clubs of a literary type when, according to many accounts, he spent much of the evening lost in his own thoughts. The following explanation may be ventured—at some stage in the conversation a remark caught his interest and he followed the thought on and on and became completely lost in the pursuit. Later, when he had acquired some celebrity, it became usual to attract his attention and to draw him into the discussion by a direct question or by provocative statements. In such occasions he frequently

---

[1] C. Colton, *Hypocrisy*, Tiverton, 1812, pp. 43-4. [2] Amicus in *The Bee*, iii, p. 5.
[3] J. V. T. Greig, *Letters of David Hume*, 1932, i, p. 280.
[4] See below, p. 137.   [5] See below, p. 135.   [6] See below, p. 131.

explained his view in detail, which accounts for the reports that his conversation resembled a lecture. It is not improbable that on an average of a number of meetings, he spoke less than the majority of his fellow members.

Most of those whom he met at Edinburgh and whose names are known are connected with some one of the courses of lectures he delivered. Those who have been noted as attending his course on Jurisprudence in addition to Wedderburn [1] and William Johnstone (Sir William Pulteney) were his friends from boyhood, James Oswald of Dunnikier, who contributed even more than Hume to the formation of his early views on economic questions, and John Callander, who was by profession an advocate, though most of his time was spent on literary and antiquarian investigations. He printed through Foulis in Glasgow a specimen of his annotations of Milton. These ran to nine folio MS. volumes and gave rise to a literary controversy in the nineteenth century. He translated De Brosses' *Collections of Voyages to the Southern Hemisphere*, which translation was published in 1766. As the translator of the New Testament his name is remembered from his principle of retaining, in his English version, the exact order of the Greek. Having become Secretary for Foreign Correspondence of the Society of Antiquaries on its foundation, he left to its library a number of manuscripts of his unpublished works.[2] John Davidson, W.S., was another friend of this period. He had been admitted in 1749 and wrote several tracts on Scottish legal antiquities, later becoming Crown Agent Depute and Keeper of the Signet 1778-97.[3] There are extant a few short but very cordial notes from Adam Smith to him.[4] Tytler records the name of John Millar, afterwards Professor of Law at Glasgow, as a member of this class.[5] Later he became a close friend of Adam Smith amongst his colleagues at Glasgow.

A considerable proportion of the younger ministers of Edinburgh also attended Adam Smith's lectures. William Robertson, who has been already mentioned, was one of these. Unlike the others, his interest was in the course of Jurisprudence, which resulted, later, in a certain amount of friction between him and Adam Smith to which reference has already been made.[6] Hugh Blair was another who at a subsequent date had the loan of Adam Smith's lectures for a literary course which he gave from 1759. A Professorship of Rhetoric and Belles Lettres having been established at the University of Edinburgh in 1762, Blair

---

[1] Lord Chancellor of England, 1793 ; Earl of Rosslyn, 1801.
[2] R. Chambers, *Biog. Dict. of Eminent Scotsmen*, 1855, i, 464-5.
[3] *History of Soc. of Writers to the Signet*, 1890, under " John Davidson ".
[4] See below, p. 267.   [5] A. F. Tytler, *Memoirs of Henry Home of Kames*, i, p. 190.
[6] See above, p. 55.

was elected to it. Another who may have been influenced by these lectures was Gilbert Stuart. Believing that Robertson—at least so the tale went in the coffee-houses of Edinburgh—had prevented his election to one of the law chairs at the University, he wrote a *History of Scotland from the Reformation to the Death of Queen Mary* and *A View of Society in Europe in its Progress from Rudeness to Refinement*, in both of which leading authorities are attacked and Robertson with special virulence.[1] In the second edition of the latter book he prints a letter from an American historian which is still more severe on Robertson. Adam Smith, on the other hand, is accepted as sound. Though Robertson is not mentioned by name, from the context he is the writer " with no tincture of philosophy " and " wanting in penetration ". His confusion is said elsewhere " to be evident and palpable ". " Though the scheme of the *History of Charles V.* is so comprehensive " it is remarkable that " amidst a wide variety of other omissions, there is not even the slightest consideration of knight service and the knight's fee ". There is such " glaring plagiarism from Guicciardini and Antonio de Solis that were each to claim their share of the doctor's works little indeed would remain to support the colossal size of his present fame ".[2]

It has been shown above that the supposed introduction of Adam Smith to Hume by Hutcheson in 1740 did not take place.[3] It was at Edinburgh that the first meeting—the foundation of a life-long friendship—happened. Adam Smith was, possibly, slower than Boswell to grasp that Hume was " an extraordinary man " and " a very proper person for a young man to cultivate an acquaintance with ".[4] Hume had been abroad during the earlier part of Adam Smith's residence in Edinburgh ; and when he returned to Scotland in 1750, he was living at Ninewells in Berwickshire. It must have been during one of his visits to Edinburgh, before Adam Smith moved to Glasgow in September or October 1751, that the two men met, as is distinctly stated by Callander.[5] At the same time the tone of the letters of 1752 and 1753 shows that, while they may have been attracted, as yet there was no intimacy between them.

In almost every relation of life Adam Smith was fortunate. He had the gift of inspiring friendship in those whose affection was most worth having. As far as it counted with him, his connections amongst influential people were both numerous and important. There was a particularly close and tender tie between him and his mother, and he was blessed in that she was spared to be with him till

---

[1] John Kay, *Edinburgh Portraits*, 1842, i, p. 95.
[2] Gilbert Stuart, *View of Society in Europe*, Edin., 1792, pp. 207, 319, 346, 386 and iv.
[3] See above, p. 34.   [4] C. B. Tinker, ed., *Letters of James Boswell*, 1824, i, p. 2.
[5] Edin. Univ. Libry. MSS. La II, 451/2.

very near the end of his life. In one direction he failed. None of the ladies he sought in marriage (for there appear to have been more than one) accepted him. Stewart mentions an attachment early in life,[1] the beginning of which may date from the time of his return from Oxford or while he was in Edinburgh. If so, this lady is unlikely to have been the " Maid of Fife " to whom his thoughts turned when he was in Paris in 1766.[2] If a tale, related by the late Sheriff Æneas Mackay, is not too good to be true this lady's name was " Jean ". According to that account, Adam Smith, meeting in Edinburgh a lady to whom he had once paid his addresses, did not recognise her until his cousin, Miss Douglas, said to him— " Don't you know, Adam, this is your ain Jeannie ? "[3]

[1] D. Stewart, *Memoir of Adam Smith*, Edin., 1811, p. 150.   [2] See below, p. 110.
[3] *Sketch of the History of Fife and Kinross*, Edin., 1890, p. 209.

CHAPTER VI

ADAM SMITH'S SETTLEMENT IN GLASGOW

John Loudon, the Professor of Logic at the University of Glasgow under whom Adam Smith had matriculated, died on 1st November, 1750.[1] Succession to this Chair was exactly the type of opening which Adam Smith had been seeking, and there can be little doubt that he took steps to have his name brought before the electors. The vacancy was considered on 19th December. It is strange, as compared with the proceedings on the appointment of a successor to Adam Smith himself fifteen months later (when, largely owing to Hume being involved, there are very full particulars of the candidates and how their claims were advanced), that there appears to be no record of any other competitors—indeed nothing beyond the official account which is printed elsewhere.[2] It is likely that others came forward, but failed to secure any strong support, and it may well be that the statement, given to the Press, that he was appointed unanimously in January 1751, may be not merely literally, but really, accurate.[3] Apart from the reputation of his lectures at Edinburgh, he had the strongest possible support, from Henry Home, Lord Kames, from Archibald, third Duke of Argyle, through his cousin, William, who had been secretary to the second Duke, and who was still a trusted adviser of the family.[4] It may be taken that the Dalrymples, a very influential connection with many ramifications, were also supporting him. With such powerful backing his election was almost a matter of course, and this in spite of the fact that he was unable to begin his duties till the next session. Though leave of absence had been granted him till then, he made the journey from Edinburgh to attend a few of the more important University meetings.[5] When the new session began in October 1751, Thomas Craigie, who had become Professor of Moral Philosophy in succession to Hutcheson, was ill; and his work was divided between Adam Smith and three other Professors. Craigie died at Lisbon on 27th November; and, when the news had been received at the end of the year,

---

[1] University MSS., vol. 55, p. 57.
[2] See below, p. 138.
[3] *Glasgow Courant*, 7th January, 1750-1.
[4] See below, p. 396 note [8].
[5] Thus he attended the Principal's or College meeting on 29th May, 1751, was absent on 10th June, present on 17th June, absent 26th June and 24th July—Univ. MSS., vol. 37.

Adam Smith exchanged to the vacant Chair.[1] At this period such transferences were not uncommon. In Adam Smith's case the chief motive was a preference for the subject, though there was a very small advantage in the salary. It is not easy to say what his total emoluments were. First, there was his fixed salary; this was 800 merks Scots, being £533 6s. 8d. Scots or, say, £44 10s. sterling. Besides this fixed salary there were some small additions to it, and it is interesting that one of the many generous things he did enables these to be recovered. When he left Glasgow in 1764 he was given leave of absence, and he could have retained his salary till the beginning of the next session. In order to help his successor, he dated his resignation as at April 1764, which meant that the incoming Professor received half a year's income but with scarcely any duties, for these had been arranged up to the end of session 1763-4. An account made up for Thomas Reid, who followed Adam Smith, shows that, including additions from funds of the Archbishopric and Subdeanery—terms which will be explained later—the augmented fixed salary was £601. 6s. 8d. Scots or just over £50 sterling.[2] So far this was much the same as that of the Professor of Logic. In addition to it, the Professors of Moral Philosophy and Natural Philosophy had a proportion of the graduation payments of those taking the degree of M.A. The larger part of a Glasgow Professor's income at that time depended on the fees of students. Reid expected to receive £100 sterling in his first session.[3] Adam Smith may have had a similar amount towards the end of his Professorship, but it is improbable that it was reached in the early years of his appointment. For instance, in May 1753, he and his successor in the Chair of Logic, James Clow, reported that their classes were so far diminished that they proposed to discontinue them, if the Faculty approved.[4] Then, in time, he became entitled to a house, rent free. The value assigned to these houses in the Professors' Court varied from £9 to £13 a year, which difference depended on their quality and which explains why there were so many removals in this Court.[5] Finally, it was the custom for Professors to take students into their houses or, as appears in at least one case, when a Professor had no more room, he put some of those he was to board into College rooms and they came to his house for meals and possibly for extra tuition. This seems to have been the ground for the disapproval by the Faculty of the number of rooms held by James Moor in the Inner Court for the use of students living with him.[6] It is known that Adam Smith received £100 a year during each of the two years that the Hon. Thomas Fitzmaurice, the younger brother of Lord Shelburne,

[1] See below, p. 139.
[2] University MSS., Loose Papers in Safe in Strong Room, Drawer G. 4.
[3] T. Reid, *Works* (ed. Hamilton), 1872, i, p. 40.   [4] Univ. MSS., vol. 37, p. 183.
[5] See below, Appendix V.   [6] University MSS., vol. 37, p. 87.

who became Prime Minister, lived under his care.[1] The names of others who boarded with him have not been recovered, with the exception of Henry Herbert, who appears in a letter below as Lord Porchester.[2] It is thus impossible to say what Adam Smith's total income from his office was. It may have been as low as £150 and as high as £300, according as the accessory earnings varied. It was lower at the beginning and higher towards the end. These figures only have reality in relation to the cost of living. It remained low, as it had been in the time of Adam Smith's father, but from 1740 and particularly after 1745, it was rising in the West. Beef was then 1½d. to 2d. per lb., butter 2½d. per lb., eggs 1d. per doz., a hen 4d. The wages of maids were 20s. the half-year and an apron, men servants received £3 to £4 a year. Miss Muir of Caldwell, who gives most of these figures, mentions that, by 1790, they had increased three times.[3]

At this period there was not a house for each Professor, and the tracing out of the changes in Adam Smith's address involves a number of complications. These have been discussed elsewhere,[4] and all that is necessary for the present narrative is to summarise the result. During his first session in residence (1751-2) it seems that he lived in chambers in the College, probably in the Inner Court, where a junior Professor, who was a bachelor, could have rooms. In May 1752, he may have moved into a house in the Professors' Court as the tenant of a Professor who did not wish to occupy it himself. In any case, by 1756, he became entitled to a house, rent free, and he is recorded then as being in occupation of the one in which it has been suggested he had lived previously as a tenant. As he became more senior, he moved twice to better houses.

There had been great changes in the staff during the eleven years in which Adam Smith had been away. Of the six Professors with whom he had come in contact only two survived—Simson in Mathematics and G. Rosse (Humanity). Of the whole twelve there were only three who had been in office in 1740. It will be necessary at a later stage to consider with some detail the personalities of

---

[1] See below, pp. 240-54. Another letter written from St. Mary's Hall, Oxford, on 26th February, 1762, is of no interest except in one small point. By his long residence at Balliol, Adam Smith had overcome the Scotticisms which were a difficulty to many of his literary compatriots. Fitzmaurice mentions that he had heard the style of the *Theory of Moral Sentiments* criticised owing to the phrase " the absence of even a haunch button " (p. 372) occurring in the description of the effect of missing something we expected to find, as for instance the want of this button in a suit of clothes.

[2] See below, pp. 293-4. The fact that he boarded with Adam Smith is established by another letter dated 11th September, 1763, in which he asks that letters addressed to him at Adam Smith's house should be forwarded to him at Aberdeen.

[3] *Caldwell Papers* (Maitland Club), 1854, Pt. I, pp. 261, 270.

[4] See below, Appendix V, where the plan shows the houses he occupied as far as can be ascertained.

several of the Professors in relation to important transactions in which Adam Smith was very closely concerned, and it will be clearer if the attempt to picture the characters of those involved is postponed so as to include several who were elected after Adam Smith and before 1761. There is very little to be added to what has already been said of the buildings. The new library was not yet ready. Owing to difficulties in drainage and, perhaps, faults in construction, it was damp and was not yet in use ;[1] indeed, after Adam Smith had been some time in Glasgow, he had a share in the moving of the books to it and in their arrangement. There are many indications that the College was showing signs of wear or of insufficient maintenance in the past, one of the most striking being a resolution in 1731 that the Professors who had charge of the students' rooms should uplift the rents and use the money, so collected, for putting them in good repair " for the better entertainment of the students and particularly for putting windows in them by degrees "[2]—it was a Spartan age.

The class room in which Adam Smith followed Hutcheson and Craigie was the upper part of the block of buildings which divided the outer from the inner Court.[3] It is the larger block on the spectator's left in Plate IV and on his right in Plate VI which is viewed from the opposite direction, and shows the side fronting the inner Court. Reid followed Adam Smith's arrangements, and the hours of teaching were 7.30 a.m. to 8.30 a.m. for lecture to the public class, 11 a.m. to noon for lecture to the private class. From noon the first class was examined on the lecture. The 7.30 o'clock class and that at noon met each day from Monday till Friday. The 11 o'clock class was held, usually, on three days a week.[4] On Saturdays the students were required to attend in the forenoon for the correction of minor offences against discipline. Those of a more serious nature were dealt with by a higher Court. In addition, he took great pains in advising his students in the choice of a career and in the fitting of themselves for it.[5] Occasionally, too, there were special lectures to the few students whom he took to board in his house and whose studies he supervised [6] or to others such as Lord Cardross, afterwards the Earl of Buchan. It was not only the education of students recommended to him which he directed with very great care ; but, as is shown in the case of the Hon. Thomas Fitzmaurice, the son of the Earl of Shelburne, who lived in his

[1] University MSS., " Journal of the Committee for carrying on the Finishing of the New Library ".
[2] University MSS., vol. 35, p. 69.
[3] D. Murray, *The Old College*, 1927, p. 144.
[4] T. Reid, *Works*, ed. Hamilton, 1872, i, p. 39.
[5] J. Ramsay, *Scotland and Scotsmen*, 1888, i, p. 463.
[6] See below, p. 70.

house for two years, he was most careful of their health and took great pains in writing full details of any illness, even if trifling, which they contracted.¹

The full and exact description of the subject-matter of the lectures, both in the class of Logic and Moral Philosophy, which has been printed by Stewart and Rae, leaves little to add on this head.² It is clear that, although Adam Smith had either a manuscript or very extensive notes, he worked out each day's lecture apart from, and largely independent of, this material. Otherwise his hesitation at the beginning and his adaptation of his treatment to the response of the " student with a plain but expressive countenance " would be meaningless. Something remains to be said as to the form of his lectures. Comparing Hume and Adam Smith as public speakers, Alexander Carlyle said " they were equal—David never tried it, and I never heard Adam but once, which was at the first meeting of the Select Society, where he opened up the design of the meeting. His voice was harsh and enunciation thick, approaching stammering." ³ Dr. Wodrow wrote that " the lectures, which were the first form of the *Theory of Moral Sentiments*, did not please Hutcheson's scholars so well as that to which they had been accustomed. The rest of his lectures were admired by them and by all, especially those on money and commerce." ⁴ Lord Buchan said that, when he was at Glasgow, " Adam Smith's lectures were my highest delight and comfort. With that wise and good man I read privately his commentaries on the Law of Nature and the Law of Nations, and had access to those papers which, being in an imperfect state at the time of his death, he caused to be destroyed." ⁵ Millar, himself a noted lecturer, even if he expresses himself with the caution of a lawyer, is no less emphatic. One feels that, with men like Alexander Carlyle, Dr. James Wodrow and some others, there is a reserve, where they praise, which detracts from anything favourable they say. The reason is to be found, in part, in the fact that such lukewarm contemporaries of Adam Smith had been students of Hutcheson, who had taught them to expect lectures which would " touch the heart ", eloquently expressed, and that even more so in Latin than in English. The grounds of this expectation may be tested from a specimen taken from the conclusion of

---

[1] Letters from Adam Smith to Lord Shelburne, 10th March, 12th March, 17th March, 19th March, 11th November, 18th November, 1760—Papers from the Bowood Library, in the possession of the Marquis of Lansdowne. Beyond noticing the evident promptitude with which Adam Smith wrote on these occasions, it is unnecessary to print these letters. They show the same solicitude and efficiency as that given by Rae relating to an illness of the Duke of Buccleuch at Paris in 1766 —*Life*, pp. 222-4.

[2] D. Stewart, *Memoir*, 1811, pp. 12-16 ; Rae, *Life*, pp. 56-7.

[3] A. Carlyle, *Autobiography*, 1860, p. 279.

[4] Univ. Libry. Glas., Murray MSS., Buchan Papers—Correspondence, ii, p. 169.

[5] *Ibid.*, Diaries, under 1763.

Hutcheson's inaugural lecture—Macte igitur estote virtute, juvenes dilectissimi, seculi hujus spes, atque venientis, spero, decus futurum, naturam atque Deum ducem sequimini, honestis animos studiis intendentes, et multifariam rerum utilium prudentiam condentes, quam deinceps in officiis omnibus honestis, temperatis, modestis, fortibus, reipublicæ nostræ atque generi humano profuturis depromatis."[1] Adam Smith was able to speak, if less eloquently, much more to the point. Further, the damning, faint praise comes almost altogether from ministers who could not forgive Adam Smith's intimacy with Hume and especially his letter painting Hume's character in most favourable colours. They failed in the insight and the charity of Mrs. Cockburn, the authoress of a version of *The Flowers of the Forest*. She wrote to Hume : " the cloven foot for which thou art worshipped I despise ; yet I remember *thee* with affection. I remember that, in spite of vain philosophy, of dark doubts, of toilsome learning, God has stamped His image of benignity so strong upon thy *heart*, that not all the labours of thy head could efface it."[2]

Another duty of a Professor at Glasgow was to take part in the business of the academic body. This was more varied and intricate than its income would suggest. Certain complications arose through events connected with the history of the University. Some of these may be touched on briefly. The Bull of Pope Nicholas V., dated 7th January, 1451, establishes a *studium generale*, and in the same year the University was established. Its history during the next century does not concern the present account except in so far as, having been an ecclesiastical foundation, it was almost ruined by the Reformation, the whole income being thereby reduced to £300 Scots. The beginning of an improvement came in 1577 when King James VI. made a grant to it of the rectory and vicarage of the parish of Govan and also a new charter, commonly known as that of the *Nova Erectio*, to which it will be necessary to refer later. Early in the next century the tithes of two parishes were vested in the academic body to which, in 1641, the temporality of the bishopric of Galloway was added. From Cromwell came the revenues of the Deanery and Sub-deanery of Glasgow. The mediaeval College had become ruinous and during the Interregnum the buildings as shown in Plate IV were erected and were finished soon after 1662. The Restoration brought another change of fortune through the diversion of the revenues of the Bishopric of Galloway, and a great debt was incurred. There was a gradual restoration of prosperity after the Revolution. In 1693 Glasgow, like each of the

---

[1] *De Naturali Hominum Socialitate, Oratio Inauguralis*, Glasgow, 1730, p. 24. There was another edition in 1756.
[2] R. Chambers, *Traditions of Edinburgh* (1868), p. 72.

72   ADAM SMITH, AS STUDENT AND PROFESSOR

other three Scottish Universities, received £300 a year from the Bishop's rents. This grant, as affecting Glasgow, was secured on the revenues of the Archbishopric of Glasgow, and in 1697-8 William III. granted a tack or lease of these revenues, *i.e.* the University was subject to an annual payment to the Treasury and was entitled to retain the remainder of the receipts. The lease, which is sometimes alluded to in the documents which follow as " the Archbishopric ", was continued for a long period, and, while very beneficial to the University finances, it involved much more work than the net income would have required, in so far as the University was compelled to collect almost twice as much as it was entitled to retain, besides coming under an obligation to account for its stewardship to the Treasury, as regards this tack, and to the Scottish Barons of the Exchequer for another part of the grant from the Crown. In these circumstances it will readily be understood that the amount of business was very considerable. While the actual collection of teinds, rents and casualties was in the charge of the factor, the appropriate governing body had to determine policy and to arrange for the internal audit of accounts, as well as that before the two Government offices already mentioned. Adam Smith will be found concerned in both of these activities.[1] In the case of properties such as the College itself and others near it, the Professors took charge. In the second half of the eighteenth century the buildings, though built of stone, were beginning to show signs of decay, and much of Adam Smith's time went in work of this kind—as for instance in connection with the Principal's house.[2] In addition, there were meetings to carry on the educational work of the place. Immediately one asks how these were arranged, there looms the shadow of the great constitutional question, which disturbed the University from 1761 for many years, and in the first stages of which Adam Smith exercised a moderating influence.[3] In order to clear the ground it is necessary first of all to expose an error of both the present writer and Rae.[4] This was the idea that the friction which in fact developed from 1761 existed from 1751, and that it arose from the distinction between the " gown " and the other Professors.[5] Rae's account is much the most picturesque and detailed, describing how the " gown " Professors held meetings separate from the other Professors with resulting quarrels. Nothing of the kind existed at this period. What has happened is that nineteenth-century conditions have been transported back to a period at which they were impossible. The decision of the Court of Session which imposed a disability on the Regius Professors (*i.e.* the non-gown Professors) was still far in

---

[1] See below, pp. 151-9. [2] See below, pp. 140-9. [3] See below, Chapter VII.
[4] W. R. Scott, *Francis Hutcheson*, p. 61 ; Rae, *Life*, p. 70.
[5] Rae, *Life*, p. 69 ; Scott, *Hutcheson*, p. 61.

the future. There was as yet no discrimination against them. A resolution in 1764 " for the appointment of a Committee to consider how far new Professors, appointed by the King, may or may not be admitted to the privileges and emoluments of the College "[1] remained without result, and all the Professors met as one body. The *Report of the Royal Commission* of 1836-7 is decisive. It states that " there are no traces of such a distinction (that is in the sense of various discriminations against the Regius Professors) having existed before the beginning of the present century ".[2]

The government of the University at the time Adam Smith became a Professor was based on that of Bologna with a Rector,[3] then elected by the students and Professors, who was the chief administrative official—the Chancellorship being an honorary office. The Rector held a Court at which the Principal and Professors sat as his assessors. There is much confusion in the names given to this and other meetings which import elements of controversy into mere description, and it will be simpler to call this the " Rector's meeting "—a method of nomenclature which is indicated by Adam Smith.[4] Next was the meeting over which the Dean of Faculty presided and a third at which the Principal was chairman. It was the practice for the last to deal with routine administration, both educationally and financially. In regard to the business of the University and the College, as far as possible, every expense was reduced to a fixed sum, and this meeting had the duty of seeing that the stated amounts were properly expended. The Rector's meeting (at least during the second half of Adam Smith's tenure of his Chair) dealt with any surplus as regards finance, with all questions in which anything new had arisen and with serious breaches of discipline. The procedure as to qualifications for degrees was divided between the meetings of the Dean and the Principal. If no point of difficulty arose the candidates for the M.A. degree had their qualifications settled by the latter. Exceptional cases and all Doctors' degrees were dealt with by the Meeting of the Dean of Faculty. Finally there was a check on the current finance and administration by the approval of accounts by the Rector, the Dean of Faculty and the Minister of the " High Kirk ", or the Cathedral, who were the Ordinary Visitors of the University.

Adam Smith was a member of each of the three meetings mentioned. It will be seen from the minutes of the University relating to him which are printed below, that he served on many Committees. There may be some doubt as to the

---

[1] University MSS., vol. 31, p. 17.   [2] *Report on Glasgow*, 1839, p. 32.

[3] In the documents of the period (*e.g.* below, p. 229) he is styled " Rector Magnificus "—the modern equivalent is " Lord Rector ".

[4] See below, p. 205.

wisdom of printing these records, since they probably differ little from those relating to any Professor of the period who had the same business ability. When rightly understood they seem to be of quite exceptional importance in the study of Adam Smith's life at this period. There is an immense amount of work to be fitted into the thirteen years he was at Glasgow, and it is vital to know how much time he had to do it. For this purpose it is necessary to be able to form an opinion whether a particular committee on which Adam Smith served required only a single meeting or a dozen. Reid wrote in 1764 that he had committee meetings " commonly four or five times a week ".[1] This was exceptional. In Adam Smith's time they increased in number after 1761, but it may be estimated that on an average they did not amount to more than one a week or at the most three in a fortnight. Also, these records contain a long unpublished report—that on the powers of the Rector and Principal [2]—which shows Adam Smith in a new light and which could not be understood without the events which preceded it. Another matter of interest in these records is of a different nature. Alike to the man of humour and to the cynic it was a jest that anyone, so absent-minded and so unworldly that he got someone else to buy the corn for his horse, should be accepted by the world as an authority on Political Economy. It might have been expected that the general explanation of Rae [3] would have disposed of this misconception. Since it persists, and that in quite unexpected places, it seems the only thing to do is to present the evidence in detail. This is another example of a saying about the propaganda of war time, that if a lie got twenty-four hours' start, the truth never quite caught it up.

There appear to be two issues involved—absent-mindedness and a want of acquaintance with business and administration. The first of these will be touched on later ; it is with respect to the second that the University records are of great value. At that time there were several members of the staff who had good business heads. It was not in this respect they failed. Without multiplying examples, it will suffice to quote the case of a foundation made by Hugh Boulter, Archbishop of Armagh, through Francis Hutcheson. The revenue in 1935 was just 124 per cent. on the original capital.

What is now known of Adam Smith's family shows that very many of them had marked administrative ability, and these records indicate that he was far from being an exception. We can follow him first employed in small, troublesome tasks. Having discharged his part well, he was often entrusted with the conclusion of the whole matter. As time went on he was used in more responsible and

---

[1] T. Reid, *Works*, ed. Hamilton, 1872, i, p. 40.
[2] See below, Chapter VII, and pp. 203-15.
[3] Rae, *Life*, pp. 67-86.

PROFESSORIAL DUTIES AT GLASGOW

difficult work, so that, in the end, there was no part of the business of the University in which he had not a share.[1] Some of his responsibilities came by the custom of seniority such as Quaestor for the Library, but his election as Dean of Faculty did not. It was frequently held during the first half of the century by a person not a Professor, in many cases the Dean was chosen by a plurality of votes: Adam Smith was elected unanimously. He was called on when anything required diplomatic handling, as for instance a difficult negotiation with the Town Council. When in his later years accounts had to be cleared with the Treasury or the Barons of the Exchequer of Scotland he was deputed for the task, and the endorsements on the wrappers and the numbers on the vouchers in his own handwriting show that he prepared these for a number of years earlier. There were several distinguished mathematicians amongst the Professors, but a special technique was required which Adam Smith had mastered. It looks as if the University depended so much on him that the statements of the crops of 1765, 1766 and 1767 under the tack of the Archbishopric were held back from audit until he had returned from France. Certainly the existing statements for these years are in a handwriting which closely resembles that of Adam Smith. It may have been that he visited Glasgow and drew it up. From the point of view of Accountancy, it is a curious document—one total bringing out a fraction $\frac{323}{480}$ of a penny.[2]

One of Adam Smith's official duties had the odd result of subjecting him to the attack of a pamphleteer. This was William Thom, the minister of Govan. He had a lawsuit with the University (which he lost) over a matter of a chalder of meal in the amount of his stipend, and there was scarcely any act of, or any absence of action by, the University which did not form a text for one of his pamphlets or letters. In a *Letter containing a Defence of the College of G——w against an insidious attempt to depreciate the Ability and Taste of its Professors* he has many sarcastic things to say about an address presented to the King in 1762 on the birth of the Prince of Wales. In a pretended apology it is stated that " the address was paltry, ill wrote, unsuitable, disaffected, stupid, ignorant, misspelt, full of improprieties and ridiculous blunders ". *Donaldsoniad : J——N D——N detected* continues the tale that " a learned gentleman " who is given all Adam Smith's characteristics, offered " to encounter personally the public ridicule which, it is said, the address had caused ". " And ", the tract adds, " in a trans-

---

[1] Affairs relating to the Church (other than those of a business nature) are excepted.

[2] University MSS., Muniment Room, Drawer G. 4 of Safe. The fraction quoted arises from the accounts at the University being kept in Scots currency, even merks Scots, which were converted into Sterling for the Government audit.

port of gratitude it was voted upon the spot to dubb him D—— of L—— which was executed with all convenient speed." [1] Probably all this did not occasion Adam Smith much concern. The event has its amusing side. Evidently Thom had heard some rumour of Adam Smith being asked to write an address. The record below [2] will show that he had got the facts inverted. It was the previous address of 1760 which Adam Smith had drafted, for that of 1762 he was one of a small committee. Probably what gave rise to the whole nonsensical statement was that Adam Smith was granted the degree of LL.D., and the Address was signed and sent for presentation towards the end of the month of October, 1762.

These facts testify to Adam Smith's efficiency, but there was much more in the situation than this. He had in his daily life the sympathy which he developed as an ethical principle. He thought the best of his colleagues,[3] and they met his favourable opinion, more or less, by living up to the good that he saw in them. Also he was perfectly objective in considering always the good of the University. Others brought forward proposals which were openly or veiledly in their own personal interests, or, what is more subtle and in fact, if carried too far, a refined form of egoism, the interests of their departments. It was never so with Adam Smith. He never made any proposition which, even remotely, could fall under either of these heads. The only instance where he did something for a friend was when he proposed William Robertson, the historian, for the degree of D.D., which was fully justified on the merits of the case. His admirer, Lord Cardross, afterwards Earl of Buchan, received the same degree in 1763, but Adam Smith did not promote it.

This characteristic was something which was peculiar to Adam Smith to the extent which he possessed it, and it even transfigured his countenance. It is noticeable that two writers, who differed so much in temperament and outlook as Alexander Carlyle and Dugald Stewart, both draw attention to it. The former speaks of his unbounded benevolence, adding that " his smile of approbation was truly captivating ",[4] and the latter of how, in the society of those he loved, his features were often brightened " with a smile of inexpressible benignity ".[5] A smile both " captivating " and of " inexpressible benignity " seems to the present generation mere hyperbole. It is fortunate that like the rather protruding lower lip—in the latter recalling the same characteristic, but with a different expression, in the Hapsburgs—this was a trait of his branch of the Douglases which has appeared occasionally since. As described by Mrs. Bannerman of Edinburgh,

---

[1] W. Thom, *Works*, Glasgow, 1799, pp. 351-61. [2] See below, p. 160.
[3] This point is developed more generally in Chapter VIII, pp. 99-100.
[4] A. Carlyle, *Autobiography*, 1860, p. 281. [5] D. Stewart, *Memoir*, 1811, p. 117.

in one of the family whom she still remembers, the whole face seemed to light up and glow with an inner light expressing kindliness and the greatest goodwill. It would require someone very fast-bound in selfishness or in his own fixed opinion when Adam Smith turned what might perhaps be called, in the deepest meaning of the word, " a Christmas face " to him to remain obstinately perverse. It is certain that, more and more, he influenced the other members of the Professoriate, and that his opinions were respected by them.

His absence of mind was the result of his power of intense concentration. This, which was natural to him, was developed by Alfred Marshall by a technique of his own which was intentionally discontinuous.[1] Such a faculty is not uncommon in men who have thought deeply. And it is to be remembered that it operates in two directions. If, for instance, Adam Smith were immersed in searching for the origin of antonomasia,[2] subject to what is said below, he might appear to be totally unconscious of some interesting, or even unique economic event. Conversely, when his whole attention was directed to something practical, he saw much more in that situation than others who witnessed it at the same time. In addition to this Dugald Stewart adds a hint of another quality which is much more rare. He wrote in 1791-2 : " I have often however been struck, at the distance of years with the accurate memory (of Adam Smith) of the most trifling particulars, and am inclined to believe, from this and other circumstances, that he possessed a power, not perhaps uncommon among absent men of recollecting, in consequence of subsequent efforts of reflection, many occurrences which, at the time when they happened, did not seem to have sensibly attracted his notice ".[3] The quality Stewart records would imply a capacity of retentiveness also far in excess of the average. Some psychologists consider that capacity, " as a physiological quality, is given once for all with a man's organisation, and which he can never hope to change ".[4] Whether it is fixed in quantity for each individual is not important in the present enquiry. What appears to emerge is that while Adam Smith had very great powers of concentration, those of retentiveness did not exactly balance them, but were still greater. So far as interest entered into the situation the scope of Adam Smith's is relevant. It seems that he may have had an awareness of two trains of events, one of which required his whole power of concentration, yet the other was retained and could be recalled on a subsequent occasion. Stewart's description is of special interest as showing, by his own

---

[1] A. C. Pigou, ed., *Memorials of Alfred Marshall*, 1925, pp. 4, 5.
[2] " Considerations concerning the first Formation of Languages ", in *Theory of Moral Sentiments*, 1892, p. 509.
[3] D. Stewart, *Memoir*, 1811, p. 114.   [4] James, *Principles of Psychology*, i, p. 664.

actual experience with Adam Smith, that the power of recall was very marked, though one would wish to know where the initiative lay. That power would be stronger if Stewart brought up the subject than if it was started by Smith himself. Perhaps this is one of those cases where the artistic imagination may come nearest to the truth. The following description of the memory of a character in fiction —a violinist—may be compared with that of Stewart. " Jake remembered every detail of the transaction which had taken place in Mr. Mountain's office four years ago, though he had not been in the room for part of the time and had appeared lost in his own meditations when it was over. ' Darling ', said Désirée, ' I never dreamt that you knew it could be brought back again. I never dreamt it would be possible.' ' Oh ' said Jake, ' I didn't know then—at least I only *heard*. But when I looked in my mind I remembered. You and Dick talked about it in the taxi.' ' But you weren't listening.' ' I told you ', said Jake, with the impatience he showed on the rare occasions when he attempted to explain his mental processes, ' I *heard*. And when I wanted to remember, I did.' "[1] There is a direct contrast to Adam Smith's method of working with an amanuensis and that of Scott, whose ideas ran far ahead of the pen of the writer. In this case also there was the faculty of carrying on two trains of thought, apparently at the same time. Robert Hogg, a nephew of the author of the *Ettrick Shepherd*, thus described how he wrote from Sir Walter's dictation. " His thoughts flowed easily and felicitously, without any difficulty to lay hold of them or to find appropriate language. . . . He sat in his chair from which he rose now and then, took a volume from the bookcase, consulted it and restored it to the shelf—all without intermission in the current of ideas, which continued to be delivered with no less readiness than if his mind had been wholly occupied with the words he was uttering. It soon became apparent to me, however, that he was carrying on two distinct trains of thought, one of which was already arranged and in the act of being spoken while, at the same time, he was in advance considering what was afterwards to be said. This I discovered by his sometimes introducing a word which was wholly out of place—*entertained* instead of *denied*, for example—but which I presently found to belong to the next sentence, perhaps four or five lines down."[2]

The University was only a part of Adam Smith's life at Glasgow. The town was his laboratory. In the middle of the eighteenth century it was a remarkable blend of the old and the new. The history of the last hundred years had left enduring traces which were being modified slowly, and sometimes painfully, by a new spirit and by new conditions. The memory of religious persecution in the West before the Revolution had resulted in a somewhat stern and rigid control of

---

[1] Naomi Royde-Smith, *Jake*, 1935, p. 237.   [2] Lockhart, *Life of Scott*, 1838, vii, p. 41.

life by the ministers. The kirk session became the arbiter of morals and, to some extent, even of manners. Young women were warned not to live alone and were told that they would be taken notice of " unless they got honest men or took themselves to service "—an order which might have been less ambiguously expressed. Nor might women, whether married or unmarried, come to the kirk with plaids about their heads lest they should sleep unnoticed during the sermon.[1] Stage plays were anathema. Robert Wodrow, the Church historian, noted with great satisfaction that in 1727 a company of actors who came from Edinburgh to produce " The Beggar's Opera " did not make " so much as to pay their music ".[2] The whole range of invective was directed against the theatre. It was " the temple of Beelzebub, the Devil's Home, the pavilion of Satan, the Temple of Belial, the temple of Satan, the pit of Hell ",[3] references which are of interest in relation to Adam Smith's action when it was proposed to build a theatre in the city in 1762.[4] Such stringent control sometimes had the inevitable consequence of producing a hypocritical outward conformity, as, for instance, in the case of a calico printer who invited the official, who had arrived to stamp his goods, to breakfast and long family prayers, during which his industrious apprentice was busy in affixing the official seal,[5] which had been left in the warehouse. Nor was the general state of the town satisfactory. Robbery with violence was common. In 1750 the city was described as much infested by thieves; and, although a house-to-house visitation was made and many suspected persons taken up, the evil continued and in 1754 fifty gentlemen, " observing the increase in vice and wickedness, have raised a fund to bring offenders to condign punishment ". This effort did not effect a permanent remedy, and in 1764 the Hall of the Town Council was burgled and an attempt made to fire it, whereby " goods to a considerable value were spoiled and burned ".[6] Thus the picture of the times is one of strong lights and some deep shadows.

The serious and religious spirit of the age found expression in the old motto of the city—" Let Glasgow flourish by the preaching of the Word ". And flourish it did. From 1730 to 1770 remarkable progress was made. The opening of the tobacco trade with the plantations after the Union established a commerce which from small beginnings became immense. The Clyde imported tobacco

[1] J. Strang, *Glasgow and Its Clubs*, 1857, p. 143 (notes).
[2] F. G. Fyfe, *Scottish Diaries*, p. 387.
[3] Walter Baynham, *The Glasgow Stage*, Glasgow, 1892, pp. 4-15.
[4] See below, p. 165.
[5] J. Strang, *Glasgow and Its Clubs*, 1857, p. 352 (note).
[6] *Glasgow Courant*, 7th January, 1750; 3rd February, 1752; 2nd December, 1754. *Glasgow Journal*, 26th April, 1764.

and other colonial products, the greater part of the former being re-exported. In order to pay for these imports, manufactures, large and small, sprang up which supplied all, or almost all, the wants of the settlers. Saddlery and leather goods were prominent amongst these, and Glasgow had several tanneries—one of which is said to have been the largest in Europe—where a strange adventure befell Adam Smith, as is related elsewhere.[1] Through a fire at the Custom House in which the local records were lost, there remain only stray figures which had been extracted earlier. These are sufficiently impressive. In the year 1771-2 over 45 million lbs. of tobacco were imported, of which only a small part was retained for home consumption, the remainder being re-exported to the Continent.[2] At this time between 54 per cent. and 55 per cent. of the total import of tobacco into Great Britain came to the Clyde.[3] It is easy to imagine that, following the early enquiries of Adam Smith on economic questions which have been described in Chapter V, the intense activity of such a diversified industry would make a very great impression on a mind so receptive as his. Indeed, many of the observations which he then made were used as illustrations in *The Glasgow Lectures*, and that, too, in some cases where Glasgow is not expressly mentioned.[4]

The growth of commerce had a great effect in enlarging men's outlook. The district within reach of the Clyde began to cease to be provincial and was taking a wider outlook. The West, and through it the remainder of the country, was being brought into touch both with the Old World and the New. Such a profound change could not fail to have a great effect on manners. The tobacco trade dominated industry. The size of ships was not quoted in tons, but in hogsheads. After the disturbance of the Rebellion was over the standard of life began to rise very rapidly. In view of what has been said about the poverty of the country before the Union, it is clear that the financing of such a great commerce presented much difficulty. This was met partly by delayed payment for tobacco and partly by the aid of the banks. Still, with a continually increasing trade, the profits made in the first twenty-five years were needed for the expanding businesses. After that it became possible to use some part of them in improvement of the amenities of life. Previously the traditional domestic habits had been continued, so that the family of a man of consideration, either in business or a profession, was content with a flat of four or five rooms—the one sitting-room being reserved for

---

[1] See below, p. 324 note [3].
[2] J. Gibson, *History of Glasgow*, 1777, pp. 213-234. The re-exports were about 40 million lbs.
[3] J. Strang, *Glasgow and Its Clubs*, 1857, p. 33 (note).
[4] D. Murray, *Early Burgh Organisation in Scotland*, i, pp. 451-5.

occasions of special importance ; while at other times meals were served in a bedroom.[1] In the second quarter of the century those strange figures of eighteenth-century Glasgow—the tobacco lords—began to appear in their scarlet cloaks, and to build self-contained houses outside the narrow limits of the city as it was then. In the ten years of Smith's absence there was a very great change in the appearance of the district. Looking down from the high ground near the University, recently completed mansions of merchants and others in the course of building came into view. Some of these merchants had the idea of establishing a club with the object of enquiring into trade in all its branches. Andrew Cochrane, acknowledged to have been Glasgow's greatest provost and who was an extensive merchant, was the founder. It was he who furnished Adam Smith with many of the facts and some ideas which, eventually, found a place in *The Wealth of Nations*. By a most brilliant piece of historical reconstruction the late Dr. David Murray has re-created the membership of this Club during its early years—the existing Adam Smith Club of Glasgow, which continues on something like the same principles, having no documents except those of very recent date. This club, according to Dr. Murray, was in existence prior to 1743. It was not thoroughly established when the Rebellion came, and Cochrane was fully occupied in protecting the city from the most exorbitant demands of the Prince and the Highland host. For some time afterwards he was endeavouring—and with considerable success— to wring compensation for the citizens from the Government in London. When the club was re-started after the Rebellion the following have been identified by Dr. Murray as having been almost certainly members. In addition to the founder, Alexander Speirs who imported one-twelfth of the total import of tobacco to Europe, John Glassford whose turnover was half a million a year, and James Ritchie, another well-known merchant. At a later period Professor Wight and W. Cunningham were included. Others, who were probably members, were George and John Murdoch, both provosts, Robin Bogle, Thomas Dunmore, Walter Stirling, Alexander and Richard Oswald.[2] Adam Smith became a member very soon after his arrival at Glasgow, and it was not long before he was very intimate with Cochrane, who has the distinction of being the first to recognise Adam Smith's economic ability, by securing his admission as an honorary burgess

---

[1] Adam Smith states that, when he lived at Glasgow, scarcely anyone had more than one servant—*Glasgow Lectures*, p. 155.

[2] D. Murray, *Early Burgh Organisation in Scotland*, i, pp. 446-50. There is also included by Dr. Murray John Dalrymple, later Sir John and a Baron of the Exchequer. Dalrymple was a member of the Literary Club, to which he was probably introduced by Adam Smith. If he was a member of this club he probably joined it later than Smith and through him. The members of the club, whose names are given above, were all either prominent in civil life or eminent merchants. Particulars of their careers are given by Dr. Murray.

of the city, or as the formula went, a burgess, *gratis*.[1] It was to the commercial club or Cochrane's Club that he read the most important paper, known as the " Lecture of 1755 ". One result of the activities of this club was a serious consideration of questions of principle as affecting trade which extended far beyond the members. The Foulis firm of printers were issuing books relating to the subject ; and, when Adam Smith came to Glasgow, he found these books in the shops and there were numerous advertisements in the Press. For instance, in March 1751 Foulis had a column advertisement which included Law, *On Money and Trade* ; Gee, *Trade and Navigation* (both of which were issued the previous year) ; *Proposals for a Council of Trade in Scotland*, Petty's *Political Arithmetic*, Josiah Child *On Trade*, Berkeley's *Querist*, etc. Towards the end of the year another bookseller, Baxter, was advertising *A Theory of Commerce and Maritime Affairs* and Postlethwayt's *Dictionary of Commerce* in 6d. parts.[2] These advertisements of varied lists of books of economic interest continued, though those of Foulis became less frequent as he was more and more involved in his Academy of Arts.

Rae gives an excellent account of the other clubs to which Adam Smith belonged, namely the Literary Society, founded in 1752, of which he was an original member and to which he contributed " an Account of some of Mr. David Hume's Essays on Commerce " at the third meeting on 23rd January, 1752,[3] and the first two parts of what became his Essay on the Imitative Arts.[4] There was also the very interesting social club, founded by Robert Simson, which met at the village of Anderston, near Glasgow. In Edinburgh he was elected a member of the Philosophical Society on its revival in 1752, he was one of the founders of the Select Society in 1754, and also of the Poker Club in 1762.

The membership of these clubs involved further demands upon Adam Smith's time, in addition to that required for his College duties. The Anderston Club met on Saturdays, and it was the custom for the College members, when the corrections of that day were over, to walk to the meeting place, dine, have their discussion, and return in the late afternoon. This club met each week. The Literary Club also met weekly, its day being Friday. The Trade or Political

---

[1] Bannerman MSS., Univ. Libry. Glasg., the original burgess ticket, dated 3rd May, 1762. He was also an honorary freeman of Edinburgh and Musselburgh. He was admitted to the latter on 26th September, 1767, with his former pupil, the Duke of Buccleuch, and Chief Baron Ord.

[2] *Glasgow Courant*, 25th March, 1st July, 30th September, 23rd December.

[3] R. Duncan, *Notices illustrative of the Literary History of Glasgow*, 1831, p. 132. Rae makes the year 1753, and therefore his reference to the advance copy of a new edition of the *Essays* should be deleted.

[4] See below, p. 112

Economy Club, again, had meetings each week—the day not being known. During the session Adam Smith cannot have attended the Edinburgh clubs frequently. He could only go if his being there on University business coincided with a meeting. Thus, if he was regular in attendance, his clubs at Glasgow would account for an afternoon and two evenings in the week during the session. As has been shown, he had little free time in the morning, perhaps enough to visit the Library and see new books or select those to be sent to his house. As to the afternoons, when College meetings were held, these fell unequally in different years, the probability is that he would have rather less than an average of two each week during term. On the whole, one gathers the impression that he would have had time to do a certain amount of reading, but that the serious part of his study and writing would have to be relegated to the long vacation, which was fully four months. Even this estimate might require some modification if the view of John Dalrymple of Cranstoun be accepted as to Smith's " indolence ". In a long letter he wrote to Foulis in 1757 he uses the word twice, in one case speaking of it as " usual ".[1] Hume, who knew him better, though he often complains of unanswered letters, recognised that, when Smith was involved in a particular enquiry, it was useless to try to divert him from it.

[1] R. Duncan, *Notices of Literary History of Glasgow*, 1831, pp. 23, 28.

CHAPTER VII

THE CONSTITUTIONAL QUESTION IN THE UNIVERSITY OF GLASGOW, 1761-1764

There remains one episode in the career of Adam Smith, while he was at the University of Glasgow, which is not only of very great interest but also, unfortunately, of considerable complexity. As to the first—it provides a memorandum composed by Adam Smith, which relates to education, and thus is the companion picture to that on the training for the medical profession which was written in 1774.[1] The earlier document is the more important since it raises issues which were fundamental in the administration and finance of Scottish Universities in the eighteenth century. From the biographical point of view it confirms what has already been said as showing the important place which Adam Smith had won amongst his colleagues, and especially his powers of conciliating and reconciling different and even opposed arguments and opinions on academic policy. At the same time it is difficult to understand the part which Adam Smith was called upon to assume, without appreciating both the character and even the peculiarities of the chief persons involved and also a number of events in the history of the University, some of which extended back about two centuries before the time of Adam Smith.

There can be no doubt that in the situation which has to be discussed, the personal idiosyncrasies of the chief actors played a considerable part. In the middle of the eighteenth century there were at Glasgow a Principal and twelve Professors. In 1760 a thirteenth—that of Astronomy—had been added. This was the only Chair established between 1718 and 1807. The first incumbent of this Professorship was Alexander Wilson, who had designed and founded the types for the printing press of the Foulises. Of the other twelve Professors, besides Adam Smith, several were famous in their own subjects. Joseph Black, the discoverer of latent heat, was appointed Professor of Medicine in 1756, and the next year he exchanged this Chair for that of Anatomy, which had been held by William Cullen, who had a large part in establishing the medical schools of Glasgow and Edinburgh. The election of John Millar to the Professorship of

[1] J. Thomson, *Life, Lectures and Writings of William Cullen*, Edin., 1859, i, pp. 473-81.

Civil Law in 1761 finds its place in one of the documents printed below.[1] He had attended Adam Smith's lectures on Jurisprudence at Edinburgh and, as Professor at Glasgow, he soon won an exceedingly high reputation. Lord Cockburn speaks of his " magical vivacity " which, however, failed to lighten the pages of his book *Concerning the Origin and Distinction of Ranks in Society* (1771). Dr. David Murray gave a long list of students who had come to Glasgow in order to study under him, and who became judges, diplomatists and statesmen.[2] Simson, the mathematician, retired in 1761 and was followed by James Williamson, who did not publish anything. James Clow, the successor of Adam Smith in the Chair of Logic, suffered in reputation through a curious concatenation of circumstances. A student named Woodburn had stated in one of the College debating societies, which was named " the Parliament of Oceana ",[3] that " more good was to be got by attending the theatre than the drowsy shops of Logic and Metaphysics ". For this disrespect he was tried in the Rector's Court and admonished.[4] The admonishment was soon forgotten, but " the drowsy shop " was long remembered as a characterisation, supposed to be apt, of the unfortunate Clow's lectures. As a matter of fact, he was a man of great ability, having been chosen, quite possibly on the recommendation of Adam Smith, to edit the highly important works of Simson, in which, amongst other reconstructions of Greek Mathematics, that of the Porisms was included.[5] In one sense Clow, as a scholar, was handicapped by his other qualities. He succeeded Adam Smith in advising on the business of the University, and, as these duties increased, they absorbed more and more of his time and energy.

The remaining seven Professors fall into two groups—one numbering four, which affords little of interest and the other which presents some striking complexities of character. The first included Robert Trail who was appointed Professor of Oriental Languages in 1761 and was translated to the Chair of Divinity six weeks later. His settlement in the parish of Kettins coincided with the Rebellion of 1745, and he was kidnapped by a mob led by a man wearing a white

[1] See below, p. 200.

[2] D. Murray, *Old College of Glasgow*, 1927, pp. 221-2.

[3] There are many references to this society in the papers of Lord Buchan—the Murray MSS., Univ. Libry. Glasg.

[4] [W. Thom], *The Trial of a Student in the College of Clutha*, Glasgow, 1768.

[5] R. Simson (ed. R. Clow), *Opera quædam reliqua, scilicet Apollonii Pergaei de sectione determinata libri ii restituti, duobus insuper libris aucti : Porismatum liber : de Logarithmis liber : de limitibus quantitatum et rationum Fragmentum*, Glas., 1776. The reason for stating that Adam Smith may have suggested Clow as the editor was that the book was printed at the cost of Philip, second Earl Stanhope, who was a friend of Adam Smith, and was in correspondence with him at the time when an editor was being chosen—Rae, *Life*, pp. 191, 193, 266, and below, p. 273 note [4].

cockade. In 1771 he was associated with Boswell in the reception of General Paoli.[1] His name is preserved as the nominal leader of one of the parties in the dispute in the University. It was over the appointment of William Wight, Professor of Church History, as Chaplain of the University in 1765, that this dispute began. His contemporaries were unanimous in their praise of his charm of manner. Alexander Carlyle, his cousin, described him in 1759 as " young, handsome, learned, eloquent and witty ",[2] and Lord Buchan said he was " a man of genius, of polite literature and of singular sweetness in his manner ".[3] Hume added, if less enthusiastically, that " he was a sensible, good-humoured gentleman-like fellow and as orthodox as you could wish ".[4] George Muirhead, Professor of Humanity, assisted his colleague, James Moor, in the preparation of the celebrated edition of Homer which was issued by the Foulis Press. The last member of this group was Thomas Hamilton, Professor of Medicine.

The three remaining personalities were William Leechman, John Anderson and James Moor. Leechman had been appointed Professor of Divinity, after a great contest, being in the opinion of Francis Hutcheson " the only right Professor of Theology in Scotland ".[5] His biographer, James Wodrow, describes " the great multitude of students " which attended his classes, but this, in the end, is reduced to " a larger number than in any other Divinity Hall in Scotland ".[6] Certainly, as a lecturer, he was not unworthy to rank with Simson, Smith, Cullen, Black and Miller. In 1761 he was appointed Principal of the University. It is difficult to determine how far he was responsible for the troubles which he encountered in that office. There is not the slightest doubt that he was a man of high character, and no charge, with the faintest semblance of substance, can be sustained either against his uprightness or his honour. The traditional view is that he was a good man struggling with the adversity heaped upon him by the evil disposition of several of his opponents. Human affairs would be much simpler if in every difficulty the situation could be neatly arranged so as to present pairs of opposites which could be labelled " right " or " wrong ". Where Leechman appears to have created needless difficulties for himself and for the University was through his singleness of purpose. Where there were alternative methods of reaching a certain goal, he was only able to see one, though the other might have been the

[1] H. M. B. Reid, *Divinity Professors in the University of Glasgow*, Glas., 1923, pp. 264-5.
[2] MSS. of the Duke of Buccleuch at Dalkeith House—Townshend Collection.
[3] University of Glasgow MSS.—Murray Collection—Lord Buchan's Diaries and Letter Book, 1763.
[4] J. Y. T. Greig, *Letters of Hume*, Oxford, 1932, ii, p. 303.
[5] W. R. Scott, *Francis Hutcheson*, Cambridge, 1900, p. 93.
[6] J. Wodrow (ed.), *Sermons of William Leechman*, London, 1889, i, pp. 29, 70.

more suitable line of approach, not necessarily in itself, but in relation to other standpoints which should have been conciliated, if that was possible. Also, and in part arising from this trait of character, he seems to have overlooked that, when differences of opinion arose, it was not sufficient to carry his point, but that it was desirable to win over those who were temporarily opposed to him, otherwise the division was in danger of becoming permanent. Then, too, as will be seen, he was not altogether happy in the judgements which he formed of those with whom he was associated. In this respect his loyalties sometimes led him to trust subordinates when a knowledge of the circumstances would have indicated, clearly, that this was no longer wholly judicious.[1] In the account of his life it is indicated that he experienced " a peculiar trouble " when he became Principal, in the financial administration of the University which is explained " through his having been little accustomed to business in his former life ".[2] But he had been seventeen years a Professor, and, as has been seen, twelve of this body had to manage all the affairs of the University, so that there had been a very protracted apprenticeship in that work.

John Anderson seems to have been born to trouble as sparks fly upward. In 1754 he had been appointed Professor of Oriental Languages, and three years later he was elected Professor of Natural Philosophy, on which occasion Adam Smith joined in a protest against the impropriety of his taking part in his own election.[3] It is perhaps easiest to form an impression of his character and temperament by beginning with what he was not, rather than what he was. He had little disposition towards the advancement of Science by independent investigation. While Watt and Black were enquiring into the properties of steam, there is no trace of Anderson having shown an interest in the enquiry. The chief direction in which he experimented was in Ballistics and Projectiles. It was on his initiative that many books on these subjects were added to the Library during the second half of the eighteenth century; and, towards the end of his life, he invented a gun in which the recoil was deadened by air which was stored in the carriage. After the British Government had declined the invention, it was accepted by the Executive of the French Revolution, as " the Gift of Science to Liberty ".[4] As a lecturer he had a gift of popular exposition, and he was proficient in demonstrating his experiments. The claim, which has been advanced on his behalf—that he was a pioneer in extending higher education to the working classes—cannot be substantiated. The credit of this development belongs, not to Anderson, but to George Birkbeck who started, almost accidentally, a class which numbered as many

---

[1] See below, p. 96.
[2] J. Wodrow (ed.), *Sermons of William Leechman*, i, p. 77.
[3] See below, p. 189.
[4] J. Coutts, *History of the University of Glasgow*, 1909, p. 320.

as 500, in 1800, a date which was four years after the death of Anderson.[1] When the latter was in his prime he could make himself most pleasant to anyone whom he wished to influence or whom he met casually. He was very fascinating as long as he got his own way. If he failed in this, he was liable to allow his ungovernable temper to have full sway, when he sometimes said things which were not only cruel but beyond the bounds both of good manners and good feeling. There are far too many cases in the University Records of his accusing other members of the College of tampering with the minutes, accompanied with innuendoes of embezzlement and forgery. Nor was it only his colleagues who came under his displeasure. When he became irritated with his students—in some cases with those who became eminent later [2]—he was quite extraordinarily injudicious. As a single instance from a number the case of James Prossor may be mentioned. While this youth was attending Anderson's class and was in a hurry to leave, he stepped over a rail. The Professor seized hold of him and forced him backwards so that he was in danger of being seriously injured by a row of pointed iron spikes. Prossor offered to apologise for what he had done amiss, but intimated at the same time that Anderson should apologise for the rough usage to which he had been subjected. The next day Anderson applied, without success, for a file of soldiers to arrest Prossor. Failing in this, he gathered a number of rough men who seized the student and lodged him in the common jail in a room where ordinary criminals were detained. Apart altogether from the remarkable absence of restraint and considerations of elementary justice, such action hit the University in a very tender place, for it claimed to exercise complete jurisdiction over its own members, and the invoking of outside assistance, altogether apart from the want of justification for it, was regarded as very serious infraction of the privileges of the Rector and his Court.[3] It is little wonder that, after a number of somewhat similar incidents, the University was compelled to suspend Anderson from the exercise of *jurisdictio ordinaria*.

James Moor in several respects is the enigma amongst the contemporaries of Adam Smith at Glasgow. He was the " ingenious lad " who collaborated with Hutcheson in the translation of Marcus Aurelius which was published by Foulis in 1742.[4] In 1746 he succeeded Alexander Dunlop as Professor of Greek. The

[1] *Glasgow Mechanics Magazine*, ii, pp. 410, 442; iii, p. 12; D. Murray, *The Old College*, 1927, p. 115; Graham Wallas, *Life of Place*, pp. 122-3.

[2] As, for instance, Simon Jefimovich Desnitzsky, who became Professor of Roman Law and Russian Jurisprudence at the University of Moscow; see below, Appendix VII.

[3] As an instance, in 1670 this Court tried a student who was charged with murder. He was acquitted—J. Coutts, *Hist. of Univ. of Glasgow*, 1909, p. 156.

[4] The first two books were by Moor, the remainder by Hutcheson—R. Duncan, *Literary History of Glasgow*, 1831, p. 49.

essays which he read to the Literary Society of Glasgow [1] give the impression that Moor was rather the type of the " elegant " scholar than that of the editor of texts. It was his connection with the Foulises—Robert was his brother-in-law—that led to the latter occupation making so great demands on him. The revision of the text of Homer for the edition of Foulis was undoubtedly a very great strain. It is said that the work extended over a great part of the night and Moor formed the habit of keeping himself wakeful and alert by consuming large quantities of strong tea and coffee. This had unfavourable reactions on his nervous system. The less charitable, such as Thomas Reid,[2] attributed his uncertainty of temper to intemperance. Like Anderson, he had trouble with his students, and, in the end, had to resign his Chair through an attack which he made upon one of them. In the meetings of the University he was liable to take offence upon the slightest occasion. His judgement was fluctuating, and it is difficult to discover the reasons which led to some of the proposals and protests which he made. The latter were frequent, but there was this difference between Anderson and Moor. The dignity or the interest of the former was likely to be the occasion of an outburst if it seemed that either was threatened, even remotely. With Moor it is difficult to find any reasonable basis for some of his actions. Thus, in given circumstances, it is the easiest thing in the world to see how Anderson would act, but Moor's course was often quite unpredictable.

It was on such personalities that Adam Smith had to exercise his powers as a moderating and conciliating influence.

The other factor in the situation was the series of difficulties which had arisen in the government of the University. It is unfortunate that these occurred at the period of its history about which least is known. The histories of Reid and Coutts are not sufficiently detailed to present a complete picture. The *Munimenta*,[3] which give all the more important documents and many other records, do not continue beyond 1727, while the Appendix to the *Report of the Commission of 1826* carries some of the accounts and statements back to 1777.[4] It was in the second half of the fifty years, which are partially unchronicled, that the difficulties emerged, though, like many things in the life of Universities, the ultimate origin was very much earlier. The charter of *Nova Erectio* of 1577 contemplated the

---

[1] " On the Influence of Philosophy on the Fine Arts ", " On Historical Composition " read 1752, " On the Composition of the Picture described in the Picture of Cebes ", read 1754, published in *Essays read to a Literary Society*, 1759 ; *A Vindication of Virgil*, read 1761 and published separately in 1766.

[2] T. Reid, *Works* (ed. Hamilton), 1872, i, p. 40.

[3] *Munimenta Alme Universitatis Glasguensis* (Maitland Club), 1854.

[4] *Report and Evidence of the University Commission of 1826*, ii (Glasgow).

work of the University as being carried on by Regents,[1] of whom one was the Principal Regent, but who for a long time afterwards took his share in the teaching. Later the Principal Regent became a Principal who had no regular duties in the giving of instruction. At the beginning of the eighteenth century the Principal was John Stirling, who held office from 1701 to 1728. He was remarkably adroit and succeeded in giving effect to his policy on occasions when the majority of the College was opposed to it. One of his methods was to keep himself well informed as to the whereabouts of the Regents even during vacations, and he called a meeting when he was assured that a sufficient number of his supporters would be available. The Visitation of 1727 (which, incidentally, transformed the Regents into Professors) made regulations which were designed to obviate this and similar abuses,[2] but the fear of dictatorial powers in the hands of the Principal was a very real one during the ensuing forty years, and explains much that would otherwise be obscure in the government of the University during that period. It was this dread which was the basis of changes in procedure which resulted in much difference of opinion and division at a later stage. Neil Campbell had succeeded Sterling as Principal. In 1752 he became paralysed and was unable to take any further part in University business. The last meeting at which he presided was on 24th July, 1752. It has been shown that the chief meetings for the transaction of business were those presided over by the Rector, the Dean and the Principal. According to the regulations of the Visitation of 1727 during a vacancy in the Principalship or in the event of his failure or inability to call a meeting at the quarterly dates, specified by the Visitation, this duty devolved upon the senior Regent of Philosophy, now a Professor.[3] Moor was in this position at the time, and for over four years he continued to summon the quarterly meetings and to preside at them. Though the Faculty met, more and more business was transferred to the Rector's meeting. In 1755 Moor took offence for no adequate reason, and, after 7th November, 1755, no further meetings of the Faculty were held until 6th November, 1761. It was unfortunate that the rules of the Visitors in 1727 did not provide for a refusal of the senior Professor of Philosophy to summon a meeting. The right of any three Professors to demand of the Principal or senior Regent that a meeting should be convened was permissive not obligatory.[4]

[1] A Regent had certain students allotted to him. He taught these all the subjects included in the curriculum, as it then existed.

[2] *Munimenta*, iii, p. 572.

[3] The Professors who represented the Regents of Philosophy were those of Natural Philosophy, Moral Philosophy, Logic, and Greek. Adam Smith followed Moor in the order of seniority.

[4] It might be urged that, since the Statutes of the Visitation of 1727 ordained quarterly meetings, these should have been held. Even the day of each of these meetings was fixed by the Visita-

UNIVERSITY POLITICS

Another change in the conduct of business had important constitutional reactions. In the long list of Deans of Faculty from the foundation up till 1731 there were only five occasions when this office was filled by a Regent or a Professor. Then from 1732 to 1767 there comes a succession of Professors, broken from 1746 to 1750 by two ministers.[1] Further, it had been the custom to elect, as Rector, some person of position who resided in the neighbourhood, and who was able to preside at his Court frequently or, at least, with reasonable regularity. In 1754 there was a change, after which date the Rector rarely attended, except for his installation, and his duties were discharged by a Professor, as Vice-Rector. These circumstances removed the check on administration imposed by the Ordinary Visitors, who, it will be recalled, were the Rector, the Dean of Faculty and the Minister of Glasgow. For a period of over ten years the acting Rector was a Professor, the Dean of Faculty was another and for fifty years the Minister of Glasgow was, at the same time, the Principal of the University. Thus the intention, in instituting Ordinary Visitors, as the normal check on the current administration of the Principal and Professors, was rendered wholly illusory.

Neil Campbell, the bedridden Principal, died on 22nd June, 1761, and the commission appointing Leechman as his successor reached Glasgow on 11th July.[2] He had served no less than four years as Dean of Faculty and two years as Vice-Rector without making any objection to the procedure as it existed at that time. In his new position he at once determined not only to restore the functions of the Principal's meeting—as he was fully entitled to do—but also to extend even further the dominance of the Professoriate under his leadership, thus marking a significant advance towards establishing what, as Sir William Hamilton said, " all theory and all experience prove to be the worst and the most corrupt depositaries of academical patronage, namely a self-elective body of Professors ".[3]

The stage is now set, and the chief actors have been introduced. If the action has dragged hitherto, it becomes more dramatic with the appearance of one of the chief characters—Adam Smith. On 27th June, 1761, it had been decided to hold a Rector's meeting on 15th July. When that date came Leechman wrote on the morning of the day fixed, that unless the Rector was present in person no meeting could be held, for he (Leechman) had already resigned his

tion and therefore they should have been convened despite any opposition Moor might have offered. Since Adam Smith was next in seniority to Moor, it seems that he cannot be absolved from some responsibility in the matter. He should have moved and have obtained the consent of any two Professors (not necessarily " gown " Professors) to fix an hour and draw up the agenda.

[1] *The University of Glasgow, Old and New*, Glasgow, 1891, pp. 19-20.
[2] *The Glasgow Journal*, 25th June and 16th July, 1761.
[3] *Works of T. Reid* (ed. Hamilton), 1872, i, p. 43 (note).

office as Vice-Rector on hearing that he had been appointed Principal. Since the meeting had been called, the Professors met to consider the situation. Adam Smith, being Dean of Faculty, acted as Præses. It was carried unanimously that the meeting having been legally convened, it had a right to transact the business on the agenda. Then there were consultations, as a result of which Adam Smith went backwards and forwards between the Faculty Room and Leechman's house with various proposals designed to meet the objections of Leechman who remained obdurate in his study. At one point it seemed that Adam Smith's diplomacy had prevailed, for Leechman was brought to offer to consider attending the meeting " as Vice-Rector " provided that the election of a Professor of Oriental Languages (which was an item on the agenda) should not take place that day. In this tentative proposal he appears to have had two objects in view; he may not have been in favour of the candidate who would have been elected, and there may have been floating in his mind, in a rudimentary form, the policy he later succeeded in forcing through, namely that elections of Professors should be made in future at the Principal's meeting and not at that of the Rector, as had long been the practice. Adam Smith having won the consent of his colleagues to this condition, returned to Leechman only to discover that he still refused to attend. It was then resolved to continue the meeting.[1] At this period the Earl of Errol was Rector and there had been no time to communicate with him. In any case, it was the custom that the Rector nominated a Vice-Rector in person. It seems that the propriety of the action both of Leechman and Adam Smith may be doubted. The former had not been admitted as Principal nor had he yet qualified before the Presbytery as he was bound to do before acting as Principal. Therefore he was still entitled to act as Vice-Rector, and the date of his resignation should have been, not that of his letter, but such time as his successor as Vice-Rector was appointed or as he was admitted Principal, whichever first happened. Nor was Adam Smith's position a happy one. It will be remembered that this meeting was the Court of the Rector at which he might be represented by the Vice-Rector. The Professors were merely assessors, and therefore in the absence of both Rector and Vice-Rector no assessor could take the place of either. Adam Smith's claim to act may have been that, as Dean of Faculty, he was one of the Ordinary Visitors of the University, and, as such, might take the place of the Rector or Vice-Rector in an emergency. Having taken the risk of continuing the meeting, Adam Smith's troubles were far from ended, since when Simson, who was still Clerk, was asked to send the Minute Books, he refused to do so. Then an emergency Clerk was added to the emergency Chairman, and the business was able to proceed. Matters

[1] See below, pp. 200-1.

were regularised by a meeting on 26th August, over which the Rector presided, and which approved of all the proceedings on 15th July.[1]

The meetings, at which the Principal was in the chair, were resumed, and at once a difficulty arose as to the character of business which, since 1755, had been transacted at the Rector's meeting and which should now be transferred back to that of the Principal. The Professoriate had changed so much since 1752 that, when Simson had retired at the end of the session 1760-1, there was scarcely anyone whose memory went back to the state of affairs before the illness of Neil Campbell. There were only two—Moor, whose judgement was unreliable, and Adam Smith, who had been a Professor during only one session while Campbell was able to act as Principal. Thus there was a tendency to accept the method of administration, which had developed in the last six years, as being the natural and normal order. On 19th April, 1762, a Committee was appointed, under the Chairmanship of Adam Smith, to report by 12th August upon the respective powers of the Rector and the Principal. The resulting report, which was drawn up by Adam Smith and is printed below,[2] involved a considerable amount of research, since it was necessary to examine and interpret the charters and statutes, to scrutinise the minutes and ascertain what had been the practice as far back as the existing records extended. This work must have constituted his chief occupation during the spring and summer of 1762.

In the preparation of this report Adam Smith was faced with two difficulties, one of which was fairly obvious, while the other is more obscure. In the first place the most important charter—that of the *Nova Erectio* of 1577, which was drawn up by George Buchanan, was far from clear upon the particular points that Adam Smith's committee had to determine. In the second place it was inevitable that the restoration of the functions of the Principal should revive the old fears as to an encroachment on the rights and privileges of the Professors. Thus, in order to allay the friction, which already had begun to develop, it was advisable to exercise the greatest powers of persuasion in order to obtain general acceptance of a method of government and administration that was in accordance with, or at least not contrary to, the charters and statutes. The difficulties were exceedingly great. There was a strong body of opinion amongst the majority of the Professors that the financial administration and the appointment of Professors should be continued in the Rector's Court or the University meeting. On the other side, Leechman urged that these classes of business were the province of the Principal's, the College or the Faculty meeting. Adam Smith's solution was

[1] See below, p. 201. It is significant that Leechman did not attend this meeting.
[2] See below, pp. 203-15.

to restore what he maintained had been the general practice before 1752, namely, that the Principal's meeting should be responsible for routine administration and finance subject to the control of the Ordinary Visitors and the Rector's meeting for the disposition of surplus revenue. There is one striking omission. The independent check on finance through the supervision of the Rector, Dean of Faculty and the Minister of Glasgow was rendered illusory by the two former being Professors and the failure of the third to act. He may have thought that this point was sufficiently covered by a quotation from a protest of Simson in 1755, in which, amongst other matters which the report does not accept, it is stated that the visitorial function of the Rector (not the Vice-Rector) should be restored. At the same time neither this protest nor the report takes account of the growing practice of electing a Rector who, by reason of his other engagements, was precluded from performing, personally, the duty of checking the somewhat voluminous accounts which was implied in the duty of the Ordinary Visitors.

There is one significant omission in Adam Smith's report. It was the custom for the Professors, not only to act as assessors at the Rector's meeting (at which the Dean of Faculty was entitled to be present) but also to vote. Though precedents could be found confirming this practice, no authority from the charters or statutes is adduced for it. This point evidently had weight with the Court of Session in the judgement which it pronounced in 1771 and which is printed below.[1] The Court of Session gave to the Principal's meeting the right to appoint Professors and to administer all the funds, subject to the control of the Ordinary Visitors. In the ensuing fifty years the Rectors became more and more eminent, including great lawyers, such as Lord Presidents and Lord Justice Clerks of the Court of Session, Lord Chief Barons of the Exchequer, a Scottish Commissioner of Customs in Adam Smith, statesmen such as Henry Dundas, Viscount Melville, Edmund Burke and Lord Brougham. Their public engagements rendered it impossible to give any real attention to their visitorial duties, with the result that the power of the Professoriate was extended and confirmed.

There is no record of the diplomacy by which Adam Smith secured a preponderating support for his scheme. Considering the numerous cross-currents of opinion and the diverse and far from amiable temperaments of some of the Professors, it shows him in a new light as a most able conciliator. Further, his efforts just fell short of achieving the very remarkable triumph of securing complete unanimity. How this resulted was a strange and remarkable accident. Moor had been appointed to put forward the case of the Rector, so that full account should be taken of it. He undertook this charge in a forensic spirit, refusing to

[1] See below, p. 208.

accept any of the points made by the Committee.[1] He was supported by Muirhead, the Professor of Humanity. The meeting on 13th August, 1762, overruled all his conclusions.[2] What makes this action the more extraordinary is that, when the issues came to be heard in the Court of Session, both Moor and Muirhead will be found to have changed round and, after advocating, in the earlier occasion, the maximum powers for the Rector, were then equally extreme on behalf of the Principal.[3] The total number of persons affected comprised the thirteen Professors and the Principal. If the Rector be added, it would bring it up to fifteen. All the others, with the exception of Moor and Muirhead and another, who was absent from the meeting and whose opinion at this time was not known,[4] concurred in the finding of the Committee.

The attainment of such a large measure of unanimity from very diverse and to some extent discordant elements was a most striking demonstration of the tribute paid by his colleagues to the singleness of purpose of Adam Smith. In other respects the whole incident may be regarded either as a preface or as an episode relatively complete in itself. From the first aspect it would be the introduction to the action of Declarator in the Court of Session in which the powers of the Rector and Principal formed one of the issues and which was decided in 1771. The underlying conditions were far from being continuous, and thus this early concordat may perhaps be taken as standing by itself. The whole atmosphere changed very soon after the moderating influence of Adam Smith was withdrawn, when the situation deteriorated very rapidly with the result that friction soon became most acute, and the sides taken were determined less by principle than by quarrels on other and much lesser matters. There is some doubt whether the advice which was tendered to the University by Thomas Miller, who was then Lord Advocate and also Rector, that a friendly [5] action should be instituted in order to determine the dispute, was well founded. It presupposed that what was involved was a question of the construction of documents. If, as seems on the whole probable, the material was insufficient, the better course would have been a Royal Visitation or Commission, which was precisely the last thing that

[1] It seems probable that the reply to Moor's criticism that only two of the original members of the Committee signed the report to which two other names had been added was that the other original members of the Committee were away during the Long Vacation, and Adam Smith obtained authority to add others who were in Glasgow during that period.

[2] See below, p. 215.

[3] *Additional Information for Dr. William Leechman and other Pursuers*, 1769 (Glasgow Univ. Libry., Y. 7. b 19), p. 28.

[4] See below, p. 224.

[5] The action of 1771 was friendly in much the same sense as a " friendly " football match at which the players indulge in a free fight.

anyone of those concerned desired. The papers in the action, which eventually developed, were most voluminous, those which were printed extended to over 600 pages. They contain one rather amusing feature, namely, the efforts of the disputants, who were now each the exponents of an extreme position, to explain away their acceptance of the report which Adam Smith had drawn up.[1]

Sometimes a small spark kindles a great fire. It was so with another series of events in which Adam Smith was concerned and which, at the beginning, was so inconspicuous as to be liable to escape notice in the University records which follow. It has been shown that Adam Smith's services were in great demand in the University in connection with the accounts. He and others were far from satisfied with the principle which was adopted. This, under an appearance of great simplicity, concealed several dangers. The transactions related to successive crops of the lands comprised in the Archbishopric and the Sub-Deanery. It seemed very simple to treat all intromissions as a cash account which was not closed until the whole crop had been realised and the rents for the period paid. The result was that the Factor might have in his hands, on the same date, sums belonging to two or three years. Adam Smith foresaw the risk (which eventually matured in a loss to the University of a comparatively large sum) that a deficiency on one account might be made good from the crop of a later year. This is the explanation of the large number of treatises on bookkeeping which were added to the Library during this period. From 1756 to 1763 there are various recommendations as to the form in which the accounts were to be kept, and, as far as can be judged, with small result.[2] If Adam Smith had remained, there can be little doubt that the position would have been amended, and that without any undue pressure or recrimination. When he went away, the matter was allowed to drop for a number of years. It may be guessed that Leechman had full confidence in Morthland, the factor, and did not feel the need for a radical change of method. In the Processes of Declarator of 1771 and 1772 Anderson had been on the same side as Leechman, but it was not long before they quarrelled. Anderson then took up the point which Adam Smith had made concerning the accounts, but in a manner totally different. Whereas Adam Smith's approach had been marked by courtesy and good feeling, Anderson's was exactly the reverse, and he was soon at odds with most of those with whom he had formerly been associated. After some heated exchanges in the University meetings, he initiated another process in the Court of Session in 1775. One effect of the previous case had been that the function of the Rector (in person), the Dean of Faculty, and Minister of Glasgow as Ordinary Visitors in the audit of the revenue and the disposal of the

[1] See below, pp. 222-5.   [2] See below, pp. 159-60.

surplus was insisted upon, with the result that the Court of Session remitted the dispute to these Visitors, who announced their decision (known as the " Shaw Park Decree ") in 1776.[1]

Mention of the last date leads to the reflection that, while Adam Smith was fortunate in many things, he was not least so in the time of his resignation. It is possible that had he remained at Glasgow, he might have been able to prevent or at least mitigate, the continual disputes and processes at law which continued all through his lifetime. On the other hand, if he had been involved in these conflicts, even if the bitterness of them had been lessened, it would have affected him as it did Reid, in making great demands on his scanty leisure. He would have lost the stimulus of his intercourse with the Physiocrats and the broadening of his outlook by foreign travel. Thus, had he remained, the publication of *The Wealth of Nations* might have been endangered ; and, if it had appeared, it would, under these circumstances, inevitably have been a much less admirable book.

The circumstances of Adam Smith's appointment as tutor to the Duke of Buccleuch and the touching farewell to his students have been often described. The terms of his engagement were more favourable to him than those which have been recorded. It appears from one of his receipts at Dalkeith House that he received £500 a year while he was travelling with the Duke and an annuity of £300 a year. He left Glasgow about the middle of January, as appears from a letter written by Joseph Black on the 23rd of that month that he had been at that time some days away from home.[2] Another letter, ten days later, from John Millar, explains a matter which has hitherto been in doubt.[3] The expressions of Reid, whether in his writings or in his letters, are much less cordial to Adam Smith than might have been expected. Giving full weight to differences on Philosophical theories, one would have expected more appreciation than the letters show for the department to which he succeeded and which had been greatly extended by Adam Smith. It now appears that Adam Smith and his friends had been exerting their influence to secure the election of Thomas Young, who was carrying on the class, as his successor. Evidently Reid remembered that Adam Smith had not only failed to support him, but had actively promoted the interests of another, and certainly a much less distinguished candidate.

[1] See below, pp. 225-8. University MSS., vol. 44 ; *Process of Declarator 1775*, printed 1778 (Glasgow University Libry., BO 4—e—19).
[2] See below, p. 256.
[3] See below, p. 257.

CHAPTER VIII

ADAM SMITH AMONG HIS FRIENDS

If we try to picture Adam Smith as he lived amongst his colleagues and friends, carrying on the various avocations which have been described in the previous two chapters, the available information is scanty. There are, however, two remarks in the *Memoir* by Dugald Stewart which, if their full meaning could be extracted, are of the very greatest importance. Both are connected with his conversations either at his Clubs or other intimate gatherings. In one it is said " the opinions too, which, in the thoughtlessness and confidence of his social hours, he was accustomed to hazard on books and on questions of speculation were not uniformly such as might have been expected from the superiority of his understanding and the singular consistency of his philosophical principles. They were liable to be influenced by accidental circumstances and by the humour of the moment ; and, when retailed by those who only saw him occasionally, suggested false and contradictory ideas of his real sentiments. On these, however, as on most other occasions there was always much truth, as well as ingenuity, in his remarks ; and if the different opinions, which at different times he pronounced upon the same subject, had been all combined together, so as to modify and limit each other, they would probably have afforded materials for a decision equally comprehensive and just." [1] There is no doubt that, between Smith's death and the delivery of the *Memoir* as a lecture to the Royal Society of Edinburgh and again between that date and the annotated edition in 1811, many strange and unqualified views were attributed to him, but these are always divorced from the context, which robs them of any real significance.

In another passage Dugald Stewart recorded a somewhat similar impression, but in a more guarded form. Millar had told him that Adam Smith contemplated a treatise on the Greek and Roman Republics as to which it is remarked that " his observations would have suggested new and important views concerning the internal and domestic circumstances of those nations ". He continues : " the same turn of thinking was frequently in his social hours applied to more familiar subjects ; and the fanciful theories which, without the least affectation of ingenuity,

[1] Ed. 1811, pp. 115-16. Stewart probably had in mind reports of Adam Smith's conversations, such as those which appeared in *The Bee*.

he was continually starting upon all the common topics of discourse, gave to his conversation a novelty and variety which were quite inexhaustible ".[1] Here it is to be noted that what is considered a fanciful, or even an extravagant, statement depends on the receptivity and the intelligence of those who hear it. A flash of inspiration is too dazzling for minds which are not attuned to receive it. Dugald Stewart was an industrious Professor and a kind laird, but one fails to find in him the divine spark. He, and others like him, may have heard some of the finest expressions of Adam Smith's genius and refused them as not being what they expected from him. This suggestion is based, in part, on the survival of what is believed to be one of these, which in spite of his friends found its way into *The Wealth of Nations*. It was the vision of a federated Empire—" the golden dream ", " a new Eldorado ".[2] There the project of such an Empire is seen as a vision but that of one who was both a mystic and severely practical. A conception of grandeur is worked out in its representative, fiscal and social aspects with the careful minuteness of the Dutch genre painter.

The second of the *obiter dicta* of Stewart relates to Adam Smith's estimate of character. " The opinions he formed of men upon a slight acquaintance were frequently erroneous ; but the tendency of his nature inclined him much more to blind partiality, than to ill-founded prejudice." And again, " in judging of individuals, it sometimes happened, his estimates were in a surprising degree wide of the truth. . . . When he attempted in the flow of his spirits to delineate those characters which, from long intimacy he might have been supposed to understand thoroughly, the picture was always lively and expressive and commonly bore a strong and amusing resemblance to the original when viewed under one particular aspect, but seldom, perhaps, conveyed a just and complete conception of it in all its dimensions and proportions." Another Edinburgh Professor, John Robison, writes in a similar strain. " When Joseph Black returned to his *Alma Mater Academica* as a Professor, he was immediately connected in the strictest friendship with the celebrated Dr. Adam Smith ; a friendship which became more and more intimate and confidential through the whole of their lives. A certain simplicity of character, with an incorruptible integrity, which was acutely sensible to the smallest indelicacy or incorrectness, was instantly seen by each of these friends in the character of the other, and riveted the bond of their union. Dr. Smith used to say that no man had less nonsense in his head than Dr. Black, and he often acknowledged himself obliged to him for setting him right in his judgement of character,

---

[1] Ed. 1811, p. 52.

[2] Cf. J. S. Nicholson, *A Project of Empire*, 1909, p. 206 ; W. R. Scott, " Books as Links of Empire ", in *Empire Review*, xxxviii, pp. 766-7.

confessing that he himself was apt to form his opinion too generally from a single feature."[1] Alexander Carlyle is more concise but more emphatic. " Adam Smith ", he wrote, " knew nothing of characters, and yet was ready to draw them on the slightest invitation. But when you checked or doubted, he retracted with the utmost ease, and contradicted all he had been saying."[2] The last sentence is in complete contradiction to the report that, after condemning a politician of the period in presence of one of his relatives, he said, " Deil care, deil care, it's all true ". The latter story, which is told by Lord Brougham,[3] is much more consistent with what is known of Adam Smith. Also, with reference to statesmen, it has to be borne in mind that the chapter of Adam Smith's life which had been lost and is now, in large measure, recovered—that is his employment during the time he spent in London in 1766-7 [4]—affords much light on one aspect of the case. When he was in close touch with Members of the Cabinet and spending a considerable amount of time in the house of the Chancellor of the Exchequer, he could hardly have failed to acquire many sidelights on the character and the acts of prominent persons which were far from being matters of common knowledge. For the rest—that he was slow to think evil—can scarcely be charged against him as a defect of character.

In view of the report of three witnesses of repute, what, it may be asked, becomes of " the impartial spectator " ? As is frequently shown in the *Theory of Moral Sentiments*, he is the arbiter who sits on the seat of judgement of the inner man. But, if that judge is capricious and generally unreliable, what is the worth of his verdict ? It surely weakens the theory if its promulgator must say, " Follow not my example, but my preaching ". Is the impartial spectator in the spirit of the plain man likely to be less fluctuating in his sentences ? The validity of the conception, as an ethical criterion, does not fall within the plan of the present book, but the fineness of Adam Smith's sympathy and his power of judgement are of supreme importance in several aspects of his economic work, so that the issue which has been raised is of very special import.

It is unfortunate that materials for the life of Adam Smith are so few—often the testimony to an event comes from only one or, at most, two sources—that it is impossible to subject them to a really critical examination. In this case, however, it happens to be possible. It will be seen in the next chapter [5] that, on the

[1] J. Robison, *Black's Elements of Chemistry*, Lond. 1803, i, p. xxxiii.
[2] A. Carlyle, *Autobiography*, 1860, p. 279.
[3] Lord Brougham, *Lives of Men of Letters*, 1846, ii, pp. 122-3.
[4] W. R. Scott, " Adam Smith at Downing St.", in *Economic His. Rev.*, Oct. 1935.
[5] See below, pp. 118-20.

appearance of Robertson's *History of Charles V.*, Adam Smith's friends accused him of plagiarism. A similar charge had previously been made against Adam Ferguson in connection with his book on Civil Society.[1] These events were ten to fifteen years later than complaints of the same kind which occasioned Adam Smith's paper in 1755. Stewart was in the difficulty, whatever his opinions on the subject may have been, that Robertson was the Principal of his University and Ferguson the colleague whose subject was closest to his own. He would have been considered wanting in *esprit de corps*, unless he had made some defence against what was regarded in Edinburgh as an attack on the University, through the assailing of two of its most prominent members. The position of Alexander Carlyle was much the same. He was very closely associated with Robertson in the General Assembly and had many reasons to be grateful to him : Ferguson was his close friend. In addition one feels in his case there was some slight jealousy of Adam Smith's intimacy with the family at Dalkeith, and there are a few rather venomous touches in his references to Smith. Accordingly, there is good reason to take both reports with a very considerable amount of reserve.

The question of what grounds there were for Adam Smith's charges of plagiarism will be discussed later ; and, in the meantime, it may be observed that there is a difference between the allegation of extravagance in expression and that of an inability to form a true judgement of character, in so far as the former is limited to chance expressions at social meetings or in the heat of discussion at a club, while the latter is general—as in fact it must be in the circumstances which have been described. There is one test which can be applied, namely, the evidence afforded by Adam Smith's opinion of his contemporaries as it has come down to us—this is a much more definite criterion than views on books or historical characters. Now what is amazing is that these are not only sound, but prescient, and this applies whether they were favourable or unfavourable, though, in the latter case, instances are likely to be scarce. Amongst those he found himself drawn towards were men of great ability and at the same time of high character. A distinction is to be made between the time when he had become celebrated and his acquaintance was sought by those most prominent amongst statesmen, authors, and artists, and the earlier period at which his reputation was still to be established. The following instances have been collected from this earlier part of his life. From his school days on through life, in spite of occasional disagreements, he was very friendly with John Oswald, Bishop of Raphoe ; with Robert Adam, the great architect ; John Drysdale, twice Moderator of the General Assembly ; and his cousins, Patrick Ross and David Skene, who rendered good service in the Army and both

---

[1] A. Carlyle, *Autobiography*, 1860, p. 285.

became Generals. His Glasgow and Oxford friends have been mentioned already.[1] At Edinburgh he had the courage to appreciate David Hume and to be proud of their friendship in face of a certain amount of unpopularity which it brought to him. Of his contemporaries as a young man, there were Alexander Wedderburn, whose early legal studies he encouraged and which eventually led to the position of Lord Chancellor; William Johnstone, better known as William Pulteney (the name he adopted by deed poll), both for his tracts on finance and even more honourably as " a man who never gave a vote which he did not in his heart believe to be right ". There were also his brother, George Johnstone, Governor of Florida; John Dalrymple, Hydrographer of the Admiralty; Sir John Dalrymple of Cranstoun, a Baron of the Scottish Exchequer; Hamilton of Bangour, the poet; and Henry Mackenzie, the author of *The Man of Feeling*. Amongst his colleagues as Professor he was the lifelong friend of Cullen, Black and Millar. Of the young men (who came to him as students at an age when it requires a faculty of divination to guess what they may become) his estimates were astonishingly successful. These include Henry Herbert, who was successful in politics and was created Baron Porchester and, later, Earl of Carnarvon, and Henry Erskine, well known as a lawyer and as Dean of the Faculty of Advocates (1788-1796).[2] To the friends of his later life who are mentioned by Rae, two may be added, John Bruce, Professor of Logic at Edinburgh (1744 to 1786), the Historiographer of the East India Company and author of its *Annals*, and Hugh Cleghorn, Professor of Civil History at St. Andrews (to whom he bequeathed a substantial legacy), and who was instrumental in obtaining information which resulted in the capture of the Island of Ceylon from the French.[3] These were men who had powers to do great things in the world, but he was no less careful about those whose opportunity or whose environment was narrow. Quite the most enthusiastic letter of recommendation which he wrote was not for a man who might become a great statesman, or an able lawyer, or a famous scientist, but for a valet and courier who had served him well.[4] He writes in favour of an " ingenious mechanick " who was a candidate for the post of Overseer of the King's Works, the moment he hears that the office has become vacant.[5] Nor is it to be thought that he was always enthusiastic. Critical

---

[1] See above, pp. 34-7.

[2] Henry Erskine was not a student of Adam Smith, but he had arranged some time before he left Glasgow that the boy should come there to take classes at the University. Henry Erskine was a brother of Lord Cardross and Lord Chancellor Erskine.

[3] Cf. *History of the Speculative Society of Edinburgh*, 1845, p. 102.

[4] See below, p. 264.

[5] Letter to Dr. Garthshore, 18th June, 1784—Homer B. Vanderblue, *Adam Smith and the " Wealth of Nations "*, Boston, Mass., 1936, p. 6.

letters have a small chance of being preserved. The adoration of Boswell for celebrated names has caused one to be recorded in which Adam Smith used the well-known phrase that the recipient was " happily possessed of a facility of manners ".[1] Though Lord Cardross was a devoted admirer of Adam Smith, the judgement of the latter on him was not far removed from that of Sir Walter Scott. To a recommendation made to Adam Smith, when Commissioner of Customs, of a person for the post of boatman, he replied that he refused to support him, for " he was a shortsighted land-lubber ".[2]

When these estimates of character are weighed, it seems a reasonable conclusion that, so far from being " in a surprising degree wide of the truth ", they show penetration, fairness and, in some cases, quite remarkable powers of anticipation.

Another aspect of Adam Smith's relations with persons whom he met and helped was that with the brothers Robert and Andrew Foulis. As in the case of Watt, it was partly one of general helpfulness, partly, at a later stage, requiring some moral courage in the giving of salutary advice which was known to be unpalatable. This Adam Smith is believed to have done.

The brothers Foulis had attended Hutcheson's class and he encouraged them to establish themselves as printers. They were authorized to style themselves " Printers to the University "; the Faculty gave them the use of rooms in the College and in a few years a Press was established which ranks in that very select class of those justly celebrated in Europe during the eighteenth century.[3] Having made remarkable progress in printing, one of the brothers, Robert, had the idea of establishing an " Academy of Arts ", which was the first of the kind in Britain. The University aided the scheme by lending part of the new Library as a studio for the training of its students.[4] Foulis had travelled widely on the Continent. He brought back many works of art and also engaged teachers of drawing, painting, sculpture and engraving. Thus the scheme took shape as a School of Art, an Art Repository (for the sale of pictures, etc.) and an Academy. The exhibition, being the chief activity of the last, was established in a most ingenious way. The College was lent for this purpose on the occasion of the Coronation of George III on 22nd September, 1761, and each year thereafter till 1775 on his birthday, when pictures were exhibited, not only in the Halls, but also in the Inner Quadrangle. The Plate No. VI will be of interest when it is remembered that Adam Smith visited

---

[1] *Journal of a Tour to the Hebrides*, 1886, v, p. 19 (note).

[2] Letter dated Sept., 1782—Caxton Head Catalogue.

[3] James MacLehose, *Glasgow University Press*, 1931, pp. 149-82.

[4] There is a drawing of the Library Hall, when put to this use, by David Allen, one of the artists who were trained there. It is engraved in *Old Glasgow*, by Andrew MacGeorge, 1880, p. 302; also in *Glasgow University Press*, by Dr. James MacLehose, p. 188.

some of these exhibitions and may have been one of the figures, more or less interested, which are shown in the Court. The touch of incongruity, characteristic of the age, in which there are bonfires very close to the pictures and rockets being fired near, is noticeable.

When it became apparent that the Academy was draining the life-blood of the University Press, Adam Smith is believed to have warned Foulis of his danger. The scheme was impossible without support from public funds. John Dalrymple suggested that Adam Smith should draw up a memorial to this end, but it is not known if he actually prepared it. Scotland was, as yet, too poor to provide a market for pictures and statuary, though curiously enough, such is the force of example, in 1756 John Smith, a frame-maker, is found advertising a sale of pictures and prints,[1] the date being only two or three years after Foulis' Academy had been opened. In addition to the narrowness of the market it was discovered, to the great disgust of the founder, that there was only a very small demand for subjects of a Scottish character, or for the work of Scottish artists. Everyone wanted something from abroad, or at least with a foreign name. In this, eighteenth-century Glasgow was not so very different from modern London. Foulis was forced to sell imported pictures and to set his students to copying the works of old masters which were in various castles and mansion houses in Scotland. Prints were sold at what appear to be absurdly low prices, from 1d. to 6d. The difference between the Scottish and foreign etchings was that where the price was the same the latter were much smaller. Local prints measuring about 2 ft. in length were priced at 4d. to 6d.[2] In the end the Academy of Arts not only failed but in its fall dragged down the printing business, to the great damage of British typography.

The failure of Robert Foulis, the surviving brother, occurred in the same year as the appearance of *The Wealth of Nations*, when Adam Smith had been away from Glasgow for twelve years ; and yet, by a strange and involved series of circumstances, it had a very definite relation to the story of his life. There are many evidences of the great influence which he exercised at Glasgow, both in the University and the city. While it was partly personal, it survived his departure, and that in two remarkable cases. It must surely have rarely happened that the notes of a Professor's lectures have been copied, and the copy paid for, two years after his resignation.[3] Yet this was so in the case of the *Glasgow Lectures*, the

[1] *Glasgow Journal*, 22nd March, 1756.

[2] *Catalogue of Pictures, etc., of the Academy of Arts*, Section " Prints ". As to the foreign engravers, if Foulis secured the plates of the exquisite little etchings of De Laune, they would have been so worn as to yield valueless impressions. Perhaps this Academy is responsible for the occurrence of these impressions from very worn plates in Great Britain.

[3] The history of the MS. as far as can be ascertained will be found in Bonar, *Library of Adam Smith*, 1932, pp. 211-14.

PLATE VI. EXHIBITION OF THE GLASGOW ACADEMY OF ART IN THE COLLEGE
on the King's Birthday, 1762, by a student of the Academy.
(From an impression, selected by Foulis, now in the Mitchell Library, Glasgow.)

title of the manuscript being dated 1766.[1] Then in 1768 a group of students selected him as a candidate for the Rectorship. He did not succeed, though returned in 1787.[2] Rae sums up this influence as follows : " his opinions became the subjects of general discussion, the branches he lectured on became fashionable in the town, the sons of the wealthier citizens used to go to College to take his class though they had no intention of completing a university course, stucco busts of him appeared in the booksellers' windows, and the very peculiarities of his voice and pronunciation received the homage of imitation.[3] No reference is given, and it appears that the sentence quoted is a mosaic of recollections and impressions collected from several sources. What is of special interest is the reference to a bust of Adam Smith having been in existence when he was still young. The excellent study of the late Mr. J. M. Gray records only one thoroughly authentic portrait of Adam Smith, namely, the Tassie medallion in its three variations.[4] Incidentally, it may be remarked that one of these, which appears elsewhere in this volume (Plate No. XIV), seems to me to give a better idea of what Adam Smith looked like when it was made, than that which has been reproduced so many times. He had had a very serious illness during the winter of 1786-7 which was the beginning of the disease which carried him off less than four years later.[5] When he sat for Tassie he had gone to London to consult Hunter, the celebrated physician. Therefore at the time the medallion was modelled he was distinctly failing. It is natural to wish to have some representation of him when he was at his best, and Rae's reference to busts of him being in Glasgow apparently indicates that there actually were such. The brevity of the statement is tantalising. After a long search the source of it was eventually found in an obscure note in Strang's *Glasgow Clubs*, according to which " Dunlop and Wilson were the most fashionable bibliopoles in the town. Their windows were ornamented with stucco busts of Adam Smith, David Hume and other literati."[6] The statement is undated, but there is no trace of this firm having been in business at the time Adam Smith was in Glasgow,[7] their first advertisement of books which has been traced being in 1773. They succeeded to the position of leading booksellers in the city

[1] This manuscript is in the University Library, Glasgow.

[2] D. Murray, *The Old College*, 1927, p. 327.

[3] Rae, *Life*, pp. 59, 60.

[4] J. Bonar, *Library of Adam Smith*, 1932, pp. xix-xxviii ; J. M. Gray, *James and William Tassie*, 1894, p. 146.

[5] Rae, *Life*, p. 402.

[6] Ed. 1857, p. 83. The remainder of Rae's summary is based on Stewart's *Memoir*, p. 16.

[7] In the newspapers of that period there are very many advertisements of booksellers, but the firm of Dunlop and Wilson is not among them.

on the failure of the Foulises. While others in this trade were unable to make any display in their windows owing to their shops being in dark recesses in the district known as the Saltmarket, Dunlop and Wilson established their business in a corner house one side of which faced on the Trongate and the other on the Candleriggs, then a fashionable part of the town. No newspapers giving advertisements are available for the two years before 1778, but in the first number of the *Glasgow Mercury*, dated 8th January of that year, they join with other booksellers in announcing the publication of Scruton's *Practical Counting House*. There is no date discoverable as to when these busts first appeared in their windows or, what is important, if duplicates were for sale. Since the Glasgow Academy of Arts produced a number of plaster busts, it is reasonable to suppose that Dunlop and Wilson purchased a part of the stock of the Foulises. The examples were not very numerous. Those in plaster included Homer, Plato, Virgil, Cicero, Livy, Seneca and Marcus Aurelius. Amongst modern writers the plaster busts were of two sizes, as is shown in the following table :

Name	Size and Prices	
	1 ft. 4½ in. to 1 ft. 5½ in.	11½ in.
Shakespeare -	6/- unvarnished, 8/- varnished	2/- unvarnished, 2/6 varnished
Milton -	4/- ,, 5/6 ,,	2/- ,, 2/6 ,,
Dryden -	6/- ,, 8/- ,,	—
Newton -	6/- ,, 8/- ,,	—
Prior -	6/- ,, 8/- ,,	—
Pope -	6/- ,, 8/- ,,	—

There is no trace of any Scottish writer except Hutcheson, their first patron, who was represented, not by a bust, but by a medallion. This was modelled by Isaac Gosset under the care and direction of Basil Hamilton, afterwards Earl of Selkirk, and was cast in bronze at Florence by A. Selvi. The Selvi bronze is circular, 3¾ in. in diameter. The Foulises produced it in plaster, measuring 5 in. by 4 in., at 2s. 6d., or in wax at 7s. 6d. The Tassie medallion of the same design was 3⅝ in.[1] It follows that, when Dunlop and Wilson added Hume and Smith

[1] Catalogue of the Glasgow Academy in R. Duncan, *Notices and Documents illustrative of the Literary History of Glasgow*, 1831, pp. 113-14 ; J. M. Gray, *James and William Tassie*, 1894, p. 118. There is at the South Kensington Museum (Ceramics Dept.) a cast of a gem presented by Max Rosenheim which is catalogued under the name of Adam Smith. As regards the resources of

to their collection, they must have caused these busts to be cast. A good deal turns upon the date at which this was done. If before 1787, we have a new portrait bust of Adam Smith which would be most valuable as showing him at an earlier age than the Tassie medallion and before the illness which has been mentioned. This firm was in business up to the death of Adam Smith, and, if the bust was modelled later than the Tassie, it is almost certain to have been based on it. Adam Smith is always disappointing the apparently reasonable expectations which are formed in the absence of actual evidence. So far as these go, they point to the bust being done at the earlier date. The failure of the Foulises, the publication of *The Wealth of Nations*, and the death of Hume all came within about a year, and the first event would release, and at the same time place in great want, the artists and modellers employed by the Academy of Arts. There are no clear indications of a connection between Adam Smith and any artist other than Tassie or of how sittings might have come about. Nothing is known of the circumstances in which the picture of his mother was painted.[1] It might be conjectured that, in order to relieve the distress caused by the closing of the Academy, he gave commissions for this painting and for a bust of himself. But, as regards the portrait, it appears to have been done at an age considerably earlier than that which Margaret Smith had reached about 1777. Adam Smith had accompanied Burke to Glasgow in April 1784,[2] and he had been there early in the previous year.[3] From the frequent references to his friends at Glasgow in his letters it is evident that he maintained very close relations with them. Thus it appears probable that he may have made several visits to Glasgow after the publication of *The Wealth of Nations* and before 1783, more especially between 1776 and his appointment as Commissioner of Customs two years later. This period is that which seems to be the most probable one for the modelling of the bust. Thus there is no difficulty in supposing that sittings could have been arranged. On the other hand, if the bust was later than the Tassie medallion, it would not have been necessary (as far as is known) for the sculptor to have gone to Edinburgh.

It is needless to say that all these problems would be solved by an inspection of the bust. Every possible method has been tried to trace an example of it. Not only have advertisements been inserted in the Press and an article, with illustra-

---

Glasgow in portraiture it may be added that amongst the effects of James Moor, Professor of Greek, there was what is described in the inventory as " a miniature picture of Dr. Simson in silver "—MSS. Univ. Libry. Glasgow—Murray MSS.—Papers relating to R. & A. Foulis, p. 483.

[1] Reproduced in J. Bonar, *Library of Adam Smith*, 1932, p. xxii.

[2] Rae, *Life*, p. 388.

[3] Letter, Adam Smith to George Baird, written from Glasgow, 7th February, 1783, in the possession of Professor Hollander, Baltimore, U.S.A.

tions, contributed to the *Glasgow Herald*,[1] but application has been made to many whose ancestors might have been expected to have purchased a copy, but so far without success. It is to be hoped that, if this bust has survived, the efforts of the Directors of the National Portrait Gallery and of the Scottish National Portrait Gallery (both of whom are greatly interested) to find an example will be crowned with success.

There is only one further remark to be made on this subject. In the account of the portraits of Adam Smith contributed by J. M. Gray to Dr. Bonar's *Library of Adam Smith* there is reference to the " Muir " portrait. Since that article was written it has changed hands and is now owned by Mr. J. H. Romanes, W.S., of Edinburgh. The present position is somewhat more favourable to its authenticity than when Mr. Gray wrote. Mr. Cursiter, the Director of the Scottish National Portrait Gallery, has been studying this picture for years, but his investigations, which have involved much research, are not complete. Stated very briefly, the present state of the data is as follows. There is the question of technique as an indication of date. That is uncertain where the period to be covered is short, for, since it is admitted that the picture is intended for Adam Smith, there is no long interval between the age at which he appears in the picture and the latest date at which it could have been painted. If the artist could be discovered and his movements known, what is the outstanding problem might be decided, namely, whether the picture was done during Adam Smith's life or after his death. Mr. Cursiter has made considerable progress along these lines, including the procuring of some documentary evidence, but, while further discoveries might clinch the matter, they might destroy the conclusions so far based on the available evidence. The matter is one for very highly skilled experts, and a decision must wait their verdict. In the meantime it may not be wholly inappropriate to add some personal impressions. First, while not venturing to dispute Gray's conclusions as a whole, I am disposed to query one of them, namely, that it is founded on the Tassie medallion (Gray, No. 356). It seems to me there are a number of small, but by no means negligible, differences. These are difficult to describe and are only apparent when the picture and the medallion are placed side by side. For instance, the chin of the painting is appreciably longer and more prominent than that in the Tassie ; more interesting is the fact that the lower lip shows a definitely greater prominence. This is significant. As has been pointed out, that was a marked family trait ; and, so far, it is probable that the picture is a better representation of Adam Smith than the medallion. At the same time this does not prove that the picture was painted from life. But it does seem to indicate that, if it was painted after Adam

[1] " Portraiture of Adam Smith ", issue of 13th February, 1935.

Smith's death, the artist must have had a vivid recollection of his subject. This new fact has a relation to the technical enquiry, for it tends somewhat strongly to fix the date of execution at the latest possible date not very long after 1790. Another circumstance is rather curious. The painting cannot be judged by the reproductions of it. These, for some reason, give quite a different impression from that produced by the original. There is a photogravure by Messrs. Doig, Wilson and Wheatley of Edinburgh and a small process block as a frontispiece to the *Economic Studies of a Lawyer* by Mr. Romanes, the owner. Being dissatisfied with both, I had another photograph of the picture made with a view to including a reproduction in the present volume. While perhaps some improvement on the others, it did not satisfy me. Its character may be judged to some extent by the Press copy of it to illustrate the article on the " Portraiture of Adam Smith " which has been already mentioned.

It was during the period while Adam Smith was in Glasgow that he again fell in love, and was again disappointed. Dugald Stewart records that " he was for several years attached to a young lady of great beauty and accomplishment ".[1] This lady died unmarried. She was alive " a considerable number of years " after 1793, but had died by 1811. The following passage from a letter written in 1766 shows that in France Adam Smith remained faithful to his Scottish love, who is there described as " a maid of Fife ", while the friends of the Duke of Buccleuch found considerable interest in the extent to which the " sympathy " of various frequenters of the salons had turned to him as well as the manœuvres of the dashing Marquise who had come to Abbeville from Paris for his sake.[2] The name of the writer of the letter is unknown. He was evidently a young Scotsman who had been a long time in France (as is shown by his fluency in the language) and who moved in good society. His main purpose is to obtain news of the Duke's movements. He is doubtful if an answer from the Duke himself would be forthcoming and addresses a playful appeal to Adam Smith. The form of the letter is determined by the fact that the writer had just completed a journey from Paris to Toulouse on which he had, as a travelling companion, a Capuchin monk, which suggests his writing in the character of an ecclesiastic, and he signs as " Le Gr[and] Vic[aire] Eccossois, fait en congregation le 18 Fbre, 1766 ".

" Et toi, Adam Smith, Philosophe de Glascow, héros et idole des high-broad Ladys,[3] que fais-tu, mon cher ami ? Comment gouvernes-tu La Duchesse d'An-

[1] D. Stewart, *Memoir*, 1811, p. 150.

[2] W. W. Currie, *Memoir of James Currie*, London, 1831, ii, pp. 318-9.

[3] This early example of a term anticipating the modern " high-brow " is unknown to the compilers of the *New Oxford Dictionary*. They agree that the manuscript reads, quite clearly, " high-broad ", but the particular reference has not yet been discovered.

ville et Mad. de Bouflers, ou ton cœur est-il toujours épris des charmes de Mad. Nicol et des appas tant apparens que cachés de cette autre dame de fife que vous aimiéz tant ? Ne puis-je recevoir de vos nouvelles, milord ? Si vous ne vouléz pas écrire vous-même, parce que vous êtes paresseux ou parce que vous griffonéz comme un chat ou, ce qui est pire, comme un duc, si Adam Smith ne veut pas m'écrire par les mêmes raisons, si l'honorable M. Scot garde aussi le silence, dites au moins à quelcun de votre maison de me mander quelque chose de votre part ; je suis chargé de savoir si vous devéz rester à Paris cet hyver ou si vous alléz courir le monde, j'ai promis de m'en informer. Si les ecrivains vous manquent, vous avéz mon ami et Cousin, Duncan le Piper, qui me mandera en Erse tout ce que vous voudréz me faire savoir, et m'enverra un morceau digne de fingal, d'oscian ou de Mac Ullin." [1]

[1] MSS. of the Duke of Buccleuch at Dalkeith House.

CHAPTER IX

ADAM SMITH'S STUDIES, 1751-1763

In the three previous chapters Adam Smith's life at Glasgow has been described from what may be called the external side, showing him in Chapters VI and VII discharging his duties as a Professor, and in Chapter VIII as he appeared to his intimates. This one will aim at picturing his intense mental activity during this period. In it three landmarks stand out, separated by intervals of about four years, namely, the lecture given to the Club of Andrew Cochrane and his contributions to the *Edinburgh Review*, both in 1755, the publication of the *Theory of Moral Sentiments* in 1759, and the draft of *The Wealth of Nations* which may be assigned to the second half of 1763.

The fuller particulars of the Edinburgh Lectures, which have been pieced together in Chapter V, show that he brought to Glasgow a considerable amount of material in the form of addresses, and great importance is to be assigned to the fact that imbedded in the course on Jurisprudence there was already a considerable amount on Economic questions, some of which reappeared, almost word for word, in *The Wealth of Nations*, though, necessarily, with important additions. The portions which have been discovered [1] do not contain any passages which point clearly to his characteristic doctrine of *laissez faire*, but there is no reason to doubt his own explicit statement in the extracts already quoted,[2] as also Dugald Stewart's testimony that the fundamental principles of *The Wealth of Nations* were delivered in lectures at Glasgow in the session of 1752-3—that is, the first year he was Professor of Moral Philosophy.[3] Accordingly his great initial discovery was already made and had been written before he came to Glasgow, though, as will be shown later, it was confirmed and partially completed there.

It is possible to suggest some of the stages which led to this discovery. It has been shown elsewhere that, in one sense, Adam Smith's central principle was an easy deduction from the prevailing Naturalism of the eighteenth century, according to which " the natural " was what was fixed and permanent in the cosmos and in the mind of man. It was what was $\phi\acute{\upsilon}\sigma\epsilon\iota$ as opposed to what was $\nu\acute{o}\mu\omega$.[4] People

---

[1] See below, pp. 379-85.　　[2] See above, p. 54.
[3] *Memoir*, 1811, p. 97.　　[4] *Transactions of the British Academy*, x, pp. 439-42.

are so accustomed to think in watertight compartments that it remained for Adam Smith and the Physiocrats to make this application of the current Naturalism at the same time, indeed almost in the same year. But each had a different line of approach, and this may, in part, account for the great fruitfulness of Adam Smith's rendering of a principle which was in large measure common to both. The development of his economic system would have proceeded more easily and symmetrically if he had adopted this general application of Naturalism rather than a more specialised method which was in fact less direct, but which explains much in the form of his early work. This was determined by his training. It has been shown that when he was about fifteen he was reading Grotius.[1] At that time his teacher, Francis Hutcheson, was using, as one of his text-books, the edition by Gershom Carmichael, his predecessor, of Puffendorf's *De Officio Hominis et Civis*;[2] Barbeyrac's edition was also referred to. Puffendorf's book dealt with Jurisprudence. In it the ethical and economic sections are few. Of the latter the longest is the chapter in Book I, *De Pretio*. Carmichael added in notes and appendices about one third concerned with Ethics. Hutcheson reversed this order by writing a system of Moral Philosophy in which he included a certain amount of Jurisprudence and Economics. In Adam Smith's final course at Edinburgh he returned to Carmichael's treatment of Puffendorf, making his course one of Jurisprudence (as it was continued in the *Glasgow Lectures*) within which there were large ethical and economic parts. In this way the origin of the method of treatment becomes clear.

The avenue of approach to Adam Smith's main discovery—in which he was not helped by Hutcheson—is somewhat more involved. In Grotius and Puffendorf, as also with Richard Cumberland,[3] the *Lex Naturæ* or *Lex Naturalis* was made the foundation of the whole juridical system. The same year (1748) that Adam Smith was writing his final course of Edinburgh lectures Montesquieu's *Esprit des Lois* was published. It is best, perhaps, to retain the term *Lex Naturalis*, since the modern term " Law of Nature " or " Natural Law " has quite a different meaning. Indeed, it is interesting to observe that the tendency to narrow the term from what was permanent primarily in man (Montesquieu) or permanent in both man and the outer world to the last—or to Nature in the modern sense— began to show itself early in England. Thus in 1694 George Dawson, who followed Hooker and Sanderson, distinguished four kinds of laws : (1) the law of

---

[1] See above, p. 34.

[2] This is established by a copy, in the possession of the author, which bears the signature of Archibald Roberton, dated 1742. Roberton matriculated at Glasgow in 1738, became an advocate, inherited the property of Bedlay and died in 1798.

[3] *De Legibus Naturæ Disquisitio Philosophica*, 1672.

Divine Operations, such as Creation and Providence; (2) the law of all natural agents, "*which is properly the Law of Nature*"; (3) the law under which angels act, "the law celestial"; (4) the law "which man works by, which is called the law of Reason".[1]

Carmichael developed the ideas of Puffendorff by extending the conception of the *Lex Naturalis*. Thus he wrote "Legibus itaque naturalibus, non unum, ut cl. auctor, sed tria fundamentalia praecepta, substernimus, Deum esse colendum, innoxiam cuique suam utilitatum quaerendam, et socialitatem fovendam". Under the heading "de colenda socialitate" he adds, "notamus esse quasdam utilitates aut voluptates, quas homines, vel ex suis actionibus, vel ex rebus externis, vel ex actionibus aliorum hominum, possunt capere".[2] Hutcheson developed this idea further when he wrote, " 'Tis plain each one has a natural right to exert his powers, according to his own judgment and inclination, for these purposes in all such industry, labour or amusements as are not hurtful to others in their persons or goods, while no more publick interests necessarily requires [*sic*] his labours or requires that his activities should be under the discretion of others. This right we call *natural liberty*. Every man has a sense of this right."[3] It will be noted that the first part of this extract comes near to an outline of Adam Smith's central principle. Everything depends on the weight given to the qualifications which are appended. That this was a case where a scholar just reaches the threshold of a great truth and then turns back may be judged from another doctrine of Hutcheson. "The populace", he writes, "often needs also to be taught, and engaged by laws, into the best methods of managing their own affairs and exercising their mechanick arts; and, in general, civil laws more precisely determine many points in which the Law of Nature leaves much latitude."[4] That was precisely the point between Hutcheson and Adam Smith. The latter was consistent in his interpretation of natural liberty. The *Lex Naturalis* prescribed it—and, from the point of view of principle, there was nothing more to be said.

In view of the divergence of Hutcheson and Adam Smith as to the scope of natural liberty, it is clear that the wide interpretation of it by the younger man did not, in itself, afford a sure foundation for an economic system. So far the basic principle was essentially deductive. But in the Edinburgh lectures, as is shown

---

[1] *Origo Legum*, Lond., 1695, p. 11.

[2] Gershom Carmichael (ed.), *Puffendorfii De Officio*, 1724, p. 60.

[3] F. Hutcheson, *System of Moral Philosophy*, 1755, i, p. 294.

[4] F. Hutcheson, *Introduction to Moral Philosophy*, 1764, ii, p. 350. One wonders if this was one of the points of distinction between the theories of Hutcheson and Smith which was stated in "a very perspicuous manner" by Joseph Black, who was a student, a colleague and a close friend of Adam Smith—J. Robison, *Lectures of Joseph Black*, Edin., 1803, i, p. xx.

by the testimony of Callander and Dugald Stewart's extracts from the lecture of 1755,[1] Adam Smith had added an inductive confirmation, which was based on historical evidence, by which he endeavoured to show that the general effect of State direction of commerce had been to slow down the rate of economic progress. Parts of this enquiry have been preserved in *The Wealth of Nations* in Book III. In fact, wherever the word " opulence " occurs, we may be sure that we are reading some of Adam Smith's earliest work. Besides which there may be other cases in which it had been changed to " wealth " at some one of the many revisions to which the MS. was subjected. His residence at Glasgow and his close intercourse with many of the leading merchants there opened up a further striking verification and at the same time laid the foundation of the critique of Mercantilism in the fourth book of *The Wealth of Nations*. When the eighteenth century began, Scotland was excluded, by a series of Acts of the English Legislature, from the Colonial trade. After the Union, this restraint was removed, and, by every test, the advance in prosperity, particularly in the West, was remarkable, and even spectacular. Here, then, it seemed that there was something approaching a valid experiment for the verification of an hypothesis, and confirming it up to the hilt. There can be no doubt as to the facts, but a question arises as to the range of the observation. If a closer examination of the situation is made, it will be seen that the economic and social progress was not through the abandonment of Mercantilism, but within it. The statistics, already quoted,[2] show that a very great part of the development depended on the re-export trade and that this was secured by Mercantilism. It is a curious fact that the summit of the wave of prosperity coincided almost exactly with the period when Adam Smith was at Glasgow. As early as 1765 (nearly two years after he had left for France) Reid was writing that " the temper of our northern colonies makes our mercantile people look very grave ".[3] Five years later the position had become serious. The War of Independence interrupted the trade; and, when peace was established, it could not be restored on the former basis. In 1778 the total overseas trade of Scotland had contracted by as much as 58 per cent., and that of the Clyde had fallen even more. Adam Smith, who at this date was still at Kirkcaldy, cannot have missed such important events, indeed there is some reason to think that they may have affected him personally through his having helped relatives or friends who had suffered in the crisis.[4] Following his own principles he may have been confident that the capital and labour displaced would ultimately find employment which would be, at least, not less remunerative. If this was his estimate of the situation,

[1] See above, pp. 54, 101.
[2] See above, p. 80.
[3] T. Reid, *Works*, 1872, i, p. 43.
[4] See below, p. 276 note [2].

it was confirmed by events, for by 1791 the overseas trade of Scotland had almost reached the level of 1771 and that without any appreciable aid from the Industrial Revolution.[1] Afterwards the improvement was exceedingly rapid and was almost continuous up to the Civil War in America.

It has been convenient to include in this preliminary review the influence of the observations, which Adam Smith made at Glasgow, on the opening of the American trade to Scotsmen. Apart from that, the remaining data enable an estimate to be framed of the character and the form of the work which he had done at Edinburgh and the general content of that which he had then in writing. During his first session at Glasgow (1751-2) when he was Professor of Logic, he cannot have had much time for study since, in addition to the work of that Chair, he took part in the teaching of Moral Philosophy, during the illness of Craigie. At the same time he was evidently following up his studies in Jurisprudence (which, for him, at this date included Political Economy), for on 23rd January, 1752, he lectured to the Literary Society, which has been mentioned previously, on Hume's Essays on Commerce. Millar's account of the lectures first in Logic and later in Moral Philosophy, which he communicated to Dugald Stewart, gives a very clear picture of them. He began with a brief account of formal logic, and this can be followed from the text-book of the period compiled by G. C. (possibly Gershom Carmichael) the preface of which is dated from Glasgow College, October 1, 1722. The edition, printed at Edinburgh in 1736, entitled *Breviuscula Introductio ad Logicam ; studiosæ Juventutis (in academica in primis Glasguensi) primis usibus accommodata* is a booklet measuring five-and-a-quarter inches by three-and-a-half inches and comprising 61 pages. The remainder of the session was assigned to lectures on literary criticism. Stewart makes out an ingenious case for this method of treatment, on the basis that, since thought is communicated by speech and writing, the best way of ascertaining the operations of the mind is by analysis of the form in which these find expression.[2]

From October 1752 onwards Adam Smith was Professor of Moral Philosophy ; and, again according to Millar, he lectured on Natural Theology, Ethics and Jurisprudence—the latter, as Stewart records, from his first session with the Moral Philosophy class, including his economic work. There is no information as to whether he had any material already written for the first of these courses.[3] If he had not this would require some preparation. Otherwise he had the lectures

---

[1] *Economic History Review*, ii, pp. 292-3.   [2] D. Stewart, *Memoir*, 1811, pp. 12, 13.

[3] The references by David Douglas and John Millar (see below, pp. 312-13) to a " metaphysical work " arouse much curiosity. These might, possibly, relate to " Principles which direct Philosophical Enquiries " which appeared in the *Essays*, or else to an unknown manuscript.

which he had given at Edinburgh covering much of his course in Ethics and Jurisprudence; and, accordingly, he had a considerable amount of the time, left by his other engagements, available for his own studies. As yet he ranged over his whole wide field of literature, philosophy, law and economics. He had the advantage of the University Library within a minute's walk from his house, he could borrow books from it to any reasonable extent. The resources of this Library, when Adam Smith used it, are described in detail below (Part II, § I). When he visited Edinburgh to see his friend Hume, the latter would place the whole resources of the Advocates' at his disposal. He had thus three ways of securing new books, either through the two libraries mentioned, or by adding them to his own collection. At this time it is not improbable that he secured access to the most expensive volumes in the former, and bought sparingly for his own library.

It has already been shown that in the years from 1752 to 1755, in addition to general reading and keeping in touch with new literature at home and abroad, Adam Smith was giving some attention to economic enquiries. Also it is possible that he was testing the resources of the University Library in history; since it will be found later that he was recommending the purchase of more recent works in this subject. Then, too, he was spending some of his time on the legal side of Jurisprudence. Thus we find him in 1752 taking part in selecting from a large collection of law books those which would be useful to the library, and once more at a subsequent date making recommendations for the filling of gaps and adding recent editions or new publications relating to law.

Further light on the more general character of his reading is obtainable from his contributions to the short-lived *Edinburgh Review* during the year 1755. The critique of Johnson's *Dictionary* is connected with his work on literary criticism and it has a unity with the *Letter* sent to the editors through his pupil and friend Alexander Wedderburn, in so far as in both there is an insistence on "the arranging and methodizing" of knowledge.[1] This is the characteristic of the French *Encyclopédie* to which special attention is drawn, and which is recommended for imitation by British scholars. It is probable that for the purpose of this letter Adam Smith consulted the copy of the volumes, then issued, at the Advocates' Library, since the work was not acquired by the University Library at Glasgow until the time of Adam Smith's quæstorship from 1758 to 1760,[2] and there is no trace of his having bought a copy for himself.[3] This fact is of some interest, since

[1] *The Edinburgh Review for the year 1755*, 2nd Edition, with Notes, 1818, p. 125.
[2] See below, p. 179.
[3] In the photographs of the complete MS. Catalogue of Adam Smith's Library in 1781—for which I am very greatly indebted to the Economic and Engineering Departments of the Imperial University of Tokyo—this book does not occur.

it tends to suggest that the illustration of pin-making may have been incorporated into the MS. after 1760. Unless a copy had been made of the whole long description in the *Encyclopédie*, it would have been difficult to work in, unless Adam Smith had the actual text before him. Rae has given a full account of the circumstances which led to the foundation of the *Review*, and the reasons for the suspension of publication.[1] The opposition to it was more powerful and vociferous than Rae allows for, as may be gathered from the following contemporary attack on it. " 'Tis a printed muster roll—a sorry temple of fame—a sure guide to infallibility—a mole ey'd performance, no male or female author can distinguish their own offspring in it—'Tis a new Papal Chair, a sort of paper credit—a draught, a prison and a pillory and an indecent attack on human liberty." Adam Smith did not escape. It is said that the specimen which the reviewer had given of Johnson's *Dictionary* " is dark and almost unintelligible ".[2]

To the same year, 1755, belongs the lecture to the club founded by Cochrane and which has been already referred to. Before considering it and the causes which led to its being written, it is advisable to discuss another somewhat mysterious paper, written or owned by Adam Smith, which is mentioned twice by Dugald Stewart. In his *Lectures on Political Economy* it is stated that the division of price into the component parts of rent, wages and profits of stock had been suggested to Adam Smith by James Oswald of Dunnikier " as appears from a manuscript of Mr. Smith's now in my possession ".[3] What was the period intended by the word " now " ? Stewart's *Lectures* were partly reconstructed from notes taken by his students and the *terminus ad quem* may be fixed by the session 1809-10.[4] Then in Stewart's *Memoir of Adam Smith*, in the first note to the edition of 1811, it is stated again that Adam Smith owed much to Oswald, and tribute is paid to his economic knowledge on the basis of " a paper of Mr. Smith's which I have perused ". It may be taken that both references relate to the same document, which was in Stewart's possession at some period when he was lecturing on Political Economy. The second reference does not show whether in 1810-11 he still had this document or not. It might perhaps be inferred that he had by that time returned it to the source from which it had been borrowed. Whether the manuscript containing the reference to Oswald was the same as that of the lecture of 1755 or whether these were distinct papers is a problem of considerable importance both in relation to the development of Adam Smith's thought and also

[1] *Life of Adam Smith*, pp. 124-5.
[2] *A New Groat's Worth of Wit for a Penny : or An Analysis or Compend of the Edinburgh Review*, pp. 3-5.
[3] *Works*, 1856, ix, p. 6. [4] D. Stewart, *Works*, 1845, viii, p. vii.

as, possibly, throwing light on the fate of the lecture of 1755. The most natural conclusion is that there was only one document which was the lecture, and in it one of the "discoveries"[1] Adam Smith claimed was the distributive division of rent, wages and interest, coupling this with an acknowledgement of his indebtedness to Oswald. This would place the enunciation of the principle by Adam Smith as early as 1755. On the other hand, if there were two documents, the date might be as late as 1768 when Oswald's health broke down. The draft of *The Wealth of Nations*, which is printed below, simplifies this question for—if we had only the *Glasgow Lectures*—it would be difficult to admit that Adam Smith had this distinction clearly in mind. The draft shows plainly that it was quite explicit in that later revision. Considering that the *Lectures* are a student's notes it would be over-refinement to suggest that Oswald's contribution was a separate document, communicated to Adam Smith some time between 1760 and 1763 but which was only incorporated in the draft and not, as yet, in the manuscript of the *Lectures*. Whichever alternative is adopted the evidence is quite distinctly in favour of Oswald's communication having reached Adam Smith and having been used by him before he went to France.[2]

Previous references to the lecture of 1755[3] will show the curious conditions under which Stewart came to treat it. Inevitably he could not be in complete *rapport* with readers later than his own generation. From what is said it is natural for these to follow the brief account thinking of some writers who had used material from Adam Smith's lectures or conversations, without permission or even acknowledgement. Since the protest was made locally, it is not unlikely that one type of borrowing Adam Smith may have had in view was in the literary articles which appeared from time to time in papers such as the *Glasgow Journal* and *Glasgow Courant*. On the other hand, what Stewart had in mind—and what determined his treatment—were the charges of plagiarism, made twelve to fifteen years later against his own colleagues, Ferguson and Robertson. This explains the extreme restraint of the account, which would have been unnecessary if he had really in his mind events which had happened nearly forty years before the *Memoir* was first printed. Under these limitations Stewart's account of the whole incident becomes the most skilful piece of writing in his works. Any charge of plagiarism made by Adam Smith or his friends must relate to his lectures on literary criticism, ethics, jurisprudence and economics. Now what Stewart did was most ingenious. He states that the lecture

---

[1] As Stewart points out, Adam Smith had been anticipated by Petty—*Works*, ix, p. 6.
[2] See below, pp. 318-19, for the date of the "Draft" mentioned in the text.
[3] See above, pp. 55, 101.

was directed against unacknowledged borrowings; and, in order to establish priority, Adam Smith gave a fairly long list of his new ideas. When, however, Stewart gave examples, he carefully omitted any reference to a subject in respect to which plagiarism had been alleged, both before and after 1755. The *Theory* had been published and therefore there is no mention of Ethics, nor of literary criticism, since it was with regard to this that the charge was made before 1755, nor to Jurisprudence for the later charges related to it. This left only the economic part of the lectures, and it was a selection from the references in these to which the examples were confined. Carlyle had a separate defence of his friend Ferguson, who claimed that, in his case, there could have been no plagiarism since " he owned he had derived many notions from a French author, and that Smith had been there before him ".[1] The reference here is to the *History of Civil Society*, which appeared in 1767, and the French author intended was no doubt Montesquieu, though the point of view in Adam Smith's lectures on Jurisprudence was quite independent.

The question remains what grounds there were for the charges of plagiarism. Intrinsically, the answer is of little importance, but it is of interest in the light that it reflects back upon Adam Smith's character. As far as can be judged from the scanty material available, both Robertson and Ferguson borrowed from Adam Smith's lectures without any acknowledgement. What is strange is that he had no disposition to hold back any of his ideas, so as to preserve to himself the credit of priority in publication. It is known that not only had he lent the manuscript of his literary lectures to Blair, but, when some of his friends complained that the manuscript had been incorporated into Blair's course with much freedom, Smith was reported to have said, " He is very welcome, there is enough left ".[2] It appears that what lay behind Adam Smith's complaint against both Ferguson and Robertson was that he had been treated by each with a lack of the candour and open dealing which he had a right to expect from men who professed friendship to him. He met them frequently, and it would only have been mere courtesy for each to have asked him if he intended to continue his studies in Jurisprudence with a view to publication. Adam Smith had secured the degree of D.D. for Robertson in 1758 and it may have been that if he visited Glasgow to have it conferred, he stayed with Smith in the College. The closing pages of the *Theory* (1759) point to the need for a treatment of the development of Jurisprudence, which would indicate to those who had attended Adam Smith's lectures at Edinburgh that this would be his next task, and it seems probable that he was contemplating a book upon it. Robertson will be found in June 1759 urging Adam Smith to

[1] *Autobiography*, 1860, p. 285.   [2] Rae, *Life of Adam Smith*, p. 33.

write a history of Philosophy,[1] while on 25th October of the same year Robertson wrote to Charles Townshend that he had been preparing for Charles V., " and I shall soon begin to write ".[2] Evidently by this date he had been consulting authorities for quite an appreciable time. Under such circumstances, it was not unreasonable that Adam Smith should feel that he had been treated in a manner which was wanting in consideration.

It may be that one forms an exaggerated idea of the importance of the lecture of 1755; but, even so, it is now the most outstanding document, still to be discovered, relating to the life of Adam Smith and the growth of his system. The chances of the manuscript being in existence are far from favourable. There are a number of possibilities. First, was there an " Oswald " document in addition? If so, Stewart might be understood to have said that it was no longer in his possession in 1810-11. If, on the other hand, the documents were not two but one, in other words, that the reference to Oswald occurred in the lecture of 1755, the same result would seem to follow. But, if Stewart no longer had the manuscript, it does not seem that he returned it to David Douglas, Lord Reston. Not only has there never been any trace of it in the possession of the Bannerman or the Cunningham families, but enquiries amongst the lawyers of various branches of these families failed to find any reference to it in the many inventories which were made of the papers and books. On the whole, one is forced to the conclusion that Stewart failed to return the manuscript. His son, Colonel Stewart, gave some documents of a mathematical nature to the United Service Club and burned all the rest. It is to be feared that this manuscript was included in the fire. There is just a gleam of hope. Stewart may have lent it to some friend, or at some time, while it was in his possession, a copy may have been made.

The next four years—approximately from 1755 to 1759—were devoted mainly to the writing and the publishing of the *Theory of Moral Sentiments*. " Mainly ", it may be noted, because Adam Smith, having made himself familiar with the historical works in the University Library, was beginning to recommend more recent books and also others on geography and travel. From what has already been said,[3] it will be plain that in the Edinburgh Lectures there had been a considerable amount of ethical material, and the fragment remaining shows that passages from it were transferred, verbally, to the *Theory*. This material required to be made into a connected treatise, and it is not possible to say at what date the book was begun. The composition of it extended over a considerable time, for,

[1] See below, p. 239.
[2] Duke of Buccleuch's MSS. at Dalkeith House, Townshend Section.
[3] See above, p. 58.

as Adam Smith himself said, he was a very slow worker, and the Earl of Buchan stated that parts of the book were read as lectures to the Literary Society of Glasgow as well as " an Essay on Language ", by which is probably intended " the Considerations concerning the first Formation of Languages " subsequently appended to the *Theory*.[1]

The place of this book in the history of British Philosophy has been frequently discussed, most recently by Dr. Walther Eckstein and Dr. James Bonar.[2] In addition the volume has a striking, though indirect, biographical significance. Quite unconsciously, in it, Adam Smith is revealing some of his own personal characteristics which qualified him to become an outstanding economist. The basis of the sympathy of the impartial spectator was the power of imaginative transposition by which he thought we are enabled to see the motives and the surroundings of another person as they appear to that person himself and " in fact change not only circumstances but persons and characters with him ".[3] There can be no doubt that Adam Smith possessed this faculty to a quite remarkable extent. He may, and probably did, err in attributing it in the same degree to other people, and to that extent the foundation of his ethics is impaired. Accordingly, the greatest value of the *Theory* at the present day is the revelation which it provides of the author's own mental processes. At the same time, this imaginative transposition is not only an " outgoing " towards the personality of others. There is also a return by which circumstances and actions are judged. From the biographical standpoint perhaps too much has been made of the element of sympathy. It is always that of an impartial spectator, clearly showing that Adam Smith's sympathy was not merely sentiment, which may easily become a positive vice in economics, though not perhaps an altogether unnatural reaction from the alleged inhumanity of " the economic man ". Adam Smith found in himself the essential precedent of a judicial attitude, such as that of an impartial spectator of the facts and circumstances as they had been clarified and illuminated through the power he possessed of immersing himself in the thought and surroundings of all sorts and conditions of men.

Rae gives a vivid description of the immediate success of the *Theory of Moral Sentiments* on its publication in the spring of 1759.[4] In certain events which followed, the chronology of his account, if not altogether erroneous, is subject to considerable doubt. The first meeting of Adam Smith with William Fitzmaurice,

[1] University of Glasgow MSS.—Murray Collection, Extracts from Lord Buchan's Diaries and Letter Book, 1763.
[2] Adam Smith, *Theorie der Ethischen Gefühle*, Leipzig, 1926 ; *Moral Sense*, 1930.
[3] This is dealt with more fully in *Transactions of the British Academy*, x, pp. 443-4.
[4] Rae, *Life of Adam Smith*, pp. 141-51.

second Earl of Shelburne and afterwards Marquis of Lansdowne, was not in 1761,[1] but in 1759, as appears from the letter printed below.[2] This is a small matter. More important is the time at which occurred the fracas between Dr. Johnson and Adam Smith. Rae places this also in the year 1761; but, were it not that Boswell reports Johnson as having said that he had met Smith before 1763 and " they did not take to each other ",[3] a more probable date is about five years later when, as is now known, Adam Smith was living in London for about six months.[4] As it turns out, he had done a good deal in the previous ten or fifteen years to ensure a somewhat hostile reception from Johnson. In reviewing the *Dictionary* in 1755 he had been very critical. It is true that he gave unstinted praise to its unique character as the unaided work of one man, as distinguished from the long-continued co-operative labours devoted to similar works abroad. On the other hand, he must have touched Johnson in a tender place when he censured the whole plan as being wanting in logic, and there is a suggestion that the linguistic theory was not sound. Authors are far from welcoming criticism even when it is constructive—and least of all Johnson. Further, in some of his lectures he had said that the *Rambler* was characterized " by heaviness, weakness and affected pedantry ".[5] Still worse was the remark " of all writers, ancient or modern, he that keeps off the greatest distance from common sense is Dr. Samuel Johnson ".[6] It is Boswell who records the remark about the *Rambler* under the date 21st September, 1762, but he may have communicated this and other sayings of Adam Smith to Johnson at an earlier date or they have been repeated by someone else.

It seems that it is an error of Rae to describe the story as " demonstrably mythical in most of its circumstances ".[7] A critical examination of it shows that there is a close resemblance to Stewart's account of the lecture of 1755, for, here as there, two similar events, which had happened at very different times have been telescoped together, and related as if they were one occurrence. Johnson and Adam Smith met in the 'sixties and had a violent disagreement. It has been shown that, when some of the remarks made in the Glasgow classrooms came to Johnson's ears, Adam Smith could scarcely expect anything but a very warm reception. That incident is complete in itself. Later, after the appearance of the *Letter giving an Account of the Death of David Hume* in 1777, Boswell met John

[1] Rae, *Life of Adam Smith*, p. 153. [2] See below, p. 240.
[3] *Boswell's Life of Johnson*, ed. G. Birkbeck Hill, 1887, i, p. 427.
[4] W. R. Scott, " Adam Smith at Downing St." in *Econ. Hist. Rev.*, vi, pp. 79-89.
[5] Geoffrey Scott (ed.), *Private Papers of James Boswell from Malahide Castle*, i, p. 70.
[6] Edin. Univ. Libry. MSS., La 451/2. [7] Rae, *Life of Adam Smith*, p. 157.

Anderson, the Glasgow Professor of Natural Philosophy. From what has already been said about his character [1] it is evident that he was a born trouble-maker; and, if he did not find a tense atmosphere, he was fertile in creating it. Brought in contact with Boswell's puckish humour, something explosive was likely to result. After the meeting Boswell wrote on 9th July, 1777, to Johnson urging that, in view of " the poisonous productions of the age ", of which the *Letter* was an example, " it was an excellent opportunity for Dr. Johnson to step forth ".[2] No doubt " the Doctor " did step forth, but not on an occasion when Adam Smith was present. Scott and others, in order to round off the tale, appended the second event to the first, which, by making the chronology impossible, has thrown doubt on the whole circumstances. The violent disagreement certainly happened; and in 1761, if Boswell is right in his date. The condemnation of Adam Smith's alleged approval of Hume's scepticism about 1777, but in his absence, almost certainly happened also, but not only the times but also the influences which moved Johnson were totally different.[3]

The third and final four years of Adam Smith's time at Glasgow—from 1759 to 1763—began with a period of ill-health, due largely to a chill. Dr. Cullen found him looking so ill in Edinburgh that he warned him he would not survive the winter unless he took a holiday and riding exercise. Accordingly he rode to York, spent some time with Lord Shelburne at Wyecombe and returned by the western roads.[4] Later he made an expedition to Inveraray to visit the Duke of Argyle.[5] When he was able to return to his studies he concentrated on Jurisprudence, including Political Economy, which is clearly forecasted in the last two pages of the *Theory*. Stewart states that after its publication Adam Smith contented himself with a short summary of Ethics when lecturing to the Moral Philosophy class and then spent the rest of the time on Jurisprudence.[6] This is exactly confirmed by the *Glasgow Lectures*, which would require the greater part of a session for their delivery in the fuller form which is condensed in the notes which remain.

To some extent the course of Adam Smith's studies at this period may be traced by the books added to the University Library on his recommenda-

---

[1] See above, p. 87.

[2] *Boswell's Life of Johnson*, ed. G. Birkbeck Hill, 1887, iii, p. 119.

[3] Professor Abbot—the discoverer of the Fettercairn MSS.—has been good enough to tell me that, according to his recollection, these papers do not contain any reference to the incidents discussed above, nor, indeed, is Adam Smith mentioned in them.

[4] See below, p. 253; Letter of Adam Smith to Lord Shelburne, 11th November, 1760—Papers from the Bowood Library, in the possession of the Marquis of Lansdowne.

[5] See below, p. 251.   [6] Stewart, *Memoir*, 1811, p. 60.

tion. The collection of more modern histories was completed. Several volumes of travel were added. A few new law books and some of the more expensive economic books or books having an economic reference, such as the French *Encyclopédie* (between 1758 and 1760) and James Postlethwayt's *History of the Public Revenue*, immediately after its publication in 1759. The final step, as regards this period, was taken when the economic material was removed from the lectures on Jurisprudence for separate treatment. The circumstances which led to this momentous decision are mentioned in more detail in the introductory note to the edition of the resulting draft which is printed below and the date there assigned to it is the late summer of 1763.[1] It is curious that the selection of a tutor for the young Duke of Buccleuch resulted in Adam Smith's decision to write a distinct economic work (in the first instance for a public of only one person) which became the groundwork of *The Wealth of Nations*.

Increasing knowledge of Adam Smith's life and surroundings has led to a revision of the views of his relation to the Physiocrats which have been held from Dugald Stewart to Thorold Rogers.[2] Then, when in 1895-6 the late Professor Cannan identified, and accepted as authentic, the manuscript copy of a student's notes of the " Lectures on Justice ",[3] opinion has moved in the opposite direction towards an increasing recognition of Adam Smith's independence. That movement should be reinforced almost as much by the discovery of what has been called " an early draft of *The Wealth of Nations* " as by that of the *Glasgow Lectures*. For it is highly significant that the chief points which Cannan indicated as having been obtained by Adam Smith from intercourse with the Physiocrats are to be found, if in a partially developed form, in the recently discovered draft.[4] In Part II, Section I, 1, reasons are given which show that it is most unlikely he was acquainted with any of the characteristic writings of the Physiocrats before he went to France. Now that the manuscript Catalogue of his library as it was in 1781, which is at Tokyo, can be collocated with Dr. Bonar's *Library of Adam Smith*, it is possible to speak with more confidence, since we have the list of all his books at a period subsequent to the publication of *The Wealth of Nations*. The manuscript Catalogue does not add many to the list of economic books. What it does suggest—and that very definitely—is that the volumes Adam Smith brought back from France were acquired very largely through personal relations and recommendations. To that extent there is something of an accidental

---

[1] See below, pp. 318-19.
[2] His edition of *The Wealth of Nations* appeared in 1869.
[3] Adam Smith, *Lectures on Justice* (ed. E. Cannan), 1896.
[4] See below, pp. 319-20 ; cf. *Economic Journal*, xlv, pp. 433-6.

character in this portion of his library. Thus his friend Bonnet at Geneva is represented by five items, Condillac by six, D'Anville by no less than eleven, and Mably by eight. In some ways the case of the *Ephémérides* is very significant. The first number was issued on 4th November, 1765, and publication continued till 1772. Adam Smith had the three years 1767, 1768, 1769 only.[1] Going farther, the *Encyclopédie* of which (as mentioned above) the volumes, so far issued, had been added to the University Library in Adam Smith's time at Glasgow contained Quesnay's article on " Fermiers " but the section in the *Glasgow Lectures* where *métayage* occurs seems to be quite independent. There is the further question whether he might not have gained some knowledge of the tenets of the Physiocrats from periodical publications, which he certainly read. Except for foreign literary reviews which suggested titles of books to be ordered for his own library or for that of the University, he does not seem to have had a high opinion of these. The Library received the *Transactions* of all the chief academies, but again he did not place much reliance on them.[2] Here it is necessary to distinguish between French influence generally and that of the Physiocrats in particular. While the latter cannot be shown to have reached him at this early period, the former undoubtedly did exert an effect, but one that united with, and was absorbed by, other formative powers. It was not only that he was acquainted with Cantillon, if not at this time with the actual book which may have been added later to his library, certainly with the extracts from it which had appeared in

[1] Higgs, *Bibliography of Economics*, 1751-1775, Nos. 3363, 3978.

[2] *Edinburgh Review for the Year 1755*, 1818, p. 123. Another possibility is that such knowledge might have reached him through Hume. The *Political Discourses* were translated into French in 1753 and, again, in 1754 (Hill Burton, *Life of Hume*, i, p. 363). In 1759 John Stewart wrote that Turgot was one of Hume's admirers in France (Greig, *Letters of Hume*, ii, p. 348), and, when Hume was in Paris, they discussed various questions together, as appears from Turgot's letter of 23rd July, 1766 (Hill Burton, *Letters of Eminent Persons*, p. 130). Mirabeau had criticised Hume's views on luxury in *L'Ami des Hommes*, the first edition of which appeared in 1756. A copy had been sent to Hume, but it had not reached him, and in July 1757 he was writing both to Millar and the Abbé le Blanc asking each to obtain one for him (Greig, *Letters*, i, pp. 257, 259). Owing to the war, the procuring of French books was very difficult at this time (see below, p. 173). As yet Mirabeau had not joined the Physiocratic group, an event which occurred in 1758-9 (Weuleresse, *Mouvement Physiocratique*, i, p. 58). It was in the latter year that he incorporated the Tableau Économique into the sixth part of *L'Ami des Hommes*. One might be inclined to expect that Hume, and through him Adam Smith, would have known of the new movement. While it is impossible to reach complete certainty, the available evidence is negative. There is no further reference to Mirabeau, or indeed to French economic questions, in Hume's correspondence till he went to France. If Adam Smith had heard of the book and it had interested him, he would, in all probability, have ordered it for the University Library, but this was not done. Then again, when Hume met members of the Physiocratic Group in Paris, he formed an unfavourable opinion of them as appears from a letter written to Morellet in 1769—" I hope that in your work you will thunder them, and crush them, and pound them, and reduce them to dust and ashes ! They are indeed the set of men the most chimerical and most arrogant that now exist, since the annihilation of the Sorbonne " (Greig, *Letters*, ii, p. 205). See also below, p. 298 note [1].

Malachy Postlethwayt's *Dictionary of Trade and Commerce*, but he was affected very much more by the general trend of enlightened opinion in France; so that, while his work at Glasgow cannot be shown to have been influenced by the Physiocrats, at the same time it is true that both they and Smith drew a part of their respective inspirations from the same sources or sources closely akin, and that some of these were French.

There is one consequence of Adam Smith's meeting with the Physiocrats which may be stated with a fair degree of certainty. If " the useful work "— " so well advanced " by January 1764—to which John Glassford, the eminent Virginia merchant, alluded in a letter printed below,[1] was the draft of *The Wealth of Nations*, it was inevitable that the new facets of the subject presented by the writings of Quesnay and his friends, as well as by personal intercourse with them, would give Adam Smith much more material, and, instead of the proposed book being ready soon after 1764, a further twelve years were required to finish it. Between the completion of the draft, as it now exists, several months elapsed before he left Glasgow. It must be a matter of uncertainty whether the chapters summarised were abstracted from an existing manuscript or were prepared from previous notes but were in anticipation of what was yet to be written in a form ready for the printer. In any case, Glassford's statement indicates that he had learnt from Adam Smith himself that the book was " well advanced ", which to a practical man must have meant " in sight of publication ". First of all Adam Smith decided to include much new material he had obtained in France. When he returned he had brought with him at least four boxes of books which were to be insured for £200 for the journey from London to Kirkcaldy.[2] After these additions had been made, the work of the Physiocrats had suggested the analysis of a number of economic conditions in England as they had already treated similar ones in France. Also, the world had not stood still and there were further problems, which had recently become prominent, to be examined. As he himself explains,[3] from 1773 (when he went to London on other business) until the book was published, he remained there, almost constantly, working at the British Museum and, perhaps, some other libraries. It is in this way that the interval of some twelve years between the preparation of the manuscript, almost ready for the printer in 1764, and final publication is accounted for.

[1] See below, p. 258.

[2] *Economic Journal*, viii, p. 402. The date of the letter is 25th March, 1766, but the true date may be a year later.

[3] See below, p. 283. Rae, *Life*, pp. 256-7, gives the time at which many of the last parts of the manuscript to be finished were written.

PART II

DOCUMENTS

§ A—OFFICIAL AND LEGAL PAPERS.

I. *Commission to Adam Smith as Clerk of the Court Martial of Scotland, 18th April, 1707.*[1]

ANNE R.

Anne by the Grace of God Queen of Scotland, England, France and Ireland, Defender of the Faith, &c^a. To our trusty and well beloved Adam Smith Greeting We reposing trust and confidence in your loyalty and fidelity have nominated, constituted and appointed and by these presents doe nominate, constitute and appoint you during all the days of your life time, To be Clerk of the Court Martial or Councill of War of all our forces within our ancient Kingdom of Scotland, levied or to be levied, in place of John Dalrymple who has now demitted that office, with power to you to constitute a Depute to serve under you therein. You are therefore with all care and diligence by yourself or your Depute to exercise the said place and office of Clerk to the Court Martial of our Forces and to enjoy all Priviledges and Casualities belonging thereto allowing for yourself and your Depute aforesaid seven shillings and six pence sterl. per diem to be paid out of the funds appointed or to be appointed for payment of our forces in our said Kingdom and we hereby grant unto you full power, warrant and authority to doe and perform all things belonging to the said office as fully and freely in all respects as the nature of the said trust doth require.

Given at our Court at Kensington the 18th day of Aprill, 1707 and of our Reign the 6th year.

By her Ma^{tys} Command,

LOUDOUN.

II. *Will of Adam Smith, W.S., Comptroller of the Customs at Kirkcaldy, dated 13th November, 1722.*[2]

At Kirkcaldy the 25th day of January, 1723, in presence of David Simpson one of the present baillies of the said burgh compeared personally James Barclay Writer in the same as Procurator for the deceased Adam Smith after designed who gave in the Disposition and Assignation under-written desiring the same to be insert and

---

[1] Public Record Office, State Papers Domestic, Scotland, Warrant Book, 23, pp. 276-7. Here the Commission is for the Court Martial. In the Will of Adam Smith, W.S., which follows, he describes himself as Clerk of Courts Martial: the reason being that he succeeded in extending his office so as to include Regimental as well as General Courts Martial.

[2] Register of Deeds, Kirkcaldy. I am much indebted to Mr. William Hutton, M.A., LL.B., the Town Clerk, for having extracted this document for me.

Registered in the Burgh Court Books of the said burgh therein to remain for conservation conform to the clause of registration under-written which desire the said baillie judging reasonable therefore decerned and ordained the same to be done conform to the said clause of registration and of which Disposition and Assignation the tenor follows :

Be it known to all men by these presents, me, Adam Smith, Clerk of the Courts Martial and Councils of War in Scotland and Controller of His Majesty's Customs at Kirkcaldy, for the love, favour and affection I have and bear to Hugh Smith my only lawful son and the persons after named to have given, granted and disponed likeas with and under the reservations, provisions, power and faculty underwritten give grant and dispone to the said Hugh Smith my only lawful son his heirs and assignees whomsoever which failing to the child or children procreat or to be procreat betwixt me and Margaret Douglas my present spouse and their heirs or assignees which failing to William Walker, Dyer, Burgess of Aberdeen and William Smith, Steward to his Grace the Duke of Argyle, my nephews, equally, their heirs or assignees whomsoever, heritably and irredeemably All and Haill that tenement of foreland [1] under and above with the pertinents and timber shop of the same which sometime pertained to Adam Smith, Merchant in Aberdeen, my uncle, and thereafter to James Smith his son, thereafter to Mr. Alexander Smith Postmaster General of Scotland, my brother, and adjudged from him by Margaret Crichton his relict and Mr. James Robertson Minister at Echlestone [2] her husband and disponed by him to me as the said Disposition dated the 26th of December, 1712, which tenement of land lies within the Burgh of Aberdeen on the west gate of the castle gate thereof betwixt the lands of the heirs of the deceased Andrew Galloway Merchant in Aberdeen on the west and the lands sometime of the deceased John Craighead and now of Alexander Troup Merchant in Aberdeen on the south and the King's Common Wayes on the east and north parts, together with all right I have or can pretend to the same.

(Here follow the clauses of infeftment.)

And Moreover Witt Ye Me for the causes foresaid to have given, granted and disponed likeas with and under the reservations, provisions, power and faculty under-written, I hereby give, grant and dispone to and in favour of the said Hugh Smith and his foresaids, which failing the child or children procreat or to be procreat betwixt me and the said Margaret Douglas and their foresaids, which failing the said William Walker and William Smith equally and their foresaids All and Sundry goods and gear, jewels, gold and silver coined and uncoined, household plenishing and furniture and others whatsoever presently pertaining and belonging

---

[1] This tenement with its pertinents was opposite the site on which stands the Town House, Aberdeen. As to its history see Appendix II.

[2] *I.e.* Eddleston in the Presbytery of Peebles—*cf.* Hew Scott, *Fasti*, 1915, i, p. 272.

DOCUMENTS—OFFICIAL AND LEGAL

to me or which shall pertain and belong to me at the time of my decease and together with all debts and sums of money resting and owing to me or which shall be resting and owing to me the time of my decease by whatsoever person or persons by bond, bill, ticket, debt, compt book or any other manner of way whatsoever.

(There follows a long list of sums due on bond on heritable property and on government stocks. The former (including penalties left blank, at the usual rate) amounts to 12,500 merks due by Alexander Gibson of Durie, Andrew Ramsay of Abbotshall, Dr. Robert Hay of Strowie, John Chalmers of Pitmedden, the Earl of Southesk, Alexander Carnagie of Bonniemoon, James Oswald of Dunnikier, Sir John Malcolm of Invertiel, Hugh, Earl of Loudoun, John Douglas of Strathenry.[1] The latter amounts to about £580 sterling, the chief item in which is " the sum of £200 Sterling bestowed upon the Fourth Subscription of South Sea Stock ".[2] Also an amount, unspecified, due by the Government to him as Clerk of the Courts Martial.)

Providing Always likeas it's hereby expressly provided and declared that the said Hugh Smith and his foresaids which failing the other persons above mentioned shall be bound and obliged likeas by their acceptance they bind and oblige themselves to pay my haill just and lawful debts which shall be resting to me the time of my decease and particularly to implement and fulfil the haill obligements contained in the Contract of Marriage betwixt me and the said Margaret Douglas due and performable by me, thir presents being granted but prejudice thereto in any sort.

(There follow clauses reserving testator's life rent, power of revocation, substitution and surrogation.)

And Moreover I hereby nominate and appoint the Honourable William Dalrymple of Glenmuir,[3] the Honourable Mr. John Clark, one of the Barons of Exchequer,[4] Mr. John Clark, Doctor of Physick in Edinburgh,[5] Mr. James Oswald

[1] The sum of 3000 merks was " an obligement " by John Douglas of Strathenry in the contract of marriage between the testator and Margaret Douglas, dated 17th November, 1720.

[2] Adam Smith, W.S., purchased this stock on the recommendation of his nephew, William Smith. The subscription lists were opened on 4th August, 1720, at 1,000. The writ of *Scire facias* (which resulted in a great fall in the price of the stock) was issued on 14th August—University of Glasgow MSS., Bannerman Papers, William Smith to Adam Smith, W.S., 30th August, 1720. Cf. W. R. Scott, *Joint Stock Companies*, iii, pp. 323-4.

[3] Son of Colonel William Dalrymple, M.P. for Ayr in the last Scots Parliament, a Commissioner for the Treaty of Union, a Commissioner for the Equivalent (married Penelope, Countess of Dumfries), grandson of the first Earl of Stair. He succeeded his mother in the Earldom of Dumfries and his brother James, as third Earl of Stair. His aunt married Hugh, Earl of Loudoun. She was noted as a great improver of the policies of Sorn Castle in Ayrshire and is said to have reached the age of 100.

[4] The Diarist. He succeeded his father as Sir John Clerk of Penicuik : born 1676, studied at Glasgow University 1693-4 and proceeded to Leyden : Commissioner for Enquiry into the Public Accounts and for the Treaty of Union, trustee for Manufactures : besides the *Diary* he was the writer of many pamphlets : F.R.S. : died 1755.

[5] Cousin to Sir John Clerk of Penicuik : a Vice-President of the Edinburgh Philosophical Society, President of the Royal College of Physicians, Edinburgh, 1740 : " one of the most cele-

of Dunnikier,[1] John Douglas of Strathenry,[2] William Caddell of Fossochee, Writer to the Signet,[3] Hercules Smith, Collector of the Customs at Kirkcaldy,[4] Archibald Arnott, Surgeon there,[5] Mr. William Smith, late Regent in the College of Aberdeen [6] and William Smith, Steward to His Grace the Duke of Argyle [7] and William Walker,[8] Dyer in Aberdeen and Mr. John Steill, Minister at Camnoch,[9] three thereof or the major part in life for the time shall be a quorum, to be tutors and curators to the said Hugh Smith during his minority and in case any child or children of my present marriage shall exist, I hereby nominate and appoint the said Mr. James Oswald, John Douglas and William Smith, Henry Millar of Pourin.[10] . . . Skene of Pitlour[11] and Robert Douglas,[12] brother of the said John Douglas, whereof any three a quorum with Margaret Douglas my spouse whom I hereby appoint

brated physicians that has appeared in Scotland since Pitcairn ". In the Laing MSS. there is a collection of letters from Simon Fraser, Lord Lovat, in which there are many references to him. He died in his chair while reading Horace in 1757. At a meeting in the Hall of the Royal Infirmary of Edinburgh Cullen paid an eloquent tribute to his character and professional qualifications—J. Thomson, *Life and Writings of W. Cullen*, 1859, i, pp. 525-36. He described himself as a cousin of Hugh Smith, a connection which was probably through the mother—John Clerk to James Oswald, 28 Jan. 1723. Bannerman Papers.

[1] Dean of Guild, Kirkcaldy, 1702-7 ; Provost, 1713-15 ; M.P., Kirkcaldy, 1702-7 (when he voted consistently against the Union) ; for Kirkcaldy Burghs, 1710-15. He died not long after Adam Smith, W.S. His son, also James, was Commissioner of the Navy, a Lord of the Treasury and Treasurer of Ireland.

[2] The elder brother of Margaret Smith, wife of the testator ; see Appendix IV.

[3] Writer, appointed, jointly with John Boyle, Clerk to the Commissioners of the Signet in 1711, admitted as W.S. in 1713, died Nov. 1728.

[4] Cousin of the testator ; for particulars see Appendix I.

[5] Probably a connection of one of the branches of the well-known Fife family of Arnot and some relation of the wife of the testator ; her grandfather was descended from Robert Arnot of Fernie, who having married Margaret Balfour, Baroness of Burleigh, changed his name to Burleigh ; see Appendix IV.

[6] Cousin of the testator, studied at King's University, Aberdeen, M.A. 1684, Governor to Lord Charles Hay in 1693, succeeded Alexander Litster as a Regent of Marischal College in the same year. Though returned in the Poll Book of 1696 as having " no wife, child or servant " he married Elizabeth, daughter of Robert Paterson, Advocate in Aberdeen, and had at least one son. Being an active Jacobite, he was deposed by the Royal Visitation of 1717—*cf.* Appendix I.

[7] Deputy to Adam Smith, W.S., when he was Clerk of Courts Martial, private secretary to Hugh, Earl of Loudoun, Steward and subsequently Secretary to the Duke of Argyle, a secretary of the office of Ordinance and Yeomen of the King's Wine Cellar, honorary burgess of Glasgow (1716), of Edinburgh (1738), of Aberdeen (1741) ; died 1753—*cf.* Appendix I.

[8] A nephew of the testator, related to two provosts of Aberdeen, married Janet Middleton, the daughter of one Principal of the University and granddaughter of another : a prominent Aberdeen merchant : died 1766.

[9] Husband of a sister of the first wife of the testator.

[10] Possibly a brother-in-law of the wife of testator. Pourin was an estate in Fife not far from Strathenry ; a relative of the David Millar who was the schoolmaster of Adam Smith, the future economist.

[11] David Skene of Pitlour in the parish of Strathmiglo, Fife, also near Strathenry. He was a member of the family of Halyards, Fife, which was a branch of the Skenes of Skene in Aberdeenshire. He married Jean Douglas on 25th July, 1718.

[12] A younger brother of the wife of the testator.

tutor and curator to her said child or children *sine qua non* to be tutors and curators to my said children of this marriage if they shall exist during their pupilarity and minority ; Declaring Always that the said tutors and curators shall not be liable for omissions but only for their actual intromissions with their respective minors' means and estate ; and further that they shall not be liable *in solidum*, but each one for his own intromissions allenarly ; And lastly hereby declare that albeit their presents with the writs above disponed be found lying by me or in the hands of any confident person the time of my decease, yet the same shall be als valid as if they had been delivered, any law or practice to the contrary notwithstanding ; Consenting to the registration hereof in the Books of Council and Session or others competent therein to remain for conservation and constitutes the said James Barclay, Writer in Kirkcaldy, my procurator, etc. In witness whereof (written on stamped paper by William Charters, Clerk of Kirkcaldy, by way of book consisting of six pages in folio) I have subscribed this and the five preceding pages at Kirkcaldy the 13th day of November, 1722, before these witnesses, the said Mr. James Oswald and William Charters and James Barclay, Servant to the said William Charters, witnesses, also to the marginal note in the fifth page and the other marginal note in this sixth page. Subscribing Adam Smith, James Oswald, witness, William Charters, witness, Ja: Barclay, witness.

III. *Abbreviate of Retour of Adam Smith as heir of his father.*[1]

Enquiry in the Burgh Court of Kirkcaldy 9th September 1724 before a jury who find that the deceased Adam Smith, Comptroller of the Customs at Kirkcaldy father of Adam Smith only son begotten between him and Margaret Douglas his wife died at the King's faith and peace and that the said Adam Smith is lawful and nearest heir of provision of his said father in terms of disposition by him dated 13 November 1722, recorded in the Burgh Court Books of Kirkcaldy 25th January 1723 and that he is of lawful age [2] (Service recorded 29th March 1727).

IV. *Decreet Arbitral, 22nd March, 1739—10th January, 1740.*[3] *Clearing of Accounts between Hercules Smith, Junr., representing the late Hercules Smith, Collector, and Adam Smith, a minor, by his Curator Adam Smith, representing the late Adam Smith, W.S., Comptroller.*

By 1738 Hercules Smith, Collector of Customs at Kirkcaldy, was dead, and his son of the same name, a merchant at Kirkcaldy, claimed, on behalf of himself and

[1] Register of Service of Heirs, Register House, Edinburgh.

[2] "The sixth head is Whether the pursuer be of lawful age, wherein we must distinguish betwixt ward-holdings and other holdings, blench, feu or burgage ; for in these any age is lawful age : but in ward-holdings, because the superior, by virtue of the ward, hath the profit of the land, during the heir's minority ; therefore they cannot enter till their majority, at which time only the heir is of lawful age, which in men is twenty-one years complete and in women fourteen years complete." Stair, *Institutions*, Bk. III, Tit. v, 39, 3rd Ed. (1759), p. 493. These provisions were altered by the Act of 1847.

[3] Register of Deeds, Kirkcaldy, found and extracted by Mr. William Hutton, Town Clerk.

four sisters, that in the adjustment of accounts of the Customs, as between the late Adam Smith, W.S., Comptroller, and the late Hercules Smith,[1] Collector, there were monies owed by the former to the latter. It is clear that there had been an apportionment of the estate of Adam Smith, W.S., between his sons Hugh and Adam, and the claim, if maintained, would devolve upon the last.

Adam Smith, the son, was still a minor, and another Adam Smith had been added to the number of his curators. This Adam Smith had been a clerk in the Customs under Adam Smith, W.S., the Comptroller, in 1722-3.[2] After the death or resignation of his successor in this office, Adam Smith, the former clerk, succeeded. By 1740 he had become Collector and in that year he was appointed Inspector General of the Outports. He was living in 1742, when he was admitted a Burgess of Aberdeen, but had retired and purchased a house in Edinburgh before 1752.

On 7th September, 1738, Hercules Smith, Jun., and Adam Smith, Collector, appeared, with their lawyers, before Baillie Thomas Brown, and it was agreed to submit the matters in dispute to arbitration. James Barclay, the Provost, and William Campbell, Lands Valuer of the Customs at Kirkcaldy, were selected by the parties to arbitrate. On 20th October they had failed to agree, and James Clark, Collector of Excise at Kirkcaldy, was chosen as oversman or umpire. He delivered his award on 10th January, 1740, in the following terms as recorded in the Register of Deeds, Kirkcaldy.

"The Decreet Arbitrall of Mr. James Clark oversman, nominated by the within and above [named] William Campbell and James Barclay, arbiters in the within submission, having accepted the determination of the same and having considered the claims and answers of both parties with the vouchers and fully heard them thereupon after mature deliberation having God and a good conscience before my eyes, I give and pronounce my Decreet Arbitrall as follows, videlicet, I find that after just count and reckoning betwixt the within Hercules and Adam Smiths there is justly resting by the within Adam Smith as Curator and taking burden upon him for Adam Smith [3] to the within Hercules Smith for himself and in name of his sisters within named a net balance of £7 Sterling which sum I decern and ordain the said Adam Smith to pay to the said Hercules Smith and upon payment I decern and ordain both parties mutually to discharge one another of all compts, reckonings, clags and claims, differences and debts, presently standing betwixt them; And I ordain both parties to stand and abide at and obey and fulfil my present Decreet Arbitrall under a penalty of £5 sterling to be paid by the faillzier to the observer or willing to observe attour performance and I ordain this my Decreet Arbitrall to be registered conform to the within clause of registration.

[1] See Appendix I.
[2] Salary Lists of the Customs at Kirkcaldy, 1722-3, General Register House, Edinburgh.
[3] *I.e.* The future economist.

" In witness whereof I have subscribed thir [sic] presents at Kirkcaldy the 29th day of January, 1739[-40], before these witnesses, William Charters, Clerk of Kirkcaldy and Robert Fraser, writer hereof [sic] subscribing Hercules Smith, Adam Smith, J. A. Clark, William Charters, witness, Robert Fraser, witness."

V. *Gen. Retornatus Adami Smith Fratri*, 1750. *Adam Smith, heir to his brother, Hugh.*[1]

The General Retour bears that Inquest was made in the Court of the Burgh of Kirkcaldie in the Court House thereof on December 15th, 1750, in presence of John Currie, Provost ; James Mackie and James Higgie, Baillies ; by virtue of a Brieve from Chancery issued to the Provost and Baillies of the said Burgh. The following just and faithful citizens, John and George Barker *non cleros* and head Baillies of the said Burgh ; James Boswell, Spirit Merchant, Alexander Kymer and William Salisbury, Merchants ; David Scott, Weaver ; William Tomson and James Holdram, Writers, Archibald Webster, Tailor ; William Campbell, Burgess ; John Durham, Surgeon Apothecary ; Robert Gilmour, Shoemaker ; Thomas Millar, Senior, Apothecary ; William Baxter, Signwriter, having been sworn with their great oath say That the late Hugh Smith lawful son of the deceased Adam Smith, Custom House Clerk at Kirkcaldy [Autigraphi Regiarum Custumarum Kirkaldie] Brother consanguinean of Adam Smith, one of the offspring procreated between the deceased Adam Smith and Margaret Douglas his spouse, died ; and that the said Adam Smith is nearer lawful heir of the said Hugh Smith, his brother consanguinean, by virtue of a disposition of date November 13th, 1722, made and executed by the deceased Adam Smith ——— ; and that the said Adam Smith is of lawful age.

The general Retour is signed and sealed by Robert Drysdale, Town Clerk of Kirkcaldy, And the extract thereof is made from the principal by William Smith, Public Depute Clerk of the said Chancery of Robert Kerr, Keeper of the Seal.

VI. *Sasine—Sale of Foreland in Aberdeen by Adam Smith*, 1757.[2]

1757, May 14. Sasine in favours of Hugh Gordon, watchmaker in Aberdeen, by virtue of a disposition containing procuratory of resignation dated at Glasgow 20 April last past, made and granted to said Hugh Gordon by Mr. Adam Smith, Professor of Moral Philosophy in the University of Glasgow, lawful son of the deceased Adam Smith, Clerk of the Courts Martials and Councils of War in Scotland, and Comptroller of H.M. Customs at Kirkaldie, procreate between him and Mrs. Margaret Douglas, his second wife,[3] heritable proprietor of the tenement of

---

[1] General Register House, Edinburgh.

[2] Aberdeen Burgh Sasines, Register House, Edinburgh, under above date. Entered previously on the same day is the Sasine in favour of Adam Smith, which had, evidently, not been effected on the death of his brother, Hugh.

[3] It is usual for the wife to be given her maiden name in Scottish legal documents.

land underwritten. Sasine is given of All and Whole that tenement of Foreland under and above with pertinents and timber shop of the same, lying within the Burgh of Aberdeen, on the west gate of the Castlegate thereof, between the lands of the heirs of the deceased Andrew Galloway, merchant in Aberdeen, now of Patrick Cushnie, Merchant, on the West, and the lands some time of the deceased John Craighead, thereafter of Andrew Troup, merchant in Aberdeen, now of John Morice, baxter, on the south and the King's common ways on the east and north parts with free entry and exit thereto ; together with all heritable right, right of title, claim, interest property, possession or other right and title whatsoever, which the said Mr. Adam Smith his predecessors or authors had, have, might or could claim or pretend thereto. Procurator in name of the deceased Adam Smith, James Thomson, Town Sergeant in Aberdeen, Procurator in name of Adam Smith, younger, William Nicoll, advocate in Aberdeen : witnesses to the giving of sasine Roderick McCulloch, Robert Robertson and William Troup, three of the Town Sergeants of Aberdeen, Notary Public—Robert Thomson.

§ B—ADAM SMITH AS STUDENT, 1737-1749

I. *The Matriculation of Adam Smith at the University of Glasgow,*
14*th November*, 1737.

Nomina Discipulorum Classis tertiæ [1] qui hoc Anno Academiam intrarunt sub Praesidio Magistri Johannis Loudoun.

      Adam Smith F: Adam Smith Generosi in Kirkaldy in Com. Fife.[2]

II. *Minute of Adam Smith's appointment as a Snell Exhibitioner.*

4*th March*, 1740.[3]

  This being the day appointed for Electing two Exhibitioners upon Mr. Snell's mortification to be presented to Baliol College, Oxford, Charles Sootie, Brother

---

[1] The numbering of Classes was a relic of the Regent system and it was abandoned in 1761. The order was the fifth class Humanity (Latin), the fourth Greek, the third Logic. Moral Philosophy should have been second and Natural Philosophy first, but these numbers were not used, since a student was permitted to take these last two classes in either order. It will be observed (p. 138) that the Logic Class was also known as the " Semi Class ".

 The conditions of matriculation at this period require some explanation. Only students who were proceeding to a degree in Arts were required to matriculate and any others who wished to vote at the election of the Lord Rector. Further, a student proceeding to the M.A. degree might matriculate in any year of his course. Thus the year of matriculation is not necessarily the undergraduate's first year at the University. The question whether Adam Smith came to Glasgow earlier than 1737 is discussed in Part I, chapter iv.

[2] It will be seen from the facsimile of part of this page of the Matriculation Album that Adam Smith's name stands first. It was the custom at this period to arrange names alphabetically in the order of the Christian names.

[3] University MSS., vol. 27, p. 133.

PLATE VII. BALLIOL COLLEGE

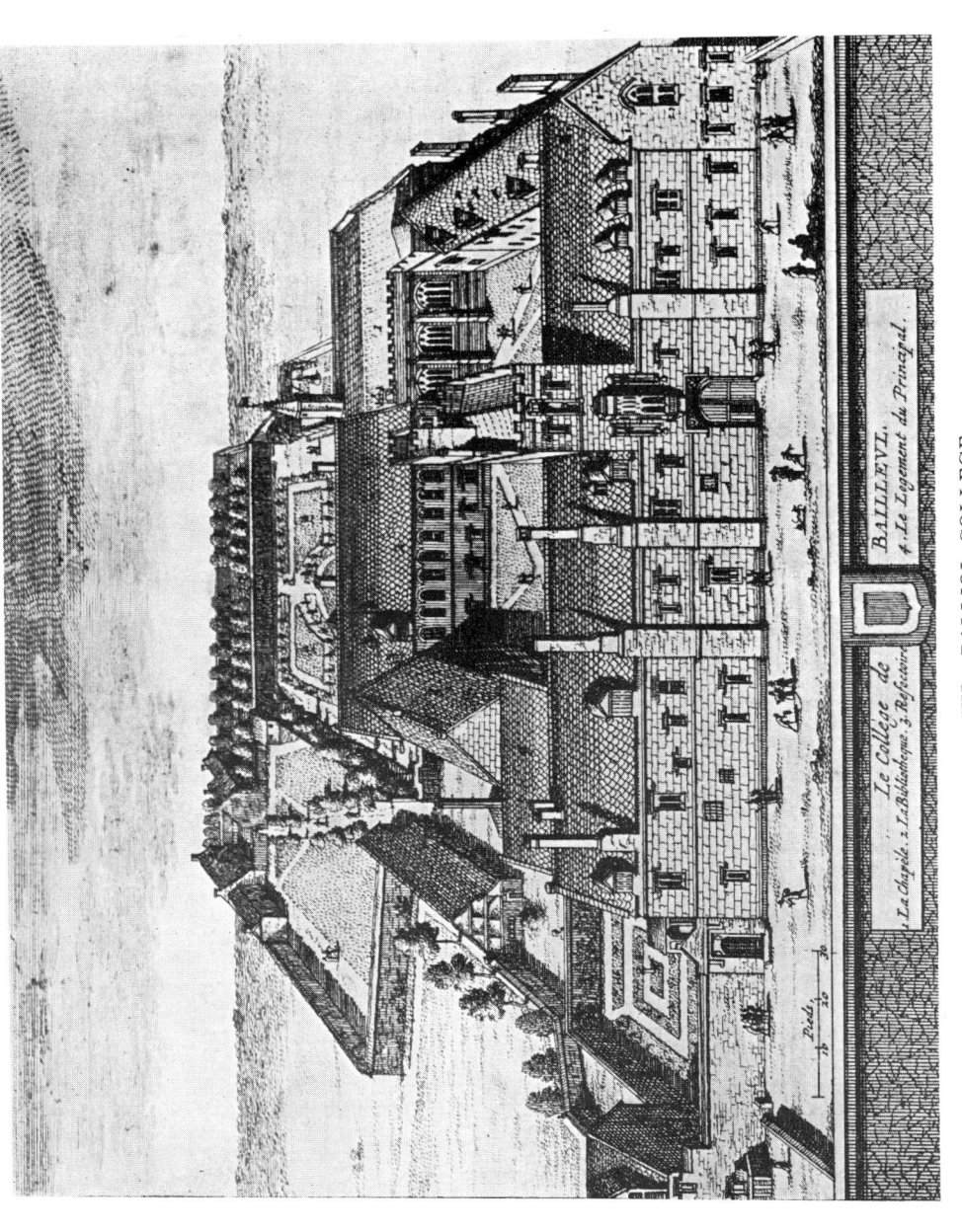

(From a print in *Les Delices de la Grand' Bretagne, & de l'Irlande.* Leyde, 1707, by James Beeverell, based on Loggan's view of 1675.)

German to Sir George Sootie of Balgon, Baron^t. And Adam Smith son to the late Adam Smith at Kircaldie were unanimously chosen to fill the two vacant Exhibitions. And a Præsentation to each of them is ordered to be got readie by the Clerk in order to be Signed and Sealed.

III. *Letter of Resignation of the Snell Exhibition.*

4th February, 1749.[1]

Edinburgh feb: 4: 1748/9   I Adam Smith one of the Exhibitioners on M^r. Snells foundation in Baliol College in Oxford do hereby resign into the hands of the Revd Dr Leigh, Master of the said college, all right & title I have to an Exhibition on the said foundation   as witness my hand

ADAM SMITH

IV. *Minute of Resignation in Records of University of Glasgow.*

28th April, 1749.[2]

The Principal produced an Intimation from the Master and Fellows of Baliol College in Oxford dated the 15th April Current giving notice that there is one Exhibitioner to be elected into Mr. Snell's foundation—in room of Adam Smith A.M. who has resigned.

§ C—APPOINTMENT OF ADAM SMITH TO PROFESSORSHIPS AT UNIVERSITY OF GLASGOW.

I. *Professor of Logic.*

9th January, 1751.[3]

Sederunt Sir John Maxwell Rector Mr. Neil Campbell Principal, Mr. Will: Craig Dec. Fac. Mr. Will: Leechman S.T.P. Rob: Simson Math.P. Mr. Rob: Dick P.P. Mr. Geo: Rosse H.L.P. Dr. Rob: Hamilton A.B.P. Mr. Ja: Moor. L.Gr.P. Mr. Tho: Craigie P.P. Dr. Herc: Lindesay I.C.P. Dr. Will: Cullen Med.P. Mr. Will: Ruat LL.O.P.[4]

An University meeting being duly summoned and convened according to the appointment of the 19th Decr. last to Elect a person to succeed the late Mr. Low-

---

[1] Balliol College Register, see facsimile, p. 366.

[2] University MSS., vol. 37, p. 72. As to Adam Smith and the degree of Master of Arts, see Part I, chapter iv.

[3] University MSS., vol. 28, pp. 49, 50.

[4] The Chairs and the date at which each occupant was appointed will be found at p. 224. Four of them were in succession to the Regents prior to 1727. One of these was Greek, and the other three were Logic, Moral Philosophy and Natural Philosophy. These were known as Professors of Philosophy and are indicated in the Sederunt by the letters " P.P." The designation " A.B.P." recalls the fact that at this time Anatomy and Botany were conjoined. A separate Professorship of Botany was founded in 1818.

doun as Professor of Philosophy to teach the Semi Classe ; and the vote being put Who shall be elected in place of Mr. Lowdoun,[1] Mr. Adam Smith son to Mr. Adam Smith in Kircaldie was unanimously Elected. And the University meeting Did and hereby Do Nominate and Elect the said Mr. Adam Smith to be Professor of Philosophy to teach the Semi Classe in this University, and Enact that upon his Acceptance of the Universitys Invitation, and giving sufficient proofs of his fitness for the said office, and his Admission following thereupon, he shall brook and enjoy all the Emoluments and Privileges belonging to the said office.

The Clerk is appointed to write to Mr. Smith now at Edinburgh and send him an Extract of his Election, and desire him to be here as soon as his affairs can allow him, in order to his being admitted. And appoint that he make a Dissertation De Origine Idearum as a tryal of his qualification for the place,[2] which the Clerk is by this Post to notifie to him, and to desire him to acquaint the University of his resolutions by first post.

16th January, 1751.[3]

Sederunt Sir John Maxwell Rector Mr. Neil Campbell Principal, Mr. Will: Craig D.F. Mr. Will: Leechman S.T.P. Rob: Simson Math.P. Mr. Rob: Dick P.P. Mr. Geo. Rosse H.L.P. Dr. Rob: Hamilton A.B.P. Mr. Ja: Moor L.Gr.P. Mr. Tho: Craigie P.P. Dr. Herc: Lindesay I.C.P. Dr. Will: Cullen Med.P. Mr. Will: Ruat LL.O.P.

An University meeting being duly summoned and convened Mr. Smith read the Dissertation De Origine Idearum which he had been appointed to make and the same being unanimously approved of and having signed the Confession of Faith

---

[1] See above, p. 32. In the " Register of Provision for Widows and Children of Professors " (MSS., vol. 55, p. 57), it is recorded that Loudon was admitted as a Regent on 28th March, 1699. His office was changed to a Professorship in 1727. He died on 1st November, 1750. There is, however, a note on the fly-leaf of MSS. vol. 39, part II, being " An Account of the Ordinary Revenue," in which it is stated that he taught in the University for fifty-three years. It appears that he may have acted as deputy for one of the Regents for a short time prior to his own appointment.

[2] In 1690 the Commissioners of Visitation made strict rules that no one was to be admitted as a Master or Regent without a previous " trial ", which in the seventeenth century consisted of a disputation upon subjects which had been assigned to each of the candidates. The Commission of 1716-17 commented with severity on the practice which prevailed at Marischal University, Aberdeen, of accepting Regents on the nomination of the Patron, but without trial. At Glasgow the direction of the Commission of 1690 was carefully observed for some years. In that year a public disputation was held to select a Regent. Nine candidates appeared, one of whom was Loudon and another William Jameson who had been blind from birth. The contest extended over a fortnight, and, in the opinion of the moderators or arbiters, there was not one of the nine who had not proved himself worthy to be elected. A list of selected candidates was drawn up, and from it one was chosen by lot. The others received a premium of £5 sterling each. Besides Loudon, two others, James Knibloe and the William Jamieson already mentioned, obtained appointments in Universities within a few years. It was not long before the test became to a large extent a matter of form. The appointment depended in fact on the previous vote, not on the Dissertation—*Munimenta Alme Universitatis Glasguensis*, 1854, ii, pp. 350-52 ; P. J. Anderson, *Records of Aberdeen Universities Commissions*, 1716-17, p. 15.

[3] University MSS., vol. 28, pp. 50, 51.

before the Presbytery of Glasgow, in order to his admission he took the usual Oath de Fideli viz :

Ego Adamus Smith cooptatus in numerum Magistrorum Academiæ Glasguensis Promitto Sancteque Iuro, me favente Dei gratia, muneris mihi demandati partes studiose fideliterque obiturum, et in hujus Academiæ rebus ac rationibus gerendis, ac promovendis, et commodis ac Ornamentis augendis Nihil reliqui ad summam fidem et diligentiam facturum, Nec ante sexennium, nisi impetrata venia ab iis quorum interest, stationem hanc deserturum, et omnino non nisi consultis, et ante sex menses præmonitis Academiæ moderatoribus, finito etiam anni curriculo, discessurum.   ADAM SMITH.

After which he was solemnly received by all the members Mr. Smith having represented that his business required him to return immediately to Edinburgh,[1] and the meeting being well informed of its being necessary he should do so, freely allowed him to go, and he appointed, with their consent Dr. Lindesay to teach his Classe during his absence.

JOHN MAXWELL RECTOR
ROB: SIMSON CL. UNIV.

II. *Professor of Moral Philosophy.*

2nd January, 1752.[2]

A few posts ago the Professor of Divinity had a letter from Lisbon with the Melancholly Account of the death of Mr. Craigie a most worthy and usefull member of this Societie upon the 27th November last, and the meeting are to consider maturely how to supply the vacancy with a fit person.

22nd April, 1752.[3]

This being the day appointed for Electing a Professor of Moral Philosophy in place of Mr. Craigie, the Question was put who shall be Professor of Moral Philosophy, and Mr. Adam Smith Professor of Logick in this University was Elected unanimously. And the University meeting Did and hereby Do Nominate and appoint the said Mr. Adam Smith to be Professor of Moral Philosophy in this University and Enact that upon his declaring his willingness to agree to this Translation and his acceptance of the Universities Invitation, and his Admission following thereupon he shall brook and enjoy all the Emoluments and Privileges belonging to the said office under the restrictions after mentioned, and shall retain the precedency he has at present.

---

[1] The business was to carry on the course of public lectures he was delivering in Edinburgh. It was this particular course which is specifically mentioned in the lecture he gave to the club in the city in 1755 (see above, Part I, chapters VIII and IX)—Dugald Stewart, *Biographical Memoirs*, 1811, p. 101.

[2] University MSS., vol. 28, p. 73.   [3] University MSS., vol. 28, pp. 80, 81.

And the University meeting Declare that the said Translation is to take place expressly upon condition that Mr. Smith agree to content himself with the salary and Emoluments of his present Profession of Logick untill the tenth of October next, tho' he should be admitted before that time and Dr. Lindesay and Mr. Ruat having been sent to Mr. Smith (who is indisposed this day) to enquire at him if he agreed to these conditions, upon their return they reported that he agreed to them.

This day Sennight a meeting is appointed to be held half an hour after three in order to admit Mr. Smith; and the meeting will then take into consideration the filling the Profession of Logick and name a day for Electing a Professor.

29th April, 1752.[1]

Mr. Adam Smith in Præsentia agreed to the conditions required of him in last minute, and thereupon was Admitted Professor of Moral Philosophy; and was formally received as such by the members.

1st November, 1753.[2]

The meeting appoint the money received from Mr. Loudoun's and Mr. Craigie's Scholars after their death, shall be divided among the Several Masters who taught their two Classes during their Sickness, and after they died, in proportion to the time they taught, and they are desired to fix their several Quotas against the next meeting.

26th November, 1753.[3]

According to the appointment of last meeting the four Masters concerned in teaching the morality class as there-mentioned, report that they have agreed to divide the Fees equally.

§ D—ADAM SMITH AND ADMINISTRATION OF THE PROPERTY OF THE UNIVERSITY.

I. *The Back Courts of the Professors' Houses next the Garden.*

10th October, 1751.[4]

Mr. Moor Dr. Cullen and Mr. Smith and Dr. Dick are appointed to view the back Courts belonging to the two houses next the garden to see in what manner they may be most conveniently separated, being now in one.

---

[1] University MSS., vol. 28, p. 82. [2] University MSS., vol. 28, pp. 104, 105.
[3] University MSS., vol. 28, p. 107.
[4] University MSS., vol. 37, p. 141. These were Nos. 1 and 2 on the plan on p. 420.

II. *The Dangerous State of the Principal's House.*

15th May, 1754.[1]

The Professor of Divinity, Robert Simson, Mr. Moor, Dr. Cullen and Mr. Smith are appointed a Committee to inspect the Principal's house, and to consult workmen and tradesmen about the rebuilding it, and to bring in plans and estimates for that purpose.

24th June, 1754.[2]

The Committee named to bring in a Plan of the Principal's house gave in Plans and a report and are likewise appointed to get an exact Plan of the buildings contiguous to it, and are empowered to employ proper persons to make the Plans and empower the said Committee to cause the Principal's old house to be pulled down, and every member who comes to the Committee is to have a vote.

21st May, 1755.[3]

Mr. Moor, Dr. Cullen and Mr. Smith are appointed to get a proper person to inspect with them the ground of the Principal's house, and to report upon Monday next at one of the clock.

24th Nov., 1756.[4]

An University meeting being duly summoned and convened, Mr. Ruet and Mr. Smith are appointed to call Mr. Dreghorn the Architect and with him examine the ground upon which part of the Principal's house stands, that a report may be made to the meeting, whether the void space will admit of a convenient house for the Principal, and that two plans be made out, the one of a separate house on the said empty space, the other on the supposition that what yet stands of the Principal's house is to make a part of the building ; and an Estimate of the expense is to be given in with each plan.

11th February, 1757.[5]

It was resolved to make a proper addition to what remains standing of the Principal's house, and Mr. Smith and Mr. Anderson were appointed to consult

---

[1] University MSS., vol. 28, p. 114.

[2] University MSS., vol. 28, p. 116. There were alarming reports as to the state of this house. On 1st April, 1752, the roof of the old part of the building was declared to be " very infirm ". On 26th March, 1754, the case had become more urgent, the south wall being in danger of falling, the house being described as now ruinous and unsafe to dwell in (vol. 28, pp. 78, 111 and vol. 38, p. 17). What made matters difficult for the Committee was that Campbell, the Principal, had had a stroke in 1752, and the Faculty offered £20 a year to enable him to move to a house in the town (vol. 38, p. 19).

[3] University MSS., vol. 28, p. 144.   [4] University MSS., vol. 28, p. 199.

[5] University MSS., vol. 28, p. 207.

142   ADAM SMITH, AS STUDENT AND PROFESSOR

with Mr. Dreghorn and bring in a plan of such an addition to the next University meeting.

10th March, 1757.[1]

The plan for rebuilding the Principal's house in terms of a former minute was laid before the meeting, and tuesday next is appointed for considering the said plan at 3 o'clock afternoon ; and likewise for inquiring into the State of Dundonald's mortification.

15th March, 1757.[2]

The meeting desires to hear Mr. Dreghorn the Architect upon the plan of the Principal's house and appoint an University meeting on Thursday at 3 o'clock afternoon for that purpose. Mr. Smith is appointed to desire Mr. Dreghorn to be present.

17th March, 1757.[3]

An University meeting being duly summoned and convened, the meeting, after an opportunity had been given to every member to put what questions he pleased to Mr. Dreghorn, determined to make an addition of one single room in each story to what is just now standing of the Principal's house according to the last plan given in by Mr. Dreghorn. Mr. Smith is appointed to desire Mr. Dreghorn to give an Estimate of the Expence of the plan, that it may be put into execution as soon as possible.

19th March, 1757.[4]

An University meeting being duly summoned and convened, upon reading the last Minute Mr. Moor protested against the resolution of building the Principal's house according to the plan there mentioned for reasons to be given in next meeting, and thereupon took Instruments [5] in the Clerk's hand, to which Protest Dr. Lindesay and Mr. Muirhead adhered, and took Instruments.

Robert Simson dissents from the resolution of building the Principal's house as soon as possible.

25th March, 1757.[6]

An University meeting being duly summoned and convened ; At the desire of the members who protested about the building of the Principal's house at the

---

[1] University MSS., vol. 28, p. 211. [2] University MSS., vol. 28, p. 212.
[3] University MSS., vol. 28, p. 213. [4] University MSS., vol. 28, p. 213.

[5] " Taking instruments " is a Scottish legal practice which may involve the drawing up of a dissent or protest by a Notary Public. It is equivalent to the lawyer's letter of to-day—D. Murray, *Legal Practice in Ayr and the West of Scotland in 15th and 16th Centuries*, 1910, p. 56. Dr. David Murray was a member of the University Court for the very long period from 1903 to 1927 ; and on occasion he preserved the old practice by " taking instruments " in due form.

[6] University MSS., vol. 28, p. 216.

DOCUMENTS—UNIVERSITY PROPERTY

last meeting, that affair is allowed to be reconsidered on tuesday next at three o'clock.

29th March, 1757.[1]

An University meeting being duly summoned and convened, the affair of the Principal's house is delayed till next meeting.

8th April, 1757.[2]

The meeting having again taken the building of the Principal's house into consideration the Question was put Whether to build a separate house, or to build an addition to the part of his house yet standing, and it carried by majority of votes to build an addition. Mr. James Moor, Dr. Lindesay and Mr. George Muirhead dissented from this resolution, and desired their dissent to be recorded.

The Question was put Whether an addition of one room should be made to each story of the Principal's house, or if the whole space to the street should be built up; and it carried so by majority to make the addition of one room. Mr. James Moor and Dr. Lindesay dissented and required their dissent to be recorded. Mr. Anderson is appointed to get an estimate of the Expence of this addition as soon as possible.

14th April, 1757.[3]

Mr. Anderson is appointed to get from Mr. Allan Dreghorn a copy of the particulars upon which his general Estimate of the expences in building the Principal's house at £398 is founded.

26th April, 1757.[4]

Mr. Smith and Mr. Anderson are appointed to settle with Mr. Dreghorn agreeably to the Estimate given in by him, everything that relates to the building of the Principal's house.

6th May, 1757.[5]

The Estimate for making the addition to the Principal's house offered by Mr. Dreghorn was approved, and it was agreed that mutual obligatory letters shall be given by the University and him agreeable to a Scroll given in, for immediately beginning the building. And Robert Simson is hereby authorised to grant Precepts upon the factor Mr. Morthland for the money which may be necessary, according as the building advances.

10th May, 1757.[6]

The obligatory missives both with regard to the addition to be made to the Principal's house, and the Building the observatory were read, and were by

[1] University MSS., vol. 28, p. 217.
[2] University MSS., vol. 28, p. 219.
[3] University MSS., vol. 28, p. 221.
[4] University MSS., vol. 28, p. 222.
[5] University MSS., vol. 28, p. 225.
[6] University MSS., vol. 28, p. 225.

appointment signed by the Vice-Rector and Clerk in name of the University on the one part, and by Mr. Dreghorn on the other in Præsentia, as were also particular Estimates according to which these two buildings are to be executed.

III. *Report on Dr. Lindesay's House.*

27th June, 1757.[1]

Dr. Leechman Mr. Smith and Dr. Black are appointed a Committee to visit Dr. Lindesay's house, and see what things are insufficient or wanting, and to report to the next meeting.

IV. *Report on Four Houses (Nos. 3-6) in the Professors' Court.*

26th June, 1758.[2]

Mr. Smith is appointed along with any Masters in town to consult tradesmen about a proper way of removing the dampers in the four houses on the side of the new Court, and to get an Estimate of the Expence.

V. *Repairs to the Principal's House and to three in the Professors' Court.*

12th August, 1762.[3]

Mr. Smith, Mr. Moor, Mr. Hamilton and Mr. Wilson are appointed a Committee to order any Reparations yet necessary in the Principals and Mr. Andersons and Mr. Millars and Mr. Hamiltons houses.

VI. *Repairs to the House occupied by William Ruat.*

23rd April, 1762.[4]

Mr. Smith & Mr. Clow are appointed a Committee to inspect the House at present possessed by Mr. Ruet & to report what reparations appear to them to be necessary.

---

[1] University MSS., vol. 28, p. 237. This was the new house on the High St. which had been chosen by Lindesay in succession to Dr. Hamilton in 1752 (vol. 28, 6th May, 1752).

[2] University MSS., vol. 28, p. 266.

[3] University MSS., vol. 30, p. 163. Anderson's house was No. 3 (see p. 420). Millar was in the back Divinity house formerly occupied by Adam Smith. " Mr. Hamilton " was Thomas Hamilton, who was appointed Professor of Medicine in 1757. He succeeded Joseph Black both in the Chair and the house.

[4] University MSS., vol. 30, p. 140. The name " Ruat " is spelled in various ways in this and subsequent entries. The form adopted above is that of his own signature to the Professor's oath.

PLATE VIII (*a*). GLASGOW COLLEGE, OUTER COURT
The Lion and Unicorn Stair and the Cloisters.

PLATE VIII (*b*). GLASGOW COLLEGE
The Professors' Court as it was about 1839. In the time of Adam Smith the nearest house on the spectator's left had not been built, and there was a pump in the middle of the grass rectangle. (From J. B. Hay, *Inaugural Addresses of Lord Rectors*, 1839.)

DOCUMENTS—UNIVERSITY PROPERTY

VII. *Transfer of the Principal's house from the Widow of the late Principal to William Leechman, his Successor.*

11*th May*, 1762.[1]

The Principal, Mr. Smith & Mr. Clow are appointed a Committee to consider of a proper answer to Mrs. Campbells last demand and to report to the next meeting.

VIII. *Repairs to the Anatomy Room.*

9*th June*, 1757.[2]

Mr. Smith Mr. Anderson and Dr. Black are appointed to visit the Anatomical chamber and Examine what reparations are necessary and to report.

27*th June*, 1757.[3]

The reparation of the Anatomy Class is ordered according to the Estimate given in by Mr. Hamilton.

IX. *Encroachments on College Lands and Nuisances.*

21*st May*, 1755.[4]

Mr. Smith and Mr. Clow are appointed to inspect the Incroachments upon the College lands bordering upon the Molendinar burn, as also the dunghill in the Weavers Vennel laid close to the College houses or the garden walls etc., and to take the proper measures to remove and prevent any damage to the College, and to get a visit of the Magistrates, and also of the Dean of Guild, if needfull.

X. *Alteration of Bridges on the Molendinar to lessen Flooding.*

26*th June*, 1755.[5]

Mr. Moor and Mr. Smith are appointed a Committee to direct the enlarging of the two arches in the College wall over the burn at the foot of the weavers vennel to prevent the inundation of it on the houses there and the College gardens.

---

[1] University MSS., vol. 30, p. 147. Mrs. Campbell had been asking for delay and was making difficulties in vacating the Principal's house.

[2] University MSS., vol. 28, p. 227.   [3] University MSS., vol. 28, p. 236.

[4] University MSS., vol. 28, p. 143. The Molendinar flowed through the College Garden in the hollow mid-way between the Observatory and the Blackfriars Lands. The general direction appears in the view reproduced, Plate III. In Scotland a "vennel" is a narrow passage—not, as in the North of England, a sewer. It is the equivalent of a wynd. Rae in adopting the English meaning has the distinguished support of the former Kaiser in the caustic comment of the latter on the function of Lord Esher.

[5] University MSS., vol. 28, p. 150.

K   S.A.S.

26th June, 1755.[1]

Mr. Moor and Dr. Cullen and Mr. Smith or any two of them are appointed to cause the bridge of deals over the burn a little above the foot of the weavers' vennel to be taken away.

XI. *Stopping a Road over the College Lands.*

26th April, 1758.[2]

An University meeting being duly summoned and convened, Dr. Lindesay and Mr. Smith are appointed to wait upon Mr. Thomas Miller to consult him about stopping the road from the Dyeing house upon the Dovehill cross the burn upon the College ground without the south east corner of the great garden.

XII. *Apparatus and Accommodation for the Natural Philosophy Class.*

11th April, 1755.[3]

Whereas by a minute of the Faculty meeting dated the third of June 1754 Dr. Dick was allowed to expend one Hundred pounds Sterling upon Instruments, part of which was due from an allowance in the Tack of the Archbishopricke now expired, and what was over was expressly laid on the new Tack of the Archbishopricke which is expected and the Dr. having laid out on his own risque the Sum of Seventy three pounds one Shilling Ninepence Sterling beyond the said Hundred pounds for Instruments according to an account laid before the Society, which the University meeting considering think the Instruments to be very proper and necessary and therefor from a desire to encourage this branch of Natural knowledge, Do agree to advance also this additional Sum upon the faith of the said new Tack. But it is hereby expressly declared that this shall be no precedent for any member of the University being allowed to lay out money at his own hand without the order of the University.

Which minute the meeting agreed to, and at the same time appointed Dr. Dick to draw up an Inventory of all the Instruments for Experimental Philosophy in his custody, with an account of the condition they are in.

A precept was ordered to be drawn to pay what remains due of the money for the Instruments purchased by Dr. Dick amounting to £73.1.9d. sterling.

22nd October, 1757.[4]

Mr. Moor and Dr. Black are appointed to inspect the Instruments belonging to Experimental Philosophy and to deliver them over to Mr. Anderson who is

---

[1] University MSS., vol. 28, p. 151.   [2] University MSS., vol. 28, p. 259.
[3] University MSS., vol. 28, p. 139.
[4] University MSS., vol. 28, p. 243. As to John Anderson's appointment to the Professorship of Natural Philosophy, see pp. 188-90.

appointed to sign a list of all he receives, which signed list is to be given in to the first University meeting.

Mr. Smith and Mr. Clow are appointed a Committee to look out for a proper room for holding these Instruments, as the room where they are at present is too small.

10th May, 1758.[1]

An University meeting being duly summoned and convened, the Committee appointed in October last to examine the Experiment room and Magistrand Classe reported that it will be necessary to put shelves and presses in the Experiment room, to make new benches, and forms in the Classe, and to carry a partition from the back of the door to the opposite wall, in order to make a closet with shelves and other necessary things. And the University meeting hereby order it to be done.

20th October, 1758.[2]

William Anderson's account of wood and work in repairing the Natural Philosophy Class and Instrument room was read and Robert Simson Mr. Smith and Dr. Black are appointed to examine it and report.

XIII. *Repairs of the Mathematical Class Room and a New Chemical Laboratory.*

26th June, 1762.[3]

Whereas the Gentlemen of the Committee appointed on the 13th of May last to consider of the Reparations necessary for the mathematical class are to be seldom in town this vacation the meeting appoint Mr. Smith & Mr. Moor to meet with Mr. Williamson & confer with him on the Reparations he proposes and to bring in an estimate of the same to the meeting which is to be held on the 12th of August next.

20th April, 1763.[4]

The Meeting having taken into their consideration the former Minutes of the University of the 11th & 13th May 26th June & 12th August last by the first of which a Room which has been for some years in the Possession of Mr. Foulis was assigned to Mr. Williamson for a Mathematical Class, and having likewise considered a Memorial presented to them by Mr. Foulis containing reasons for his being continued in the Possession of that Room. They are unanimously of opinion

---

[1] University MSS., vol. 28, p. 261. The Class is called "the Magistrand" because usually the last before graduation as M.A.

[2] University MSS., vol. 28, p. 268.   [3] University MSS., vol. 30, p. 157.

[4] University MSS., vol. 30, p. 230.

that Mr. Foulis holds the Possession of the said Room at the Pleasure of the University only but in regard of his great services to the University & the situation of his Academy for painting and in regard that Mr. Williamson has voluntarily declared his willingness to pass from the said Minutes upon his being provided in another convenient room for his Class ; They agree that Mr. Foulis shall continue in the meantime in the Possession of the afores^d. Room & that Mr. Williamson shall be provided in the most convenient Room that can be found for his Class & they appoint Dr. Smith, Mr. Anderson & Dr. Williamson a Committee to look thro' the different Rooms in the College for that Purpose & to report.

10th May, 1763.[1]

The Committee of last meeting upon the Mathematical Class gave in their Report & several Proposals were made thereupon. The Meeting appoint Dr. Smith, Dr. Leechman Dr. Trail Dr. Black & Dr. Williamson a Committee to consider of these Proposals & bring in their report to an University Meeting hereby appointed to be held upon Saturday next at 11 o'clock forenoon.

14th May, 1763.[2]

The Meeting heard the Report of the Committee of last meeting upon the Proposals relating to the Mathematical Class, and after deliberation it was the opinion of the meeting that the best thing the University could do at present provided their Funds will admit of it, is to build a new & Compleat Laboratory and convert the present Laboratory into a Mathematical Class.

1st March, 1764.[3]

The Minutes of the different meetings concerning the building of a new Laboratory and fitting up the present one for a Mathematical Class were read over in the presence of the Rector and were adhered to by the Meeting who hereby resolve to set about the same with all convenient speed ; provided always that the expence of the Laboratory shall not exceed the three hundred and fifty Pounds sterling and that the present one shall be fitted up for a Mathematical Class with all proper frugality, which was recommended in general to the Meeting by the Lord Rector.

XIV. *Curator of the College Rooms.*

26th June, 1760.[4]

Mr. Smith and Mr. Clow are Elected Curators of the College Rooms for the ensuing year.

[1] University MSS., vol. 30, p. 233.
[2] University MSS., vol. 30, p. 234.
[3] University MSS., vol. 31, p. 13.
[4] University MSS., vol. 33, p. 100.

11th November, 1762.[1]

The Curators for the College Chambers gave in an information of the state of the said Chambers. The Principal, Mr. Moor and Dr. Smith are appointed a Committee to speak with Mr. Foulis and Mr. Watt and see if they can part with any of the Rooms which they possess at present.

16th November, 1762.[2]

The Committee appointed last meeting to speak with Mr. Foulis and Mr. Watt were not ready to report.

21st December, 1762.[3]

The Committee of the 11th November last to speak to Mr. Foulis and Mr. Watt were not yet ready to report.

3rd February, 1763.[4]

The Principal, Dr. Smith and Mr. Moor are appointed a Committee to search the College Records for the grounds upon which Mr. Foulis possesses the several rooms he has in the College and to report.

XV. *The Fencing Academy.*

22nd December, 1761.[5]

A meeting being duly summoned and convened by the Principal, a scheme for an Academy of dancing, fencing and riding to be established at Glasgow under the direction of the University was taken into consideration, and Mr. Smith is appointed in name of the Masters to acquaint Lord Errol the Rector of their design, and to desire his assistance, and Mr. Anderson and others as they may have opportunity are appointed to acquaint such of the neibouring gentlemen as are thought will be favourable to the plan.

14th June, 1766.[6]

The Meeting appoints the low room, next to Robert Cross's House, to be set apart for a fencing Room for College people only. The Floor of it to be laid with pavement of free stone and a new window to be put into it, towards the principal's Garden.

---

[1] University MSS., vol. 38, p. 48. In 1741 R. Foulis had a room in the College to show his stock of books. The Committee in the text did not succeed in arresting his desire for expansion, since, in 1770, he had six additional rooms besides garrets. The circumstances in which the University from 1757 enabled Watt to carry on his inventions are well known—J. MacLehose, *The Glasgow University Press*, pp. 157, 164.

[2] University MSS., vol. 38, p. 49.   [3] University MSS., vol. 38, p. 51.
[4] University MSS., vol. 30, p. 220.   [5] University MSS., vol. 38, p. 36.
[6] University MSS., vol. 31, p. 152.

21st April, 1767.[1]

The Committee appointed by the same Meeting to examine the Proposal and Estimate for building a Fencing School report, that it is proposed to build it, with old stones belonging to the College, on the Vacant Ground between the Door to the Church Yard, and the Door to the Principal's Garden, that the whole Expence of every thing relating to it shall not exceed Twenty Pounds, and that if the Meeting shall agree to execute the proposal, the Dean of Guild's Consent to rest the Roof of the Fencing School upon the Wall of the Church Yard must be obtained.

§ E—QUESTIONS OF FINANCE AND LAW ARISING OUT OF THE ADMINISTRATION OF THE UNIVERSITY PROPERTY.

I. *Proceedings at a typical Faculty Meeting.*

24th May, 1753.[2]

Sederunt : Mr. James Moor Præses L.G.P. Mr. George Rosse H.L.P. Dr. Herc. Lindesay I.C.P. Dr. Will. Cullen Med.P. Mr. Will. Ruat H.E.P. Mr. Ad. Smith P.P. Dr. Rob. Dick P.P. Mr. Ja. Clow P.P.

Mr. Rosse was chosen Clerk pro tempore.

Mr. Morthland is appointed to write to Mistress Craigie that the College is to pay up the Four Hundred pounds sterling owing to her children either at Lammass or Martinmass next and to ask at which of these terms she would choose to have it.[3]

The Faculty having conversed with Mr. Morthland on the state of the College Revenue the Question was put whether at the end of two years the College may safely venture to incurr an expence of Five Hundred pounds sterl. and it was carried in the affirmative.

Mr. Moor desired to have it marked that he protested against minuting the above decision for reasons to be given in next meeting, and thereupon took instruments in the Clerks hands.

Next the Question was put whether the said Five hundred pounds should be applyed to the building another house, and it was carried in the affirmative.

Mr. Moor desired it might be marked that he protested also against this decision for reasons to be given in next meeting.

[1] University MSS., vol. 31, p. 212.

[2] University MSS., vol. 37, pp. 182-3. This was what is known as a Faculty meeting, composed of the Principal and Professors, at which the Principal presided. Neil Campbell, the Principal, had a stroke and the last of these meetings he attended was on 24th July of the previous year. James Moor, as the senior " gown " Professor, became Præses under the award of the Visitation of 1727. As will be seen there arose later a very complicated dispute as to the powers of this meeting and another known as the Rector's Meeting—see above, Part I, chapter VII, also below, pp. 200-5.

[3] Craigie had built a house on a vacant site in the Professors' Court. He died soon afterwards and the University paid £400 for the house.

PLATE IX. THE FORE HALL OF THE OLD COLLEGE
(From an old photograph.)

Mr. Rosse and Dr. Lindesay desired to have it marked that they did not vote in either of the above questions.

The members who voted in the above Questions desired to have it marked that they considered the above minute as an opinion to be submitted to the first University meeting.

30th May, 1753.[1]

Reasons of Mr. Moors First Protest.

1. Because he thinks that an opinion or conjecture of what the College funds may amount to at a future period of time is, in itself, a thing needless to be recorded.

2. Because he thinks it at present particularly improper to make a publick record how ample the funds of the College will be at the very period at which their present Tack of the Archbishopricke expires, when at the same time they are to solicite a renewal of that Tack ; and such solicitation must be founded upon the circumstances which the College funds will then be in.

3. Because he thinks this minute is, in fact, inconsistent with the tenour of the Memorial already presented on the part of the College to the Duke of Argyll in order to their obtaining the said renewal, and therefor may furnish a handle for being refused that renewal.

4. Because he thinks the opinion contained in the minut is ill founded, both as it contradicts the said Memorial, and as it is only an opinion of some Junior members, to which all their Seniors present, not only refused their assent, but took care to have their refusal recorded.

II. *Fixing the Payment by College " vassals."*

14th May, 1755.[2]

Dr. Hamilton, Robert Simson, Mr. Smith and Mr. Clow or any two of them are appointed to send for Robert Barclay the College Writer, and settle what ought to be payed by George Nisbit and Robert Mathie at their entring the College vassals for the land they have bought near Limmerfield in the Toothie, and that both for their own Entry and for William Caldwell's their Authors, all being singular successors to Alexander McEwen the souldier who was the last that entred with the College.

[1] University MSS., vol. 37, p. 183.

[2] University MSS., vol. 28, p. 141. Scottish land tenure retained its feudal origin to a more marked degree in the eighteenth century than at present. A feu was a grant by a superior to a vassal—thus Balfour in his *Practicks* (c. 1578) heads this section with the title " Of Superiouris and Vassillis". The tenure admitted of what were known as casualties on the occurrence of various events, that is an exceptional payment in addition to the annual payment reserved in the grant. It was probably some form of casualty which this committee was to determine as to the amount—cf. *Encyclopædia of the Laws of Scotland*, XIV, pp. 271-4.

III. *A Question of Law concerning a Feu in Virginia St., Glasgow.*

26th February, 1756.[1]

An University meeting being duly summoned and convened, Dr. Lindesay, Mr. Smith and Mr. Clow are appointed a Committee to draw up a Memorial to be laid before Mr. Ferguson of Pitfour, Advocate concerning the affair of the feu of the two acres in Longcroft now partly in Virginia Street and partly in Mr. McDual's garden mentioned in the minuts of 2nd December last, in order to get his opinion whether the College can, *bona fide*, quit the said feu, and without being in hazard to be brought to an account by their superiors, or whether they cannot.

IV. *A Question relative to the Charge for certain Salaries in the Accounts.*

15th April, 1755.[2]

An University meeting being duly summoned and convened, Mr. Morthland's Accounts of the ordinary revenue for Crop 1752 which had been examined by the Committee, were now signed by the Masters and factor in presence of the Magistrates, viz., Provost George Murdoch and Baillies George Carmichael, William Craufurd and James Glen and the Vouchers which had also been examined were put into their proper places in the Charter chest.

Mr. Clow protested and took instruments in the Clerk's hands against allowing 50 merks to both Mr. Robert Dick and Mr. Moor as Eldest Regent, and signed the Accounts with this exception, which is also to be understood in all future Accounts he signs.

V. *Accounts of the Sub-Deanery as between the present and the late factor.*

11th June, 1755.[3]

Mr. Moor, Dr. Cullen, Mr. Smith and Mr. Clow are appointed to examine Mr. Morthland's Account of the Grassums of the Subdeanry, and the Account of

---

[1] University MSS., vol. 28, p. 167. This entry relates to the building of large country houses by successful merchants. Before 1745 what is now Virginia St. was a garden used for growing vegetables. In 1753 the ground was feued by Andrew Buchanan, the Provost, who built a handsome mansion, standing in its own grounds. Part of the ground was sub-feued to Archibald Buchanan of Silverbanks who built a house on it, which eleven years later was sold to the Thistle Bank as its chief office—*History of Glasgow*, 1872, pp. 1027-8. James Ferguson was raised to the Bench as Lord Ferguson of Pitfour in 1764.

[2] University MSS., vol. 28, p. 139. From the account above (Part I, chapter VI) it will be seen that the College Revenues were charged with fixed salaries to the Professors. The basis of Clow's protest was that the Professors who succeeded the former regents received equal salaries except for the addition of the sum mentioned to the two who were senior as to date of appointment. It shows the low scale of payments at the period that the amount of 50 merks Scots amounted to approximately £2 16s. sterling.

[3] University MSS., vol. 28, p. 146. The grant of the revenues of the sub-deanery originated from the time of Cromwell. In 1670 Charles II. confirmed it by a Charter under the great seal.

DOCUMENTS—UNIVERSITY FINANCE 153

his Intromissions with Mr. Wood's rests, and of his own rests, and his Accounts of mortifications.

VI. *The Mortification of the Duchess of Hamilton.*

2nd December, 1755.[1]

Dr. Hamilton, the Professor of Divinity, Dr. Lindesay, Mr. Smith and Mr. Clow or any two of them are appointed a Committee to examine the Accounts of the Dutchess of Hamilton's mortification, since the last that were passed by the Duke or his doers, and draw up a state of the same to be presented to His Grace and his doers. And Dr. Hamilton, Dr. Lindesay and Mr. Smith are appointed to wait on his Grace after the Accounts are settled, and let him know they are ready to be laid before his Commissioners and doers.

23rd December, 1755.[2]

There being about £500 Sterling of College money to come into the Factor's hands at Whitsunday next, the meeting appoint that sum to be applied towards refunding the money belonging to the Countess of Forfar's mortification borrowed by the College.

23rd December, 1755.[3]

Mr. Smith, Dr. Dick and Mr. Clow are appointed to bring in a state of the Countess of Forfar's mortification and a plan to put it upon a better footing, that an application may be made to the Parliament, at the same time with the other for the Dutchess of Hamilton's, to get these Regulations allowed.

23rd December, 1755.[4]

The meeting being advised by their Lawyers, that neither the purchase of Thornly Park by the money belonging to the Dutchess of Hamilton's mortification recorded in the minuts of 26th Nov. 1753 ; nor the Regulations for meliorating the

---

Grassums were a payment by a tenant to his landlord at the grant or the renewal of a lease—*Encyclopædia of the Laws of Scotland*, 1929, vii, p. 501. Wood had been the University factor or agent, who was succeeded by Morthland.

[1] University MSS., vol. 28 p. 155. In 1694 Anne, Duchess of Hamilton and Châtelherault, mortified a sum of 18,000 merks Scots (or £1000 sterling) for the foundation of three Bursaries for Students of Theology—*Deeds instituting Bursaries, Scholarships in the College and University of Glasgow*, 1850, pp. 102-17.

[2] University MSS., vol. 28, p. 158.

[3] University MSS., vol. 28, p. 158. The Countess of Forfar was Robina, daughter of Sir William Lockhart of Lee and grandniece of Oliver Cromwell. She mortified in 1737 £500 sterling to educate five boys from five parishes at the grammar school in Glasgow and afterwards at the University—*Deeds instituting Bursaries, Scholarships in the College and University of Glasgow*, 1850, pp. 167-76.

[4] University MSS., vol. 28, p. 157.

said mortification brought in by the Committee mentioned in the minuts of the 5th February last, can be effectually made and appointed without the Authority of an Act of Parliament : Therefore the University meeting appoint the Committee who by the minut of the 2nd of Dec. last are to wait upon His Grace the Duke of Hamilton, to assure him that the University will readily concurr with his Grace in applying for and obtaining an Act of Parliament to empower them to purchase these or any other lands with the money belonging to the said mortification, and to obtain the Authority of Parliament for such Regulations for the meliorating of the same, as shall be agreed upon by his Grace and the University.

30th December, 1755.[1]

Mr. Smith being to go to Edinburgh to-morrow the meeting appoint him to carry in the Vouchers of the Accounts of the Dutchess of Hamilton's mortification, from the year 1713 when the Accounts were last signed by the Dutchess, and empower him to meet with Mr. Archibald Stewart the Duke of Hamilton's Doer, in order to get the said accounts passed, and also to go along with him to Mr. James Ferguson, Advocate, to concert with him the form of a Bill to be brought into Parliament for the purposes mentioned in the minuts of the 23rd Dec. current.

5th January, 1756.[2]

An University meeting being duly summoned and convened, Mr. Smith reported that he had shewn the Books of the Accounts of the Dutchess of Hamilton's mortification, and the vouchers of the same to Mr. Andrew Steuart, who declared his satisfaction with the Accuracy both of the Accounts and vouchers ; and that Mr. Steuart and he had advised with Mr. Ferguson about the Bill to be brought into Parliament mentioned in last minuts, and that Mr. Ferguson was to prepare the form of such a Bill.

2nd March, 1757.[3]

The meeting appoint the Clerk to write to Mr. Ruat that the majority desire that at the 2^d reading of the Bill, or if it be already read a second time, he shall at the 3^d reading of it propose to have it altered so as it may be agreeable to the terms proposed by the Presbytery of Hamilton in their minut already sent up to him.

Mr. Smith is appointed to write an answer to the letter of the Presbytery of Hamilton addressed to Dr. Leechman.

[1] University MSS., vol. 28, p. 160.   [2] University MSS., vol. 28, p. 160.

[3] University MSS., vol. 28, p. 209. The Bill, mentioned in the previous minutes, was now before Parliament, and Ruat, who was then in London, was requested to attend at the House of Commons for the purpose mentioned. The Bill became law in 1758. The Act is printed in *Deeds instituting Bursaries, Scholarships, &c., in the College and University of Glasgow*, 1850, pp. 109-25, 109-18.

23rd February, 1758.[1]

Robert Simson, Mr. Smith and Mr. Clow are appointed a Committee to Examine the Accounts of the Dutchess of Hamilton's mortification and to report to the University meeting to be held on Thursday the 23rd instant.

VII. *A Feu Duty of* 12^d. *Scots.*

14th December, 1756.[2]

It was reported to the meeting by Messrs. Moor, Lindesay and Smith and Robert Barclay the College writer that in consequence of an order of Faculty dated 18th Dec. 1755 they had consulted Mr. Thomas Miller Advocate upon the Memorial presented by Provost Buchanan and William McDoual of Castle Sempil Esq. concerning the sale of the feu duty of twelve penny Scots yearly payable to the College out of their two acres in Long Croft long ago feud by the College to David Scot and having laid the necessary papers before Mr. Miller he advised the sale at such a number of years purchase as could be agreed on, and that the College were in perfect safety to grant a Disposition thereof; and conform thereto a Disposition being made out by the said Robert Barclay was presented to the meeting and approved and signed and committed to the said Robert Barclay to receive the price being 100 years purchase of the feu Duty and at the same time to receive from Messrs. McDoual and Buchanan a Discharge of the real Warrandice upon the teinds of Daldouie granted in Security of the said Feu. Mr. Clow dissented from this Deed of the Societie and desired his Dissent to be marked in the minuts.

VIII. *Clearing the Accounts of the Revenue of the University.*
(a) *The Archbishopric before the Barons of Exchequer.*

25th June, 1760.[3]

Nine years Accounts of the Tack of the Archbishopricke beginning with Crop 1749, and ending with crop 1757, having been made out and laid before the meeting by Robert Simson, they appoint him and Mr. Clow and Mr. Smith to take out the vouchers of the said accounts for the first six years of them, and also the vouchers for the Instruments purchased for Experimental Philosophy and Astronomy and any others that may be necessary, and appoint Mr. Smith to wait upon the Barons of Exchequer at their Midsummer term to get these Accounts passed,

---

[1] University MSS., vol. 28, p. 253.

[2] University MSS., vol. 28, p. 202. By Act of Parliament of 1672 the University was authorized to sell small feu duties—J. Coutts, *Hist. Univ. of Glasgow,* 1909, p. 151; *cf.* above, p. 152.

[3] University MSS., vol. 30, p. 17. As to the tack or lease of the Archbishopric see above (Part I, chapter VI). These are the accounts which have been referred to, pp. 72-5. A summary of them is preserved at the General Register House, Edinburgh, in Exchequer Declared Accounts, Pipe, 1730-1760.

and it is recommended to him to get an allowance of three Bolls two firlots for the lands of Possil and Knapperly from the payment of which Mr. William Craufurd the proprietor was exempted by a Decreet of the Court of Session; and also endeavour to get an allowance for the Instruments that have been purchased, out of the Balance of the Accounts.

25th July, 1760.[1]

Mr. Smith being obliged to leave Edinburgh on Account of his health, Mr. Moor is appointed in his place to wait on the Barons of Exchequer to clear the Accounts of the Archbishopricke.

(b) *The Ordinary Revenue before the Treasury.*

16th June, 1761.[2]

As Mr. Smith proposes to go to London this vacation, the meeting authorize him to get the Accounts of the ordinary revenue and subdeanry for Crops 1755, 1756, 1757 and 1758 cleared with the Treasury, and appoint Robert Simson to make up these Accounts as soon as possible. And Mr. Smith is further appointed to meet with Mr. Joshua Sharpe and to settle with him the Accounts of his Intromissions with the rents of the lands mortified to the College by Dr. Williams; as also to enquire into the state of the Division of Mr. Snell's mortified Estate with respect to Coleburn farm and the affair of the Prebends of Lincoln etc. with any other particulars necessary for the University to know, particularly the £500 of costs of suit agreed to be payed by the Lesee to the University.

27th August, 1761.[3]

Doctor Robert Simson brought in the Accounts of the University Revenue for the years 1755-56-57-58 which were read and delivered in presentia to Mr. Adam Smith in order to his presenting them to the Treasury of Great Britain and obtaining a certificate of the sum superexpended as usual.

The Accounts were as follows

Account of the ordinary Revenue of the University of Glasgow for the Crops of years 1755, 1756, 1757, 1758 encluding the hundred pounds sterling granted to

---

[1] University MSS., vol. 30, p. 22; as to Adam Smith's illness at Edinburgh see below, p. 253.

[2] University MSS., vol. 30, p. 57. The profit from the tack of the Archbishopric was treated as extraordinary Revenue and, as such, liable in the first place for the deficit on the Ordinary Revenue. The accounts of the latter, which have been preserved, are contained in MSS., vol. 39, Part II, which ends in 1745. It is probable that the next volume, having been required as a production in one of the Court of Session cases (see pp. 222-8), was not returned to the muniment room. As to the Snell Exhibition see Part I, chapter iv, and below, pp. 161-3. Mr. Joshua Sharpe was acting for the University at this time in the long Chancery Suit with Balliol College.

[3] University MSS., vol. 30, pp. 71-2.

supply the deficiency of the Revenue, together with the Annual Expences of the said University for these years with which the said Revenue is burthened. Humbly presented to the Right Honorable the Lords of His Majesties Treasury according to the Directions given by Her Majestie Queen Anne under the Great Seal dated at Windsor the 16 Day of December 1713 Whereby Her Majestie appropriates one hundred pounds for supplying the Deficiency of the said Revenue.

By the Account sent up to the Right Honorable the Lords of His Majesties Treasurie Anno 1756 this University was found to have expended more than their Revenue in the year 1713 and the following years to the end of 1754 the sum of £509. 10. $5\frac{5}{6}$ £509. 10. $5\frac{5}{6}$

	The Universities Revenue	Expences
Anno 1755 -	£1996. 10. $5\frac{5}{6}$	£2252. 6. $0\frac{5}{6}$
1756 -	2973. 8. $1\frac{5}{6}$	2947. 10. $6\frac{5}{12}$
1757 -	842. 7. $9\frac{5}{6}$	2545. 19. $11\frac{5}{6}$
1758 -	1692. 5. 8	1880. 11. $6\frac{1}{2}$
	7504. 12. $1\frac{1}{2}$	9626. 8. $1\frac{7}{12}$
		7504. 12. $1\frac{1}{2}$

Superexpended in the above four years - 2121. 16. $0\frac{1}{12}$ 2121. 16. $0\frac{1}{12}$

Superexpended from 1713 to 1758 both inclusive - - 2631. 6. $5\frac{11}{12}$

15th October, 1761.[1]

An University meeting being duely summoned and convened Mr. Smith reported that he had laid the accounts of the University for the years 1755, 1756, 1757, & 1758 before the Treasury and produced the certificate of the Treasury signed by Mr. West Secretary finding that the University had expended above their Revenue for these & the preceding years the sum of £2631. 6. $5\frac{11}{12}$ the Certificate is dated the 15th of September 1761.

Dr. Simson is ordered to give a precept to Mr. Smith for four guineas expended by him in fees in procuring the above certificate.

28th January, 1762.[2]

Mr. Smith is appointed to write to Lord Erroll to apply to the Earl of Bute for a New Privy Seal for the two hundred & ten Pounds of Queen Annes Bounty settled by her upon this University & to desire the distribution to be made in the same Manner as formerly.

---

[1] University MSS., vol. 30, p. 78.   [2] University MSS., vol. 30, p. 119.

IX. *The University repays a loan to the Ship Bank.*

27th May, 1762.[1]

John Pender offers to lend the College the sum of two hundred pounds, sterl. the Principal, Mr. Smith & Mr. Moor are appointed to sign a bill or bond for the said sum & to see that Mr. Morthland employ the money to extinguish an equal sum due by the College to Messrs. Dunlop, Houston & comp. Bankers in Glasgow.

2nd June, 1762.[2]

The Principal, Mr. Smith & Mr. Moor reported that in consequence of the appointment of the 27th of May last they did this day sign a Bill to John Pender for two hundred pounds sterl. and the meeting has just now received a letter from Mr. Morthland informing them that he has this day paid in the said two hundred pounds to the Bank & got the Payment marked on the Back of the College Bill in evidence of which he has sent the following note

Mr. Matthew Morthland   Glasgow 2^d. June 1762

You have this day paid me two hundred pounds sterl. which I have received in part of the College Bill of £380 sterl. 23^d. Jany. 1760 to the Bank

Sic Subscrib.   Alex^r. Morson for D.H. & Comp.

X. *Loan by the University to Distressed Russian Students.*

11th August, 1762.[3]

The University meeting having taken into consideration the state of the two Russian Gentlemen sent to this University by the recommendation of Lord Mansfield communicated by the Earl of Errol, And having been informed that for sometime past, probably on account of the confusions in which the Government of Russia has been involved, they have been disappointed of their remittances which they had reason to expect from Russia, the Meeting unanimously think it a duty incumbent upon them to advance money to these two Gentlemen untill their remittances shall arrive. And therefore desire the Principal to Grant a Precept to

---

[1] University MSS., vol. 30, p. 149. This loan was made by the Ship Bank, the first of the Glasgow Banks, which started business in January 1750—*Banking in Glasgow during the Olden Time*, Glasgow, 1884, pp. 8-11.

[2] University MSS., vol. 30, pp. 151-2.

[3] University MSS., vol. 30, p. 162. Simon Jefimovich Desnitsky and Ivan Andreevich Tretiakov. Both received the degree of LL.D. by examination in 1767. The previous year Desnitsky was one of a number of students who were in the bad books of John Anderson. The latter excluded him from the " band " in the Chapel as the Choir was then called. Desnitsky consulted another student, Alexander Ferguson, who advised him to insult Anderson. This action brought the students into trouble. Desnitsky was compelled to apologise in the *Comitia* while Ferguson was sentenced by the Rector " to be taken immediately to prison by the beadle for a little time "— J. Coutts, *History of the University*, 1909, pp. 222-3. For the later career of both Russian students see, below, the Appendix VII, by Professor Alexseev.

each of them upon Mr. Morthland for twenty pounds sterling. And appoint Mr. Smith Mr. Anderson and Mr. Williamson or any two of them a Committee to issue precepts for money, if they shall think it necessary before the meeting of the College in October next.

27th October, 1762.[1]

An University meeting being duely summoned & convened. Doctor Smith delivered from the two Russian Gent^n. the sum of Forty pounds sterling which had been advanced to them by the minute of the 11th August last. The said sum was sent from the table to the Factor & the obligation of the two Gent^n. was put into Doctor Smiths hands to be given up to them.

XI. *Examination of the old Valuation of the Lands of Yoker.*

16th December, 1763.[2]

The Principal, Dr. Trail Dr. Smith and Mr. Millar are appointed a committee to examine into an old Valuation of Sir James Maxwells Lands of Yowker and Blawarthill, of which a copy is delivered to the said Gentlemen.

XII. *The System of Keeping the University Accounts.*

9th March, 1756.[3]

The Committee upon the Factor's Accounts gave in a Memorial concerning them, and the meeting appoint the Factor to draw up his Accounts in conformity to it.

3rd April, 1756.[4]

An University meeting being duly summoned and convened, Mr. Morthland's Accounts of the ordinary revenue Crop 1753 which had been examined by the Committee were now compared with the books, and the vouchers of them received

---

[1] University MSS., vol. 30, p. 204. [2] University MSS., vol. 38, p. 63.

[3] University MSS., vol. 28, p. 169. The system of account keeping occasioned some discussion and later a case in the Court of Session and action by the Ordinary Visitors, see below, pp. 225-8. The method was quite obsolete, being based on an effort to keep the account open until the crop was sold and all rents paid. As will be noticed above, p. 155, this involved a delay of three years or more. Adam Smith prepared the accounts for submission to the Scottish Barons of the Exchequer, as is shown by his endorsement and the wrappers of his special paper on the accounts for the crops of 1756 and afterwards. It is evident he was anxious to introduce a better method. Some of his colleagues were hard to convince, amongst them the Principal. The question aroused discussion, as is shown by the number of books on accounting added to the Library. Adam Smith's education of his colleagues was proceeding tactfully when he resigned. One of his converts was Anderson, who then continued the matter, but in a hectoring manner, with the result of inducing much friction leading to legal proceedings.

[4] University MSS., vol. 28, p. 177.

in presence of Provost Geo. Murdoch, Baillie Robert Christie, Baillie James Spreal, Baillie James Whytlaw, and the said Accounts were signed by the Masters and factor in their presence. And the vouchers were put into the Charter Chest.

And after the Magistrates had gone away, Mr. Morthland's Accounts of the Subdeanry and also of the Archbishopricke for Crop 1753 both which had been examined by the Committee, were now compared with the books and the vouchers of them received, and the Accounts were signed by the Masters and the factor ; and the vouchers of both Accounts were put into their proper places in the Charter Chest.

Mr. Morthland having gotten credit in the Accounts of the Subdeanry for Crop 1753 for Eight hundred fifty two pounds Scots which is designed to be stocked out at Interest to replace Robert Simson's Bond of the like value, Mr. Morthland gave his Bill to Dr. Hamilton Vice Rector payable at Martinmas next. And the said Bill is laid up at the end of the vouchers of the Subdeanry.

14th April, 1763.[1]

Dr. Smith Mr. Hamilton and Mr. Millar are appointed a committee to desire from Mr. Morthland a sight of the Ledger which he was ordered last year to keep for the Inspection of the Masters and to certifie to him the Resolution of the Meeting to have that order put in execution.

1st June, 1763.[2]

Mr. Hamilton & Mr. Millar, who had called upon Mr. Morthland to enquire whether he had kept a Ledger according to the orders of the University, reported that he says he has kept a book of that kind which he imagines will give satisfaction to any of the Masters who chuse to look into it. Dr. Smith, Mr. Clow Mr. Hamilton & Mr. Millar are appointed a Committee to inspect the said Book & report.

XIII. *Examinations of the State of the Dundonald Mortification.*

28th October, 1763.[3]

An University meeting being duely summoned and convened
Dr. Smith Mr. Clow and Dr. Trail or any two of them are appointed a Committee to examine into Lord Dondonald's mortification and prepare a state of it to be laid before a subsequent meeting in order to be transmitted to Lord Dondonald for regulating the future payment of the Bursary.

[1] University MSS., vol. 38, p. 57.   [2] University MSS., vol. 30, p. 238.
[3] University MSS., vol. 31, p. 4. These bursaries (being four in Philosophy and three in Theology) were instituted by William, first Earl of Dundonald and his son, Lord Cochran, in 1673—*Deeds instituting Bursaries, Scholarships, &c., in the College and University of Glasgow*, 1850, pp. 67-76.

DOCUMENTS—SNELL EXHIBITIONS

§ F—SOME TRANSACTIONS RELATING TO THE SNELL EXHIBITIONS AT BALLIOL COLLEGE, OXFORD, 1756-1762

29th April, 1756.[1]

An University meeting being duly summoned and convened, Mr. Ruat who came home from London on the 27th current reported that he had gotten a Decree passed before the Master of the Rolls whereby Dr. Williams' Estates in Hertfordshire and Essex which by the Deed of Lease and Release of the date 172 had been conveyed only to the Professors named therein, was now conveyed by this new Deed of Lease and Release which are dated the 3rd and 4th of December 1755 to the present Professors of this University and their heirs for ever with same limitations; and the meeting appoint Dr. Rob. Hamilton, Rob. Simson, Dr. Lindesay, Mr. William Ruat and Mr. Smith a Committee to peruse the said Deeds, and make such an Extract from them as is proper to be recorded in the University records for preservation.

2nd November, 1756.[2]

The meeting appoint Dr. Lindesay, Mr. Rouet and Mr. Smith a Committee to draw up a Memorial and letter to Mr. Joshua Sharpe concerning the Baliol affair, both of which are to be laid before the Faculty on friday or at farthest on monday next for their approbation.

5th November, 1756.[3]

An University meeting being duly summoned and convened, the scheme given in by Mr. Snell's four Trustees in Oxford, the Vice-Chancellor, Provost of Queen's College, President of St. John's, and Master of Baliol College; as also the additional Articles given in by the Master and Fellows of Baliol College; as also a Scroll of a letter to Mr. Joshua Sharpe containing remarks upon that Scheme and the additional articles, and objections against them and the said letter was unanimously approved of and is to be signed by the Clerk, who at the same time is to desire Mr. Sharpe to write without delay what steps are proper and necessary to be taken by the University for the finishing of what relates to the whole of this affair in the best manner and the letter is to be sent off this post.

25th July, 1760.[4]

There was produced an Intimation by the Master and Fellows of Baliol College under their Common Seal, of a vacancy of one of Mr. Snells Exhibitioners, it is dated the 25th June last and was received by Mr. Smith the 3rd of July current and a meeting is appointed to be held on Wednesday the 6th of August next in

---

[1] University MSS., vol. 28, p. 179. As to the position of the Snell Exhibitions at this time, see above, Part I, chapter IV.

[2] University MSS., vol. 28, p. 195. [3] University MSS., vol. 28, p. 195.

[4] University MSS., vol. 30, p. 22.

order to Elect an Exhibitioner to fill the said vacancy, and the Clerk is to acquaint the absent members of this appointment.

16th June, 1761.[1]

Mr. Smith is appointed to write to Dr. Smith at Oxford, and inform him of the motives for sending up so young a student as George McClellan to be Exhibitioner on Mr. Snell's mortification, that he may lay them before the Master and Fellows of Baliol College.

15th October, 1761.[2]

Mr. Smith gave an account of the state of our affair with Baliol College & the Lessee of Mr. Snells Mortification. He is desired to write to Mr. Sharp to consult Mr. Wedderburn concerning the propriety of makeing a separate agreement with the Lessee & at the same time to write to Mr. Wedderburn his own views of that matter. He is likewise desired to write to Doctor King to use his interest with Baliol College to come to an agreement with this University & with the Prebendaries of Lincoln.

11th June, 1762.[3]

Mr. Smith communicated several remonstrances from the Exhibitioners at Oxford upon the present state of those exhibitions & an university meeting is appointed to be held on Monday at 3 o'clock afternoon to consider of this matter.

14th June, 1762.[4]

The Meeting according to appointment took the affair of Baliol College into consideration & having read several of the last letters from Mr. Ruet & Mr. Sharp and deliberated upon the present state of that affair ; Appoint Mr. Smith to write to Mr. Sharpe by next post & desire him to inform the University what steps have been taken since his last letter of the 8th March last & to press him earnestly to take all possible steps to bring that affair to a speedy conclusion. Mr. Smith received an extract of Mr. Sharps said letter & is to lay a copy of his letter to Mr. Sharp before the next University meeting.

9th November, 1762.[5]

Dr. Smith read a letter from Mr. Wedderburn upon the subject of the Baliol exhibitions, in which he promises to write more fully in a short time.

---

[1] University MSS., vol. 30, p. 57. Dr. Smith was John Smith, born *c.* 1721, matriculated 1736, Snell Exhibitioner 1744, B.A. (Oxon.) 1748, D.Med. 1757, Savilian Professor of Geometry at Oxford from 1766 to *c.* 1797—Addison, *Matriculation Albums*, 1913, No. 554.

[2] University MSS., vol. 30, p. 78. Alexander Wedderburn was later Lord Chancellor. There are several of his letters in § P.

[3] University MSS., vol. 30, p. 153.   [4] University MSS., vol. 30, p. 154.

[5] University MSS., vol. 30, p. 208.

DOCUMENTS—TOWN AND GOWN

7th December, 1762.[1]

A letter was read from Mr. Bruce, one of the Oxford Exhibitioners, to Dr. Smith, informing him that the agreement & termination of the Disputes with Baliol College are to be finally concluded before Christmas next. The Principal & Dean of Faculty are appointed a Committee to enquire & report as soon as possible to an University meeting What Claims the University may have upon Balliol College or the Charity Estate that the best methods may be taken to make them effectual.

§ G—THE UNIVERSITY AND THE CITY
I. *Students and Petty Customs.*

27th December, 1757.[2]

Mr. Smith reported that he had spoken to the Provost of Glasgow about the Ladles exacted by the town from students for meal brought into the town for their use, and that the Provost promised to cause what had been exacted to be returned, and that accordingly the money was offered by the Town's Ladler to the students.

II. *Protests against the Erection of a Play-house in the City.*

14th/25th October, 1752.[3]

An University meeting being duly summoned and convened the following Regulations concerning Students who are under Graduates were read and unanimously agreed to by the meeting:

---

[1] University MSS., vol. 30, pp. 212-13.

[2] University MSS., vol. 28, p. 249. This was a local tax of the nature of an octroi duty, a type of public burden of which traces remained in Scotland till a comparatively recent date. Originally the tax was exacted in kind, being taken by a ladle, and hence the official collecting it was called " the ladler ". It was claimed that the members of the University were exempt under the various charters. The difficulty seems to have arisen through the tax having been farmed. In 1739 the revenue from ladles and dues in the meal market was 5,250 merks, or about one-quarter of the total revenue of the city—G. Eyre-Todd, *History of Glasgow,* iii, p. 178. The difficulty seems to have arisen through a new lessee (or tacksman, as this official was called in Scotland) having come into control of the petty customs. Thus, earlier in the year, the following public announcement was made by the Provost and Burgh Council—" the dues of multures of the meal market, tron, weighhouse, bridge, key and cran are to be set by public roup to the highest bidder "—*Glasgow Courant,* 23rd May, 1757. Evidently the incoming tacksman found it convenient to ignore the privileges of University, and the hardship would arise when the students arrived for the opening of the session in October. It was usual for many of them to bring supplies of oatmeal and other provisions, which, previously had been passed into the city free of this tax. Adam Smith was in an excellent position to secure favourable consideration of the case of the University. From 1744 to 1760 the Provostship, with two exceptions, alternated between Andrew Cochrane and his brother-in-law, John Murdoch. It was the former who played a judicious part when the Jacobite troops occupied the city from 26th December, 1745, to 3rd January, 1746, and the two went to London to recover the amount then levied on the burgesses. Cochrane was the founder of the economic club to which Adam Smith belonged—D. Murray, *Early Burgh Organisation,* I, p. 446.

[3] University MSS., vol. 28, p. 89. The local attitude to the theatre is dealt with above in Part I, chapter VI. The reason for the action of Adam Smith and other members of the University was to avoid riots.

1mo. That no Student shall be present at Assemblys, Concerts, Balls etc. for dancing or other publick diversions oftener than thrice in one session, and that each time an express allowance from the Master with whom he studies or with whom he lodges shall be necessary, which is not to be granted before the first of April. The penalty to be one Crown.

2do. That no Student under age shall keep a horse during the Session, unless authorized by parents or friends.

3^{tio}. That no Student shall wear lace in Session time, after this present Session of the College.

4to. That no Student shall enter into any Societie of Free Masons, and if already entered shall not attend their meetings during Session time, under penalty of expulsion.

5to. That no Student shall at any time go to any publick Billiard Table, under penalty of half a Crown the first time.

6to. That all students shall be obliged to Matriculate under penalty of not being allowed to attend the Lectures of any Master.

9th March, 1756.[1]

An University meeting being duly summoned and convened, A Libel which had been delivered to the Vice-Rector was read in which complaint is made against Neil McNeil who attends some private Classes, and Godwin De Haney in the semi Classe that they had entered into Mr. Seymour's dancing school upon friday the 5th current in disguise and had a pistol with them which they attempted to discharge in the school and thereby occasioned great disturbance ; and William Rolland in the semi-Classe, by his own confession, was along with them ; the University meeting in order to deter the students from such irregular behaviour, ordered them to be fined in proportion to the degree of their guilt which appeared upon their Examination, viz : Neil McNeil to be fined in Twenty shillings sterling Godwin De Haney in Fifteen shillings and William Rolland in ten shillings, and that the whole be given to Mr. Seymour in consideration of the loss he sustained by them and they are ordered to be rebuked next Saturday in the Common Hall before the Comitia ; and also to give bond to the University under the penalty of ten pounds sterling that they shall for the future no ways disturb or molest Mr. Seymour or his School.

25th November, 1762.[2]

The Principal, Dr. Smith, Mr. Clow, & Dr. Trail are appointed a Committee to confer with the Magistrates concerning the most proper methods of preventing

---

[1] University MSS., vol. 28, p. 168. There is no record of either student having graduated. Neil MacNeil was the only son of a British shipbuilder, and Godwin de Haney came from Jamaica. Both matriculated in 1754. The name of William Rolland does not appear amongst those of the matriculated students.

[2] University MSS., vol. 30, p. 209-10.

the Establishment of a Playhouse in Glasgow & the same Committee are desired to procure all the information in their power concerning the Priviledges of the University of Oxford with regard to preventing any thing of that kind being established within their bounds, & in what manner those priviledges are made effectual.

3rd December, 1762.[1]

The Committee appointed last meeting to think of the most proper methods of preventing the establishment of a Playhouse in Glasgow & to Meet with the Magistrates upon that Business, not being ready to report, are desired to continue their diligence & report to an University meeting which is hereby appointed to be held on Tuesday the 7th Inst. at 3 o'clock afternoon.

7th December, 1762.[2]

The Committee appointed to think of the most proper methods of preventing the establishment of a Playhouse & to meet with the Magistrates, gave in their report which was approved of & they are desired to continue their diligence & report further to an University meeting which is hereby appointed to be held on Saturday the 11th Inst. at 10 o'clock forenoon.

11th December, 1762.[3]

The Committee of last meeting upon the Playhouse gave in a scroll of a memorial which is proposed to be sent on the part of the University & City of Glasgow to the Lord Advocate, which was approved of.

The same Committee are appointed to lay the said Memorial before the Magistrates for their approbation & to draw up a scroll of a letter to be sent along with it & which is to be considered in an University meeting hereby appointed to be held on Tuesday next the 14th Inst. at 3 o'clock.

14th December, 1762.[4]

The Committee upon the Playhouse reported that they had communicated the Memorial to the Magistrates who had approved of it & were to meet again tomorrow with the said Committee for the dispatch of that Business.

6th January, 1763.[5]

The Principal read a letter from the Kings Advocate in answer to one wrote to him by order of the University upon the affair of the Playhouse. Dr. Smith, The Principal Mr. Clow Dr. Trail Mr. Moor & Mr. Millar are appointed a Committee to enquire into the extent of the antient Priviledges & Jurisdiction of the University in order to answer some doubts & difficulties in the said letter; and in the mean

[1] University MSS., vol. 30, p. 211.
[2] University MSS., vol. 30, p. 212.
[3] University MSS., vol. 30, p. 213-14.
[4] University MSS., vol. 30, p. 214.
[5] University MSS., vol. 30, p. 218-19.

time the Principall is appointed to write to the Advocate to signifie the earnest desire of the University & City of Glasgow to prevent the establishment of a Playhouse in this Neighbourhood.

16th March, 1763.[1]

The Committee appointed to converse with the Magistrates concerning the Playhouse, Reported, that the Magistrates & Inhabitants of this City were willing in consequence of some encouragement received from his Majestys Advocate to enter into a Prosecution against the Players in case they should come to act Plays at Glasgow, provided the University concurr with them. The University therefore by this Minute declare their resolution to enter into such Prosecution in concurrence with the Magistrates & Inhabitants of Glasgow.

26th June, 1763.[2]

The Principal, Dr. Trail and Mr. Muirhead are appointed a Committee to meet occasionally with the Magistrates of Glasgow during the Present Vacation and to concurr with them in the most proper steps for preventing the establishment of the Playhouse in this Place.

20th March, 1764.[3]

As it is reported that Plays are to be acted in this Town before the end of the Present Session the Principal Dr. Trail Mr. Clow and Mr. Muirhead are appointed a Committee to meet with the Magistrates and concurr with them in all proper measures to prevent it.

§ H—CEREMONIAL ADDRESSES AND A PRESENTATION

I. *To King George III*.

4th November, 1760.[4]

Mr. Smith is desired to bring a draught of an address to his Majestie to be laid before the meeting.

1st December, 1760.[5]

A draught of an Address to His Majestie was read and approved, a fair copy is appointed to be written out and signed tomorrow at 3 o'clock when an University meeting is hereby appointed to be held.

2nd December, 1760.[6]

As the Address to the King was not ready for signing, it is appointed to be signed at a meeting appointed to be held on Thursday next at 3 o'clock afternoon.

[1] University MSS., vol. 30, p. 225.
[2] University MSS., vol. 31, p. 3.
[3] University MSS., vol. 31, p. 18.
[4] University MSS., vol. 30, p. 28.
[5] University MSS., vol. 30, p. 31.
[6] University MSS., vol. 30, p. 32.

4th December, 1760.[1]

The Address to His Majesty was read and signed, and Mr. Moor is appointed to transmit it to the Earl of Errol at London to be delivered to the Duke of Montrose Chancellor of the University to be presented by him and Lord Errol to His Majesty, and Dr. Leechman is appointed to write to the Duke of Montrose, and Mr. Moor to the Earl of Errol in the name of the University for this purpose. The tenor of the Address is as follows :

To the King's most Excellent Majesty

The Humble Address of the Chancellor, Rector, Dean of Faculty Principal and Professors of the University of Glasgow.

We Your Majesties most dutiful and Loyal subjects the Chancellor, Dean of Faculty, Principal and Professors of the University of Glasgow most humbly beg leave to condole with your Majesty on the sudden and unexpected death of our late most Gracious Sovereign, Your Majesties Illustrious and Royal Grandfather.

The United Kingdoms of Great Britain must always reverence the memory of a Prince under whose equitable and just administration they have enjoyed so much internal peace and security, and whose long and prosperous reign has been concluded by a series of events which have both enlarged the Dominion and augmented the renown of the British nation.

We beg leave at the same time with hearts full of the most respectful affection, to congratulate Your Majesty upon your happy accession to the Throne of these Kingdoms.

Your Majesties faithfull subjects cannot avoid conceiving the most flattering hopes of happiness from the reign of a Prince born and educated among themselves, accustomed to their manners, acquainted with their laws, fond of their Constitution, and desirous to govern them as becomes a generous, a martial, and a free people to be governed.

Such is the high opinion which Your Majesties now united and most affectionate subjects universally entertain of Your Majesties magnanimity and disinterested virtue, that they have the firmest conviction that you desire, that you wish to govern them in no other manner, that the privileges of your subjects are as dear to you as the Prerogatives of your Crown, that you glory in being the King of a free people, and that far from being jealous of that ardent spirit of Liberty which naturally animates the breast of every Briton, it is your generous ambition to cherish and support it.

All the members of your Majesties dutiful and loyal University regard it as their chief merit that they have always been sincerely and warmly attached to the Protestant Succession in your Majesties illustrious family, that they have always

[1] University MSS., vol. 30, pp. 32-4. The Duke of Montrose was William the second duke. The Earl of Errol (James the 13th Earl) was Lord Rector, November 1760 to November 1762.

considered the Law which established it, as the surest Basis of the Religion and Liberty of Great Britain, and that they have constantly endeavoured to inculcate upon the youth entrusted to their care, such sentiments of Loyalty as it becomes the Subjects of a Monarchy founded on the principles of Liberty to entertain.

26th October, 1761.[1]

The Meeting appoint the Principal Mr. Moor and Mr. Smith to draw up an address to the King upon his Marriage.

18th October, 1762.[2]

The Principal, Mr. Moor, Mr. Smith and Dr. Trail are appointed a committee to draw up an address to the King upon the Birth of the Prince of Wales.

28th October, 1762.[3]

The address to his Majesty was signed & delivered to Dr. Smith that he might transmit it to Lord Errol & request of him likewise to sign & forward it to the Chancellor of the University.

II. *Adam Smith, on behalf of the University, delivers a Copy of Foulis' Homer for Presentation to the King of Sicily.*

10th January, 1764.[4]

His Sicilian Majesty haveing been graciously pleased upon the application of Sir James Gray to order copies of the Antiquities of Herculaneum to be sent to the several Universities of Scotland the meeting agree to send a copy of the large Homer to His Majesty and another to Sir James Gray and appoint Dr. Moor and Mr. Muirhead to draw up a proper letter of thanks to his Majesty, which is to be sent up to London to be delivered with the Books by Dr. Smith to Sir James Gray.

ADAM SMITH PRÆSES.
JOSEPH BLACK CL. UNIV.

§ I—THE UNIVERSITY LIBRARY

I. *Its Resources in the Time of Adam Smith.*

The minutes concerning the Library, which follow, will be clearer if elucidated by a summary of its position and character at this period. The privilege of the Copyright Act of 1709 resulted in considerable accessions, so that the space available in the College, erected during the Civil War, proved insufficient. The new Library, which was begun when Adam Smith was a student, was at length finished, though, as will appear, there were various imperfections in its construction. Mean-

---

[1] University MSS., vol. 30, p. 86.
[2] University MSS., vol. 30, p. 203.
[3] University MSS., vol. 30, p. 207.
[4] University MSS., vol. 31, p. 11.

while the books acquired had been stored in the Professors' houses and in 1745 a beginning was made in moving them to the new building.[1] Ten years later Adam Smith was one of those commissioned to examine the volumes, still remaining in the Old Library, to decide which of them should be removed to the new one.

Besides the right to books, registered under the Copyright Act, the Library was augmented from three other sources : (1) gifts, (2) the income from benefactions for this purpose and (3) revenue from students and graduates appropriated for the purchase of books.

(1) *Gifts.*—While these were not numerous, they were important. In 1693 David Campbell, a bookseller at Boston, New England, presented Elliot's *Indian Grammar*, 4to, Cambridge, Mass., 1666 ; *The New Testament, translated into the Indian Language*, 4to, Cambridge, Mass., 1661 ; *The Bible in the Language of the Indians of Virginia, translated by John Elliot*, 4to, Cambridge, Mass., 1663, and London, 1680, being a complete collection of these extraordinarily rare books. Queen Anne presented eleven volumes of Rymer's *Foedera*, 1704-10, and the King of Naples *Antichità di Ercolano*. Of more personal interest in relation to Adam Smith was the gift by the Duke of Argyle in 1753 (to whose brother Adam Smith's cousin had been secretary) of Leupold's *Theatrum Machinarum*, eight volumes, and in 1770 by his former pupil, the Duke of Buccleuch, *Ionian Antiquities*.

(2) *Benefactions.*—The Barrowfield Fund is of interest in several ways. John Orr had been a student of Divinity who turned to a commercial career. At one time he was in serious financial difficulties from which he was relieved by loans from his friends—amongst whom were three Professors—Dunlop, Robert Simson and Loudon. Later, when he had prospered, remembering this timely aid and his interest in learning, he presented in 1730 £500 sterling, the interest on which was to be expended, in the first instance, on writings of Greek or Latin authors before A.D. 350 which were not already in the Library, after which other books might be purchased. This fund is known as " the Barrowfield ", after an estate he had purchased which had been the residence of John Walkinshaw, whose daughter, Clementina, was associated with the Young Pretender. Her daughter, Charlotte Stewart, Duchess of Albany, was " the bonnie lass of Albany " of Burns.[2] " The Principal Stirling Fund " was bequeathed by the donor after whom it was named. In 1727 the sum left to the University was 3,000 merks Scots, to be payable after the death of his widow, which occurred in 1738.

(3) *Revenue from students and graduates.*—(*a*) *Undergraduates* : Owing to the re-arrangement of the Library, this contribution had been suspended for several years. It was restored in 1754. All students, except those in the Humanity Class or who were exempted on the ground of poverty, were compelled to pay a " stent " to the Library for four years. This was not a flat rate but varied according to their

---

[1] J. Coutts, *History of the University of Glasgow*, 1909, p. 254.
[2] J. F. S. Gordon, *View of the City of Glasgow*, pp. 606, 752, 753.

means and position, which were estimated by one of their number, known as a "stent master"—a salutary device against ostentation. The rates were modest, 2s., 2s. 6d., 3s., 4s. or 5s. according as they were rated.

(*b*) *Graduates :* In the sixteenth century it was the custom for graduates to testify their gratitude for the teaching they had received or for their success in graduating by presenting important books to the Library. In some cases the value is recorded, such as amounts varying from £18 to £60 Scots.[1] In the eighteenth century by 1748 half of a fee of £20 for the degree of D.D. was payable to the Library; the like proportion of £15, the fee for LL.D., £2 from the fee of M.D.,[2] and from Masters of Arts 5s. sterling was required. Examinations were ceremonious. The bedellus conducted the candidate to the celebrated Black Stone chair, but the examinee was not permitted to sit on it until he had handed in the receipt for his payment of the fee for the Library. These payments will be found illustrated in the Quæstor's accounts of Adam Smith which are appended.

The Library was well supplied with books in Theology, and the Barrowfield fund enabled it to purchase good editions of the classics, ranging from Aldines and other celebrated presses to approved editions as these were issued. In fact, the Quæstor at the time Adam Smith was appointed Professor in 1751 found it difficult to expend the income on the primary function of the fund and had turned to manuscripts, amongst which was the Glasgow Octateuch. Ancient Philosophy was well represented and modern Philosophy moderately. In the first half of the eighteenth century a collection of mathematical books was built up. Law and Medicine were being cultivated. Modern Literature was almost a blank. There was scarcely a book in the German language, though an effort was made to be abreast of the latest developments of Continental scholarship through keeping the Transactions of various Academies up to date. These included the French Academy in its divisions of Science, Surgery, Inscriptions and Belles-Lettres, and also the Russian and the German Academies.

The number of volumes was not large. In 1691 the total was 3299 (of which 1271 were folios). By 1760 the total was 5643.[3] When a catalogue was printed in 1791 the number of entries in it for these volumes was very much larger owing to the great quantity of authors contained in some of the collections such as P. Pithoeus, *Historiæ Francorum*, fol., Francof., 1596; B. Vulcanus, *Gothicarum et Langobardicarum rerum scriptores*, 12mo, Lug. Bat., 1617; B. Straccha, *Tractatus varii de mercatura, rebusque ad mercaturam pertinentibus*, fol., Amst., 1669; *Collection of State Tracts*, 3 vols., fol., Lond., 1705-7; J. G. Graevius, *Thesaurus antiquitatum et historiarum Italiae*, 30 tom., fol., Lug. Bat., 1704-25; J. G. Eccardus, *Corpus*

---

[1] W. P. Dickson, *Glasgow University Library*, 1888, pp. 6, 7.

[2] It will be seen from Adam Smith's accounts below, that he sometimes obtained more.

[3] W. P. Dickson, *Glasgow University Library*, 1888, p. 31. The number of volumes in Adam Smith's Library in 1781 was more than a third of that in the University Library in 1760.

Historicum Medii Ævi, Lips., 1723 ; L. A. Muratorius, *Antiquitates Italicæ medii Ævi*, 6 tom., fol., Mediolani, 1738 ; J. R. Wegelinus, *Thesaurus rerum Suevicarum*, 4 tom., Lindaugiae, 1756-60.

The first year Adam Smith was in Glasgow he was placed on committees connected with the Library, and he was intimately concerned with it during the greater part of the period he was at the University. The books which can be traced to his recommendations are of interest as showing the direction of his studies during this period. It appears that in June 1752 Foulis, the printer and bookseller, had secured the offer of a large library of books in law and medicine. The Committee succeeded in making a bargain by which duplicates were avoided, and the volumes added to the Library were almost altogether in law, being fairly recent, chiefly quartos, bound in vellum or calf. It shows the low price of second-hand books at this period that the average price per volume came to just over 9d. There were 161 books, in 174 volumes, costing £7 sterling. As a contrast new books were relatively dear. As will be seen, Adam Smith gave more, when he was Quæstor, for Ferreras, *Histoire général de l'Espagne*, 10 tom., 4to, Paris, 1751, which cost £8 8s., while seven volumes of *L'Encyclopédie* and binding came to £19 15s. It is noteworthy that, while really important books, which would now be classed as economic, were purchased soon after they were published, the largest accessions, traceable to Adam Smith, were the latest histories of foreign countries. It was in this manner that he laid a broad and firm foundation for the economic enquiries which he carried out while at Glasgow.

This leads on to the final division of this section. The most patient and thorough work of Dr. Bonar on *The Library of Adam Smith* is invaluable for sources and references in *The Wealth of Nations*. As regards his work at Glasgow, the University Library was only a minute's walk from any of the three houses which he occupied there. Since it can be stated, confidently, that at this time he depended on that Library and that his own was far from the size to which it grew afterwards, the resources of the former are of great interest as regards the most convenient authorities available to him at this period. It is fortunate that its state can be ascertained almost exactly at any given date in the eighteenth century. In 1791 the University had a catalogue printed by Andrew Foulis. The dates of the books in it show, approximately, the time they were likely to have been added. Further, the MS. Quæstors' statements give a dated list of the books ordered by each Quæstor. That of Adam Smith is appended.[1] Cannan bases his notes of references in the *Glasgow Lectures* on the Catalogue of the Advocates' (now the National) Library. In order to obtain more direct access to the sources of Adam Smith's early work, a list of books of interest to him, with the dates at which each was added while he was at Glasgow, was prepared. It was of considerable size and it seemed, on reflection, that the above explanation and others which have been

---

[1] See below, pp. 178-84.

given elsewhere in this volume will suffice for most purposes, all the more since Cannan's reconstruction of the sources of the *Glasgow Lectures* comes very close to the books available at Glasgow, many of which were added to the Library at Adam Smith's suggestion. Two improvements may be suggested. The new facts in Chapter IX enable many of the authorities for the sections on the " Slow Progress of Opulence " to be recovered from those used by Robertson in his *History of Charles V*. Also, as a small point, in the specially legal portion, it seems that Adam Smith used the larger treatises rather than some smaller handbooks which Cannan quotes—this again depends on the extant recommendations of books for the Library.

It may have seemed to the careful reader that one point has been omitted in the foregoing account, namely a reference to the " Catalogue of books belonging to Adam Smith in 1761 " as reported by Dr. Bonar in his *Catalogue of the Library of Adam Smith*, 1932, p. 214. That manuscript, which is at Tokyo, was of considerable importance to the present enquiry, as it ought to show whether he owned any book by one of the Physiocratic group in 1761. By the courtesy of Professors Kawai and Tanabe of the Imperial University, Tokyo, Professor Kamo of the same University was good enough to arrange for a photographic copy of each of the 103 pages of this manuscript. In places the ink is faded, which accounts for a misreading of the date (as supplied to Dr. Bonar), which is 1781 instead of 1761.[1] The reproduction being available, it becomes possible to complete the picture of Adam Smith's library. There are, of course, a number of additions, but nothing of outstanding importance, which shows, incidentally, the value of the close watch which has been kept for a number of years on the appearance in booksellers' catalogues for books associated with Adam Smith. As was to be expected, this manuscript fills all the gaps which previously existed in the bibliography of Cannan to *The Wealth of Nations*, and adds a few more sources. Another matter is interesting. The number of books which are dated after Adam Smith left Glasgow in the two Catalogues taken together is most impressive. This suggests that it would have been hardly worth making a Catalogue of his books in 1761. It is curious also how many titles of volumes appear which he had recommended for the Glasgow University Library. It is evident that, while he was there, he depended on the Library copies. Later, when he was working at Kirkcaldy, he found he needed them for reference and bought the same books for himself. Thus it may be taken that the Library was, in large part, formed after he left Glasgow.[2]

These considerations afford some light on the final problem as to whether

---

[1] See the reproductions of the title page and a page of the body of the document, below, pp. 390-1.

[2] As an instance, the Library copy of Jethro Tull's *Horse-hoeing Husbandry* is dated 1733 : Adam Smith's 1762. It is probable this was bought after he returned from France, since Mr. Higgs (*Bibl. of Economics*) does not record an edition between 1762 and 1775.

Adam Smith had read any Physiocratic book before he went to France. It is true that in his Library were three books of Mirabeau, *Théorie de l'impôt*, 1760, *L'Ami des hommes*, 1763, and *Philosophie rurale*, also 1763. While there cannot be complete certainty, the balance of probability is that these were acquired, with many other French books, mainly economic, while he was in France. It is most significant that, in the Catalogue of the University Library of 1791, no name of any member of the Physiocratic group occurs. As already stated, the chances are that, if any such book had been ordered, it would have been for the University Library, not for that of Adam Smith. It has also to be borne in mind that the Seven Years War was in progress from 1756 to 1763, which rendered direct importation almost impossible and introduced new risks into that from neutral countries. As an instance, French ships intercepted commerce near the entrance to the Firth of Clyde. In March 1760 it was possible for spectators on the hills of Kintyre to witness a brilliant action off the Mull of Galloway in which three British frigates encountered the same number of French ships. Both squadrons were almost equal in guns, yet after an engagement of thirty-four minutes the largest French vessel, *Belleisle*, struck her flag, and very soon afterwards another, *La Blonde*.[1] Thus it is natural that the purchases of French books, on behalf of the Library, were few. During the approximate period of the war only forty-one books in French were obtained. Two cannot be identified in the catalogue. Of the remaining thirty-nine, no less than seventeen were printed outside France. It shows the stress of the times that one of these was the Boileau, published by Foulis in 1759. This leaves twenty-two works printed in France. The great majority of these were second-hand. One indeed went back to 1600. There were only six which had been issued, either in whole or in part, since the beginning of the War. They were, relatively, very costly. Most of them, as for instance the French *Encyclopédie*,[2] Deguignes, *Histoire des Huns, des Turcs et des Mongols*, and a book of Du Monceau du Hamel were probably recommended by Adam Smith, and were obtained, in spite of the high cost, as being necessary immediately for the studies on which he was then engaged.

II. *Minutes*.[3]

2nd January, 1752.[4]

The meeting appointed the books, formerly named and not yet purchased to be bought this year, and the Committee formerly named, viz. the Professor of

---

[1] *Glasgow Journal*, 10th March, 1760.   [2] Published 1751-57.

[3] The Quaestors were Leechman 1746-51 (who added books and MSS., chiefly Theological but some Classical), Moor 1751-3 (literature, mainly classical), Lindesay 1753-5 (miscellaneous), Cullen 1755, Ruat 1756-8, Adam Smith 1758-60. While Smith was nominally Quaestor for two years, he really acted for five. As will be seen (p. 176) he wound up Cullen's Quæstorship; Ruat was away for his period of two years except for about three months and again Adam Smith acted.

[4] University MSS., vol. 49, p. 58.

Divinity, Robert Simson, Mr. Rosse, Mr. Moor the present Quæstor are appointed to examine the former list of books and compare them with the Catalogue in the New Library to see what books have been named and not yet purchased, so also to determine what books are proper to be bought with what may remain unexpended of the interest of the above fund [*i.e.* the Barrowfield Fund].

26th June, 1752.[1]

Whereas the Collection of stents [2] from the publick classes for the publick Library has for some years been intermitted, the Faculty appointed the classes to be stented as usual immediately after the publick Examination, and that no collection for private Libraries [3] shall be made before the publick.

The Library keeper is appointed to attend in the Library betwixt twelve and two o'clock, and betwixt three and four from the 10th of Octr to Candlemass ; and during the rest of the Session from twelve to three and from three to five o'clock, and from 10th June to 10th October once a week upon Wednesday from ten to two.

The Committee named 26th June, 1751[4] are appointed to bring in Regulations concerning the management of the publick Library which were then committed to them to prepare, as also to communicate with the magistrates on the subject then mentioned in the minutes of that day.[5]

Whereas the ordinary funds for the publick Library are indebted considerably to Barrowfields fund and Principal Stirling's [fund] the present Quæstor [James Moor] is appointed to repay them at the rate of £10 Sterling per an.

Robert Simson Dr. Hamilton Mr. Moor the present Quæstor, Dr. Lindesay Dr. Cullen and Dr. Dick and Mr. Rosse and Mr. Smith are empowered to name what books in Law and Physick in Mr. Foulis last Catalogue are proper for the Library and to purchase them.

4th January, 1753.[6]

Robert Simson Mr. Moor and Dr. Lindesay are appointed to consider and bring in a proper method for preventing the books in the new Library from being spoiled by the moisture of the room.

26th June, 1753.[7]

Dr. Cullen and Mr. Smith are appointed with the Questor to call in and get payment of any sums that are owing to or may become due to the funds of the Library, and to settle the whole bygone accounts against the 10th of October next.

---

[1] University MSS., vol. 33, p. 72.   [2] *i.e.* a levy which must be paid, see above, p. 169.
[3] *i.e.* the Class Libraries.
[4] The same persons, appointed for another Committee, with the addition of Dr. Hamilton.
[5] Relating to the duties of the Librarian, whose salary was provided by the city.
[6] University MSS., vol. 49, p. 59.   [7] University MSS., vol. 33, p. 76.

DOCUMENTS—UNIVERSITY LIBRARY

26th December, 1753.[1]

Dr. Lindesay is appointed to have seventeen pounds ten shillings of the money gotten in from Mr. Loudon's scholars and the remainder to be given towards making a private Library for the Logick Class.

22nd January, 1754.[2]

The faculty appoint the drains about the new Library to be cleared, and the heap of earth on its north end to be removed ; both these being absolutely necessary for removing the moisture from the Library.

24th June, 1754.[3]

The Faculty having considered that the laying of a Stent on the students in order to purchase books for the publick Library has been intermitted for several years by reason of transporting books from the Old Library to the New, and putting them in order in it as also making Catalogues of them, which took up a considerable time, it was now unanimously agreed that all the students, whilst gown students or others in whatsoever Faculty except those in the Humanity Class, shall, if of the lowest condition, pay two shillings sterling, except there're quite unable which is left to the discretion of their masters to determine, and the better sort two shillings and six pence, three shillings, four or five shillings as their condition can allow. And it is appointed that this stent shall be collected immediately for this year, and every year afterwards in the month of January before any Stent for the private Librarys is laid on ; and that every individual after paying it for four years shall be free from paying it for the future.

26th June, 1754.[4]

The order made upon the 26th of June last year appointing Dr. Cullen and Mr. Smith to get payment of any sums owing to the funds of the publick Library is renewed and Mr. Clow is added to the Committee.

26th May, 1755.[5]

Mr. Moor, Dr Cullen and Mr. Smith and Dr Dick or any two of them are appointed to visit the Old Library to see what books in it ought to be put into the new Library, and to put those which are to remain in the Old Library into a convenient order and so as to be secured sufficiently.

---

[1] University MSS., vol. 28, p. 112.   [2] University MSS., vol. 38, p. 15.

[3] University MSS., vol. 33, p. 79. The gown students (or " Togati ") were not strictly coextensive with those in the Faculty of Arts, though this is intended. The students were similarly stented prior to graduation. In 1764 according to the roll of the Stent Masters (*i.e.* the students elected some of their number to fix the rates as regards individuals) the students were rated some at £5 5s., some at £4 4s., £3 3s., £2 2s. and £1 11s. 6d., occasionally reducing the last to £1 10s., but these stents were in connection with graduation and included more than the Library " stent ".

[4] University MSS., vol. 33, p. 81.   [5] University MSS., vol. 28, p. 145.

26th December, 1755.[1]

Dr. Cullen present Quæstor being to leave the University, Mr. Smith is appointed Quæstor from the time he gives up his charge of that office untill the 26th of June next.

5th January, 1758.[2]

Mr. Smith and Mr. Buchanan are appointed to examine Dr. Lindesay's Quæstor's Accounts, and to see the Books put into the Library, and inserted into the Catalogues.

26th April, 1758.[3]

Mr. Smith and Mr. Buchanan are appointed to see the Books in Dr. Lindesay's the former Quæstors hands put into their proper places in the Library.

26th June, 1758.[4]

Mr. Adam Smith was unanimously elected Quæstor to the publick Library.

17th January, 1759.[5]

Mr. Muirhead gave in an Account of the binding of the Books gotten from Stationers' Hall and some others, discharged by Mr. Foulis amounting to twelve [pounds] six shillings and seven pence ½d. Sterling which sum he received by order of a former minute of the University meeting from the several masters undermentioned *viz* £3 from Mr. Smith £6 from Mr. Clow £3. 7. 6 from Mr. Anderson and the balance was paid by Mr. Muirhead to Mr. Smith, present Quæstor.

26th June, 1759.[6]

Mr. Adam Smith was unanimously elected Quæstor for the next year.

4th March, 1760.[7]

The Committee appointed to examine the Quæstor's Accounts given in by Mr. Smith, viz : one year of Dr. Cullen's Quæstorship commencing the 26th June 1755 and two years of Mr. Rouet's from 26th June 1756 to 26th June 1758, reported that they had carefully examined these Accounts and found them justly stated, and the Balance over expended to be Ten pounds three shillings ten pence sterling and the Accounts are ordered to lie upon the table till next meeting.

---

[1] University MSS., vol. 33, p. 88. Adam Smith witnessed Cullen's resignation of the Chair of Medicine on 23rd March, 1756—Univ. MSS., vol. 28, p. 171.

[2] University MSS., vol. 28, p. 251.   [3] University MSS., vol. 28, p. 259.
[4] University MSS., vol. 33, p. 92.   [5] University MSS., vol. 33, p. 95.
[6] University MSS., vol. 33, p. 97.

[7] The reason Adam Smith presented three years Quæstor's account before his own period of office was that Cullen resigned to go to Edinburgh. Ruat was in Glasgow only during three months of the period of his Quæstorship and Adam Smith acted for him—University MSS., vol. 30, p. 2.

DOCUMENTS—UNIVERSITY LIBRARY

20th March, 1760.[1]

Mr. Smiths Quæstors accompts are to be cleared next meeting.

29th April, 1760.[2]

Robert Simson and Mr. Clow are appointed to examine the Accounts of the money payed for Binding College books by Mr. Muirhead and to add the same to the two years Quæstors Accounts of Mr. Rouet's Quæstorship given in by Mr. Smith.

12th May, 1760.[3]

An University meeting being duly summoned and convened, Dr. Cullen's Quæstors Account from 26th June 1755 to 26th June 1756 which was entrusted by him to Mr. Adam Smith in order to get it passed, after having been examined by the Committee was now passed the charge amounting to Fifty four pounds fourteen shillings eight pence sterling and the discharge to fifty six pounds seventeen shillings sterling and the balance due to the Compter being two pounds two shill: four pence sterl. was ordered to be payed by Mr. Rouet the succeeding Quæstor, and Dr. Cullen and Mr. Smith are hereby Discharged of that years Accompt.

Also Mr. Rouet's Quæstors Accompt for the two years from 26th June 1756 to 26th June 1758 which were entrusted to Mr. Smith having been examined by the Committee was now passed, the Charge amounting to ninety seven pounds five shillings four pence sterl. and the Discharge to ninety six pounds nineteen shill: one penny $\frac{1}{2}$d. sterl. ; and the balance due to the Compter being six shillings two pence $\frac{1}{2}$d. was ordered to be payed to Mr. Smith the succeeding Quæstor.

3rd November, 1760.[4]

Mr. Moor and Mr. Muirhead together with the Quæstor Mr. Smith are appointed a Committee to consider what Books are proper to be bought on Barrowfields fund this year, and to report what books are proper to be bought of the catalogue given in by Mr. Foulis.

3rd December, 1762.[5]

Dr. Smith, Dr. Trail & Mr. Williamson are appointed a Committee to examine into the State of the College Manuscripts & think of a proper manner of preserving them.

10th May, 1763.[6]

Dr. Smith gave in his accounts as Quæstor from 26 June 1758 to 26 June 1760 which are committed to Dr. Leechman & Mr. Clow for Examination.

---

[1] University MSS., vol. 30, p. 4.
[2] University MSS., vol. 30, p. 8.
[3] University MSS., vol. 30, p. 9.
[4] University MSS., vol. 29, p. 3.
[5] University MSS., vol. 30, p. 211-12.
[6] University MSS., vol. 30, p. 233.

S.A.S.

19th May, 1763.[1]

The Committee of the 10th Inst. upon the Quæstors accounts reported that they found them just & the said accounts are hereby admitted as such. The Total of the charge amounts to ninety eight Pounds ten shillings & ten pence Sterling; The discharge to one hundred & sixteen Pounds one shilling & eight pence. The Ballance due to the Compter being seventeen Pounds ten shillings & ten pence was ordered to be paid to Dr. Smith by the succeeding Quæstor—And Dr. Smith is desired to put up the Books properly in the Library & enter them in the Catalogue and as Dr. Smith has long executed the office of Quæstor he is allowed to take the assistance of an Amanuensis—The above accounts & vouchers are left in the Clerks Hands.

10th January, 1764.[2]

The Principal is appointed to give Dr. Smith a Precept upon Mr. Morthland for the sum of Seventeen Pounds ten Shillings and ten pence Sterl. being the ballance of Dr. Smith's accounts as Quæstor which were passed in the University meeting 19th May last. And Mr. Morthland is appointed to retain this sum from the first money he pays to the Quæstor for the use of the Library.

III. *Dr. Smith's Quæstor Accounts from 26th June*, 1758, *to 26th June*, 1760.[3]

This contains the Sect. of Barrowfields Fund to be inserted into the Book for this fund.[4]

College of Glasgow Debtor to Barrowfields fund for two years Rent during the Quæstorship of Adam Smith viz from 26 June 1758 to 26 June 1760 - - - - - - - - -	50	0 0
Creditor to the Same.		
By the Ballance of what was expended upon the said fund during the three preceding years - - - - - -	3	15 6
By Dion Cassius, Reimari, 2 vol. - - - - -	3	15 0
By Desguignes [Deguignes], Histoire des Huns, 5 vol. - -	4	4 0

[1] University MSS., vol. 30, p. 235. [2] University MSS., vol. 31, p. 11.

[3] University MSS., Drawer I—2. This MS. is in Adam Smith's own hand, which a French intimate described a few years later as " griffonéz comme un chat ". Unless the Essay (which is described in Part I, chapter iv) entitled " Enquiry into the Laws which govern the Conduct of Individuals in Society " is in Adam Smith's own hand, this account (consisting of 8 pp. folio) is the most extensive piece of his penmanship amongst the University manuscripts. The account is more systematic than those of his predecessors. Each receipt is marked with the large " N " with a number that appears on the MS. of the draft of *The Wealth of Nations*. Clow, the next Quæstor, followed Adam Smith's model and his Account is marked " Kept as a model for drawing up Quæstor's Accounts ".

[4] The meetings of the Committee for this fund and the books purchased by the income from it are copied in vol. 49 of the University MSS.

DOCUMENTS—UNIVERSITY LIBRARY

By Giannone, Historia Civile di Napoli, 4 vol	2	12	0
By Ferreras, Histoire d'Espagne, 10 vol.	8	8	0
By The State Historians of Venice, 10 vol [1]	5	5	0
By The Abregé Chronologique of Meseray [Mezeray], 3 vol	1	5	0
By the Supplement to the same		8	0
By L'Histoire de la France par le père Daniel, 7 vol.	3	13	6
By Reveries de Saxe [Saxe, Maurice Comte de—Ses reveries, ou memoires sur l'art de la guerre, fol., Haye, 1758]	1	10	0
By Kippaxes translation of Ustaritz's [Uztariz] discourse of the commerce & finnances of Spain, 2 vol.		12	0
By Du Hamel [2] sur la Culture des Terres, 5 v.	1	0	0
By Reports to the House of Commons on weights and measures		5	0
By Binding the same		2	6
By Postlethwait's History of the Public Revenue	2	8	0
By binding the same		6	6
By Bushing's [Büsching's] Geography, 6 vol.	4	10	0
By binding the same		18	0
By L'Encyclopedie, 7 vols [3]	18	0	0
By Binding the same	1	15	0
	64	13	0
Ballance due to the College upon deducting the above charge	14	13	0

[1] This title is translated. It is Istorici delle cose Veneziane i quali hanno scritto per pubblico decreto. 10 tom., 4to, Ven., 1718-22. It is edited by Marcantonio Cocceio Sabellico. *Cf.* Bonar, *Library*, 1932, p. 162.

[2] The library was well supplied with the works of this writer—M. du Monceau Duhamel.
 Traité des arbes et arbustes, qui se cultivent en France en pleine terre, 2 tom., 4to, Paris, 1755.
 Des Semis et plantations des arbes, 2 tom., 4to, Paris, 1760.
 Traité de l'exploitation des bois, 2 tom., 4to, Paris, 1764.
 Traité de la culture des terres (as above), 5 tom., 12mo, Paris, 1753-7.
 Eléments d'agriculture, 2 tom., 12mo, Paris, 1762.
 Traité de la conservation des grains et en particulier du froment, 12mo, Paris, 1754.
 Histoire d'un insecte qui devore les grains de l'Angoumois, 12mo, Paris, 1762.
 Moyen de conserver la santé aux equipages des vaisseaux, 12mo, Paris, 1759.
 Art du charbonier, fol., Paris, 1761.
 Art de chandelier, fol., Paris, 1761.

[3] The set was 17 vols., but the original invoice shows that seven volumes were charged for on 4th December, 1759. Adam Smith scrutinised the accounts carefully, *viz.*, in one of Gavin Hamilton dated 2nd July, 1759, he deducted £3 0s. 6d. on the following grounds : " In the within account there is an overcharge of three £ and six pence, occasioned by charging four voll. of the Berlin Memoirs too much, to wit : two tenth Vol. of which only one was sent and that imperfect also the eighth and ninth vol: which had been paid before. There are also charged three numbers of Commentarii de rebus in medicina gestis too many. Each vol. of the Berlin memoirs is 12 Shil : and each number of the Commentarii is 1s. 6D. The whole sum overcharged therefor is £3 6D, so that the real amount of this Acct. to the Library is £21 9s. 6D."

College of Glasgow Debtor to Principal Stirlings fund for two years Rent during the Quæstorship of Adam Smith, viz. from 26 June 1758 to 26 June 1760 - - - - - - 16 13 4
For a Ballance on the accounts of the three preceding years - - 6 2 0

22 15 4

Creditor to the same
By Dom. Calmet's Commentaire sur La Sainte Bible, 8 vol. - 8 8 0
By [Goguet, A. Y.] L'Origine des Loix, des Arts et des Metiers, 6 vol. - - - - - - - - - - 18 0

Total discharge - - - 9 6 0
Ballance due to the fund - - - - - - - - 13 9 4

College of Glasgow Debtor to the other Ordinary funds of the Library during the above two years Quæstorship of the said Adam Smith.
By Dr. Dawson's degree - - - - - - - 5 0 0
By Dr Plumer's Degree - - - - - - - 2 10 0
By another D$^{r's}$ Degree - - - - - - - 2 5 0
By eleven Masters of Arts - - - - - - 2 15 0
By one years Collection of the Ethic Class - - - 4 17 0
By another of the same - - - - - - - 4 13 0
By one years collection of the Logic Class - - - 3 0 0
By another of the same - - - - - - - 2 14 6
By two years collection of the Physic Class - - - 4 3 0

Total Charge - - - - 31 17 6

Creditor to the same.
By the Ballance of what was over expended upon the said funds during the three former years - - - - - 12 12 6
To be deducted from this Ballance three years collection of the Greek Class paid up by Mr. Moor while the former Accounts were on the table - - - - - - - 10 0 6

Real Ballance - - - - 2 12 0

By Acta Eruditorum Lipsiæ 1758 - - - - - - 10 0
By binding the same - - - - - - - 2 0

DOCUMENTS—UNIVERSITY LIBRARY

By Acta Eruditorum Lipsiæ 1759		10	6
By Commentarii de rebus in Medicina gestis vol. 9. Part 2, 3 & 4		4	6
By vol. 6 Part 2 & 3 of the same book		3	0
By vol. 8 Part 1 & 2 of the same book		3	0
By the six first Volumes of the Memoires de L'Academie de Berlin	4	4	0
By vol. 13 of the same book		14	0
By binding the six first vol: of the above Book[s] at two shillings each Vol:		12	0
By Stair's Institutions New Edition	3	6	0
By Fountainhall's Decisions	2	2	0
By binding the same		4	0
By Dalrymple's Decisions		16	0
By Harcarse's Decisions [Sir Roger Hog of Harcarse]		15	0
By Bacon's New Abridgement of Law, 4 vol.	6	6	0
By Gilbert's Reports		16	0
By Gilbert on Evidence		6	0
,, on Ejectments		6	0
,, Cases in Law and Equity		7	0
,, Uses and Trusts		7	0
,, Practice of Chancery		6	0
,, Practice of Common Pleas		6	0
,, Law of Executions & History of the King's Bench		6	0
,, On Tenures		6	0
,, On Replevins		6	0
,, on Devises		5	0
,, on Rents		4	0
By Dugdale's Origines Juridiciales		18	0
By Fortescue de Laudibus legum Angliæ		1	6
By Lambard's Archeion [or a discourse upon the high courts of Justice in England 12mo, Lond. 1635]		1	6
By Cay's Abridgement of the English Statutes	3	0	0
By Bullenbroke's & Belcher's Abridgement of the Irish Statutes with four Appendices	1	13	10
By Baretti's New Italian Dictionary 2 vol	2	5	0
By Oeuvres Politiques de St. Pierre 17 vol	3	0	0
By Annales Politique du Meme 2 vol		7	0
By Boscovich De Solis ac Lunae defectibus		12	6
By [Anon.] Parallelle [Parallele] des Tragiques Grec & François [12mo Lyon 1760]		2	6

By [Brosse] L'Histoire des Navigations Australes 2 vol.	1	10	0
By Simlerus de Republica Helvetiorum [Lugd. Bat. 1627 Cum supplementis variorum Tiguri, 1634]		5	0
By [Roy, Pierre le] Satyre Menippee 3 vol		10	6
By The Life of Clarendon 3 vol		18	0
By Lee's Captures of War		4	0
By Hesiodi Opera Greek & Lat. [probably ed. by T. Robinson, 4to, Oxon., 1737]		14	0
By Alembert Traité de L Equilibre des fluides		14	0
Reflexions sur les Vents		10	0
Traité de Dynamique		9	0
Théorie des Fluides		7	0
Recherches sur Les Equinoxes		7	0
By binding the above five Volumes at 2 Shill: per Volume		10	0
By Binding Haller Icones Anatomicæ [Iconum anatomicarum fasciculi VIII, fol. Gottingen, 1743-56]		5	6
,, ,, Acta Petropolitana tom. 12 [Commentarii Academiæ Scientiarum Imperialis Petropolitanae 4to]		2	6
,, The Ruins of Balbec [Wood, R. The Ruins of Balbec, otherwise Heliopolis in Coelosyria, fol. max. Lond. 1757]		8	0
By Bergeron's Recueil des Voyages [faits en Tartarie, en Perse et allieurs 2 tom 4to Leide, 1729]		12	0
By Binding Voet de duellis			7
,, ,, ,, de jure militari			8
,, ,, Matthæius Canonicum [Matthaeus Ant. Manuductio ad jus canonicum 8vo Lug. Bat. 1696]			7
,, ,, Apologie de Newton		1	6
These four last books in the list formerly given in to the Library but their binding neglected to be charged.			
By a box for Carriage		2	0
By carriage of different parcels [1]			
By binding Acta Lipsiæ, 1759, Memoires de Barlinval 1 vol. also vol 6 & 7 of commentarii de rebus in medicina gestis		6	0
Total Discharge	48	4	8
To Total charge	31	17	6
Ballance due to College	16	7	2

[1] Evidently Adam Smith made the Library a gift of the cost of carriage.

Charge against Adam Smith as Quæstor to the College of Glasgow
from 26 June 1758 to 26 June 1760.

Barrowfields fund	50	0 0
Principal Stirlings fund	16	13 4
Dr. Dawson's Degree	5	0 0
Dr. Plumer's Degree	2	10 0
Another Doctor's Degree	2	5 0
Eleven Masters of Arts	2	15 0
One years Collection of the Ethic Class	4	17 0
Another of the same	4	13 0
One years Collection of the Logic class	3	0 0
Another of the same	2	14 6
Two years collection of the Physic class	4	3 0
	98	10 10

Discharge of the foregoing Acc^t.

By Ballance due to the Counter upon a former account		5 6
By Kincaids Account 1760	32	4 0
By Another of the same	8	10 0
By a third of the same	10	7 0
By an Account of Hamilton & Balfour	35	1 6
By another of the same	1	1 0
By an account of Stalker		10 6
By an account of same	1	2 0
By a binding Account of Foulis	1	16 0
By another of the same	2	17 0
By a third of the same	1	7 0
By an account of William Miller	8	8 0
By an account of Andrew Miller	2	7 0
By Bushings [Büsching] Geography 6 vols 4to	4	10 0
By Cay's Abridgement of the English Statutes	3	0 0
By the Abridgement of the Irish Statutes	1	13 10
By a fourth Account of Foulis		15 4
By binding Acta Lipsiæ, 1759, Memoires de Berlin vol. 13, & Commentarii de rebus in Medicina gestis vol: 6 & 7		6 0
Total discharge	116	1 8
Total Charge	98	10 10
Ballance due to the Counter	17	10 10

General Account

College of Glasgow D^r to Borrowfields	-	-	-	-	-	50	0	0
,, ,, ,, ,, to Principal Stirlings	-	-	-	-	22	15	4
,, ,, ,, ,, to the other funds	-	-	-	-	-	31	17	6
		Total	-	-	-	-	-	104	12	10

College of Glasgow Creditor.

To Barrowfields fund	-	-	-	-	-	-	-	-	64	13	0
To Principal Stirling	-	-	-	-	-	-	-	-	9	6	0
To the other funds	-	-	-	-	-	-	-	-	48	4	8
									122	3	8
	Ballance due to College from the different funds								104	12	10
Adam Smith Debtor to the College	-	-	-	-	-	-	98	10	10
	Creditor to the same	-	-	-	-	116	1	8
	Ballance due by the College	-	-	-	-	17	10	10

[Receipt by Librarian for Books in the Previous Lists]
    Received the above.

THOMAS CLARK.

[Donations]
    Received Robinson's History [William Robertson, History of Scotland], 2 vols 4to and Historical Review of Pensilvania presents for the Library.

THOMAS CLARK.

§ J—ADAM SMITH, DEAN OF FACULTY.[1]

20th October, 1758.[2]

    Mr. Smith represented to the Faculty that the Rev. Mr. William Robertson one of the Ministers of Edinburgh was a person of great worth and learning, and

---

[1] As to the place of the Dean of Faculty in the University organisation of the period, see above, Part I, chapter VII. The meetings at which he presided were concerned with the courses of study and the granting of degrees. Since, however, the system of examination for the M.A. degree worked automatically, it was only any case presenting exceptional circumstances that came before the Dean. His meeting paid special attention to the conditions and the grant of doctorates.

[2] University MSS., vol. 33, p. 94. This was the only degree promoted by Adam Smith. Robertson had attended his lectures in Edinburgh and both were members of the Select Society founded in 1754. Robertson's *History of Scotland* was published in 1759. Adam Smith's action regarding honorary degrees differed from that of Hutcheson, who proposed many. At the same time he had a standard of merit, for he protested vigorously when Clothworthy O'Neil, then High Sheriff of Antrim, applied for an M.A. degree, on the ground that he had failed to pass sufficient examinations.

DOCUMENTS—THE DEAN OF FACULTY

remarkable for his uncommon ability both in speaking and writing, and very well deserved to be taken notice of by this University by conferring an Academical Degree upon him, and the faculty knowing this representation to be just, unanimously resolved to give him the Degree of Doctor in Divinity ; and a Diploma for this purpose is ordered to be expeded for him.

26th June, 1760.[1]

Sederunt Dr. Hercules Lindesay J.C.P.D.F. Dr. William Leechman S.T.P. Rob. Simson Math. P. Mr. Jas. Moor L.Gr.P. Mr. Ad. Smith P.P. Mr. Ja. Clow P.P. Mr. Jo. Anderson P.P. Dr. Jos. Black Med.P. Mr. Tho. Hamilton A. et B.P. Mr. Ja. Buchanan LL.O.P. Mr. Alex. Wilson Ast.Pr.P.

This being the Statute day for Electing the Dean of Faculty, Mr. Adam Smith P.P. was unanimously chosen Dean of Faculty for the ensuing year.

Mr. Smith having accepted the office of Dean of Faculty did in Præsentia take the usual Oath de Fideli viz :

Ego Adamus Smith Philosophiæ Professor Electus Decanus Facultatis hujus Academiæ, sancte polliceor me in munere mihi demandato studiose fideliterque versaturum.

ADAMUS SMITH.

After which he was solemnly received by all the members.

HER. LINDESAY D.F.
ROB. SIMSON Cl. Fac.

Eodem tempore sederunt ut supra Mr. Smith being in the chair.

The following list of students was named to be presented to the Right Hon[ble] the Barons of Exchequer out of which their Lordships are desired to name one to enter the logick Classe the 10th of October next as Bursar upon King Williams mortification,[2] viz :

William Richardson	Patrick Campbell	Robert Inglis
Godfrey McCalman	Colin Campbell	Douglas Hamilton

Mr. James Clow was unanimously elected Quæstor to the publick Library.

ADAM SMITH, Dean Fac.
ROB. SIMSON, Cl. Fac.

26th June, 1761.[3]

This being the Statute day for Electing the Dean of Faculty Mr. Adam Smith was unanimously chosen for the ensuing year.

---

[1] University MSS., vol. 33, p. 100.

[2] Founded by King William III, 28th December, 1695—*Deeds instituting Bursaries, Scholarships in University of Glasgow*, 1850, pp. 126-9.

[3] University MSS., vol. 33, p. 105.

Mr. Smith having accepted the office of Dean of Faculty did in Præsentia take the usual Oath de fideli viz :

Ego Adamus Smith Philosophiæ Professor Electus Decanus Facultatis hujus Academiæ, sancte polliceor me in munere mihi demandato studiose fideliterque versaturum.

ADAM SMITH.

After which he was solemnly received by all the Professors.

18th August, 1761.[1]

A meeting of Faculty being duly summoned and convened, Dr. Leechman protested against the meeting as not legal, and against all the resolutions of it as null and void, because the absent Masters had not been summoned, and thereupon took instruments in the hands of the Clerk ; and Robert Simson adhered to the above protest and took instruments.

The meeting overuled the objection and proceeded to the business for which they were summoned viz: Robert Simson is required by the meeting to bring in written proposals to be laid before the Rector's meeting to be held the 26th instant concerning the manner in which, and the persons by whom the Mathematical Classes are to be taught during the ensuing Session with certification that if he does not this meeting recommends it to the University meeting to take the matter wholly into their own consideration. Robert Simson (tho' he does not acknowledge the legality of this meeting) desires that he may have eight days after the 26th of this month to consider the proposal made to him which was overuled by the meeting.

ADAM SMITH D.F.

26th June, 1762.[2]

A Faculty meeting being duely summoned and convened

This being the Statute day for electing the Dean of Faculty Mr. James Clow P.P. was unanimously chosen Dean of Faculty for the ensuing year. And Mr. Clow having accepted the Office did in præsentia take and subscribe the usual Oath de fideli viz :

Ego Jacobus Clow Philosophiæ Professor, electus Decanus Facultatis hujus Academiæ sancte Polliceor me in munere mihi demandato studiose fideliterque versaturum.

JAS. CLOW.

Upon which he was solemnly admitted and received by all present.

ADAM SMITH D.F.

[1] University MSS., vol. 33, p. 105-6. The reasons behind Leechman's protest will appear in the next section. See also a more general point of view in Part I, chapter VII.

[2] University MSS., vol. 33, p. 109.

DOCUMENTS—THE DEAN OF FACULTY

21st October, 1762.[1]

Sederunt Mr. James Clow P.P.D.F. Dr. Willm. Leechman Prin^l. Dr. Robt. Trail S.T.P. Mr. James Moor L.G.P. Mr. Geo. Muirhead L.H.P. Mr. Thos. Hamilton B. & An.P. Mr. Alex. Wilson A.P.P. Mr. John Millar LL.P. Mr. Willm. Wight, H.H.P.

A Faculty meeting being duly summoned and convened

The meeting considering Mr. Adam Smith's universally acknowledged Reputation in letters and particularly that he has taught Jurisprudence these many years in this University with great applause and advantage to the Society do unanimously resolve to conferr the Degree of Doctor of Laws upon him and appoint a Diploma to be accordingly expeded for that Purpose.

JA^s. CLOW D.F.
JOSEPH BLACK CL. UNIV.

10th March, 1763.[2]

A Faculty Meeting being duly summoned and convened The Principal, Dr. Trail, Mr. Moor, Dr. Smith, Mr. Muirhead and Mr. Anderson, with any other Masters who chuse to join them are appointed a committee to consider of all Proposals relative to the Qualifications of Students who are to be admitted to degrees in Arts and to examine the Statutes relating to this subject.

26th April, 1763.[3]

A Faculty Meeting being duely summoned and convened

The consideration of the affair concerning the Regulation of Degrees is deferred till this day eight days at 3 o'clock afternoon.

3rd May, 1763.[4]

A Faculty Meeting being duely summoned and convened

The Meeting did not think it proper to make any new regulations at present concerning the conferring of degrees in Arts.

18th May, 1764.[5]

1mo No foreign [*i.e.* non-Scottish] student who has never been in any other University shall be admitted to a trial for a Degree in Arts untill he has regularly

---

[1] University MSS., vol. 33, p. 110. [2] University MSS., vol. 33, p. 113.
[3] University MSS., vol. 33, p. 113. [4] University MSS., vol. 33, p. 114.
[5] University MSS., vol. 33, p. 124. These regulations show the special point which was under consideration at this time. The question dates back to the time of Hutcheson. There was no way in which students in Ireland who were not members of the Irish Church could obtain higher education there. A number of "Academies" sprang into being—one of which was carried on by Hutcheson. On his becoming a Professor he obtained concessions for such students when they came to Glasgow, whereby they were allowed credit for the time spent at the institutions at which they had been previously. Experience showed some of these students were ill prepared, and these regulations were designed to correct the existing laxity.

studied for two sessions in this University and has attended in a gown the two classes of Natural and Moral Philosophy each in one session successively, besides being qualified to undergo an examination in the other parts of Philosophy and the Languages.

2° Any foreign student coming from another University shall produce a certificate of his standing and behaviour in that University and shall have studied six months in this before he can be admitted to tryall.

3 Every candidate for a degree in Arts, whether Scotch or Foreigner shall undergo an examination in Vergil and the first Decad of Livy, as a proof of his knowledge of the Latin Language, and in Xenophon's Memorabilia and the first . . . books of Homer's Illiad for Greek.

4° Any candidate may, if he chooses be examined upon Mathematics or any other branch of academical knowledge and have certified in the Diploma his proficiency in that branch and his having been taught it here when that is the case.

Mr. Anderson protested and took instruments.

§ K—TRANSACTIONS RELATING TO PROFESSORS.

I. *The Translation of John Anderson from the Chair of Oriental Languages to that of Natural Philosophy.*

13th February, 1755.[1]

An University meeting being duly summoned and convened, a letter was read from the Primate of Ireland directed to the Principal by which he in a very civil but earnest manner makes application to the Principal and other members that they would allow Mr. Anderson to stay another winter with Mr. Campbell in France, providing his office can be supplied by one of the Masters during his absence; and the meeting considering that the granting of the Primate's desire may be of great advantage to the Societie, and that the refusing of it may be attended with ill consequences to the University, resolved to allow Mr. Anderson to be absent another winter; and appoint Dr. Leechman, Robert Simson and Mr. Smith a Committee to draw up a civil letter to the Primate and acquaint him that the University has granted his desire, to be signed by the Clerk in name of the University, and sent off next post, and appoint the same persons to draw up a letter to Mr. Anderson to be signed as the other and sent off at the same time, to acquaint him with granting this allowance.

[1] University MSS., vol. 28, p. 134. The Archbishop of Armagh is Primate of all Ireland : the Archbishop of Dublin, Primate of Ireland. The " Primate " is usually applied to the former. George Stone filled this office from 1747 to 1765. The Archbishop of Dublin, 1743-65, was Charles Cobb. " Mr. Anderson " was John Anderson who had been appointed Professor of Oriental Languages in 1754. The following minutes relate to his translation from this Chair to that of Natural Philosophy. The " Mr. Campbell " of the minute has not been identified.

6th September, 1757.[1]

The vacancy of the Profession of Natural Philosophy was taken into further consideration ; and the Question being put name a day for the Election of a Professor, or delay ; it was carried by a majority, Delay. Messrs. Moor, Lindesay, Smith and Black protested against Mr. Anderson's being allowed a vote in the above Question, for reasons to be given in at next meeting, and took Instruments thereupon.

And the Question being next put what day the consideration of the vacancy should be resumed ; It was carried by the Rector's casting vote, for the thirtieth day of the present September. Mr. Moor in his own name, and in name of all who should adhere to him protested against this resolution as illegal void and null because carried by the Rector's casting vote including Mr. Anderson's vote. Dr Lindesay and Mr. Smith adhered to this protest, as did Dr. Black.

20th October, 1757.[2]

An University meeting being duly summoned and convened, the consideration of the vacancy of the Profession of Natural Philosophy was resumed in consequence of the minut of the 6th of Sept. last, as a Quorum of the members could not be made upon the 30th of Sept. and the meeting considering how long this affair has already been under deliberation, and that the Session of the College commenced ten days ago, besides that a number of students are waiting in town with a view of attending the study of Natural Philosophy, and considering further that all the members of the University meeting are now in town and have been regularly summoned to attend, except Dr. Lindesay ; the meeting appoint the morrow at twelve o'clock for Electing a Professor of Natural Philosophy as absolutely necessary in the present circumstances of the University.

Mr. Moor protests against the above resolution and against meeting to-morrow as illegal void and null because made in violation of and contrary to the only Rules by which the Societie proceeds in filling up a vacant Profession, and because Mr. Anderson a Candidate was allowed to vote in the said resolution, and for other reasons to be given in at the first legal meeting, and thereupon takes Instruments and craves Extracts.

Mr. Smith likewise protests against the Election of a Professor of Natural Philosophy to-morrow as being too early after the last day of deliberation to give warning to the absent member, and as such precipitation may establish a precedent which in future times may have bad consequences. He likewise protests against Mr. Anderson's voting in any Question concerning an Election where he himself is a Candidate.

[1] University MSS., vol. 28, p. 238. The Lord Rector at this time was Patrick Boyle.
[2] University MSS., vol. 28, p. 240.

Dr. Black adheres to Mr. Smith's Protest, and Mr. Muirhead adheres likewise to it in so far as concerns the precipitating the day of Election, as being contrary to standing rules of the Societie.

21st October, 1757.[1]

An University meeting being duly summoned and convened, and this being the day appointed for Electing a Professor of Natural Philosophy in place of Dr. Dick who died the 22nd of May last, the Question was put who shall be Professor of Natural Philosophy, and Mr. John Anderson Professor of Oriental Languages was elected.

And the University meeting did and hereby do Nominate and Appoint the said Mr. John Anderson to be Professor of Natural Philosophy in this University, and Enact that upon his declaring his willingness to agree to this translation, and his acceptance of the Universities Invitation, and his admission following thereupon, he shall brook and enjoy all the Emoluments and Privileges belonging to the said office under the restriction after mentioned, and shall retain the precedency he has at present.

The University meeting Declare that the said Translation is to take place expressly upon condition that Mr. Anderson agrees to the terms mentioned in Mr. Robert Dick's demission with respect to the said Mr. Dick's retaining the whole of the salary during his life.

Mr. Smith desired it to be marked that he did not vote in the foregoing Election, but that this proceeds from no objection to Mr. Anderson, in whose Election he would willingly have concurred with the majority of his Colleagues ; but only because he regards the method of proceeding as irregular in consequence of his yesterday's Protest, and as what may establish a proceeding which is liable to the greatest abuse, and still protests that this practice shall never be carried into a precedent in any time coming, and thereupon took Instruments.

Dr. Black declared that he was entirely of the same sentiments with Mr. Smith, and adhered to his Protest, and thereupon took Instruments.

Mr. John Anderson being sent for agreed in praesentia to the Translation, and formally declared his resignation of his office of Professor of Oriental Languages, and his Acceptance of the Universities Invitation upon the conditions above mentioned, and thereupon Did in order to his admission take the usual Oath de Fideli.

II. *The Case of William Ruat, Professor of Church History.*

Adam Smith was concerned with this question only in its later stages, but it may have had some influence in determining his own action in the resignation of his Chair. William Ruat matriculated in 1730. He was tutor first to Sir John Max-

[1] University MSS., vol. 28, p. 241.

well of Pollok and then to Murray of Broughton.[1] He was elected Professor of Oriental Languages in 1751, being admitted on 2nd January, being a fortnight senior to Adam Smith who was admitted on the 16th.[2] The next year he was translated to the Chair of Ecclesiastical History. His interests were rather practical, than scholarly. Samuel Kendrick wrote to James Wodrow that Ruat " was not of the literary class and I do not remember him ever giving lectures while he was Professor of Church History.[3] He gave his energies to the business of the University and, particularly, to the Chancery suit relating to the Snell Exhibitions which had already been in progress since 1738. In 1754 the University appointed him to go to London to forward its interests and, more especially, to expedite the proceedings. " He was absent in London, Oxford and Warwickshire for a period of two years, three months and seven days prior to 26th June, 1756, attending to the interests of Glasgow College in the suit", and his expenses amounted to £687. He was sent up again in December 1756, and did not return till the spring of 1759, at an outlay of £318 ".[4] He was thanked on several occasions for his extraordinary pains and the greatest diligence in the conduct of this affair.[5] He handed in an account of his expenses for the second visit to London on 28th April, 1759 ; he was again thanked on 3rd May, and on the 16th he presented a letter from the Earl of Hopetoun in which leave was asked in order that he might go abroad at once as tutor to Lord Hope.[6] This request was the less acceptable, in the circumstances, through an offer being made, if it was granted, to provide £400, the interest on which was to be applied as a contribution to the salary of an astronomical observer.[7] Leave of absence was refused,[8] whereupon Ruat went on the Continent. Early in 1760 Ruat's conduct was considered and, as will be seen, his office was ultimately declared vacant, which, since it was a Crown appointment, resulted in the complications which are detailed in the later minutes.

2nd February, 1760.[9]

Upon which a Second Vote being put Declare Mr. Ruats office vacant or not it carried to declare the office vacant. Against which determination as well as any sentence that may pass in consequence of it Dr. Leechman Dr. Simson Mr. Clow & Mr. Anderson entered a protest in their own name & in name of all who shall adhere to them whether present or absent for reasons to be given in writing to the

---

[1] Murray MSS. (University Library), Buchan MSS. Papers relating to R. & A. Foulis, f. 151.
[2] University MSS., vol. 55.
[3] Dated 27th April, 1808, in Papers Relating to R. & A. Foulis, Murray MSS.
[4] W. I. Addison, *The Snell Exhibitions*, 1901, p. 22 ; University MSS., vol. 28, pp. 111, 189.
[5] University MSS., vol. 38, p. 28 ; vol. 28, pp. 284, 287.
[6] University MSS., vol. 28, p. 284.
[7] J. Coutts, *History of University of Glasgow*, p. 230.
[8] University MSS., vol. 28, p. 289.   [9] University MSS., vol. 29, p. 12.

next meeting; & they further protest that no extract or notification of this sentence shall be given without inserting their protests & reasons.

7th February, 1760.[1]

Dr. Lindesay Mr. Moor & Mr. Smith are appointed a Committee to draw up answers to the above reasons, and an University [Meeting] is appointed to be held on Monday next at three of the clock afternoon to receive these Answers & for other affairs of the University.

4th November, 1760.[2]

Mr. Smith presented a letter to the University meeting from the Earl of Errol which was read; and a meeting is appointed to be held on friday next at 12 o'clock to consider it.

11th November, 1760.[3]

An University meeting being duly summoned and convened, the meeting proceeded to determine on the letter from Lord Errol to Mr. Smith the tenor of which is as follows

London Oct^r· 27th. 1761.

Dear Sir

I am this moment come from Lord Bute, and he desires me to inform the University that the Kings orders are that you immediately vacate Mr. Rouets place de novo, and that every thing may be done in a legal way, as soon as that is done His Majesty will appoint a Successor. There is a necessity of complying with this else it may be of the worst consequences to the University. I could do no more, I said all that was possible but to no effect. One thing Lord Bute told me is that he is engaged to no body, but that the man who is recommended as the fittest for filling the place properly will be his man. I beg to hear from you soon on this subject, and I likewise hope our address will be sent up immediately.[4] With my compliments to all my friends I ever am, Dear Sir,

Most sincerely yours,

Sic Subs.   Erroll.

---

[1] University MSS., vol. 29, p. 19.   [2] University MSS., vol. 30, p. 92.

[3] University MSS., vol. 30, pp. 95-6. John, 3rd Earl of Bute, was First Lord of the Treasury, the Earl of Errol was Lord Rector of the University, James Ferguson was raised to the Bench as Lord Pitfour. James Burnett of Monboddo also became a Scottish judge in 1767. He was connected with Adam Smith through his daughter having married Alexander Walker in 1755 who was a son of William Walker, one of Adam Smith's tutors and curators (see below, p. 276). Burnet was one of the counsel in the noted " Douglas Cause " and he went to Paris to take evidence there on behalf of the claimant. The latter succeeded in his suit and was elevated to the peerage in 1790 as Baron Douglas. His youngest daughter, Mary Sidney, married in 1821 Robert Douglas of Strathenry—a second cousin of Adam Smith. See below, Appendix IV.

[4] This was the address to George III. on his marriage, mentioned above, p. 166.

DOCUMENTS—RELATING TO PROFESSORS

And the meeting have this day resolved to send in Mr. Smith and Mr. Millar to Edinburgh to consult two Advocates viz. Mr. James Ferguson of Pittfour and Mr. James Burnet of Mountbodie upon the legality of the Sentence of the University meeting of the 2nd of February 1760 by which Sentence the Professorship of Ecclesiastical History in this University was declared vacant, particularly upon the following Queries

Query 1st. Does the want of the formality of a summons invalidate the Sentence of the University in the particular circumstances of the affair of Mr. Rouet?

Query 2nd. Is the action of deserting his office after leave of absence had been refused relevant to infer the censure that is passed upon the conduct of Mr. Rouet in the body of the Sentence?

Query 3rd. Ought this Sentence in order to have effect, to have been formally intimated to Mr. Rouet, and even supposing it in all other respects legal and formal?

Query 4th. If the Sentence of the University is informal or irrelevant in any of these respects what is now the proper or legal method of proceeding in order to vacate the office de novo?

And Mr. Smith and Mr. Millar are allowed to carry in the University book in which the transactions relating to that affair are narrated.

20th November, 1761.[1]

Mr. Smith and Mr. Millar gave in the signed opinion of Mr. Ferguson and Mr. Burnet containing their answers to the Queries concerning Mr. Rouet's affair, which are as follows,

Answers to the Queries proposed for the University of Glasgow.

We have considered the proceedings had by the University upon occasion of Mr. Rouets withdrawing from his charge. And in answer to the First Querie We are of opinion that the want of a notification to Mr. Rouet was a material defect in the proceedings had against him on account of his absence. And that this was very properly taken notice of before granting a new presentation. Even a private Patron ought to be satisfied of the modus vacandi before he fills the office, and still more was this proper in the case of a Royal Presentation.

To the Second Querie We are of opinion that Mr. Rouet's deserting his office after leave of absence had been refused by the University was relevant to infer deprivation, And to vacate the office. But as to any farther censure or reflection upon his conduct, we should rather have advised it to be left out of the Sentence.

To the Third Querie, If Mr. Rouet had been certiorated before the proceedings had against him in the University meeting, we do not think it would have been

[1] University MSS., vol. 30, pp. 97-8.

necessary to have intimated the sentence to him after it was pronounced, as it would then have been incumbent upon him to appoint some person to appear in his behalf and inform him of the proceedings. But the want of that previous certioration was the material defect in this case as already observed.

To the Fourth Querie When a Professor resides on the place there is no difficulty in proceeding against him for any offence before the University Court in terms of the Statutes, as in that case it is easie to give him a proper certioration to appear and offer what he has to say in his defence.

But when he has retired out of the Kingdom the matter is more difficult. There is no Civil Court that can cite people who are abroad to appear before them except Court of Session. And they cannot delegate their jurisdiction to any other Court against a principal defender tho they are in use to grant letters in supplement against Witnesses. They may assist other Judges to explicate the Jurisdiction the law has given them, but they cannot give them any new jurisdiction and therefor when a party absent is to be tryed before an University meeting, the only certioration he can get is by a letter which may be transmitted to a Gentleman in the country where he is and if he refuses to acknowledge the receipt of it under his hand, all the evidence that can be held is a declaration from a Gentleman of Character to whom it was transmitted concurred in by the Witnesses who were present at the delivery; after which it is not probable that the absent member would deny the delivery when it could be so easily proved by his Oath.

At the same time, We must own that this proceeding is not strictly legal and if there is reason to apprehend an after challenge, the proper way to secure against it, is to execute a summonds against him before the Court of Session at the Mercat Cross of Edinburgh, Pier and Shore of Leith, referring to his Oath the fact of his being refused leave of absence, and of his going abroad and still continuing abroad. and if he appears, the case will be tryed. If not, We are of opinion that the decree which will pass in course on the summonds will be effectual, as the grounds of deprivation are undoubtedly relevant, and also proven by his being holden as confessed after being cited in the proper manner the Law of the Country prescribes.

Tho the citation is of itself sufficient to support the decree in point of law, yet it would be very proper at the same time to acquaint the party by a letter which will make any after attempt to challenge it be thought highly unfavourable as well as destitute of any foundation in Law.

This is the opinion of Sic Subs. James Ferguson Ja: Burnet. Nov. 13. 1761.

These answers are to be taken into consideration on tuesday next, and a meeting is hereby appointed to be held upon tuesday at a quarter before four o'clock afternoon in the Charter room for that purpose.

Mr. Smith and Mr. Millar gave in an Account of their expences, amounting to twelve pounds sixteen shillings ninepence sterling which is ordered to lye upon the table.

26th November, 1761.[1]

The University meeting having in respect to his Majesties command taken into consideration the minute of the second of February 1760 whereby the Profession of Ecclesiastical History was declared vacant, and whereby likewise Mr. William Ruat was declared to be no longer a member of this Society; and being informed by Council learned in the law, that there were several informalities in their method of procedure, & being willing to give satisfaction to the most scrupulous, and desirous of nothing but to support the Discipline of the University against the attack which was lately made upon it, and to get the place filled according to the most Gracious promise of His Majestie, aggree to reverse the said Minute of the second of February 1760 whereby the Profession of Ecclesiastical History was declared vacant and whereby likewise Mr William Ruat was declared to be no longer a member of this Society.

The said Minute is therefore hereby declared to be reversed in the whole and in every part of it, and the University Meeting Resolve to Proceed De Novo against Mr. Ruat in the most formal manner which a regard to their Statutes and the independency of their Constitution will admitt of.

Mr. Moor and Mr. Muirhead protested against this resolution of reversing at present the sentence against Mr. Ruat.

13th August, 1762.[2]

The Principal laid before the meeting a letter from Mr. Robert Barclay inclosing an order from Mr. Ruat empowering the said Mr. Barclay to demand uplift and Discharge all Salaries that might be due to him to the date of his demission 19th Jan[ry.] 1762. The Principal is desired to acquaint Mr. Barclay that the University Meeting will give him an answer as soon as possible.

As Mr. Smith is going to Edinburgh tomorrow he is desired to Consult the Lord Advocate upon this business or if he be engaged to Consult Mr. Ferguson.

III. *The Case of James Moor, Professor of Greek.*

This might well be called the " strange case " of Moor. It is not amongst the regular minute books of the University meetings, but in a separate volume, marked to be held *In retentis*. The record presents a picture of judicial proceedings, in which many of the usual rules of procedure were quite ignored.

It will be seen that, as a result of the investigation into the terms of the charters

---

[1] University MSS., vol. 30, pp. 102-3.

[2] University MSS., vol. 30, p. 165. Thomas Miller was the Lord Advocate. He was elected Lord Rector on 25th November, 1762 (see p. 216). The result of the matter was that Ruat resigned his Professorship. It is pleasant to record that he carried on negotiations for the University in London, *gratis*, in 1766 and 1767, and it appears that he remained on good terms with Adam Smith—Rae, *Life*, p. 85.

and the customs of the University, in which Adam Smith was concerned and which are printed later,[1] discipline was maintained by two different bodies—in the case of minor offences by the Principal and Professors and in more serious matters by the Rector's meeting or Court in which the Rector adjudicated with the Dean of Faculty, the Principal and Professors as his Assessors. In the absence of the Rector it was a question, which had been raised and was debated during the ensuing sixteen years, whether all the powers of a Rector could be exercised by the Vice-Rector. It was not until later that the constitution of a Court for purposes of discipline by a Vice-Rector had been seriously contested. As to rules of procedure, Adam Smith relied on the advice of John Millar, as both a member of the Court and as legal Assessor. Millar, as has been shown above,[2] was one of the most brilliant teachers of law of his time, but his experience of practice as an advocate had been extremely short, since only sixteen months elapsed between his having put on the gown of an advocate and the exchanging of it for that of a professor.[3] The whole conduct of the case required direction, and, as far as the report extends, matters were pronounced upon in the decision upon which evidence had not been received. Millar should have supplied the defect whether it was in procedure, or in the record. On the other side, the whole treatment of a very difficult case is an outstanding example of Adam Smith's loyalty to the best interests of the University and at the same time shows the utmost consideration for an often lovable, if sometimes erring colleague.

Probably no one at this interval of time can disentangle the complexities of the characters of Anderson and Moor. In reference to the latter it has been suggested [4] that the severity of his studies had produced a neurasthenic condition, marked by great excitability and frequent outbreaks of temper upon what was very small provocation. The symptoms were in some respects similar to those of intoxication, and the habits of the time made this apparently the obvious explanation. Intemperance may have been present but it is not improbable that, if so, it was caused by the neurasthenic condition already mentioned. In any case there was a certain amount of scandal which imported many extraneous questions into the enquiry.

The whole matter arose from a somewhat trivial cause. In the spring of 1763 Moor was lecturing in the afternoon when he was interrupted by the noise made outside by some students of Anatomy. He rushed from his class-room and remonstrated with the offenders in a somewhat violent manner. It was alleged that he struck one with his cane, threatened to whip the other two and gave orders to the porter to put the three in prison.[5] Apparently the students kept out of his reach and, no doubt, were disrespectful to a greater or less degree. Moor called upon Adam

---

[1] See below, pp. 204-5.   [2] See Part I, chapter VII.
[3] A. F. Tytler, *Memoirs of Henry Home, Lord Kames*, 1807, i, p. 199.
[4] See above, Part I, chapter VII.
[5] There was a room in the tower, in which students were sometimes detained.

Smith, as Vice-Rector, to hold a meeting of the Rector's Court to take cognisance of what " he considered most insolent and audacious behaviour ". The first of eight meetings was held on 4th June, 1763, and the last on the 16th. The evidence showed that, through whatever cause, Moor on the occasion under discussion was not in control of himself and was the victim of ungovernable rage. Thus, from being the complainant, he became in effect the defendant. It was this fact which accounts for his protests on matters of procedure. From the point at which Millar asked whether Moor was under the influence of liquor, the character of the whole testimony began to shift. Previously the students, who had been summoned, were concerned in defending themselves against the charges which had been made by Moor. Now their evidence was directed towards exonerating him from the suggestion of intoxication. The following record of the proceedings on 8th June gives a sufficient picture of what was most characteristic in the conduct of the investigation:

6th June, 1763.[1]

Coll. Glasgow, 6th June 1763.

Sederunt Dr. Adam Smith P.P. Vice Rector Dr. W$^{m.}$ Leechman Principal Mr. James Clow P.P. Dean of Faculty Dr. James Moor L.G.P. Mr. George Muirhead L.H.P. Dr. Joseph Black Med.P. Mr. Thomas Hamilton Bot. et An. P. Dr. Alexander Wilson A.P.P. Mr. John Millar I.C.P.

An University Meeting being duly convened according to appointment Dr. Moor gave in the following Representation viz

Whereas Mr. Moor, when he came to the University Meeting, on Saturday last, did expect, and still thinks he had reason to expect, that the Meeting would have followed the forms of proceeding established and authorised by the Constitution and practice of this University ; and whereas, by the advice of the Gentleman to whom the Vice Rector chose to apply for direction in the form of proceeding, Mr. Moor, to his surprise, found that the Meeting departed entirely from their own Constitution and practice, and followed the forms of other Courts of a quite different constitution and instituted for quite different ends, and to which other Courts there lyes an appeal from any decision, in such cases, given by an University Meeting ; Which innovation obliged Mr. Moor to demand a question, and this question being carried against him by the votes of the Principal Doctor Black Mr. Hamilton and Mr. Millar, against those of the Dean of Faculty, Mr. Muirhead and Mr. Wilson ; and whereas Mr. Moor apprehends that the said Gentlemen by whose votes that question was carried were not, at that time, sufficiently aware of the usage of the University Meeting in such matters Therefore Mr. Moor begs leave to assure them that he can produce a great number of instances in proof of what he now asserts, and particularly he lays before them at present a case exactly similar, as he thinks,

[1] University MSS. XXIX (121), pp. 5-7. The " gentleman " mentioned in the report was John Millar.

to the present case, hoping they will be pleased to take it immediately into consideration, before they proceed further. Monday June 6th 1763
(Signed)   JA. MOOR.

Upon which the vote was put whether such of the remaining witnesses as are students shall be examined upon Oath, or shall give in a Declaration which is to be signed by the Vice Rector and the Declarant—It carried for the Declaration—Dr. Smith Mr. Hamilton Mr. Millar & Dr. Black dissented from this resolution 1st Because they apprehend that by examining such of the students upon Oath as are willing to give their Oath and are above the age of fourteen years, the Meeting are more likely to learn the whole of the truth ; the respect for an Oath obliging them to declare what they might conceal if there was a declaration only. $2^{ly.}$ Because the Meeting had already begun by examining upon Oath at the desire of the other party one student adduced as a witness by Dr. Moor. And $3^{ly.}$ Because this resolution was taken in the presence of Dr. Moor, tho' he did not vote, but in the absence of the other parties.

The students were called in and having brought council along with them they were desired to remove untill it should be debated whether Council was to be admitted or not. And the vote having been put, in their absence it carried to admit Council. Upon which Dr. Moor craved a delay untill he could also have the benefit of Council, which accordingly was granted   And a University Meeting is hereby appointed to be held to-morrow at four o'clock afternoon at which the parties with their witnesses are ordered to attend.

Dr. Moor protested against the resolution of admitting Council in this case, because he thinks it contrary to the constitution and subversive of the discipline of this University, and of which not one single instance can be produced for upwards of these three hundred years even from the original foundation of the University, and hereupon takes instruments and craves Extracts.

Mr. Muirhead and Mr. Wilson likewise protested against the above resolution as a thing quite new and unprecedented in this Society subversive of its discipline and tending to introduce endless trouble and confusion and hereupon take instruments and crave Extracts.

The students having been again called in the above minutes were read to them Upon which they protested against that resolution of the Meeting by which it was resolved that such of the witnesses as are students should for the future be examined not upon Oath but in the way of a signed declaration and hereupon take instruments and crave Extracts.

Signed   ADAM SMITH Vice Rector.

No evidence in support of some matters which were introduced into the early proceedings is to be found in the record, though they are given weight in the preface to the finding of the Court. The members of it evidently felt that Moor, on certain occasions, had been unfit to exercise discipline with reasonable judgement and restraint. In addition, though as to this no evidence was adduced, they seem to have been convinced that he was setting a bad example and was lowering the repute of the Professoriate.

In its finding the Court recapitulated the charges which had developed from the enquiry. There were " loud reports " that Moor behaved in an indecent and irregular manner, that he was frequently disordered by liquor to such a degree as was visible to masters, students and servants, that he pretended to exercise College discipline when in that condition, that he had not the sense of shame which he ought to have for the offensive behaviour with which he was charged. There is no definite pronouncement as to how far these charges were proved or not. What impressed the Court, and is recorded, is Moor's mixture of assurance and petulance during the proceedings. The decision was that " he was to be rebuked and admonished in the strongest and most solemn manner ".[1]

However irregular the procedure was, the influence of Adam Smith can be traced in the effort to uphold the fair fame of the University and at the same time to afford every possible opportunity for amendment in conduct of a colleague who was in fault in certain respects, at least. For this reason he was able to prevail on the other members of the Court that the report of the enquiry should not be incorporated in the official minutes, but should be copied into a separate book and held *in retentis*. If Moor gave no further cause for complaint, the whole matter would be buried in oblivion. But, if he offended again, the minute was available for production on a second charge. It is unfortunate that circumstances arose in which these papers were required. Less than ten years later Moor's ungovernable temper once more brought trouble to the University and to him. In November 1772, a student in his class-room aroused his displeasure. He seized one of the tall, heavy, wooden candlesticks which stood on the floor beside his desk and struck the student on the head with it. This case was the subject of a long enquiry with the result that Moor was compelled to resign his chair in 1774.[2]

§ L—ADAM SMITH, VICE RECTOR.
I. *Adam Smith, Præses.*

3rd *June*, 1761.[3]

Mr. Smith was elected Præses of the meeting to attest Dr. Leechman's subscription of the Article in the Register for the Widow's Scheme of the date of his admission.

[1] University MSS. XXIX (121), p. 19.

[2] J. Coutts, *History of the University*, 1909, pp. 310-11.

[3] University MSS., vol. 30, p. 55. William Leechman, Professor of Divinity and Vice-Rector, was appointed Principal by King's Letter dated 6th of July. The " Widows' Scheme " referred to above was one established by Act of Parliament in 1743 (17 Geo. II, cap. 2), contributions to which

II. *The Legality of Adam Smith's Procedure Questioned.*

15th July, 1761.[1]

Sederunt Mr. Adam Smith Professor of Moral Philosophy and Dean of Faculty. Mr. James Moor Professor of Greek & Eldest Regent. Mr. George Muirhead Professor of Humanity. Dr. Joseph Black Professor of Medicine. Mr. Thomas Hamilton Professor of Botany, and Anatomy. and Mr. Alexander Wilson Professor of Astronomy and Observer.

An University Meeting being duely summoned and convened in consequence of the appointment of the university meeting on the 27th of June last and of a mandate signed by the Vice-Rector summoning the members in consequence of the said appointment to meet this day at eleven o'clock before noon in order to admit Mr. John Millar to be Professor of Law and to elect a Professor of Oriental Languages and for other affairs of the University: which Mandate was accordingly regularly intimated yesterday to all the Members in town. And Doctor Leechman who came to town yesterday having thought fit this day between the Hours of ten and eleven to write to Mr. Professor Smith the following letter

" To Mr. Adam Smith Professor of Moral Philosophy
in the University of Glasgow

GLASGOW July 15th 1761.
" Sir,
I acquaint you and the other Professors by this that unless the Rector himself is to be present in the Meeting to preside there can be no meeting today as I have already resigned the Office of Vice-Rector. I likewise by this inform you that His Majesty has been graciously pleased by his Royal letter dated at St. James's the 6th of July to nominate me to be principal which I have also intimated to the Lord Rector and as soon as it can be done shall qualifye before the Presbytery and desire the Rector to call a meeting for my admission. Please to communicate this to all the Gentlemen my collegues.

I am Sir your most obedient humble Serv[t.]
Sic Subscribitur WILL. LEECHMAN."

The Meeting having taken this into consideration were unanimously of opinion, that having been legally summoned and convened they had a right to

---

were compulsory. Each Principal or Professor was required to sign on admission to a new office. Thus Adam Smith signed twice (Univ. MSS., vol. 55). This signature of Leechman was in anticipation of his formal admission. It may be of interest to note that James Moor had his goods seized at the instance of the managers of this Fund for failure to pay his contributions. There were also other creditors (Univ. Library, Buchan Papers, R. & A. Foulis Collection, p. 483).

[1] University MSS., vol. 30, pp. 62-5. The involved circumstances determining Leechman's action and the subsequent enquiry into the respective powers of the Rector and Principal are discussed above, Part I, Chapter VII.

proceed upon the business for which this meeting was legally appointed and summoned.

Before however they came to this Resolution they sent many messages to Doctor Leechman intreating and requiring his presence. Mr. Smith once brought a message from Doctor Leechman that if the meeting would agree not to proceed to the election of a Professor of Oriental Languages this day, Mr. Leechman would take it into consideration whether he should come and preside as Vice-Rector at the meeting. The Meeting tho they were sensible of the inconveniencies which might attend this proposal yet being desirous to yield to their Collegue for the sake of harmony agreed not to proceed to the Election this day provided Mr. Leechman would come and preside as Vice-Rector in order to admit Mr. Millar and for other Business of the University. Mr. Smith haveing carried this Message to Doctor Leechman brought back for answer a final refusal to come to the meeting in order to preside as Vice-Rector.

The Meeting in consequence of this final Refusal resolved to proceed upon the business for which they were summoned and accordingly elected Mr. Adam Smith Dean of Faculty to be præses of this meeting and Dr. Joseph Black to be clerk pro tempore. The Præses then sent to Doctor Simson for the University Books, Doctor Simson himself not being present, but the said Doctor Simson absolutely refused to send them.

The meeting then proceeded to their business.

III. *Confirmed by the Rector.*

26th August, 1761.[1]

Sederunt The Right Honorable The Earl of Erroll Rector Mr. Adam Smith P.P.D.F. Doctor Robert Simson Math.P. Mr. James Moor L.G.P. Mr. James Clow P.P. Mr. George Muirhead L.H.P. Mr. John Anderson P.N.P. Doctor Joseph Black Med.P. Mr. Thomas Hamilton Anat. et Bot. P. Mr. Alexander Wilson Astr.P.P. Mr. John Millar I.C.P.

An University meeting being duly summoned and convened The Meeting having taken into their consideration the Proceedings of the Meeting of the fifteenth of July last declared their approbation of the said Meeting's Procedure and order the Minute to be recorded in the University Book in order that the proceedings of that day may never afterwards be controverted. Doctor Simson Mr. Clow & Mr. Anderson desire it to be marked that the Rectors consent to the Election of any of the Masters is absolutely necessary both from the Kings Charter of new Erection in 1577 and from the constant practice of the University and that an Election made now in presence of the Rector would be the best way to prevent the Election of 15th of July last being made a precedent but if it be confirmed by the Rector's

[1] University MSS., vol. 30, p. 66.

consent now given it is proper to be declared that it shall not be brought into precedent for the future.

IV. *The Respective Powers of Rector and Principal.*

19th April, 1762.[1]

As some doubts had arisen concerning the respective Powers of the Rector & Principal—The Meeting appoint Mr. Moor to give in the claim on the side of the Rector supported by proper Vouchers from the Charters, Statutes & practice of the College ; And the Principal to do the same on his side And they are empowered to call for Charters, Statutes & any other papers which may be necessary, from the Clerk.

The Meeting farther Appoint The Dean of faculty, Dr. Trail, Mr. Clow, Mr. Muirhead, & Mr. Miller a Committee to receive the said claims & to report & that their first Meeting shall be on Monday next in the Charter Room half an hour after five o'clock P.M. with power to adjourn.

28th May, 1762.[2]

The Principal protested that as the Committee appointed to enquire into the Respective Rights of the Rector & Principal had yet made no report this confirmation shall not prejudice any of the Rights which shall be found to belong to the Principal.

The above mentioned Committee are ordered to prepare & bring in their report to an University meeting to be held on the 12th of August next at twelve o'clock at noon.

V. *Adam Smith's Report on the Powers of Rector and Principal.*

13th August, 1762.[3]

Sederunt Mr. James Moor V.R. L.G.P. Dr. William Leechman Prin[l.] Mr. Adam Smith P.P. Mr. George Muirhead L.H.P. Dr. Joseph Black Med.P. Mr. Alexander Wilson A.P.P. Mr. John Millar I.C.P. Mr. Pat. Cumin LL.Oo.P. Mr. James Williamson Math.P. Mr. William Wight H.H.P.

An University Meeting being duely summoned and convened. Eodem Die hora IV p.m. Sederunt ut Supra.

---

[1] University MSS., vol. 30, pp. 135-6. Moor succeeded Leechman as Vice-Rector and held office till the expiration of the Earl of Errol's term of office in November. Thereupon Adam Smith was elected Præses of the Rector's meetings, being formally nominated Vice-Rector immediately Millar was installed as Rector (p. 216). He remained Dean of Faculty till 26th June, 1762 (p. 186).

[2] University MSS., vol. 30, p. 150.

[3] University MSS., vol. 30, pp. 164-84. Moor did not carry out his part of the minute of 19th April. When August 12 came he had no report ready, but borrowed that of the Committee in order to reply to it. The charter cited was printed as an Appendix in the *Memorial for Dr. Leechman*

DOCUMENTS—POWERS OF RECTOR, ETC. 203

The Report of the Committee given in yesterday was returned by Mr. Moor and is as follows

Report of the Committee appointed to enquire concerning the respective powers of the Rectors & Principals meetings, And to Report to the University meeting to be held on the 12th of August 1762.

The Committee appointed to enquire concerning the respective powers of the Rectors and Principals meetings and to Report to the University meeting to be held on the 12th of August 1762, Find,

1$^{mo.}$ That, with regard to Discipline, by the Express words of the Charter of New Erection by James the Sixth of Scotland dated 13th July 1577, the ordinary Jurisdiction over all the members of the College seems to be vested in the Principal. The words are, " Gymnasiarcham autem pium et probum hominem inprimis esse oportet cui totum collegium et singula ejus membra subesse oporteat, cui in singulas collegii nostri personas jurisdictionem committimus ordinariam." (a)

(a) Jura leges instituta etc. fol. 43.

2$^{do.}$ That this ordinary jurisdiction of the Principal is, in the same Charter, by words equally express, declared to be subordinate to that of the Rector and his meeting. There are three different passages in the above mentioned Charter which plainly establish this subordination of the Principal to the Rectors meeting. The first of these is as follows. " Resideat vero [Gymnasiarcha scilicet] in dicto Collegio, neque inde pedem moveat ad longinquiorem aliquam profectionem, nisi re cum Rectore academiæ, Decano facultatis, et cæteris suis Collegis Regentibus communicata et venia impetrata graviore aliqua de causa aut evidenti collegii commodo. Quod si Gymnasiarcha sine licentia legittime petita et obtenta per triduum extra Gymnasii septa pernoctaverit, volumus ut muneri ejus, quod eo casu vacare pronunciamus, alius idoneus modo infrascripto sufficiatur." (b)

(b) ibid. eod. fol. 43.

The second passage comes immediately after the recital of the several duties of the Principal and is as follows—" Et sic quidem præ-

---

against Dr. Trail and Others (Glas. Univ. Liby. DQ 2, 25, pp. 71-5) and in a better form in *Munimenta Alme Universitatis Glasguensis*, 1854, i, pp. 103-13. (As to the word " Alme " in above title, it may be remarked that in the MS. records of this period " æ " rarely appears). Adam Smith's references to the MS., entitled " Jura Leges ", indicate a somewhat miscellaneous volume, many extracts from which are printed in their proper sequence in *Munimenta*, vol. ii. In vol. i of the same book the " Jura Leges " is referred to as " No. 7 of the Clerk's Press ". It contained a copy of the Charter of James VI which is quoted above and which shows signs of having been collated with the original (*Munimenta*, i, p. xxi).

The general situation, in which this dispute arose, is described above in Part I, chapter VII.

fectum collegii nostri vitam suam instituere volumus, qui si negligentior fuerit in suo munere et quæ sunt ei per specialem erectionem injuncta non impleverit, neque resipiscere velit, cum ter admonitus fuerit per academiæ Rectorem, Decanum facultatis, Collegii Regentes aut eorum majorem partem, sed in malos mores proclivis fuerit, iisdem auctoribus exauctorabitur, quos prius in electione locum habere decrevimus." (c)

(c) *ibid. fol.* 44.

The third passage comes immediately after the recital of the different duties of the several Regents, who were at that time three in number, and is as follows " Eorum, [Scilicet Regentium], electio, præsentatio, et admissio, penes Rectorem, Decanum facultatis et Gymnasiarcham esto, qui bona fide nostram institutionem sequuti, de quam optimis et doctissimis præceptoribus collegio providebunt, qui adolescentes docendo scribendo declamando disputando quam diligentissime in palestra literaria exerceant. Potestas autem emendandi et corrigendi dictos Regentes erit penes dictum gymnasiarcham cui etiam potestas erit eosdem collegio ejiciendi si postpositis eorum officiis ter ut dictum est admoniti resipiscere noluerint cognita tamen causa et adhibito consilio Rectoris et Decani facultatis." (d)

(d) *ibid. fol.* 45.

By the two first of these passages it is evident that the Principal himself was subject to the jurisdiction and liable to the Censure of the Rector and Dean of faculty joined with their ordinary assessors the Regents or moderators of the College ; and by the last of these passages it appears, First, That the Principal could proceed to inflict some slighter Censures upon such of the Regents as were deficient in their duty without the assistance of the Rector and Dean of faculty, As the Charter, immediately after declaring that the Right of Election belongs to the Rector, Dean of faculty and Principal, adds, " That however the power of Censuring and Correcting shall be in the Principal." " Potestas autem emendandi et corrigendi dictos Regentes erit penes dictum Gymnasiarcham." And Secondly That the Principal could not proceed to inflict any more severe sentence, such as that of extrusion, without the assistance and advice of the Rector and Dean of faculty, the cause being examined in their presence and the Rector consequently as supreme magistrate of the university presiding in the meeting. The jurisdiction of the Principal, therefore, it would appear, could extend only to smaller matters such as might fall within that ordinary jurisdiction mentioned in the first quoted passage. But that the higher and more extraordinary jurisdiction could belong to the Rector and his court only.

$3^{tio.}$ That neither the Rector nor Principal nor Dean of Faculty have at any time either claimed or exercised any arbitrary authority or jurisdiction nor have ever attempted to decide in any important affair of the Society but in the presence and with the Consent of their proper assessors or of the major part of them and that consequently whatever opinion this Committee has already given or shall hereafter give concerning the powers of the Rector, Principal or Dean of faculty is always to be understood concerning the powers of the respective meetings or Courts of the Rector, Principal or Dean of faculty, and not concerning the powers of these several magistrates when alone and seperated from their respective assessors.

4$^{to.}$ That with regard to the administration of the College revenue the ordinary management of it is by the express words of the same Charter Committed to the Principal and his ordinary Colleagues and assessors the Regents of the College. The words which declare this follow immediately after the recital of the duties of the oeconomus or provisor, who was to Collect the College Revenues, Sue the College Debtors, and provide necessaries for the College table. They are as follows. " Is autem, [scilicet oeconomus], tenebitur in singulos dies rationem reddere emptorum et importatorum Gymnasiarchæ et reliquis præceptoribus præsentibus nequa in re minima fraus fiat collegio. Quotidianæ enim rationes in animadversaria redactæ magno erunt familiæ usui porro præceptores ipsi unacum oeconomo tenebuntur rationem reddere administrationis quater in anno Rectori Decano facultatis et Ministro urbis Glasguensis, qui operam dabunt Calendis Octobris Calendis februarii Calendis maij Calendis augusti ut quam exactissimo Calculo omnia subducantur quorum etiam conscientias compellamus ut omnia recte et secundum nostram intentionem in dicto collegio administrata esse videant et in ordinem sua auctoritate redigeant [sic] et quater in annos Singulos dictis rationibus subscribant quæ tum solummodo authenticæ habebuntur. Eorumque consilio quicquid fuerit residui, sive ex hac nostra fundatione sive ex vetera erectione id omne in alios usus Gymnasii non prætermittendos impendatur." (e)[1]

(e) *ibid. fol.* 45, 46.

By this passage it evidently appears that the respective powers of the Rector and Principal with regard to the administration of Revenue were perfectly similar to the respective powers of the same magistrats with regard to discipline. That the ordinary management was in the Principal and his Colleagues or assessors the Regents, under the controul however of the Rector and Dean of faculty by

---

[1] The conclusion of this extract is condensed according to the Charter as printed in *Munimenta*, i, p. 111.

whose advice the surplus revenue which remained after paying the sallaries of the several officers of the College and maintaining the College table, was to be employed.

The Committee having found the power and jurisdiction of the Principal as subordinate to that of the Rector, thus far established in the Charter of New Erection 1577, proceeded next to enquire how far this power and jurisdiction had been confirmed or abrogated by the subsequent custom and practice of the University And in consequence of this inquiry finds,

$1^{mo.}$ That from the time of Principal Gillespie who was admitted in the 1653, down to the year 1755, it is acknowledged by all parties that the Principal was in the use of holding meetings in which the Rector was not present, and in which, notwithstanding, agreed part of the College business of all kinds was transacted, And $2^{do.}$ That this practice of a hundred years standing seems to be fully confirmed supported and authorized by the statutes of the last visitation 1727,[1] which, tho made to restrain the powers of the Principal within proper bounds, by the whole tenor of them, however, Suppose that the Principal has an undoubted power of Calling and presiding in meetings for the dispatch of College business, Thus page 7 It is enacted as follows. " And the Commission Statutes appoints and ordains that in all time coming the minutes of all meetings of faculties shall at the next Sederunt to be held the following day be made up and adjusted, and after being fully settled shall be fairly entered in the faculty book and signed by the Principal and Clerk, without prejudice to the Faculty at the first meeting if they can all conveniently stay so long together to settle adjust and subscribe the minutes in the book.

That the Clerk shall be obliged to mark all dissents and protests with the reasons of them and to give extracts thereof when required.

That what shall be concluded by the majority in any meeting of the faculty shall take effect and be signed by the Principal or preses and that the Principal or Preses shall have liberty to mark his dissent notwithstanding of his Signing the minute if he be of a contrary opinion to what is concluded.

That the vicarious right of administration in case of the Principals absence or of the vacancy of that office, Is and shall be in the Person of such of the four Regents sciz : Of the Three Professors of Philosophy and Professor of Greek as is or shall be of eldest standing in the said University for the time And that in the case foresaid the

[1] *Munimenta*, ii, pp. 569-81.

DOCUMENTS—POWERS OF RECTOR, ETC.

eldest Regent shall have the right of Calling and presiding in all meetings and of doing every thing which the principal could do.

That in all the several meetings of the Masters of the University the Majority of the Constituent members shall be a Quorum.

That to all faculties the members be duely Summoned by the bedall the day preceding the meeting.

That the Principal or eldest Regent when required by any three of the Masters by write under their hand expressing the causes, shall call a faculty and in case of his refusal they the said three may themselves call a faculty and the faculty Convened may in the Principal and eldest Regent's absence chuse a Preses.

And that any three masters may in like manner call a faculty in case of the absence of the Principal or that his office be vacant and in case of the absence of the eldest Regent.

That there be four ordinary faculty meetings held every Session consisting of the Principal and all the Professors of the University, To witt, Upon the first friday of November, Second friday of January, Last friday of March, and last friday of Aprile, at three of the Clock in the afternoon of the said respective days, in the Common hall or in the Faculty room without prejudice to the Principal in his right of office or to the eldest regent or to the three members as aforesaid to call meetings as occasions require.

That in case of the absence of the Principal and eldest Regent upon any of the four stated days above mentioned That the meeting may Choice its own preses And that the Principal, eldest Regent or preses shall not in any meeting have a double vote but only the Single Casting vote."

By the whole tenor of the above statutes it is evident that the Principal is Supposed to have a power of Calling and presiding in meetings of Faculty for the dispatch of College business. This power accordingly was, as has already been observed, exercised by the Principal or in his absence by the eldest Regent without any Challenge or interruption till the year 1755. The late Principal Campbell was at that time indisposed, having some years before that been struck with a Palsey which from the moment in which it seised him rendered him incapable of attending to the business of the Society. For sometime after this misfortune had befallen the Principal, Mr. Moor, called and presided in faculty meetings according to the directions of the above statute of visitation. These faculties however appear to have met more rarely towards the end of the year 1754. And through the whole of the year 1755, there are but two of these meetings recorded in the faculty book one in January the other in November, from which time down to the Sixth of November 1761, sometime after Dr. Leechman in consequence of the death of the late Principal Campbell, had been presented to the office of Principal, there are no meetings of this kind in which the Principal or eldest Regent had the right of presiding, recorded in the Faculty book. During the whole of this interval, the University meeting in which the Rector or his Deputy the Vice Rector have the right of presiding, transacted the whole business which had before that been divided between those two different meetings.

On the 11th of Aprile 1755, about the time when this change was beginning or rathere some little time after it had been begun, Mr. Moor the eldest Regent gave in the following paper to the University meeting held that day. "That whereas this meeting had been summoned to pass the factors accounts, he had just now put the members in mind that the Accounts of the Archbishoprick had hitherto passed in meetings of Faculty held by the Principal or eldest Regent and that the Conveyance of the Tack was to the Principal and Masters without mention of the Rector and therefore proposed that these accounts should be passed this year in the same manner as formerly ; to which proposal the meeting did not agree ; and that therefore he did not subscribe the said accounts."

Immediately after this paper inserted by Mr. Moor there follows in the Minutes of the same University meeting the underwriten answer to it by Doctor Simson. "Robert Simson desires it may be inserted in the minutes that by the Charter of Erection of the College granted by King James the 6th in 1577, the Rector and Dean of Faculty are appointed visitors of the College and in particular are constituted auditors of all accounts of the Revenue ; so that even any accounts of the branches of it that are not disponed to them but to the Principal and Regents only, for instance the Teinds of the parish of Govan, are to be audited by them, and without their subscribing them are not authentick, as is plain from the express words of the foresaid Charter of Erection ; And the Subdeanery accounts and those of the Archbishoprick are for the same reason to be audited and signed by them ; tho by the seldome attendance of the Rector, and unacquaintedness of the Deans of Faculty in former times with the College affairs, the same has been for most part neglected ; but ought to be brought in practice. Besides there are no meetings appointed by the Statutes, or the Erection above named, to be held by the Principal except meerly for the Exercise of Discipline ; the Calling of meetings by the Principal for any other business being an innovation crept in by the Election of Rectors that lived at a distance from Glasgow and who on that account could not hold meetings so frequently as the College affairs required."

At the time when these two papers were given in the late Doctor Robert Hamilton was Vice Rector and continued to be so till his death which happened on the 15th of May 1756. In consequence of which on the 9th of June following Doctor William Leechman was appointed Vice Rector and continued to be so with very little interruption till 1761, when he resigned that office upon his being presented by his Majesty to the office of Principal. In consequence of his resignation Mr. Moor was appointed Vice Rector who had likewise before that exercised the same office by the appointment of Mr. Milliken at that time Lord Rector of the University, for a few months during the absence of Doctor Leechman who had taken a journey to England for the recovery of his health. During this whole period of about six years, in which the Rectors meeting transacted the whole business, which it had formerly divided with the Principals meeting, the Rector himself very rarely attended and the Vice Rector therefore generally presided.

The Committee observe upon the above mentioned paper given in by Mr. Simson which gave occasion to the Change before taken notice of, that Mr. Simson appears to have been mistaken when he asserted " that there are no meetings appointed by the statutes or by the Erection above named to be held by the Principal, except meerly for the exercise of discipline." Since by the Statutes of the last visitation 1727, above quoted, It is expressly ordered " That there be four ordinary Faculty meetings held every Session consisting of the Principal and all the Professors of the University, viz. upon the first friday of November, Second friday of January, last friday of March and last friday of Aprile, at three of the Clock in the afternoon of the said respective days, in the Common hall or in the Faculty room, without prejudice to the principal in his right of office, or to the eldest Regent, or to the three members as aforesaid to call meetings as occasions require." The Statutes of the last Royal visitation in 1727, must surely be allowed to be statutes.

Mr. Simson appears likewise to have been mistaken when he asserted " That by the Charter of New Erection no meetings were appointed to be held by the Principal except meerly for the exercise of Discipline ", Since by the words of that Charter formerly quoted the Oeconomus, who then did the whole business which is executed

S.A.S.

at present by the College Factor, is ordered to Account every day to the Principal and Regents; who being thus constituted the ordinary auditors of his accounts are consequently appointed to hold meetings for that purpose.

It has been alledged indeed that the Commissioners of this Commission of visitation were unacquainted with the antient statutes and Practice of the University and that it was in consequence of this ignorance that the statutes above quoted were enacted by them.

The Committee beg leave to observe upon this 1st. That Supposing this to have been really the case it would follow that it might be extremely proper for some Subsequent Commission of Visitation to repeal those statutes as founded upon a mistake, but that it cannot be competent for any Court which is unquestionably inferior to the Commission of visitation to dispense with the observation of those statutes upon pretence that this Court judged those Commissioners to have been ill informed with regard to the antient practice and constitution of the University. There could be no proper subordination of one Court to another if the inferior Court could at any time take upon them to dispense with the orders of their Superiors upon pretence that their Superiors had been ill informed. The University meeting is a Court unquestionably inferior and Subordinate to a Royal Commission of visitation which with regard to the University meeting is endowed with absolute legislative power. The university meeting therefore cannot be authorized at their own hands to redress any real or Supposed grievance which they may imagine has been imposed upon them by such visitation. To obtain the redress of any such real or Supposed grievance they must apply to some authority which is as much above such Commission of visitation as the Commission of visitation is above the University meeting, that is, either to the Sovereign Courts of Justice, to the King in Council, or to the King and Parliament. Supposing therefore that there was the Clearest evidence that the Commissioners of last visitation had been ill informed with regard to the antient constitution and practice of the University it would not follow that the University meeting had any right to dispense with the observation of those statutes.

But 2dly. It does not appear to the Committee that the Commissioners of last visitation were in any respect ill informed with regard to the Antient Constitution and practice of the University or that in authorizing the Principal to call and Preside in meetings of Faculty they authorized any innovation. What they have done in this respect seems perfectly conformable to the Regulations in the Charter of New Erection by James 6th 1577, by which the same or an equal authority is conferred upon the Principal as has already been observed. The only reason which has yet been alledged to prove that this Authority of the Principal is an innovation is, that before the time of Principal Gillespie (*g*) 1653, there are not in the university books any records of meetings of faculty held by the Principal in which the Rector does not appear to have been present. But it will by no means follow that no such meetings were held because no record of them has been preserved in the University books. To be convinced of this nothing more is necessary than a very general inspection into the confused and disorderly manner in which the minutes of all meetings are recorded in that old parchment book which contains the chief transactions of the society from the New Erection till many years after the time of Principal Gillespie. In that book it is very common to find a transaction inserted between two other transactions of which the latest had happened a hundred years before it. For example at the bottom of the page (*f*) which comes immediately after the New Erection 1577, is inserted the Record of the admission of the present Mr. Robert Dick 1714. Upon turning that page you find the next transaction dated 1586. (*h*) In the page immediately after, the transaction which follows is dated 1600. (*i*) From the nature of things the University must have made many transactions between these two last mentioned of which there is no record in that book. This account of a part of the three pages which immediately follow after the record of the New Erection may serve as a Specimen of the whole book. Without going further than the same three pages we may find clear evidence that the society were not in these times accustomed to enter Minuts into any books even of very important transactions and consequently that the want of a minut cannot be any proof that there were no such transactions. The transaction last mentioned [in] 1600, for example, is not a Minut of any meeting but the Copy of a deed by which the Principal and Masters with the Consent of the Rector and Dean of Faculty convey certain Lands in few-farm to the persons therein named. There is no minute of Faculty authorising this. It had, it seems, been at that time the Custom of the society to content themselves when they entered into any transaction of this or any other kind to consider the deed itself to be laid up in the Charter Chest as sufficient evidence of the transaction and not to trouble themselves with keeping any regular authenticated Journal of their proceedings. Long after this

(*g*) *jura leges instituta etc. fol.* 91, *also folio* 92, 94, 100, 101, 102.

(*f*) *jura leges instituta etc. fol.* 47.
(*h*) *folio* 48.
(*i*) *folio* 49.
See also *folio* 100, 110, 112, 113.

time, and even long after the time of Principal Gillespie, Principal James Fall who was admitted 1684 seems to have been the first who began any regular Journals of the affairs of the Society. This Journal he wrote with his own hand in his own Closet as it was Convenient for him. It contains an account of the affairs of the Society from the 29th Sept$^r.$ 1684 to the 8th of September 1690 when he was deprived of his office for refusing to take the oaths to King William. This Journal tho' very imperfect and altogether unauthenticated contains a more distinct and connected account of the affairs of the Society than any thing that is to be met with of an earlier date. The Title of it is, " Affaires relating to the College of Glasgow from my entry thereto to be principal writen with my own hand as they occured by me, Ja. Fall." He concludes it with the following words. " If they who Succeed me think fit to follow out and continue this brief narrative of the affairs relating to the College they may be useful and profitable to posterity. If not I have done my part. At Glasgow this 8th day of September 1690. Ja. Fall." [1] The continuation of this Journal was thought to be a matter of so much consequence that Principal William Dunlop who succeeded Principal Fall declares in the page immediately following that he is resolved to pursue it. " Finding ", says he, " this Commendable method of transmitting the affairs of the University to the view of those who shall succeed us, I am resolved to follow the same Since I have succeeded to the office of Principal of this University and to do the same with my own hand. Will. Dunlop prin^l." He continues it however no further than January the 2d 1691. And even the two last articles of that Continuation appear to be in a different hand. Besides this Journal there are in Principal Dunlops time pretty distinct and well authenticated Minuts in a book by themselves which end March 1st 1694. Principal John Stirling [2] Succeeded Principal Dunlop and was admitted September 18th 1701. He likewise declares at the end of Mr. Dunlops Journal that he proposes to continue so useful a method of recording the affairs of the University. " The late Principal Mr. Dunlop, says he, having been so much taken up with public affaires that he could not get his design of transmitting the account of the University affairs to such as should Succeed him accomplished, and finding no memoirs in his sons hands for continuing the Account begun by him I am constrained to begin where he left. John Stirling." He concludes it in the year 1702 with these words. " Having

---

[1] This Report (and also that of Dunlop) is printed in *Munimenta*, iii, pp. 689-96.
[2] *Munimenta*, iii, pp. 506-602.

been careful since the time of my entry to keep record of the Proceedings of the Faculty by taking minuts of all material things that past I judge this way of recording things less necessary than in Doctor Fall's time. I therefore resolve to continue it no longer. John Stirling." This important Journal of these three Principals consists of Eighteen pages in folio. The minuts in Principal Stirlings time appear to have been kept with much more accuracy and exactness than they had ever been before as will be evident upon a very Slight inspection of that book which contains the records of the society from the time of his admission to the 26 february 1717. Even in his time however the records of three distinct meetings viz of that in which the Rector presides, of that in which the Dean of Faculty presides, and of that in which the Principal presides, are all kept in one and the same book and follow one another according to the order of time. This too seems to have been pretty much the case from the time of the New Erection down to the time in which Mr. Simson was made Clerk to the university who introduced order and method into the affairs of the Society in this respect as well as in many others. We must except however a very short period viz from November 1642 to December 1648 in which there appears to have been kept a very regular Dean of Facultys Book which is still extant.

From this short account of the method in which the transactions of the society were recorded it would be very easy to infer that we cannot conclude with any certainty that there were no meetings of a certain kind because in the antient Books of the Society there appeared no Minuts of any such meetings. And the University has in this respect been no worse than almost all other Courts which have generally Subsisted a Century or two before they have fallen upon a proper regular and orderly method of preserving the records of their proceedings.

The Committee further beg leave to observe that to allow the Principal or his meeting a Jurisdiction and a Share in the management of the Revenue of the College Subordinate and liable to the Controul of the Rector and his meeting cannot in any respect abridge the liberty of the society or the independency of any person in it. From the nature of Subordinate Jurisdiction there must always be an appeal from the inferior to the Superior Court after Sentence past in the former, and even before sentence if upon complaint made by any party concerned it appeared to the Superior Court that things were not likely to be carried on in the most candid and equitable manner in the inferior Court, it might be lawful for the Superior Court to Stop proceedings and to call up the matter before themselves in the manner of a Certiorari or advocation.

The Committee further observe that from the time in which the records of each meeting have been kept in separate books the distribution of the respective business seems in general, tho' perhaps with some exceptions, to have been as follows. First to the Rectors meeting fell the Elections of masters, the employment of the Excrepence of the Revenue and the final passing and approving of the annual accounts of the ordinary Revenue. As the Rector and Dean of Faculty are by the Charter of Erection declared the auditors of all accounts, those of the Subdeanery and Archbishoprick ought likewise to be past in the same meeting, tho the practice has not in this respect been so uniform.

2dly. To the Dean of facultys meeting fell the conferring of degrees, the care of the Library, the Election of the Kings bursars 26th of June, and in general every thing relative to Learning.

3dly. To the Principals meeting fell all the other ordinary affairs of the College.

4^{thly}. The Election of a member to the General Assembly has sometimes been made in the one meeting and sometimes in the other: As it is the Election however of a Representative to the whole incorporated body it seems properly to belong to the Rectors meeting.

5^{thly}. Bursars upon those bursaries to which the Society has the right of presentation have sometimes been Elected in the Rectors and sometimes in the Principals meeting, perhaps because the words of the Mortification sometimes convey them to the Rector principal and masters, and sometimes simply to the Principal and Masters. This at least would seem the properest foundation for such a distinction. The same Rule ought to be followed with regard to the Registration of presentations to such bursaries as are in the Gift of other patrons. In whatever book however the presentations to such bursaries may happen to be recorded it should seem that the bursar ought to be equally secure in the possession of the Charity. The Right of Registration should in general not seem to be worth the disputing since it can only increase the business without in the smallest degree augmenting the authority of the meeting.

6^{thly}. Tho' certain bursaries may be mortified to the Principal and Professors, without any mention of the Rector, and that consequently the right of presentation to these bursaries belongs properly to the Principals meeting, yet that upon complaint of unfair and illegal proceedings in such elections such as that all the masters had not been summoned, or the like it should seem reasonable that the Rectors meeting may call the matter before themselves, and if such complaint shall appear to have been well grounded, award a more proper method of proceeding in a new Election to be made in the Principal's meeting.

At the College of Glasgow 10th August 1762.

Sic Subscribitur ADAM SMITH
JOSEPH BLACK
JOHN MILLAR
ALEX^R. WILSON

13th August, 1762.[1]

Mr. Moor at the same time gave in his objections to as much of it as he had time to peruse and compare with the records and they are as follow.

Objections to the Report given in yesterday, the 12th of August 1762 to the University Meeting.

1. Its title is " The Report of the Committee &c." Whereas that Committee consists of five members and this report is signed by two only of these five, The other two Gentlemen who sign along with them not being of the appointment.

2. It takes no notice of the original records of the University for above 100 years, tho' a pretty large extract from them had been laid before the Committee and seemed to be approved by them.

Mr. Moors objections were read and considered one by one by the meeting and all of them over ruled. After which the Question was put agree to the Report of the Committee or not—It carried to Agree.

Upon which Mr. Moor made the following protest.

In behalf of the Lord Rector of the University Mr. Moor for himself and in name of all who adhere protests against this agreement of the present meeting, to the Report given in to the meeting of yesterday for reasons to be given in due time

---

[1] University MSS., vol. 30, pp. 184-201. No minute has been found changing the membership of the Committee. The two who signed the report and were nominated on 19th April, 1762, were Adam Smith and John Millar. Later references show that the report of the Committee was drawn up by Adam Smith. Moor's second objection is supported by the citation of a number of passages from the records of the University. There is no object in printing these, since, as evidence against the Report they are admittedly incomplete, while in the *Information for Dr. Robert Trail against Dr. Leechman* (Univ. Lib. DQ. 2, 25) the quotations are most voluminous, adding greatly to those extracted by Moor.

manner and form. And hereupon takes instruments in the Clerks hands and Craves extracts.

VI. *Adam Smith confirmed as Præses and, later, as Vice-Rector.*

25th November, 1762.[1]

A Letter was given in from the Lord Advocate by which he declares his acceptance of the Office of Rector of this University & as he is under a necessity of going up to London at present recommends Dr. Smith to preside in University meetings untill his Lordship can be admitted & appoint a Vice-Rector. The above letter came the 16th instant in answer to an express sent off the day of Election & it was ordered to be kept in retentis.

Doctor Smith the Præses is appointed to summon the next meeting, & the Præses of every meeting is to summon the next meeting thereafter in like manner, untill the Admission of the Rector.

25th March, 1763.[2]

The Principal gave in the reasons of his Protest, as mentioned in the last meeting, the tenor of them is as follows.

1$^{mo.}$ He protested against referring the affair of Tollcross Teinds to the University meeting because there was no difficulty in the affair to make such a reference necessary.

2$^{do.}$ Because the meeting to which it was referred has no jurisdiction or power of any kind. For as the Rector is not yet admitted, there can be no Vice-Rector or any other person who has power to transact Business in his name, so that the meeting is absolutely unconstitutional.

3$^{tio.}$ Tho' the Rector were admitted and present in person, there lies no appeal from the Faculty to any Court in which he presides and determines by a majority of votes.

4$^{to.}$ Because the whole Teinds of the Subdeanry (in which the Teinds in question lye) are given to the Principal and Professors, without being subjected to the controul either of Rector or Dean of Faculty.

Dr. Trail Dr. Smith and Mr. Moor are appointed a Committee to answer the Principals Reasons of Protest.

---

[1] University MSS., vol. 30, pp. 209-10. The Lord Advocate was Thomas Miller of Barskimming and Glenlee (see p. 217). He was born 3rd November, 1717, admitted advocate 1742, Joint Sheriff Principal City of Glasgow 1748, Solicitor of Excise 1755, Solicitor-General 1759, Lord Advocate 1760, Lord Justice Clerk 1766, Lord President of the Court of Session, in succession to Robert Dundas of Arniston, 1788, and was created a Baronet in the same year. He died 27th September, 1789—Brunton and Haig, *Senators of the College of Justice*, pp. 530-1 ; G. W. T. Omond, *Lord Advocates*, 1883, ii, pp. 68–72.

[2] University MSS., vol. 38, p. 56.

Coll. Glasg. xix^{no}. Aprilis MDCCLXIII [1]

Habitis Academiæ Comitiis Vir amplissimus Thomas Miller de Barskimmen Armiger, & Regiarum Causarum Apud Scotos Procurator, Munus Rectoris Magnifici ad quod electus fuerat in Se suscepit et hoc Juramento se obstrinxit.

Ego Thomas Miller promitto sancteque polliceor, Me in Muneris Mihi demandati ratione obeunda, studiose fideliterque versaturum

THO: MILLER RECTOR.

Eodem Tempore assessores nominavit Moderatores Academiæ & Apparitorem nominavit Joannem Bryce

THO: MILLER RECTOR
JOSEPH BLACK CL. UNIV.

Eodem Die, Meridie
Sederunt   The Right Hon^{bl} Thomas Miller Rector & the rest ut supra,

The University Meeting which had been adjourned being again convened. The Rector read over the Minutes of the University Meetings which had been held since his election & consented to & approved of them; and by the advice & with the consent of his assessors appointed Doctor Adam Smith P.P. to execute the Office & to have the full Power of the Rector during his Absence.

An University meeting is appointed to be held to-morrow at Twelve o'clock.

THO: MILLER RECTOR
JOSEPH BLACK CL. UNIV.

VII. *Further Discussions on the Powers of Rector and Principal.*

28th October, 1763.[2]

The Principal adds in his own name that he dissents, for the following further reasons.

" 1$^{mo.}$ That the Resolution complained of was taken in an unconstitutional meeting. For the Principal and masters being uncontroverted Proprietors and administrators of the Colleges Revenue, it belongs to the Principal to call meetings of Faculty to deliberate about the disposal of College money, and when the Faculty

---

[1] University MSS., vol. 30, pp. 228-9. One of the matters upon which controversy was beginning was the question whether the Vice-Rector could exercise " the full power " of the Rector. The adoption of this form by as eminent a lawyer as Thomas Miller is of interest. It will be noted that when Adam Smith as Rector appointed a Vice-Rector (see p. 231) to exercise the full power of the Rector with the exception of the Visitorial power and certain powers relating to mortifications.

[2] University MSS., vol. 31, p. 7. This protest relates to the proposed Chemical Laboratory. As this was to be erected by means of surplus revenue the proposal came before the Rector's meeting with Adam Smith presiding, as Vice-Rector. This meeting, after considering the state of the Revenue, decided that a Laboratory may be built and directed Dick, Lecturer in Chemistry, to prepare plans at a cost not exceeding £350 sterling. Leechman and Clow dissented. Adam Smith answers the protest in the next extract.

has deliberated, it belongs to them to call the Visitors of the College for their advice and concurrence; But it does not belong to the Rector, either in the Capacity of head of the University or in the Capacity of Visitor of the College to call any meeting about College money in which he presides and determines by majority of Voices.

" $2^{do.}$ Because it may surely be doubted whether the Vice-Rector is a Visitor of the College but only the Rector himself for tho' the Rector, by the Statutes of the University may appoint a Vice-Rector to act in his absence in all University affairs, yet he cannot appoint him to act for him in College affairs, because the Rector is not a Visitor of the College ex officio but by the special and particular appointment of the foundation Charter. The Sherrif of the County might have been appointed a visitor, but tho he could have appointed a Depute Sheriff to act in his absence in County Business, yet that Depute would not have been a Visitor of the College, And the Nova Erectio makes no mention of a Vice-Rector.

" And $3^{tio.}$ Independent of these Reasons, when we have the happiness of a Rector of such established Reputation, not only for worth but abilities in Business as the present, it seems to be decent, prudent and just to take his advice in such momentous matters as that of disposing a considerable sum of College money, in the circumstances above represented. And therefor as neither the Rector nor Dean have yet given their consent to the disposal of the money in question, the Principal reserves to himself the power of laying the whole matter before the Rector in Person and the Dean, as Visitors of the College, Qui omnia bene administrata esse videant."

31st October, 1763.[1]

" And with respect to that part of the Reasons which refers to the Rector he begs leave to remark that neither the Principal nor any other Person, in the Meeting in which the Resolution was taken, made any objection on account of the Rector's absence. It appeared to the Majority a step highly proper and becomeing the present Reputation of this University to further countenance the study and Teaching of a Science which is one of the most usefull and solid, and which is dayly comeing into greater esteem ; and there seemed to be no particular necessity for giving the Rector himself any trouble upon this occasion, tho there is no Person in the Society who has not a proper value for his advice, and who will not pay the proper regard to it."

As a Meeting could not be held on the 1st of August for want of a Quorum, The Memorials drawn up by the Committee appointed the 10th May and 26th June last to collect the facts relating to the Powers and Office of the Rector and Principal were now read to the Meeting ; and the Principal and Dr. Smith are

[1] University MSS., vol. 31, pp. 8, 9.

appointed to wait upon the Lord Rector to deliver to him the said memorials and to confer with him and desire an University Meeting upon the subject.

ADAM SMITH VICE RECTOR.

2nd November, 1763.[1]

Sederunt The Right Honourable Thomas Miller, Rector ; Dr. Willm. Leechman Prin^l. Mr. James Clow P.P.D.F. Dr. Robt. Trail S.T.P. Dr. James Moor L.G.P. Dr. Adam Smith P.P. Mr. Geo. Muirhead L.H.P. Mr. John Anderson P.N.P. Dr. Jos. Black. Med.P. Mr. Thos. Hamilton B. & An.P. Dr. Alex^r. Wilson A.P.P. Dr. James Williamson Math.P. Dr. Willm. Wight H.H.P. Mr. John Millar L.L.P.

An University Meeting being duely summoned and convened

The Meeting considered the two Memorials given in to last meeting, and direct their Agent to lay them before the Rector and Mr. Ferguson, Dean of the Faculty of Advocates in Edinburgh, for their opinion.

THOMAS MILLER RECTOR
JOSEPH BLACK CL. UNIV.

COLL. GLASG: Die xv^to. Novembris
MDCCLXIII[2]

Habitis Academiæ Comitijs, electus est hujus Academiæ Rector Magnificus in Annum sequentem Vir amplissimus et Honorabilis Thomas Miller de Barskimmen, Armiger et Regiarum Causarum apud Scotos Procurator

Adam Smith Vice Rector
Joseph Black Cl. p.t. in Com. elect.

2nd December, 1763.[3]

An University meeting being duely summoned and convened Dr. Smith was elected Præses.

10th June, 1766.[4]

The Memorial concerning the Jurisdiction of the Rector signed by Dr. Moor and Dr. Smith, consisting of 52 Pages, and the principal's answers to the said Memorial consisting of 20 pages, which had been laid before Mr. Millar, now Lord Justice Clerk, were returned to this Meeting by Dr. Williamson, and were laid up in the Charter Chest.

---

[1] University MSS., vol. 31, p. 9.   [2] University MSS., vol. 31, p. 10.

[3] University MSS., vol. 31, p. 10. Adam Smith was Vice-Rector at the meeting on the 15th November till his successor was elected. Miller was re-elected, but was not present. It is a question whether Adam Smith should have signed as Vice-Rector after the election had taken place. It was necessary, according to precedent, that the Rector should be admitted ; then, if necessary, he could appoint a Vice-Rector to act for him in his absence. This is the last Rector's meeting which Adam Smith attended as a Professor. The Rector not having been admitted as yet, he is elected as Præses. It shows that he had the confidence of his colleagues, since there were many opportunities to have chosen another person to preside.

[4] University MSS., vol. 31, p. 135.

§ M—ADAM SMITH'S RESIGNATION.

8th November, 1763.[1]

Dr. Smith represented that some interesting Business would probably require his leaving the College some time this Winter and made the following Proposals and request to the Meeting

1$^{st.}$ That if he should be obliged to leave the College without finishing his usual Course of Lectures he should pay back to all his Students the fees which he shall have received from them and that if any of them should refuse to accept of such fees he should in that Case pay them to the University.

2$^{dl.}$ That whatever part of the usual Course of Lectures he should leave unfinished should be given gratis to the Students by a Person to be appointed by the University with such Salary as they shall think Proper which Salary is to be paid by Dr. Smith. The Faculty accepts of the above Proposals and hereby unanimously grant Dr. Smith leave of absence for three months of this Session, if his Business shall require it, and at such time as he shall find it necessary.

1st March, 1764.[2]

A letter was given in from Dr. Smith the Tenor of which follows
Addressed " To the Right Hon$^{ble.}$ Thomas Miller, Esq$^{r.}$
His Majesty's Advocate for Scotland

My Lord,
I take this first opportunity, after my arrival in this Place, which was not till yesterday to resign my Office into the hands of Your Lordship, of the Dean of Faculty, of the Principal of the College and of all my other most respectable and worthy collegues. Into Your and their hands therefor I do hereby resign my Office of Professor of Moral Philosophy in the University of Glasgow and in the College thereof, with all the emoluments Privileges and advantages which belong to it. I reserve however my Right to the Salary for the current half year which commenced at the 10th of October for one part of my salary and at Martinmass last for another; and I desire that this Salary may be paid to the Gentleman who does that part of my Duty which I was obliged to leave undone, in the manner agreed on between my very worthy Collegues and me before we parted. I never was more anxious for the Good of the College than at this moment and I sincerely wish that

---

[1] University MSS., vol. 33, p. 118, printed by Rae, *Life*, pp. 167-8.

[2] University MSS., vol. 31, p. 13. This letter is addressed to Thomas Miller as Rector (see above, p. 219). Rae, *Life*, pp. 141-4, describes the events leading up to Adam Smith's appointment as tutor to the Duke of Buccleuch. Charles Townshend discussed the question at a meeting with Adam Smith in Glasgow in the summer of 1763 (see p. 384 note [3]); then followed Townshend's letter of 25th October, 1763—Rae, *Life*, pp. 164-5. This letter has been printed by Rae, *Life*, p. 172, and the tribute to Adam Smith's work as a Professor by Stewart, *Memoir*, 1811, p. 64.

whoever is my Successor may not only do Credit to the Office by his Abilities but be a comfort to the very excellent Men with whom he is likely to spend his life, by the Probity of his heart and the Goodness of his Temper.

I have the Honour to be my Lord, your Lordship's
most obed[t.] and most faithfull Servant

Paris 14th Feb. 1764.   Signed   ADAM SMITH.

The Meeting accept of Dr. Smith's Resignation in terms of the above letter, and the Office of Professor of Moral Philosophy in this University is therefore hereby declared to be vacant. The University at the same time cannot help expressing their sincere Regret at the Removal of Dr. Smith, whose distinguished Probity and amiable qualities procured him the esteem and affection of his Collegues ; whose uncommon Genius, great Abilities and extensive Learning did so much Honour to this Society ; His elegant and ingenious Theory of Moral Sentiments having recommended him to the esteem of Men of Taste and Literature thro'out Europe ; his happy Talents in illustrating abstracted Subjects and faithfull assiduity in communicating usefull knowledge distinguished him as a Professor and at once afforded the greatest pleasure and the most important instruction to the Youth under his Care.

5th May, 1764.[1]

The Meeting haveing deliberated upon the Vacancy and upon the several candidates appoint an University Meeting to be held on Tuesday the 22[d.] curr[t.] at 12 o'clock to proceed to the Election of a Professor of Moral Philosophy.

22nd May, 1764.[2]

This Meeting haveing on the 5th Inst. been appointed for the election of a Professor of Moral Philosophy, the Vote was put and Doctor Thomas Reid Professor of Philosophy in the Kings College Aberdeen was elected : The University Meeting therefore did and hereby Do elect him to the vacant Profession of Moral Philosophy and the Rector is requested to write to Doctor Reid in the name of the meeting to acquaint him with his election and desire him to accept of the Office.

[1] University MSS., vol. 31, p. 24. See Part I, chapter vii, and the letters printed below (pp. 256-7) as to Adam Smith's interest in the election of his successor.

[2] University MSS., vol. 31, p. 28.

§ N—EXTRACTS FROM DOCUMENTS PRODUCED BY THE PARTIES IN THE ACTION FOR DECLARATOR IN THE COURT OF SESSION, 1766-1771, RELATING TO THE REPORT ON THE JURISDICTION OF THE RECTOR, 1762, AND OTHER ISSUES RAISED IN THAT PERIOD.

I. *Pursuer's Information.*[1]

Your Lordships will be informed, that in the year 1762, the disputes with regard to the powers of the rector, and principal, &c. having by this time arrived at such a height as to create very great embarrassment in carrying on the business of the University, a committee of which two of the defenders, viz. Doctor Robert Traill, and Mr. John Miller professor of law, were members, was appointed to examine into the constitution and ancient practice of the university. At the distance of about four months, a report was given in by this committee which is subscribed by Mr. John Miller, and also by Dr. Joseph Black, who was a defender when the present process was raised, and was approved of by the majority of an university meeting, at which all the defendants except Dr. Trail, were present, not one of them dissenting or making any objection to it whatever. This report, made by these very learned gentlemen, and which it must be presumed contained their real sentiments at the time, after the most diligent search into the records of the university, contradicts almost every word of what the defenders are now pleased to advance in their information.

When treating of this meeting composed of the principal and masters, and the powers competent to it, the report contains the following passages : " *That, with regard to the administration of the college-revenue, the ordinary management of it is, by the express words of the same charter*, (nova erectio), *committed to the principal and his ordinary colleagues and assessors the regents of the college.* The words which declare this follow immediately after the recital of the duties of the œconomus or provisor who is to collect the college-revenues, sue the college debtors, and provide necessaries for the college-table : [here the clauses in the *nova erectio* founded on by the pursuers are taken in]. By this passage it evidently appears, that the respective powers of the rector and principal, with regard to the administration of the revenue, were perfectly similar to the respective powers of the same magistrates, with regard to discipline : *That the ordinary management was in the principal and his colleagues or assessors the regents ; under the controul however of the rector and dean of faculty, by whose advice the surplus-revenue which remained after paying the salaries of the several officers of the college, and maintaining the college table, was to be employed.*

The committee having found the powers and jurisdiction of the principal as

---

[1] University MSS., vols. 41 and 43. *Additional Information for Dr. William Leechman and others against Doctor Robert Trail and others March* 9 1769 (University Library Y7—b. 19). Adam Smith's name is not mentioned, though he wrote the Report, possibly through his having resigned.

subordinate to that of the rector thus far established in the charter of new erection 1577, proceed next to enquire how far this power and jurisdiction had been confirmed, or abrogated by the subsequent custom and practice of the University ; and in consequence of this inquiry, find, *primo That from the time Principal* Gillespie was admitted in the year 1653, down to the year 1755, it is acknowledged by all parties, that the principal was in the use of holding meetings in which the rector was not present, and in which notwithstanding a great part of the college-business *of all kinds was transacted ; and, secundo, That this practice, of a hundred years standing, seems to be fully confirmed, supported and authorised by the statutes of the last visitation 1727,* which, tho' made to restrain the power of the principal within proper bounds, by the whole tenour of them, however, suppose that the principal has an undoubted power of calling and presiding in meetings for the despatch of college business." [Here are inserted the clauses of the statutes of royal visitation.] " By the whole tenour of the above statutes, it is evident that the principal is supposed to have a power of calling and presiding in meetings of faculty for the dispatch of college business. *This power accordingly was, as has already been observed, exercised by the principal, or, in his absence, by the eldest regent, without any challenge or interruption till the year 1755.* The late Principal Campbell was at that time indisposed, having some years before been struck down with a palsy, which, from the moment in which it seized him, rendered him incapable of attending to the business of the society. For some time after this misfortune had befallen the principal, Mr. Moor called and presided in faculty meetings, according to the above statutes of visitation. These faculties, however, appeared to have met more rarely towards the end of the year 1754." And with regard to the practice during Principal Stirling's time the report goes on thus : " The minutes during Principal Stirling's time appear to have been kept with much more accuracy and exactness than they had ever been before, as will be evident upon a very slight inspection of that book which contains the records of the society from the time of his admission to the 26th of February 1717. Even in his time, however, the records of three distinct meetings, viz. of that in which the rector presides, of that in which the dean of faculty presides, and of that in which the principal presides, are all kept in one and the same book : This too seems to have been pretty much the case from the time of the new erection, down to the time in which Mr. Simson was made clerk of the University, who introduced order and method into the affairs of the society in this respect, as well as in many others."

It can hardly be thought that the gentlemen who made up the report, and gave it to the meeting as containing the genuine sentiments of the Committee, and as a result of the accurate enquiries which they had made, could have afterwards authorized their counsel to aver before your Lordships that, till the time of the revolution, no such meeting existed as that composed of the principal and regents, except for exercising the ordinary discipline over the gown-students.

II. *Defender's Reply.*[1]

To put an end to disputes prejudicial to the welfare and tranquillity of the society a committee was appointed " to examine the statutes and practice of the university, with regard to the jurisdiction and powers of the rector, principal and dean of faculty, and to report."

The aim of the committee in their report was to reconcile, as far as possible, the opposite opinions of their brethren. Their intention was to suggest terms of accomodation to the contending parties, and, by proposing mutual concessions, to terminate disputes pernicious to their common welfare. They therefore proposed a certain distribution to be made of the university business between a meeting in which the rector or his deputy should preside, and another in which the principal should preside. To this conciliatory report, all the members of the society, except two, agreed ; and the defenders cannot help thinking that it would have been more expedient for the university still to have adhered to it, than to have involved themselves in expensive litigation.

Although, after a more accurate investigation of the University records, the opinion of this committee has been discovered to be, in some respects erroneous, yet it will be observed it was in almost every article contrary to the present claim of the pursuers, and particularly did not admit of any negative or visitorial power in the rector and dean of faculty.[2] Notwithstanding this, all the pursuers then in the university agreed to it, except two Dr. James Moor, and Mr. George Muirhead, who protested against it *as derogatory from the rights and privileges of the rector*, whom these gentlemen *then* understood to have a right to preside in all meetings concerning the management of the revenue.

III. *Further Memorial from Pursuer.*[3]

This report differing so widely from what the defenders now maintain, they would willingly explain to be merely a conciliatory proposition of the committee, such as might bring together the contending parties in the university.

The reverse of this appears in every line. What is quoted above, it is impossible to dispute, contains not the sentiments of the committee with regard to what *ought* to be the practice for the future, but their deliberate opinion, expressed as clearly as words can do it, of what had been the practice in times past. When the enquiries were made previous to this report, the minds of the persons engaged had not yet

---

[1] *A Memorial for Dr. Robert Traill and others against Dr. Leechman and others*, 9th January, 1770, p. 125 (Univ. Library, Y7—b. 19). This is expanded from a previous statement of 1769 by the same parties in *Additional Information for Dr. Robert Traill*, p. 44.

[2] This is an error, since such powers are mentioned in the Report more than once (see above, pp. 205-8). It is curious that, both here and in the Report, the name of the minister of Glasgow is omitted. He is included in the Judgement of the Court of Session, see below, p. 225.

[3] *Memorial for Dr. Leechman and others against Dr. Robert Traill*, 9th January, 1770, p. 43 (Univ. Library, Y7—b. 19).

LIST OF RECTORS, DEANS OF FACULTY, PRINCIPALS AND PROFESSORS AT THE UNIVERSITY OF GLASGOW, 1751-1776.

NOTE.—The Rector was elected on the 14th of November, the Dean on 26th of June. If a Rector was unable to attend the meetings of his Court he appointed a Vice-Rector when he was installed. In such cases the name of the Vice-Rector is printed below that of the Rector. An arrow indicates a transference from one Chair to another.

P = a pursuer in the action of Declarator; 1766-71, and D = a defender; P₁ = a pursuer in the action of Declarator in 1775 and D₁ = a defender in that action and before the visitors at Shaw Park, 1775 and 1776.

Year	Rectors	Deans of Faculty	Principals	Divinity	Greek	Logic	Moral Philosophy	Natural Philosophy	Mathematics (1691)	Humanity (1706)	Oriental Languages (1709)	Civil Law (1712)	Medicine (1712)	Church History (1716)	Anatomy (1718)	Astronomy (1760)	Year
1751	Sir John Maxwell, Bart., of Nether Pollok	William Leechman	Neil Campbell (1728)	William Leechman (1744)	James Moor (1746-74)	Adam Smith (1751)	Thomas Craigie (1746)	Robert Dick (1751)	Robert Simson (1711)	George Rosse (1735)	William Ruat (1751)	Hercules Lindesay (1750)	Robert Hamilton (1742)	William Anderson (1721)	William Cullen (1751)	—	1751
1752	William Muir of Caldwell	William Leechman				James Clow (to 1787)	Adam Smith				↓ William Ruat					—	1752
1753	William Muir of Caldwell	George Rosse								George Muirhead						—	1753
1754	John Boyle, Earl of Glasgow Robert Hamilton (Prof. of Medicine), V.-R.	George Rosse								George Muirhead (to 1773)	John Anderson					—	1754
1755	John Boyle, Earl of Glasgow R. Hamilton, V.-R. (to June 1756)	Robert Simson														—	1755
1756	Patrick Boyle William Leechman, Prof. of Divinity, V.-R., from June 1756	James Moor											Joseph Black		Robert Hamilton	—	1756
1757	Patrick Boyle William Leechman, V.-R.	James Moor											Thomas Hamilton (to 1781)		Joseph Black (to 1766)	—	1757
1758	James Milliken of Milliken William Leechman, V.-R.	Hercules Lindesay					John Anderson (to 1796)			James Buchanan					—	1758
1759	James Milliken of Milliken William Leechman, V.-R.	Hercules Lindesay														—	1759
1760	James Hay, Earl of Errol William Leechman, V.-R.	Adam Smith														Alex. Wilson (to 1784)	1760
1761	Earl of Errol William Leechman, V.-R. James Moor, V.-R.	Adam Smith	William Leechman (to 1786)	Robert Traill (to 1775)							Robert Traill Patrick Cummin	John Miller (to 1801)					1761
1762	Thomas Millar of Barskimming Adam Smith, Praeses and V.-R.	James Clow												William Wight (to 1778)			1762
1763	Thomas Millar Adam Smith, V.-R.	James Clow															1763
1764	William Muir of Caldwell James Clow, V.-R.		Leechman	Traill	Moor	Clow	Thomas Reid	Anderson	Williamson	Muirhead	Cummin	Millar	Hamilton	Wight	Black	Wilson	1764
1766-71			P	D	P	P	P	P	D	P	D	D	—	D	—	P	1766-71
1775-6			D₁	—	—	D₁	P₁	P₁	D₁	—	—	D₁	—	—	—	P₁	1775-6

been inflamed with the violence attending legal disputes ; and it is probable, that they really had in view to discover what was the true constitution and ancient practice of the University. Had this continued to be the only object of these gentlemen in their later inquiries it perhaps might have been found that they would not have departed so far from the opinions which they then entertained.

IV. *Decision in the Process of Declarator, November 22, 1770.*[1]

The Lords of Council find and declare,

1. That the whole revenue and property of the College of Glasgow (excepting such mortifications for bursars, and other uses which are otherwise conveyed) is, by the Foundation Charter, granted by King James VI. *anno* 1577, and by the other subsequent charters and grants, and the Statutes of the College, vested in the Principal and Masters of the said College ; and that the sole right and administration thereof belongs to them, the said Principal and Masters ; and consequently, that the Court of the Rector and his assessors, have no legal power or authority whatever to meddle with, or dispose of the College money, or revenue of the College, in all time coming.

2. That the Rector, and Dean of Faculty of the University of Glasgow and the Minister of the Town of Glasgow, are, by the said Foundation Charter, appointed Visitors of the said College ; by whose advice and consent only, or of a majority of them, all the surpluses of the College revenue, after paying the Master's salaries, and other standing burdens, are to be disposed of, and applied to pious and necessary uses of the College. And, therefore, That in all time coming, all acts and deeds whatsoever of the said Administrators, in disposing of such surpluses, shall be held to be null and void ; unless they bear that they were done by the express consent of the said visitors, or the majority of them.

3. That, agreeable to the said Foundation Charter, the Principal and Masters, as Administrators, are bound to lay the accounts of their administration of the Revenue of the College before the said Visitors, for their examination ; and that, without the approbation of the said visitors, the said accompts shall not be held valid and authentic.

For Leechman and others Dean, Lockhart, Sol[r], H. Dundas, R. Blair.
For Trail and others Ad[v], Montgomery, Macqueen, Cullen, Crosbie.

V. (*a*) *Sederunt at the first of the meetings of the Ordinary Visitors at Shaw Park.*[2]

at Shaw Park, Oct. 10th. 1775.

The ordinary Visitors of Glasgow College being met according to their adjournment of the third current. Present, The right honourable Lord Cathcart,

[1] *Decisions of the Court of Session*, Nov. 1769 to Jan. 1772, vol. li, Edin. 1803, pp. 142-146.

[2] Process of Declarator MDCCLXXV concerning the Management of the Revenue of Glasgow College. Printed MDCCLXXVIII (University Library, DO4—e. 19).

S.A.S.

Lord Rector, Mr. John Corse, Dean of Faculties, Mr. John Hamilton, Minister of Glasgow.

(b) Decree of the Ordinary Visitors at Shaw Park, October 12, 1775.

We, the ordinary Visitors of the College of Glasgow in consequence of the process of Declarator of Mr. John Anderson, against Dr. Robert Traill and others, having been remitted, by an interlocutor of Lord Elliock Ordinary,[1] pronounced by him on the 1st of August, 1775, agreeable to the desire of both parties, to be taken under cognisance, and decided by us, with a recommendation to proceed accordingly, with all convenient dispatch, FIND, DISCERN, AND DECLARE, That the Statutes of the Royal Visitation of the year 1727, are the rule to be observed by the College of Glasgow, in all points to which they extend ; that according to the said statutes, the accompts with the Factor ought to be kept in the regular way of book keeping ; that the Factor ought to sign each page of his accompts, and make oath upon them in terms of the statute ;[2] and to keep an exact Cash-Book, Journal, and Ledger, and make the same patent to the Masters, or any of them.

FIND AND DECLARE, That altho the above articles are precisely ordained by the statutes, and ought to have been strictly observed since the last Royal Visitation in the year 1727, they were not attended to by the Principal and Professors then in office, and that their successors have continued till this day in the ancient tract.

FIND AND DECLARE, That from hence forwards, the statutes ought to be rigidly observed, and enforced by the Faculty in the above, as well as in all other articles.

FIND AND DECLARE, That the Faculty ought to oblige their Factor, in order that his accompts may be kept in the regular, established, and universally received way of book keeping, to charge himself with the whole revenue of the College, discharging himself by his disbursements, by deductions, and by such rests as he has endeavoured by legal diligence to recover, or with respect to which he has been authorised by an order of the Faculty to grant delay ; such deductions and rests neither being objects of intromission nor of omission, for which he alone and his Caution [3] are answerable : and that he should charge himself, in the first article of the next accompt, with the sum of the said rests, as well as deductions, in order that whatever may, by further diligence, be recovered, may accrue to the credit of the College and the University.[4] But let it be observed, that we expect, that when the Faculty shall find it proper to grant indulgence, as aforesaid, to any of the per-

---

[1] James Veitch of Elliock, admitted advocate 1738, travelled on the Continent and became a friend of Frederick the Great; Sheriff-Depute of Peebles 1747, M.P. for Dumfries 1755-60, elevated to Bench in 1760 as Lord Elliock—Brunton and Haig, *Senators of the College of Justice*, p. 525.

[2] *Munimenta Alme Universitatis Glasguensis*, 1854, ii, p. 575.

[3] " Caution " here and below is the term in Scots Law for a surety.

[4] This was the main point urged by Anderson—University MSS., vol. 44.

sons liable in payment to them, they will do it with such caution, as that the interests of the College shall not be materially hurt thereby ; and that their indulgence to one, where it may be proper, may not open a door to others, where it may not be proper. In which view we recommend it to their consideration whether it may not be wise and prudent, that equality may be preserved, and that they themselves may be relieved from improper solicitations, to give to their Factor a general order in writing, authorizing him to suspend diligence against all persons liable in payment to the College, till such term, beyond the legal term, as they shall think proper, and shall have been approved of by the Visitors, when consulted by them ; and to take that opportunity of declaring, that that being the utmost latitude they can assume in the administration of an estate not their own, they are not at liberty, in any instance, to grant further indulgence : which order will place the Factor, and his caution, in the same point of security against the charge of omission, in case he does diligence at the term prescribed to him ; as if, without the order, he had done it at the legal term.

FIND AND DECLARE, that the Faculty ought to oblige the Factor to give in an exact signed list of rests, specifying and describing them, and distinguishing those on which he has done diligence, for the three [1] respective branches of the revenue, at every clearance ; whereby a full and single accompt may arise yearly, and the whole estate and condition of the University may appear at one view : and that they ought, from time to time, to expunge such deductions as are no longer necessary to be continued in their accompts, in order that the balance may be struck with as much exactitude as possible.

FIND AND DECLARE, That the Factor, who, according to the Statutes, is obliged to make up his accompts yearly, or oftener, if required, has bound himself in his factory, to make them up, and give them in, on the 12th. or 13th. of November, yearly ; but, after maturely considering what has been advanced by parties on this head, appoint the Faculty to make him give in his accompts for the Cropt 1775 on the 15th. or 16th. of March, 1777 ; and to observe this method in all time thereafter, that they may have sufficient leisure to examine and pass the said accompts yearly, before the vacation of the College ; leaving it with the Faculty to accompt with the Factor for crops 1773 and 1774, at the terms which shall to them appear most convenient for all concerned.

FIND AND DECLARE that such demands as the Factor has lately, and on former occasions, made of annual sums of money, over and above his yearly salary of sixty pounds sterling, are inconsistent with the statutes, and therefore inadmissible, and that the Faculty should oblige the Factor to give them, at every clearance, as full a discharge as he receives from them : and also directs the Faculty to discontinue,

---

[1] At this time these were the Ordinary or Original Revenue, the Tack of the Archbishopric and Revenue from the Sub-deanery. Later supplementary income and Exchequer Precepts were added—*Commission of 1826 and 1830 for Visiting the Universities of Scotland*, 1837, ii, pp. 304, 317-27.

in the docquets granted to their factor upon such occasions, the following clause, now in use to be inserted in it, viz. " But also, by these presents, empower him and his foresaids, to uplift and receive what is resting and owing unpaid by those liable in payment for the cropt and year   and to appropriate the same to his own use, in respect he has made thankful payment to us thereof, excepting the above balance, as said is," as such clause can have no place in accompts kept in the method appointed by this Decree.

CATHCART, Rector.
JOHN CORSE, Dean of Faculties.
JOHN HAMILTON, Minister of Glasgow.

(c) Decision on Reclaiming Petition against the Decree passed at Shaw Park on 12th October, 1775.[1]

Glasgow College, March 28th, 1776.

Present the right honourable the Lord Rector, the rev. Mr. John Corse, Dean of Faculties, and the rev. John Hamilton, Minister of Glasgow, Ordinary Visitors of Glasgow College.

THE VISITORS having taken under their consideration, the reclaiming petition against their Decree, made at Shaw Park on the 12th of October last, with the other papers presented to the Visitors, and proceedings had upon them. And having heard Principal Leechman, Mr. Clow and Mr. Millar in support of the reclaiming petition, and Dr. Reid and Mr. Anderson in support of the Decree, are of opinion, to refuse the reclaiming petition; and do refuse it accordingly; and so recommend to the Faculty to prepare and authenticate a proper mode, or form, for the Factor exhibiting a general annual accompt; agreeable to the directions, spirit, and intendment, of the Decree, and the form of the Docquet or discharge proper to be annexed to such accompt.

JAMES MONTGOMERY,[2] Rector.
JOHN CORSE, Dean of Faculties.
JOHN HAMILTON, Minister of Glasgow.

§ O—" ADAMUS SMITH, RECTOR MAGNIFICUS ".
I. *Elected by the four Nations, 1787.*

MDCCLXXXVII.[3]

Apud Collegium Glasguense die decimo quinto Novembris.

Comitiis Universitatis legitime citatis programmate Vice Rectoris et in aula publica legitime habitis.

---

[1] Process of Declarator MDCCLXXV concerning the Management of the Revenue of Glasgow College, Printed MCCLXXVIII—University Library, DO4—e. 19, p. 17.

[2] A Baron of the Exchequer in Scotland.   [3] University MSS., vol. 72, p. 36.

Professor Young electus est clericus comitiorum in annum sequentem.

Statutis de eligendo Rectore Magnifico perlectis et Academicis in quatuor nationes legitime divisis harum unaquaeque more solito Dominum Rectorem hujus Universitatis in annum sequentem eligebat.

Vir admodum honorabilis Dominus Adamus Smith L.L.D. e curatoribus, rebus portorii dirigendis praefectis, unus, et in hac Academia quondam Ethicis [sic] Professor, suffragiis omnium quatuor nationum electus est Rector Magnificus hujus Universitatis in Annum sequentem quod more solito et solenni in Comitiis promulgatum est.

10th June 1786 signed by us according to appointment of Senate of this date } ARCH: DAVIDSON
PAT WILSON CLER: SEN.

II. *Acceptance of Election.*

20th November, 1787.[1]

The Principal laid before the Meeting a Letter from Adam Smith L.L.D. Lord Rector elect in which he declares his acceptance of the office the tenor whereof follows

" Reverend and Dear Sir,

" I have this moment received the honour of your letter of the 15th instant. I accept with gratitude and pleasure, the very great honour which the University of Glasgow have done me in electing me for the ensuing year to be the Rector of that Illustrious Body. No preferment could have given me so much real satisfaction. No man can owe greater obligations to a Society than I do to the University of Glasgow. They educated me, they sent me to Oxford, soon after my return to Scotland they elected me one of their own Members, and afterwards preferred me to another office, to which the abilities and virtues of the never to be forgotten Dr. Hutcheson had given a superior degree of illustration. The period of thirteen years which I spent as a Member of that Society I remember as by far the most useful, and, therefore, as by far the happiest, and most honourable period of my life ; and now, after three and twenty years absence, to be remembered in so very agreeable manner by my old friends and protectors gives me a heartfelt joy which I cannot easily express to you.

I shall be happy to receive the commands of my Colleagues concerning the times when it may be convenient for them to do me the honour of admitting me to the office. Mr. Millar mentions Christmass. We have commonly at the board of Customs a vacation of five or six days at that time. But I am so regular an attendant that I think myself entitled to take the play for a week at any time. It will be no inconvenience to me, therefore to wait upon you at whatever time you

[1] University MSS., vol. 72, p. 38.

please. I beg to be remembered to my Colleagues in the most respectful and most affectionate manner; and that you would believe me to be, with great truth, Reverend and dear Sir

Your and their most obliged
most obedient and most humble servant
(Signed) ADAM SMITH.

Edinburgh
16.Nov.1787
The Rev^d. Dr. Archibald Davidson
Principal of the College, Glasgow.

III. *Installation and Appointment of a Vice-Rector.*

MDCCLXXXVII.[1]

Apud Collegium Glasguense die Decimo nono Decembris :

Comitiis Universitatis legitime citatis programmate vice Rectoris et in Aula publica legitime habitis.

Vir admodum honorabilis Dominus Adamus Smith L.L.D. e curatoribus, rebus portorii dirigendis praefectis, unus, et in hac Academia quondam Ethices Professor, munus Rectoris Magnifici, ad quod electus fuerat, in se suscepit et hoc Juramento sese obstrinxit.

Ego Adamus Smith promitto sancteque polliceor me in muneris mihi demandati ratione obeunda studiose fideliterque versaturum.

ADAMUS SMITH

Eodem tempore Assessores nominavit Decanum Facultatum hujus Universitatis, praefectum Collegii Glasguensis, et omnes Professores in eodem Collegio.

Apparitorem nominavit Johannem McLachlan

ADAMUS SMITH RECTOR.

Glasgow College 19th Decr. 1787.

Present   Adam Smith L.L.D. Lord Rector
The Reverend Dr. Alexander Hutcheson D.FF.

Dr. Archibald Davidson	Dr. Thomas Reid P.M.P.
Principal	Mr. William Richardson L.H.P.
Dr. Robert Findlay S.S.T.P.	Mr. John Young L.G.P.
Mr. John Millar I.C.P.	Dr. Hugh McLeod H.E.P.
Mr. Patrick Cumin L.O.P.	Mr. William Hamilton A. et B.P.
Dr. James Williamson	Mr. Patrick Wilson A.P.P.
Math.P.	Mr. George Jardine P.P.

A Meeting of the Senate being duly summoned and convened.

The Lord Rector by the advice and with the consent of the Senate appoints Mr. William Richardson Professor of Humanity to execute the office and to have

---

[1] University MSS., vol. 72, p. 39.

the full Power of the Rector in his absence ; except the Visitorial Power given the Rector by the Nova Erectio, and such other Powers as are given to the Rector, in particular Deeds of Mortification, without any mention of the Rector.

IV. *Re-appointed*, 1788.

MDCCLXXXVIII.[1]

Apud Collegium Glasguense die vigesimo septimo Novembris.

Comitiis Universitatis legitime citatis Programmate vice Rectoris et in Aula publica legitime habitis.

Vir Admodum honorabilis Dominus Adamus Smith L.L.D. e curatoribus rebus portorii dirigendis praefectis, unus, et in hac Academia quondam Ethices Professor, munus Rectoris Magnifici, ad quod electus fuerat, in se suscepit et hoc Juramento sese obstrinxit.

Ego Adamus Smith promitto sancteque polliceor me in muneris mihi demandati ratione obeunda studiose fideliterque versaturum.

ADAMUS SMITH

Eodem tempore assessores nominavit Decanum Facultatum hujus Universitatis, praefectum Collegii Glasguensis, et omnes Professores in eodem Collegio.

Apparitorem nominavit Johannem McLachlan.

ADAMUS SMITH RECTOR.

Glasgow College 27 Novr. 1788.

Present   Adam Smith L.L.D. Lord Rector
The Reverend Dr. James Meek D.F.F.

Dr. Archibald Davidson Princ^l.	Dr. Alexander Stevenson Med.P.
Dr. Robert Findlay S.S.T.P.	Mr. William Richardson L.H.P.
Mr. John Millar I.C.P.	Mr. John Young L.G.P.
Mr. Patrick Cumin L.O.P.	Dr. Hugh Macleod H.E.P.
Dr. James Williamson Math.P.	Mr. William Hamilton A. et B.P.
Dr. Thomas Reid P.M.P.	Mr. Patrick Wilson A.P.P.

Mr. George Jardine P.P.

A Meeting of Senate being duly summoned and convened.

The Lord Rector by the advice and with the consent of the Senate appoints Mr. William Richardson Prof^r. of Humanity to execute the office and to have the full Power of the Rector in his absence ; except the visitorial Power given the Rector by the Nova Erectio and such other Powers as are given to the Rector in particular Deeds of Mortification without any mention of the Vice Rector.

---

[1] University MSS., vol. 72, pp. 60-1. It will be noted that in the nomination of a Vice-Rector in 1787 there are certain exceptions to his exercise of the power of the Rector, amongst them control of mortifications without any mention of the Rector. In the corresponding nomination of 1788 the proviso is " without any mention of the Vice-Rector "—the word " Vice " having been inserted by Adam Smith himself.

§ P—LETTERS FROM, TO, OR RELATING TO ADAM SMITH

I. *Adam Smith to William Smith " at the Duke of Argyle's House in Brutin St."* [1]

Oxon: Aug 24, 1740.

Sir,

I yesterday receiv'd your letter with a bill of sixteen pounds enclos'd, for which I humbly thank you, but more for the good advice you were pleas'd to give me. I am indeed affraid that my expenses at college must necessarily amount to a much greater sum this year than at any time hereafter, because of the extraordinary and most extravagant fees we are obliged to pay the College and University on our admittance; it will be his own fault if any one should endanger his health at Oxford by excessive Study, our only business here being to go to prayers twice a day and to lecture twice a week.

I am, dear Sir,
Your most oblig'd Servant,
ADAM SMITH.

II. *From Adam Smith to his Mother.* [2]

Adderbury
Oct. 23, 1741

Dear Mother,

I have been these fourteen days last past here at Adderbury with Mr. Smith; the Place is agreeable enough, and there is a great deal of good company in the town.

In my last letter I desir'd you to send me some Stockings, the sooner you send 'em the better. I have taken this opportunity to write to you, and to give my service to all friends, tho' as you see, I have not very much to say,

I am,
Dear Mother, your most Affectionate son,
ADAM SMITH.

---

[1] Bannerman MSS., Univ. Libry. Glasg. William Smith was, at this time, Secretary to John, second Duke of Argyle. He was a tutor and curator of Adam Smith (see above, p. 35). Some particulars of his career are given in Appendix I.

[2] Bannerman MSS., Univ. Libry. Glasg. The "Mr. Smith" mentioned in this letter is the William Smith to whom Adam Smith had written in the previous August. In view of what has been said elsewhere, the address, Adderbury, is of great interest. A year later the eldest daughter of the Duke of Argyle married Francis, Earl of Dalkeith. It was her son, the Duke of Buccleuch, with whom Adam Smith went to France from 1764 to 1766. The letter engaging him was written from Adderbury—Rae, *Life*, p. 165.

III. *Adam Smith to his Mother.*[1]

[Balliol]   May 12th [? 1742]

Dear Mother,

I take this opportunity of writing to you by a Gentleman of my acquaintance who sets out for Scotland tomorrow. The Certificate of my age which I mentioned in my last Letters will not be necessary so soon as I then expected ; if you have not sent already, it will come in full time if you give [it] to Mr. Smith [2] when he returns from Scotland. I told you in my last to inform Mr. Smith that one of the £40 Exhibitions would shortly be vacant, in case that he intended to make interest for any of his friends. It will not however be vacant so soon as I expected. The Gentleman who carrys this to Edinb^{gh} (one Mr. Preston [3]) I have been very much oblig'd to. He will probably be at Kirkcaldy and will wait upon you before he leaves Scotland.

I am Dear Mother
Yours &c.
A. S.

IV. *Alexander Wedderburn to Adam Smith.*[4]

Baliol College,
Oxford March 20 [? 1754].

Dr Smith,

I should endeavour to make my way to you by an Apology for not having wrote during so long a period as we have been absent from each other, were I not perfectly satisfied That It must be unnecessary. Though I have not heard once from you since we parted, I make very little Doubt that I have been frequently in your Thoughts. I judge so, because amidst all the variety of Objects which have since, I may rather say distracted than, interested me, I have always in my best hours of Reflexion had my Thoughts turned towards you. If you judge by the

---

[1] Bannerman Papers, Univ. Libry. Glasg.

[2] Probably the William Smith mentioned in the previous letters.

[3] The Exhibition shortly expected to be vacant appears to have been a Snell held by the John Preston alluded to in the next sentence. He was a younger son of Sir George Preston, Bart., of Valleyfield. His resignation took effect in 1743. The next vacancy did not occur till 1747.

[4] Bannerman MSS., Univ. Libry. Glasg. This letter is not without difficulty. Assigning it to Alexander Wedderburn, afterwards Lord Loughborough and Earl of Rosslyn, involves an extension of the time he spent in England as recorded by John Lord Campbell in *Lives of Lord Chancellors*, 1847, vi, pp. 13-15. Wedderburn was a student at Glasgow in 1748. He attended Adam Smith's lectures in Edinburgh probably in 1750-1, and, then or before, Adam Smith had given him great encouragement. Wedderburn had a desire to qualify for the English bar and entered at the Inner Temple on 8th May, 1753. On this occasion he only remained a few weeks in England. It was probably the next year, under the circumstances explained later in the letter, that he visited Balliol, whence he wrote. Campbell mentions that Adam Smith frequently corresponded with him.

same Rule, you will not infer from my Silence either Neglect or Forgetfulness. You may very possibly conclude that I have been Giddy, Idle and dissipated and I am afraid w^h great Truth. The only Merit I can pretend is the being sensible of my Follies, even whilst I was most engaged in them and the having at length made my Escape from them. You have inquired, I dare say, sometimes about me and have very like been Told I was perfectly Idle and followed nothing but pleasure. I have not studied enough to be able to contradict This intirely, but I have paid some little Attention to the Courts of Law here and have even read a little of my Ld Coke. My acquaintance at London was grown so large and was so much more engaging than my Business that I could not well carry on both in the same place. I have had Resolution enough to leave Town and am now at your old habitation, Oxford, where the acquaintances I have found are so totally different from those I have left that my Studies run no risk of being much interrupted. It has occurred to me since I came here that, on the plan I should wish to pursue, I could make one of the Scotch Exhibitions very serviceable to me. I make no Ceremony in mentioning it to you nor no preamble but that I believe it would be an Advantage to me and that you would be of the same opinion, if I had time to lay all the Circumstances before you. One of Them, Dr. Smith's,[1] must be vacant soon in course. There is another which will in all probability be vacant, as the Gentleman is thought to be in the utmost Hazard. I am sufficiently qualified by my standing and should have some Friends at Glasgow. Do you think I should have any Difficulty in getting The Nomination? It is a Thing I would rather wish to be offered than to ask and that, at any rate, I would not seem to take too much pains upon nor ask w^h the least chance of a Disappointment.[2] I have not mentioned this to anyone but yourself, nor shall I till I hear from you. If it is necessary, to prevent a pre-engagement, to take any Step in it, you can be the best judge, only I should wish to be as little mentioned in it as possible and, especially while my Father[3] is not acquainted w^h

---

[1] John Smith was born at Maybole, Ayrshire, c. 1721, matriculated at Glasgow 1736, at Balliol 1744—B.A. 1748, M.A. 1751, B.Med. 1753, D.Med. 1757 (from St. Mary's Hall). He vacated the Snell exhibition in 1755. A. Carlyle speaks of him as "an eminent practitioner". He was elected Savilian Professor of Geometry in 1766—W. I. Addison, *Snell Exhibitioners*, 1901, p. 45. The gentleman " in the utmost hazard " of the next sentence cannot be identified with any certainty. In spite of Mr. Addison's great labour on the history of these early exhibitioners, considerable gaps remain. It is true that there were two vacancies in 1755. Besides that through the resignation of John Smith, there was another by that of Alexander Campbell, but if he was the Alexander Campbell of the Council of Bengal, he was not in great hazard through illness. Could he have been sent down, as he resigned three years before the expiration of his exhibition?

[2] There was an election in 1750. Then there were two in 1755—" Mr. Bruce ", possibly James Bruce, son of William, Earl of Elgin, and George Wilsone, of whom there are no particulars except that he was third son of William Wilson, writer, in Stirlingshire. There is no trace of his career at Oxford.

[3] Peter Wedderburn, admitted advocate 1715, assessor of City of Edinburgh and secretary to the Excise, raised to the Bench as Lord Chesterhall in 1755, died 1756.

my Intentions. I know you don't love College Business but this, I hope, can scarcely be an affair of any Trouble.

    Believe me, my Dr Smith, with the same affection as ever,
                Your Sincere Friend,
                                ALEX^r WEDDERBURN.

Shall I hear from you soon?

    V. *From Adam Smith, Collector of Customs at Alloa, to Adam Smith, Professor at Glasgow.*[1]

                                            Alloa,
                                    27 Augt. 1754.

Dr Cusine,

    I have your favours the answer to which has been retarded by my being for some days in the Highlands. I am sorry you did not know when I left London. I would have wrote you again upon the subject in question after I came to Scotland, but I have only seen the Gentleman with whom I was to commune on the matter and am to see him again in a few dayes. I gave the Duke of Argyll a Memoriall anent some of my own affairs which his Grace said he would consider and upon which my answer much depends, but if your friend expects such easy purchase, he will be mistaken in me for my Office here is above 200 Pounds [2] per ann: and I do not think I would resign it under ten years purchase. I would have advised you when I came to Edin^b which was in the end of June but I did not apprehend your friend would have proceeded a step till you heard from me. The Duke was gone from Edin^b before I came there, therefore I could not know his opinion of the affair I laid before him. If I knew the small office your friend has in view I could tell you if it would suit his Taste, and in ten Dayes time I can give you this Gentleman's.... I have in view in ten days and with respect to my own you will see my situation.

    I intend to go into the Shyre of Air in a month's time to see Lord Dumfries and some others. I think you would not be the worse to take a jant that way, it would be good for your health, and amuse you.

    Our compliments to my Aunt Jane,
                      Dr. Cus.
                            Yours most Sincerely,
                                    ADAM SMITH.

---

[1] Papers of Miss Cunningham, Hereford. The writer of the letter was born in Aberdeen in 1711. In 1752 he had a wife and four children—MS. " List of the Officers of the Customs and Salt Duty in Scotland ", Register House, Edinburgh.

[2] It is generally understood that the actual income of a Collector was double the official salary. This Adam Smith in 1752 received £30 a year as Collector of Customs; he had an equal amount as Collector of the Salt Duty, and he may have had other smaller offices. Thus his estimate of the actual income appears to be considerably overstated, but he was in the position of a vendor—and an Aberdonian.

VI. *Adam Smith to William Johnstone.*[1]

Glasgow,
19 August 1758.

Dear Johnstoune :

 I am much obliged to you for your attention in mentioning me to Mr. Elliot.[2] I have the greatest desire to see him but have been looking in the map & find Minto above three score mortal miles from Glasgow the nearest way you can go to it. This abates my ardor a good deal. However I shall take the affair ad avisandum.

 I send you enclosed a portion of a letter I received last night from Captain Gordon ; it is of an early date, but it had come under cover to another Gentleman who was out of the way. It is [n]ot what I expected. I had told him that we might make a demand upon him for one or two hundred pounds & tho he gives me here an unlimited commission we must not abuse generosity but confine our demand to a sum within the largest of the two, & the more within it the better. Show this letter to John Hume & if you can to James Russell ; & let me know by next post if possible what sum will be wanted from him.[3]

 I ever am, Dear Johnstoune, ever yours

ADAM SMITH.

VII. *From Adam Ferguson to* ———.[4]

London, Aprile 17th 1759.

Dear S^r,

 I have just received your obliging letter and notwithstanding the other Prospect Home[5] mentioned to you, which is precarious, I will make some enquirys about what you mention. When I heard some time ago that Mr. Ruat was engaged to go abroad with Lord Hope I was told at the same time that he had obtained leave to keep his Professorship but that The D. of Argyle had insisted upon having the salary for some other purpose of a public nature during his absence.[6] If that matter is intirely at the disposal of people here, my information

---

[1] Pierpont Morgan Library, New York. As to William Johnstone, see above, p. 63.

[2] Probably Gilbert Elliot—see below, p. 239.

[3] Possibly this paragraph relates to the Glasgow Academy of Art. In the end of 1757 there were schemes for providing funds for this undertaking. One method was that supporters of it subscribed certain sums in return for which each was entitled to works of art equal in value to the amount of his contribution. Dalrymple wrote that he proposed to consult " Mr. Elliot " about this scheme while in London during the spring of 1758—*Notices and Documents illustrative of the Literary History of Glasgow*, 1831, pp. 28, 84, 85. The " John Hume " mentioned was John Home, author of *Douglas*.

[4] Bannerman Papers, Univ. Libry. Glasg.

[5] Author of *Douglas* and other poems. The two prospects are detailed in Rae, *Life*, p. 142.

[6] The circumstances relating to Ruat's Chair are recorded above, pp. 190-94.

is probably right, yours seems to imply that the College will interpose and in that case the matter may be still uncertain. I have seen your Brother once or twice with John Home and that acquaintance has given me great pleasure, he has a great deal of Lord Elibank's ingenuity of whom he talked by the hour with great understanding.[1]

You'll have heard of J. Dalrymple's [2] Scuffle. It raised a sort of Laugh against the Scotch Lawyers, but Jack by good luck had none of the ridicule but what was forced upon him. The other sent a Challenge to hinder his pleading a cause in which it seems he himself was formerly employed in Scotland. Jack went first to Mr. Elliot to advise about this comical situation, who remitted him to Sir Henry Erskine and by him the answer to the Challenge was dictated viz. That as he was engaged to plead the cause in question on the Wednesday following he could not in honour expose his Life till he had acquitted himself of that trust, that afterwards he would be ready [to] wait upon him. After sending this answer Jack stepped in to the Coffee house where he met his antagonist and being pressed to an immediate engagement, declined it upon Sir Harry's principle and was called Scoundrel and Coward upon the Spot, which provoked him to draw and a Scuffle ensued in which the Combatants tumbled over chairs but were prevented from doing more mischief by some gentlemen from the other end of the room who attended them up Stairs and made up the Quarrel before they parted. I send you this account partly to amuse you in case you have not heard it so particularly, and partly on Jack's account because such things are often misrepresented.

We have scarcely heard of any thing this winter but Scotch authors. We have been impatient for Smith's book some time and I was vexed to hear Miller had some doubts about publishing it this season, however you will probably know more of that from himself. There is a History of Gustavus published, which looks as like Hume and Robertson on the outside as can be conceived but it is the most amazing stuff that ever was seen. Remember me to all Friends at Edinburgh and Glasgow. I am, Dear S^r with the most sincere affection,

Your most faithfull and most humble servant,

ADAM FERGUSON.

[1] The reference to the brother of the recipient of the letter gives a hint as to who he was. Amongst ministers Ferguson's chief friends were Drs. Robertson, Blair, Drysdale, Cleghorn, A. Carlyle, Ballantyne and Logan, and amongst laymen Patrick, Lord Elibank, Gilbert Elliot of Minto, Wedderburn, afterwards Lord Loughborough, Mure of Caldwell and W. Johnston, later Sir W. Pulteney. Evidently the person to whom Adam Ferguson wrote sent the letter to Adam Smith, on account of the allusion to him at the end. He may well have been Mure of Caldwell, who had been Rector from 1752 to 1754.

[2] Author of *An Essay towards a General History of Feudal Property in Britain*, 1757, and other works; afterwards a Baron of the Exchequer.

VIII. *Andrew Millar to Adam Smith.*[1]

Presented of Mr. Smith's "Theory of Moral Sentiments" in half binding—Earl of Bute—Earl of Hardwicke—Dr. Markham—Mr. Selwyn—Earl of Shelburne—Lord Mansfield—Mr. Hume—Ld Lyttleton—Dr. Warburton—Mr. Elliot—Mr. Wedderburn—Mr. Jennings—Duke of Argyle—Mr. Walpole—Mr. Burke—Dr. Birch—Charles Townshend Esq.—Mr. Solicitor General.[2]

Dear Sir, London, 26 April 1759.

I rec^d ye errata w^c are printed and I made ½ sheet of Contents, w^c makes ye whole book 34 Sh[eets] a cheap 6^s vol b^d especially considering ye Matter w^c I am sure is excellent

The above 18 copys have been d^d by ye order of Messrs Hume, Wedderburn and John Dalrymple. I think of 2 more to ye authors of ye Rivews w^c will make 20. I Propose 10 of them in a Present to you and ye other is to be charged 2£, the price to B[ookselle]rs taking a n^o as they were only delivered to the Persons in blue Paper & boards so ye 3^d of ye difference is to be by Kincaid & Bell p^d y^o & ye other 2. 3^{ds} of the copy right by me.

Mr Rose at Kew, whom Rouet[3] knows well, took 25 copys to dispose amongst his friends, y^t I have no sort of doubt of this Impression being soon gone though it will not be published till next week, before w^c I shall ship Mr Kincaid w^c I hope will sail next week w^t convoy.

Mrs Millar joins w^t me in our kind remembrance of y^r Mother y^o and all friends, and I am

D S^r

Y^{rs} most sincerely

AND. MILLAR.

IX. *William Robertson to Adam Smith.*

My Dear Sir, Ed^r 14th June, [? 1759].[4]

Our friend John Home arrived here from London two days ago. Tho' I dare say you have heard of the good reception of the *Theory* from many different

---

[1] Bannerman MSS., Univ. Libry. Glasg.

[2] Several of these names appear in Hume's letter to Adam Smith of 12th April, 1759, and the chief facts about them are given in Professor Greig's notes in *Letters of Hume*, i, p. 303. Of the others, whose names have not yet occurred, Dr. Birch (1705-66) was the author of the *History of the Royal Society* and many other works. George Augustus Selwyn (1719-91) was the wit and friend of Horace Walpole. "Mr. Jennings" is Soame Jenyns and "Mr. Solicitor General", Charles Yorke (1722-70), who was appointed to this office on 8th December, 1756; he became Attorney General in 1762 and finally Lord Chancellor, though he only held the last dignity for a few days in January 1770.

[3] This reference is of interest as showing that Ruat and Adam Smith remained on friendly terms after Adam Smith had to take the steps against him which have been already described, pp. 190-94.

[4] Bannerman MSS., Univ. Libry. Glasg.

people, I must acquaint you with the intelligence Home brings.[1] He assures me that it is in the hands of all persons of the best fashion ; that it meets with great approbation both on account of the matter and stile ; and that it is impossible for any book on so serious a subject to be received in a more gracious manner. It comforts the English a good deal to hear that you were bred at Oxford, they claim some part of you on that account. Home joins with me in insisting that your next work shall be on some subject less abstruse. I still wish you would think on the History of Philosophy. I write this in great haste as Johnstone is waiting me that we may go to walk. When shall we see you in town ?
I ever am yours most faithfully
WILLIAM ROBERTSON.

X. *Gilbert Elliot of Minto to Adam Smith.*[2]

London,
14th Nov^r, 1758.

Dear Sir,
I have of late had a good deal of conversation with Lord Fitzmorris [3] about the education of his Brother who is now at Eaton and I believe about fifteen or sixteen years of age. He thinks his Brother too young to go abroad ; and, as he left Oxford himself about two years ago, has no sort of inclination to send him to that University. After stating to him, as well as I could, the nature of our Universitys and the advantage, I thought, his Brother might draw from being put under your direction, he came to a resolution of advising his Father, Lord Shelburn to follow that course. His Lordship has agreed to it, and I have undertaken to open it to you and to learn as soon as possible whether it

[1] As to John Home's movements about the time this letter was written *cf.* Life prefixed to Collected Ed. of his *Works*, 1822, i, p. 58, and A. Carlyle, *Autobiography*, 1860, p. 398. The Johnstone mentioned at the end may have been the same person as that noted above, p. 102.

[2] Bannerman Papers, Univ. Libry. Glasg. Gilbert Elliot, afterwards third baronet of Minto (1722-77), the grandson of a Senator of the College of Justice and son of a Lord Justice Clerk, was distinguished as a statesman, poet and philosopher. As the first he obtained the approval of Walpole, who described him as one of the ablest members of the House of Commons. Scott praised his poems, particularly the ballad " Amynta ", and Hume paid attention to his criticism of his theories.

[3] Lord William Fitzmaurice, son of Hon. John Fitzmaurice, who was a grandson of Sir William Petty and inherited his estates ; he was created Earl of Shelburne in 1753. His son, Lord William, succeeded, as second Earl, in 1761. He reached the rank of General in the Army, and entered politics. After filling several offices, he was appointed Prime Minister in 1782, in succession to the Marquis of Rockingham, and was created Marquis of Lansdowne in 1784. He had one brother, the Hon. Thomas Fitzmaurice, who matriculated at Glasgow in 1759, then went to Oxford where he graduated M.A. in 1764. He became a barrister and sat in Parliament for Co. Kerry 1763-8, Calne 1768-74, Wycombe 1774-80. He was High Sheriff in 1781. He married Mary O'Brien, Countess of Orkney in her own right. He died in 1793. His recollections of Adam Smith were vivid, and he always spoke of him with the greatest admiration—*Memoir of James Currie*, 1831, ii, p. 317.

be agreeable to you to undertake the charge. Lord Shelburn has an immense estate, and can afford, if he pleases, to settle ten thousand a year upon his second son, without at all hurting Lord Fitzmorris. He tells me he will not spare money but did not wish the boy should be indulged in too great an expense, which, I am affraid, has hitherto been the case. He proposes that he should be in your house and intirely under your direction, and to give you for his board and the inspection of his education a hundred pound a year, or more, if it should be thought proper. I understand he is a very good school scholar, very lively and tolerably ungovernable, but probably will not give you much trouble, as you will have the total charge and direction without any controul. If you have no objection to taking him into your house, he will come to you immediately, as Lord Fitzmorris tells me he may probably take that opportunity of runing over Scotland, paying a visit to Lord Dunmore [1] and puting his Brother upon a proper foot. I think myself that a young man of this rank coming to your University may be of advantage to it, especially as I find every thinking man here begins to discover the very absurd constitution of the English Universitys, without knowing what to do better. It is indeed possible that Oxford may a little recover itself by having lately established there a Professor for the common constitutional law of the Kingdom, and also admitted Masters for some of the exercises, which two last articles have some connection, at least, with the occupations of ordinary life, and I can hardly say so much for the usual academical institutions, little adapted for the improvement of young men either of rank or liberal views. I have little doubt but you might soon draw a good many of the youth of this part of the world to pass a winter or two at Glasgow, notwithstanding the distance and disadvantage of the dialect provided that to your real advantages you were to add the best Masters for the exercises and also for acquiring the french language, an accomplishment indispensably necessary, and which cannot be acquired either at Eaton or Westminster,[2] tho' all the children, male and female bred in their father's houses, are regularly taught both to speak and write french with tolerable facility. Pray let me have your answer as soon as possible.

Is your book in the Press or will it be there soon?

Believe me Dr Sir

Yours very faithfully

GILB. ELLIOT.

[1] John, fourth Earl of Dunmore, who had married Lady Charlotte Stewart earlier in this year.

[2] It is probably through this and similar requests that Smith is found very soon afterwards advocating the establishment, in connection with the University, of an Academy for dancing, fencing and riding—J. Coutts, *Hist. of Univ. of Glasgow*, 1909, p. 223, *cf.* above, p. 149. As to French, from 1730 the University made a small grant to a competent Frenchman to teach this language. Later one of the Professors taught French and another Italian. During this century German was neglected. The *Library Catalogue* of 1791 reveals a curious state of affairs in this respect. While there was information as to the history, the religion and social conditions in Germany, it was all in Latin. No work in German has been traced in that *Catalogue*.

CORRESPONDENCE

XI. *Adam Smith to Lord Fitzmaurice at the Earl of Shelburne's house, Hanover Square, London.*[1]

Glasgow College.
21. Feb. 1759.

My Lord,

I give you the Trouble of this Letter, tho I have nothing particular to inform you of besides what I told you in my last, that Mr. Fitzmaurice attends all his classes with the most exact particularity and gives more application to his studies than could reasonably be expected. I find him perfectly tractable and docile in every respect and I heartily wish that we may give the same satisfaction to him which he gives to all of us. I find that he is so far advanced in the Greek language that it will not be difficult to carry him on and if he continues to be as regular as at present, I believe, I can promise that against this time twelve-month he will be able to read it with ease. He masters all that he is about at present so easily that I intend in about a month hence he should begin to learn Algebra and Arithmetic with the Proffessor of Mathematics.

This country is so barren of all sorts of transactions y^t can interest anybody that lives at a distance from it that little intertainment is to be expected from any correspondent on this side the tweed. Our epistles to our friends at the capital commonly consist more in enquiries than in informations. I must therefore put your Lordship in mind of the promise you was so good as to make to me of some times letting me hear from you of what passes in the Great World, either at home or abroad. I hear there is no faction in parliament, which I am glad of. For tho' a little faction now and then gives spirit to the nation the continuance of it obstructs all public business and puts it out of the power of the best Minister to do much good. Even Sir Robert Walpole's administration would, I imagine have been better had it not been for the violence of the opposition that was made to it, which in the beginning had no great foundation. There is at present so little noise made about our own affairs y^t the Portuguese Conspiracy takes up a good part of the attention of this part of the world. I see this day in the newspapers an abstract of the evidence or rather of the facts for which these unhappy noblemen have been condemned.[2] In the end of it they found a great deal upon the presumptions of law which were against them which, as no other evidence is particularly specified, makes me fear that this horrid execution has been a little precipitate. For want of some thing else to write to your Lordship

---

[1] Papers from the Bowood Library in the possession of the Marquis of Lansdowne.

[2] The conspiracy of 3rd September, 1758, was ruthlessly crushed by the Marquis de Pombal, the Prime Minister. The Duke of Aveiro and the Marquis of Tavora were broken alive on the wheel, the sons and a son-in-law of the Duke were strangled and the wife of the Marquis was beheaded.

I am obliged to talk to you of subjects you must not only know much better than I, but which you must be quite sick of.

> I am, with the greatest regard
> Your Lordships Most Obedient and Most Humble Servant,
> ADAM SMITH.

XII. *Adam Smith to Lord Shelburne.*[1]

Glasgow,
10 Mar. 1759.

My Lord,

I have been very much out of my Duty in having so long neglected to write to your Lordship who have trusted me with so important a charge as the education of Mr. Fitzmaurice. I waited till I could say some thing to your Lordship with regard to what I expected of him which might be depended upon, and I can now venture to assure your Lordship that the fault ought to be laid to my charge if he does not turn out at least an uncommonly good scholar. There is not a poor boy in the college who is supported by charity and studies for bread that is more punctual in his attendance upon every part of College discipline. He attends different Masters for Greek, Latin and Philosophy five hours a day, and is besides employ'd with me at home between two and three hours in going over the subjects of those different lectures. He reads, too, every day some thing by himselfe and a good deal on Saturdays and Sundays when he has most leisure. He has never yet missed a Single hour, except two days that he was ill of a very violent Cholic, occasioned by cold and, I suspect, by the want of his usual exercise, which, I find, was very violent at Eton and for which he has at present no leisure. It was with the greatest difficulty that I could keep him at home for those two days. He is perfectly sober, eats no supper, or what is next to none, a roasted apple or some such trifle and drinks scarce any thing but water. There is the more merit in this part of his conduct as it is the effect of Resolution not of habit, for I find he has been accustomed to a different way of living at Eton. But your Lordships and My Lady Shelburne's [2] good advice has, I understand, produced this change. I can assure your Lordship that I have conversed with him for these two months with the greatest intimacy and that I find him every way agreeable ; full of spirit and sensibility, two qualities which are very rarely joined together. I have a great deal more to say to your Lordship, but an unexpected call obliges me to conclude this letter abruptly. I shall write to your Lordship again by next at greater Length. I have delayed writing so long that I was ashamed to delay it

---

[1] Papers from the Bowood Library, in the possession of the Marquis of Lansdowne.

[2] Mary, daughter of the Hon. William Fitzmaurice of Gallane, Co. Kerry. She was a cousin of the Hon. John Fitzmaurice (afterwards Earl of Shelburne) to whom this letter was written. They were married in 1734.

any longer, so snatched the first quarter of an hour which business of this [1] afforded me to scrawl this Letter

I am, with the greatest respect
Your Lordship's most obedient and most humble Servant,
ADAM SMITH.

XIII. *Adam Smith to Lord Shelburne.*[2]

Glasgow College,
4 April 1759.

My Lord,

I did myselfe the honour to write to your Lordship some time ago and promised to write more distinctly by next post. It was not in my Power to keep my word. A slight indisposition which has hung about me ever since, joined to a multiplicity of business which several accidents have conspired to bring upon me, have kept me either so exhausted or so hurried that till this moment I have not had one hour in which I had both leisure and spirits to sit down to write to your Lordship.

I have nothing to add to what I said to your Lordship in my Last letter concerning Mr Fitzmaurice's behaviour here. It has hitherto been altogether unexceptionable.

With regard to the Plan which I would propose for his education while he continues here; he will finish his Philosophical studies next winter; and as my Lord Fitzmaurice seemed to propose that he should stay here another year after that, I w^d propose that it should be employed in perfecting himselfe in Philosophy [3] and the Languages, but chiefly and principally in the Study of Law and history. In that year I would advise him to attend the Lectures of the Proffessor of Civil Law: for tho' the Civil Law has no authority in the English courts, the study of it is an admirable preparation for the study of ye English Law. The Civil Law is digested into a more regular system than the English Law has yet been, and tho' the Principles of the former are in many respects different from those of the latter, yet there are many principles common to both, and one who has studied the Civil Law at least knows what a system of law is, what parts it consists of, and how these ought to be arranged: so that when he afterwards comes to study the law of any other country which is not so well digested, he carries at least the idea of a system in his head and knows to what part of it he ought to refer every thing

---

[1] The letter (as the context shows) was written in great haste and several words have been interlined. That required here was overlooked.

[2] Papers in the Bowood Library, in the possession of the Marquis of Lansdowne.

[3] " Philosophy " included Natural as well as Moral Philosophy. Thomas Fitzmaurice became greatly interested in the former, but there is nothing to show whether the course in Natural Philosophy was included in Adam Smith's " plan ", as it existed at this time.

that he reads. While he attends the lectures of the Proffessor of Civil Law, I shall read with him myselfe an institute of the Feudal Law, which is the foundation of the present laws and Government of all European Nations.

In order to have him immediately under my own eye I have hurried him a little in his Philosophical studies and have made him pass the Logic Class which ought regularly to have been his first study and brought him at once into my own, the Moral Philosophy. He attends however the lectures of the Proffessor of Logic one hour a day. This, with two hours that he attends upon my Lectures, with one hour which he gives to the Proffessor of Mathematics, one hour to the Professor of Greek and another to that of Latin, makes his hours which he attends every day, except Saturday and Sunday, to be six in all. He has never yet missed a single hour, and in the evening and the morning goes over very regularly with me the business of those different classes. I chuse rather to oppress him with business for this first winter: it keeps him constantly employed and leaves no time for Idleness. The oppression too is not so great as it may seem. The Study of Greek and Latin is not at all new to him: Logic requires little attention so that moral philosophy and mathematics are the only studies which take up much of his time. The great vigour both of mind and body with which he seems to be blessed makes every thing easy to him. We have one holiday in the month which he has hitherto constantly chosen of his own accord to employ rather in learning some thing, which he had missed by being too late in coming to the College, than in diversion.

The College breaks up in the beginning of June and does not sit down again till the beginning of October. During this interval I propose that he should learn french and Dancing and fencing and that besides he should read with me the best Latin, Greek and french Authors on Moral Philosophy for two or three hours every morning, so that he will not be idle in the vacation. The Proffessor of Mathematics too proposes to teach him Euclid at that time as he was too late to learn it in the Class. That Gentleman, who is now turned seventy but preserves all the gaiety and vigour of youth, takes more pains upon M^r. Fitzmaurice than I ever knew him to do upon any Person, and generally gives him a private lecture twice or thrice a week. This is purely the effect of personal liking, for no other consideration is capable of making M^r. Simson give up his ease.

I make Mr Fitzmaurice pay all his own accounts after he has summed up and examin'd them along with me. He gives me a receipt for whatever money he receives: in the receipt he marks the purpose for which it is to be applyed and preserves the account as his voucher, marking upon the back of it the day when it was payed. These shall all be transmitted to your Lordship when there is occasion. But as My Lord Fitzmaurice left fifty Pounds here I shall have no occasion to make any demand for some time.

Your Lordship may depend upon the most religious complyance with whatever commands you shall please to lay upon me with regard to the conduct or Education of Mr Fitzmaurice.

I have been lately made to flatter myselfe with the Pleasure and Honour of seeing your Lordship in Scotland this summer. It would give the greatest satisfaction both to Mr Fitzmaurice and me. Your Lordship would then see with your own eyes in what manner he was employed and could judge better how far it was necessary either to increase or diminish the quantity of work which is now imposed upon him.

We are no strangers in this country to the very noble and generous work which your Lordship has been employed in in Ireland. We have in Scotland some noblemen whose estates extend from the east to the west sea, who call themselves improvers and are called so by their countrymen when they cultivate two or three hundred acres round their own family seat, while they allow all the rest [of] their country to lie waste, almost uninhabited and entirely unimproved, not worth a shilling the hundred acres, without thinking themselves answerable to God, their country and their Posterity for so shameful as well as so foolish a neglect. Your Lordship, I hear, is not of that opinion, and tho' you are not negligent either of the elegance or magnificence of your country Villas, you do not think that any attention of that kind dispenses with the more noble and important duty of attempting to introduce arts, industry and independency into a miserable country, which has hitherto been a stranger to them all. Nothing, I have often imagined, would give more pleasure to Sir William Petty,[1] your Lordship's ever honoured ancestor, than to see his representative pursuing a Plan so suitable to his own Ideas which are generally wise and public spirited.

Believe me to be with the greatest respect, My Lord, Your Lordship's most Obliged and most obedient Humble Servant,

ADAM SMITH.

XIV. *Lord Shelburne to Adam Smith.*[2]

Dublin,
April 26, 1759.

S^r

I have lately rec^d your letter of the 4th inst., your former of the 10th of March, came also to my hands in due time. I cannot sufficiently express my

---

[1] William Petty had three children. There were two sons—Charles, Baron Shelburne, who died 1696, and Henry, Earl of Shelburne, who died 1751—and a daughter, Anne, who married Thomas Fitzmaurice, twenty-first Lord of Kerry and first Earl of Kerry. There were two sons of the latter marriage—William, second Earl of Kerry, and John. The sons of Sir William Petty died *s.p.*, and John Fitzmaurice succeeded to the Petty estates on the death of his uncle, Henry, Earl of Shelburne. John Fitzmaurice was created Baron Dunkerrow and Viscount Fitzmaurice in the Peerage of Ireland in 1751 and Earl of Shelburne in 1753.

[2] Bannerman Papers, Univ. Libry. Glasg.

Satisfaction at the account you give me of my Son, now under your care ; the description you make of him, convinces me of your power of looking into him, so does the Scheme you chalk-out for the prosecution of his studies convince me of your judgment. Every thing confirms that you merit that Character which made me wish so much that you should take the charge of him upon you, and, if I mistake not, I shall make you much amends by assuring you that the more I reflect on the situation he is in, the more I am happy; so much so, and so satisfied both of your Ability and Inclination to do him Service that I must refuse the request you make that I should point out what I wish to have done. I can point out nothing, I can only approve of what you mean to do. The general fault I find with Oxford and Cambridge is that Boys sent thither, instead of being the Governed, become the Governors of the Colleges, and that Birth and Fortune there are more respected than Literary Merit ; I flatter'd Myself that it was not so at Glasgow and your commendation of my Son's conformity to the Discipline of the place he is in, persuades me that you think as I do, that no greater service can be done in leading to Manhood than to confirm Youth by long practice in the habit of obedience ; a power of adopting the will of another will make one Master of one's own. Œconomy seems likewise to have a just place in your attention. No fortune is able to do without it, nor can any man be Charitable, Generous or Just who neglects it. It will make a man happy under slender Circumstances and make him shine if his Income be affluent. Your Pupil comes into the World a sort of an Adventurer, intitl'd to nothing and will, if I may venture to prophesy concerning him, have more in proportion as his own wants are few. I wish him train'd to need little, not for the purpose of Accumulating, but in order to enable him to Give more. The Building which is to be raised by Him, on the foundations that I am laying, is what I cannot hope to see and what I trust, and do believe, I shall not be troubl'd about when my power to interpose shall cease. I wish him, therefore, to be convinc'd that it is His happiness, and not my own, that I have in view. I wish him to become an honourable and Benevolent man, I wish him Punctual and Sober, a lover of Method and so skill'd in Figures and in the businesses of Life, as by assisting me in my latter days, he may make me rejoice at my Labours in his early ones.

Perhaps it is not yet the Season of procuring for him some Instruction to mend his hand-writing but it is what he will want and what he is capable of receiving ; for, when he writes with care, he does it in a manner that makes me think him capable of writing well. His Genius I *have* thought, open to every thing, his perception of Images and of Lines express'd on paper, was, in the earliest part of his life, quick and clear, this makes me hope that the Study of Euclid, which you intend for him, will be of profit and not above his reach, it is, in my mind, a far better teacher of Reasoning than Logic is. If his Idleness and Volatility can be overcome, Mathematicks in general, I fancy, will be agreeable to him, and from a turn that he has to Mechanicks the Experimental parts of Natural Philosophy will, I am sure, be a great delight to him. I mention these things only to convince you that I have him and his future happiness at heart ; and, if he shall not turn out such as his Talents are equal to, be assur'd that I shall not be the more doubtful of, or the less thankful for your Endeavours.

The time of my Son's stay at Glasgow is by no means limited as you seem to think from what his Elder brother [1] told you. I wish him to stay so long as you, Sir, can endure him under your Eye and as long as he shall continue worthy of your attention ; for my part, having no view to any thing but his Improvement, nor any use to make of him until he shall be perfect in those things which I only know how to Admire, but not how to Teach, I shall rejoice at the length of his Absence from me, being much of opinion that great Evils arise by suffering Boys to become men too soon. A knowledge in the Civil Law is the best foundation he can have to introduce to that of his own Country, the study of it may make him Wise, but it is upon Your Precepts and Example in morality that I depend for making him Happy.

I can hardly flatter myself with the hope of seeing Scotland this Summer, but I think of a jaunt thither with much pleasure.

You make me very vain by approving so much my endeavour to make a part of this Country happier than I found it. If I succeed I shall make myself so. I shall be glad that Good is done, how little hand soever I may have in doing it. In the present case a very Slender share of praise is to fall to my Lot. The truth is that my Property is so scatter'd [2] and my Avocations from Every place so frequent that I cou'd only have Imagin'd the Work you have heard of, but cou'd not possibly have brought it to a likelyhood of perfection, were it not for the great and able aid I rec'd from my friend, Dr. Henry.[3] This Gentleman has had his education in your University, tho' a Native of this Country. It is an honour to Glasgow to

[1] William Petty-Fitzmaurice, see above, p. 239.

[2] The estates inherited from Petty were necessarily scattered owing to the circumstances of their acquisition. The forfeited lands in Ireland after the Civil War were allocated to meet arrears of pay to the soldiers and loans by adventurers. Petty made the survey and allocations at a specified rate. When the allocations were finished Petty found difficulty (as he stated) in obtaining his own remuneration in cash, and he was authorized to take it from surplus lands. Thus he had to receive land where such remained available. The chief papers relating to these transactions are printed in *The History of the Down Survey*, ed. T. A. Larcom, Dublin, 1851, particularly pp. 257-89.

[3] It is not easy to determine who Dr. Henry was. There were two Henrys mentioned in the University records of the period and who came from Ireland. One David, matriculated in 1701, who was probably too old by the time the letter was written. The other was William Henry, who graduated in 1720 and entered the Divinity school in the following year. The list of medical degrees is wanting and that of Doctors of Divinity is very imperfect. Francis Hutcheson was very active in promoting the claims of his Irish friends for the degree of D.D. William Henry was his contemporary and may have been one of these, or he may have procured a doctorate for another person of the name, but the terms of the letter indicate that " Dr. Henry " had been educated at Glasgow, besides receiving a Doctor's degree from the University.

have train'd up one of a Spirit so Great and so Disinterested as his in doing good to Mankind. The burthen of my late work has been borne by him and so ought the praise, if any it shall deserve. It is a pleasure to me to give this just Character of him to one of your merit. Your pupil will be glad, I hope, to hear that his friend, Dr. Henry, continues both to deserve and acquire the Esteem of Every body. I pray you to assure him of my Love and to believe me to be with much esteem, S[r]
    Your much oblig'd and very humble Servant,
                   SHELBURNE.

XV. *Adam Smith to Lord Shelburne.*[1]

                Glasgow College,
                 23 July 1759.

My Lord,

  It must give everybody the greatest pleasure to serve your Lordship, when you express so agreeably your satisfaction with every attempt of this kind, and I must return your Lordship the thanks of the University for your goodness in recommending it as a proper place of Education for the Children of your friend, Sir John Colthurst.

  The expense of board in the common boarding houses is from five to eight Pounds per quarter for each person. The expense of washing is not included in this; the ordinary rate of which is at 1[sh] 10[d] per Dozen. The expence of Masters' fees will probably amount to eight or ten Guineas for each Person. There are, besides, some other College dues which, however, will not upon the whole amount to twenty shillings per an: for each Person. Their linnen ought to be sent from Ireland where it is both cheaper and better than here. A suit of plain Cloaths of the finest cloth may be had for about five Pounds. These are all the necessary expenses which any Gentleman's son has occasion to be at while he attends upon this University. What the unnecessary expenses may be, it is impossible for me to determine. These will depend upon the young gentlemen themselves, upon the habits they have been bred up in and the injunctions that are laid upon them. Your Lordship may depend upon every attention which it can be in my power to give to whoever has the honour of being so nearly connected with your Lordships family:[2] and I shall endeavour to settle them in such a manner that I can have as exact an account of their conduct as if they were in my own house. If I am not mistaken M[r] Fitzmaurice shewed me some time last winter two letters that had been written by these two young gentlemen to your Lordship. I was greatly pleased with them as marking the

---

[1] Papers from the Bowood Library, in the possession of the Marquis of Lansdowne.

[2] Sir John Conway Colthurst, Bart., married in 1741 Lady Charlotte Fitzmaurice, daughter of Thomas, first Earl of Kerry, who was a cousin of the Earl of Shelburne to whom this letter is addressed.

sobriety, modesty and innocence of their manners; so that I have no fear of the behaviour of those who appear to have been so properly educated.

With regard to Mr. Fitzmaurice his conduct is in every respect as regular as ever. I was obliged to go to Edinburgh about a month ago, when I carried him along with me. This relaxation, which lasted about a fortnight, had no other effect than to serve [as] a short vacation to him. The day after he returned he began the same course of life which he had practised before without being at all dissipated by the amusements of Edinburgh. While he was there, indeed, he entered fully into them and I think did not miss any one public diversion, which led him into a little more expence than I expected. As this, however, is all the vacation which he will have, I did not grudge it to him nor think it necessary to check him.

I will beg your Lordship to offer my complements, tho' unknown, to Dr. Henry. I was no stranger to his character before the very honourable and generous mention which your Lordship was pleased to make of him in your letter to me. Mr Fitzmaurice shewed me last winter a letter from him which gave me an impression of his character which exactly corresponded with what your Lordship was pleased to say of him.

I am, with the greatest respect, My Lord,
Your Lordship's Most Obedient and Most humble Servant,
ADAM SMITH.

XVI. *Adam Smith to Lord Shelburne.*[1]

Glasgow College,
31 August, 1759.

My Lord,

I wrote to your Lordship about a month ago and directed my letter to Hanover Square that My Lady Shelburne might see it as it passed to Ireland. In that letter I gave your Lordship a full detail of the different Articles of expence incurred at Glasgow. I shall not at present repeat them; as your Lordship must undoubtedly by this time have received it. What your Lordship seems chiefly anxious about, the care that is to be taken of the Morals of the two young people you are so good as to recommend to our care, is undoubtedly of far the greater importance. What I would advise for this purpose is either first, that the Tutor of whom your Lordship gives so advantageous a character, should, if at all convenient, come along with them: or, secondly, that a Tutor should be appointed them here; or, last of all, that they should be boarded in some of the Proffessors' houses who are in the Practise of taking Boarders. The first expedient I look upon as incomparably the Best, nothing being equal to established

[1] Papers from the Bowood Library, in the possession of the Marquis of Lansdowne.

Authority for the government of young people. The objection against the second, is not only the expence that would attend it which would probably be considerable (as not only a fee of at least twenty or thirty Pounds a year must probably be paid to such a Tutor, but to have the proper use of him he must be boarded along with them) but likewise the extreme difficult of finding a good one : I think, however, this might be taken care of. The objection against the third expedient is likewise its expensiveness, the board taken by the Professors being ten pounds per quarter for each Person. Your Lordship will judge which of these is the most proper expedient.

Your Lordship makes me very vain when you mention the satisfaction you have had in reading the book I lately published, and the engagements you think I have come under to the Public. I can, however, assure your Lordship that I have come under no engagements which I look upon as so sacred as those by which I am bound as a member of this University to do every [1] in my power to serve the young people who are sent here to study, such especially as are particularly recommended to my care. I shall expect, whenever they are settled that your Lordship's friends will look upon my house as their home, and that they will have recourse to me in every Difficulty that they meet in the Prosecution of their studies, and that I shall never regard any application of this kind as an interruption of business, but as the most agreeable and useful business in which I can be engaged.

I shall soon have occasion for a remittance from your Lordship. The fifty Pounds, left here by Lord Fitzmaurice, are now spent and I am now about thirty pounds in advance. I shall send your Lordship upon the sitting down of the College a full account of every article of the former year's expence. The chief articles have been fees to different Masters, two suits of Cloaths, a suit of mourning and a summer suit of fustian, Books and some other necessaries. His allowance for Pocket is a guinea per month.

I am, with the greatest respect, my Lord,
Your Lordships Most obedient and most humble Servant,
ADAM SMITH.

XVII. *Adam Smith to Lord Shelburne.*[2]

Glasgow,
29 October, 1759.

(This letter consists, in the main, of an analysis of the vouchers and receipts of the expenditure by, or on account of Thomas Fitzmaurice since he came under Adam Smith's care at Glasgow. It was accompanied by two packets of vouchers. The

[1] A word has been omitted here.
[2] Papers from the Bowood Library, in the possession of the Marquis of Lansdowne.

following passage may be of interest in view of Adam Smith's reported declaration that in Argyleshire he had heard poems recited similar to those published by Macpherson as Ossian's.)

The two principal articles of which there is no account are that for a journey to Edin: and that for another to the Duke of Argyll's at Inverara. I am answerable for the first of these, as it was upon my account that he went to Edinburgh, I did not chuse to leave him behind me. I expected to have brought him back with me for fourty shill: but when I came there I was often obliged either to sup or dine at places where it was improper to carry him. When this happened to be the case, that I might be sure what company he was in in a very dissolute Town, I ordered a small entertainment at our lodgings and invited two or three young lawiers to keep him company in my absence. Inverara is two days journey from Glasgow and we happened to be misinformed with regard to [the] Duke's motions and came there two days before him during which time we stayed at a very expensive Inn.[1] At both these places I laid out the money and Mr Fitzmaurice kept the account; and, when we came home, we divided the expence between us.

XVIII. *Adam Smith to Lord Shelburne.*[2]

Glasgow,
3 Dec. 1759.

My Lord,

I received by this Post the honour of your Lordship's Letter of the 17th November with the two draughts enclosed. Your Lordship has remitted the money in the manner that is most advantageous to me. As the ballance of Exchange is almost always against Glasgow and in favour of London, all London bills commonly sell above Par and I this day received ½ per cent. advanced price for the two draughts you sent me. I should abuse your Lordship's Generosity very grossly if I took advantage of what you are so good as to put into my Power and did not declare that I think the sum you have remitted me full compensation for all the trouble I have been at with M^r. Fitzmaurice. That trouble, indeed, is very Little. I have never known anybody more easily governed, or who more readily adopted any advice when the propriety of it is fairly explained to him. Since he came here, he has been, perhaps, the most regular student in the whole University. I shall give your Lordship but one instance of it. We have a meeting of the whole University every Saturday morning for discipline; the whole business of this meeting is to enquire into the delinquencies of the former

---

[1] This may have been the occasion when (as related by Hume) Adam Smith heard a piper of the Argyleshire Militia repeating the poems of Ossian—J. Y. T. Greig, *Letters of Hume*, i, p. 329.

[2] Papers in the Bowood Library, in the possession of the Marquis of Lansdowne.

week and to punish them with some small fine. A very strict attendance upon this meeting is not insisted on and the most regular commonly think they do enough if they attend once in three times. M^r. Fitzmaurice never missed this meeting till Saturday last when he happened to oversleep himself and, as I did not go out myself that day I did not think it worth while to set him up. This absence was so remarkable that I had messages that forenoon from, I believe, half the University to enquire if he was well. I cannot give your Lordship a stronger instance how much he makes it a point of honour to observe the most frivolous parts of his duty as a student with exact regularity. He gives very good application and has a very great ambition to distinguish himself as a man of Learning. He seems to have a particular turn for, and delight in Mechanics and Mathematics which make the principal part of his business this year continuing, however, all his last year's studies except Logic. What he is most defective in is Grammar, especially english Grammar, in which he is apt some times to blunder to a degree that I am some times at a loss to account for. This, however, I expect will soon be mended.

Your Lordship will receive along with this letter two covers containing four sheets of Anecdotes relating to the King of Prussia. My Lord Fitzmaurice received them from a friend of his in Germany. He sent them to one Mr. Boyle at London, I suppose my Lord Orrery's son,[1] in order to be sent to me, whom he desired to transmit them to your Lordship that *when you had read them, you might burn them, for he was not at liberty to give a copy*. These were his Lordships words. I received them about three weeks ago and have read them over and over with great pleasure. They will, I dare to say, give your Lordship the same satisfaction. M^r. Boyle desired me to return them to him. I chose, however, to obey My Lord Fitzmaurice. The channel besides, by which M^r. Boyle proposed they should be returned did not appear to me to be perfectly secure, and he did not favour me with his direction. I would however beg of [your] Lordship not to burn them, till I can clear this up with Mr. Boyle, that if My Lord Fitzmaurice intended them to be seen by any fourth person his intention may yet be fullfilled.

I am your Lordship's Most Obliged and Most Obedient humble Servant,

ADAM SMITH.

---

[1] John Boyle, Earl of Cork and Orrery. If Adam Smith was right as to the relationship, the " Mr. Boyle " of the letter was Edmund Boyle, the third son who succeeded as seventh earl on the failure of male issue of his brothers.

XIX. *Adam Smith to Lord Shelburne.*[1]

Glasgow,
15 July, 1760.

My Lord,

I send your Lordship enclosed in the same packet with this letter Mr Fitzmaurice's receipts for the money he has got from me since the beginning of November last. The sum, you will see, is upwards of ninety Pounds. I did not propose to trouble your Lordship upon this subject till November next. But I happened unluckily to catch cold in March last and I suffered this illness, thro' carelessness, to hang about me till within these three weeks, and then thought I had got entirely the better of it. But upon going to Edinburgh about ten days ago, having lain in a damp bed in that neighbourhood, it returned upon me with so much violence that, two days ago, my friend Dr. Cullen took me aside on the street of Edinburgh and told me that he thought it his duty to inform me plainly that, if I had any hope of surviving next winter, I must ride at least five hundred miles before the beginning of September. I came home yesterday to settle my affairs which, as well as I can judge, will take me up near a fortnight. If I was in health, it would not take up two days, but at present I can give so little continued application that I have already been obliged to interrupt this letter twice in order to let the profuse sweat, which the labour of writing three lines had thrown me into, go off. I am besides obliged to employ a great deal of time in riding. I propose going the length of York and returning by the West of England as soon as my affairs will allow me. If, indeed I run down as fast for these ten days to come as I have done for these ten days past, I think I shall save myself the trouble and My Mother, who is my heir, the expence of following my friend's prescription.

As the expence of this proposed journey comes upon me a little unexpectedly I find myself obliged to begg that your Lordship would order payment immediately of the money I have advanced. Besides the money contained in the inclosed account Mr. Fitzmaurice owes three different accounts, two to different Booksellers and one to a Clothier. It will be three or four days before I can get in these different accounts. By what he tells me, they will amount to between thirty and fourty Pounds Ster: I fancy nearer the latter sum than the former. I must likewise beg your Lordship to remit the last of these sums upon Trust [2] and I shall immediately take care that the Accounts themselves be transmitted to you. I would chuse to leave him behind me free in the world and, as my intended journey will run away with all my ready cash, I cannot do it otherwise.

---

[1] Papers in the Bowood Library, in the possession of the Marquis of Lansdowne.

[2] That is, vouchers were sent for the other accounts. Adam Smith asks that, in addition to the recoupment of the sums he had advanced, he should be *trusted* with a further amount of £30 or £40 to meet bills outstanding, so that (as he explains) if his illness had a fatal termination Thomas Fitzmaurice should be free from all debt.

[The second half of the letter contains a description of Thomas Fitzmaurice's progress in his studies and the development of his character, in terms similar to the previous letters. Adam Smith concludes :]

Take him altogether he is one of the best young men I have known and, since he came here, has done more good than I ever knew anybody do in the same time. I have not the least fear that any thing will go wrong in my absence. I do not propose being away above a month. He will be in my house and have the conversation and assistance of several of my collegues whenever he pleases to call for it. Independent of this, my confidence in his own steadyness is now perfect and entire, and my illness will only be the loss of a lecture to him. Remember me in the most [? respectful] manner to Lady Shelburne. I began this letter in the forenoon, I finish it at eight at night. It has been the labour of almost a day. You may judge how often I have been obliged to interrupt it.

I am Your Lordship's Most Obliged and Most Obedient humble Servant,

ADAM SMITH.

Endorsed 15 July. 1760.
Mr. Smith of Glasgow.
Giving acc^t of his ill state of health and desiring a remittance of Money on acc^t of my son, Thomas.

I have accordingly remitted to him two Drafts on Gosling & C° for 100£ each this 30 July, 1760.[1]

XX. *Adam Smith to William Strahan.*[2]

30: Dec: 1760.

My Dear Strahan,
    The opposite leaf [3] will set before your eyes the manifold sins & iniquities you have been guilty of in printing my book. The first six, at least the first, third & fourth & sixth [4] are what you call sins against ye holy Ghost which cannot upon any account be pardoned. The remainder are capable of remission in case of repentance, humiliation & contrition. I should have sent you them sooner.

Remember me to Rose.[5] Tell him I have not forgot what I promised him

---

[1] The last figure in the day of the month is uncertain. It appears that one draft for £100 represented the fee to Adam Smith for board, teaching and general supervision, according to the original arrangement (see above, p. 240). The other draft of the same amount was to meet the advances Adam Smith had made to his pupil for the payment of his University fees and tradesmen's accounts. The Earl of Shelburne died on 10th May, 1761. Adam Smith was asked to write his epitaph.

[2] Boston Public Library.

[3] This leaf no longer forms part of the manuscript.

[4] The words " & sixth " have been interlined.

[5] Perhaps the person mentioned above, p. 238.

but have been exceptionally hurried. My Delay, I hope, will occasion him no inconveniency : if it does I shall be excessively concerned & shall order some papers left in England to be given to him. They are not what I w^d w[ish] them, but I had rather lose a little reput[a]tion with the Public as let him suffer by my negligence. It will give me infinite pleasure to hear both from him & from you. I hear much good of our King.

    I ever am, my Dear Friend, Yours,

ADAM SMITH.

Remember me to Mrs Strahan & likewise to Dr Franklin & Son.

XXI. *William Cullen (by his son Robert) to Adam Smith.*[1]

Edin^r.
24 June, 1761.

Dear Sir,

  My Papa intended to have writ you this night himself but he is this day in particular so excessively hurried that he has not a moment's time to sit down. He has therefore desired me to write for him. We are excessively sorry to hear that you have had the misfortune to lose Mr. Buchanan. My Papa desires me to inform you that if you should desire a Successor to him, a young man of very good parts of a Literary turn, one who has applied himself with Success to the Oriental Languages and one who would be contented with that Place alone, you may find such a one in Dr. Cuming's son, Peter.

    I am, Sir

    Your most humble Servant,

ROBERT CULLEN.

XXII. *Adam Ferguson to Adam Smith.*[2]

Edinburgh,
Novr 5th, 1761.

Dear S^r,

  Two or three days before I got your letter I happened to be applyed to by Mr. Alexander, Merchant, here to recommend a young man, if I knew any

---

[1] Bannerman Papers, Univ. Libry. Glasg. The transference of Adam Smith's friend, William Cullen, to the Chair of Chemistry at Edinburgh is noted above, p. 85. His son, Robert, was born about 1740 and matriculated at Glasgow in 1753. He was described by Adam Smith " as the best student he ever had " (Edin. Univ. MSS., La. II, 451-2). Afterwards he was employed as tutor by Kames and became an advocate, appearing for the defenders in the Action of Declarator 1769-1772 (see above, p. 225), Lord of Session 1796, Lord of Justiciary 1799, died 1810. James Buchanan, whose death is mentioned, had been appointed Professor of Oriental Languages in 1757 in succession to John Anderson. The vacancy was filled by the election of Robert Trail. The " Dr. Cuming " mentioned was Patrick Cumming who at this date was near the end of his tenure of the Professorship of Divinity at Edinburgh.

[2] Bannerman Papers, Univ. Libry. Glasg.

fit, to be tutor to his son. I immediately carried your letter to him and he is perfectly satisfyed with the recommendation and I am well satisfyed that, as far as relates to Mr. Alexander himself and his family, your friend will have every reason to applaud his good fortune in meeting with him. He has very right Ideas with respect to his Children and very noble ones with respect to the person whom he trusts with the charge of them. He told me, when he first mentioned this Subject that it would be a pleasure to him to meet with such a young man as he could forward through life and that he would not scruple to risk of his fortune in doing it if his subject was promising. The only difficulty with Mr. Alexander with respect to your Friend is that his view to Physic may carry him away from him sooner than he would wish. And it may be a difficulty with your Friend that the two boys of whom the charge is proposed to him are so young, the one being eight and the other six but they are equally advanced, being to begin the Latin together. He proposes that they shall attend the Public School while they have the avantage of a Tutor at home. He leaves the terms to you or me and will be inclined to increase them as the boys advance especially if that will induce a person to his mind to continue with him the full time. Remember me affectionately to J. Black and all friends with you. You'll please let me know your friend's resolution when he has determined himself. I am D^r S^r,

Your most affectionate humble Servant,

ADAM FERGUSON.

XXIII. *Joseph Black to Adam Smith.*[1]

Glasgow,
23rd Jany, 1764.

Dr Sir,

Inclosed I send you a letter from Ireland and the one to my Brother which you may deliver when you please. Mrs. Smith and Miss Douglas are perfectly well and you made your Mother very happy with the letter which came last night. She was particularly overjoyed at the hint that your stay abroad was not to be so long as you expected. She begs you will write as often as you can. I rec^d y^r line from Edinb. about Balfour[2] and as to the affair of the House, Mrs.

---

[1] Bannerman Papers, Univ. Libry. Glasg. "The house" mentioned is that Adam Smith occupied in the Professors' Court in virtue of his office. As to the conditions and circumstances see Appendix V. Evidently Adam Smith had already decided to resign his Chair and had indicated his intention to Black. T. Young is the unnamed substitute mentioned in the arrangements he made for the carrying on of his classes. Young had graduated in 1763. He is entered in the matriculation album as third son of Thomas Young of Burntisland, Fife. The next letter shows that he was a candidate for the vacant chair. Nothing seems to be known of his subsequent career.

[2] Perhaps a bookseller in Edinburgh, where Adam Smith had his letters addressed when staying there; cf. below, p. 272.

Smith will certainly be allowed to stay in it untill martinmass and it is even probable she may keep it untill the whitsunday after. T. Young performs admirably well and is much respected by the students.

Farewell and believe me,

Y^{rs} JOSEPH BLACK.

XXIV. *From John Millar to Adam Smith " to the care of Mr Andrew Miller, bookseller opposite St. Catharine Street in the Strand."* [1]

Glasgow,
Feb^{ry} 2^d. 1764.

Dr Sir,

I write this to you, with the concurrence of Dr. Black, to acquaint you of the state of our affairs since you left us. D^r. Reid at Aberdeen has been strongly recommended by Lord Kames. He is also recommended to Dr. Traill by Lord Deskford. There is great reason to believe that interest will be used from all these different quarters with Mr. McKenzie. Possibly, too, the Duke of Queensberry and Lord Hopeton will be engaged in his behalf, the consequence of which in the present state of things is altogether uncertain.

Black and I still think that Young is by far the best man, who has appeared; for Morehead refuses to accept. We earnestly beg that, if you can do any thing in counter working these extraneous operations, you will exert yourself. I cannot but say that we join also in wishing that, if you know any place where your opinion of Young would be of service, you would take an opportunity of giving it. I can assure you he needs that assistance. There is now a strong circumstance in his favour which we could not know formerly. He has taught the class hitherto with great and universal applause; and by all accounts discovers an ease and fluency in speaking, which, I own, I scarce expected. No body knows of my writing this but Black.

Yours Sincerely
JOHN MILLER.

Your mother is in good health.

[1] Bannerman Papers, Univ. Libry. Glasg. It appears from the above account that a sufficient number of the professors were prepared to offer the succession of Adam Smith's chair to Muirhead, who had been appointed Professor of Oriental Languages in 1753 and Professor of Humanity the following year. He refused it. Black and Millar were in favour of T. Young who carried on the class after Adam Smith went to France. The supporters of Reid mentioned include Robert Traill, Professor of Divinity, Lord Deskford, the eldest son and successor of James, fifth Earl of Findlater and second Earl of Seafield. Another candidate is mentioned in the *Caldwell Papers*, Maitland Club, 1854, i, p. 171, where it is said that the University was thinking of William Wight (who had been elected Professor of Ecclesiastical History in 1762) as successor to Adam Smith.

S.A.S.

XXV. *From John Glassford to " Dr Adam Smith at Tholouse ".*[1]

Glasgow, 5th Nov^r, 1764.

Dear Sir,

I have at different Times had the pleasure of hearing of your wellfare since you left Glasgow, altho' not favoured with any Letter from yourself. I hope that your Time passes agreeably and that you are bringing forward at your leisure Hours the useful work that was so well advanced here. It would be a Pity to want it longer than you find necessary to finish it to your own liking, as it may then very safely make its appearance.

This I send under cover to Mr. George Kippen [2] of this place who I expect settled at London about the Time this gets there, as he set out from Glasgow on the 29th of last Month with an Intention to go from London to France in order to pass the winter in one of the southern provinces of that Kingdom for the Benefit of his Health, which for upwards of a year has been very indifferent, but which Doctor Black [3] thinks will be greatly benefited by the exercise that he gets in this journey thither and which the Mildness of the Winter Season in the south of France will permit his taking in these Months that you know are too unfavourable here for valetudinary people to go much abroad. Mrs. Kippen goes along with Mr. Kippen as does Mr. Clawson [4] whom you have probably known at the University here and who will make an agreeable Companion to him.

You no doubt are acquainted with Mr. Kippen's Character and usefulness in Society which makes it unnecessary for me to say much in recommendation of him to your Civilities. If he fixes at Tholouse or its neighbourhood, I know that he can depend on your best advice and friendship in directing him to a proper House to lodge in that they may have as many of the conveniencies as are to be afforded to Strangers in their Situation.

You no doubt know that your friend,[5] Mr. William Smith, came to the Incle

---

[1] Bannerman MSS., Univ. Libry. Glasg.

[2] A Glasgow merchant, the son of George Kippen (who was admitted a burgess of Glasgow on 14th March, 1706) and Janet, the daughter of William Stewart, maltman. George Kippen, junior, was admitted a burgess on 22nd September, 1737, and was living in 1781—J. R. Anderson, *Burgesses of Glasgow*, 1573-1750, pp. 266, 425 ; *Glasgow Past and Present*, i, p. 581.

[3] Adam Smith's friend and colleague.

[4] Patrick Clason, matriculated 1755, M.A. 1758, tutor to Earl of Dunmore, schoolmaster at Logie, died 1811.

[5] " Friend " in this connection may imply a relationship to Adam Smith. In which case, this William Smith was probably a son of one of Adam Smith's cousins, though not of the William Smith who was a tutor and curator of Adam Smith. He had a son, William, who succeeded him as Secretary to the Duke of Argyle, and who was a witness to various documents relating to the Campbell properties between 1758 and 1772—*The Clan Campbell*, ed. Sir Duncan Campbell, Second Series, pp. 91, 122. The " Inkle factory " was one for making broad tapes. It was founded in 1732 by Alexander Harvie who managed, at the risk of his life, to bring from Haarlem two large looms and also a skilled worker in this industry. The " younger brother " of William Smith might, perhaps, have been the Adam Smith, the student at Glasgow University, who had left earlier in the same year without being known to have obtained a degree.

factory warehouse as was proposed before you left Glasgow where he gives application and seems in general very well qualified for Business of that sort. His younger Brother is gone upon a voyage in one of my ships from home to Havre-de-Grace and from thence to Maryland and back to this place with an intention to keep at sea if this trying voyage pleases him.

I refer you to some of your other Correspondents for any news that are going here. Indeed I do not remember any worth noticing to you and my now writing you, except that the Members for Scotland seem now resolved to carry through the Bill for abolishing the optional clause in Bank and Bankers' Notes the ensuing session which you know was dropp'd in the last.[1] I am with great regard
Dr Sir, Your obed^t h^{ble} Servt

JOHN GLASSFORD.

XXVI. *Adam Smith as Commissioner for taking Evidence at Toulouse in the Douglas Cause.*[2]

L'an 1765, et le 4 d'Octobre, à Toulouse, après midi, par devant nous, Adam Smith, gentilhomme Ecossois, commissaire convenu et nommé par Mess. Alexandre Mackonnochie et André Stuart, suivant notre commission, signée d'eux, et datée à Paris le 24 Mai dernier, à l'effet de prendre de Mons. l'Abbé de Colbert, vicaire-général dudit Toulouse, sa reponce sur les questions qui lui seront faites par nous ci-après, a comparu ledit Sieur Abbé de Colbert, auquel avons montré en original notre commission, lui en avons fait lecture en entier, et l'avons prié, sommé et requis de repondre verité sur chacune des questions que nous avons à

[1] The optional clause, *i.e.* for payment of bank notes in cash or notes of other banks, was not abolished till much later. Glassford was a partner in " The Glasgow Arms Bank ", founded in 1750.

[2] *Proof in the Conjoined Processes George-James, Duke of Hamilton and others against the Person pretending to be Archibald Stewart, alias Douglas—Pursuer's Proof*, pp. 431*, 1019. In this case there were irregularities in the collecting of evidence in France, a contention which was accepted in the judgement on the appeal before the House of Lords. The defender animadverted on a *Monitoire* produced before the Tournelle Chamber of the Parlement of Paris as an *ex parte* statement. This, by Order of the Archbishop, was read in all the churches of Paris. It assumed the case of the pursuer, and enjoined all persons who had knowledge of " the crime " to communicate their evidence under penalty of excommunication. The defender in the Scottish case appealed to a *Monitoire* which had been issued in the Calas case, which was afterwards proved to have assumed the guilt of an innocent person—*Memorial for Archibald Douglas of Douglas*, p. 29, and Appendix I. This was countered by an attack of the pursuer on the methods of procuring evidence which had been adopted by the agents of the defender. Where Adam Smith was called upon was in connection with the enquiries which had been made by Abbé de Colbert on behalf of the defender. As will be seen from the text above, the questions were settled by the solicitors who were acting for both parties and who were in France. Full particulars of the career of Abbé de Colbert are given by Rae. Andrew Stuart was agent for the Duke of Hamilton. He was a friend of Adam Smith, as appears below, p. 278. His colleague on the same side was John Davidson, with whom Adam Smith was intimate—see below, p. 267. Alexander Maconochie represented Archibald Douglas in France. The appearance of his name in this connection is of interest, since he was the grandfather of the James Allan Maconochie who wrote his name on the cover of the manuscript of the *Glasgow Lectures*.

lui faire, et proposer prealablement avoir prêté le serment requis en pareil cas ; lequel dit Sieur Abbé de Colbert auroit de suite prêté le serment en la forme de droit, et promis et juré dire et repondre la verité, et a signé (Signé) *S. Colbert, vic. gen.*[1]

XXVII. *Depositions sent by Madame Denis of Ferney to Adam Smith*, 1765.[2]

Samedy 7e du mois, vers les onze heures du matin, les gardes chasses de Mad^e Denis, Dame de ferney vinrent avertir que des gens du village de Saconnex chassaient au nombre de cinq dans les allées du bois de ferney qui est fermé de trois portes et qui fait partie des jardins du chateau de ferney.

Joseph Fillon charpentier, demeurant à Saconnex a déposé aujourdhui 10 x^{bre} devant le procureur fiscal, que c'était Mr Dillon qui était venu le prendre à Saconnex, avec un soldat de la garnison de genêve pour le mener chasser avec lui a ferney, que lui, Joseph Fillon, lui avait représenté que celà n'était pas permis, que Mr Dillon lui repondit que Madame Denis lui avait donné la permission et qu'il lui repondait de tout.

Quatre personnes ont déposés que Mr Dillon a dit en leur présence qu'il mettrait le feu au chateau. Trois personnes ont déposé que Mr Dillon etait venu à midy dans le village de fernex hier 9e du present mois avec quatre personnes armées de fusils et de pistolets, qu'ils sont entrés chez le garde, qu'ils l'ont cherché chez lui et dans les maisons voisines et que Mr Dillon a dit en jurant qu'il l'aurait mort ou vif. Madame Denis fait juges de ces procedés tous les gentils hommes anglais qui sont à Genêve.

Mr Dillon se plaint qu'on a tué un de ses chiens de chasse ; mais ce ne sont pas les gardes qui l'ont tué puisqu'il fut tué pendant que les gardes faisaient leur raport juridique, et qu'il le fut par les gens du village de ferney qui croyaient que ce chien appartenait à un braconier nommé Simon, du village d'Ornex, et qu'ils ne pouvaient pas savoir que ce chien avait été vendu quatre jours auparavant à Mr Dillon qu'ils ne connaissaient pas et qu'ils n'avaient jamais vu.

Il résulte de tous ces faits déposés dans le proces que Mr Dillon doit réparer

[1] It is useless to print the twenty questions asked. After those which were introductory the Abbé replied to some that he had no knowledge and to others his answer was " qu'ayant été conseil de Madame la Duchesse Douglas il ne croit pas devoir rien répondre à cette question ". The examination is signed by Colbert, Adam Smith and Sieur Palanque, who acted as Secretary.

There is some difficulty as between the date of this and the next paper. The existing account is that the journey of the Duke of Buccleuch's party from Toulouse to Geneva was of a leisurely nature. The interval seems too short for the distance to be travelled, even at a rapid rate. It is probable that the date at which Madame Denis sent the depositions to Adam Smith was considerably later than that at which they were taken.

[2] Bannerman Papers, Univ. Libry. Glasg. Ferney was the estate which Voltaire purchased in 1759, in the name of his niece, Madame Denis. It was in French territory three and a half miles from Geneva. The celebrity of Voltaire soon made it an important literary centre—L. Crouslé, *Vie de Voltaire*, 1890, i, p. 318 ; S. G: Tallentyre, *Life of Voltaire*, 1910, pp. 352, 368.

l'insulte faite à Mad[e] Denis et payer les frais du procès qui tombe sur les habitants de Sacconey.

N.B. Le garde chasse chez lequel Mr Dillon alla avec main forte à ferney, aiant voulu se dérober à sa poursuitte, s'est cassé les reins, et est en danger de sa vie.

Mad[e] Denis comptait envoier ce mémoire hier à Monsieur Schmidt ; elle avait dicté quatre mots pour être mis au bas du mémoire ; on les a par inadvertence écrit sur une lettre séparée. Mad[e] Denis répète qu'elle s'en raporte à la morale de Monsieur Schmidt, et au jugement de toute la noblesse anglaise qui est à Genêve ; elle lui présente ses obéissances ainsi que Mr de Voltaire.

a ferney,
11 X[bre] 1765.

XXVIII. *Etat des habit, linge et effet apartenant a Monsieur Smith.*[1]

Scavoire

Un habit de veloure cramoisij, veste et culotte a jartier d'or, plus une veste a fon d'or.
Un habit de ratinne, veste et culotte.
Un habit de velour ciselée rouge, veste et deux culotte.
Un habit de soy fon gris rayer, veste et deux culotte.
Autre habit de soy fon roujatre, veste et deux culotte.
Autre habit de soy Moyrée, veste et culotte.
Trois gillet de Molton.
Un habit noire doublé de satin, veste et culotte.
Autre habit noire, veste et culotte.
Autre habit noire, veste et culotte.
Autre habit noire, veste et culotte.
Autre habit noire de gros de raple, veste et trois culotte.
Un habit de camelot, deux veste et deux culotte.
Un surtout de draps gry, veste pairaille et deux culotte.
Autre surtout de draps gris, veste de soy et deux culotte.
Un gilet de pluche de soy, doublé de molton.
Trois gillet de toille de coton.
Un de basin.

Vingt huit chemise.
Ving deux colles.
Six cançons de futaine.

[1] Bannerman Papers, Univ. Libry. Glasg. This inventory was no doubt compiled by Adam Smith's servant in Paris who had previously been employed by David Hume. He was the invaluable St. Jean, who is alluded to in the letter of Smith to Hume of 13th March, 1766 (see below, p. 264). No effort has been made to correct or modify the French of the original, since, except in a few cases, it is quite clear what the writer means.

Dix bonnet de basin.
Trois de laine.
Deux de coton rayé.
Douze paires de choson.
Quinze mouchoire rouge.
Sept autre rouge avec de mouche blanche.
Dix sept paires de bas de soy blan.
Trois paire a cotte.
Onze cravatte.
Quatre paires de bas de soy noire.
Six paire de bas de laine gri blan., tout neuf.
Cinq paires de bas de laine blans rayé.
Deux autres paires de gris soy et laine.
Six paires de bas de filoselle pluché.
Trois paires de bas de pau.
Quatre paires de bas de coton blan.
Six paires de manchette d'antoilage et effilet.
Sept paires de mouseline a effilet.
Quatre paires de mouseline a grand deuille.
Quatre paires de pleureuse.
Trois paires de manchette de mouseline brodé.
Deux paires de manchette a dantelle.
Une plise fouré.
Une rindegotte de draps.
Un manchon de martre.
Un etuit de chagrin gerny de six rasoire, pierre, cuire, sixsau [ciseaux] et pince.

XXIX. *Adam Smith to David Hume.*[1]

[Undated. ?August 1765.]

My Dear Friend,
    Nothing has alarmed us so much among all the late extraordinary changes, as Ld Hertford quitting Paris and Ld George Lenox being appointed

---

[1] Bannerman Papers, Univ. Libry. Glasg. It is rather a puzzle how this and three other letters to Hume come to be in the possession of Adam Smith's successors. This one is badly written, even for Adam Smith, but it was not a draft as is shown by its being addressed to Hume at the English Embassy and is marked as having passed through the post. It would appear that it was dashed off immediately the news of the changes at the Embassy was received. Since Hume in the letter, correctly dated 5th September, alludes to the satisfaction Smith expressed in the improvement of his pupil, that letter is a reply to this one from Smith (*cf.* Greig, *Letters of Hume*, i, p. 521). Then Smith answered Hume's proposal to live in France (which is also in the letter of 5th September) by that which follows. Another fact, still more curious, is that amongst the papers of the Bannerman and Cunningham families there are no letters from Hume. J. H. Burton,

secretary to the English Embassy. Let me beg to know immediately if you leave Paris likewise, and if any proper provision has been made for you. We propose being in Paris by the beginning of November and it will be the greatest disappointment to the Duke of Buccleugh not to find you there. He has read almost all your works several times over, and was it not for the more wholesome doctrine which I take care to instill into him, I am afraid he might be in danger of adopting some of your wicked Principles. You will find him very much improved.

I should be glad to know the causes of this astonishing change. It appears at present quite a riddle to me unless the Queen is supposed to take a little more upon her than usual. I beg to hear from you as soon as Possible.

I ever am, my Dearest Friend,
Yours entirely,
ADAM SMITH.

XXX. *Adam Smith to David Hume.*[1]

[Undated. ? September or October 1765.]

My Dear friend

It gives me the Greatest pleasure to find that you are so well contented with your present situation. I think, however, that you are wrong in thinking of settling at Paris. A man is always displaced in a forreign Country, and notwithstanding the boasted humanity and politeness of this Nation, they appear to me to be, in general, more meanly interested, and that the cordiality of their friendship is much less to be depended on than that of our own countrymen. They live in such large societies, and their affections are dissipated amongst so great a variety of objects, that they can bestow but a very small share of them upon any individual. Do not imagine that the great Princes and Ladies, who want you to live with them, make this proposal from real and sincere affection to you. They mean nothing but to gratify their own vanity by having an illustrious man in their house, and you would soon feel the want of that cordial and trusty affection which you enjoyed in the family of Lord and Lady Hertford, to whom I must beg to be remembered in the most dutiful and respectful manner. Your objections to London appear to me to be without foundation. The hatred of Scotchmen can subsist, even at present, among nobody but the stupidest of the People, and is such a piece of nonsense that it must pall even among them in a twelve month. The clamour against you on account of Deism is stronger, no doubt, at London where you are a Native and consequently may be a candidate for every thing, than at Paris where, as a forreigner, you possibly can be a candidate

(*Life and Correspondence of Hume*, i, p. ix) relates that when the collection of Hume's letters, now at the Royal Society of Edinburgh's Rooms, was being formed, Adam Smith's heirs contributed letters from Hume to Adam Smith, receiving these in exchange.

[1] Bannerman Papers, Univ. Libry. Glasg. It will be noted that Adam Smith answers, point by point, the arguments of Hume's letter—Greig, *Letters of Hume*, i, p. 521.

for nothing. Your Presence dissipated in six month's time much stronger prejudices in Edinburgh, and when you appear at Court, in open day light, as you must do upon your return, and not live obscurely at Miss Elliot's [1] with six or seven Scotch men as before, the same irresistible good temper will, in a very few weeks dissipate much weaker prejudices at London.[2] . . . In short I have a very great interest in your settling at London, where, after many firm resolutions to return to Scotland, I think it is most likely I shall settle myself.[3] Let us make short excursions together sometimes to see our friends in France and some times to see our friends in Scotland, but let London be the place of our ordinary residence.

Before you set out from Paris I would beg of you to leave me some letters to honest men and women. You may leave them either with Foley, Thellason and Neckar [4] to be delivered on my arrival at Paris.

The Duke desires to be remembered. . . .

XXXI. *Adam Smith to David Hume.*[5]

Hotel du Parc Royale,
13, March, 1766.

Dear Hume,

I am much obliged to you for recommending your Servant to me.[6] He is without exception the best I ever had in my life and I have always been very well serv'd. The main Purpose of this letter is to recommend the bearer to your Protection. He has served the Duke of Buccleugh with the most acknowledged fidelity ever since he came abroad, and has been driven out of his service by the jealousy and ill humour of Cook, the Duke's Maitre d'Hotel. I will answer both for his honesty and his good nature which is such that I should have thought it impossible for any human creature to dislike him. He is very young and is on that account thoughtless and sometimes negligent. His great perfection is as a travelling Servant. If it falls in your way, easily, and without giving yourself any trouble, to recommend him to a proper place in England, you may perfectly depend upon his possessing all the above mentioned qualities in a very high degree. His name is David Challende—he is a Suisse.

[1] In spite of Adam Smith's advice, his next letter to Hume is addressed to him at Miss Elliot's, Lisle St. Leicester fields.

[2] Three or four lines have been lost here and similarly at the end of the letter.

[3] This intention was afterwards abandoned and he wrote later of his passionate longing to rejoin his old friends—Greig, *Letters of Hume*, i, p. 521 (note).

[4] Foley was a banker in Paris : Thélluson and Neckar were partners in another banking house, the latter retired in 1772 and entered politics, in which he attained to high office as a financier. He fell in 1790 and was arrested.

[5] Bannerman Papers, Univ. Libry. Glasg.

[6] The servant who received this high character was named St. Jean—Greig, *Letters of Hume*, ii, p. 6.

PLATE X. ADAM SMITH'S HOUSE IN KIRKCALDY, DEMOLISHED IN 1834
(From a water colour in the Adam Smith Class Library, Dept. of Political Economy, University of Glasgow.)

You are much wanted in Paris. Everybody I see enquires after the time of your return. Do not, however, for God's sake, think of settling in this country but let both of us spend the remainder of our days on the same side of the Water. Come, however, to Paris in the meantime and we shall settle the plan of our future life together.

I ever am, my dear friend, Yours

ADAM SMITH.

XXXII. *Adam Smith to [Andrew Millar ?].*[1]

Kirkaldy,
30 August, 1767.

Dear Sir,

I send you enclosed a bill for twelve Pounds eleven Shillings. When it is paid, and it is due more than a fortnight ago, I will begg the favour of you to deliver [two Pounds ?] eleven shillings to Dr Morton,[2] Secretary of the Royal Society, which he has been so good as to lay out for me. To the best of my Remembrance I owe you about or near ten Pounds, the shilling or two that is either under or over we shall adjust at meeting. I must beg the favour of you to present my most respectful complements to Dr Morton & to tell him how much I think myself [indebted ?] to him for his many [civilities ?]. There is no need for taking any receipt from him. Remember me likewise to M^r & Mrs. Miller & to all other friends.

I ever am, Dear Sir,
Most sincerely yours

ADAM SMITH.

XXXIII. *Adam Smith to [Lord Hailes].*[3]

Kirkaldy
23 May, 1769.

My Lord,

I return your Lordship your two manuscripts, having taken a copy of that upon prices,[4] as your Lordship permitted me to do it.

[1] In the possession of Professor J. H. Hollander, Baltimore, U.S.A.

[2] Charles Morton (1716–99), Fellow of the Royal Society 1752, Secretary 1759. On the establishment of the British Museum, appointed under-librarian of the manuscript and medal department, succeeding Dr. Maty in 1776 as principal librarian. His chief work was an edition of Whitelock's *Embassy to Sweden* (1772).

[3] In the possession of Professor J. H. Hollander, Baltimore, U.S.A. Though the name of the recipient of this letter is not given, it can be ascertained to have been that of Sir David Dalrymple, Bart., Lord Hailes—a Scottish judge from 1766 to 1792. Adam Smith had written to him on 5th March asking for the loan of the " papers on the prices of provisions in former times " (Rae, *Life*, p. 247). Also he was one of the guardians of Elisabeth, Countess of Sutherland, whose case is mentioned in the letter.

[4] Amongst the Bannerman Papers (Univ. Libry. Glasg.) there is the MS. " Prices of Corn, Cattle &c. in Scotland " which has been mentioned above (p. 59). The question arises whether this

I have not the Latin copy of the LL of Malcolm by me ;[1] but Skene appears to have understood one passage differently from your Lordship. It is Chap. 3 S. 5. " Item, for ilk man not found the time of the Attachment the Crowner sall remain at his house quhere he dwells, be the space of ane day & ane nicht ; & sall have his reasonable sustentation for himself & twa of his servants ; & for twa other men brought with him to be witness ; & for his Clerk twa Shillinges & sall take na mair." According to this Passage as here translated & pointed ; the reasonable sustentation is for the five persons, & the twa Shillings is the fee of the Clerk. If the twa Shillings are to be understood to be the value of the reasonable sustentation, it is for six persons which is 4d. a piece. 4d. is the day wages of a Master mason of free stone as appointed by the statute of Labourers of the 25 of Ed. III. This therefore would not in those days have appeared an unreasonable sustentation for a Crowner & five Attendants.

I last week happened to see the case of Lady Sutherland, your Lordships ward.[2] There is at present depending before the Parliament of Paris a process of the same kind between the Marechal of Clermont Tonnerre & the Countess Lannion for the Honours & estate of Clermont in Dauphine. The Lady is much connected with some of my friends who have sent me all her papers.[3] There is a good deal of affinity between her case & that of the countess of Sutherland. Both turn upon the

manuscript is that alluded to in the letter or is earlier or later. As is usual, it is in the hand of an amanuensis, but with a correction by Adam Smith. Though it contains a reference to the annual salary of the coroner of Aberbrothock in 1488, there is nothing in it as early as the circumstances discussed in the second paragraph of the letter. So far, it seems probable that this paper was different from that alluded to above. This need occasion no surprise in view of Adam Smith's habit of accumulating papers, usually by others, on any subject at which he was working—as, for instance, in the case of Public Finance. It might be as early as the Edinburgh Lectures. As to this, the handwriting differs from that of the other portions of these lectures, though at first sight the paper seems similar to that of the economic fragments. While that containing the sentences on the Atonement has the watermark " Pro Patria ", which is illustrated on Plate XIV, the other two bear the garter ribbon crowned, with the motto enclosing a lion rampant, grasping a trident. The counter-mark is G. R. with a crown. The paper of the MS. on the " Prices of Corn " seems to be the same ; but, when closely examined, it will be found that there are slight differences in the watermark. Instead of the motto, within the ribbon, the space is occupied by an ornament, and the counter-mark is different, being the letters H. H. This paper is not found amongst Adam Smith's MSS. before he went to France but occurs later, as for instance in the drafts of the letters to Anker and Holt, which were written in 1780. Thus it is possible that this MS. may be late.

[1] *I.e.* the Acts of Malcolm II. (1005–1034). The reference is to the English edition of the *Regiam Majestatem Scotiæ* which appears in the catalogue of Adam Smith's Library in 1781 as " the Old Laws and Constitution of Scotland". Apparently, at the date of letter, either his Library did not include the Latin edition or it had been lent. Bonar's *Catalogue* records the Latin, but not the English version.

[2] This case was decided by the House of Lords in favour of the Countess on 21st March, 1771. The Catalogue of Adam Smith's Library in 1781 gives the *Case* of the claim, Bonar's Catalogue the *Additional Case*. Adam Smith's friend, Alexander Wedderburn, was leading counsel for the Countess, which may explain how Adam Smith came to have a copy of the " Case."

[3] There is no trace of this case in the Catalogue of Adam Smith's Library in 1781, nor amongst his papers.

PLATE XI. THE BUREAU

which probably belonged to Adam Smith's father and which contained the MSS. mentioned in his letter to Hume, 16th April, 1773, and from which the majority of them were removed for destruction. (In the possession of Mrs. Bannerman, Edinburgh.)

antiquity of female honours and female feifs. If your Lordship thinks they can be of any use I shall send them by the Carrier next week.

I have the honour to be
Your Lordship's obliged and Most humble Servant,
ADAM SMITH.

XXXIV. *Adam Smith to John Davidson, W.S., Castlehill, Edinburgh.*[1]

Kirkcaldy,
11 March, 1771.

Dear Sir,

Your friend, Cowan, has not done justice to my watch.[2] Since I came to this side of the water, she runs down as fast as I wind her up. The latch, I suspect, is either much damaged or lost altogether. I suppose he had given her to some of his apprentices. I must now beg that he will take the trouble to look at her with some care himself.

I am, my dear Sir, most faithfully and affectionately yours
ADAM SMITH.

XXXV. *Adam Smith to John Davidson, W.S.*[3]

Kirkcaldy
undated (? 1771 autumn)

My Dear Sir,

I should be glad to see the Duke of Buccleugh before he leaves this country. I should therefore be much obliged to you if you would let me know when he returns to Dalkeith and how long he proposes to stay there.

If you see Andrew Stewart[4] you may tell him that I am longing to see him, as he promised me a visit.

I intended about a week ago to make a long visit to my friends on your side of the water. I had got wind in my stomach which I suspected a little dissipation might be necessary to dispel. By taking three or four very laborious walks I have got intirely rid of it, so now I shall not leave my retreat these six months [to come].[5]

I ever am, my Dear Sir, most faithfully and affectionately yours,
ADAM SMITH.

---

[1] Edinburgh University Library, MSS. Div. 11/191. As to Davidson, see above p. 63.

[2] If Adam Smith was wearing this watch when he was stopped by a highwayman, as is mentioned below, p. 274, he was no longer troubled with its irregularities.

[3] Edinburgh Univ. Libry. as above.

[4] Andrew Stewart was both a Writer and Commissioner of the Signet. He was admitted to the former office in 1759.

[5] Owing to breaking of the seal a few words are missing.

XXXVI. *Dr. John Roebuck to Adam Smith, 27 Suffolk St., Charing Cross, London.*[1]

Bo'ness,
Novr 1, 1775.

Dear Sir,
    I have so long delayed writing that I blush to take the Pen. Yet I know you will believe me when I say if my writing would have been of real service to you no consideration should have made me omit it. Since I left London I have not enjoyed good Health, but have been dul and inactive and yet not so ill as to be confined to the House or to take Medicines. I have trusted to indolence and temperance to restore me to health and have therefore attended only to absolutely necessary Business.

    On my return home I found Mr. Miller rather more tractable than I expected. My concerns, however, suffered a good deal by my absence, not for want of either knowledge or industry in my son, John, who truly executed his part to admiration, but for want of sufficient Authority which necessitated him to yield to the Controul of my Trustees when I might have resisted sometimes. I think Mr. Miller disposed to [be]have candidly according to his knowledge : at other times I find it difficult to refrain from contrary sentiments. I am daily, however, becoming more independent. These reflections to ourselves, I should weary you with the subject if I was placed in your easy Chair.

    Business and want of good Health has so confined me to Kinneil [2] that I have nothing but News Paper Politicks to furnish me with a little Zest which has roused me to write the inclosed Paper, I will not say in answer—for I did not chuse to be personal—but on occasion of the publication of Mr Burk's Letter to Mr —— of Bristol.[3] I sent it last Post to a friend to put it in some of the Papers (of

---

[1] Bannerman MSS., Univ. Glasg. Libry. John Roebuck (1718–94), inventor, went to school at Northampton, studied medicine at Edinburgh and Leyden where he graduated as M.D. in 1752, made a number of inventions and advised manufacturers in the Midlands on matters relating to Chemistry and Mechanics, founded the Carron Iron Works, the first furnace being blown in on 1st Jan., 1760. In order to assist the development of this enterprise he took a lease of coal mines and salt works near Borrowstounness or Bo'ness. This undertaking proved unprofitable, and Roebuck became involved in difficulties. He was retained as manager by his creditors, and it is this position which is alluded to at the end of the first paragraph of his letter.

[2] Kinneil House was a residence belonging to the Duke of Hamilton which was included in Roebuck's lease. It was there that in 1764 a working model of Watt's engine was put together. In the neighbourhood of Carron Watt erected his first engine, the patent for which had been secured in 1769. In the course of his experiments he had become indebted to Professor Joseph Black for £1,200. Roebuck paid this debt and became a partner of Watt in the development of the steam engine. When his difficulties increased, he was compelled to sell his interest in the invention to Boulton, hence the establishment of the firm " Boulton and Watt ". Kinneil House had several literary associations at a later date, one of which is that it was there Dugald Stewart wrote his *Philosophy of the Human Mind*. As recently as 1936 several ancient mural paintings were discovered there.

[3] The manuscript of this letter is damaged in places, as, for instance, in the last figure of the date. There can be little doubt that this is a " five," not an " eight." In any case the reference in

course without mentioning my name). But perhaps it may not see the light. I have inclosed you a Coppy of a Letter from Capt. Lowne with the Characters of some of the Boston Politicians, though the Pictures are not well painted yet I am inclined to think they are not much unlike the Originals.

I this day received the King's speech which delights me much, as I perceive the Ministry are now exerting a proper spirit.

I some time ago received a coppie of a letter to T. R. by which I perceive both you and Mr. W. have been attentive to my interest. In hopes it will take place I have been instructing Ben. in some branches of Chymistry so as to enable him to carry on Business with advantage soon after his arrival

I hoped by this time to have seen your Name in the Papers. The meeting of Parl^t is the proper time for the Publication of such a work as yours. It might also have been of general use in influencing the opinion of many in the American contest.

Mrs Roebuck sends her kind comp^{ts} to you.

I am, Dear Sir, ever your Affect^{te} Friend and Humble Ser^t

JOHN ROEBUCK

XXXVII. *Alexander Wedderburn to Adam Smith.*[1]

6th June, 1776.

My Dear Smith,

Your reflections a month ago upon the bad advices from America are all confuted by the favourable accounts lately received, which prove that our preparations have been seasonable, our plans wise and the execution of them in all departments of government active and vigorous. The next westerly wind may possibly establish your doctrines [2] because Quebec is not taken and General Lee is, and because five American frigates were not able to beat an old twenty gun ship, we are wonderfully well pleased with ourselves.[3] I have neither desponded very

the text presents some difficulty. Edmund Burke wrote no letter which complies with the description in the text. The nearest is that addressed to a gentleman of Bristol—Mr. Samuel Span—which is dated 23rd April, 1778. There was another Burke, named William, a relative of the statesman, whose writings were attributed to Edmund, and who was mentioned as one of the possible writers of the *Letters of Junius*. William Burke was contributing letters to the newspapers at this time, particularly to the *London Evening Post*, and it may be one of these to which Roebuck refers. He is mentioned in another connection below, p. 300.

[1] Bannerman MSS., Univ. Libry. Glasg.

[2] This may not have been intended seriously, but Wedderburn very nearly proved himself a true prophet. The Declaration of Independence was signed on 4th July.

[3] On 6th March, 1776, Admiral George Douglas, in command of the *Isis* man of war and two frigates, forced his way through the ice of the St. Lawrence and landed supplies at Quebec. For this service he received a baronetcy and appears in another connection later (p. 307 note [1]). The raising of the investment took place on 6th May. The old twenty-gun ship was the *Glasgow*, which, in company with a tender, met five American frigates near the Bahamas. *Glasgow*," after a very sharp engagement ", in which her tender was captured, escaped. The capture of General Lee is ante-

much nor been at all elated by any accounts from America, But I have a strong persuasion that, in spite of our wretched Conduct, the mere force of govern^t, clumsily and unsteadily applied, will beat down the more unsteady and unmanageable Force of a democratical Rebellion. Fortune must be very adverse to us indeed if distraction, folly, Envy and Faction should not fight for, as well as against us. So much for Politicks, of which at this time of the year I always have a perfect distaste, but I never felt it so strong as at present, were the session to open at this moment I know no man with whom I am fit to act except our friend, Herbert.[1] Would it, in your opinion, be justifiable in any man and, if so, would it be fit for me to take up the system of pursuing my own Ideas without the least attention to the sentiments or situations of other People ? I am at present disposed to think that this is the best line a man can follow, provided he acts so as to show that it is system, and not caprice which directs him.

I saw some of your French friends. Suard[2] was my old acquaintance, a very reasonable man, well informed and free from prejudices, Necker's conversation shows that he is very rich and accustomed to be heard with complaisance.[3] I did not take him to be very profound, even in the subjects he has had the greatest opportunity of knowing. He seems to think that a " Book of Rates " is a good method of augmenting the industry of a country, a great quantity of coin a certain proof of wealth and that a nation is the poorer for all the manufactures bought of foreigners. He will not be a convert to your System, for he is in possession of three or four terms that are of too much use in all his arguments to be easily dropped and that you do not much employ. Corn is with him " La matiere

---

dated. He was surprised at Baskinridge with his staff on 13th Dec., 1776, and made prisoner—*Gentleman's Magazine*, 1776, p. 158,* 1777 [p. 7], C. Stedman, *History of the American War*, Lond., 1794, i, pp. 170, 226.

[1] Wedderburn's position in relation to his colleagues at this time was very uncertain. Some years before his political character had been assailed in the " Rosciad " ;

> To mischief trained, e'en from his mother's womb,
> Grown old in fraud, though yet in manhood's bloom,
> Adopting arts by which gay villains rise
> And reach the heights which honest men despise,
> Mute at the bar, and in the senate loud,
> Dull 'mongst the dullest, proudest of the proud,
> A pert prim prater of the Northern race,
> Guilt in his heart, and famine in his face.

At this time his real grievance was that he had been disappointed of " a judicial office of a decent rank " accompanied by a peerage—Campbell, *Lives of the Lord Chancellors*, 1847, vi, pp. 60, 121. The " Herbert " mentioned was Adam Smith's former pupil, who appears in a later letter (p. 293) as Lord Porchester.

[2] Jean Baptiste Antoine Suard (1734–1817) at one time edited the *Gazette de France*, author of *Exposé succinct de la contestation . . . entre M. Hume et M. Rousseau* (1766), *Variétés Littéraires* (1768), collaborated in translations of Robertson's *Charles V.* and *History of America*, editor of La Rochefoucauld's *Maximes*.

[3] See above, p. 264.

premiere ", coin " Le tresor Publique " and by a dextrous application of the various literal and figurative senses of these phrases, he is very successfull in every argument. I was unlucky in not meeting Mad^e Necker, but I could not prevail on Mrs W. to make a Party for her, and had only the men.

I remember you mentioned two Books to me that would be of service to Sir Ja^s Erskine and I have forgot the titles of them.[1] If they occurr to you, I should be very glad to have them, as I must in a few weeks find some employment for his University.

I saw a very chearfull Letter from D. Hume, who I am happy to hear from other accounts is not likely to leave you any commission for a considerable time.[2]

I ever am, My Dear Smith,
Yours most sincerely
AL. WEDDERBURN.

XXXVIII. *Adam Smith to David Hume.* [3]

Kirkaldy,
Fifeshire,
16 June, 1776.

My Dear Friend,
I am very sorry to learn by Mr. Strahan that the Bath Waters have not agreed with you for some time, so well as they appeared to do at first. You have

---

[1] Sir James Erskine, son of Wedderburn's only sister, who succeeded his uncle, the writer of this letter, by special remainder as second Earl of Rosslyn. He was born in 1762, entered the Army, became a Lieutenant-General (1803) and died in 1837. When this letter was written the boy was still at Edinburgh Academy, and his uncle was considering his going to the University.

[2] An allusion to Adam Smith being Hume's literary executor.

[3] Bannerman Papers, Univ. Libry. Glasg. This letter has been printed in an anonymous *Sketch of the Life and Writings of Adam Smith*, which was written by J. R. McCulloch. According to a note by the author in the Editor's copy only 50 specimens were printed for distribution to friends. For this reason and also because there are several differences as between the printed copy and the actual manuscript of the letter, it seems worth the re-printing. It is possible McCulloch used a transcript. If he had had access to this collection of the Bannerman papers, he could scarcely have failed to appreciate their importance. As to the circumstances, Adam Ferguson wrote to Edward Gibbon on 18th April, 1776 : " I am sorry to tell you that our respectable friend, Mr. Hume, is still declining in his health ; he is greatly emaciated and loses strength. He talks familiarly of his near prospect of dying. His mother, it seems, died under the same symptoms ; and it appears so little necessary, or proper, to flatter him, that no one attempts it. I never observed his understanding more clear, or his humour more lively. He has a great aversion to leaving the tranquillity of his own house, to go in search of health amongst inns and hostlers. And his friends here gave way to him for some time ; but now think it necessary that he should make an effort to try what change of place and air, or any thing else Sir John Pringle may advise, can do for him"—R. Chambers, *Biographical Dict. of Eminent Scotsmen*, 1856, ii, p. 289. Hume accepted the advice of Adam Smith and other friends and tried a journey, dying at Edinburgh shortly after his return on 25th August—Greig, *Letters of Hume*, ii, pp. 449–50.

found one Medicine which has agreed with you ; travelling and change of air. I would continue, if I was you, during the continuance of the fine Season the constant application of that medicine without troubling myself with any other, and would spend the summer in sauntering thro' all the different corners of England without halting above two or three nights in any one place. If before the month of October you do not find yourself thoroughly re-established, you may then think of changing this cold climate for a better, and of visiting the venerable remains of antient and modern arts that are to be seen about Rome and the Kingdom of Naples. A mineral water is as much a drug as any that comes out of the Apothecaries Shop. It produces the same violent effects upon the Body. It occasions a real disease, tho' a transitory one, over and above that which nature occasions. If the new disease is not so hostile to the old one as to contribute to expell it, it necessarily weakens the Power which nature might otherwise have to expell it. Change of air and moderate exercise occasion no new disease : they only moderate the hurtful effects of any lingering disease which may be lurking in the constitution ; and thereby preserve the body in as good order as it is capable of being during the continuance of that morbid state. They do not weaken, but invigorate, the power of Nature to expel the disease. I reckon it probable that the Bath waters had never agreed with you, but that the good effects of your journey not being spent when you began to use them, you continued for some time to recover, not by means of them, but in spite of them. Is it probable that the Buxton waters will do you more good ? The Prescription supposed most likely to do good is always given first. If it fails, which it does nine times in ten, the second is surely likely to fail ninety nine times in a hundred. The journey to Buxton, however, may be of great service to you, but I would be sparing in the use of the water.

I am greatly obliged to you for your letter and for the unlimited confidence which you repose in me.[1] If I should have the misfortune to survive you, you may depend upon my taking every possible measure which may prevent any thing from being lost which you wish should be preserved.

> I ever am, my Dearest Friend,
> Most faithfully and affectionately Yours,
> ADAM SMITH.

I go to Edinburgh the day after tomorrow, and it will be some weeks before I return to this town. I will, therefore, beg of you to direct to me to the care of Mr. John Balfour, Bookseller.

---

[1] This refers to Hume's letter to Adam Smith written from London 3rd May, 1776. Professor Greig (*Letters of Hume*, ii, p. 317) appends the relevant clause of Hume's will in which all his manuscripts were bequeathed to Adam Smith with full power over all his papers " trusting to that intimate and sincere friendship which has ever subsisted between us."

PLATE XII. RELICS OF ADAM SMITH

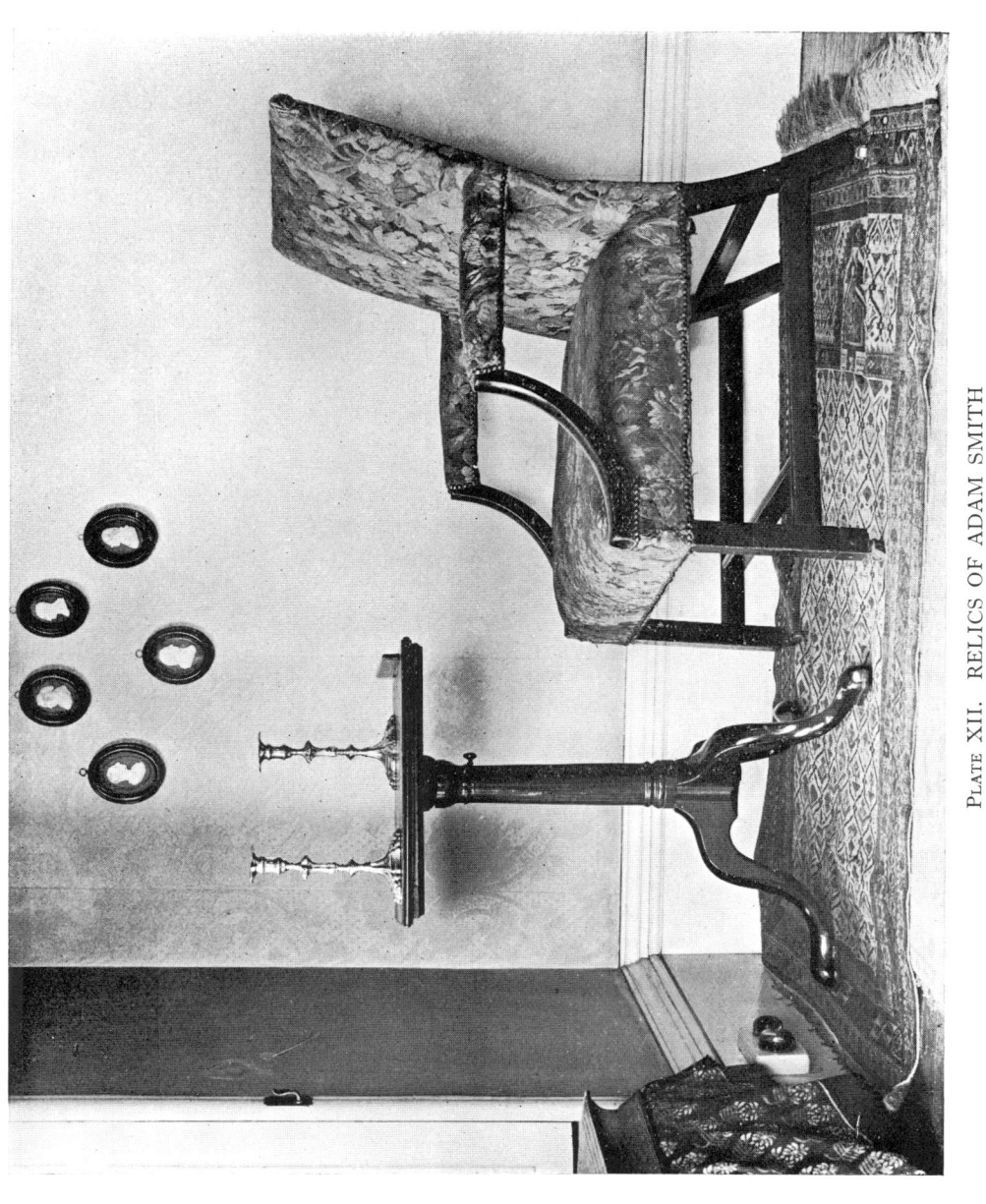

Four Tassie Medallions of his friends, mentioned by Rae, with a fifth of Adam Smith himself: his armchair, reading-desk, silver candlesticks and snuff box. (In the possession of Mrs. Bannerman, Edinburgh.)

XXXIX. *Adam Ferguson to Adam Smith*, " *at Mr. Home's House in Suffolk St. London.*" [1]

Edinburgh,
April 12th, 1777.

My Dear Smith,

I heard from Mr. Chalmers [2] of your being again entangled in my disagreeable affairs and have since received your own letter enclosing one from my Lord Stanhope to you. I have been greatly at a loss on this occasion for want of My usual Counsellor, Mr. Davidson.[3] After mature consideration it appears to my friends here, as well as to myself, that a requisition to produce the original of Earl Stanhope's letter to me, dated at Paris April 6th, 1774, may be a matter of Course in Business. But that it may proceed likewise from some degree of suspicion that my Copy of this Letter, particularly that transcribed in my own hand writing and sent to the Earl of Chesterfield [4] in January last is not exact. That, if the original letter were by any Accident lost this suspicion might produce Insinuations of which I should, in that case, have no direct refutation. And that in this view of the matter I ought not to expose this letter to any avoidable accident whatever. If my Lord Chesterfield declare his Intention, in case my Copy is verified by the original, to fullfill the condition which will Relieve my Lord Stanhope of his obligation, I will, if he give me leave, without loss of time, go to London and wait upon his Lordship with the original Letter. In the mean time I send by this post Copys of this and two other letters from my Lord Stanhope to me, Collated and Attested by a Notary Public and By The Lord Provost of Edinburgh, in hopes that this may be sufficient. These Copys go in a Packet to Mr. Chalmers who will communicate them to you and otherwise employ them for any purpose they can serve. I return you with this Lord Stanhope's letter to yourself and send to His Lordship the Copy he desires in my own hand writeing very sorry that any difficulty should hinder me from sending the Original.

I am, my Dear Smith,
Your most affectionate and humble servant,

ADAM FERGUSON.[5]

[1] Bannerman Papers, Univ. Libry. Glasg.   [2] George Chalmers (1742-1825).
[3] John Davidson, W.S., a friend of Adam Smith; see above, p. 267.
[4] Adam Ferguson had been elected Professor of Natural Philosophy in the University of Edinburgh in 1759, which Chair he exchanged for that of Moral Philosophy in 1764. In 1773 the Earl of Chesterfield (who was then a young man, having succeeded Philip, the 4th Earl and author of the *Letters*, in 1773) arranged with Ferguson that they should go together on a tour of the Continent, which continued till 1775. During the absence of Ferguson his duties at Edinburgh were discharged by Dugald Stewart. Adam Smith met Earl Stanhope when he was at Geneva, and they found they had many common interests—indeed it was Stanhope who made possible the printing of the unpublished writings of Adam Smith's teacher, Robert Simson, the Glasgow Mathematician. Earl Stanhope consulted Adam Smith, at a later date, on a tutor for his ward the Earl of Chesterfield, and Adam Smith recommended Ferguson—Rae, *Life*, pp. 193, 266-7. That recommendation brought Adam Smith into the discussion mentioned in Ferguson's letter.
[5] The tone of this letter confirms other information that Adam Smith no longer felt he had any grievance against Ferguson for unacknowledged borrowings which have been mentioned in Chapter IX.

XL. *Alexander Wedderburn to Adam Smith.*[1]

30 Oct[r] 1777.

My Dear Smith,

I have long intended to answer your Letter which I received very regularly, but in a situation where I could not give you the least Intelligence about Mr. Nelthorpe.[2] That part of your Letter is now as much out of date as the account of your mercy to the highwayman, in which I suspect there was a little mixture of Prudence ; nor I am convinced that the ardour of your Man's Courage would have misdirected his Pistol, and if he had shot, I shou'd have been in more pain for your danger than the highwayman's.[3]

I believe I may venture to assure you that neither of the two Gentlemen you recommend so warmly will succeed M[r] Menzies. [4] I am sorry that I did not know how much you interested yourself in their favour before I received the D——[ss] of Br's note, which I immediately conveyed to L[d] North, and I am afeared it has had its full effect. I have often heard of that ladys interfering in Business never fail to spoil it. This Dutchess, meaning no doubt very well, runs counter to your recommendation very unluckily, disappoints you of the pleasure of seeing either a very able or a very jolly Comm[r] of the Customs, and deprives one of these Gentlemen of the more substantial pleasure of enjoying a very good office.[5]

If you do not come up to London directly and for some months at least, keep Mr. Nelthorpe in countenance. I shall as little forgive the Dutchess for meddling in this business, as you ought to do.

There is a Packet arrived from Howe [6] which has been two months upon its

[1] Bannerman MSS., Univ. Libry. Glasg. Wedderburn was now Solicitor General.

[2] William Nelthorpe was appointed a Commissioner of Customs in 1774. It appears that he had been a candidate for another office.

[3] This is the only allusion to the episode of Adam Smith and the highwayman. There is no letter from Adam Smith to be found in the papers of Wedderburn which survive in the Rosslyn collection. The servant mentioned may have been Robert Reid who had left Adam Smith's service before the death of his mother in 1784. When Reid wrote a letter of condolence on 11th Sept., 1785 (Bannerman Papers), he was living at Miramichi in the province of New Brunswick, Canada, and was coroner for the district.

[4] Archibald Menzies had been appointed a Commissioner of Customs in 1770, his office was vacant in 1777. This letter is to be read in conjunction with that of Sir Grey Cooper. It is not clear whether Wedderburn's is rather heavy humour, or whether Adam Smith did, in the first instance, advocate the claims of others. He may have been recommended in the first instance by the Duke of Buccleuch and followed that recommendation by a formal letter of application. Another competitor was Archibald Henderson, who, on Adam Smith's appointment, was granted a pension of £400 a year. It is said Adam Smith offered to exchange his salary of £500 a year for Henderson's pension—MSS., Edin. Univ. Liby.—La. II, 451/2.

[5] This and the next letter are difficult to interpret. Both appear to be ironical. Apparently Adam Smith supported another candidate or candidates. The Duke of Buccleuch intervened as appears from Adam Smith's letter printed below. The Duchess mentioned by an initial may be B——r or B——h, the final letter differing little in Wedderburn's hand. In any case, it appears that Adam Smith sent a formal application on his own behalf, which is that to which Grey Cooper refers.

[6] Either Viscount Howe or Major General Howe who were in command on sea and land in the operations in America.

passage. People seem pleased with the accounts but I do not know what they are, having only been a few hours in town.

I ever am, my Dr Smith, Yours most sincerely,

AL. WEDDERBURN.

XLI. *Sir Grey Cooper, Bart., to Adam Smith.*[1]

Parliament Street,
Novr 7, 1777.

Dear Sir,

I assure you with great sincerity and truth that I am much flattered and pleased with your letter which was delivered to me last week by our friend, Mr Solicitor general [2] and who at the same time was so good as to show me one he has received from you on the same subject. There is a character of sentiment in these letters so very different from the applications and sollicitations which I have been long accustomed to receive that the Singularity and novelty of it gave me uncommon pleasure. When you sollicited the appointment of your friend's son to the Collectorship of Grenville Harbour I remember well the zeal, the assiduity and the warmth of heart with which you recommended him, and I reflect with satisfaction that it was in my power to second your wishes and to contribute my good offices to give success to that application : you now sollicit a place at the Board of Customs at Edinburgh for another Person ; but, in this case, instead of a warm and eager application, I find nothing But Phlegm, Composure and Indifference. It is, however, fortunate that the person whom you so faintly support, does not want yours or any other great man's recommendation ; and, tho' you seem to have no very high opinion of him, his merit is so well known to Lord North and to all the world that (alas what a Bathos !) he will very soon, if I am not very much mistaken, be appointed a Commissioner of the Customs in Scotland.

I am, Dear Sir,
With much esteem and regard your faithfull, Humble Servant,

GREY COOPER.

XLII. *Adam Smith to Mr. Spottiswood.*[3]

Kirkaldy,
21 Januy. 1778.

Dear Sir,

I do not know how to express my thankfulness to you for voluntarily undertaking to transact my business at the treasury. A man of honour who undertakes to

---

[1] Bannerman Papers, Libry. Univ. Glasg. The writer was at this time Secretary of the Treasury, he became a Commissioner of the Treasury in 1783 and died in 1801. This letter is in reply to Adam Smith's application for the post of Commissioner of Customs at Edinburgh.

[2] Adam Smith's friend, Alexander Wedderburn. As to the tone of letter see note above, p. 274.

[3] The Pierpont Morgan Library, New York. Spottiswood was a nephew of Strahan.

execute a trust for another often thinks that he cannot save his money too much. This may be for the honour of the trustee but is not always for that of the truster. You rate the fees at 90 or 100 pounds. Every one else tells me they amount to 150 or 160 pounds. May I beg that I may have no dispute with the Clerks of the treasury and that every thing may be paid as liberally as it usually is by other people.

I am with the highest sense of your kindness, Dear Sir,
    Your most obliged & most obedient Servant,
                 ADAM SMITH.

XLIII. *Adam Smith to William Strahan.*[1]

Edin.
5 Feb. 1778.

Dear Sir,

I received the Commission on Monday the 2nd inst; four days after my name had appeared in the *Gazette*. I am assured there is scarce an example of any such Commissions coming to Edinburgh in less than four weeks after that publication. I do not know in what manner to thank you for your friendly diligence in procuring me this ready dispatch, which at this moment happened to be of very great consequence to me.[2] I am much afraid it may never be in my power to make you any proper return, I can only assure you that I shall always retain the most lively sense of your very great kindness.

    I ever am, Dear Sir,
    Your most obliged and most obedient humble Servant,
                 ADAM SMITH.

XLIV. [*John Macpherson?*] *to Adam Smith.*[3]

Kensington Gore,
28 Nov. '78.

My Dear Sir,

I meant to have written you long since, and wished to have communicated some public news, that might have, at least, amused you as much as a common

---

[1] University of London—Goldsmiths' Libry.—Coll. of Autograph Letters, f. 111. William Strahan was M.P. for Malmesbury borough—J. Nichols, *Literary Anecdotes*, 1812, pp. 390-5.

[2] Apart from special circumstances Adam Smith should have been comparatively well off. He had a pension of £300 a year from the Buccleuch estates and, in addition, he inherited his father's property subject to the provision for his mother. It may be guessed that he had advanced money to some of his friends who were in difficulties through the troubles in America. These may have been in Glasgow or Aberdeen. His former tutor, William Walker of Aberdeen, was now dead, and his son, Alexander, was compelled to execute a deed of assignment in favour of his creditors in 1783. The children of Adam Smith, the Collector of Customs at Alloa, who was then deceased, are included as bondholders. There is, however, no mention of the greater Adam Smith—Deeds at the Town House, Aberdeen; Rae (*Life*, pp. 253-4) mentions, in this connection, the failure of Banks in 1772, and suggests that the Buccleuch family were involved and that Adam Smith was endeavouring to extricate them.

[3] Univ. Glas. Libry.—Bannerman MSS. This letter, as it now exists, consists of a sheet of 4 pp. 4°. It continued on another sheet (which contained the signature) and is now lost. I am much

Advertiser. But tho' I have been much at the first Source of Intelligence, and tho' I know almost all that can be known yet have I little to tell you. You perhaps Remember the Speech which I spouted for the Premier at your Table at 2 in the morning of the Day I left Edin^r. It was so well relished, that you would have found from it all the Features of what was afterwards spoken in the House. It was a lucky Co-incidence with times and Sentiments.

I had a most ample Discussion with Ld. N[orth] at Bushy Park on my Return from Scotland. I will get him to do something Essential for the Nabob. We went over all India, America, Scotland and England. I pledged your Authority about importing part of the Dead Treasure of Calcutta.[1] He felt the Authority with Respect, but hesitated about a measure so novel. He thought the Treasury of Bengal was a kind of Bank. Finding the necessity of remaining in office, he is become more manly, and his speech the first day of the Session was in a firmer tone than usual. He was inquisitive about your Duke [2] and the Advocate .[3] To my astonishment he had all the little History of Edin^r and in rather a wrong light. It seems you have awaked some new ideas about improving the Revenue. For he said the absurdity of enforcing the prevention of Contraband Trade in America was evinced from the Difficulties of it in the faithful Kingdom of Scotland,[4] as appeared by late Representations.

Your Letter to the Attorney General [5] he spoke of to me with warmth, and I

---

indebted to Professor Namier for the identification of the writer. The hand is that of John Macpherson, who was M.P. for Cricklade from April 1779 to May 1782. In Add. MSS 38213. f. 6 (Brit. Mus.) there is one of his letters, written to Charles Jenkinson and dated from Kensington Gore 2nd Jan., 1780, the script of which is the same as in the above. John Macpherson (1745-1821) was the chief figure in the controversy concerning the debts of Mohammed Ali, nabob of the Carnatic, and the case of the Nabob of Arcot. He had gone to India in 1767, becoming a writer in the service of the East India Co. in 1770. In 1776 he was dismissed from his post in India. In 1781 he was appointed by Lord North to a seat on the Supreme Council at Calcutta. In 1785, being senior member of the Council, he was appointed Governor-General in succession to Hastings. He was created a baronet in 1786—*D.N.B.*

No member of Parliament of the period is recorded amongst the rate-payers of Kensington Gore. It seems that some householder there let rooms to M.P.s. Governor George Johnston, who was M.P. for Appleby in this Parliament, also lived at Kensington Gore, whence he wrote a letter on 10th Mar., 1779 (*MSS. Earl of Carlisle*, 15 *Rept. Hist. MSS. Com.*, Pt. VI., p. 421). While James Macpherson, of Ossian fame, was member for Camelford he, too, lived for six years in Kensington Gore.

[1] Cf. *Wealth of Nations*, ed. Cannan, i, pp. 211, 267.   [2] Duke of Buccleuch.

[3] Henry Dundas, later Viscount Melville, ; see correspondence with Adam Smith below, pp. 302-4.

[4] Cf. A specimen of a circular letter, issued by the Scottish Commissioners of Customs, signed by the Commissioners (including Adam Smith) and dated 4th Jan., 1782, to officers preventing smuggling—" Instructions to David Collins Esq., Commander of H.M.S. *Alfred*—Goldsmiths' Libry., Univ. London. A similar letter, dated 28th May, 1783, and also signed by Adam Smith and the other Commissioners, was catalogued in 1936 by Goodspeed's Bookshop, of Boston, U.S.A.

[5] Alexander Wedderburn, *see* above, p. 270 (note). The debate described was that of 26th November, 1778, on the King's Speech, reported in *Parliamentary Register*, xl, pp. 1-64.

hope to turn it to our mutual good. I have since dined twice with him, and he is to taste my Magnums at Kensington Gore soon. Of all the Speakers and *Men* who distinguished themselves on the 26th he shone most and with most Efficacy. I sat near Mr A^w Stuart [1] and Robinson [2] while he was speaking, and we all felt his commanding Superiority. All the Gloss Reasoning and prismatic figures in Burke's long Speech, as well as the more solid vehemence of Foxes harangue he broke down as you would a Pile of glasses with the sweep of your arm. He covered the Minister by desiring to lay open his conduct, and he drew the House to the original Motion amidst the firmest conviction of his own Position. Ld. North felt the Telamonian Shield as well as the Edge which at once protected him and galled his opponents. This is no Exaggeration, and I believe North for the first time feels Regard, where before he had only Respect. I have aided the impression by even an accident. . . . .

XLV. *Le Duc de la Rochefoucauld to Adam Smith.*[3]

Verteuil
6. Aout, 1779.

C'est ici, Monsieur, au fond d'une Province où sont situées nos terres, et où le voisinage de ma garnison m'a permis de venir passer quelque tems avec ma mere, que me sont parvenus votre lettre du 15. Mai et l'ouvrage posthume de votre digne ami que vous avez eu la bonté de m'envoier. Il est tel que son esprit aussi délicat que profond, et sa manière de penser fort connue devoient le faire présumer en voiant son titre ; je l'ai lu avec un véritable plaisir ; on ne peut pas mieux plaider le *Scepticisme*, mais comme il le dit lui même, s'il y a de véritables *Sceptiques*, ils sont en bien petit nombre, et cette doctrine ne convient qu'à bien peu de gens : je vous

---

[1] Andrew Stuart (d. 1801) sat in this Parliament for Lanarkshire. He was second son of Archibald Stuart of Torrance. He was a Writer of the Signet and with John Davidson, another friend of Adam Smith, prepared the case of the Hamiltons in the celebrated Douglas Cause. Wedderburn was one of the prominent counsel when the case came before the House of Lords. Stuart's action in the matter led to a duel with Edward Thurlow (afterwards Lord Thurlow, who was a counsel on the Douglas side) and to his biting *Letters to Lord Mansfield*, 1773.

[2] John Robinson, Member for Harwich borough, Secretary of the Treasury.

[3] Bannerman MSS., Univ. Libry. Glasg. This letter is to be read in conjunction with that of the same writer, dated 3rd March, 1778, and which is printed by Dugald Stewart and by Rae. It is of interest as affording a solution of a difficulty which the latter found in Stewart's account of the circumstances (*Life of Adam Smith*, pp. 340-1), namely that it was only *eventually* Adam Smith thought he had done injustice to the author of the *Maximes*. This letter shows that this was admitted at once. At the same time, there was evidently some reason why the alteration could not be made in the fifth edition of the *Theory* which was issued in 1781. The explanation Dugald Stewart was to give to the Duc de la Rochefoucauld, when the former visited France in 1789, was not that Smith had at length resolved on the emendation, but to recount the circumstances which delayed the fulfilment of the promise, made in 1778-9, until the sixth edition, published in 1790, just before the death of Adam Smith.

avoue que je ne le suis point sur l'existence d'un Etre premier, et je crois qu'il seroit très avantageux que tout le monde crût à son existence dépouillée des accompagnemens dangereux que la superstition y a joints dans presque tous les pais ; mais je ne voudrois pas que l'on regardât son existence comme si peu liée avec ce qui se passe ici bas. Mais je m'aperçois que, insensiblement, j'entre en matière sur un sujet bien au dessus de mes forces, ce qui appartiendroit à l'Auteur de la *Théory of Moral Sentiments*.

Je reçois avec bien de plaisir l'annonce de la nouvelle Edition que vous préparez de cet excellent ouvrage ; je pousserai l'indiscrétion jusqu'à vous en demander un Exemplaire quand il paroîtra : et si les changemens que vous y aurez faits, exigeoient une nouvelle Edition française, et que M. l'Abbé Blavet [1] ne la donnât pas, j'aurois peut être la témérité de reprendre mon entreprise, mais il faudroit que j'y fusse autorisé par votre aveu, et par l'assurance que vous voudriez bien revoir la traduction avant qu'elle vît le jour.

Je suis ici dans un lieu qu'a beaucoup habité mon grand pere, Auteur des Maximes, et je vous dois en son nom des remercimens de la justice que vous voulez lui rendre, et qu'il mérite : la réputation de son esprit est bien établie, et celle de son cœur a été injustement attaquée, car il étoit honnête homme, et croioit à la vertu qu'il pratiquoit. Il a fait comme beaucoup d'Auteurs, il a trop generalisé les conséquences d'un principe vrai ; et Diderot me disoit un jour au sujet de son livre, que le moien de lui éviter les reproches qu'il a quelquefois encourus, c'étoit de l'intituler, *Réflexions Morales, à l'usage des Cours*.

J'ai reçu en même tems que le vôtre un autre Exemplaire de l'ouvrage de M. Hume par un de ses neveux que j'ai connu il y a quelques années à Metz, et qui étoit alors Militaire ; je voudrois bien lui en témoigner ma reconnoissance, mais j'ignore son adresse ; si vous pouvez me mander où et par quel moien je pourrois lui faire parvenir une lettre, je vous en serais infiniment obligé.

Ma mere me charge de vous faire ses complimens ; recevez, je vous supplie, l'expression sincere de tous les sentimens d'estime et d'attachement avec lesquels j'ai l'honneur d'être, Monsieur, votre très humble et très obeissant Serviteur,

Le Duc de la Rochefoucauld.

[1] The first French translation of the *Theory* was issued at Paris in 1764. Blavet's translation was issued in 1774. He also translated *The Wealth of Nations*. Dr. David Murray applied the Italian phrase *tradottore traditore* to Blavet's translation (*French Translations of the Wealth of Nations*, Glasgow, 1905, p. 4), but Adam Smith himself wrote to Blavet in 1782 saying that he had discouraged the Comte de Nort, a colonel of infantry in the French Army, from attempting another French translation, and that he did not propose to authorise any but that of Blavet. At a later date the translations of Blavet were subjected to extensive revision with the assistance of M. Guyot of Neufchatel (a friend of Adam Smith) and the Abbé Morellet. *Ibid.*, pp. 8, 9.

XLVI. *Adam Smith to Peter Anker, Consul General of Denmark in Great Britain.*[1]

(Adam Smith's copy relative to the Danish Translation of *The Wealth of Nations* in the hand of an amanuensis.)

[? October 1780]

Dear Sir,

It gave me very great pleasure to find that I had not been altogether forgotten either by you or by your valuable friend, Mr. Holt. I can plead no other excuse for having delayed so very long to answer your very obliging letter, except the great number of occupations in which I am necessarily involved by the duties of my office and by my own private affairs. I did not chuse to answer your letter till I had answered Mr. Holt, which required more time than I have commonly to spare. I have at last taken the liberty to inclose to you my answer to his letter which I must beg the favour of you to transmitte to him.

I have likewise taken the liberty to desire Mr Cadell to deliver to you three copies of the second edition of my book ; I hope you will be so good as [to] accept of one of them as a memorandum of old friendship and transmitte the other two to Mr Holt, the one as a memorandum of the same kind to him, the other as a present to Mr Dreby who has done me the honour to translate my Book into your language.

It gives me great pleasure to hear from you that the armed Neutrality of the northern powers [2] does not mean to be hostile to Great Britain. Notwithstanding, however, the very high respect which I have for your authority, I must acknowledge that I dread a great deal from it, and hope very little. But whatever may happen in

---

[1] Bannerman MSS., Libry. Univ. Glasg. The Danish translation appeared in two volumes in 1779-80. Smith's letter to Strahan and Rae's explanations give a full account of the circumstances —*Life*, pp. 355-6. I am much indebted to Professor Axel Nielsen of Copenhagen for the following particulars of the translator and how the translation came to be made. " Frantz Dræby, born at Copenhagen in 1740, went to Christiania (now Oslo), Norway, in 1766 as tutor to the sons of one of the most prominent merchants there, James Collet. Dræby went with the two young Collets on a tour to France and Germany from 1773 and in 1776 they arrived in England, where they stayed some time. At the end of his engagement Dræby became a Secretary to the Norwegian Bureau of the Department of Commerce in Copenhagen, in which Department were Andreas Holt and Karsten Anker who were both in higher positions. Since the families of Collet and Anker were intermarried, it was probably through this influence that Dræby secured his appointment. That of a secretary was the lowest in which a University graduate was placed." Professor Nielsen is of opinion that it was Holt or Anker who recommended Dræby to make the translation, but it may have been that Dræby had heard of the new book in England and was anxious to translate it, whereupon his superiors and the Collet influence secured the subscribers which made it possible for the book to appear. Professor Nielsen continues : " The relations between England and Norway at this time were much closer than those between England and Denmark. This is the reason why the three names connected with the translations are those of Norwegians, and also for the special mention of the Norwegian subscribers which occurs in the Preface of the translation "—*Cf.* Hans Degen, " Om den Danske Oversættelse af Adam Smith " in *Nationaløkonomisk Tidsskrift*, 1936, pp. 223-32.

[2] In 1778 France concluded an alliance with the United States, which was joined by Spain later in the year. It was the exercise of " the right of search " by the Navy which caused the armed neutrality of the Northern Powers.

the disposition of our respective Nations towards one another, I trust no alterations will ever happen in those of our private friendship.

I have the honour to be with the highest respect and esteem,
Your most affectionate humble servant

P.S. I am not sure if my address to Mr Holt at Copenhagen is sufficiently distinct. After sealing the letter you will be so good as to supply what is defective.

XLVII. *Adam Smith to Andreas Holt, Commissioner of the Danish Board of Trade and Economy.*[1]

(Adam Smith's copy of his letter relative to the Danish translation of *The Wealth of Nations*, in the hand of an amanuensis.)

[? October 1780]

Dear Sir,

I am ashamed of having delayed so long to answer your very obliging letter ; but I am occupied four days in every week at the Custom House ; during which it is impossible to sit down seriously to any other business : during the other three days, too, I am liable to be frequently interrupted by the extraordinary duties of my office, as well as by my own private affairs and the common duties of society.

It gives me the greatest pleasure to hear that Mr. Dreby has done me the distinguished honour of translating my Book into the Danish language. I beg you will present to him my most sincere thanks and most respectful comp^{ts}. I am much concerned that I cannot have the pleasure of reading it in his translation, as I am so unfortunate as not to understand the Danish language.

I Published more than two years ago a second edition of the " enquiry concerning the Wealth of Nations," in which, though I have made no material alteration, I have made a good number of corrections, none of which, however, affect even in the slightest degree the general principles or Plan of the System. I have by this Post directed Mr Cadell to deliver two copies of this second edition to your friend and pupil Mr Anker, of whom I have taken the liberty to ask the favour of transmitting them by the first convenient opportunity to you. I hope you will be so good as to accept of one of them for yourself and present the other, in my name, to Mr. Dreby.

I do not pretend that this second edition, though a good deal more correct than the first, is entirely exempted from all errors. I have myself discovered several inaccuracies. The most considerable is [2] in vol. 2, page 482 where I say " In England, for example, when by the land-tax, every other sort of revenue was supposed to be assessed at four shillings in the pound, it was very popular to lay a

[1] Bannerman MSS., Univ. Libry. Glasg.

[2] The reference to the second edition is ii, p. 481 ; *cf.* Cannan, ed. *Wealth of Nations*, 1904, ii, p. 351, note 2.

real tax of five shillings in the pound upon the salaries of offices which exceeded a hundred pounds a year, those of the judges and a few others, less obnoxious to envy, excepted." The tax upon such salaries amounts, not to five shillings only, but to five and six pence in the pound, and the salaries of judges are not exempted from it. The only salaries exempted are the pensions of the younger branches of the Royal family, and the pay of the Officers of the Army and Navy. This blunder which so far as I know is the grossest in the whole Book and which arose from trusting too much to memory, does not in the least affect the reasoning or conclusion which it was brought to support.

I have not thought it proper to make any direct answer to any of my adversaries. In the second edition I flattered myself that I had obviated all the objections of Governor Pownal.[1] I find, however, he is by no means satisfied, and as Authors are not much disposed to alter the opinions they have once published, I am not much surprised at it.

The anonymous author of a pamphlet concerning national defence, who I have been told is a gentleman of the name of Douglas, has written against me.[2] When he wrote his book, he had not read mine to the end. He fancies that because I insist that a Militia is in all cases inferior to a well regulated and well disciplined standing Army, I disapprove of Militias altogether. With regard to that subject, he and I happened to be precisely of the same opinion. This Gentleman, if I am rightly informed of his name, is a man of parts and one of my acquaintances, so that I was a little surprised at his attack upon me, and still more at the mode of it.

A very diligent, laborious, honest Man of the name of Anderson has published a large quarto volume concerning improvements;[3] in this volume he has done me the honour to employ a very long chapter in answering my objections to the bounty upon the exportation of Corn. In volume second page 101 of the first edition, I happened to say that the nature of things had stamped a real value upon Corn which no human institution can alter. The expression was certainly too strong, and had escaped me in the heat of writing. I ought to have said that the nature of things had stamped upon corn a real value which could not be altered merely by

---

[1] Adam Smith proposed in 1777 to call on Pownall and evidently thought he had convinced him—*Cf.* Rae, *Life*, pp. 318-19. Pownall's tract was *A . . . Letter to Adam Smith, being an Examination of several Points of Doctrine laid down in his " Inquiry into the Nature and Causes of the Wealth of Nations,"* 4°, 1776; W. Cunningham," Economic Doctrine in the Eighteenth Century " in *Economic Journal*, i, pp. 91-2. In Pownall's *Letter* there were several criticisms of Adam Smith. If these were accepted and the necessary alterations made, Pownall urged that *The Wealth of Nations* should be used in all schools as a text-book. A translation of the *Letter* was appended to the Danish translation —*Undersøgelse om National-Velstands Natur og Aarsag*, ii, pp. 683-75.

[2] *A Letter from a Gentleman in Edinburgh to his Grace the Duke of Buccleugh on National Defence, with some Remarks on Dr. Smith's Chapter on that Subject in his Book, entitled " An Enquiry into the Nature and Causes of the Wealth of Nations,"* London, 8°, 1778. The Preface is signed with the letters " M. T."

[3] James Anderson, *Observations on the Means of Exciting a Spirit of National Industry*, 4°, 1777.

altering its money price. This was all that the argument required, and all that I really meant. Mr. Anderson takes advantage of this hasty expression and triumphs very much by showing that in several other parts of my Work I had acknowledged that whatever lowered the real price of manufactur'd produce rais'd the price of rude produce and consequently of corn. In the second edition I have corrected this careless expression, which I apprehend takes away the foundation of the whole argument of Mr. Anderson.

It is not worth while to take notice, even to you, of the innumerable squibs thrown out upon me in the newspapers. I have, however, upon the whole been much less abused than I had reason to expect, so that in this respect I think myself rather lucky than otherwise. A single, and, as I thought, a very harmless Sheet of paper, which I happened to write concerning the death of our late friend, Mr Hume,[1] brought upon me ten times more abuse than the very violent attack I had made upon the whole commercial system of Great Britain. So much for what relates to my Book.

I was much intertained with the account, which you was so good as [to] send me of your travels into Iceland, and of the different situation you have been in since I had the pleasure of seeing you in France, and was very happy to find in the end that you had obtained so comfortable and honourable an establishment at Copenhagen. The revolution in the administration of your Government, which you mention, I always believe to have been conducted with great prudence and moderation, and to have been indispensably necessary for the preservation of the State. It gives me great pleasure to hear the agreeable accounts which you give me of the young Prince and of the very proper manner in which hè is educated.

Since I had the pleasure of seeing you, my own life has been extreamly uniform. Upon my return to Great Britain I retired to a small town in Scotland, the place of my nativity, where I continued to live for six years in great tranquillity and almost in complete retirement. During this time I amused myself principally with writing my " Enquiry concerning the Wealth of Nations," in studying Botany (in which, however, I made no great progress) as well as some other sciences to which I had never given much attention before. In the Spring of 1773 a proposal, which many of my friends thought very advantageous, was made to me to go abroad a second time.[2] The discussion of this proposal obliged me to go to London, where the Duke of Buccleugh was so good as to dissuade [me] from accepting it. For four years after this London was my principal residence, where I finished and published my book. I had returned to my old retirement at Kirkaldy and was employing myself in writing another Work concerning the imitative arts ; when, by the interest of the Duke of Buccleugh, I was appointed to my present office ; which, though it requires a good deal of attendance, is both easy and honourable, and for my way of living sufficiently beneficial. Upon my appointment I proposed to surrender

[1] *Cf.* Rae, *Life*, pp. 295-314.   [2] As tutor to the Duke of Hamilton—Rae, *Life*, p. 258.

the annuity which had been settled upon me by the Tutors of the Duke of Buccleugh before I went abroad with him, and which had been renewed by his Grace when he came of age, as a thing for which I had no farther occasion. But his Grace sent me word by his Cashier, to whom I had offered to deliver up his bond, that though I had considered what was fit for my own honour, I had not considered what was fit for his, and that he would never suffer it to be suspected that he had procured an office for his friend, in order to relieve himself from the burden of such an annuity. My present situation is, therefore, fully as affluent as I could wish it to be. The only thing I regret in it is the interruptions to my literary pursuits, which the duties of my office necessarily occasion. Several Works, which I had projected are likely to go on much more slowly than they otherwise would have done.

Wishing you every sort of happiness and prosperity, I have the honour to be with the highest respect and esteem, Dear Sir,
Your most affectionate, humble Servant.

XLVIII. *From Henry Mackenzie, author of the* Man of Feeling, " copy of my second letter to Mr. Carmichael in 1781".[1]

Dr Smith, whom I reckon the first of our writers both in point of genius and information, is now revising both his " Theory of Moral Sentiments " and his " Essay on the Wealth of Nations." In the new editions of both (which are to be published in the Spring) there will be considerable alterations and improvements. He has, lying by him, several essays, some finished, but the greater part not quite completed on subjects of criticism and Belles Lettres, which, when he chooses to put them to the world, will, I am confident, nowise derogate from his former reputation as an author.

XLIX. *Henry Mackenzie to Adam Smith, No. 27 Suffolk St., Charing Cross, London.*[2]

Edin^r
7th June, 1782.

Dear Sir,
　　The inclosed Letter will serve as my Apology and explain the Reason for my troubling you once more with a Letter. It happens, whimsically enough, that it should be on a similar Subject with my last. This second Application I could not well avoid, without giving some offence to a Man whose Genius, as well as the warmth and goodness of his Heart, I respect, and who being of the *Genus irritabile vatum* is, I am afraid, somewhat easily offended.

[1] National Library, Edinburgh, Mackenzie's Autograph Letters, MS. 646, No. I, f. 7.
[2] Bannerman MSS., Univ. Libry. Glasgow. Henry Mackenzie (1745-1831), author of *The Man of Feeling*, promoter of and chief contributor to *The Mirror*. He acted on behalf of Adam Smith's literary executors in preparing his *Essays* for publication—see below, p. 314.

He left his *Runnamede*[1] two days with me. I gave it such a Perusal as the Leisure of those two Days would allow, sufficient to judge of its general Effect on my Feelings, but by no means equal to the forming any critical opinion upon it. I offered, however, to the Author, when he called again for his Tragedy, some Observations I had made on the leading Incidents of the Piece, some of which I thought faulty ; on the other hand, I gave the Commendation I thought they merited to certain Passages and added in gen^l that, if it were now to be brought on the Stage, the Spirit of Liberty it breath'd might catch an Audience, and that some of the Declamation of it, which critically speaking I might find fault with, was such as I had seen procure loud applause in an English Theatre. These were the observations which produced the inclosed Letter from Mr. Logan, w^h I take the Liberty of sending to you, to save a long Narrative which would be awkward to me and possibly not very intelligible to you. My Opinion of it (which Mr Logan does me the honor of supposing might have some Influence with you) is nearly as above, allowing for that Delicacy which the " sturdiest Moralist " must temper his Truth with in speaking to an Author of his works.

I hope your former Indisposition has been long quite removed and that you have escaped the Influenza which has raged in London and now begins here. About 240 of the S. Fencibles are down with it.[2] Our weather is now milder and I hope may blunt its Effects with us.

I am, Dr Sir, with greatest Regard your most obed^t Servt

HENRY MACKENZIE.

L. *John Logan to Henry Mackenzie.*[3]
(*Enclosed in the previous letter.*)

Leith.
June 6th, 1782

Dear Sir,

Your suggestion to me that *Runnemede* [sic] and particularly some scenes of it are calculated to make an Impression upon the Stage has put a scheme into my head which I shall explain. Dr. Smith is to continue in London for some time, he is acquainted with Sherridan, and much connected with some of his friends and Patrons, and tho' he is not a politician, his opinions in affairs of Literature will have its weight. I shall write to him this Evening and desire his assistance in introducing it upon the stage.

He has seen *Runnamede* and tho' he expressed his approbation of it as a poem in terms that I would not chuse to repeat, he seemed to doubt of its being adapted

---

[1] As to the author, J. Logan—see below, p. 304.

[2] Adam Smith had become an honorary captain of the Trained Bands of Edinburgh on 4th June of this year—Rae, *Life*, p. 374.

[3] Bannerman MSS., Univ. Libry. Glasg.

to the English Stage. If you will take the trouble to write to him and express the same favourable opinion you did to me, I will look upon it as a very great Obligation. His letters are directed to the British Coffee House, near Charing Cross. If any other path to the Theatre occurrs to you, it will make me exceedingly happy if you will mention it, as I have many reasons for wishing that, if possible, it could be introduced to the Stage this winter.

I hope you will excuse me for giving you this trouble and believe me to be,
Dear Sir, your faithful humble Ser^t,

J. LOGAN.

LI. *T. Cadell to Adam Smith.*[1]

London,
December 12th, 1782.

Dear Sir,

I was favoured with yours of the 7th and communicated its contents to our friend, Strahan, who desires his best Compliments. I am happy to hear you are preparing for a new Edition of the " Wealth of Nations "—the delay will, I am afraid, prevent our publishing this new Edition this Winter. We will, however, set about it as soon as we receive the Copy ; and, if we cannot get [it] in time to publish before the Town is empty we will postpone it to the meeting of Parliament in the ensuing Winter. I heartily approve of selling the Additions separate, but as they will be very valuable we must, if possible, prevent their being sold but to those who purchased the Book. I have nothing further to add but that I remain with great respect and regard,

Dear Sir, your obliged and affectionate, Humble Servant,

THO. CADELL.

Will you be so obliging to let your servant deliver the enclosed to Dr. Stedman.[2]

LII. *Adam Smith to William Strahan.*[3]

Custom house,
Edinburgh, 22 May, 1783.

My Dear Strahan,

I have for these several months been labouring as hard as the continual interruptions, which my employment necessarily occasions, will allow me. I now only wait for some accounts which my friend, Sir Grey Cooper[4] was so good as to

---

[1] Bannerman MSS., Univ. Libry. Glasg.

[2] John Stedman, M.D., author of *Physiological Essays and Observations*, Edin., 1769, and editor of Horace's *Ars Poetica*, 1782.

[3] In the possession of the Pennsylvania Historical Society.   [4] See above, p. 275.

promise me from the treasury, in order to compleat all the Additions which I propose to make to my third edition. This Edition will probably see me out and I should therefore chuse to leave it behind me as perfect as I can make it. The Principal additions are to the second vol., some new arguments against the corn bounty, against the Herring buss bounty, a new concluding Chapter upon the mercantile System, a short History and, I presume a full exposition of the Absurdity and hurtfulness of almost all our chartered trading companies.[1] I expect to be able to finish it in about a month after I receive the treasury accounts which are now preparing. I must correct the press myself and you must, therefor, frank me the sheets as they are printed. I would even rather than not correct it myself come up to London in the beginning of next winter and attend the Press myself. Remember me to Cadel, to Rose and to Griffiths. I long to have more dinners at the Packhorse. If you have any literary news, I should be glad to hear it. I should likewise be glad to know your judgement concerning the present state of our affairs.

I ever am, My Dear friend, most affectionately yours,

ADAM SMITH.

LIII. *From George Dempster to Adam Smith.*[2]

London,
18th Decr, 1783.

Dear Sir,

Will you forgive my troubling you with the enclosed. It is the Effusion of a very gratefull Heart, and the writer a good man and deserving officer.[3]

I dare say you have heard of a smuggling Committee, lately appointed. I promised to Mr. Eden, our Chairman, that I would drop you a hint of the intention of the Committee to desire the favour of your attendance in Town after the Holidays. Strange Events have since happened which render doubtfull the existence of the House itself and, of course, of all its Committees even to the beginning of the Holidays. So far as I can judge there is as great a probability of your seeing some of the Committee in Scotland as of the Committee seeing you in London.[4] Should, however, the present surmises of a dissolution prove groundless, the Committee will be indebted to you for your Ideas of the most effectual means to prevent smuggling which, by all the Information we have received, has come to an alarming

[1] Cf. *Wealth of Nations* (ed. Cannan), i, p. xv, and ii, pp. 223-48.

[2] Bannerman MSS., Univ. Libry. Glasg.

[3] If the enclosure mentioned is extant, it is difficult to identify it. In the same bundle there is a memorandum on naval tactics, which is unsigned, but which analyses several naval engagements, the latest of which is dated 12th April, 1782.

[4] The anticipated dissolution of Parliament did not take place until the spring of 1784—*Letters of George Dempster*, edited by J. Ferguson, 1934, pp. 123-31.

height, threatening the destruction of the Revenue, the fair trader, the Health and Morals of the People,

I am, with most sincere respect,
Dear Sir, Your most obedient and most humble Servant
GEORGE DEMPSTER.

LIV. *Adam Smith to John Davidson Esqr., Castlehill.*[1]

Tuesday, 25 Feb^y,[2] 1783.

Dear Sir,
William Donald Landwaiter doing duty at Greenock but standing on the establishment at Port Glasgow is dead. Gabriel Millar will be presented by this nights post. But our presentation will be of little weight unless he is supported by better interest,

I ever am &c.
ADAM SMITH.

Endorsement in two other hands. Gabriel Millar was appointed at the recommendation of the Duke of Hamilton to an office, which was suppressed, and he was therefore disappointed—The Duke therefore now requests Millar's succeeding to the vacancy at Port Glasgow—

Mr. And^w Stuart inform'd that the office of Landw^r at Glasgow was given to Mr Ewart the 2 Ins^t Month.

J. N.   J. N. B.[3]

LV. *Adam Smith to* —— (*Draft in Adam Smith's own hand*).[4]

[? after 1783.]

My Dear Sir,
After making you wait a fortnight, in expectation of an account from the excise which I have not yet received, I at last sit down to answer your very obliging letter, not one bit better informed than I was an hour after I received it. As soon as I get more information you shall have it.[5]

---

[1] In the possession of Professor E. R. A. Seligman, New York. Andrew Stewart (who is mentioned in the endorsement) was " doer " for the Duke of Hamilton. He, with John Davidson (to whom the letter is addressed), was the solicitor for the Hamilton interest in the Douglas Cause.

[2] The month of the date is overwritten. The other word was April.

[3] The initials given above as " J. N. B." are very doubtful.

[4] Bannerman MSS., Libry. Univ. Glas. There is no indication of the recipient of the letter of which this is a draft. From the letter to George Chalmers which follows (pp. 294-5) he must have been one holding high office, as otherwise permission would have been required for the communication of official information.

[5] Amongst the Bannerman Papers there is a document of one page, headed " Calculation of Loss to the Revenue in North Britain from the Abuse of Small Stills, " which may be that referred to. It was estimated there were 1,000 small stills and the duty lost was calculated to be £182,000.

By the 1ˢᵗ George III. cap. 1. sect. 8 all the duties and revenues which were payable to the late king during his life in Scotland were reserved to his present Majesty, over and above the £800,000 per an. granted to him from the aggregate fund.

By the 10ᵗʰ Anne cap. 26, sect. 108, all the duties of customs and excise at that time payable in Scotland were made liable to the expense of keeping up the three courts of Session, Justiciary and Exchequer.

In consequence of the first of these clauses, not only the rents of the Crown lands and the feudal casualties arising in Scotland, but the produce of all fines and forfeitures and consequently all seizures, the new subsidy, the Hereditary and temporary excise, as well as several other branches of revenue are, by our Barons of Exchequer, considered as making part of the private estate of the king to be disposed of in what manner he pleases and consequently applicable to pensions and Gratuities.

In consequence of the second of these clauses combined with the first, if those private funds should be so far exhausted by pensions and gratuities as not to be sufficient for the maintenance of the 3 courts, the same Judges consider all the different branches of customs and excise, payable in Scotland in 10ᵗʰ of Queen Anne, as liable to make up the deficiency.

The pensions upon the civil list of Scotland at the death of the late king did not, I have been assured, much exceed four thousand pounds a year. They at present amount to upwards of eighteen thousand pounds a year. I should have enclosed a list of them, had I not known that it was sent up quarterly to the treasury.

The amount of the civil establishment in Scotland during the last year has been as follows.

Michaelmas quarter,	1782	£15,550 . 1 . .
Christmas,	1782	16,798 . 12 . 1
Lady day,	1783	16,615 . 15 . 5½
Midsummer,	1783	17,915 . 2 . 1½
		66,879 . 10 . 8

Whatever part of the funds, which are considered as the private property of the king, is not exhausted by pensions is applied to the payment of the three courts and the other necessary charges of the civil establishment of Scotland. So far as those private funds are not sufficient for the purpose, the deficiency is supplied by having recourse to the subsidiary funds applicable to the same purpose by the above clause in the 10ᵗʰ of Queen Anne. The remainder of those subsidiary funds is remitted by the order of the boards of Customs and Excise to the Receivers general of those respective revenues in England.

The enclosed account will sufficiently explain to you the nature of the funds under the management of our board which are applicable to the Civil List, and the manner in which they are applied. In a post or two I shall probably be able to send you a similar account of those under the management of the Excise.

LVI. *Adam Smith to William Strahan.*[1]

Custom house,
Edinburgh, 10 June, 1784.

My Dear Sir,

I return you the Proof, which, indeed, requires little correction, except in the pointing and not much in that. I received the fair sheets by the Coach, and sent Robertson of Dalmenie his parcel. I [am] much pleased with the Paper and letter, and am obliged to you for sending the fair sheets rather by the cheap conveyance of the Coach rather than by the expensive one of the Post. I should be glad, however, to receive the proofs of the Manuscript part by the Post as the speedier conveyance ; and, if it gives you much trouble to provide franks, I shall willingly pay the postage. I should immediately have acknowledged the receipt of the fair sheets ; but I had just then come from performing the last duty to my poor old Mother ; and, tho' the death of a person in the ninetieth year of her age was no doubt an event most agreeable to the course of nature ; and, therefore, to be foreseen and prepared for, yet I must say to you what I have said to other people, that the final separation from a person who certainly loved me more than any other person ever did or ever will love me ; and whom I certainly loved and respected more than I shall either love or respect any other person, I cannot help feeling, even at this hour, as a very heavy stroke upon me. Even in this state of mind, it gives me very great concern to hear that there is any failure in your health and spirits.[2] The good weather, I hope, will soon re-establish both in their ordinary vigour. My old friends grow very thin in the world, and I do not find that my new ones are likely to supply their place. I shall be very anxious to hear from you as soon as your conveniency will permit.

Remember me to M[r] and M[rs] Spottiswood and to all other friends, and believe me to be, My Dear friend,

Most faithfully and affectionately ever yours,

ADAM SMITH.

[1] In the possession of the Pennsylvania Historical Society.

[2] Strahan refused to stand for re-election as an M.P. in 1784 owing to the state of his health. He died on 9th July, 1785.

PLATE XIII. EXAMPLES OF THE PARROT ORNAMENT IN SCOTTISH BOOKBINDING

The volume in the centre is the copy of the 5th Ed. of *Moral Sentiments*, presented by Adam Smith to Henry Dundas. It is bound in marbled calf. That on the left is a Holy Bible, Cambridge, 1792, bound in red morocco, with the badge of George, Prince of Wales. That on the right is also a Holy Bible, Edinburgh, 1772, in blue morocco with a dedication by Kincaid the printer to Lady Janet Dundas. (Library, University of Glasgow.)

LVII. *Adam Smith to* [*T. Cadell?*][1]

Custom house,
Edinburgh,
10 August, 1784.

Dear Sir,
I received last week all the Volumes of the Philosophical transactions [2] which I wanted except the Volumes 70, 71, and the first part of 72. I received the second part of 72 and both parts of Volume 73.[2] I am much obliged to you for the trouble you have been at; those still wanting, I suppose will come when the Society meets.

I wrote to Strahan desiring a few presents to be made in my name before Publication,[3] viz to Lady Louisa MacDonald, to Lords Stanhope, Mahon, Loughborough & Sheffield; to these let me add a Sixth to Sir Grey Cooper. The copy to Lady Louisa to be finely bound and Gilt; the rest in boards. I should likewise be glad you would send me six copies in boards (by the first Leith ship) to be distributed to some of my friends here.

I received the leaf that was wanting in Chesterfield's miscellanies;[4] but you say nothing to me about the french translation by the Abbè Morellet which I am very anxious to see.[5] I have another french translation by the Abbè Blavet.

Remember me to all friends and believe me to be,
My Dear Sir, Most faithfully Yours,

ADAM SMITH.

---

[1] In the possession of Professor J. H. Hollander, Baltimore, U.S.A.

[2] Adam Smith had 21 vols. of these Transactions, which were those of the Royal Society—Bonar, *Library*, 1932, p. 141.

[3] This was the third edition of *The Wealth of Nations*, which, though issued at the end of the year, had been ready earlier—Rae, *Life*, p. 362. Of the recipients Lady Louisa MacDonald was the wife of Sir Archibald MacDonald, who was appointed Solicitor-General in this year; Earl Stanhope is mentioned above, p. 273; Lord Mahon was his heir, who succeeded as third earl in 1786; Lord Loughborough is Alexander Wedderburn, who had been one of those attending Adam Smith's lectures at Edinburgh; Lord Sheffield was the first earl, the executor of Gibbon and the author of many economic pamphlets; Sir Grey Cooper is mentioned above, p. 275.

[4] The Miscellaneous Works in 4 vols, 1779, which were in Adam Smith's Library—Bonar, *Catalogue*, 1932, p. 45.

[5] Rae (*Life*, p. 359) describes the circumstances which prevented the printing of Morellet's manuscript translation. That of Blavet, mentioned in the next sentence of the text, was often attributed to Morellet. The explanation of Adam Smith's request may be either that he had heard from some of his friends in France that Morellet had begun a translation on receiving a copy of the book from Lord Shelburne, and it was not unreasonable to assume that, after four or five years, it would have been printed, or it may have been that from some source he had learnt of another translation issued at La Haye in four vols., the first two being dated 1778 and the second two 1779, and that he may have thought this was by Morellet—*cf.* D. Murray, *French Translations of The Wealth of Nations*, 1905, pp. 9-13.

LVIII. *Adam Smith to [T. Cadell?]*[1]

Custom House, Edinburgh
16 Nov[r] 1784.

Dear Sir,
  For these several weeks past I have been looking for a letter from you by every Post, in answer to the last I wrote you. I see that you have executed my commissions, as I have received the thanks of some of the persons to whom I had begged the favour of you to send copies.[2]

  To those which in my former letter I desired you to deliver as presents from the Authour I must beg the favour of you to add four more: one to Lord Shelburne[3]; and three to the Marquis de Bombelles[4]; one to the Marquis himselfe, one to the Duke of Rochefoucault; and one to the Dutchess Chabot, the sister of the Duke of Rochefoucault and the daughter of the Dutchess D'Anville. My Lord Shelburne will be so good as to deliver the three copies to the Marquis de Bombelles, who will be so good as to deliver at Paris the two copies for the Duke of Rochefoucault and the Dutchess Chabot. Remember me most respectfully and affectionately to Strahan & believe me to be,
    Dear Sir,
      Ever Yours,
        ADAM SMITH.

LIX. *Adam Smith to Revd. Dr. James Monteath, Barrowby, near Grantham.*[5]

Customhouse, Edinburgh
22 feb : 1785.

My Dear James,
  I received your very kind and friendly letter in due course; and have no hesitation to recommend the University of Edinburgh in preference to any other.[6] It is at present better provided in Professors than any other Society of the kind that I ever knew; and it is likely soon to be still better provided than at present. While my own residence, besides, is here, which is now very likely to be for life, I

---

[1] In possession of the late Professor Foxwell, Cambridge.

[2] The third edition of *The Wealth of Nations*, mentioned in the previous letter.

[3] See above, p. 239.

[4] Marc Marie Bombelles (1744-1821), in the diplomatic service, an émigré, fought with the Royalists. On the restoration of the Bourbons took orders and was bishop of Amiens.

[5] Papers of Sir W. F. Stuart Menteth, Bart., Mansefield House, Ayrshire.

[6] The Principal was William Robertson, the historian. Others already mentioned are John Bruce (Logic), Dugald Stewart (Moral Philosophy), Adam Ferguson (Mathematics), John Robison (Natural Philosophy), A. F. Tytler, afterwards Lord Woodhouselee (Civil History), William Cullen (Physic), Joseph Black (Chemistry). To whom may be added Allan Maconochie, afterwards Lord Meadowbank (Public Law). It was at Meadowbank House that the MS. of the *Glasgow Lectures* was found, and the volume contains the signature of James Allan Maconochie who was the son of the above Allan Maconochie, first Lord Meadowbank.

would fain flatter myself I may be of some use in rendering both your stay here agreeable and your son's useful. I approve entirely of your attending your son [1] to the place of his education yourself as his principal Governour and Preceptor. I consider it as the most sacred as well as the most important duty of a father. But I disapprove altogether of your proposal to resign your Living. It may happen that Scotland may not turn out to be so agreeable a place of residence either to you or to your family as you at present hope; and it will certainly be more prudent to take a trial of us for a year or two at least, before you take the final and irrevocable resolution of giving up altogether your connection with your present neighbourhood and abode. You have hitherto been so religiously exact in the performance of all your pastoral duties, that you are well entitled to demand a vacation for at least three or four winters in order to attend upon the education of your son. I give you this caution, much against my own interest and inclination, and merely for Conscience sake. You are now, except one or two old Cousins,[2] the oldest friend I have now remaining in the world, and it gives me the most unspeakable satisfaction to think that I have some chance of ending my days in your Society and neighbourhood.

I ever am, My Dearest friend, your most affectionate and most faithful,
humble servant,

ADAM SMITH.

LX. *Lord Porchester to Adam Smith.*[3]

Highclere,
August 24th, 1785.

My Dear Smith,
Least you should be surprised with the sudden appearance of a little Czar in black presenting a letter to you desiring your acquaintance, I must apprize you that on the receipt of the enclosed Letter I have just sent to Doctor Ogle, Dean of Winchester,[4] a Letter of introduction to you; he is a very worthy, respectable Man, as little of a high priest as a priest can possibly be and a great deal more of a Republican than will ever lead the Dean to a Bishoprick, a very Zealous man in every thing he undertakes and will at any time sacrifice his interest to his Principles

---

[1] Charles Granville Stuart Menteth, created a baronet in 1838.

[2] Colonel Douglas, Miss Janet Douglas, Colonel Patrick Ross and Miss Ross of Innernethy.

[3] Bannerman MSS., Univ. Libry. Glasg. Henry Herbert (b. 1741) had been a student of Adam Smith at Glasgow, where he matriculated in 1762, having been previously at Christ Church, Oxford. He was M.P. for Wilton from 1768 to 1780. He was created Baron Porchester of High Clere in 1780 and Earl of Carnarvon in 1793. His wife, who is mentioned towards the end of this letter, was Elizabeth, daughter of Charles, first Earl of Egremont. He was appointed Master of the Horse in 1806 and died in 1811.

[4] Newton Ogle, D.D., third son of Dr. Nathaniel Ogle of Kirkley Hall, Northumberland, born 1726, married Susanna, eldest daughter of Dr. John Thomas, Bishop of Winchester. Porchester was a true prophet, since Ogle never became a Bishop. He was deputy Clerk of the Closet to the King and subsequently Prebendary of Durham. He succeeded to the Kirkley property in 1762.

which are all strongly tinged with a Republican cast. I shall really be much obliged to you for any civility you can, without inconvenience to yourself, show him. He is Brother to Admiral Sir Chaloner Ogle, married the daughter of the late Bishop of Winchester from whom he got great preferment in the Church and would have long ago been higher but for his uncourtly disposition, never having been able to resist showing his Enthusiasm in any cause coloured with Publick Liberty.

I hope you continue in perfect Health and happiness and not idly bent to keep the results of your Studies to yourself. Lady Porchester desires to be remembered to you and with me wishes you would persuade yourself to come up and spend one of your vacations here with us, for I think you have arranged your attendance on your official Duties so as to have several months in the year to spare. In the strange arrangement of this world one lives daily with People one cares little about and does not see above once [in] an age those one esteems most.

Pray remember me kindly to all your Family, not forgetting my good friend Miss Douglas.

I remain, my Dear Smith,
with the greatest esteem and regard, most faithfully and
affectionately Yours,

PORCHESTER.

LXI. *Adam Smith to George Chalmers, Berkeley Square, No. 31, London.*[1]

Custom House,
Edinburgh,
10 Nov. 1785.

Sir,

I received the honour of your very polite and obliging letter of the 3rd Nov^r, and shall be very happy to give you every information in my power towards perfecting so very useful and comfortable a work as your estimate.[2] The two accounts you wish for are official accounts which have been annually transmitted to the treasury in consequence of an annual order for that purpose. It is contrary to the practice of this Board to communicate accounts of this nature to any private person without particular order or permission from a secretary of the treasury. The slightest card from Mr. Rose either to me, if he will do me that honour, or to any other member of our Board will procure you that and any other information in our power to give without a moment's delay.

[1] National Library, Edinburgh, Watson Coll. MSS, No. 680.

[2] *The Estimate of the comparative Strength of Great Britain* was first published in 1782. There were further editions in 1786, 1794, 1802, 1804, 1812. In a copy of the edition of 1782, presented by Chalmers to Adam Smith, there is an inscription " the Author requests Dr. Adam Smith to accept this enlarged and corrected copy of his Estimate as a mark of his high respect". As to the explanation of the words " enlarged and corrected copy " and eulogistic references to *The Wealth of Nations* in the body of the work—see J. Bonar, *Library of Adam Smith*, 1932, pp. 43-4.

The accounts of tunnage of British shipping entered and cleared out from the ports of Scotland does not comprehend the Coast trade. The accounts of that trade may easily be had from the year 1779. It cannot easily be had from the year 1759.[1]

The late reverend Mr. Webster,[2] of all the men I have ever known the most skilful in Political Arithmetic, had made out what seemed a very accurate account of the Population of Scotland as it stood in the year 1755. He had collected the lists of births, burials and marriages in all the different Parishes in Scotland. In many of the parishes he had got the people counted accurately. In others he had got the lists of what are called examinable persons, that is, of people who are fit to be examined before the Kirk Session in the Scotch Catechism, Children of seven and eight years of age are considered as examinable persons. In several parishes he had got the ages of all the different inhabitants ascertained. He had computed the numbers in the Parishes where he had got only the lists of the Births, Burials and Marriages by those in the Parishes which were in nearly similar circumstances and had been accurately counted. This account filled a pretty large Volume in folio. About ten years ago I had the use of this account for many months. By it the whole number of souls in Scotland amounted to little more than 1,250,000. The same Gentleman a few months before his death told me that he had stated the numbers too low; and that, upon better information, he believed they might amount to 1,500,000, according to the best of my recollection. I acknowledge, however, I cannot be very positive about the precise number mentioned in this verbal information. If he has left any papers behind him upon this subject which I can either get access to, or get any distinct account of, I shall immediately inform you. You know that I have little faith in Political Arithmetic and this story does not contribute to mend my opinion of it.

I am very much flattered by your good opinion of my book. There is no man living whose approbation I set more value upon.

I have the honour to be with the highest respect and esteem, Sir, Your most obedient and most faithful humble Servant,

ADAM SMITH.

[1] There is a large collection of Customs Papers bound in a great vellum folio, which was presented to the Glasgow University Library by Dr. Bonar in 1931. Many of these documents relate to shipping. Document No. 13 may be a draft of that prepared for Chalmers or a correction of the figures supplied to him. It is significant that Adam Smith writes, the particulars "cannot easily be had from 1759", and this paper begins with that year and continues till 1788, showing that the return was continued consecutively. It is endorsed "sent" [to London] "24, Dec. 1788."

[2] The MS. "Account of the Number of the People in Scotland in the year, 1755" is in the National Library, Edinburgh. There is also a copy at the General Register House, Edinburgh. The author, Alexander Webster (c. 1707-84), had already joined with Revd. Dr. Robert Wallace in promoting a scheme for pensions for widows of ministers of the Church of Scotland which was based on returns of marriages and the age at death of ministers. This scheme was established by Act of Parliament in 1742 and still exists. The enquiries made amongst the parishes facilitated the preparation of the "Account". In the later editions Chalmers quotes a figure of 1,555,663 for the population of Scotland in 1775—*Estimate*, 1812, p. 387 note.

LXII. *Adam Smith to George Chalmers.*[1]

Mr. Smith's most respectful compliments to Mr. Chalmers. He sends him the tunnage account corrected in the way he wished. The other accounts which he wanted will be forwarded with all possible dispatch on Monday or tuesday next at farthest Friday, 3rd Dec^r, 1785.

LXIII. *Adam Smith to [William Strahan].*[2]

Edinburgh,
13 feb, 1786.

Dear Sir,

I must beg the favour of you to endeavour to employ Sharp[3] for three or four weeks to come in the best way you can, till we have time to look about us. I see he does not spell well, which alone must make him a bad compositor. I have wrote him an encouraging letter, as his letter to me expressed great dejection of spirits. I have, however, (as you will see by the enclosed, which I beg you will read) taken notice of this defect. If in the meantime you could recommend him as clerk to any Warehouse keeper, an employment for which you think him qualified, I should be much obliged to you.

I beg you will employ one of your best compositors in printing the new edition of my book. I must beg that a compleat copy be sent to me before it is published that I may revise and correct it. You may depend upon my not detaining you above a week. I should likewise be glad to know when I may draw for the money; I wish to conclude the transaction, least Mr Cadell should take another fit of the ague and make another request which may not be so well received as the former.[4]

I ever am, Dear Sir, Most faithfully yours,
ADAM SMITH.

---

[1] National Libry. Edin. Miscellaneous Letters and Papers (George Chalmers Coll.) 2. 1. 15, f. 60.

[2] In the possession of Professor J. H. Hollander, Baltimore, U.S.A.

[3] In the Bannerman Papers at Glasg. Univ. Libry. there is a letter from Buccleuch Sharp, dated 5th Feb., 1786, stating that he was employed as a printer by Strahan, but he wished a change of occupation. He was anxious to do copying for Adam Smith.

[4] Reference to the terms between Adam Smith and Cadell (see below, p. 314) shows that profits on the first two editions were divided between them. The payment for copyright took effect from the third edition. The last sentence of the letter seems to indicate there was some delay in remitting the amount due to the author.

CORRESPONDENCE

LXIV. *Adam Smith to [Sir John Sinclair of Ulbster].*[1]

Edinburgh,
11 April 1786.

Dear Sir,

I took the liberty to write you some weeks ago a pretty long letter which I should be glad to hear you had received; and that you have, from the bottom of your heart, forgiven the very great freedom which I have used with you.

In that letter I said that I had no particular remark to make upon what you had said concerning sugar. Upon further recollection, however, I suspect you are wrong with regard to the prices of Muscovado Sugar. I never have bought any of that sugar for family use,[2] so that I have no personal experience of the price. I remember, I think, having told you that during the late war I used to pay fourteen and fifteen pence for the same sugar which I now buy for eight pence and nine pence. I wish you would make some further enquiry concerning the prices of Muscovado Sugar. It certainly could never be so low as a penny a pound. When I lived at Glasgow a hogshead of Muscovado Sugar was valued at importation from thirty to thirty six shillings the hundred weight of 112 lib. The pound could not be sold, at this rate, under four or five pence; I am told that it sells at present for six pence; The sugar which I principally make use of is what good Housewives call breakfast Sugar and which I buy at the price above mentioned [of] eight pence or nine pence a pound.

I heartily congratulate you upon your late acquisition of Title;[3] and hope I may still live to see you arrive at still higher honours.

I ever am
My Dear Sir
Most faithfully and affectionately Yours
ADAM SMITH.

[1] State Historical Museum, Moscow. The name of the recipient of this letter is not given. As to the reasons for assigning it to Sinclair see the last sentence.

[2] Adam Smith had a special interest in sugar, as is shown by the following anecdote: " Being a bachelor, his household was managed by his cousin, Miss Jeany Douglas, a stern old maid, of whom the philosopher is said to have stood so much in awe, that, though fond of a lump of sugar, (perhaps for the excitement of his physical system during study), he had to watch till her back was turned, before venturing to snatch it from the tea table."—*Minor Antiquities of Edinburgh*, 1833, p. 253. A slightly different version of the tale is given by Sir Walter Scott; *cf.* Rae, *Life*, p. 338.

[3] John Sinclair of Ulbster was created a Baronet on 14th February, 1786. Sinclair and Smith were in contact by 1777 (Rae, *Life*, pp. 343, 382, 394, 417). Also in this year Sinclair made a very extensive journey in the north of Europe, during which he visited St. Petersburg—G. E. Cokayne, *Baronetage*, v, p. 248. Another title of the same year is of interest to students of Adam Smith. William Green, who was chief engineer at Gibraltar, was created a baronet in June. His mother was named Helen and she was a sister of "Adam Smith of Aberdeen". This Adam may possibly have been a son of the William Smith of Aberdeen who was a tutor and curator of the economist, or he may have been the Adam who was Collector at Alloa (see above, pp. 132, 235), who was born in Aberdeen, maintained his connection with the city and lived there after his retirement. He

LXV. *Adam Smith to the Abbé Morellet.*[1]

Edinburgh,
May, 1786.

Dear Sir,

After so long an Interruption of our correspondence, I should have been afraid to put you in mind of an old acquaintance, if I had not understood from our most valuable friend the Marquis of Landsdown,[2] that you still did me the honour to remember me with some degree of kindness. It is in consequence of this that I now venture to introduce to your acquaintance, my particular friend, Mr John Bruce, Professor of Logic [3] in the University of Edinburgh. He accompanies on his travels Mr Dundas, a young gentleman of great modesty and propriety of manners and of great application to his studies and to all his other duties, the son of the gentleman who may be considered as our present Minister for Scotland.[4] Give me leave to recommend them both to your advice and protection during whatever stay they may think proper to make in your Capital.

Give me leave to condole with you on the many heavy losses which the Society, in which I had the Pleasure of seeing you about twenty years ago, have sustained through the death of so many of its greatest ornaments, of Helvetius, of Mr Turgot, of Mademoiselle D'Espinasse, of M^r D'Alembert, of Mr Diderot.[5] I have not heard of Baron d'Holbach these two or three years past. I hope he is happy and in

---

invested money in the district, as for instance in a loan to his connection, William Walker (*cf.* above, p. 276). He was dead in 1763, in which year his son, William, was made a burgess, and some of his daughters were living at Aberdeen early in the nineteenth century.

[1] In the possession of Professor J. H. Hollander, Baltimore, U.S.A. The saying of Hume, quoted above p. 125 note (2), shows an expectation, or at least a hope, that Morellet should reduce the Physiocrats " to dust and ashes ". Recurring to what was said at that place it is perhaps worth adding that the Advocates Library had no copy of any Physiocratic book before Adam Smith went to France. It is true that the Catalogue records *L'Ami des Hommes*, 6 tom., 1758. That is before Mirabeau joined the Physiocrats. This is the edition issued à la Haye chez Benjamin Gilbert. The volumes are dated i-iii, 1758 ; iv, 1759 ; v and vi, 1762, and vol. vi contains the " Tableau Economique." This seems to be in direct contradiction to what has been said above. The explanation is that the book only reached the library in 1771. I am obliged to Dr. Meikle for burrowing into the old registers to settle this point, which is of considerable interest.

[2] See above, p. 292, where he appears as the second earl of Shelburne. He was created Marquis of Lansdowne in 1784.

[3] John Bruce (1744-1826), Professor of Logic, 1774-86, travelling tutor to Robert Dundas (the pupil mentioned in the letter), who succeeded his father, Henry Dundas, as second Viscount Melville. Bruce was employed under Henry Dundas in the Board of Control of Indian Affairs and became Keeper of the State Paper Office and Historiographer of the East India Company. In the latter capacity he wrote the *Annals* of the Company. He belonged to the family of Bruce of Earl's Hall, Fife, and died at an estate he owned near Falkland.

[4] Adam Smith was fortunate in his relations with the two most influential men in Scotland during the eighteenth century. John, Duke of Argyle, was his early patron and he enjoyed the friendship of Henry Dundas.

[5] For an account of this circle see Rae, *Life*, pp. 194-231.

good health. Be so good as to assure him of my most affectionate and respectful remembrance, and that I shall never forget the very great kindness he did me the honour to shew me during my residence at Paris. Excuse this very great freedom, and believe me to be, with the highest respect & esteem,
   Dear Sir, Your most obliged and most obedient Servant,
                ADAM SMITH.

LXVI. *Adam Smith to Thomas Cadell*.[1]

             Edinburgh,
             7 May, 1786.

Dear Sir,
  This letter will be delivered to you by my very intimate and particular friend Mr John Bruce.[2] He has a work upon moral Philosophy which, tho' he and I differ a little as David Hume and I used to do, I expect will do him very great honour.[3] It is as free from metaphysics as is possible for any work on that subject to be. Its fault, in my opinion, is that it is too free of them. But what is a fault to me may very probably be a recommendation to the Public. It is extremely well written; with simplicity and perspicuity every where, and in proper places with warmth which becomes the subject. I most earnestly recommend it to your attention.
  I ever am, Dear Sir, Most faithfully yours,
                ADAM SMITH.

LXVII. *Adam Smith to " John Bruce, Esq. chez Mons. de la Serriere, Rue de Tossez, St. Jacques à Paris"*.[4]

             Edinburgh,
             3rd Oct^r., 1786.

My Dear John,
  After begging your pardon for having so long delayed[5] writing to you, at last I send you the letter I promised to Professor Meiner. My mortal aversion to letters of compliment and ceremony has been the principal cause of the delay.

---

[1] Pierpont Morgan Library, New York.

[2] Professor of Moral Philosophy at Edinburgh, afterwards Historiographer of the East India Company.

[3] Published in 1786 under the title *Elements of the Science of Ethics, on the Principles of Natural Philosophy*.

[4] General Register House, Edinburgh.

[5] Adam Smith had written to Bruce on 7th Sept., 1786 (who was then in Edinburgh), saying that he had much private business on hand and begging a postponement of his reply to Bruce's request.

Remember me most affectionately to your Pupil,[1] and believe me with the greatest love and regard, My Dear John, most faithfully and sincerely yours,

ADAM SMITH.

LXVIII. *Adam Smith to [Lieutenant-Colonel Alexander Ross].*[2]

Edinburgh,
13, Decr. 1786.

My Dear Sir,
When I had the honour to wait upon you immediately before you left Scotland, I told you that there was only one man in India whom I would presume to recommend to your particular countenance and protection ; viz, your name sake Lieut^{nt} Collonel Ross, chief Engineer upon the Madras Establishment. A very particular circumstance obliges me to depart from this resolution. My old and most valuable friend, Mr William Burke,[3] was appointed deputy paymaster General to the King's forces in India when his Cousin, Edmund, was paymaster general. He still continues to enjoy that office. May I most earnestly recommend him, not only to your notice and kindness, but even to your friendship. I am sure you will find him worthy of it. You never knew an honester hearted fellow ; social, convivial, perfectly good-natured and quite frank & open ; naturally the friend of every man that stood in need of a friend. He is a real man of Business, of excellent abilities ; and, as he went out to India after the first intimation of Lord Pigot's affair[4] arrived in England, he must by this time have acquired a

---

[1] " I hope Mr. Dundas will not be offended at Mr. Bruce for allowing Bob to see me during my stay at Paris. He grows most amazing like his father every day ; with some difficulty I prevailed on him to talk French—it was bad, but I hope will improve before he goes home. He has likewise got a dancing master which he stands much in need of."—Mrs. E. Fawkener to the Duke of Buccleuch, 28th July, 1785, amongst Papers of Henry, the third Duke, at Dalkeith House.

[2] Harvard College Library. This letter was discovered lately by Dr. A. H. Cole of the Baker Library amongst the pages of a first edition of *The Wealth of Nations*. Through the facts that, as appears from the third line, the letter was written to someone named Ross and that it went to India (it is endorsed " received by the *Princess Royal* : answered 16th Aug./87 by the *Ravensworth* "), it is evident that the recipient was Lt.-Col. Alexander Ross, who entered the Army in 1760, served as aide-de-camp to Lord Cornwallis during the American War, was appointed Deputy Adjutant-General in Scotland in August 1783 and served in a similar capacity in India. He was promoted Colonel in 1793, Surveyor-General of Ordnance in 1795, Lieutenant-General in 1802 and General in 1812. The *Correspondence of Cornwallis* was edited by his son, Charles Ross, who mentions, as an instance of intimacy between his father and his chief, that in 1859 there were more than 400 letters extant which had been written between 1782 and 1805 by Cornwallis to his father. As to Patrick Ross, Chief Engineer at Madras, see the next letter but one.

[3] On 2nd Dec., 1789, Cornwallis wrote : " I have ever since I have been in India treated William Burke with the greatest possible attention and I have done him some little favours, such as Ensignies in the King's service to his friends. But it is impossible for me to serve him essentially, that is, to put large sums of money in his pocket, without gross violation of my public duty and doing acts for which I should deserve to be impeached "—*Correspondence*, i, p. 450.

[4] Governor of Madras 1775, suspended two members of the Council 1776, arrested and imprisoned by the suspended members, died in prison 17th April, 1777.

great knowledge and experience in the Affairs of that country. You will, I imagine, find few men more capable of giving both good information and good advice.

I need not tell you how much all your friends in this country lament and regret your absence. Nothing but the acquisition of distinguished honour and Glory can ever compensate the comfortable situation you left behind you, or make amends for your separation from all the love and friendship you enjoyed in this country. Wealth and preferment are most inadequate compensations. But as I know that nothing but your generous Attachment to your friend, Lord Cornwallis,[1] could have separated you from us, I have no doubt of your acquiring the only adequate compensation for what you have lost. I had the pleasure of seeing Lord Cornwallis twice at the Earl of Bristol's. He probably will not recollect me. If he does, I beg to be remembered to him in the most respectful manner. I have the honour to be, with the most perfect love and esteem, My Dear Sir,
Your most affectionate and most faithful, humble Servant,
ADAM SMITH.

LXIX. *From Adam Smith to Joseph Black.*[2]

London,
9 May, 1787.

My dear Doctor,
This letter will be delivered to you by the Baron de Baert, a french Gentleman of great distinction and greater information.[3] He is a great traveller and has visited a country unknown to all other travellers that ever I met with, the Southern frontier of the Russian Empire from Kion to Astrakan and Casan. I beg you will make him acquainted with Hutton and with every other person you think can amuse him.

He is recommended to me by the Duke of Rochefoucault, the gentleman in France to whom I owe the greatest obligations
I ever am, My Dear Doctor, most faithfully Yours
ADAM SMITH.

[1] Served in America under Howe and Clinton, Governor-General and Commander-in-Chief, Bengal, 1786, concluded treaty with Tippoo Sahib 1792, returned to England 1792, Governor-General of India 1804, died 1805.

[2] Letters and Papers of Joseph Black in the possession of Miss J. E. S. Black, S. Farnborough. The only other allusion to Adam Smith in Black's correspondence is a postscript in a letter from N. Cappe, York, dated 6th Nov., 1788, in which he and his family send " kind and respectful salutations " to him. There is a scrap containing names of " Three books, recommended by Smith : Cours et Etudes pour son Altesse, Prince de —— par M. de Condillac, Mosheim's Church History, Vertat, Father Paule." The first of these appears in the Catalogue of Adam Smith's library in 1781 under the title of " Cours d'Etude pour l'Instruction du Prince de Parme " in 12 vols.

[3] Alexandre Balthazar François de Paul de Baert (*c.* 1750-1825), author of *Tableau de la Grande Bretagne et d'Irlande* (1800) and other works.

LXX. *Henry Dundas to Adam Smith.*[1]

India Board,
21st March, 1787.

Dear Smith,

I received your letter this forenoon. Ross[2] was certainly injured, but Sir Archibald Campbell will do him justice. I would have persevered against the Court of Directors, but I was suspicious they would have carried their bad humour as far as to dismiss him from their Service, so that by protecting him farther I might have ruined him.

I am glad you have got vacation. Mr. Pitt, Mr. Greenville and your humble servant are clearly of opinion you cannot spend it so well as here. The weather is fine, my villa at Wimbledon a most comfortable, healthy place. You shall have a comfortable room; and, as the Business is much relaxed, we shall have time to discuss all your Books with you every evening. Mr. Greenville, who is an uncommonly sensible man, is concert in this request.

Yours faithfully,

HENRY DUNDAS.

---

[1] Bannerman Papers, Univ. Libry. Glasg. It was partly in response to this invitation that Adam Smith went to London in the following month. Partly, also, as is stated by Rae—*Life*, p. 404—to consult John Hunter as to the state of his health. It was at the house of Dundas during this visit that, on Smith's entering a room, where Addington, Grenville, Pitt and Wilberforce had assembled to meet him, they stood till Smith was seated because, as Pitt said, they were all his scholars. With regard to Wilberforce it is noted in the Buchan MSS.—Correspondence, ii, p. 171—that Clarkson mentions as " a great honour to the University of Glasgow that it should have produced, before any public agitation of this question [*i.e.* the abolition of the slave trade], three Professors all of whom bore their public testimony". These were Francis Hutcheson, Adam Smith and John Millar.

[2] The Ross mentioned was Adam Smith's cousin, Patrick Ross, son of Patrick Ross, Innernethy, Perthshire—Rae, *Life*, p. 361, and below, Appendix IV. In 1770 Patrick Ross was a Captain, and on 17th January of that year he was appointed Chief Engineer at the Fort of St. George, with the rank of Lieutenant-Colonel. On several occasions he applied for an advance in rank, and the particular difficulty, which occasioned Adam Smith's intervention, will appear from Paragraph 26 in the East India Company's Despatch to the Governor and Council at Fort St. George, dated 8th July, 1785. " In reply to the 283rd paragraph of your Select letter, dated 5th. September, 1782, relative to the request of your Chief Engineer, Lieutenant-Colonel Ross, we cannot help expressing our very great surprise that, after we had twice put a negative upon his application for advanced rank previous to his departure from England, he should have been induced soon after his arrival at Madras to renew his application to you. In his letter to your Board of the 1st July 1782 he states we had permitted him ' to return to his rank in the service which is next before Colonel James'. But Colonel Ross must have known that we permitted him in the very words of our Resolution " to return to his rank of *Lieut. Colonel and Chief Engineer at Madras*, but that he was not allowed to rank in the Infantry Corps on that Establishment ". And that on his subsequent request to rank as Colonel in the Army by Brevet we resolved not to comply therewith. His urging you therefore to a compliance with a request, which we had previously decided on, was highly disrespectful to us, and we direct you to acquaint Lieut. Colonel Ross of our disapprobation of his conduct on this occasion". Sir Archibald Campbell was Governor and Commander-in-Chief of the Province from 3rd September, 1786, to February 1789. The intervention of Adam Smith, through Dundas, proved successful, and Patrick Ross eventually retired with the rank of General.

LXXI. *Adam Smith to Henry Dundas.*[1]

Buckingham St.,
York Buildings, No. 12.
Wednesday 18 July 1787.

Dear Sir,

When I took the liberty to recommend to your protection my friend and near relation, Mr. Robert Douglas,[2] $Lieut^{nt}$ in the 58th regiment of foot, you was so good as to desire me to write you a letter to put you in mind of the Circumstances of his case. It is in consequence of this conversation that I take the liberty to trouble you at present.

He is the son of Coll. Robert Douglas of Strathendrie, the oldest friend and one of the nearest relations I have now living in the world. His two elder Brothers, $Lieut^{nt}$ Coll. Douglas of the Guards and John Robert Douglas of the corps of Engineers are both officers of merit. His younger brother, Charles Douglas, got a commission in Lord McLeod's regiment, some years after Robert had joined his regiment at Gibraltar. But McLeod's being a new raised regiment Charles's first commission was a Lieutenancy, and he had very soon an opportunity of purchasing a company in the same regiment. He was reduced to half pay at the peace, but had soon after an opportunity of exchanging into full pay with an officer who wished to retire and is now a Captain in Gibraltar. It is his elder Brother, Robert, an older officer and, I believe, an officer of very great merit still remaining a lieutenant. Both brothers served during the whole siege of Gibraltar, and were both present in the sally commanded by General Ross. During the continuance of the siege Robert's friends had several opportunities of purchasing a company for him, which they were very well disposed to embrace, but they were told, I think very properly, that he could not be removed from his regiment while in actual service. His service, therefore, has stopt his preferment instead of promoting it. For his character as an officer and a Gentleman I can safely refer you to all those whom he has served either with or under ; particularly, Sir George August Elliot, General Boyd and General Ross.

I believe I told you that one of Adair's places, Chelsea Hospital is in the gift of the paymasters, the other or rather the recommendation to it in that of the Secretary at War. Chelsea Hospital is the best of the two, but both would be best of all ; and nothing is too good for our friend John. In the giving away of these Places, the King, I understand, sometimes interferes.

Believe me to be, with the highest sense of your kindness, Dear Sir, your most obliged and most faithful humble Servant,

ADAM SMITH.

[1] National Library, Edinburgh, Melville Papers MS. 4 (f. 53).
[2] The Robert Douglas here mentioned and other members of the family are recorded in Appendix IV.

LXXII. *John Logan to Adam Smith.*[1]

London, 20th Augt '87.

Dear Sir,

I am happy to hear from Mr. Mackenzie that you have got down to Edinburgh in good health. There is an old acquaintance of mine, Dr. Rutherford, a Dissenting Clergyman and Master of an Academy at Uxbridge who is publishing " A View of antient History " by subscription. He is a good natured friendly Man and there is something interesting in his situation. Soon after he began the business of teaching, he was called to visit one of his former pupils who was in a fever. The boy died in his arms, and at the same time the Father was arrested for the sum of fifteen hundred pounds and would have been carried to prison if Dr. Rutherford had not been Security for him, who had the whole to pay. This was probably a London trick, but embarrassed Rutherford very much. Independent of this consideration, the book will not only be a good one but the very best on the subject. May I, therefore, hope that you will do him the honour to be one of his subscribers? The book is to be published in three volumes, large octavo, but I only ask the favour of you to subscribe for the first. If you could interest the family of Buccleugh in this affair, I would look upon it as a great favour, their names would be of great service to the keeper of an Academy.

The King of Prussia and our Court seem determined to support the Prince

---

[1] Bannerman MSS., Univ. Liby. Glasg. John Logan (1748-88), at one time a minister of the Scottish Church, was well qualified for a place in both Disraeli's *Quarrels of Authors* and *Curiosities of Literature*, for every one of his works involves either a controversy or a problem. He published in 1770 a collection of the Poems of his College friend Michael Bruce (who had died young), and at intervals ever since there has been an intermittent controversy as to whether he held back some of Bruce's writings which he issued later as his own. Amongst these is the " Ode to the Cuckoo ", which was described by Burke as " the most beautiful lyric in our language". One of the pieces of evidence cited in this dispute is that of Professor Davidson, which has a connection with Adam Smith's family. It was when returning from a visit to Colonel Douglas of Strathenry that Davidson, while passing through Kinnesswood, said he saw a letter of Bruce in which there was a reference to this ode. When Logan was a candidate for the Chair of Civil History at Edinburgh in 1780 he asked Carlyle to recommend him to " Home, Adam Ferguson and Dr. Smith". The next year he wrote from London that he was " in great habits with Dr. Smith", and it will have been seen that he asked Adam Smith's help in getting his play, *Runnamede*, introduced to the stage, p. 285. The Chamberlain intervened to prevent the play being acted in London on account of references to liberty which were considered injudicious. Chambers states that the *View of Antient History* was written by Logan, though published under the name of Rutherford—*Dict. of Eminent Scotsmen*, iii. p. 492. It appeared in two volumes in 1788-91, and reached a third edition in 1809. The above letter was sent with variations to other persons—as for instance to A. Carlyle—J. Mackenzie, *Life of Michael Bruce*, 1905, pp. 174-6. The attempt to excite sympathy with " Rutherford " in order to procure subscriptions is characteristic. In the last year of his life he issued a pamphlet *A Review of the Principal Charges against Mr. Hastings*, for publishing which Stockdale was prosecuted on the ground of infringing the privileges of the House of Commons. He was acquitted. Adam Smith thought better of Logan than several of his modern critics and he considered his *Poems* and *Elements of the Philosophy of History* deserving of a place in his library—Bonar, *Library of Adam Smith*, 1932, p. 104, and MS. catalogue of 1781.

PLATE XIV. ADAM SMITH IN HIS 64TH YEAR, 1787
In the antique manner by Tassie (Gray, No. 357).
(From the collection of Sir Edmund Findlay, Bart.)

of Orange, at the same time I have no apprehension of a war. The Duke of York is figuring away here at present and is very popular, which is not wonderful when we consider the Character of the Royal Competitors he has to struggle with.

Lord George Gordon [1] has returned to London and what is more extraordinary has become a Jew. He lodges at the house of my Taylor, goes to the synagogue on Saturdays and eats no meat but what is killed by the Jews. He is said to be making love to a rich Jewess, but I expect his plans are deeper and that he intends to set up as Messiah, a trade which has never been very successful. He set up a hideous and horrid roar when he was circumcised.

I set off to the country this day to remain for a fortnight which makes me shorten my letter.

Believe me to be ever, Sir, your most faithful hu^{ble} Servt

J. LOGAN.

LXXIII. *Adam Smith to* ⸺.[2]

Edin.
11 Oct^r, 1788.

Reverend and Dear Sir,

This letter is to introduce and to recommend to your attention three Spanish Gentlemen.

Collonel Francis Xavier Tyrry
Dr John Andrew de Temes y Prado
Don Francis Codon.

They are men of letters and are travelling for their instruction and improvement. Dr Temes is Rector of the University of Valladolid. They all speak french intellegibly. The Collonel even begins to make himself be understood in English. They are well informed men and their conversation will not be disagreeable to you. You are, I imagine, by far the best modern linguist among us, and I, therefor, have taken the liberty to give you this trouble; which I hope you will excuse,

I ever am, Reverend and Dear Sir,

Most faithfully and affectionately yours,

ADAM SMITH.

---

[1] Lord George Gordon at this time was in the midst of his disorderly appearances in London. In 1786 he took up the case of Cagliostro and the Diamond Necklace. In 1788 he was committed to Newgate for five years.

[2] New York Public Library.

LXXIV. *Adam Smith to the Revd. Dr. James Monteath, Closeburn Castle, Dumfriesshire.*[1]

Edin :
16, Sept^r, 1788.

My Dear James,

Your Letter gave my [2] very great pleasure as it both informed me of your good health and as it gave me the hope of seeing you here in the end of October or beginning of November. Millar seldom comes into Glasgow till the beginning of November; but he will be able to receive your son and you at his country house [3] just as conveniently as at his town house; and you and he may speculate about his farm.

Poor Miss Douglas [4] has been confined to her bed now for some time. Without any hope of recovery, she preserves her usual spirit and Chearfulness, directs the affairs of the family, which she expects to leave in a few days, with as much care and distinctness as ever; and, tho' sorry to part with her friends, seems to die with satisfaction and contentment, happy in the life that she has spent, and very well pleased with the lot that has fallen to her, and without the slightest fear or anxiety about the change she expects so soon to undergo.

We are much obliged to you for your Game; but do not send any more. Nobody in the family can eat them, and we do not at present entertain Strangers. About the end of the first week of Septr Miss Douglas said to me, " If you do not receive game in a day or two from your friend, Monteath, I shall believe that he is either not well, or not in the country". They arrived next day.

Remember me to the Ladies and the Young Gentlemen and believe me to be, with the greatest love and regard, My Dear James,

Ever Yours

ADAM SMITH.

LXXV. *Adam Smith to the Reverend Dr James Stewart Monteath Closeburn Castle.*[5]

Canongate,
2 feb., 1789.

My Dear James,

As soon as I received your letter I sent for Mr Angier, who could not then give me any such distinct and satisfactory answer concerning the time in

---

[1] Papers of Sir W. F. Stuart-Menteth, Bart., Mansefield House.

[2] A word omitted or else a mistake for " me ".

[3] The " town house " was that in the College where Millar was still a Professor. The " country house " was Milheugh, which remains in the possession of a branch of the family. Though some of Millar's books are there, no papers or letters relating to him have been found by the family.

[4] His cousin, Miss Janet Douglas.

[5] Papers of Sir W. F. Stuart-Menteth, Bart., Mansefield House.

CORRESPONDENCE

which he proposed to be at Glasgow, as was worth the communicating. I sent for him last week again, and he breakfasted with me this morning when he assured me he would be at Glasgow by the middle of next month. He said he would then be willing to charge himself with the cure of your son and, upon his leaving Glasgow in the beginning of May, to accompany him for some weeks to your house in the country. I have no doubt about the propriety of your accepting this proposal. He is much charmed with our friend, Charles's temper and Disposition.

I am much obliged to you for your enquiries about the Binghams : [1] they are very satisfactory and comfortable. I have had a very proper and very affecting letter from the Young Lady, which, however, I have not answered. She is young and I am not sure of her discretion. If Sir Charles, and if still more Lady Douglas should ever hear that I correspond with her, and disapprove of their conduct, it would put it totally out of my power to render her the smallest service. I expect them both here every hour when I hope to do her effectual service.

We are all longing for you at the Club, and, if you will take up your quarters with me, David's Bed is at your service.

Remember me most respectfully to Mrs Monteith and Miss Monteith and believe me to be, My Dearest James,
Most faithfully yours,

ADAM SMITH.

[1] This casual reference gives an unexpected light on Adam Smith's power of conciliation in circumstances very different from those which have been previously noted. His intervention arose in the following manner. He had a friend, Admiral Sir Charles Douglas, Bart. They were distantly related—Adam Smith being descended, through his mother, from the fifth Earl of Morton and Sir Charles Douglas from the sixth Earl. While Sir Charles had rendered good service in the Navy, having forced the passage of the St. Lawrence to relieve Quebec in 1776, he had not a happy manner with others in the service and was frequently embroiled both with his superiors and with civilians. Lady Douglas was very much " the wife of the Admiral of the Station ". The eighteenth century had its " revolting daughters", one of whom was their child, Lydia Marianna, who, when nineteen years of age, married on 10th Nov., 1788, Revd. Richard Bingham, a Fellow of New College, Oxford. The marriage was against the wishes of the parents, who were highly incensed. The young couple applied to Adam Smith in order that he should use his good offices to effect a reconciliation. The letter from the bride is not in existence, but from a later one (Bannerman MSS., L. M. Bingham to Adam Smith 20th Feb., 1789) it appears that he was successful in obtaining permission for her clothes and effects to be given to her. The father seemed likely to remain obdurate. He wrote to his sister Mrs. Baillie on 19th Feb., 1789 (Bannerman MSS.), that he was coming to Edinburgh, adding " in the meantime, I premise, that no disagreeable things are to be so much as spoken of ! And that nobody is so much as to make mention to me of any thing of my undutiful eldest daughter ! She being severed for ever and for ever from the parent stock ". Sir Charles died on 10th March, 1789. Adam Smith's anticipation of the attitude of Lady Douglas seems to have been confirmed, since the notices of this family in early issues of the Peerage include the name Lydia Marianna, but there is no mention of her marriage. It may be added that the married life of the pair was probably not devoid of some excitement. Richard Bingham became perpetual curate of Trinity Church, Gosport, in 1790 ; Vicar of Great Hale, Lincolnshire, in 1796 ; Prebendary of Chichester Cathedral in 1807. He spent six months in the county gaol at Winchester from 26th Nov., 1813, for having, illegally, obtained a licence for a public house when no such house was in existence. In 1829 he published by subscription the third edition of Joseph Bingham's *Origines Ecclesiasticæ*—Boase, *Modern English Biography*.

LXXVI. *Revd James Stuart Menteath to Adam Smith.*[1]

Closeburn Castle
20th Ap^l, 1789.

My Dear Adam,
From your sensibility of Soul you will easily conceive the pleasure that your most obliging Favour of the 15th gave me, and entirely relying on Professor Millar's authority and no less on good David's for the great Service done to my Son by Mr. Angier,[2] I have this Day written to Mr Erskine desiring Him to send you 43 guineas which I must beg the favour of you to pay Mr. Angier on my Acc^t, as likewise my most grateful Thanks and to tell Him that I rec^d His Letter, which I sh^d have answered myself but did not know where a Letter might find Him. Mr. Angier's Fee for a Cure is 50 guineas, now, as I had given Him 10 guineas for his attendance on my Son this time twelve months I presume that He will think the 40 guineas now a full Payment, but if you find He expects 50 for what He has lately done I will beg the favour of you to give him them. The 3 guineas is on acc^t of his Expenses while He was at Glasgow.

What you say with respect [to] yourself as to money Matters is equally applicable to me. We have both much larger Incomes now than at a former period, but I am not quite certain that either of us is more happy than we were then. Solomon sith, " He that increaseth Knowledge increaseth Sorrow "; this may be true, but I am not quite so certain of it as I am of this that He, who increaseth Property, increaseth Trouble. This I experience daily.

I am not quite determined about going to Glasgow for my Son, but if I go shall certainly return by Ed^r and do myself the pleasure of seeing you.

My best Respects attend your Sunday nights' Friends and believe me to be with great truth,
My Dear Adam, Your ever most obliged and most affectionate,
JA^s STUART MENTEATH.

---

[1] Bannerman MSS., Liby. Univ. Glasg. See above, p. 39. It will be noted that the name is spelled in different ways by the writers of the letters.

[2] The son of the writer—Charles Granville Stuart-Menteath—matriculated at Glasgow in 1788. It appears from the context that, before going to the University, he had been in need of professional treatment and that this had to be continued when he was living with John Millar, which was arranged by Adam Smith with the help of " the good David ". From the next letter it may perhaps be inferred that Angier's treatment was to remedy some impediment of speech. C. G. Stuart-Menteath became Vice-Lieutenant of Dumfriesshire. He was created a Baronet in 1838, and claimed to be head of the house of Menteath, a claim contested by Dalyell of Binns. He died in 1847.

LXXVII. *Adam Smith to Rev^d Dr. James Stewart Monteath, Closeburn Castle.*[1]

Edin. 9 May 1789.

My Dear James,

David returned to me on Saturday the 2nd inst. The first question I asked him was concerning your son. He said, your son was wonderfully improved by Angier's instructions; but that after Angier had left him, he (David) thought he had fallen back a little. He said your son's industry was prodigious; and that, as their rooms were adjoining, he heard your son every day practising Angier's lessons aloud, some times as early as five in the morning. I was excessively vexed at this intelligence; and, as soon as I could see Angier, complained to him of it. He said the habit might not be compleatly confirmed; but that, whenever he was in the same place with Mr. Monteath, he was willing to attend him without fee or reward. I received the inclosed letter from him this morning in confirmation of this. Angier was perfectly satisfied with the 43 guineas. I had not lain out of the money above half a minute when James Dundas repaid it.

Ever yours

ADAM SMITH.

LXXVIII. *Adam Smith to Thomas Cadell.*[2]

Custom House
Edinburgh, 31 March, 1789.

Dear Sir,

Since I wrote to you last I have been labouring very hard in preparing the proposed new edition of the Theory of Moral Sentiments. I have even hurt my health and been obliged to return, within these few days, to my usual attendance at the Custom house (from which the indulgence of my colleagues had excused me), I may say principally for the sake of relaxation and a much easier Business. Besides the Additions and improvements I mentioned to you, I have inserted, immediately after the fifth part, a compleat new sixth part containing a practical system of Morality, under the title of the Character of Virtue. The Book now will consist of seven Parts and will make two pretty large 8vo. Volumes. After all my labours, however, I am afraid it will be Midsummer before I can get the whole Manuscript in such proper order as to send it to you.[3] I am very much ashamed of this delay; but the subject has grown upon me. I would fain flatter myself that your Profit from the additions will fully compensate the loss you may have suffered by the delay. Let me hear from you as soon as you conveniently can. Remember me to Strahan and Believe me, ever yours,

ADAM SMITH.

[1] Papers of Sir W. F. Stuart-Menteth, Bart., Mansefield House.

[2] In the possession of Professor J. H. Hollander, Baltimore, U.S.A.

[3] The sixth edition which appeared in 1790 before Adam Smith's death—*cf.* Bonar, *Library of Adam Smith*, 1932, pp. 169-70.

LXXIX. *Adam Smith to David Douglas.*[1]

Edin.
21 Jan. 1790.

My Dearest David,

I have many apologies to make to you for having neglected so long to write to you. You will not, I know, impute it to any want of regard or affection but to an increased shaking in my hand which renders writing more and more inconvenient for me.[2] Your day of tryal [3] will probably be some day in May as, it is proposed, I understand to bring a new act of Parliament altering the day of meeting for the court of Session from the 12th day of June to the 12th or some other day in May. You may, I believe, rest satisfied that nobody will get before you.

The illness of Mr Hamilton [4] gives me the greatest concern. His death, which God forbid, would be an irreparable loss to the College of Glasgow.

I saw Mr Herbert [5] at Dalkeith ; but I only saw him. He was so good as to call on me at Edinburgh. But I had the ill Luck to miss him. Be so good as to deliver the inclosed letter to him ; it is an invitation to spend some part of the summer with us at Edinburgh. By putting up a bed in our Drawing room we can very easily accomodate him.

I should be glad to hear how the Greek goes on. I suppose by this time you are far advanced in the Odyssey. Mrs Ross and Miss Ross are both in their usual state of health, as is likewise your Brother, the Col¹, who is here just now on his way to London.[6] Remember me to Mr and Mrs. Miller, to Mr James and to all the rest of the family.

I ever am, my Dearest David,
Most affectionately yours
ADAM SMITH.

---

[1] In the possession of Professor J. H. Hollander, Baltimore, U.S.A.

[2] What Adam Smith writes is illustrated by the specimens of his writing during the last four years of his life.

[3] *I.e.* for admission as an Advocate.

[4] William Hamilton, Professor of Anatomy, had studied under Black, Cullen and William Hunter. His illness proved fatal and he died in his thirty-second year. His eldest son was Sir William Hamilton, Professor of Logic and Metaphysics at the University of Edinburgh.

[5] Probably the eldest son of Adam Smith's former pupil, Henry Herbert, who had been elevated to the peerage as Baron Porchester in 1780, and who corresponded with his former professor ; see above, pp. 68 note ², 293.

[6] Susannah Ross was a niece of Adam Smith's mother (see below, p. 414). She may have been dead at the date of this letter, in which case the Mrs. Ross mentioned would have been her daughter-in-law, the wife of Colonel Patrick Ross who is alluded to in a letter quoted by Rae, *Life*, p. 361. Colonel Douglas was the Colonel William Ann Douglas mentioned below, p. 415.

LXXX. *The Duke of Buccleuch to Adam Smith.*[1]

Gros. Sq.,
24th. Feb. 1790.

My Dear Sir,

I took the first opportunity in my power of speaking to Mr. Dundas about Dr. Cullen's daughters. The enclosed letter will give you pleasure and I have no doubt public satisfaction. Ministers seldom gain much credit by granting of Pensions, but in this case, I am sure, Mr. Pitt and Mr. Dundas will be much commended.

I hope this fine weather will restore you to your usual strength, I wish you could go to Dalkeith House for some time, I am sure the Country air and gentle exercise will be of service to you. I need not tell you how much I am interested in whatever concerns you. I should be ungrateful if I did not feel, as I do, with regard to your health and happiness. We have long lived in friendship, uninterrupted for one single moment, since we were first acquainted.

I hope soon to hear from you,
Yours sincerely,

BUCCLEUGH.

LXXXI. *From John Millar to David Douglas, " Panmure House, Cannongate", Edinburgh.*[2]

Milheugh,
10 Aug^t, 1790.

My Dear Sir,

I am much obliged to you for the particulars of which you give me an account, both with respect to our late worthy friend, and to yourself. I could easily have supposed it was not an object with Mr. Smith to make money, but if he had not been remarkably inattentive to that article, as he was a man of no personal expense, he must have made much more than he has done.[3] As it is, I sincerely think you have enough for any good purpose. You have little enough to excite you to activity in business, and what is abundantly sufficient to enable you to carry

---

[1] Bannerman Papers, Univ. Libry. Glasg. The pension for the daughters of Dr. Cullen is in response to the request made by Adam Smith to the Duke of Buccleuch and others mentioned by Lord Buchan—Rae, *Life*, p. 433.

[2] Bannerman MSS., Univ. Libry. Glasg. The writer of this letter is Adam Smith's pupil and friend, the Professor of Law at Glasgow.

[3] The true explanation is given by D. Stewart on the authority of Miss Ross, Adam Smith's cousin—" some very affecting instances of Mr. Smith's benificence, in cases where he found it impossible to conceal entirely his good offices have been mentioned to me by a near relation of his, Miss Ross, daughter of the late Patrick Ross, Esq. of Innernethy. They were all on a scale much beyond what might have been expected from his fortune, and were accompanied with circumstances equally honourable to the delicacy of his feelings and the liberality of his heart "—*Memoir*, p. 106 (note).

it on with proper frugality. I mean without encroaching upon the library, which you certainly will be disposed to retain undiminished.[1] I should think your best scheme would be, upon your putting on the gown, to buy a small house, for which you have already more furniture than will be sufficient, and to procure an *elderly* female servant for your house-keeper. In this way you may live very comfortably, and as frugally as you please. You will easily perceive that I have it in view to eat a bit of toasted cheese with you of an evening. These are the only entertainments you should give for many years to come, unless it be a dinner to a favorite *writer*, or rather a writer who makes a favorite of you.[2]

I regret the fate of the MSS. though I am not surprised at it. If they were unfinished, it was judicious to prevent their coming before the public, because an author who has acquired a high reputation has much to lose, but little to gain by any new publication. If a man has written one book of merit, everyone thinks that it requires nothing but industry to write another. But if he falls off, the first was a lucky hit. It would have been happy for John Hume,[3] that he had never written any thing but " Douglas". I am far from imagining, however, that Mr. Smith's MSS. would have conveyed any such idea. Indeed I *know* the contrary. They would have conveyed the same marks of genius, a genius of the highest order, perhaps with less correctness, or at least with some inequality in the composition.

It will give me the greatest pleasure to contribute any hints to Mr. Stuart[4] with regard to Mr. Smith's professorial talents, or any other particular you mention, while he remained at Glasgow—with this proviso, that Mr Stuart shall use the utmost freedom with every article and make the whole entirely his own, as far as he makes use of it. I shall expect to hear soon from you or Mr. Stuart, at what time I should be ready.

I am glad to hear that a part of Mr. Smith's writings are likely to see the light— for I hope you and your privy council[5] will use all the latitude you can upon that side of the question. Of the discourses which he intended upon the imitative arts, he read two to our Society at Glasgow,[6] but the third was not then finished. I wish it may be finished now. Of all his writings, I have most curiosity about the

---

[1] This was done by David Douglas. The subsequent history of the library is traced by Dr. James Bonar, *Libry. of Adam Smith*, 1932, pp. xvii, xxx-i.

[2] *I.e.* a solicitor. David Douglas was about to begin practising at the Scottish Bar.

[3] The name is now written " Home." It is usually pronounced " Hume " and was often written in that form.

[4] *I.e.* Dugald Stewart. Millar's contribution appeared in Stewart's *Memoir*.

[5] Joseph Black and James Hutton—Smith's literary executors—assisted, as appears later (p. 314), by Henry Mackenzie.

[6] This was the Literary Society of which Millar was a member. No notice of the papers mentioned in the text is to be found in the extracts from the first volume of the minutes which were printed in *Notices and Documents illustrative of the Literary History of Glasgow*, 1831, pp. 132-5.

metaphysical work you mention. I should like to see his powers of illustration employed upon the true old Humean philosophy.[1] You have not, I hope, given up thought of a visit to us this summer. I can easily imagine [2] ... you have felt for some time must have ... to your studies with much effect. That, however, is a circumstance of little moment. Perhaps it may be as well to admit a little further dissipation before you buckle to for the winter. You have been so regular hitherto that you need not be afraid of yourself. I have been constantly at home, and shall, in all probability, continue for the rest of the summer. Everybody here desires to be remembered to you.

I am ever, My Dear Friend, Yours Sincerely

JOHN MILLAR.

LXXXII. *Lord Loughborough to* (?) *David Douglas.*[3]

Sir,

14th Aug^t, 1790.

I should have written an earlier Answer to the Letter I was favoured with upon a very affecting subject, but you will easily conceive that a reluctance to enter upon it would long suspend my resolution. Tho' the Loss of my much esteemed friend must be deeply felt by all who knew Him, no one has more reason than yourself to lament it. His regard for you was very strongly marked in the last conversation I had with Him, and I shall always feel it a duty to shew every attention in my power to one so much connected with Him.

The disposition of his unprinted Works is exactly what I expected as he told me it was his determination to destroy the greater part of them, and He particularly excepted the History of Astronomy and his Treatise on the imitative Arts.[4] The last I had seen when he was in London, but, I understood it had since received some alterations. The first I had not seen for many years, but understood from conversation that he had been employed in correcting it.

You will undoubtedly be most solicitous that any publication may correspond to the reputation his name has so justly acquired and I shall be very glad to be informed when any intention of publishing any part of his works is to take place. If you should come into any part of the Kingdom where I happen to be, I trust you will be no Stranger to my House.

I am, Sir, w^h great regard,

Y^r Obedient Humble Servant,

LOUGHBOROUGH.

[1] There is no trace of this MS.

[2] As in some other cases, parts of the letter have been lost in the breaking of the seal.

[3] Bannerman Papers., Univ. Libry. Glasg.

[4] These two Essays were more complete than the other posthumous publications. The first extends to 93 pp. in the first edition of the *Essays on Philosophical Subjects* (pp. 1-93). That "On the Imitative Arts" comes fourth and amounts to 52 pp. The first two parts are in a revised form, but Part III., which deals with dancing, is very far from complete.

LXXXIII. *From T. Cadell to Henry Mackenzie.*[1]

London, Decr 21, 1792.

Dear Sir,·
I am to acknowledge the rec^t of your favour of the 12th and I am much surprised to find you did not receive my former Letter on the subject of Mr. Smith's posthumous work—this Letter I wrote from Eastbourn August 31 in answer to yours of the Second. [It] has long been a fixed rule with Mr. Strahan and myself not to [se]t a value upon Literary works—we receive the Author's proposal and then Judge whether we can accept or not—but in this case, such is our respect for the memory of Mr. Smith and such is our confidence in you, my Dear Sir, that we are induced to submit the following offer to your consideration, viz. that the first Edition be printed in Quarto and to consist of one thousand copies for which we will pay three Hundred pounds, and in case the Book should be printed again we agree to pay a further sum of two Hundred pounds. On referring back to our agreement with Mr. Smith we find that we shared the profits of the Quarto Edition with the Author; [2] that, when the Book was established, we paid for the property £300 for the term of 14 years, and a further sum of £300 in case the Author lived to assign his second term of 14 years, which you know he did. As the work, now to be published, can only be assigned for 14 years, we flatter ourselves the offer we now make will be acceptable. We should prefer printing in London, if equally agreeable to you.[3]

Mr. Strahan desires his affectionate Compliments, and I remain, Dr Sir,
Your ever obliged and most Humble servant,
T. CADELL.

Cannot we have a Portrait of Dr Smith's—I much wish to add his to my list.[4]

[1] Bannerman Papers, Univ. Lib. Glasg.

[2] It appears from a letter which Adam Smith wrote to Strahan on 13th November, 1776 (Rae, *Life*, p. 308), that he had then received "£300 of the copy money of the first edition".

[3] As compared with what was paid Adam Smith and his executors for the two books mentioned, Robertson is said to have received more than £600 for his *History of Scotland* and £4500 for the *History of the Reign of Charles V.* An opponent in the Assembly calculated that the latter sum worked out at 2d. per word—Kay, *Edinburgh Portraits*, 1842, i., p. 94.

[4] A good reproduction of the Tassie Medallion (with wig) was added to the 1811 Edition of Stewart's *Memoir* of Adam Smith.

PART III

AN EARLY DRAFT OF PART OF
THE WEALTH OF NATIONS
(*c.* 1763)

INTRODUCTION

The manuscript which follows may fairly be described as an early draft of *The Wealth of Nations*. The lectures which Adam Smith gave at Glasgow after the publication of the *Theory of Moral Sentiments* were on Jurisprudence, in which there were five " general parts "—two of these being economic. The manuscript which is printed below was intended to be an economic treatise, and nothing else. It begins with a chapter, headed the second, entitled " The Nature and Causes of Public Opulence ". It is evident that the unwritten first chapter would have corresponded to the Introduction of *The Wealth of Nations* and would have provided the plan of the book.

The finding of the manuscript came about in the following way. Amongst a number of quests for further information concerning Adam Smith it seemed possible that, since he had been tutor to Henry, third Duke of Buccleuch, there might exist some letters which would help in one or more of the enquiries which are discussed in the present volume. His Grace the late Duke, not only gave me every facility, but also provided most valuable information which contributed very materially to the ultimate success of the search. While some information came from his other seats, Dalkeith House proved most fruitful.

The negotiations relating to the tutorship were initiated by Charles Townshend, the second husband of the Countess of Dalkeith, who was the mother of Henry, the third Duke, to whom Adam Smith was tutor from 1764 to 1766. Townshend died in 1767, when Chancellor of the Exchequer, and his papers were collected from Downing Street and his town house and sent to his country residence at Adderbury ; whence, on the death of the Countess, they were brought to Dalkeith House, where they have been kept together ever since. The manuscript is amongst these papers. There is a certain appropriateness in its home, since Dalkeith at one time belonged to the head of the branch of the Douglas family from which Adam Smith's mother descended [1] till it was sold in 1642 by William, eighth Earl of Morton, to Francis Scott, second Earl of Buccleuch.[2]

There are clear indications of how this manuscript came to be written and why it was amongst Townshend's papers. Rae records that Hume wrote to Adam Smith on 12th April, 1759, that Townshend had said to Oswald that he would put the Duke of Buccleuch under the care of the author of the *Theory of Moral Sentiments*, at the same time warning Smith of the instability of many of Townshend's projects.[3] Time went on,

---

[1] See below, Appendix IV.

[2] A. F. Steuart, *Dalkeith, its Castle and its Palace*, Edin. 1925, pp. 27-9.

[3] *Life of Adam Smith*, pp. 141-8. When Townshend was Secretary for War he was attacked in a pamphlet, *A Letter to the Right Honourable Ch . . . s T . . . nd Esq.*, London, 1763, p. 4, for what was alleged to be a radical change of policy, in the following terms : " In what manner, Sir, shall we

Smith had been to Dalkeith House and Townshend had visited him in Glasgow,[1] but nothing had been fixed. In view of what Hume had written and the impression of brilliance with a trace of instability which Townshend had produced on shrewd Scotsmen during the time he had been resident at Dalkeith in 1759-60,[2] Adam Smith evidently devised means of keeping himself before Townshend's mind, and something which arose out of conversations between them no doubt gave him an occasion to prepare this manuscript and send it to Townshend.

The manuscript is written on stout, handmade paper, in double folio sheets. The handwriting is that of an amanuensis, and it is almost certainly that of the College scribe who copied, amongst many other University documents, the long report by Adam Smith embodying the findings of the Committee of 1762 on the powers of the Rector and Principal.[3] It was revised by Adam Smith, who numbered the sheets, consisting of four pages each, $N.1$, $N.2$ up to $N.12$, thus making forty-eight pages containing 11,951 words.[4] There are also many other alterations by Adam Smith, and an effort is made to reproduce the character of the manuscript in type by printing the words and letters in Adam Smith's hand in italics. The manuscript is not complete. Each page has a catch-word and page 48 brings it to the quotation from " old Cato " which occurs in the *Glasgow Lectures* towards the end of the part treating of Agriculture in the " Slow Progress of Opulence "[5] which is " 1mo ". The catch-word is " 2do of ", which shows that the first of the missing pages was that which treated of the slow progress of arts and commerce. The reasons for the separation of the concluding sheets and their fate are discussed below.[6]

It will be observed that the manuscript has a character of its own. The first chapter —that is the one entitled " Chap. 2 "—treats of Division of Labour and corresponds to Chapters I and II of *The Wealth of Nations*. Indeed, except for some paragraphs which have been moved to other parts of the work and to which reference will be made later, the material has been taken almost verbatim into the later book, subject to verbal changes.

---

account for your present total change of character, rather indeed a direct contradiction to all your former sentiments and conduct. By what arguments is the reasoning of years in a few short days confuted ? Is it from the variety of genius, the flexibility of spirit, or the natural uncertainty of all human understanding that we thus start from one extreme to the other ? Or, instead of these subtle and metaphysical refinements, does it not merely simply proceed from first admiring our own parts and then raising the admiration of others by shewing the facility with which we can dispute and argue, and only not convince, on both sides of a question."

[1] See below, p. 324 note [3].

[2] Townshend had a scheme of changing his seat in Parliament and becoming member for Edinburgh. He was anxious to obtain the support of the Duke of Argyle, who had very great interest in Scotland. A friend, John Dalrymple, after attending the Duke's levee wrote on 1st September, 1759, to Townshend that " in the good, cautious, Scottish manner not a man would say good or ill of you ". Dalrymple broke the ice with a vivid description of Townshend's doings at Dalkeith, but all that he could report was that Argyle said " You was perhaps the cleverest man in the Kingdom "—Buccleuch MSS., Townshend Collection.

[3] Printed above, Part II, § L, V, pp. 202-15.

[4] The top of the first page, with Adam Smith's numeral and some other alterations by him, is reproduced on p. 386.

[5] P. 229. The corresponding portion of *The Wealth of Nations* is Book III, Chapter ii.

[6] P. 356 note [2].

such as the alteration of expressions sometimes, in the case of adjectives reducing, but in other cases increasing, the emphasis. Contrary to what might be expected, in repeating this manuscript in *The Wealth of Nations* there has been compression, rather than expansion as frequently happens when an earlier work is incorporated into a later one. The remaining Chapters are represented by rather detailed summaries. While thus less full than the *Glasgow Lectures*, they are of considerable interest as showing how close and integrated the argument is. Chap. 3 is concerned with Price, Chap. 4 with Money, Chap. 5 jumps to " The Slow Progress of Opulence ".

Is this manuscript that of the *Glasgow Lectures* or an early revision of these ? Many reasons point to the latter. The *Lectures* contain a few statements, which are scarcely of a nature to have been introduced extempore and are not to be found in the manuscript. It would have been necessary for Adam Smith to dictate the summaries of chapters and he might well have introduced some of the other differences which distinguish the manuscript from the *Lectures*. It may have been that further study and the use of his material in teaching had given him ideas not in the lectures which the reporter summarised. That course must have been given in the session 1762-3,[1] and it follows that the probable date of the revision, represented by this manuscript, would be 1763, probably the summer or later.[2]

It has been shown above,[3] that there had been at least three previous revisions of Adam Smith's economic material. In this later revision there is the epoch-making decision to separate it completely from the treatment of Jurisprudence in which it had been previously embedded. Only slightly less important is the very much greater prominence which is given to questions of Distribution here as compared with the report of the *Glasgow Lectures*. It is conceivable that these passages *were* in the *Lectures* and that they were either ignored or condensed to such an extent as to be scarcely recognisable, but the compiler of the notes has been found to have been exceptionally accurate in all other parts of his work, so that it seems a rather gratuitous assumption that he was fully adequate elsewhere and failed in this one particular, and not only in one place, but in several.[4] Still, whether these passages were in the lectures or were added to them in this revision, the outstanding fact is that the extent to which Adam Smith dealt with Distribution at this stage is much greater than has been supposed, and the scope and penetration of this treatment are noteworthy.

Professor Cannan in describing the relation of the *Glasgow Lectures* to *The Wealth of Nations* says that " the dissertations on the division of labour, money, prices and the causes of the differences of wages in different employments, evidently existed very nearly in their present form before Adam Smith went to France, and the scheme of distribution, on the other hand, was wholly absent. It is plain that Smith acquired the idea of the necessity of a scheme of distribution from the Physiocrats, and that he tacked

---

[1] An experiment made by an expert note-taker proves that it is not possible that the notes could have been taken in the part of the next session during which Adam Smith was at Glasgow.

[2] The differences between the *Glasgow Lectures* and the manuscript, on the supposition that the reporting was fairly uniform for each day, which may not have been the case, would probably have come about January, if they had been in the lectures and omitted by the note-taker.

[3] See Part I, Chapters V and IX.

[4] This question is discussed in *Economic Journal*, September, 1935.

his own scheme (very different from theirs) on to his already existing theory of prices."[1] Elsewhere he says that "there is no trace whatever in the lectures of the scheme of distribution which *The Wealth of Nations* sets forth".... "There is nothing at all about capital in the lectures and stock is not given an important place, while there is no mention whatever of that distinction between productive and unproductive labour which is fundamental in *The Wealth of Nations*."[2] No one could have expected that, when the lectures have been dated in the Session 1762-3, so near Adam Smith's departure for France, there should have been the revision represented by the manuscript now under consideration. Thus in these quotations there are two elements of time, namely, that represented by the *Lectures* and the period between the delivery of them and Adam Smith's departure to France. As regards the first of these, account has to be taken of that statement of Dugald Stewart, previously discussed, in which Smith stated that James Oswald had suggested to him the division of price into rent, profit of stock and the payment of labour.[3] If that is dated before 1764 Adam Smith's views on Distribution must have been more advanced than the summary by Cannan suggests. However that may have been, there can be no question that the present manuscript contains much more on Distribution than is to be found in the *Lectures*. There is a very definite scheme, a conception not only of a National Dividend, but of a real National Dividend, and in the example of pin-making this is considered as distributed amongst the members of a " great society ", though, it is true, that, for purposes of illustration, this is taken as consisting of 100,000 families. There will be found the division as between profit and wages, while rent is mentioned several times elsewhere. It is curious that on the first page of the manuscript the distinction between productive and unproductive labour stares one in the face.

It is of much interest that in this revision, where apparently for the first time he treated Distribution seriously, he endeavours to work it in with his account of Production. There are grounds for thinking that in Adam Smith's earliest treatment of economic questions he followed Hutcheson's order fairly closely.[4] That is retained in the *Lectures* and in the present revision of them. Arrangement of his material was always a difficulty with Adam Smith.[5] As regards Distribution, his first attempt was to show how as wealth was produced it was distributed. Later, he must have felt that this left too

---

[1] *Glasgow Lectures*, p. xxxi.   [2] *Glasgow Lectures*, p. xxviii.
[3] See above, Part I, Chapter IX.   [4] W. R. Scott, *Francis Hutcheson*, p. 235.

[5] A very remarkable instance of this problem of arrangement, which troubled him for more than forty years and provoked much controversy, was mentioned by himself. This related to the celebrated sentences on the Atonement. There is no reason to doubt Adam Smith's own statement that they were withdrawn in the sixth edition of the *Theory* (1790) because they were misplaced. Rae mentions (*Life*, p. 429) that the manuscript, containing these sentences, was found in a volume of Aristotle in the year 1831. Whether Rae intended it or not, this has been taken to mean that the fragment discovered was a part of the *Theory*. It was not, being the part of the Edinburgh Lectures which is described in Part I, Chapter V. This MS. begins with the conclusion of a discussion which is that " duty for its own sake " is " the natural and proper object of love and reward ". As first written this lecture went on to examine in some detail the principles of legal sanctions. At an early revision the sentences on the Atonement were inserted. This obviously was not a happy arrangement. In the *Theory* the passage was expanded and made to close Part II, Section II, Chapter iii. Then follows Section III, which discusses the influence of fortune upon the sentiments of mankind, which is far from being an ideal collocation.

much to be assumed involving many things that had not yet been explained.[1] As a result the distributive portion of *The Wealth of Nations* came to be treated with " price ".

Professor Cannan spoke of economic ideas having crossed the Channel many times while *The Wealth of Nations* was being composed, " and it is as useless, as it is invidious to dispute about the relative shares of Great Britain and France in the progress effected ".[2] Already Adam Smith (while he was at Glasgow) was in close touch with French Literature. Though he knew of Cantillon's *Essai*, either directly or through Postlethwayt's *Dictionary*, and had some acquaintance with the early volumes of the *Encyclopédie*, the more complete knowledge of the state of his library and that of the University render it highly improbable that he was acquainted with any work of the Physiocrats during this period.[3] He was fully conversant with the chief sources from which they reached the general standpoint which they, in large measure, shared with him. There the question might well be left, but there is a long-standing tradition in favour of a very direct Physiocratic influence upon Adam Smith. One group of alleged instances of this has been shown not to apply. But it is easy to think of anyone who clings to that traditon admitting, and gladly accepting, all that has been said about the character of the Distributive element in the manuscript, but placing its date after the meeting between the Physiocrats and Adam Smith. After all, the evidence, as to date, is based on a question of handwriting, and this is a matter open to differences of opinion. But the evidence is much more than this. Townshend died on 4th September, 1767. When Adam Smith returned from France towards the end of the previous year, he remained for six months collaborating with Townshend in the circumstances which have been explained elsewhere.[4] There would have been no need under such conditions to have prepared this manuscript. Accordingly, if it was written after the meeting with the Physiocrats, it must have been done in France, and it is difficult to suppose that an amanuensis with a characteristic British handwriting would have been available there. In fact, as previously stated, the hand is very definitely that of one of the scribes of Glasgow University. Confirmation comes from a most unexpected quarter. If, as Adam Smith himself said, he was a beau in his books, he was the complete dandy in his writing-paper. He not only had the very best handmade paper, but that which was commonly used by Government departments. In the muniments of the University of Glasgow there are a number of specimens, even used as covers for documents with endorsements by Adam Smith, and the manuscript now under consideration is written on this type of paper. It was of Dutch manufacture, since, though it was claimed as far back as 1695 that good, white writing-paper was being made in England,[5] that imported from Holland and France was preferred during almost the whole of the eighteenth century. That on which Adam Smith wrote bore watermarks similar to those of the paper which had been used by his father,

---

[1] As one reads the distributive sentences in the paragraphs on pin-making there is a most vivid sense of this difficulty. Hence the alternative statement of the problem in terms of a commodity distribution (pins) in order to meet the absence of any explanation of the nature of money and price.

[2] *Wealth of Nations* (ed. Cannan), i, pp. *xlvii, xlviii*.   [3] See above, Part II, § I.

[4] W. R. Scott, " Adam Smith at Downing St., 1766-7 " in *Economic History Review*, October 1935, pp. 79-89.

[5] W. R. Scott, *Joint Stock Companies*, 1911, iii, p. 67.

322 ADAM SMITH, AS STUDENT AND PROFESSOR

and it was the same as that used in Government offices. There were several types of watermark. The counter-mark on the left-hand double folio sheet was a double circle about 1¾ inch in diameter enclosing a laurel wreath, within which there is G.R. crowned. The royal cypher does not necessarily indicate that this paper was made for official use. It may have reference to the duty on imported paper. In any case there seems to have been no difficulty in members of the public purchasing it, provided they paid the high price. At the same time it is of some significance that this type of paper was used in Government offices, by Adam Smith and members of his family, while it scarcely ever occurs in letters written to him. There were varieties in the watermark on the other half sheet, (1) The ribbon of the garter with the motto, within which are the royal arms —this is about 3½ inches high. (2) An elliptical picket fence on which Britannia seems to sit, though no doubt she is on a throne. In her right hand she grasps a spear on which is what appears to be a cap of liberty with which she protects a lion rampant, crowned. The motto is *Pro Patria*. This mark measures 3½ inches by 4 inches, and Mr. Edward Heawood tells me that it is of Dutch origin. (3) A ribbon, crowned, with a motto which seems to read *Pro Patria eiusque Libertate*, inside which is a crowned lion, rampant and regardant, grasping a spear. The mark measures 4 inches by 3 inches, and the paper is of Dutch manufacture. Each of the twelve sheets of the manuscript bears this third watermark. There can be no question of this paper being brought to France or purchased there, since the letters he wrote while abroad were on paper of an altogether different type. There are some written from Toulouse, all on a thin paper, some unwatermarked, some with a dolphin. Most of his letters from Paris were on a paper of the character he had used in Scotland, but marked with the name of the celebrated Dutch paper-making firm Vanderlay. The watermark was a ducal crown with either a flag or a double 4 on a mound and the name in large capitals. The concurrence of a paper which Adam Smith is known to have used at Glasgow with a Glasgow amanuensis makes it certain that the manuscript was written there.

THE MANUSCRIPT

N.1. CHAP. 2.[1]

Of the nature and Causes of public *opu*lence.[2]

The unassisted labour of a solitary individual, it is evident, is altogether unable to provide for him, such food, such cloaths and such lodging, as not only the luxury of the great, but as the natural

---

[1] In the manuscript there is no first chapter. Adam Smith numbered each double folio sheet of four pages in his own hand and this is No. 1. There are no italics in the manuscript, and an attempt has been made to reproduce in type its general character by printing Adam Smith's additions and alterations in italics.

[2] The first three letters of " opulence " have been erased and written again by Adam Smith— probably to change the initial letter from a capital to a small " o ". The use of this word, both in the *Glasgow Lectures* and in the present manuscript, is striking. On the whole Adam Smith appears to give it a meaning akin to national wealth. Johnson in his Dictionary defines it as " wealth, riches, affluence," while " opulently " is described as " richly with splendour ". The term is also used by

PLATE XV. ONE TYPE OF WATERMARK IN THE OFFICIAL PAPER USED BY ADAM SMITH WHILE HE WAS AT GLASGOW
(Register House, Edinburgh.)

DRAFT OF "THE WEALTH OF NATIONS" 323

appetites of the meanest peasant, are, in every civilized society, supposed to require. Observe in what manner a common day labourer in Britain or *in* [1] Holland is accommodated with all these, and you will be sensible that his luxury is much superior *to* [2] that of many an Indian prince, the absolute master of the lives and liberties of a thousand naked savages.[3] The woolen coat which covers the day labourer, as coarse and *rough* [4] as it may appear to be, could not be produced without the joint labour of a multitude of artists. The Shepherd, the Grazier, the Clipper, the Sorter of the Wool, the

Hume as equivalent to wealth. It appears that early in the eighteenth century the meaning of amplitude was only beginning to be understood as implied in the word. Amongst other tendencies in this direction Adam Smith may have observed the following notice in *The Glasgow Journal* (26th February, 1759) : " Died Samuel McColl, an eminent merchant of this place, who, by his great skill and application to business, has, with a fair character, left an opulent fortune to his family." It may have been James Oswald who suggested the substitution of " wealth " for " opulence ". " Wealth " occurs rarely in the *Glasgow Lectures*, and it is noteworthy in *The Wealth of Nations* that " opulence " has been allowed to remain in passages which have been moved from this manuscript, which suggests that, in other places in the later work in which it occurs, these also represent the copying of an early form of which the manuscript is no longer in existence.

The similarity of the title of this chapter to that of *The Wealth of Nations* is both significant and striking. We have " the nature and causes " but only of public wealth. This sufficed for the immediate purpose ; though, as the argument is developed, it becomes clear that the enquiry relates not to the opulence or wealth of one nation, but of nations generally (*Glasgow Lectures*, pp. 201-11). Whether this had been recognised in the title of the manuscript, if it ever had one, can only be a matter of conjecture. It has been suggested by Mr. R. F. Jones that Adam Smith may have borrowed the phrase " Wealth of Nations " from Dryden or Johnson. There is a line in the verses of the former to " the Duchess of York on the memorable victory gained by the Duke against the Hollanders, June 3, 1665 " :

" These, where the wealth of nations ought to flow."

In Johnson's *Rambler* (1752) the phrase also occurs : " To be poor, in the epick language is only not to command the wealth of nations, nor to have fleets and armies in pay." As against the literary influence there is an economic one, which may have been the more powerful. When, later, he met the Physiocrats he would hear of " Richesse des gens ", which he incorporated into the title of his great book. The final influence of the Physiocrats is rendered certain by the following passage : " This sect (*i.e.* the Physiocrats) in their works, which are very numerous, and which treat not only of what is properly called Political Œconomy, or of the nature and causes of the wealth of nations, but of every other branch of the system of civil government "—*Wealth of Nations*, ed. Cannan, ii, p. 177.

[1] Added at the end of a line.   [2] Inserted.

[3] Through the close relation between the West of Scotland and the Plantations in North America there was much discussion in Glasgow about the Red Indians. The *Glasgow Courant* at this period had frequent letters from settlers in which many raids by Indians were recounted. Amongst gifts to the Glasgow University's Library between 1693 and 1698 were Elliot's *Indian Grammar*, 4to, Camb., 1666 ; *the New Testament translated into the Indian Language* (translated by Elliot), 4to, Camb., Mass., 1661 ; and the *Bible in the Language of the Indians of Virginia*, 4to, 1663 and 1680. " The naked savages " thus formed part of the picture. As the troubles developed in North America, some of them became our allies, and at a later revision of the manuscript " the Indian prince " was changed to the " African king " of *The Wealth of Nations* (Cannan, i, p. 14). Hume, writing of the Turkish government, speaks of the Grand Signior as " absolute master of the lives and fortunes of each individual "—*Political Discourses*, 1752, p. 121.

[4] Written over some word misspelt or in substitution for a word erased.

picker, the Comber, the Dyer, the Scribbler, the Spinner, the weaver, the fuller, the Dresser,[1] must all join their different arts in order to make out this very homely production. Not to mention the merchants and carriers, who transport the materials from one of those artists to another, who often lives in a very distant country ; how many other artists are employed in producing the tools even of the very meanest of these. I shall say nothing of so very complex a machine as the loom of the weaver or as the Mill of the Fuller ; much less of the immense commerce and navigation, the Ship-building, the sail-making, the Rope-making, necessary to bring together the different drugs made use of by the Dyer, which often come from the remotest corners of the world ; but consider only what a variety of labour is necessary to produce that very simple machine, the sheers of the Clipper. The miner, the builder of the furnace for smelting the ore, the burner of the Charcoal to be made use of in that operation, the feller of the timber of which that charcoal is made, the brickmaker, the bricklayer, the smelter, the mill[2] wright, the forger, the smith, must all club their different industries in order to produce them. If we were to examine in the same manner all the other parts of his dress and household furniture, the coarse linnen shirt which he wears next his skin, the shoes which cover his feet,[3] the bed which he lyes in and all the different parts which compose it, the kitchen grate at which he prepares his victuals, the coals which he makes use of for that purpose, dugg from the bowels of the earth, and brought to him, perhaps, by a long sea and a long land

---

[1] *Cf. Dictionarium Polygraphicum, or the whole body of Arts methodically digested*, Lond., 1735, Article " Wool " ; Chambers, *Cyclopædia*, Article " Cloth " ; *Dictionary of Arts and Sciences*, 1754, ii, pp. 625-7.

[2] An erasure at the end of the word—probably the amanuensis wrote " miln ". For the process of iron smelting in Britain in Adam Smith's time see Chambers, *Cyclopædia*, Article " Iron, forged ".

[3] Clothing, furniture and ironware, such as the kitchen grate mentioned, were made in large quantities at Glasgow, chiefly for export. In particular, leather was a very considerable industry there in Adam Smith's time. McUre in his *View of Glasgow*, 1736, mentions three tanneries—one of which was said to be the largest in Europe. These were all situated on the banks of the Molendinar burn and were thus near the College. When Charles Townshend visited Adam Smith in Glasgow, they went together to see a number of manufactories. Amongst these was one of the tan-works. Adam Smith, while pointing out some object of interest, or, as a contemporary account has it, " demonstrating the division of labour ", was standing on a plank which was used for crossing the tan-pit. He overbalanced and plunged into the nauseous pool below, composed of the fat from the hides, lime and the gas generated in the process (Edin. Univ. Libry. MSS., La. II, 451/2). Apart from the indignity of the accident, there was a very considerable element of danger, since the general condition of slipperiness made a rescue exceedingly difficult and there was a risk of asphyxiation from the fumes. On 6th February, 1935, a similar accident occurred to a worker in a Glasgow tannery, and one man lost his life while two of his mates who tried to rescue him were saved only with the greatest difficulty.

DRAFT OF "THE WEALTH OF NATIONS"

carriage, all the other utensils of his kitchen, all the furniture of his table, the knives and forks, the Delft or pewter plates upon which he serves up and divides his victuals, the many hands who are employed in preparing his bread & his beer, the plowman, the sower of the corn, the reaper, the thresher, the maltster, the miller, the brewer, the baker, with all the other artists who supply each of them with the tools of their respective trades, the glass window which lets in the heat and the light, and keeps out the wind and the rain, and all the knowledge and art which were requisite for preparing that beautiful and happy invention, without which these northern parts of the world would scarce have been made habitable, at least, by that effeminate and delicate race of mortals who dwell in them at present.[1] If we examine, I say, all *those* different conveniencies [2] and luxuries with which he is accomodated and consider what a variety of labour is employed about each of them, we shall be sensible that without the assistance and cooperation of many thousands, the very meanest person in civilized society could not be provided for, even in what we very falsely imagine, the easy and simple manner in which he is commonly accomodated. Compared, indeed, with the yet more extravagant luxury of the great, his accomodation must no doubt appear extremely simple and easy; and yet, perhaps, it may be true that the accomodation of a European prince does not so much exceed that of an industrious and frugal peasant, as the accomodation of this last exceeds that of the chief of a savage nation in North America.[3]

It cannot be very difficult to explain how it comes about that the rich and the powerful should, in a Civilized society, be better provided with the conveniencies and necessaries of life than it is

---

[1] Adam Smith was most Spartan in his mode of life. An intimate friend recorded that it was his practice, when at Kirkcaldy, to bathe daily, summer and winter, in the sea, which he said prevented his catching colds (Edin. Univ. MS., La. II, 451/2). His garden there was bounded by the sea. It may have been after bathing that on one occasion he began to meditate and emerged from his thoughts to find himself in his dressing-gown amongst the crowd of church-goers in Dunfermline.

[2] There are alterations and erasures at " those " and " conveniencies ". The amanuensis may have written " his different conveniences ".

[3] The later history of the property owned by Adam Smith's maternal grandfather affords a very remarkable confirmation of what he wrote one and three quarter centuries ago. When Mary Queen of Scots went to Falkland Palace to hunt, she sometimes made a progress by Loch Leven and spent the night at Strathenry Castle. At the present time this building is used as follows: the ground floor for storage, the first and second floors are occupied by the chauffeur and gardener respectively, the upper floor is a billiard room. Thus the apartments in which the Queen and the chief members of her suite slept now form the homes of the workers on the estate. To which it is to be added that the accommodation has been very greatly improved, as compared with what it was in the sixteenth century.

possible for any person *to provide himself in* [1] a savage and solitary state. It is very easy to conceive that the person who can at all times direct the labours of thousands to his own purposes, should be better provided with whatever he has occasion for, than he who *dep*ends [2] upon his own industry only. But how it comes about that the labourer and the peasant should likewise be better provided, is not perhaps so easily understood. In a Civilized Society the poor provide both for themselves and for the enormous luxury of their Superiors. The rent, which goes to support the vanity of the slothful Landlord, is all *earned* [3] by the industry of the peasant. The monied man indulges himself in every sort of ignoble and sordid sensuality, at the expence of the merchant and the Tradesman, to whom he lends out his stock at interest. All the indolent and frivolous retainers upon a Court, are, in the same manner, fed cloathed and lodged by the labour of those who pay the taxes which support them. Among savages, on the contrary, every individual enjoys the whole produce of his own industry. There are among them, no Landlords, no usurers, no taxgatherers.[4] We might naturally expect, therefore, if experience

[1] This was originally " it is possible for any person of a savage and solitary state to provide himself " and was altered as above.

[2] These letters were overwritten.

[3] A word was erased (probably " earned ", misspelt). " The vanity of the slothful landlord " suggests some interesting reflections, regarding the funds inherited by Adam Smith from his father. The greater part of these (see above, pp. 131-5) were lent upon bond on large estates. If the investment remained of a similar character, it would seem that Adam Smith may have regarded the interest which he received as a diminution of the resources, otherwise available, for pandering to the landlord's vanity. It is unfortunate for several reasons that the inventory of Adam Smith's estate, which is mentioned in connection with his will, is not now in existence. It would have shown how his capital was invested. If he had recalled his bonds and placed the proceeds in some of the rising Glasgow industries, there would probably be mention of it, since the names of those interested in the various enterprises of the period are known. Besides, he became liable for the annuity reserved to his mother under her marriage contract, and the trustees, being lairds, would have preferred, and indeed insisted on, investments connected with landed property. The fact that he sold land in the city of Aberdeen in 1757 is not relevant, since that sale was evidently a purely family transaction. The absence of the inventory is unfortunate in another way. While everything that is known confirms the accounts of Adam Smith's generosity in helping various persons with considerable sums, the fact that his will only specifies a sum of £650 at his bankers (Bonar, *Library of Adam Smith*, 1894, p. xvii) has given rise to an impression that this was his whole estate, and that his surplus income and anything he inherited had all gone in undisclosed gifts. Quite obviously, the transmission of the corpus of the estate was covered by other clauses of the will—the specification of moneys lent on bond, etc., being full and somewhat detailed.

[4] There is no trace of the distributive problem which is raised here in the corresponding portion of the *Glasgow Lectures* (p. 162), nor of the next paragraph in the manuscript. In the former there is a sentence : " It is the division of labour which increases the opulence of a country." This interrupts the argument, and is what the reporter recorded of a summary, introduced to retain the attention of the students in a course continued from day to day. Sir William Hamilton, Professor of Logic and Metaphysics at Edinburgh, 1836-56, made it his practice to give periodic analyses of successive stages of his argument; *cf. Lectures on Metaphysics*, 1870.

did not demonstrate the contrary, that every individual among them, should have a much greater affluence of the necessaries and Conveniencies of life, than can be posse*s*sed [1] by the inferior ranks of people in a Civilized Society.

What considerably increases this difficulty, is the consideration, that the labour of an hundred, or an hundred thousand men, should seem to bear the same proportion to the support of an hundred or of an hundred thousand, which the labour of one bears to the support of one man. Supposing therefore that the produce of the labour of the multitude, was to be equally and fairly divided, each individual, we should expect, could be little better provided for than the single person who laboured alone. But with regard to the produce of the labour of a great Society there is never any such thing as a fair and equal division. In a Society of an hundred thousand families, there will perhaps be one hundred who don't labour at all, and who yet, either by violence, or by the more orderly oppression of law, employ a greater part of the labour of the society than any other ten thousand in it. The division of what remains too, after this enormous defalcation, is by no means made in proportion to the labour of each individual. On the contrary those who labour most get least. The opulent merchant, who spends a great part of his time in luxury and entertainments, enjoys a much greater proportion of the profits of his traffic, than all the Clerks and Accountants who do the business. These last, again, enjoying a great deal of leisure, and suffering scarce any other hardship besides the confinement of attendance, enjoy a much greater share of the produce, than three times an equal number of artizans, who, under th*eir* [2] direction, labour much more severely and assiduously. The artizan again, tho' he works generally under cover, protected from the injuries of the weather, at his ease and assisted by the convenience of innumerable machines, enjoys a much greater share than the poor labourer who has the soil and the seasons to struggle with, and, who while he affords the materials for supplying the luxury of all the other members of the common wealth, and bears, as it were, upon his shoulders the whole fa*b*ric [3] of human society, seems himself to be pressed down below ground by the

N. 2.

---

[1] Here, as in other places, Adam Smith has made an alteration in the writing of the doubled " s ", probably to distinguish the first " s " from an " f "; *cf* the first sheet of the facsimile of this MS., p. 386, line 1, " unassisted ".

[2] Correction over an erasure, possibly to correct a mis-spelling " thier ".

[3] Another erasure—the amanuensis may have written " faberic "; *cf.* Hume, *Political Discourses*, 1752, p. 18, " Where riches are in few hands, these must enjoy all the power and will readily conspire to lay the whole burthen on the poor."

weight, and to be buried out of sight in the lowest foundations of the building. In the midst of so much oppressive inequality in what manner shall we account for the superior affluence and abundance commonly possessed [1] even by this lowest and most despised member of Civilized society, compared with what the most respected and active savage can attain to.

The division of labour, by which each individual confines himself to a particular branch of business, can alone account for that superior opulence which takes place in civilized societies, and which, notwithstanding the inequality of property, extends itself to the lowest member of the community. Let us consider the effects of this division of labour as it takes place in some particular manufactures, and we shall from thence more easily be enabled to explain in what manner it operates in the general business of society. Thus, to give a very frivolous [2] instance, if all the parts of a pin were to be made by one man, if the same person was to dig the mettal out of the mine, seperate it from the ore, forge it, split it into small rods, then spin these rods into wire, and last of all make that wire into pins, a man perhaps could with his utmost industry scarce make a pin in a year. The price of a pin, therefore, must, in this case, at least have been equal to the maintenance [3] of a man for a year. Let this be supposed equal to six pounds sterling, a miserable allowance for a person of so much ingenuity, the price of a single pin must have been six pounds sterling. Supposing that the wire was furnished [4] to him ready made, as at present, even in his case, I imagine, one man could with his utmost dilligence, scarce make twenty pins in a day. *2 His maintainance for a day therefore must be charged upon those twenty pins. Let us suppose this maintenance equal to ten pence, a most liberal allowance compared with the foregoing, there must be a half penny of this charged upon each pin over and above the price of the wire and the profite of the merchant which would make the price of a pin about a penny : a price which appears as nothing compared with the foregoing, but which is still extravagant, compared with that which actually takes place. For the pin-maker, in preparing this small superfluity very properly takes care to divide the labour among a great number of persons. One man straightens the wire, another cuts it, a third points it, a fourth grinds it at the top for receiving the head,

*2 *which, allowing three hundred working days in the year, will amount to six thousand pins in the year; an immense increase!*

---

[1] See p. 327, note [1].   [2] *The Wealth of Nations* reads " trifling " here.
[3] An erasure—the amanuensis may have written " maintainance " ; see six lines below, where the word is thus written and not corrected.
[4] There is an erasure and correction in the middle of this word.

three or four people are employed about making the head, to put it on is the business of a particular person, to guild the pins is the occupation of another, it is even a trade by itself to put them in the paper. When this small operation is in this manner divided among about eighteen persons,[1] these eighteen will, perhaps, among them, make upwards of thirty six thousand pins in a day. Each person, therefore, making an eighteenth part of thirty six thousand pins, may be considered as making two thousand pins a day, and supposing three hundred working days in the year, each person may be considered as making six hundred thousand pins in the year, that is each person produces six hundred thousand times the quantity of work which he was capable of producing, when he had the whole machinery and materials to provide for himself, as upon the first supposition; and one hundred times the quantity of work which he was capable of producing, when the wire was afforded him ready made as upon the second. The yearly maintenance, therefore, of each person is to be charged not upon one pin as *by*[2] the first supposition, nor upon six thousand as by the second, but upon six hundred thousand pins. The master of the work, therefore, can both afford to increase the wages of the labourer, and yet sell the commodity at a vastly lower rate than before: And pins instead of being sold at six pounds a piece as upon the first supposition, or at twelve pence a dozen as upon the second, are commonly sold at several dozens for a half penny.

The division of labour has the same effect in all the other arts, as in this frivolous manufacture, and occasions in the same manner an immense multiplication of the productions of each. In every opulent society, the farmer is nothing but a farmer, the manufacturer nothing but a manufacturer. The labour which is necessary to produce any one compleat manufacture is divided among a vast number of hands. How many different people are employed in each branch of the Linnen and woollen manufactures, from the growers of the flax and the wool, to the Dyers and dressers of the Cloth; or the bleachers and Smoothers of the Linnen! The nature of agriculture, indeed, does not admit of so many subdivisions of labour, nor of such an

---

[1] See Cannan's notes in reference to the Article in the *Encyclopédie*, v, pp. 804-8, in *Glasgow Lectures*, p. 164, notes [1] and [2]. It is possibly a small point but it may be noted that Chambers in the article on "Pin" in his *Cyclopædia* makes the number of workers successively employed on distinct operations, twenty-five, counting from the beginning of the drawing of the brass wire to the placing of the pins in their papers. In his article on "Wire" he does not specify the number of operations in the making of it, so that it is impossible to say whether the French method of the *Encyclopédie* or that described by Chambers involved the larger number of distinct processes in pin making proper.

[2] A word—probably "on"—has been erased, and "by" written in its place.

N. 3.

entire seperation of one business from another, as commonly takes place in manufactures. It is impossible to seperate, so entirely, the business of the grazier from that of the Corn farmer, as the trade of the Carpenter is commonly seperated from that of the Smith. The Spinner is always a different person from the weaver. But the plowman, the harrower, the sower of the seed, and the reaper of the Corn are often the same. The occasions for their different labours returning with the different seasons of the year, make it impossible for one man to be entirely employed in any one of these different occupations. With regard even to agriculture, however, in well cultivated Countries, the business of the thresher and the ditcher, as they can do their work through the whole year, are often considered as compleat trades, distinct and seperated from all others. It is the same case with the plow-wright and the makers of all the other Instruments of agriculture, the forgers of the scythe and reaping hook, the wheel wright, the cart & waggon maker. It is this impossibility, however, of making so compleat and entire a seperation of all the different branches of labour employed in Agriculture, which must forever hinder the improvement of this art from keeping pace with the improvements of manufactures. The most opulent nation will commonly excell all its' neighbours in agriculture as well as in manufactures ; but it will always be more distinguished by its superiority in the latter than in the former, tho' the former may be of much greater value. The Corn of France is fully as good and in the provinces [1] where it grows rather cheaper than that of England, at least during ordinary seasons. But the toys of England, their watches, their cutlery ware, their locks & hinges of doors, their buckles and buttons are, in accuracy, solidity and perfection of worth, out of all comparison superior to those of France, and cheaper too in the same degree of goodness.[2]

[1] This is probably derived from the agricultural works of M. du Monceau Duhamel, of which there are eleven of Adam Smith's period in the University Library. It was his friend and colleague, William Cullen, who was responsible for most of the collection. In 1754 or 1755 Henry Home, Lord Kames, wrote to Cullen : " How goes on your farming scheme, in particular ? In this science facts would be delightful. Your friend, at least your correspondent, Du Hamel is a ninny "—T. Thomson, *Life of William Cullen*, 1859, ii, p. 85. In the list, printed above (p. 179), of the books ordered by Adam Smith for the library when he was Quæstor from 1758 to 1760, there is Duhamel's *Traité de la Culture des Terres*. Three of the volumes have calculations in Adam Smith's hand on the end papers. Those in vol. v relate to yields of land in France, and Adam Smith noted at the end—" being something less than 2½ bolls per Scotch acre ".

[2] There is an extensive erasure at this point. It is clear that the amanuensis continued after " goodness " with a new sentence (but not a new paragraph) " it is the immense multiplication ", etc. A new paragraph was required and the two lines written were erased. This makes it evident that this MS. was dictated, rather than copied from a manuscript of the *Lectures*.

It is the immense multiplication of the productions of all the different arts, in consequence of the division of labour, which, notwithstanding the great inequalities of property, occasions, in all civilized societies, that universal opulence which extends itself to the lowest ranks of the people. So great a quantity of every thing is produced, that there is enough both to gratify the slothful and oppressive profusion of the great, and at the same time abundantly to supply the wants of the artizan and the peasant. Each man performs so great a quantity of that work which peculiarly belongs to him, that he can both afford something to those who do not labour at all, and at the same time have as much behind, as will enable him, by exchanging it for the productions of other arts, to supply himself with all the necessaries and conveniencies which he stands in need of. Let us suppose, for example, to return to the frivolous instance, which I formerly gave, that pins may be valued at a penny the hundred, which is nearly the price of some particular sorts of them. The pinmaker who, according to the foregoing supposition, could be considered as making two thousand pins a day, produces work to the value of twenty pence. Let five pence be allowed for the price of the wire, the wear of the tools and the profits of the master of the work, there remain fifteen pence for the wages of the artizan, with which he can purchase all the necessaries and conveniencies [1] of life. The case here, is the same, as if he gave five hundred pins to his master for affording him the wire the tools and the employment, and *kept* [2] fifteen hundred to himself, in order to be exchanged for the productions of the other arts which he had occasion for. For it is the same thing, with regard to opulence, whether we consider a person as posse*ss*ed [3] of a particular merchandize, or of the value of a particular merchandize.

(*a*) *I do not mean that the profits are divided in fact precisely in the above manner, but that they may be divided in such manner.*

Let us suppose, that by still further divisions of labour and improvements of art, a pin-maker could be made to produce four thousand pins a day. In this case, tho' pins were to be valued one fourth less, and to be sold for three farthings the hundred, the artizan would produce work to the value of th*ir*ty [4] pence a day. His master might have ten pence *or* [5] the value of thirteen hundred and thirty three pins for his profits and expences, and the artizan retain twenty pence or the value of two thousand six hundred and sixty seven pins for his wages. The price of the work would be diminished, and the wages of the labourer increased ; the public would be better supplyed and the workmen more amply rewarded. (*a*)

[1] See above, p. 325 note [2].
[2] A word has been erased and " kept " written in its place.
[3] See above, p. 327 note [1].
[4] Written over an erasure.
[5] Written over an erasure.

It is, in this manner, that in an opulent and commercial society, labour becomes dear and work cheap, and those two events which vulgar prejudice and superficial reflection are apt to consider as altogether incompatible, are found by experience to be perfectly consistent. The high price of labour is to be considered not meerly as a proof of the general opulence of Society which can afford to pay well all those whom it employs; it is to be regarded as what constitutes the expence of public opulence, or as the very thing in which public opulence properly consists. That state is properly opulent in which opulence is easily come at, or in which a little labour properly and judiciously employed, is capable of procuring any man a great abundance of all the necessaries and conveniencies of life. Nothing else it is evident can render it general, or diffuse it universally through all the members of the society. National opulence is the opulence of the whole people, which nothing but the great reward of labour, and, consequently the great facility of acquiring, can give occasion to. As this labour however is applied with great skill and judgement, as it is supported *by*[1] the concurrence and united forces of a great society, and over and above all this, as it is assisted by innumerable machines, it produces a much greater effect, and performs a much greater quantity of work, than in proportion to the superiority of its reward. The more opulent, therefore, the society, labour will always be so much the dearer and work so much the cheaper, and if some opulent countries have lost several of their manufactures and some branches of their commerce, by having been undersold in foreign markets by the *T*raders and artizans of poorer countries, who were contented with less profit and smaller wages, this will rarely be found to have been meerly the effect of the opulence of the one country and the poverty of the other. Some other cause, we may be assured, must have concurred. The rich country must have been guilty of some great error in its police. It must either have oppressed that particular branch of commerce or manufacture by improper customs & excises, or by the licensed insolence of the officers of revenue, frequently more vexatious than all the taxes which they levey. Or by taxing, and thereby raising the prices of the necessaries of life, it must have increased the difficulty of subsistance, and thereby have screwed up the price of labour to an unnatural height, far beyond what the opulence of the society could, of its own accord, have raised it to. Where no error of this kind has been committed, as among individuals, a rich merchant can always undersell, and a rich manufac-

---

[1] A word erased and " by " substituted.

turer under work a poor one ; so among great societies, a rich nation must always in every comp*eti*tion [1] of commerce and manufactures, have an equal, or superior advantage over a poor one.

This immense increase of quantity of work performed, in consequence of the division of labour, is owing to three different circumstances. First to the increase of dexterity in every particular workman ; secondly to the saving of the time which is lost in passing from one species of work to another ; and, last of all, to the invention of innumerable machines, which facilitate labour and enable one workman to do the business of many.

The improvement of the dexterity of the workmen greatly increases the quantity of the work performed ; and the division of labour, by reducing the work which every man has to perform to a very simple operation, and by making the performance of that operation the sole business of his life, necessarily improves, to the highest degree, the dexterity of the workman. A Smith, *who has rarely or never had occasion to make nails,*[2] tho accustomed to use his hammer in

---

[1] These letters have been written over erasures.

[2] A line has been erased and Adam Smith substituted the words underlined. Rae, in describing the boyhood of Adam Smith at Kirkcaldy (p. 8), mentions the town had a nailery or two, and there is a tradition that he was fond of visiting them. This is easy to understand, since a smithy has a species of natural atraction to boys. Even if the tradition is true, Adam Smith had much better opportunities of becoming conversant with the industry in his visits to Dunnikier, both during the life-time of James Oswald, his father's friend and his own trustee, and later, after James Oswald's death when the estate passed to the eldest son, whose name was the same and who was a close friend of Adam Smith, to whom he owed many suggestions about his economic investigations—perhaps more than he did to Hume. Dunnikier in the first half of the eighteenth century was a nailmaking village. Even at the end of the century, when through reasons explained below the industry had contracted, there were forty smiths there. This and other interesting details are contained in the edition of 1803 of Sir R. Sibbald's *History of Fife* (p. 318 note), which incorporates information from the *Old Statistical Accounts of Scotland* (xii, p. 514). " The village is better known by the name of Pathhead. It is named from its situation near a steep descent, called ' the Path '. It is divided into Pathhead proper or Dunnikier, situated on the Dunnikier estate, and Sinclairtown, situated on the Sinclair estate. . . . The chief employment in Pathhead was for a long time the making of nails. They sent great quantities to Edinburgh, to Glasgow and to the north of Scotland. Two things favoured the trade, plenty of good coals near them, and the facility of getting old iron by the ships trading from Dysart to Holland. But, when other places came to have the same advantages and nail factories were erected in different quarters, the profits of this trade diminished. Linen manufactures have been introduced since that time—in Pathhead there are forty-three smiths who make about 6 millions of nails annually the value of which is about £1,000." It is clear that by the time of this account many of the smiths had to work at other branches of their trade, since nine workers, equal to the boy Adam Smith mentions, could account for six million nails. When Adam Smith settled at Glasgow he would have heard of the Nailers' Close in the Bridgeton district. There is a water-colour of this close, with a nailer in his apron, by W. R. Maindy, in the Wylie Collection at Glasgow University. The nailers had a marked pride in their craft. In 1763 two hoemakers and a smith, employed at the Smithfield manufactory, had been charged with pilfering. The nailmakers went to the expense of inserting a long displayed advertisement in *The Glasgow Journal* of 12th May stating that they had been subjected to " public odium " through being employed in the same factory. They

a hundred other operations, which one would think not very different, can, I am informed, with his utmost dilligence, scarce make two or three hundred nails in a day, and these too excessively bad. A country smith who shoes horses, mends locks and hinges of doors, makes and mends spades, shovels and all the other instruments of agriculture, when he has no particular piece of work upon his hands, commonly employs his time in making nails. Such a person can, when he exerts himself, make about a thousand nails a day, and those too pretty good.[1] I have seen a boy, of nineteen years of age, who had done nothing else all his life but made nails, who, in twelve hours, could make two thousand three hundred nails, that is about eight times the work of the first, and more than double the work of the second. The making of a nail, however, is by no means one of the simplest operations. The same person mends the fire, blows the bellows, heats the iron,[2] forges every part of the nail and in forging

protested that their work was in a different part and quite separate from that in which hoes and axes were made. They threatened proceedings against any persons who continued to defame them.

Thus Adam Smith had the material as regards nailmaking at a very early period, though it is possible that meeting the industry in Glasgow may have revived his impressions of Dunnikier and Kirkcaldy. The balance of probability points to this illustration having been one of the first parts of *The Wealth of Nations* to be written. Reverting to the common order of treatment of economic topics by Hutcheson and Adam Smith (W. R. Scott, *Francis Hutcheson*, p. 235), in so far as it is stated that Smith referred to his notes of Hutcheson's lectures or to the *System* (p. 232) when preparing his own course at Glasgow, the use of Hutcheson's order and some of his economic material must be carried back to the last series of lectures given at Edinburgh. In those notes he found Hutcheson claiming an increase of dexterity as one of the advantages of Division of Labour, and it may have occurred to him to illustrate this by the example of nailmaking. Now that it is known that " the causes of the slow Progress of Opulence " belong to the same period, this becomes quite understandable. In fact, much of the poor arrangement and apparent discontinuity of Adam Smith's treatment is attributable to his reluctance to scrap material already written. He was even unwilling to rewrite it.

The case is different with his other detailed example of pinmaking. The *Encyclopédie* had not been published when the Edinburgh lectures were delivered. The book was not in Adam Smith's own library. He seems to have used the copies of Chambers' *Cyclopædia* at Glasgow University Library or the Advocates' Library, since his own copy was the edition of 1786. The *Encyclopédie* did not reach Glasgow University Library till Smith recommended it 1758-60. At this period he is not known to have been to London till 1761, so that the British Museum was not available to him before that date. Since he comments on the book in the number of the *Edinburgh Review* for July 1755, he must have seen at least the first volume by then. Here an interesting piece of information comes to light. Dr. Meikle, the Keeper of the National Library of Scotland (formerly the Advocates' Library), has been good enough to examine the accession registers as far as they exist. That for the years 1751-4 does not contain any record of this book. Then there is a gap from 1754 to 1763. Considering that Hume was Keeper between 1752 and 1757, it is probable that he had ordered the volumes, then published, and that some at least had arrived early in 1755. That several years elapsed before Adam Smith ordered it shows that, after writing his article, he had no pressing need for the book, until he was concentrating on economic enquiries after his *Theory of Moral Sentiments* had been published.

[1] In the parish of St. Ninian, near Perth, it was recorded in the *Old Statistical Account of Scotland*, 1794 (xviii, p. 394), that it was usual for a smith to make 1000 to 1200 nails a day.

[2] This was written " heats the iron and forges "—" and " was deleted.

DRAFT OF "THE WEALTH OF NATIONS" 335

2 notwithstanding all this, a good workman will make very near four nails in a minute.

the head is obliged to change his tools, which occasions a considerable loss of time. *2* The different operations into which the making of a pin or of a mettal button is subdivided, are all of them much more simple, and the dexterity acquired by the person, the sole business of whose life is to perform them, is out of all proportion greater. The rapidity, with which some of the operations of those manufatur*es* [1] are performed, far exceeds what the human hand could, by those who had never seen them, be supposed capable of acquiring.

The advantage, too, which is gained by saving the time commonly lost in passing from one species of work to another is very considerable, and much greater than what we should, at first, be apt to imagine. It is impossible to pass very quickly from some businesses to others, which are carried on in distant places and with quite different tools. A country weaver, who likewise cultivates a small farm must lo*se* [2] a good deal of time in passing from his loom to the field and from the field to his loom. Where the two businesses can be carried on in the same work house, the loss of time is no doubt much less. It is even here, however, very considerable. A man commonly saunters a little in turning his hand from one sor*t* [3] of employment to a quite different. When he first begins the new work he is seldome very keen or hearty. His mind does not go with it, and he for some time *rather* triffles *than* applies to *good* purpose.[4] A man of great Spirit and activity, when he is hard pushed upon some particular occasion, will pass with the greatest rapidity from one sort of work to another through a great variety of businesses. Even a man of spirit and activity, however, must be hard pushed before he can do this. In the ordinary course of business, when he passes from one thing to another he will saunter and trifle, tho' not undoubtedly in the same degree, yet in the same manner as an idle fellow. This habit of sauntering and of Indolent, careless application, which is naturally, or rather necessarily contracted by every country workman, who is obliged to change his work and his tools every half hour, and to apply his hand in twenty different manners almost every day in his life, renders him almost always very slothful and lazy, and incapable, even upon the most pressing occasions, of any vigourous application.

[1] The last two letters written over an erasure.

[2] Possibly "loss" was written; corrected as above.

[3] The "t" in "sort" has been written by Adam Smith. Changes like this are probably due to his wishing each letter to be distinct, and, if the amanuensis left one faint, Adam Smith went over it with his own pen.

[4] "Rather" is inserted, words have been erased and "than" and "good" written in their places.

Independent therefore of his want of the most perfect dexterity this cause alone must always make the quantity of the work which he performs extremely inconsiderable.

Every body must be sensible how much labour is abridged and facilitated by the application of proper machinery. By means of the *plough*[1] two men, with the assistance of three horses, will cultivate more ground than twenty could do with the spade. A miller and his servant with a wind *or*[2] water mill will, at their ease, grind more corn than eight men could do, with the severest labour, by hand mills. To grind corn in a hand mill was the severest work to which the antients commonly applied their slaves and to which they seldome condemned them *unless*[3] when they had been guilty of some very great fault. A handmill however, is a very ingenuous machine which greatly facilitates labour, and by which a great deal of more work can be performed, than when the corn is either to be beat in a mortar, or with the bare hand, unassisted by any machinery, to be rubbed into pouder between two hard stones, as is the practice, not only of all barbarous nations, but of some remote provinces in this country. It was the division of labour which probably gave occasion to the invention of the greater part of those machines, by which labour is so much facilitated and abri*d*ged.[4] When the whole force of the mind is directed to one particular object, as in consequence of the division of labour, it must be, the mind is more likely to discover the easiest methods of attaining that object, than when the attention is dissipated among a great variety of things. He was, probably, a farmer who first invented the original, rude form of the plou*gh*.[5] The improvements, which were afterwards made upon it, might be owing, sometimes to the ingenuity of the plow wright when that business had become a particular occupation, and sometimes to that of the farmer. Scarce any of them are so complex as to exceed what might be expected from the capacity of the latter. The Drill plow, the most ingenious of any, was the invention of a farmer,[6] Some miserable slave, condemned to grind corn between two stones by the meer strength of his arms, pretty much in the same manner as painters bray their colours at present,[7] was probably the first who thought of

---

[1] Evidently " plow " was written and Adam Smith altered it as above.

[2] " or " written after an erasure.   [3] Written over an erasure.

[4] " d " inserted in " abriged ".   [5] " plow ", thus corrected.

[6] *Cf.* Tull, Jethro, *Horse-hoeing husbandry ; or an essay upon the principles of tillage and vegetation*, fol., Lond., 1733—a book adopted and applied by Duhamel (p. 330 note [1]).

[7] It may be guessed that this illustration is due to what Adam Smith had noticed at the Academy of Art which had been established in the University by Foulis. *Cf.* Part I, Chapter VIII.

DRAFT OF "THE WEALTH OF NATIONS"

supporting the upper stone by a spindle and of turning it round by a crank or handle which moved horizontally, according to what seems to have been the original, rude form of hand mills; He who first thought of making the spindle pass quite through the under mill stone, which is at rest, of uniting it with a trundle, and of turning round that trundle by means of a cog wheel, which was itself turned round by a winch or handle, according to the present form of hand mills, was probably a mill wright, or a person whose principal or sole business it was, in consequence of the still further division of labour, to prepare that original, rude machine which it does not exceed the capacity of a common slave to have invented. Great advantages were gained by this improvement. The whole machinery being thus placed below the under millstone, the top of the upper one was left free for the conveniencies of the *Hop*per,[1] the feeder and Shoe, and the Crank or handle, which turned the cog wheel, moving in a Circle perpendicular to the horizon, the strength of the human body could be applied to it with much more advantage, than to any crank which was to be turned round in a Circle parallel to the horizon. These different improvements were probably not all of them the inventions of one man, but the successive discoveries of time and experience, and of the ingenuity of many different artists. Some of the more simple of them, such as the feeder and the shoe, might be the contrivances of the miller: But the more complex, such as the cog wheel and trundle, were probably the inventions of the millwright. They bear [2] the most evident marks of the ingenuity of a *very* [3] intelligent artist. He who first thought of substituting, in the room of the Crank or handle, an outer wheel which was to be t*u*rned [4] round by a stream of water, and much more, he who first thought of employing a stream of wind for the same purpose, was probably no workman of any kind, but a philosopher or meer man of speculation; one of these people whose trade it is, not to do any thing but to observe every thing, and who are upon that account capable of combining together the powers of the most opposite and distant objects. To apply in the most advantagious manner those powers, which are allready known and *which* [5] have already been applyed to a particular purpose, does not exceed the

---

[1] The first three letters have been erased and "Hop" written. The corn-mill in Adam Smith's time is illustrated and described in *Dictionary of Arts and Sciences*, 1754, iii, pp. 2075-6.

[2] The original form was "they bear in them the most evident marks", "in them" scored out.

[3] " v " in " very " written by Adam Smith.

[4] This may have been " tourned ", and the second and third letters were erased and replaced by a " u ".

[5] Written over an erasure.

capacity of an ingenious artist. But to think of the application of new powers, which are altogether unknown, and which have never before been applied to any similar purpose, belongs to those only who have a greater range of thought and more extensive views of things than naturally fall to the share of a meer artist. When an artist makes any such discovery he showes himself to be, not a meer artist, but a real philosopher, whatever may be his nominal profession. It was a real philosopher only who could invent the fire engine, and first form the idea of producing so great an effect, by a power in nature which had never before been thought of. Many inferior artists, employed in the fabric of this wonderful machine may after wards discover more happy methods of applying that power than those first made use of by its illustrious inventor.[1] It must have been a philosopher who, in the same manner first invented, those now common and therefore disregarded, machines, wind and water mills. Many inferior artists may have afterwards improved them. Philosophy or speculation, in the progress of society, naturally becomes, like every other employment, the sole occupation of a particular class of citizens. Like every other trade it is subdivided into many different branches, and we have mechanical, chemical, astronomical, Physical, Metaphysical, moral, political, commercial and critical philosophers. In philosophy, as in every other business, this subdivision of employment improves dexterity and saves time. Each individual is more expert at his particular branch. More work is done upon the whole and the quantity of science is considerably increased by it.

This [2] division of labour from which so many advantages result, is originally the effect of no human wisdom which forsees and intends that general opulence to which it gives occasion.[3] It is the necessary, tho' very slow and gradual consequence, of a certain principle or propensity in human nature, which has in view no such extensive utility. This is a propensity, common to all men and to be found

---

[1] Watt must have been in Adam Smith's mind when he wrote this passage. From 1759 Watt had been experimenting with steam and his enquiries were closely connected with those of Adam Smith's friend, Joseph Black, on latent heat. It was in 1763 that Watt, in repairing a model of the Newcomen engine, got the idea of a separate condenser.

[2] See above, p. 326 note [4].

[3] In the *Glasgow Lectures*, pp. 168-9, there is a paragraph of sixteen lines which is not represented in this manuscript. It begins " we have already shown that the division of labour is the immediate cause of opulence ", continuing with an allusion to Sesostris in relation to every man following the occupation of his father, against which it is contended that there must be a division of ranks, and ending " but it is not this which gives occasion to the division of labour "—a passage which is partially reproduced in *The Wealth of Nations*.

N. 6.

in no other race of animals, a propensity to truck, barter and exchange one thing for another. That this propensity is common to all men is sufficiently obvious. And it is equal*ly* [1] so that it is to be found in no other race of animals, which seems to be acquainted neither with this nor with any other Species of Contract. Two Greyhounds, in running down the same hare, have sometimes the appearance of acting in some sort of Concert. Each turns her towards his Companion, or endeavours to intercept her, when his companion turns her towards himself. This however is not the effect of any Contract, but arises meerly from their passions happening, at that instant, to concurr in the same object. No body every saw a dog make a fair and deliberate exchange of one bone for another with another dog. No body ever saw one animal by its gestures and natural cries, signify to another, " This is mine that yours ; I am willing to give this for that." When an animal wants to obtain something either of a man or of another animal, it has no other means of persuasion but to gain the kindness and favour of those whose service it stands in need of. A puppy fawns upon its dam, and a Spaniel endeavours, by a thousand attractions to engage the attention of *its* [2] master who is at dinner, when it wants to be fed by him. Man sometimes uses the same arts with his bretheren, And when he has no other means of engaging them to act according to his inclinations, endeavours by every fawning attention to obtain their goodwill. He has not time, however, to do this upon every occasion. So necessitous is his natural situation, that he stands at all times in need of the co-operation and assistance of great multitudes, while his whole life is Scarce sufficient to gain the friendship of a few persons. In every other race of animals each individual is almost entirely independent, and *in* [3] its ordinary and natural state has occasion for the assistance of no other living Creature. When any uncommon misfortune befals it, its piteous and doleful cries will sometimes engage its fellows, and sometimes prevail even upon man to rel*ie*ve [4] it. When such assistance, however, becomes indispensibly necessary, the Creature must generally lay its account *with* [5] perishing for want of it. Such occasions can, in the common course of things, occur but seldom, and nature, with her usual œconomy, has not thought proper to make any particular provision

---

[1] This passage was originally " That this propensity is common to all men and it is equal so ", etc. Adam Smith inserted a full stop after " obvious " and made the " a " of " and " a capital letter; " ly " at the end of " equal " inserted.

[2] Written over an erasure, possibly originally " his ".

[3] Written on an erasure.   [4] Correction of the spelling " to releive it ".

[5] Written on an erasure.

for them, any more than she has made for the relief of man when he is shipwrecked in the middle of the ocean. Her great purpose the continuance and propogation of each species, she has thought, was not likely to be interrupted by such uncommon and extraordinary accidents. But tho' an animal when once it has grown up to maturity, stands but seldom in need of the assistance of its fellows, a man has almost constant occasion for the help of his bretheren, and it is in vain for him to expect it from their benevolence only. He will be much more likely to prevail if he can interest their self love in his favour, and show them that it is for their own advantage to do for him what he requires of them. Whoever offers to another a bargain of any kind proposes to do this. " Give me that which I want and you shall have this which you want," is the plain meaning of every such offer. It is, in this manner, that we obtain from one another, by far the greater and more important part of those good offices which we stand in need of. It is not from the benevolence of the butcher, the brewer and the baker that we expect our dinner, but from their regard to their own interest. We address ourselves, not to their humanity, but to their self love, and never talk to them of our own necessities, but of their advantages. Nobody but a beggar *chuses* [1] to depend chiefly upon the benevolences of his fellow citizens. Even a beggar does not depend upon it entirely. If he did he would perish in a week. The Charity of well disposed people, indeed, *may* [2] supply him perhaps, with the whole fund of his subsistence. But tho' this principle ultimately provides him with all the necessaries of life which he has occasion for, it neither does, nor can provide him with them, as he has occasion for them. The greater part of his occasional wants are supplied in the same manner as those of other people, by treaty, by barter and by purchase. With the money which one man gives him he purchases food. The old cloaths, which another bestows upon him, he exchanges for other old cloaths which suit him better, or for lodging or for food, or for money, with which he can buy either food, cloaths or lodging as he has occasion.

As it is in this manner, by barter and exchange, that we obtain from one another the greater part of those mutual good offices which we stand in need of, so it is *this same* [3] trucking disposition which

---

[1] " Chuses " inserted.   [2] Written on an erasure.

[3] Probably written " the same ", then erased and made into the above. Adam Smith's letters were larger and more straggling than those of his amanuensis. Sometimes he overwrote a word as he wished it to be when the change meant a letter or two. This usually made an uneven and untidy result. Then, the paper being thick, he erased part of the word, or the whole of it, sometimes (as above) more than one word, and wrote what he wanted on the space thus left blank.

N. 7.

originally gives occasion to that division of labour upon which is founded the whole opulence of Civilized Societies. Among a nation of hunters or shepherds, a particular savage is observed to make bows and arrows with more readiness and dexterity than any other person. He sometimes exchanges them for venison or for Cattle with [1] his Companions; and, by degrees, comes to find that he can in this manner *procure* [2] more venison and more Cattle than if he himself went to the field to hunt them. From a regard to his own interest and ease, therefore, it grows to be his chief business to make bows and arrows; and he becomes, in this manner, a kind of armourer. Another excels in making the frames and covers of their little huts or moveable houses. He is accustomed, in this way, to be of use to those of his own tribe, who reward him, in the same manner, with cattle and with venison, till at length he finds it for his interest to dedicate himself entirely to this employment, and he becomes a sort of house Carpenter. In the same manner, a third becomes a smith; a fourth a tanner or dresser of hydes and skins, the principal part of the cloathing of savages; and thus the certainty of being able to exchange all that part of the produce of his own labour which he himself has no occasion for, for such parts of the produce of other mens labours as he has occasion for, enables every man to apply himself to a particular occupation and to cultivate and bring to perfection whatever natural genius or talent he may possess for that particular species of business.

In reality the difference of natural talents in different men is perhaps much less than we are aware of, and the very different genius which appears to distinguish men of different professions when grown up to maturity, is not, perhaps, so much the cause as the effect of the division of labour. What two men can be more different than a Philosopher and a Common porter? This difference however, seems to arise not so much from nature, as from habit, custom and education. When they came into the world, and for the first five or six years of their existence, they were, perhaps, pretty much alike, and neither their parents nor their play fellows could observe any remarkable distinction. About that age, or soon after, they come to be employed in very different occupations. The difference of what we call genius [3] comes then to be taken notice of, and widens by

[1] Originally " with some of his Companions ", then " some of " deleted.
[2] " Procure " had been misspelt and was rewritten over an erasure.
[3] Originally " the difference of what we call genius between them comes then to be taken notice of "—" between them " deleted.

degrees, till at last the vanity of the Philosopher is scarce willing to acknowledge any resemblance. But without the disposition to truck, barter & exchange, every man must have procured for himself every necessary of life which he wanted. Every man must have employed himself in every thing. All must have had the same work to do and the same duties to perform, and there could have been no such difference of employment as could alone give occasion to any great difference of character. It is upon this account that a much greater uniformity of character is to be observed among savages than among Civilized nations. Among the former there is Scarce any division of labour and consequently no remarkable difference of employments; whereas among the latter there is an almost infinite variety of occupations, of which the respective duties bear scarce any resemblance to one another. What a perfect uniformity of Character do we find in *all the heroes described by Ossian* ?[1] And what a variety of manners, on the contrary, in those who are celebrated by *Homer* ?[2] Ossian plainly describes the exploits of a nation of Hunters, while Homer paints the actions of two nations, who, tho' far from being perfectly civilized, were yet much advanced beyond the age of Shepherds, who cultivated Lands, who built cities, and among whom he mentions many different trades and occupations, such as masons, Carpenters, Smiths, merchants, soothsayers, priests, Physicians. *2 a new Paragraph.*[3] 2 It is this disposition to truck, barter and exchange which not only gives occasion to that difference of genius and talents, so remarkable among men of different professions, but which renders that difference usefull.

---

[1] These words are written over an erasure. James MacPherson published *Fragments of Ancient Poetry collected in the Highlands* in 1760, followed by *Fingal* in 1762 and *Temora* in 1763. Adam Smith had the two last (Bonar, *Library of Adam Smith*, 1932, p. 108). Though the earlier work does not appear in the MS. Catalogue of his Library in 1781, it is probable that he had it, since David Hume wrote on 16th August, 1760, " Adam Smith, the celebrated professor in Glasgow, told me that the piper of the Argyleshire Militia repeated to him all those poems which Mr. Macpherson has translated and many more of equal beauty "—J. V. T. Greig, *Letters of David Hume*, i, p. 329. It is interesting, too, to find one of his friends in France mentioning Ossian to him in 1764. No doubt these poems had been discussed between them. From the biographical point of view the reference to the Argyleshire Militia is of some importance. It is probably connected with one or more visits which Adam Smith paid to his cousin, William Smith, who had been at one time Secretary to the Duke of Argyle. As William Smith died in 1753, unless there were some other occasion on which Adam Smith met this piper (as, for instance, when he was at Inveraray in the summer of 1759—see above, p. 250), it would put the meeting, mentioned by Hume, at least seven years before the poems were printed. This allusion shows that Adam Smith's MS., printed above, was not earlier than 1760, but other considerations, quite independently, make a date as early as 1760 unlikely.

[2] Originally written " homer ".

[3] *Cf.* above, p. 328. Possibly the direction for a new paragraph may be intended for a printer, indicating an intention to publish the manuscript. A letter from John Glassford in 1764 (which is printed above, p. 258) shows that the writer was expecting an early appearance of the book.

There are many tribes of animals, which are all confessedly of the same species, upon whom nature seems to have stampt a much more remarkable distinction of genius and disposition, than any, which takes place among men, antecedent to custom and education. By nature a Philosopher is not, in Genius [1] and disposition, half so different from a Porter, as a mastiff is from a Greyhound, or a greyhound from a spaniel, or this last from a Sheep dog. Those different tribes of animals, however, tho' all of the same Species, are of Scarce any use to one another. The strength of the mastiff is not in the least supported, either by the swiftness of the Greyhound, or by the sagacity of the Spaniel or by the docility of the Sheep dog. The effects of those different geniuses and talents, for want of the power or disposition to barter and exchange, cannot be brought into a Common stock, and do not, in the least, contribute to the better accomodation of the species. Each animal is still obliged to support and defend itself seperately and independently, and derives no sort of advantage from that variety of talents with which nature has distinguished its fellows. Among men, on the Contrary, the most dissimilar geniuses are of use to one another, the different produces of their different talents, being brought, as it were into a common stock, by the general disposition to truck, barter & exchange. A porter is of use to a Philosopher, not only by sometimes carrying a burden for him, but by facilitating almost every trade and manufacture whose productions the Philosopher can have occasion for. Whatever we buy from any shop or ware-house comes cheaper to us, by means of those poor despised labourers, who in all great towns have set themselves aside for the particular occupation of carrying goods from one place to another, of packing and unpacking them, and who, in consequence, have acquired extraordinary strength dexterity and readiness in this sort of business. Every thing would be dearer, if, before it was exposed to sale, it had been carried packt and unpackt by hands less able and less dexterous, who for an equal quantity of work, would have taken more time, and must, consequently, have required more wages, which must have been charged upon the goods.[2] The Philosopher on the other hand is of use to the porter not only by

N. 8.

---

[1] Written on an erasure.

[2] Adam Smith's surroundings at Glasgow suggested and gave point to this illustration. The commerce of the Clyde consisted in the import of tobacco, the greater part of which was re-exported. The industry of the district supplied a great variety of the needs of the colonists. Many of the commodities exported were small and some were fragile. Careful packing was required to stand the difficulties of an ocean voyage in the small ships of the period and also, in most cases, several transshipments.

being sometimes an occasional Customer, as well as any other man, who is not a porter, but in many other respects. If the Speculations of the Philosopher have been turned towards the improvement of the mechanic arts, the benefit of them *may* [1] evidently descend to the meanest of the people. Whoever burns Coals, has them at a better bargain by means of *the inventor of the* [2] fire engine. Whoever eats bread receives a much greater advantage of the same kind from the Inventors and improvers of wind and water mills. [3] Even the speculations of those who neither invent nor improve any thing are not altogether useless. They serve at least to keep alive and deliver down to posterity the inventions and improvements which had been made before them. They explain the grounds and reasons upon which those discoveries were founded, and do not allow the quantity of usefull knowledge to diminish. In opulent and commercial societies, besides, to think *or* [4] to reason comes to be, like every other employment, a particular business, which is carried on by a very few people, who furnish the public with all the thought and reason possessed [5] by the vast multitudes that labour. Let any ordinary person make a fair review of all the knowledge which he possesses concerning any subject that does not fall within the limits of his particular occupation, and he will find that almost every thing he knows has been acquired at second hand, from books, from the literary instructions which he may have received in his youth, or from the occasional conversations

---

[1] Written over an erasure.

[2] Originally " a better bargain by means of the fire engine ", " the inventor of " inserted after " means of ". As Professor Cannan pointed out (*Lectures*, p. 171 note) this was the early type of steam engine invented for supplying power to pump water from coal mines. In the first English work on the coal-mining industry—*Rara Avis in Terris* or *the Compleat Miner*, written about 1681—it was said " were it not for water, a colliery in these parts [the Wear district] might be termed a golden mine ". Thomas Savery invented an engine for the purpose which was patented in 1698 and protected by a private act in 1699—*The Miner's Friend*, by T. Savery, Lond., 1702, reprinted in B. Woodcroft, *Supplement to Letters Patent and Specifications*, 1858, vol. I, pp. 114-27. This engine was deficient in lifting power and it appears its maximum was about 30 feet. Newcomen made important improvements in 1710. In 1716 engines of this type were in use for draining mines in Stafford, Cornwall, Warwick and Flint. It was introduced to a mine at Stevenston in Ayrshire in 1719— R. L. Galloway, *Annals of Coal Mining*, 1898, p. 240; N. M. Scott, " Documents relating to Coal Mining in the Saltcoats District in the first Quarter of the Eighteenth Century " in *Scottish Historical Review*, xix, p. 91. The engine is illustrated in the former work at pp. 238-9. It was when repairing the model belonging to the Natural Philosophy Department at Glasgow University that Watt discovered his separate condenser.

[3] *Cf.* Postlethwayt, *Dictionary* (1757), art. " Farming." " The discoverers of useful arts for the benefit of general commerce labour for all ages. We still enjoy the fruits of their application and industry. They have procured for us all the conveniencies of life. They have converted all nature to our use. They have taught us to extract from the bowels of the earth and even from the deeps of the sea, the most precious riches."

[4] Written over an erasure, possibly replacing " and ".   [5] See above, p. 327 note [1].

which he may have had with men of Learning. A very small part of it only, he will find, has been the produce of his own observations or reflections. All the rest has been purchased, in the same manner as his shoes or his stockings, from those whose business it is to make up and prepare for the market that particular species of goods. It is in this manner that he has acquired all his general ideas *concerning* [1] the great subjects of Religion, morals & government, concerning his own happiness or that of his country. This whole System concerning each of those important objects, will almost always be found to have been originally the produce of the industry of other people, from whom, either he himself, or those who have had the care of his education, have procured it in the same manner as any other commodity, by barter & exchange for some part of the produce of their own labour.

CONTENTS OF THE FOLLOWING CHAPTERS.
CHAP. 3^d.

Of the Rule of Exchanging or of the Circumstances which regulate the prices of Commodities. Treats of

1mo, The price which is requisite to induce the labourer to apply himself to any particular species of industry, which must be sufficient, 1st to maintain him 2dly To indemnify him for the expence of his Education to that particular business. 3dly. To compensate him for the risk he may run, either of not living long enough to receive this indemnification, or of not succeeding in the Trade let him live ever so long. Price of country labour. of Handicraft work.[2] Of Ingenious arts. Of the Liberal professions. profits of Silver mines.

2do. The price which is fixed by the *market*,[3] and which is regulated 1st. by the need or demand for any particular commodity, 2dly. by the abundance or scarcity of the commodity in proportion to that need or demand, and 3dly. by the riches or poverty of the demandants.

---

[1] Some letters erased and thus written.

[2] *Cf.* Cannan, *Lectures*, p. 174, note 1. Cantillon, *Essai*, ed. H. Higgs, 1931, p. 19. There was a copy of the *Essai* in Adam Smith's Library. Even if he acquired it in France, he would have had Postlethwayt's extracts in the *Universal Dictionary*. As early as 20th May, 1751, there was a column advertisement in the *Glasgow Courant* announcing the publication, and on 23rd December a bookseller was inviting subscriptions either for the whole work or for an issue in parts at 6d. each. On 2nd February, 1756, the second edition was similarly advertised. The price was £4 in sheets or £4 10s. bound. The University Library bought the second edition, and between 1755 and 1758 Adam Smith was instrumental in procuring for the Library Savary's *Parfait Négociant* (Amst., 1726), which had been largely used by Postlethwayt.

[3] Written over an erasure.

3^{tio}. The connection between those two prices. That the *market*[1] price can never, for any considerable time, be either above, or below, that price which is sufficient to encourage the labourer, unless there is some great error in the public police, which prevents the concurrence of labour when the price is too high, or forces a greater concurrence than is natural, when the price is too low.

4to. That as national or public opulence consists in the cheapness of commodities in proportion to the wages of labour, whatever tends to raise their price above what is precisely necessary to encourage the labourer, tends to diminish national or public opulence. of excises and other taxes upon industry. of monopolies.

5to. That there is in every country what may be called a natural balance of industry, or a disposition in the people to apply to each species of work precisely in proportion to the demand for that work. That whatever tends to break this balance, tends to hurt national or public opulence; whether it be by giving extraordinary discouragement to some sorts of industry or extraordinary encouragement to others. of the French Kings Edict against planting new vineyards[2] and of some equally absurd Laws of other nations. Of Bounties either upon the exportation or manufacture of certain goods. That they tend to render, indeed, such goods cheaper, the public paying a part of the price, but all others dearer; and upon the whole to enhance the price of Commodities. Of the Bounty upon Corn. That it has sunk the price of Corn, and thereby tends to lower the rents of Corn farms. That by diminishing the number, it tends to raise *the rent of grass farms*,[3] to raise the price of butcher meat, the price of hay, the expence of keeping horses, and, consequently, the price of Carriage, which must, so far, embarrass the whole inland commerce of the country.

Chap. 4th.

Of money, its nature, origin and history, considered, first, as the measure of value, and secondly as the instrument of Commerce.

Under the first head I have little to say that is very new or particular; except a general history of the Coins of France,[4] England &

---

[1] Written over an erasure.

[2] This illustration is wanting in the *Glasgow Lectures* and also in the corresponding passage of *The Wealth of Nations* (ed. Cannan, i, pp. 63-4). It appears to be taken from Hume's Essay " Of the Balance of Trade "—*Political Discourses*, 1752, p. 89.

[3] This was originally " that by diminishing the number of grass farms it tends to raise the rents of such farms ".

[4] Either the reporter of the *Lectures* condensed the references to French coins almost out of his notes or else, what is more probable, this was added to the manuscript of the lectures, based on

Scotland ; the different changes they have undergone ; their causes and effects. And except some observations upon, what may be called, the money prices of commodities. That human industry, being at all times equally employed to multiply both silver & commodities, and it being more in human power to multiply commodities than to multiply silver, the quantity of the former should naturally be expected to increase in a much greater proportion than that of the latter, and that consequently the money prices of commodities should, at all times, be continually sinking. That, however, things do not exactly correspond to this expectation. That in times of great barbarism and ignorance the money prices of such commodities, as are in those times to be had, are always extremely low, and for what reason.[1] That they rise gradually till the Society arives at a certain pitch of civility and improvement ; and that in its further progress from this improved state, to still greater opulence and improvement, those prices sink gradually again. That the money prices of Commodities have in general been sinking in England for near a century past, and would have sunk much more, had they not been artificially kept up by improper taxes and excises, and by some unjust monopolies. That the cheapness of commodities, in China and the Moguls empire,[2] is the necessary effect of the immense opulence of those countries, notwithstanding their great abundance of Gold and silver.

Under the second head, after explaining the use and necessity of a general instrument of commerce, or medium of exchange, and the way in which the precious metals come naturally to be made use of as such ; I endeavour to show,

1mo. That as the sole use of money is to circulate commodities, that is, food cloaths, and the conveniences of lodging, or domestic accomodation, and that as money itself is neither food cloaths nor lodging, the larger proportion which that part of the stock of any nation which is converted into money, bears to the whole ; the less food cloaths and lodging there must be in that nation ; which must, therefore, be so much the worse fed cloathed and lodged, and consequently so much the poorer and less powerful. That money, serving

data derived from books Adam Smith had caused to be added to the University Library, *e.g.* Article by de Forbonnais in the *Encyclopédie* on "Espèces", ϒ, pp. 957-70. It was the writing of this article which occasioned the production of his *Elémens du Commerce*, though the book appeared in 1754, a year earlier than the article.

[1] This is probably an instance of early material, collected for the lectures in Edinburgh, being incorporated into this manuscript. The data are of a type which coheres with the investigation in Robertson's *Charles V.*, see above, Part I, chapter V.

[2] *Cf.* Cannan's note 1, *Glasgow Lectures*, p. 165.

only to circulate commodities, is so much dead stock which produces nothing, and which may very properly be compared to a high road, which, while it helps to circulate the produce of all the grass & corn, in the country, and thereby indirectly contributes to the raising of both, produces itself neither grass nor Corn.

2do. That whatever contrivance can enable any nation to circulate the produce of its industry with a smaller quantity of money than would otherwise be necessary, must be extremely advantagious; because the quantity of money saved may be exchanged abroad for commodities, by means of which a greater number of people can be fed, cloathed, lodged, maintained & employed, the profit upon whose industry will still further increase the public opulence. That banks and bank notes are contrivances of this sort. They enable us, as it were, to plough up our high roads, by affording us a sort of communication through the air by which we do our business equally well. That, therefore, to confine them by monopolies, or any other restraints, except such as are necessary to prevent frauds & abuses, must obstruct the progress of public opulence. History of banking ancient and modern.

3^{tio}. That national opulence, or the effect of national opulence either at home or abroad, neither consists in, nor depends upon the quantity of money, or even of gold & silver that is in the country; and that no sort of preference is due to this species of goods above any other. The bad effects of the contrary opinion both in Speculation and practice. *In speculation* [1] it has given occasion to the Systems of Mun and Gee; of Mandeville who built upon them; and of Mr. Hume who endeavoured to refute them.

In practice it has given occasion,

N. 10.

1mo. To the prohibition which takes place in some countries, of exporting either coin or bullion. A prohibition, which, very happily, is always in a great measure ineffectual, and which, so far as it is

---

[1] Written over an erasure. It was probably owing to the interest in economic questions aroused by the Political Economy Club, mentioned previously (p. 81) that the Foulises reprinted a number of tracts. On 25th March, 1751, they had a displayed column advertisement in the *Glasgow Courant* of Child's *New Discourse on Trade, Proposals for constituting a Council of Trade in Scotland* (which was attributed to Law instead of Paterson), Gee's *Trade and Navigation* and Berkeley's *Querist*. Adam Smith was most unlikely to have influenced the selection, having been appointed to the Chair of Logic on 16th January of the same year, with leave of absence till the beginning of the next session. But on 8th September, 1755, there was another displayed advertisement of the same publishers and he may have had a voice in the additions to the previous list. These comprise Petty's *Political Arithmetic*, Law's *Money and Trade Considered*, Mun's *England's Treasure by Forraign Trade* and Tucker's *Naturalisation of Foreign Protestants*, with Hutcheson's *De Naturali Hominum Socialitate Oratio Inauguralis*—the last being the address he gave on admission as a Professor.

(a) THE AYRSHIRE HALF-PENNY

(b) THE PENNY OF SCOTLAND

PLATE XVI. The Head of Adam Smith on the Ayrshire half-penny and on the penny of Scotland.
(a) The Ayrshire half-penny; (b) the penny of Scotland, 1797.

effectual, necessarily tends to impoverish the country. First because whatever Gold and silver there is in any country, over and above what is sufficient to Circulate the produce of its industry, is so much dead stock, which is of no use *at all*.[1] whereas, if allowed to go abroad, it would naturally be exchanged for what would feed, Cloath, maintain & employ a greater number of people, whose industry would increase real national opulence, by multiplying the conveniencies and necessaries of life. Secondly, Because this unnecessary accumulation of Gold and Silver, renders those metals cheap in proportion to other commodities, and consequently raises the money price of every thing. This stops all industry, the peasants, manufacturers and traders of such a Country, being necessarily undersold, both at home & abroad, by the traders of other Countries in which the mon*ey*-prices [2] of things are lower. The misery of Spain and Portugal, owing, in part, for many other causes concur, to this prohibition.

2do. To the unreasonable restraints imposed upon certain branches of Commerce, and to the unreasonable encouragement given to others ; upon pretence that the one drains us of our money, we sending abroad money and getting home only goods which we consume ; and that the other enrich*es us, we* [3] sending abroad only goods and getting home hard cash. The meanness vulgarity and folly of both these conceptions. First, that every branch of Commerce which one nation can regularly carry on with another is, and necessarily must be, advantagious to both, each exchanging that which it has less need of, for that which it has more need of, each giving what is of less value in its own Country for what is of more value in the same country ; each therefore increasing its own real opulence, and consequently its own power of feeding, cloathing, maintaining and employing people. Secondly, That whatever tends to restrain the liberty of exchanging one thing for another, tends to discourage industry, and to obstruct the division of labour which is the foundation of the opulence of Society. It is allowed that all prohibitions of exportation discourage industry ; but a prohibition of importation must have the same effect. Since it is the same thing whether you forbid me to exchange my wares, at the place where I can exchange them to most advantage, or for the goods for which I can exchange them to most advantage. If you prohibit the importation of French Claret, for example, you discourage all that industry of which the produce would have been exchanged for French Claret. Whether

---

[1] Written over an erasure.   [2] Originally "monied" and corrected as above.
[3] Possibly "enriching us" was written and corrected as above.

that industry would have been exercised in making a piece of broad cloth, or in bringing Gold from the Brazils, is of no consequence to national opulence. If that Cloth *is* [1] more than the home consumption requires,[2] it must go abroad ; and if that Gold is more than the Channel of home Circulation requires, *for these are the same*,[3] or can receive, it must go abroad in the same manner, and be exchanged for something to be consumed at home, and why not for good Claret ? Thirdly, that the produce of every Species of industry which is not either destroyed by some misfortune, or taken from us by an enemy, is, must and ought to be consumed at home, either in substance, or in what it is exchanged for, after one, two, three, or three hundred exchanges : And that this is so far from either taking away, or diminishing the national profit [4] upon industry, that it is the very circumstance which renders all industry profit*able* [5] to the nation ; Since it is only by means of this home consumption that more people can be maintained & employed, or those maintained & employed before are maintained & employed more agreeably, or that the nation can, in any respect, better its circumstances. Fourthly That no nation ever was ruined by what is called the ballance of Trade being against them, but by the excess of their annual consumption, above the annual produce of their industry which would necessarily ruin them, tho they had no foreign trade at all. Fifthly, that no nation whose industry and opulence are entire can be long in want of money ; goods commanding money even more necessarily than money commands goods. Sixthly That all extraordinary encouragement given to any one branch of Commerce, breaks the natural balance of industry in commerce as well as in manufactures, and, so far, obstructs the progress of opulence. Of the British Trade to France & Portugal. That a free trade to France would tend infinitely more to enrich Great Britain than a free trade to Portugal, because, France, on account of its superior opulence having more to give could take more from us, and exchanging to a much greater value and in a much greater variety of ways, would encourage more industry in Great Britain and give occasion to more subdivisions of labour ; and that it is only passion and national prejudice which ever made any body think other*wise*.[6] The British merchant.

3^{tio}. The notion that national opulence consists in money has given occasion to the current and pernicious opinion that we can never

---

[1] Originally " was ", corrected to " is ". [2] Originally "required ", corrected as above.
[3] Inserted. [4] Originally " profite " or " profits " and changed as above.
[5] Written over an erasure. [6] Written over an erasure.

N. 11.

hurt ourselves by any expence incurred at home; because the money, being all spent among ourselves, does not go out of the country; and that, what one loses, another gets. That the difference, with regard to the diminution of public opulence, when a stock of the conveniencies and necessaries of life is wasted uselessly at home, and when either these, or the money which purchases these, is sent abroad to be wasted in the same manner, is extremely inconsiderable. Useless sea wars very near as destructive to public opulence as useless Land wars.

4to. The notion that national opulence consisted in or depended upon money, joined to another false notion that the value put upon the precious metals was a matter of institution and agreement, gave occasion to the famous System of Mr. Law.[1] That Gentleman imagined that by proper measures, the inhabitants of a particular country, might gradually be induced to affix the idea of a certain value to a certain paper currency; in the same manner, as they affix it, at present, to a certain sum of money: and even to prefer the paper to the money. And that if this was once fairly brought about, the Government, which had the issuing of this paper, might excite what industry raise, and pay what armies and fit out what fleets they thought proper, without being at any other expence but that of building a paper mill. The vanity of both these imaginations, together with the history and analysis of the principal operations of this System. South sea Scheme.[2]

CHAP. 5TH.

Concerning the Causes of the slow progress of opulence.[3]

Those causes of two kinds. First, natural impediments; and, secondly, oppressive, or injudicious Government.

---

[1] See p. 348 note 1. In the *Lectures*, as Professor Cannan points out (p. 211, note 1), the correct date for the introduction of Law's scheme to the Scottish Parliament was 1705, not 1701 as the reporter stated. In the *Const. and Finance of Companies*, iii, pp. 265-7, this and other schemes, with the general environment of the times, are described. Adam Smith continues Law's career to the rise and fall of his " System ". The authorities referred to by Cannan in his note to the corresponding passage in *The Wealth of Nations* were not available at the time this manuscript was written, but there was at hand in the Glasgow University Library *Recherches et Considérations sur les Finances de France*, 1595-1721, Liège, 1758, compiled by Forbonnais, and the critique of Law's System in the article on " Emprunts " in the *Encyclopédie*, v, p. 598.

[2] Adam Smith's father held some South Sea Stock of the Fourth Subscription (see p. 131). Anderson's *Annals of Commerce* had not reached Adam Smith when this was written. It seems probable he drew his information from Chambers' *Cyclopædia*, Articles " Company (South Sea) " and " Bubbles ".

[3] This part of the *Lectures*, subsequently incorporated into *The Wealth of Nations*, probably represents the portion which, in an early form, was first written, being based on lectures delivered at Edinburgh in the winter of 1748-9 (see above, Part I, chapter V.)

The original Poverty and Ignorance of mankind the natural impediments to the progress of opulence. That it is easier for a nation, in the same manner, as for an Individual, to raise itself from a moderate degree of wealth to the highest opulence, than to acquire this moderate degree of wealth; Money, according to the proverb, begetting money, among nations as among individuals. The extreme difficulty of beginning accumulation and the many accidents to which it is exposed. The slowness and difficulty with which those things, which now appear the most simple inventions were originally found out. That a nation is not always in a condition to imitate and copy the inventions and improvements of its m*ore* [1] wealthy neighbours; the application of these frequently requiring a stock with which it is not furnished.

The oppressive and injudicious Governments to which mankind are almost always subject, but more especially, in the rude beginnings of society, greatly increase those natural impediments, which of themselves are not easily surmounted: The oppression and errors of Government affect either I^{mo}.[2] agriculture; or, 2do. arts & commerce.

I^{mo}.[2] The great importance of agriculture and how much the value of its annual produce exceeds that of any other art. That the cultivation of Land depends upon the proportion which the stock of those who cultivate it [3] bears to the quantity of Land to be cultivated. That consequently whatever tends to prevent the accumulation of stock in the hands of the Cultivators, or to discourage them from continuing this species of industry after they have accumulated some stock in this manner, must tend to retard the progress of agriculture.

That the chiefs of an independent nation which settles in any country, either by Conquest or otherwise, as soon as the idea of private property in Land is introduced, never leave any part of the Land vacant, but constantly, from that greediness which is natural to man, seize much greater tracts of it to themselves than they have, either strength, or stock, to Cultivate. [4] From the same greediness and rapacity, being unwilling to divide the profites of this Land with any freeman, what they cannot, or will not, cultivate by their own

---

[1] Written over an erasure.   [2] "I^{mo}" "2do" inserted.

[3] Originally "who cultivate it for their own benefite bears" and "for their own benefite" being deleted.

[4] See authorities quoted by Cannan, *Lectures*, pp. 34-40, with the addition of those in W. Robertson, *History of Charles V.*, 1769, I, pp. 213-27.

strength, they endeavour to Cultivate by the strength of slaves, whom they either conquer in war, or purchase in some other way, and in whose hands no stock ever can accumulate.

Of the Cultivation by slaves.

That Land can never be cultivated to the best advantage by slaves, the work which is done by slaves always coming dearer than that which is done by freemen. Of the scanty produce and great expence of the slave cultivation among the antient Greeks and Romans. Of villenage as it took place among our Saxon and Norman ancestors; of the Adscripti Glebæ in Germany and Poland, and the Rustici in Russia, and those who work in the Coal and Salt works of Scotland.[1] That the high Cultivation of Barbadoes, and of some other sugar and tobacco Colonies, notwithstanding that in them the labour is performed almost entirely by slaves, is owing to this Circumstance, that the Cultivation of Tobacco and sugar is engrossed, the one, almost entirely by the English, the other, by the English and French, who thus enjoying a sort of Monopoly against all the rest of the world, indemnify themselves by the exorbitance of their profites, for their expensive and thriftless method of Cultivation. The great expence of slave cultivation in the sugar *Plantations*.[2] The yet more exorbitant profites of the Planter. That the Planters in the more northern Colonies, cultivating chiefly wheat and Indian Corn,[3] by which they can expect no such exorbitant returns, find it not for their interest to employ many slaves, and yet Pensilvania *the Jerseys* [4] and some of the Provinces of New England are much richer and more populous than Virginia notwithstanding, that Tobacco is, by its ordinary high price a more profitable Cultivation.

---

[1] Cannan, *Glasgow Lectures*, pp. 226-33, notes, with the addition of W. Robertson, *History of Charles V.*, 1769, I, pp. 227-32.

[2] Written over an erasure.

[3] On 6th December, 1756, the Corporation offered premiums for the importation of Indian corn to Glasgow—" the Corporation, in order to encourage the importation of grain from America for the use of the poor, offer a premium of £10 for each 1000 bushels of the first 20,000 bushels of Indian corn imported to Glasgow before August 1 next."—*Glasgow Courant*.

[4] " the Jerseys " inserted.

N. 12.

Of the Cultivation by the Antient Metayers [1] or Tenants by Steelbow. (a)

(a) *The first of these expressions is French the second, Scotch. This species of lease having been long disused in England, and even in all the tollerably cultivated parts of Scotland. I know no English word for it at present.*

That through the whole of that very small corn*er* [2] of the world in which Slavery has,[3] by a concurrence of different causes, been abolished, what naturally, and almost necessarily, came after the Cultivation by slaves, was that by the Antient Metayers or Tenants by Steelbow. To these at the Commencement of the lease, a certain number of Cattle were delivered by the Lord, to be returned in equal number and goodness at the expiration of it. With these Cattle the Tenant was to cultivate the Land, and the Lord and he were to divide the produce between them, each ch*u*sing [4] a sheaff in his turn, when the Corn was cut down and set up in sheaffs on the field. That land could never be improved to the best advantage by such Tenants. 1st. because stock could not, without the greatest difficulty, accumulate in their hands; and 2dly. because if it did accumulate, they would never lay it out in the improvement of the Land, since the Lord, who laid out nothing, was to divide the profites with them. That the greater part of the Lands in the western parts of Europe, the only corner of the world in which Slavery has ever been abolished, particularly about five Sixth parts of the Lands in France, are still cultivated by Tenants of this kind.

Of the Cultivation by Farmers properly so called.

That to those Metayers, or Tenants by Steelbow, succeeded, in some few places, farmers properly so called, or Tenants who had a lease of their lands either for life or during a term of years, for a rent certain to be paid, at first, in kind, and afterwards in money. That those Tenants seem to have been originally Metayers, in whose hands, notwithstanding many oppressions, some property had accumulated, and who were thereby enabled to stock their own

---

[1] It is interesting to compare this passage with the *Glasgow Lectures*, p. 226, where the reporter has it "a great part of France is still cultivated by tenants of steel bow and it is said that it still remains in some parts of the Highlands of Scotland." The question is whether in the lectures as delivered Adam Smith used the term "metayer". It is clear that he was acquainted with the fact of the existence of this type of land tenure in France which he could have obtained from the considerable number of books on French agriculture in the Glasgow University Library. It may have been that his lectures did not contain the word, or alternatively the reporter not catching it, and perhaps hearing that steel bow was an equivalent, wrote down the latter. In any case, Adam Smith would have obtained full information, perhaps at a later date, from Quesnay's Article on "Fermiers" in the *Encyclopédie* (vi, p. 539). "Steelbow" is mentioned in Stair, *Institutions of the Law of Scotland*, ed. 1832, pp. 108, 250, 535.

[2] Written over an erasure.   [3] "Had" changed into "has".

[4] Written over an erasure.

DRAFT OF "THE WEALTH OF NATIONS" 355

farms, and, consequently, to offer a contract of this kind to their Lord. That *such*[1] farmers, having some little stock of their own, and not being liable to have their rents immediately raised upon them, might be both able and willing to make some improvements. That they still, however, laboured under many inabilities and discouragements. That a lease of Lands, being a transaction founded upon contract, originally and naturally begot only a personal right in the Tenant, which, tho it was good against the lessor or his heirs, was not good against a purchaser. That, therefore, if a Tenant made any such improvement *of*[2] his lands as greatly increased their value, he was sure of being *turned out*[3] of his lease, either by a real, or *by*[4] a sham purchaser. Of the statutes of England and Scotland by which leases were first secured against purchasers, and that this police is almost peculiar to Great Britain. Of the many other discouragements which Tenants laboured under. Of the disadvantages of a rent paid in kind and of the difficulties, which attended the first introduction of money rents. 2 Of the arbitrary services with which all sorts of Tenants were all over Europe long burdened at the will of the Landlord. Of the Laws by which these were restrained or abolished in some Countries, of the political reasons of those Laws, and how far these services are still due in many countries. Of purveyance. Of the arbitrary and exorbitant tallages to which Tenants of all kinds were liable, and how far these still subsist in many countries. Of the taille in France and its effects upon agriculture. Of the advantage which agriculture derives in England from the Law which gives certain lease holders a right of voting for members of Parliament, which thereby establishes a mutual dependance between the Landlord and the Tenant, and makes the former, if he has any regard to his interest in the County, very cautious of attempting to raise his rents, or of demanding any other oppressive exactions of the latter. The superior liberty of the English above the Scots.

2 of leases from year to year, or will.

That the original engrossment of Lands by the chiefs of the nations has been perpetuated in Europe by three different causes. First by the obstruction which the antient feudal government gave to the alienation of Land, which, notwithstanding the almost entire extinction of that Government, is still every where embarrassed by many unnecessary forms, not requisite in the transference of any other property how valuable soever. Secondly by entails and other perpetuities. Thirdly by the right of Primo geniture. The reasons

---

[1] "Such" inserted.
[2] Originally "on".
[3] Written on an erasure (? evicted, erased).
[4] Also written on an erasure.

of the rapid progress of opulence in those Colonies in which this engrossment of Lands has been in some measure prevented, and in which the greater part of Lands are cultivated, not by farmers, but by proprietors. Of the British North American Colonies.

Of other discouragements to the Cultivation of Lands. Of tythes. Of the Prohibition of the exportation of Corn according to the antient police of almost every part of Europe. That sometime after the full establishment of the power of the Romans, a prohibition of this kind, together with the distributions which were annually made by the Government of Sicilian, Egyptian and African Corn at a very low price to the people, and which must have had the same effect to discourage home Cultivation as a bounty upon importation, gave occasion to the depopulation of antient Italy, and to the saying of old Cato, " Qui cuidam querenti quid maxime prodesset in re familiari? Bene pascere, respond*it*.[1] Quid proximum? Satis bene pascere. Quid tertium? Male pascere. Quid quartum? Arare " Cicero de off. lib 2d. at the end.

2do.   of [2]

---

[1] The last two letters have been altered. Possibly originally " respondet ".

[2] The passage from Cato appears to have been quoted from memory. The first sentence in the original is : " A quo cum quaereretur, quid maxime in re familiari expediret, respondit." The quotation is summarised in a different context in *The Wealth of Nations*, i, p. 151. The manuscript, as it now exists, breaks off at a point corresponding to p. 229 of the *Glasgow Lectures*, which contained fifty-nine pages more. Of these twenty-three pages are economic. The corresponding place in *The Wealth of Nations* is, in Cannan's edition, i, p. 370.

The existence of the catchword " 2do " (relating to the rise and progress of cities and towns) almost forces one to speculate as to what happened to the remainder. In going through the mass of the Townshend papers, no other case appeared where a piece of manuscript was deficient in this way. Two explanations may be suggested. (1) Townshend may have made some notes on the later sheets and returned those so annotated to Adam Smith, in which case, even if he retained these sheets, they would have perished with the greater part of his unpublished material. (2) It is by no means impossible that the analysis of the chapters on revenue and taxes may have suggested to Townshend his own work on the Funds which has been described in *Economic History Review*, October 1935, pp. 80-2. In that case he might well have retained Adam Smith's MS. covering this subject. It has been shown that after Townshend's death Adam Smith recovered his own papers relating to the partly completed book ; and, on this assumption, the remainder of this MS. would have been amongst them. He may have used it for *The Wealth of Nations*, if there was anything additional or an improvement on what he already had, and then destroyed it. Otherwise its fate would have been that already described.

PART IV

FACSIMILES OF THE HANDWRITING OF ADAM SMITH
AND HIS AMANUENSES

FACSIMILES OF THE HANDWRITING OF ADAM SMITH AND HIS AMANUENSES.

The following examples of Adam Smith's writing extend over a period of fifty-six years. A study of them gives some light on his method of composition and on his style. Many students of his life and work have alluded to his " round schoolboy hand ". The consequences are more important than they appear at first sight. In the letter to Cadell (which is reproduced below) he speaks of himself as " a slow, a very slow workman ". What he had chiefly in mind was—as he adds— that he " undid what he had written half a dozen times." In addition to that his type of penmanship was such that he could only write more slowly than the average person. He had a tendency to raise his pen during the writing of a short word and sometimes more than once. This was particularly marked in early youth and in his later years. Also he wrote untidily. This is marked in the letter to Strahan of 1760.[1] It is shown also in the second specimen of the manuscript of the draft of *The Wealth of Nations* and in many places in that manuscript, where, after a word had been erased, he could not get the same number of letters to fit in and, sometimes, a second erasure was necessary. This is one reason why an amanuensis was employed to provide his manuscript for the printer or to submit to his friends. Another reason, no doubt arising out of the former and his concentration on study, was that he hated the act of writing, particularly letters. In the majority of David Hume's letters to him there is usually a complaint of unanswered notes. In fact he carried this trait so far that documents at the University of Glasgow, usually in the autograph of Professors, were, in Adam Smith's case, in the hand of one of the College scribes. Two instances may be mentioned. In the matriculation roll of the University it was the custom for the student to sign his name under a general heading (the three types of these in Adam Smith's time are reproduced below) and the Professor filled in the description. It is doubtful if Adam Smith could have got it into the space available, and usually this was added by one of the scribes for him. In the long report on the powers of the Rector and Principal (above pp. 203–15), which was compiled by Adam Smith, the record of it, even to the signature, is not in his hand; while the protest by James Moor which follows is his own writing. Also, no doubt, it was the practice of Adam Smith's official friends to have the use of an official copyist, and this accentuated Adam Smith's natural disposition in that direction. The practice of dictating to an amanuensis had the effect of preserving something once written. A study of the manuscript of the draft of *The Wealth of Nations* shows that he was very skilful in changing a few letters to improve the meaning, but he succumbed to the temptation of setting his amanuensis to

[1] J. Bonar, *Adam Smith's Library*, 1932, at p. xxviii.

copy out long passages without detailed revision, hence the appearance of "opulence" in *The Wealth of Nations*, when it is evident he had intended to replace it throughout by "wealth". The result of the investigation in Part I, Chapter IX, has been to show that *The Wealth of Nations* is, in a sense, an amalgam, incorporating material written at different times, and some of it almost thirty years prior to the completion of the book. This is largely accounted for by the intervention of an amanuensis and the consequences of this. It is clear that great pains were taken to secure consistency; for, while Adam Smith reached his central and fundamental position very early, there must have been matters of detail on which his views changed. Scarcely any trace of this remains. On the other hand, the later additions were inserted into the previous manuscript with no change or a very small change in it. It was easy and simple to instruct the amanuensis where to insert a new chapter or an appendix, but the original symmetrical arrangement was impaired, with the result that the argument moves less freely and spontaneously in the final revision than it did in the earlier and less complete draft.[1]

The writing of most of the amanuenses employed by Adam Smith is reproduced in the following pages. There is one curious irregularity. While their work remains, their names are unknown. Though a specimen of the manuscript of *The Wealth of Nations* is wanting, the name of the man who was responsible for the penmanship has come to light. This appears from an obituary notice, dated March 1819, in the *Scots Magazine*, in which it is stated that Alexander Gillies " was amanuensis to Dr. Adam Smith and *transcribed*[2] for him his celebrated work, *The Wealth of Nations* ". It may be presumed that Gillies had some employment in Kirkcaldy between 1767 and 1773. In 1785 he was appointed an assistant officer of the Excise at Edinburgh. On 15th September, 1786, he was promoted to the office of Gauger. By 1797 he was an Examiner in the Ayrshire Collection, and from 6th July of that year he was Supervisor of the Kilmarnock district. In 1810 he was Supervisor in the Queensferry district of the Linlithgowshire Collection.[3] Apparently he retired soon afterwards. The *Scots Magazine* mentions that for some time previous to his death he had been supported by David Douglas, Lord Reston. It may be guessed that, not only did he hold the same rank in the service as Robert Burns, but he may have had some of the same habits, since as Supervisor at Kilmarnock he received a salary of £65 a year and his riding charges, but the income was higher. Burns in one of his letters puts the earnings of a Supervisor at £120 to £200 a year.[4] At the time this was a respectable income.

[1] *Cf.* Appendix VI.

[2] " Transcribe " is fairly accurate; since, when Gillies began, there would be a large amount of material already in writing, which was copied after alterations had been made.

[3] Excise Papers at the General Register House, Edinburgh, and *Edinburgh Almanacks*.

[4] *Letters of Robert Burns* (ed. F. H. Allen), 1927, iii, p. 227.

FACSIMILES

Signature of William Smith, Regent, Marischal University, Aberdeen (*fl.* 1669-1729), named in the Will of Adam Smith, W.S., as a tutor and curator of his elder son Hugh (from the Propinquity Book—20th June, 1699—Town House, Aberdeen).

Signatures of Hercules Smith (a tutor and curator of Hugh Smith) and of Adam Smith, W.S., the father of Adam Smith, author of *The Wealth of Nations*, from a Salary List of the Customs at Kirkcaldy, dated 25th March, 1722 (General Register House, Edinburgh).

Signature of Margaret Douglas, mother of Adam Smith (Glasgow University Library).

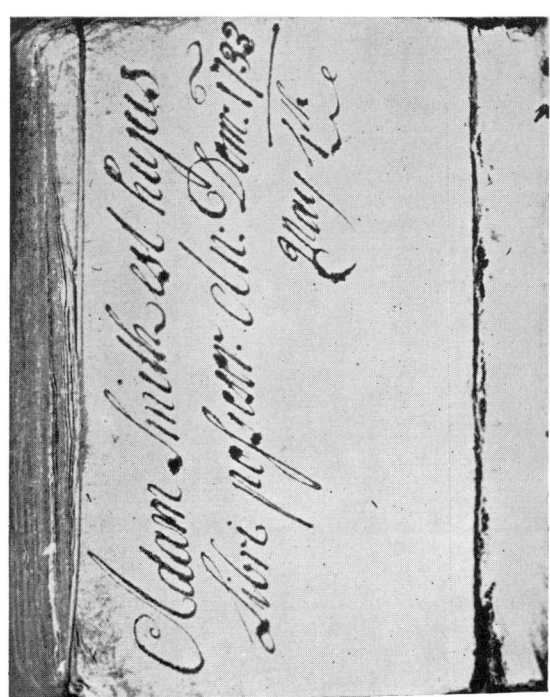

Signature of Adam Smith, when a schoolboy, in *Eutropii Historiae Romanae breviarium in usum scholarum*, 12mo, calf, Edinburgh, 1725 (Adam Smith Hall, Kirkcaldy).

Signature of Adam Smith in the Matriculation Roll of the University of Glasgow, 14th November, 1737.

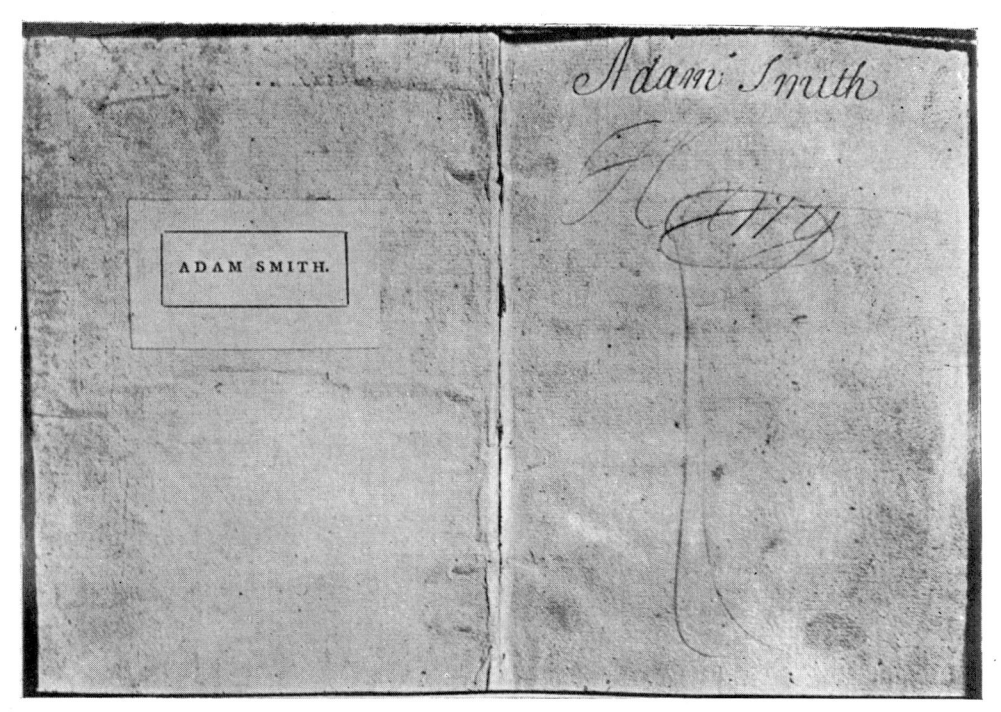

Signature of Adam Smith when he was attending the Greek class at the University of Glasgow in 1738-9 or perhaps in 1737-8; in *Epicteti Stoici philosophi Encheiridion unà cum Cebetis Thebani Tabula Heironymo Wolfio Oetingensi interprete*, London, 1670 (Glasgow University Library).

A letter from Adam Smith to his mother from Balliol (Miss Cunningham, Hereford).

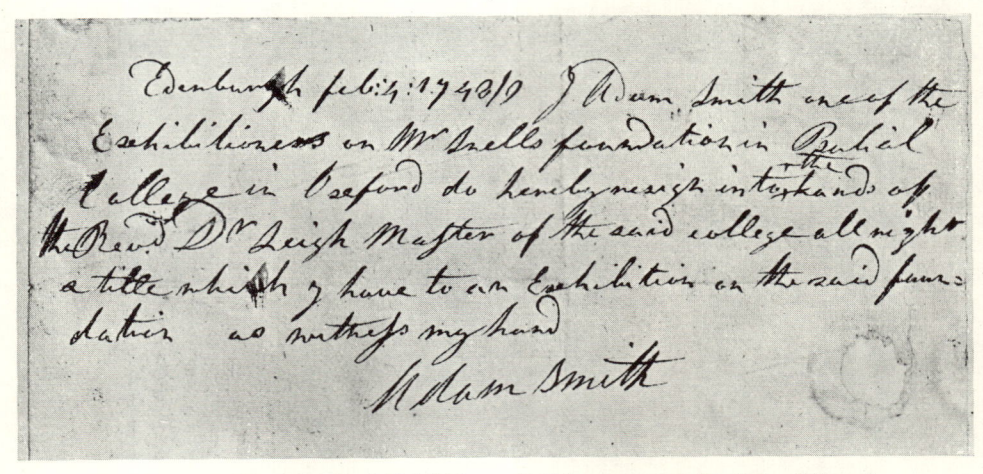

His resignation of the Snell Exhibition, 4th February, 1749 (Bodleian Library).

SIGNATURES AND INSCRIPTIONS IN BOOKS

1. To the Professor's Oath, 16th January, 1751; 2. To the Oath as Dean of Faculty, 26th June, 1760; 3. Last signature as Dean of Faculty, 26th June, 1762; 4. Signature of Minute of Meeting of 15th July, 1761, the legality of which was questioned; 5. First signature as Vice-Rector, 14th May, 1763; 6. Last signature as Professor, 10th January, 1764, he signs as Præses and not as Vice-Rector since the Rector had not been admitted; 7. As Rector, 27th November, 1788; 8. Inscription in 5th edition of *Theory of Moral Sentiments*, 1781; 9. Inscription in 6th edition of *Theory of Moral Sentiments*, 1790 (all at the University of Glasgow). The inscription in the 2nd edition of *The Wealth of Nations* in the Library is not in Adam Smith's hand, but the Duke of Buccleuch's copy of the 3rd edition is inscribed by Adam Smith.

A book with most interesting associations with Adam Smith. It was in the Moral Philosophy Class Library in 1732. It has also Adam Smith's book label, being apparently included amongst his books by mistake when such labels were being pasted in his books. The small slip is in the fold of the binding. The signature differs from that of Adam Smith. It may be that of Adam Smith, a student, who was in the Moral Philosophy Class in 1762-3 (Glasgow University Library).

Expediency of naturalisation
part 1
part 2
Letter to a friend on naturalisation
Second letter on the same subject.
Inquiry concerning spirituous
Liquors.
Reflections on the Turkey trade.
Instructions to travellers.
Dispertations on passages
of Scripture
All the above by Tucker.

Tracts by Josiah Tucker, 1751-7. Contents in Adam Smith's handwriting (Glasgow University Library).

Present state of the nation.
Observations on a late state
of the nation
Thoughts on the present Dis=
=contents.
Speech of Mr Burke 19 april 1774
Ditto 22 March 1775
Letter to Mr Burke by Tucker
Address and Appeal to the
Landed Interest by Tucker.

Political Pamphlets, 1768-75. Contents in Adam Smith's handwriting (Glasgow University Library).

1. Considerations on the present state of Public affairs by Mr Pulteney.

2. View of the Hard Labour Bill

3. Considerations on Militia's and Standing Armies. by Mr Sinclair.

4. Thoughts on the naval strength of G. Britain. by the Same.

6. Observations on McKintosh's Travels in Europe, Asia and Africa. By Joseph Price

5. Political Observations on the Population of Countries.

7. Lucubrations during a short recess.

8. Observations on the sixth Æneid of Virgil.

Contents of a volume marked "Political Tracts" in the handwriting of Adam Smith. The Tracts were issued from 1778 to 1782 (Glasgow University Library).

The Italian heroic verse is exactly the same with the English.

In both the accent ought regularly to fall upon every second syllable; that is upon the 2d. 4th. 6th. 8th & 10th.

In both, for the sake of variety, it is frequently allowable, if I may say so, to slurr an accent; that is, to let a syllable, which ought regularly to be accented, pass without an accent. The movement of such a verse taken by itself, appears less perfect ~~it seems to hobble~~ ~~if I may say so~~ and seems as it were to hobble; ~~mixed~~ with other verses, it may frequently have a better effect than if they were all perfectly regular. Thus, in the two following verses,

Let us, since life can little more supply,
Than just to look about us and to die.

The movement of the first verse appears more perfect than that of the second in which the ~~eleventh~~ 8th ~~eighth~~ syllable (and) is slurred over without an accent.

In neither can the accent ever fall upon an odd syllable, that is, upon the 3d. 5th. 7. or 9th., without spoiling the verse.

In both, the verse, where there is a double rhyme, ~~where there~~ consists of eleven syllables; where there is a

The earliest form of the Essay "on the Affinity between English and Italian Verses" (c. 1777-84, Glasgow University Library: reduced from quarto).

(371)

single rhyme, of ten only.

In Italian, double rhymes are most common; in English, single rhymes. Upon this account the greater part of Italian verses consist of eleven syllables, or are what are called Hendecasyllables; While the greater part of english verses consist of ten only. This constitutes the principal, I believe, the sole difference between them. In Italian there are in which case the verse consists of sometimes triple rhymes. I do not recollect any triple in English heroic verse. Both in English and Italian verses of eleven syllables the accent falls always upon the tenth syllable. It is the same case with the Italian verses of triple rhymes, or verses of twelve syllables: neither the eleventh nor the twelfth syllable can be accented.

The reason of this principal, or, as I think, sole difference between Italian and english verse I take to be, that in English, the greater part of words, of more than one syllable, are accented upon the last syllable; whereas in Italian the greater part of words are accented upon the syllable before the last. This circumstance necessarily makes double rhymes most frequent in the one language, and single rhymes in the other.

The rarity of double rhymes in English heroic verse makes them, when they occur, appear awkward

The earliest form of the Essay "on the Affinity between English and Italian Verses" (c. 1777-84, continued, Glasgow University Library).

and even ludicrous. Good writers therefore commonly reserve them for ludicrous occasions.

Worth makes the man, and want of it, the fellow;
The rest is all but leather or prunello.

have not the same air with the greater part of the verses of the Essay on man. In Italian heroic verse the like variety makes both single and triple rhymes have nearly the same effect. They are by good writers therefore reserved for nearly the same occasions.

In counting the syllables both of english and

The earliest form of the Essay "on the Affinity between English and Italian Verses" (c. 1777-84, concluded, Glasgow University Library).

Dear Sir

You have very great reason to wonder at my long silence. The weak state of my health and my attendance at the Custom house, occupied me so much after my return to Scotland, that tho' I gave as much application to study as these circumstances would permit, yet that application was neither very great, nor very steady, so that my progress was not very great. I have now taken leave of my colleagues for four months and I am at present giving the most intense application. My subject is the theory of moral sentiments, to all parts of which I am making many additions and corrections. The chief and the most important additions will be to the third part, that concerning the sense of Duty and to the last part concerning the History of moral Philosophy. As I consider my tenure of this life as extremely precarious, and am very uncertain whether I shall live to finish several other works which I have projected and in which I have made some progress

Letter from Adam Smith to Thomas Cadell, Bookseller in the Strand, 1788 (Glasgow University Library: reduced from quarto).

gress, the best thing, I think, I can do is to leave these I have already published in the best and most perfect state behind me. I am a slow a very slow workman, who do and undo everything I write at least half a dozen of times before I can be tolerably pleased with it; and tho' I have now, I think, brought my work within compass, yet it will be the month of June before I shall be able to send it to you. I have told you already, and I need not tell you again, that I mean to make you a present of all my Additions. I must beg, therefore, that no new edition of that book may be published before that time.

I should be glad to know how the sale of my other book goes on.

I am ashamed of the trouble I have so often given you about the Philosophical transactions. The second part of 1787 is now due to me; and the first part of 1788, if it is yet published, I should be much obliged to you if you could find a clever way of sending them

Letter from Adam Smith to Thomas Cadell (continued).

them to me.
Remember me most affectionately to Strahan and believe me to be
My Dear Sir
Edin.
15. March 1788.
Most affectionately yours
Adam Smith

Letter from Adam Smith to Thomas Cadell (concluded).

My Dear Sir

I need not, I flatter myselfe, inform you at this time, what pleasure, the late happy, (and to my own melancholy and evil boding mind, I acknowledge, unexpected) event, has given to your friends here and, I will venture to say, to all the real friends of the country. The firmness, propriety and prudence of every part of your young friends conduct must, as long as it is remembered, place him very high in the estimation of every wise and thinking man in the Kingdom.

It gives me great concern that I am obliged to put you in mind of anything that, at this time of business, can give you any trouble. But there is a very favourable report of the Scots Barons lying before the Lords of the treasury for their approbation, upon the petition of the University of Glasgow for a renewal of the Grant of the Archbishoprie. My Colleagues at Glasgow are besides very anxious about a pension to the Widow of their late friend and assistant

Adam Smith to Henry Dundas, 1789 (Glasgow University Library: reduced from quarto).

assistant in their Labours, Dr Irwin. My col=
=leagues at this board too are equally so about some=
=thing of the same kind to the Daughter of the late
Richard Gardiner, who, before ~~his~~ her fathers death had got
some hopes of something of this kind, and she now
certainly needs it more than ever. These are the
only affairs about which I wish to trouble you; and
enough you will say, of all conscience

The Earl of Icome thinks himself very much
obliged to you for your letter which I transmitted
him the moment I received it. I have every
reason, that good information (for it is good in=
=formation only) can give, to expect much good
of this young Gentleman. I ever am, with the
highest regard Dr Sir
        Your most obliged
        and most affectionate humble
        Servant
        Adam Smith

Custom house
Edinburgh
25 March 1789

Letter from Adam Smith to Henry Dundas (concluded).

...che, for an equal quantity of work, would have taken more time & consequently ~~would~~ have required more wages, which must have been charged upon the goods. The philosopher, on the other hand, is of use to the porter; not only by being sometimes an occasional customer, like any other man who is not a porter, but in many other respects. If the speculations of the philosopher have been turned towards the improvement of the mechanic arts, the benefit of them may evidently descend to the meanest of the people. Whoever burns coals has them at a better bargain by means of the inventer of the fire-engine. Whoever eats bread receives a much greater advantage of the same kind from the inventers & improvers of wind & water mills. Even the speculations of those who neither invent nor improve any thing are not altogether useless. They serve, at least, to keep alive & deliver down to posterity the inventions & improvements which have been made before them. They explain the grounds & reasons upon which those discoveries were founded & do not suffer the quantity of useful science to diminish.

As it is the power of exchanging which gives occasion to the division of labour, so the extent of this division will always be in proportion to the extent of that power. Every species of industry will be carried on in a more or less perfect manner, that is will be more or less accurately subdivided, into the different branches according to which it is capable of being split, in proportion to...

Very early economic work of Adam Smith, one of the Edinburgh Lectures.
I. Division of Labour. The Philosopher and the Porter (Glasgow University Library: reduced from folio).

(379)

to the extent of the market, which is evidently the same thing with the power of exchanging. When the market is very small it is altogether impossible that there can be that separation of one employment from another which naturally takes place when it is more extensive. In a country village, for example, it is altogether impossible that there should be such a trade as that of a porter. All the burdens which, in such a situation, there can be any occasion to carry from one house to another would not give full employment to a man for a week in the year. Such a business can scarce be perfectly separated from all others in a pretty large market town. For the same reason, in all the small villages which are at a great distance from any market town, each family must bake their own bread & brew their own beer, to their own great expence & inconveniency, by the interruption which is thereby given to their respective employments, & by being obliged, on this account, to maintain a greater number of servants than would otherwise be necessary. In mountainous & desart countries, such as the greater part of the Highlands of Scotland, we cannot expect to find, in the same manner, even a smith, or a carpenter, within less than twenty or thirty miles of another smith or another carpenter. The scattered families who live at ten or fifteen miles distance from the nearest of any of those three artisans, must learn to perform themselves a great number of little pieces of work for which, in more populous countries, they would readily have recourse to one or other of them, whom they now send for, can afford to, only upon very extraordinary occasions.

Very early economic work of Adam Smith, one of the Edinburgh Lectures.
I. Division of Labour (continued). Extent of the Market (Glasgow University Library).

(380)

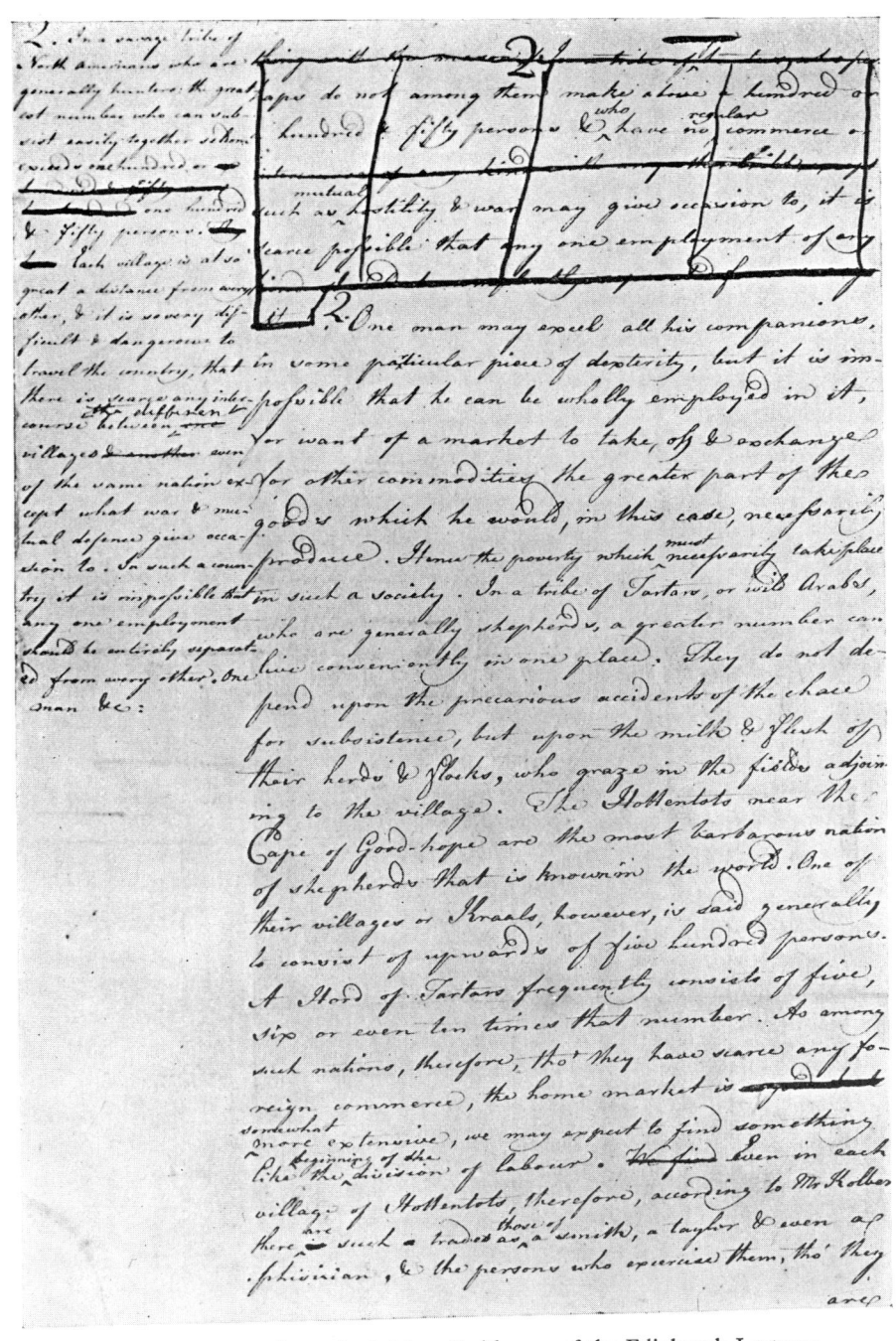

Very early economic work of Adam Smith, one of the Edinburgh Lectures.
I. Division of Labour (continued). Illustrations of Extent of the Market (Glasgow University Library).

are not entirely, are principally supported by those respective employments, by which too they are greatly distinguished from the rest of their fellow citizens. Among the Tartars & Arabs we find the faint commencements of a still greater variety of employments. The Hottentots, therefore, may be regarded as a richer nation than the north Americans, & the Tartars & Arabs as richer than the Hottentots. The compleat division of labour, however, is posterior to the invention even of agriculture. By means of agriculture the same quantity of ground not only produces corn but is made capable of supporting a much greater number of cattle than before. A much greater number of people, therefore, may easily subsist in the same place. The home market in consequence, becomes much more extensive. The smith, the mason, the carpenter, the weaver & the taylor soon find it for their interest not to trouble themselves with cultivating the ground, but to exchange with the farmer the produces of their several employments for the corn & cattle which they have occasion for. The farmer, too, very soon comes to find it equally for his interest not to interrupt his own business with making cloaths for his family, with building or repairing his own house, with mending or making the different instruments of his trade, or the different parts of his household furniture, but to call in the assistance of other workmen whom he rewards with corn or with cattle.

Very early economic work of Adam Smith, one of the Edinburgh Lectures.
I. Division of Labour (concluded). Further illustrations of the Extent of the Market (Glasgow University Library).

or ten men, & sailing from the port of Leith, will frequently in three days, generally in six days, carry two hundred tuns of goods to the same market. Eight or ten men, therefore, by the help of water carriage, can transport, in a much shorter time, a greater quantity of goods from Edinburgh to London than sixty six narrow wheeled waggons drawn by three hundred & ninety six horses & attended by a hundred & thirty two men; or than forty broad wheeled waggons drawn by three hundred & twenty horses & attended by eighty men. Upon two hundred tuns of goods, therefore, which are carried by the cheapest land carriage from Edinburgh to London there must be charged the maintenance of eighty men for three weeks, both the maintenance &, what, tho' less than the maintenance, is however of very great value, the tear & wear of three hundred & twenty horses as well as of forty waggons. Whereas upon two hundred tuns of goods carried between the same markets by water carriages, there is to be charged only the maintenance of eight or ten men for about a fortnight & the tear & wear of a ship of two hundred tuns burden. If there was no other communication, therefore, between Edinburgh & London but by land, & there as no goods could be transported from the one place to the other except such whose price was very high in proportion to their weight, could not be the hundredth part of the commerce which is at present carried on between them, nor, in consequence, the hundredth part of the encouragement which they at present mutually give to each other's industry. There could be very little commerce of any kind between the distant parts of the world. How few goods are so precious as to bear the expence of land carriage between London & Canton in China.

Very early economic work of Adam Smith, one of the Edinburgh Lectures.
II. Land and Water Carriage (Glasgow University Library: reduced from folio).

(383)

which at present carry on so extensive a commerce with one another & give consequently so much mutual encouragement to each others industry? The first improvements, therefore, in arts & industry are always made in those places where the conveniency of water carriage affords the most extensive market to the produce of every sort of labour. In our north American colonies the plantations have constantly followed either the sea coast, or the banks of the navigable rivers & have scarce any where extended themselves to any considerable distance from both. What James the sixth of Scotland said of the country of Fife, of which the inland parts were at that time very ill while the sea coast was extremely well cultivated, that it was like a coarse woollen coat edged with gold lace, might still be said of the greater part of our north American colonies. The countries of the world which appear to have been first civilised are those which lye round the coast of the Mediterranean sea. That sea, by far the greatest inlet that is known in the world, having no tides nor consequently any waves except such as are caused by the wind only, was by the smoothness of its surface as well as by the multitude of its islands & the proximity of its opposite coasts extremely favourable to the infant navigation of the world, when from the want of the compass men were afraid to quit the coast & from the imperfection of the art of shipbuilding to abandon themselves to the boisterous waves of the ocean. Egypt, of all the countries upon the coast of the Mediterranean, seems to have been the first in

Very early economic work of Adam Smith, one of the Edinburgh Lectures.
II. Land and Water Carriage (continued, Glasgow University Library).

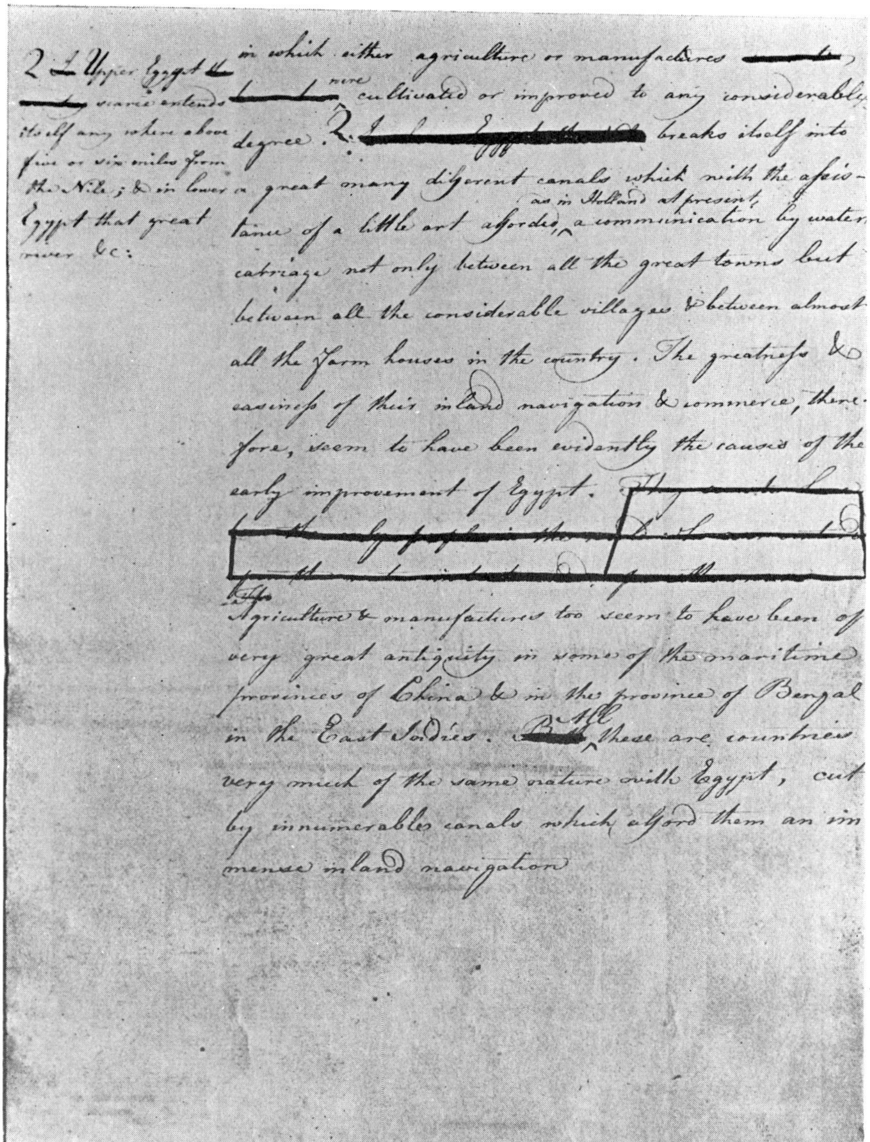

2 L Upper Egypt [redacted] scarce extends itself any where above five or six miles from the Nile; & in lower Egypt that great river &c:

in which either agriculture or manufactures [redacted] more cultivated or improved to any considerable degree. 2 [redacted] breaks itself into a great many different canals which with the assistance of a little art afforded, as in Holland at present, a communication by water carriage not only between all the great towns but between all the considerable villages & between almost all the farm houses in the country. The greatness & easiness of their inland navigation & commerce, therefore, seem to have been evidently the causes of the early improvement of Egypt. [redacted]

Agriculture & manufactures too seem to have been of very great antiquity in some of the maritime provinces of China & in the province of Bengal in the East Indies. [redacted] All these are countries very much of the same nature with Egypt, cut by innumerable canals which afford them an immense inland navigation

Very early economic work of Adam Smith, one of the Edinburgh Lectures.
II. Land and Water Carriage (concluded, Glasgow University Library).

N. 1.

Chap. 2.

Of the nature and causes of public opulence

The unassisted labour of a solitary individual, it is evident, is altogether unable to provide for him, such food, such cloaths and such lodging as not only the luxury of the great, but as the nicenesse & appetites of his meanest peasant are, in every civilized society, supposed to require. Observe in what manner a common day labourer in Britain or in Holland is accommodated with all these, and you will besensible that his luxury is much superior to that of many an Indian Prince, the absolute master of the lives and liberties of a thousand

MS. of an Early Draft of *The Wealth of Nations*—the first page "N 1", the first three letters of "opulence" and the word "to" are in Adam Smith's hand (Dalkeith House, Charter Room, Charles Townshend MSS.: part of a folio page, reduced).

MS. of an Early Draft of *The Wealth of Nations*—Sheet 3, p. iii, with marginal addition and several alterations in the text in Adam Smith's hand.

Juris Prudence

or

Notes from the Lectures on Justice, Police, Revenue, and Arms delivered in the University of Glasgow

by

Adam Smith Professor of Moral Philosophy.

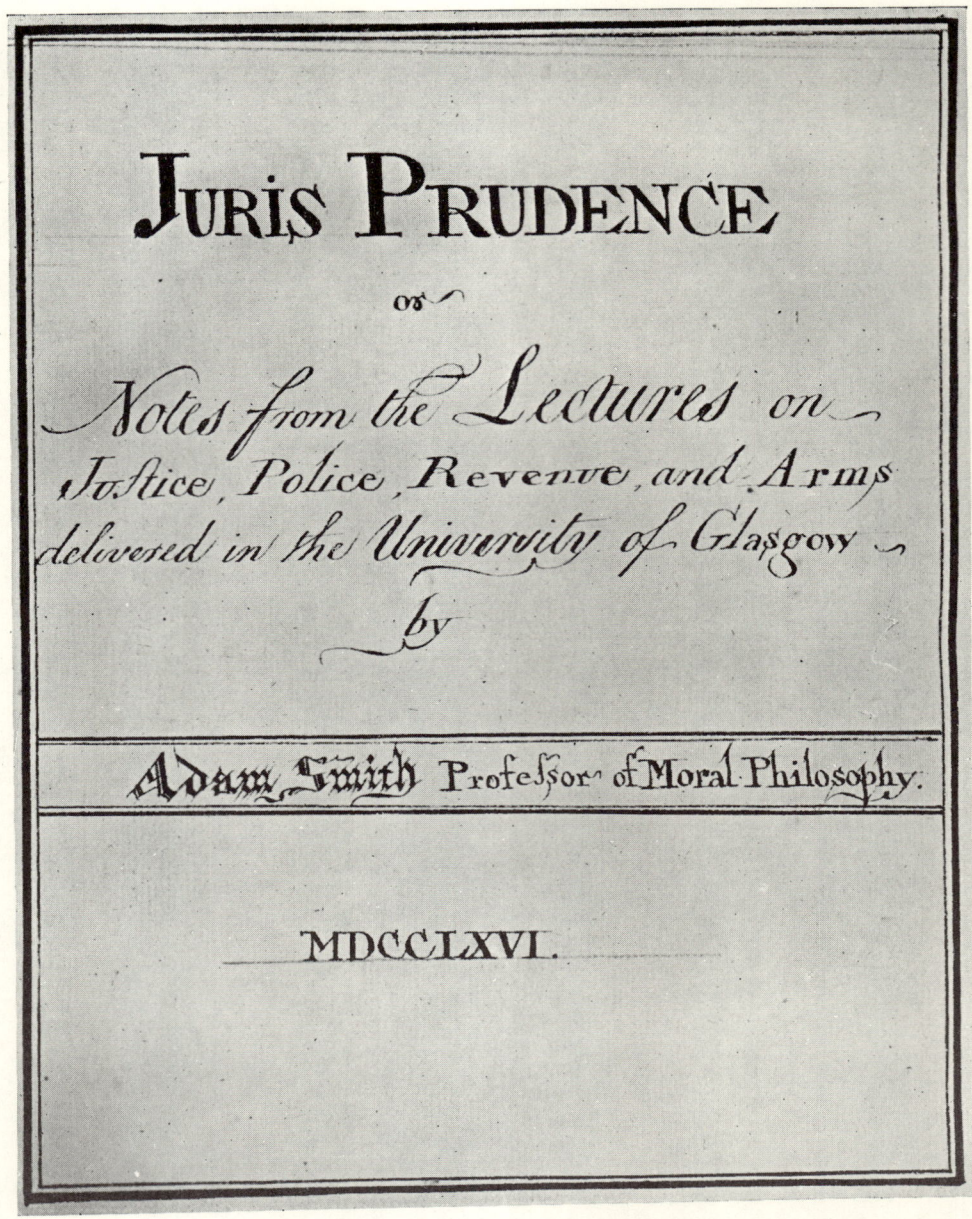

MDCCLXVI.

MS. of the Glasgow Lectures—Title-page (Glasgow University Library: reduced from quarto).

> 211
>
> For as the Establishment of Law & Government is the highest effort of human Prudence & Wisdom, the Causes cannot have a different influence from what the Effects have. Besides it is by the Wisdom & Probity of those with whom we live, that a propriety of Conduct is pointed out to us, & the proper Means of attaining it. Their Valour defends us, their Benevolence supplies us, the hungry is fed, the Naked is Cloathed by the Exertion of these divine qualities. Thus according to the above representation, all things are subservient to the supplying our three fold Necessities.
>
> In an Uncivilized Nation & where Labour is undivided, every thing is provided for, that the Natural Wants of Mankind require, Yet when the Nation is Cultivated & Labour divided, a more Liberal provision is allotted them; & it is on this Account that a common Day Labourer in Brittain has more Luxury in his Way of Living than an Indian Sovereign. The Woolen Coat he Wears requires very considerable preparations the Wool gatherer, the Dresser, the Spinster, the Dyer, the Weaver, the Taylor, & many more must all be Employed before the Labourer is Cloathed. The Tools, by which all this is Effectuated, employ a still greater Number of Artists, the Loom Maker, Miln Wright, Ropemaker, not to mention the Bricklayer, the Freesetter, the Miner, the Smelter

MS. of the Glasgow Lectures—a page of the text (Glasgow University Library).

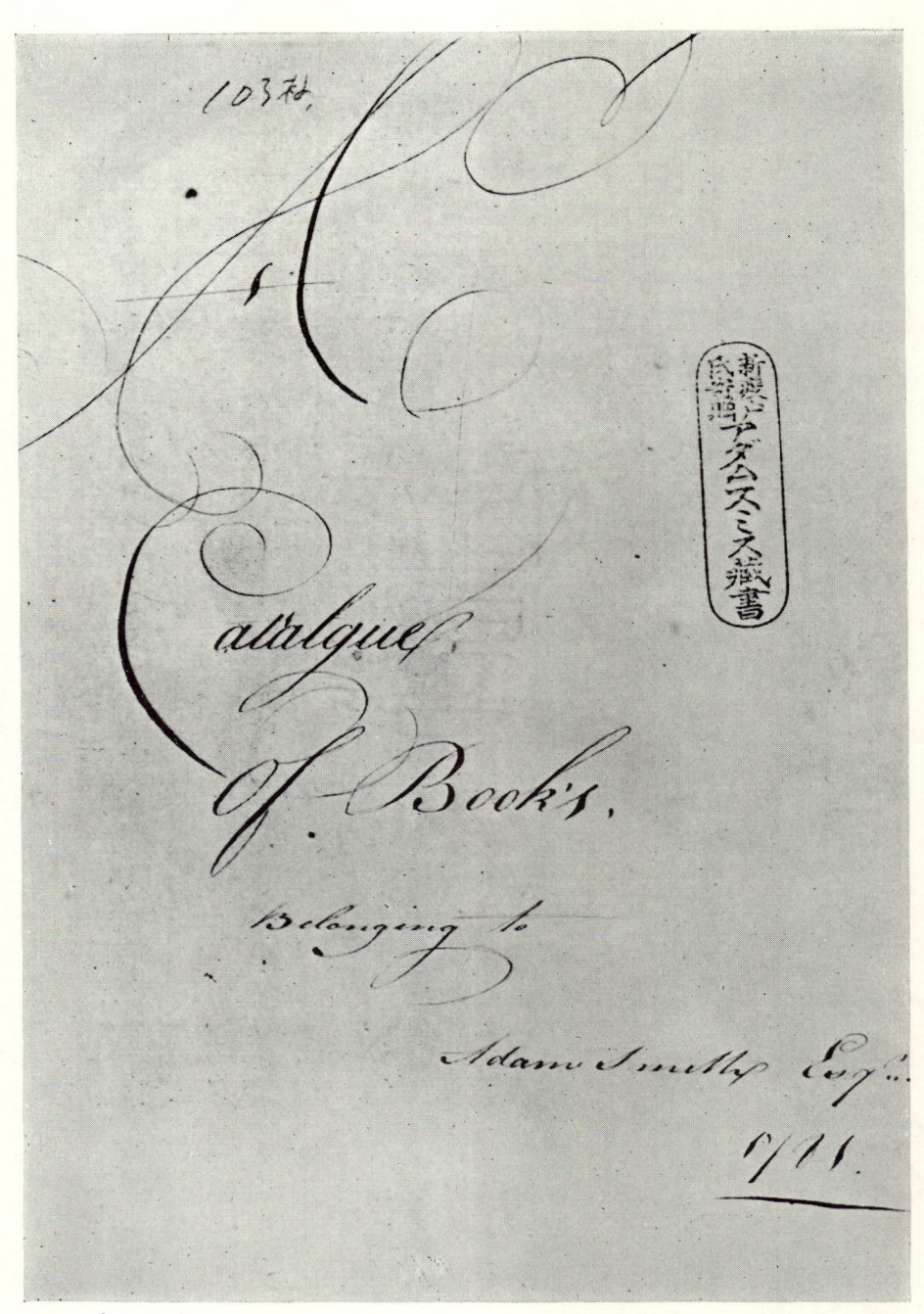

First page of Catalogue of Adam Smith's Library in 1781, at the Imperial University, Tokio (reduced from folio size).

Shelf 4th

Meditazioni sulla Economia Politica.
Elemens D'Agriculture par M. Monceau 2 Tomes
Priaries Artificielles.
Recherches sur la Valeur des Monnoies.
Essai sur la Police des Grains par Herbert.
Essai Politique sur le Commerce.
Reflexions Politiques sur les Finances, et
    Le Commerce 2 Tomes.
Examen des Reflexions Politiques sur les
    Finances et le Commerce 2 Tomes.
Essai sur la Nature du Commerce en
    General.
L'Ami des Hommes, ou Traité de la Popu-
    lation 5 Tomes.
Essais sur les Ponts et Chaussées la
    Voirie et les Corvées 2 Tomes.
L'Anti-Financier.
Le Reformateur ou Nouveau Projet.
Elemens du Commerce 2 Tomes.
Recherches et Considerations sur les Finances
    de France 6 Tomes.
Principes et Observations Oeconomiques 2 T.
Le Commerce et Le Gouvernement par
    M. de Condillac.
L'Ordre Naturel et Essentiel des Societes
    Politiques 2 Tomes
    (Lyon)

P. 41 of the Catalogue of Adam Smith's Library, 1781.

The Matriculation Roll. Types of Description of Professors. 1. 1752-55 as Magister; 2. With Degree, 1756-8; 3. From 1759 as Dominus. (Matriculation Album, Glasgow University Records.)

APPENDICES

APPENDIX I

THE SMITHS OF ROTHIEBIRSBEN, INVERAMSAY AND SEATON, ABERDEENSHIRE

The statement of Dugald Stewart that Adam Smith's father was " a native of Aberdeenshire " has been an incentive to the genealogists and antiquarians of that county towards identifying the family from which the economist descended. The search has been somewhat like that for the philosopher's stone and, through special circumstances, has hitherto been without success. The chief reason has been that there were very many of the name in the county, and there has been no clue which would connect Adam Smith, W.S.,[1] with one of these rather than with any of the others. Adam Smith himself, in causing most of his papers to be burned, seems to have started a whole chain of loss or destruction of documents which has proved an immense impediment to his biographers. There is the disappearance of the most important lecture of 1755, which, as suggested above,[2] may have been burned by Colonel Stewart, the son of Dugald Stewart. Then there may have been letters or papers in the possession of James Oswald of Dunnikier which would establish the debt of Adam Smith to him, but Colonel St. Clair Oswald informs me that, when his great grandfather, James Townsend Oswald, built the house at Dunnikier and removed from Kirkcaldy about 1770, the old papers were burned with the exception of a letter from Adam Smith, dated 19th January, 1752, N.S.[3] Brougham in his *Lives of Men of Letters* [4] refers to, and quotes extracts from, a number of letters which Adam Smith wrote from Balliol between 1740 and 1746, but, with the exception of one reproduced elsewhere,[5] these cannot now be found.[6] In 1895 Miss Mary A. Bannerman wrote a letter to *The Scotsman* in which she refers to the marriage contract of the first wife of Adam Smith, W.S., and she appears to have had the contract for his

---

[1] Since Adam Smith, the father of the economist, will be mentioned frequently, it will conduce to brevity to describe him as " Adam Smith, W.S." rather than by the offices he held, namely Clerk to the Courts Martial and Councils of War for Scotland and Comptroller of the Customs at Kirkcaldy.

[2] See above, p. 120. [3] *Memorials of James Oswald*, 1825, pp. 124-7.
[4] ii, p. 215. [5] See above, p. 366.

[6] Through the kindness of Miss Haldane I had the Brougham papers examined and no trace of these letters could be found. They originally came from the Cunninghams. It is to be feared that Brougham did not return them. Three others of this period (printed above, pp. 232-3) came from the Bannermans.

second marriage also before her.[1] The latter document cannot now be traced. Still more serious, at least as affecting the present inquiry, was the destruction by fire on 30th October, 1720, of the records of the Commissariot of Aberdeen which contained the testaments of the City and County.[2] The registers of births and marriages of many parishes during the necessary period are not now in existence. When the quest is for younger sons, it is unlikely that the sasines, or deeds relating to property, will help.

The tracing of two wills of Adam Smith, W.S.—one (revoked) dated 30th August, 1718,[3] and the other, summarised elsewhere,[4] give a considerable amount of information about his family; and in spite of the very great difficulties which have been mentioned above, this imposes the obligation of making a determined attempt to solve this age-old puzzle.

These wills mention the following relatives of Adam Smith, W.S.—his uncle, Adam Smith, who was a burgess of Aberdeen, and his son, James Smith; a brother of the testator, Alexander Smith, who had been a writer (*i.e.* a solicitor) in Edinburgh, General Collector of Taxation in Scotland[5] and was subsequently Postmaster General of Scotland.[6] He died in the winter of 1701-2. There was another brother, William, in Old Aberdeen, who was dead when the wills were drawn.[7] Two nephews are mentioned—William Walker, burgess of Aberdeen, who was related to two Provosts and who, as will be seen, was a man of importance in that city, and William Smith, who succeeded his uncle, Adam, as Secretary to the Earl of Loudoun and was, later, Steward, and afterwards Secretary to the Duke of Argyle, a Secretary to the Office of Ordinance and a Yeoman of the King's Wine Cellar.[8] There were two other Smiths mentioned,

---

[1] J. Bonar, *Library of Adam Smith*, London, 1932, p. 207.

[2] In 1927 the Marquis of Aberdeen sent to the Register House a volume of Aberdeen Testaments 1661-1747, but these do not contain any wills of Smiths which would be helpful—*Report by Keeper of Registers and Records of Scotland*, 1935, p. 18.

[3] Found amongst the papers of the late Rev. Dr. Douglas Bannerman, Inchture, Perthshire, now at Glasgow University Library.

[4] See above, pp. 129-33.

[5] Aberdeen Sasines, Gen. Register House, Edinburgh, 21st January, 1713, Adam Smith and Lily (Lilias) Drummond.

[6] See below, Appendix III.

[7] Decree of Adjudication, Crichton against Smith, 21st July, 1709, Gen. Register House, Edinburgh, Mack Office.

[8] He died at Adderbury in Oxfordshire on 23rd October, 1753. Atterbury became the seat of the Earl of Dalkeith, the father of Henry, Duke of Buccleuch, to whom Adam Smith was tutor at a later date. In 1753 the Countess of Dalkeith was in residence there. She was the eldest daughter of John, Second Duke of Argyle, and, as mentioned elsewhere, married secondly, Charles Townshend. The announcement of the death appeared in the *Glasgow Courant* of 5th November, 1753. It is certain that this notice had been drawn up by Adam Smith himself, though it is prefaced by the words " we hear from London ". No doubt (as suggested above, p. 66) William Smith had secured the influence of Archibald, the third Duke of Argyle, in favour of his cousin, Adam, when the latter was a candidate for the Philosophy Chairs at Glasgow, and he was grateful.

SMITHS OF INVERAMSAY

William, a late Regent in Marischal University, Aberdeen, and Hercules, Collector of Customs at Kirkcaldy. From other sources it is known that he had a connection, also named Adam, who was his clerk during the later years of his comptrollership of the Customs at Kirkcaldy.[1] This Adam was a tutor and curator of the author of *The Wealth of Nations* during the later part of his minority, became Collector of Customs at Kirkcaldy and Inspector of Customs for the out ports. Yet another Adam, who was Collector of Customs and Excise at Alloa, described himself as a cousin of Adam Smith of Glasgow.[2] Also in the Customs was an Alexander Smith who was born at Strachan in Kincardineshire in 1674. In 1752, though seventy-eight years of age, he was still in office at Dunbar, and was described as being infirm but capable. It is noted " he likes his cups and a wench ". There were several other Smiths in the Customs and Excise, but there is no information available to connect them with the family of Adam Smith, W.S., or that from which he derived.

The list of tutors and curators in the wills of Adam Smith, W.S., shows that he was well connected and the same conclusion is reached through his marriages.[3] This also applies to such marriages of his relatives as are known, the husbands and wives belonging to landed families, well-to-do merchants, university and professional people. The Customs and Excise at this period were both staffed from the first of these classes. Thus it is recorded that " most of the older Collectors of Customs were aristocratically connected ". [4]

It is unfortunate that no tradition as to who Adam Smith's grandfather was has survived. Mrs. Bannerman of Edinburgh attributes the loss of the information which David Douglas (Lord Reston and Adam Smith's heir) must have had to the fact that he died comparatively young and before his daughters were old enough to take an interest in this matter. The various transmissions of property in Aberdeen described as the foreland at the Castlegate (which are detailed in the next Appendix) might have been fruitful if Adam Smith, the burgess of Aberdeen and uncle of Adam Smith, W.S., had inherited it; since, in that case the sasines or registers of title would have shown the members of his family who had preceded him as proprietors. It turns out, however, that the foreland was acquired by purchase—the date being 8th July, 1675.[5]

Since Adam Smith, W.S., was much the youngest of his family and, by the

---

[1] Gen. Register House, Edinburgh—Customs, Salary accounts.

[2] See above, p. 134.   [3] See above, pp. 15, 18.

[4] MS. Report by Henry Alton on Customs and Excise Documents at the Register House, pp. 17, 18. As an instance, the bond of the Collector at Kirkcaldy who preceded Hercules Smith, John Bethune, was signed as sureties by William Morrison of Prestongrange, James Bethune of Blebo and David Bethune of Balfour. The sureties of Hercules Smith were of equal importance.

[5] Sasina Adami Smyth et Elspetae Moir ejus sponsae tenementi Magistri Jacobi Robertsone— Aberdeen Sasines at Town House, Aberdeen. It may be noted that, from the point of view of legal styles, some forms occur in this document which have not been noted elsewhere.

time he came to make his wills, his brothers were dead and also since the Christian name of his father was not known for certain, the further stages of the inquiry could be pursued only indirectly—that is by following up the parentage (where it can be ascertained) [1] of some of his relatives. On enquiry those that proved most promising were William Smith, the Regent, and Hercules Smith, Collector of Customs at Kirkcaldy. The former was Governor or tutor of Lord Charles Hay in 1693 who succeeded his father as twelfth Earl of Errol in 1704. In December 1693 William Smith was appointed a regent at Marischal University. In the Aberdeen Poll Book he is recorded as having neither wife, child nor servant.[2] These conditions did not last long for he married in 1709 Elizabeth, daughter of Robert Paterson, an advocate and commissary in Aberdeen and proprietor of Kirktown. In 1702 the Town Council made a grant for the printing of his address *Oratio in qua, Inclytæ Academiæ Marischallanæ Aberdonensis, nobilissimus Parens, illustres Mæcenates et eximii Benefactores ad annum MDCXCVI, commemorantur*—a document which remains one of the sources for parts of the history of the University.[3] He had relatives at the rival University—King's—and in 1711 he was invited to succeed his cousin, William Black, there, but he declined.[4] Like most of his family who remained in Aberdeenshire, he was a Jacobite, and during the Rebellion of 1715 he joined with almost all the staff of Marischal in presenting an address at Fetteresso to " James VIII " and he took part in electing Jacobite magistrates. As a result he was deprived of his office by the Commission of 1717. He seems to have remained in Aberdeen, and was still alive in 1729 when he appeared to establish his claim to the property and effects of his second son, Alexander, who was drowned when serving on the *Tiger*, man-of-war.[5]

[1] In the very intricate enquiries which will be detailed below I have received immense help from the late Mr. A. T. McRobert, Editor of *Scottish Notes and Queries*. It was not only that he had a very extensive knowledge of the inter-connection of Aberdeen families, which, as new facts came to light, saved me very many journeys to Aberdeen. When most of these failed, one after another, he was never discouraged. Indeed, his enthusiasm was such that when we found that the foreland, mentioned above, had come into the possession of the Corporation of Aberdeen, he was not deterred by the fact that the eighteenth-century title deeds at the Town House amounted to a mass of nine cubic feet. He worked his way through them till he found the original deed of sale by Adam Smith which, incidentally, has an excellent signature. His death occurred when all printed matter had been examined and the first results of material, still in manuscript, had come in. It was an instance of his prescience that he was then convinced that Adam Smith, W.S., had descended from some branch of the Inveramsay family (which was confirmed by data found later). He was also of opinion that the grandfather of Adam Smith, W.S., was William Smith in Dilspro (now Grandholm), who had a son, Adam, apprenticed to James Robertson for five years from Whitsunday 1656 (*Scottish Notes and Queries*, xi, p. 119). This Adam, according to that view, would be the burgess in Aberdeen, the proprietor of the foreland mentioned, see below, p. 408.

[2] ii, p. 623.

[3] *Records of Marischal College and University* (New Spalding Club), *passim*; J. P. Edmond, *Aberdeen Printers*, Part III, p. 151.

[4] *Officers of Graduates of University and King's College, Aberdeen* (New Spalding Club), p. 61.

[5] Propinquity Book—Town House, Aberdeen—3/2/1729.

The evidence relating to the parentage of William Smith, Regent, depends on what are known as " birth brieves ". These came into existence when for any reason someone wished to establish his ancestry, as for instance a Scotsman who was living abroad ; or one who was in his own country in relation to the transmission of property. The method was to carry the descent back for three or four generations and each line of descent at each stage was deposed to by the nearest relative who had knowledge of the circumstances. Thus on the parental line it was customary for an appearance to be made by a contemporary of the claimant and, if possible, by another of a previous generation. William Smith was a deponent on several occasions. On two of these, in 1697 and 1705, he appeared with John Smith of Inveramsay.[1] The latter, who was born about 1652, would represent the elder generation and William Smith (born 1669) the younger one. This link is strengthened by the case of Hercules Smith, who, like the Regent, was a son of a member of the Inveramsay family. The evidence for this, though slightly involved, is quite convincing. The father of the John Smith of Inveramsay just mentioned was also named John, and he had a brother, James, who in 1673 was described as being in Logie, by 1674 his description was " in Meikle, Fetlerlether " and in 1680 he was again in Logie.[2] It may be explained that " in " represents a tenant or tacksman—James Smith was probably the latter—while " of " indicates a proprietor of the lands or a laird. " Hercules " is a somewhat uncommon name. It is suggestive that it occurs in the families of Scott of Logie and of Brotherton. It appears probable that James Smith in Logie married one of the five daughters of Hercules Scott of Brotherton, the third son of James Scott of Logie.[3] Following the matter further, Hercules Smith became a merchant in Montrose (which is the nearest town to Logie) and in 1704 he succeeded Robert Ronald, a late Provost of the burgh, as collector of customs for that place, and his bond was signed by James Scott of Logie and Hercules Scott of Brotherton. This James Scott was the eldest son of the James of Logie previously mentioned, and elder brother of Hercules Scott of Brotherton. Thus the two Smiths who were of the generation of Adam Smith, W.S., are definitely traced to the Inveramsay family. Being his cousins,[4]

---

[1] Propinquity Book, Town House, Aberdeen, printed in the *New Spalding Club Miscellany*, v, pp. 362, 367.

[2] Aberdeen Sasines, 27th June, 1673, 8th February and 19th July, 1680, General Register House, Edinburgh ; A. N. W. Stirling, *Fyvie Castle*, 1928, p. 252.

[3] Keith S. M. Scott, *Scott 1118-1923*, pp. 194-97.

[4] It might be urged that Hercules Smith was included as tutor and curator, not as a cousin of the testator but as a friend—both being in the same service in the same place. There are several good reasons for the statement in the text. Adam and Hercules Smith were appointed to Kirkcaldy at the same time, indicating previous consultations between them and the same influence on their behalf. Also Adam Smith, W.S., had included several relatives of his second wife as curators and one of his first wife. Owing to deaths in his own family he evidently found that his surviving near relatives were comparatively few.

he must also have belonged to it. It may be possible to indicate the point at which he derived from it.

Meanwhile the more urgent question is who were the Smiths of Inveramsay ? It will be seen there is much of interest and even of romance in this side of Adam Smith's ancestry. First of all, as to the situation of the place and other lands, owned or occupied by members of this family, most of them were in the parish of Chapel of Garioch about 20 miles N.E. of the city of Aberdeen. The nearest town is Inverurie. Inveramsay is of interest since this estate contained the battlefield of Harlaw where Donald, Lord of the Isles, was defeated in 1411. The mansion house, which has now been destroyed, was about a quarter of a mile from the site of the battle. It was called Poolwalls and is believed to have incorporated parts of an old peel or keep. Further north a branch of the family was connected for a long time, as tacksmen, with the lands and mill of Tiftie or Tifty, a picturesquely situated glen not far from Fyvie Castle.

As far back as 1633 there is record of a John Smith at Inveramsay.[1] While he was a member of the family which, later, became lairds of this and adjoining lands, they did not descend directly from him. Early in the seventeenth century William Smyth at the Mill of Rothiebirsben, was in the position of being able to lend money on landed security; and, in 1625, his son, James Smith at the same place acknowledged the receipt of 1000 merks, part of a sum which had been lent on the lands of Little Warthill.[2] This James had a numerous family. One of these was John Smith, who had been a Baillie and Treasurer of Aberdeen. In 1655 George Seaton of Seaton sold the town and lands of Ardoyne and Buchanstoun with mill, pertinents and common pasture in the forest of Bennochie with houses and pendicles to John Innes, who re-sold to John Smith, son of James at Rothiebersben, which sale was confirmed in the Registry of the Great Seal.[3] In 1664 he received another charter of the lands of Rashivit, including the Peelwalls and wardhouse and the town and lands of Harlaw and lands in Legatsden.[4] These were followed by a charter from Patrick, Bishop of Aberdeen, dated 11th June, 1666, of the " toun and lands of Gordonsmilne ".[5] His successors also owned the estate of Drimmies.[6] He was a man of standing amongst his fellow lairds, as is shown by his being chosen by the heritors as one of their representatives to confer with General Monk when the Restoration was being planned. These properties made him one of lesser barons of Aberdeenshire. This term had reference to the constitution of the Scottish Parliament, which was composed of three estates. The first comprised the greater barons, who

---

[1] F. M. S., *Heraldry of Smith in Scotland*, London, 1873, p. 26.
[2] D. Littlejohn, *Records of the Sheriff Court of Aberdeenshire*, ii, p. 282.
[3] *Calendar*, 1660-1668, p. 450.   [4] *Ibid.*, p. 691.
[5] Aberdeenshire Sasines of this date, Register House, Edinburgh.
[6] J. Davidson, *Inverurie*, p. 487.

were noblemen owning very large estates. The second consisted of lairds who had a smaller, but a considerable amount of land and who met in each shire and selected commissioners to represent them at Edinburgh. The third estate consisted of the members elected by the burghs. As a matter of fact, the previous possessors of Ardoyne, Buchanstoun and Rothiebirsben had each been classed as a lesser baron.[1] John Smith was dead by 1669, and he was succeeded by his son of the same name. From this time the interest shifts to the other sons of James Smith of Rothiebirsben who had many transactions in property up to the time of the Revolution. The Inveramsay family were active Jacobites, and their fortunes declined. On the other hand, as so often happened, the cadets or their sons supported the Revolution and they increased both in influence and fortune.

There were five of these younger sons of James Smith, namely, William Smith who in 1674 was at the Mill of Tifty or Tiftie, Robert Smith of Smithieburn, James Smith in Meikle, Nathaniel Smith a burgess of Aberdeen and Patrick Smith at the Mill of Ardoyne. James Smith has already been mentioned, and there are some matters of interest relating to several of his brothers.

William Smith was evidently what was known as a tacksman—that is, a person who held land on lease, in this case under the Earl of Dunfermline of Fyvie. Usually there were small tenants on this land and a part of it was farmed by the tacksman. Of the under-holdings an important one was the Mill of Tiftie.[2] His rent under the lease in 1672 was " of mail three score and six bollis, of money one pound, of wadderis three, of lambis three, of capounis three dozen, of hennis three dozen, of pattis one lait, one miln swyne and one stone brew tallow ".[3] The total value may seem small, but three or fours years of this rent would equal, if not exceed, the 400 bolls of meal for which Macleod of Assynt betrayed the great Marquis of Montrose.[4]

When it is said a man is possessed of great determination of character, it often means that he is very far from being a pleasant person. William Smith with his wife and the Chamberlain (or Estate Agent) of Fyvie, and also his wife, became involved in the prevalent obsession of the period concerning witchcraft. They were summoned before the Presbytery on a number of occasions in 1650-1 on a charge of employing a " charmer " to cure cattle. The Chamberlain, one thinks somewhat meanly, transferred the blame to his wife ; and, though they were influential persons, the wife was compelled in the end to sit on the stool of repentance in the parish kirk. Smith and his wife strenuously denied everything

---

[1] D. Littlejohn, *Records of Sheriff Court, Aberdeenshire*, i, pp. 189, 292, 368.

[2] For the function and position of the tacksman see I. F. Grant, *Old Highland Farm*, 1769-1782, pp. 136, 142-9.

[3] *New Statistical Account*, xii, p. 325.

[4] Alex. Smith, *New History of Aberdeenshire*, i, p. 336.

and outfaced the Presbytery.[1] He next came to grips with his superior. In 1676, being offered a new lease, he tore the document violently from the notary and refused to return it.[2] In spite of this the tack was renewed to himself and his daughter, Elizabeth, who subsequently married Alexander Dunbar. Though Fyvie was forfeited in 1694, the Countess of Dunfermline renewed the lease to Dunbar in 1705.[3] It must have been a minor interest to the tacksman, since by 1700 he had succeeded to the estate of Monkshill. It is interesting to observe that William Smith, the Regent of Marischal University, was entitled to an annual rent from these lands.[4]

It was as a father that William Smith has obtained celebrity—though, unfortunately, in no favourable sense. Besides several sons, he had three daughters who were famed for their beauty. One of these was the Elizabeth already mentioned. Another was Agnes, commonly known as Nannie or Annie. In the service of the Earl of Dunfermline there was a trumpeter, Andrew Lamb or Lamie. The two fell deeply in love with each other. The parents had hopes of the "Lord of Fyvie", who was probably Alexander, third Earl of Dunfermline, as a son-in-law, and Agnes was subjected to such ill-treatment by her family that she died in 1673. This ill-starred romance has been commemorated in one of the most popular of the northern ballads—Mill o' Tifty's Annie.[5] In passing it may be remarked that Agnes or Annie Smith was not the only lady connected with this family to be celebrated in verse. Adam Smith's cousin, Alexander Walker, married Elizabeth Burnett, daughter of James Burnett of Monboddo; and, when she died, Beattie contributed an elegy to the *Scots Magazine* in 1759. Burns celebrated the beauty of her niece.

In spite of the unpopularity of William Smith after the tragic death of his daughter, he seems to have prospered. On 28th July, 1675, he had sasine of the lands of Nether Buchanstoun from his brother, James, and on 8th February, 1677, he added part of Over Buchanstoun also from his brother, while on 9th June, 1677, he purchased the town and lands of Mott of Auchterless.[6] In 1696 he and his wife Helen Black were still living.[7]

Robert Smith, the third brother, obtained a charter dated 27th November, 1670, from the Principal, Masters and Members of King's College, Aberdeen, in his own favour and that of John Smith, a Regent, and William Smith, his sons.[8] He died in 1690. His third daughter, Isobel, married Principal Row

[1] A. M. W. Stirling, *Fyvie Castle*, 1928, pp. 211-15.
[2] *Ibid.*, p. 251.   [3] *Ibid.*, p. 277.
[4] *The Jacobite Cess for the County of Aberdeen*, 1715, Third Spalding Club, p. 194.
[5] The whole circumstances have been fully detailed, together with a reprint of the ballad and collations of the more important variants by Mrs. A. M. W. Stirling in *Fyvie Castle*, 1928, pp. 238-52.
[6] Aberdeenshire Sasines under above dates at General Register House, Edinburgh.
[7] *Pollable Persons in the Shire of Aberdeen*, 1696 (Spalding Club), ii, p. 297.
[8] Sasine, 25th January, 1671—General Register House, Edinburgh.

SMITHS OF INVERAMSAY

in 1684.[1] Nathaniel, the burgess of Aberdeen, was dead in 1694, when his son, also Nathaniel, was proved his heir to house property in the city.[2] The fifth son, Patrick, who was at the Mill of Ardoyne in 1674, was deceased by 1697.[3]

The coat of arms used by this family—it was not matriculated at the Lyon Office—included a crest which was prophetic: Or, on a saltire azure between four crescents gules, a martlet of the second. Crest, a dexter hand issuing from the clouds, holding a pen. Motto, *Floret qui vigilat*.[4]

In view of what is still to come the foregoing data and some additional details may be summarised as follows:

SMITHS OF ROTHIEBIRSBEN AND INVERAMSAY

I. William Smyth of Mill at Rothiebirsben married Isobel Layng *fl.* 1611, and had at least one son.

II. James Smith also at Rothiebirsben, who married Margaret, d. of Alexander Lamb of Rothie. He had at least five sons:
1. John (see below).
2. William of Mill of Tiftie and Buchanstoun, m. Helen Black.
    (1) Alexander.
    (2) William.
    (i) Agnes.
    (ii) Elizabeth, and another daughter.
3. Robert of Smiddieburn (1622-1690), m. Margaret Lindsay.
    (1) John,
    (2) William,
    and at least three daughters, one of whom, Isobel, b. 1662, married Principal Row of King's University, Aberdeen.
4. James of Logie and Buchanstoun, m. a daughter of Hercules Scott of Logie. They had a son, Hercules Scott, Collector of Customs at Kirkcaldy, d. by 1738.
5. Nathaniel, burgess of Aberdeen, m. in 1664 Marjory Allardes or Allardyce, and they had a son:
    Nathaniel, and other children.
6. Patrick at Ardoyne m. Margaret d. of Robert Glas of Auchmenzie, d. before 1697.

Margaret m. Ninian Black in Bourtie. They had a son:
   William Black (1655-1714), Regent and Sub-Principal of King's University and Proprietor of Haddo, in which he was succeeded by his son, Patrick.

---

[1] *Scottish Notes and Queries*, vii, p. 152.
[2] Aberdeen Sasines, 10th September, 1694.
[3] *Spalding Club, Miscellany*, v, p. 562.
[4] F. M. S., *Heraldry of Smith in Scotland*, p. 25.

III. John Smith of Inveramsay, Baillie, Dean of Guild and Treasurer of Aberdeen, who died c. 1668, leaving (besides daughters) one son :
IV. John Smith of Inveramsay, b. c. 1652, d. 1750, who had :
    Patrick (see below).
    Robert, M.D. (1693-1783).
V. Patrick Smith of Inveramsay, Advocate and Procurator Fiscal in Aberdeen 1707-1716, m. Elizabeth d. of Alexander Kerr of Menie, who died in 1743 leaving,

1. David of Inveramsay, a lieutenant in the Jacobite Army in 1745 and very active, excepted from the Act of Indemnity of 1747 but through the return of a verdict of " ignoramus " at Edinburgh in October 1748 he escaped all penalties.
2. Alexander of Menie, an estate which he inherited through his mother. He was also involved in the Rebellion.
3. Andrew, also in the Rebellion. He had been taken prisoner by 2nd December, 1745.
   i. Clementina m. Hugh Gordon, Watchmaker, Aberdeen, who purchased the foreland at Castlegate from Professor Adam Smith. She and his sisters were co-heiresses of the estate of Drimmies.
   ii. Janet.
   iii. Marjory.
   iv. Rachel.
   v. Helen m. Charles Hacket, an active Jacobite. He showed great zeal in collecting the cess. After Culloden he was long a fugitive. On his marriage he settled at Poolwalls as a liferenter and became known as an " agricultural improver ".[1]

The imperfect data make it most difficult to proceed further in assigning Adam Smith, W.S., his place in the Inveramsay family. The question of the date of his birth is of prime importance. Considering the nature of the duties of a private secretary to a Scottish Minister of the period, it follows that he was young when he was selected for this office in or about 1705. Therefore it may be taken that he was born between 1675 and 1680. Next was he a first or a second cousin of Hercules and William Smith, the Regent ? As to the former there are the following data. He cannot have been a son of John of Inveramsay (III), who had died long before he was born and whose successor, John (IV), was an only son.[2] John (IV) in turn was married too late. William Smith and his

---

[1] The details of Jacobite activities are condensed from A. and H. Tayler, *Jacobites of Aberdeenshire and Banffshire in the Forty-five*, 1928, pp. 153, 287, 397.

[2] Sasine John Smith of Inveramsay, of foreland Nether Church, Aberdeen, 6th August, 1683—General Register House, Edinburgh.

wife Helen Black were already married in 1650, and both were living in 1696. According to the date of birth of Agnes Smith and the age of Helen Black, it is most improbable that they had a child in the years when Adam Smith, W.S., could have been born. But he might have been their grandchild. He could have been the son of either Robert Smith of Smiddieburn or of Patrick in Ardoyne, though in each case the date of birth would have been rather late. Waiving that objection, William Smith, the Regent, b. 1669 (and still alive in 1729), might have been the son of William or Robert, and Adam of Robert or Patrick. James of Logie is excluded as the father of Hercules, and Nathaniel (who appears to have lived and died in Aberdeen) by the statement of Dugald Stewart.

One consideration which to some extent militates against Adam Smith, W.S., having been a first cousin of Hercules and William, the Regent, is that his Christian name does not occur in any of the known descendants of the Inveramsay line. At the same time it appears fairly frequently amongst others of the name. As early as 1535 there was an Adam Smith in Dundee.[1] In the seventeenth century there follow in Aberdeenshire Adam Smith in Calsie Croft, Scottistoun, in 1607,[2] this or another Adam Smith in Scotstoun married Agnes Watson in 1631, Adam Smith who was admitted a burgess *ex gratia*, as a servitor of John Earl of Sutherland,[3] in 1623, Adam Smith in the Hill of Beltie in 1625, Adam Smith in Pervinnes in 1630, Adam Smith in Ardgrain in 1633, Adam Smith admitted burgess of Aberdeen in 1652, Adam Smith indentured as an apprentice in 1656, who became a burgess in 1664, and Adam Smith in Achath in 1689,[4] Adam Smith, Postmaster in Aberdeen in 1700.[5] In addition there is the known fact that Adam Smith, W.S., had an uncle, a burgess of Aberdeen, who was one of the later burgesses just noted. As it happens there was a John Smith, living in Seaton, which is situated where the Don makes a loop about five miles north of the city of Aberdeen. Very little is known about him except that his family complies exactly with the known conditions of that of Adam Smith, W.S. He was either a tacksman or farmer, and, as in the case of the Rothiebirsben and Inveramsay Smiths, the marriages found are with the daughters of landed people.[6] It follows that, instead of Adam Smith, W.S.,

[1] Sir R. Douglas, *Baronage*, 1798, p. 543.   [2] D. Littlejohn, *Records of Sheriff Court*, ii, 107.

[3] *Miscellany New Spalding Club*, i, p. 136. Many of Adam Smith's relatives were burgesses, usually *ex gratia*, at a later date—William Smith, the Regent (1698), Hercules Smith, Collector (1708), William Smith, Secretary to Duke of Argyle (1741), Adam Smith, Inspector of Customs (1742), William Smith, son of the Collector of Customs, Alloa (1763).

[4] D. Littlejohn, *Aberdeenshire Sheriff Court Book*, ii, pp. 284, 336 ; *Miscellany of the New Spalding Club*, i, p. 136, ii, 402, 421, 463 ; *Scottish Notes and Queries*, ix, p. 119.

[5] Rickart MS. under 7th September, 1700—Library, King's College, Aberdeen.

[6] Adam Smith, the burgess of Aberdeen, married Elspeth Moir, a daughter of John Moir of Bairnes. He, like several other members of the family, had friends at King's University—the baptism of his son Patrick being witnessed by Patrick Sandilands, a Regent and sub-Principal, and by Dr. Patrick Sibbald, Professor of Divinity.

having been a son of James Smith of Rothiebirsben, he may have been a grand-nephew, while Adam, the merchant in Aberdeen, was a nephew.

These Smiths seem to have been extremely limited in the choice of Christian names, and therefore the correspondence of two groups does not go far towards indicating identity. The case is considerably strengthened when both agree in a rather uncommon age distribution. To recall what is known concerning the family of Adam Smith, W.S. He had an uncle Adam, burgess in Aberdeen. The eldest of his brothers and sisters was a woman who married a Walker of Aberdeen. This is evident from the fact that by the time of Adam Smith's birth the Walkers were a whole generation in advance—his cousin, William Walker, having had a son, Alexander, born about the same time as Adam, the future economist. Further, Adam, W.S. (the father) must have been fifteen to twenty years younger than his brother, Alexander. About 1700 this Adam had come of age, whereas Alexander had then made a career. He had been General Collector of Taxation for Scotland and was then Postmaster General. Thus the known members of the family are the mother of William Walker, Alexander, P.M.G., William, a smith in Aberdeen, and Adam, W.S. John Smith in Seaton had a family of twelve of which several died in infancy, as is shown by the repetition of the same name, thus there were no less than three Johns. Omitting these, we have Isobel b. 1652, Jean b. 1658, Alexander b. 1662, William b. 1665,[1] James b. 1668, Barbara b. 1671, John b. 1674, and Adam b. May 6, 1679, at whose baptism the witnesses were Adam Smith the uncle, Adam Maltman, Adam Marke, Adam Morison. Very little can be ascertained about the Smiths in Seaton. There are sasines concerning a George Smith in Seaton, dated 1663 to 1667, who may have been a relative, possibly a brother of John. There are strong grounds for thinking that a James Smith, a well-known merchant in Aberdeen, was connected with the family of Adam Smith, W.S., since this James acted as attorney for Alexander Smith, the P.M.G., in taking sasine of the foreland at Castlegate. In that case his father, also James, might well be the James who was born in 1668. There is, however, another line of relationship. The second wife of Adam Smith, burgess, was Elspeth Moir, one of the co-heiresses of John Moir of Bairnes. Her sister, Bessie, married James Smith and Isobel married Thomas Jaffray of Dilspro.[2] This James may well have been both a cousin and a brother-in-law of Adam, the burgess, but there is no evidence for the former relationship. The agreement of the Christian names, order and age distribution of the family of John Smith in Seaton with that to which Adam Smith, W.S., belonged strongly indicates

---

[1] These particulars are taken from the Register of the Parish of Old Machar. John Smith may be credited with the child of someone else by error. On 15th August, 1665, he had a son, William, baptised, and on 29th October of the same year, a daughter, Janet.

[2] *Aberdeenshire Valuation Roll*, 1667 (Third Spalding Club), pp. 106-7.

that both were the same. So far as the investigation has proceeded, it would be necessary to check it by finding that the registers of the parish of Chapel of Garioch (in which most of the Inveramsay properties were situated) failed to yield such a list of names and age distribution. It is unfortunate this check cannot be applied, for these registers do not exist at the period required—those of baptisms beginning in 1763 and of marriages and deaths in 1783. Then, just when the manuscript of this Appendix was on the eve of being sent to the printer a further discovery of Bannerman Papers provided a complete documentary proof of the descent which has been established above. There is a receipt by William Smith, a writer, and the nephew of Adam Smith, W.S., previously mentioned, who acted as his clerk, in the following terms, " Edin^b. 14 Janry 1711. Received by Mr. William Smith wryter from Mr. James Craig three twenty shiling notes which I am to send north to John Smith in Seaton upon the account of Mr. Adam Smith, as witness my hand day and date above.—William Smith ". On 20th January following, Adam Smith wrote to John Craig, the writer, from London, " You likewise advise me that you have sent three pound in bank notes to my father for which you have taken my nevow's receipt which shall be good to you ".[1] John Smith died on 4th April, 1712, and old Seaton (*i.e.* James Gordon of Seaton) and other local notables were at his funeral.[2] Including the descent of John Smith in Seaton, we have the following table :

I. William Smyth in Rothiebirsben, who had sons.

II. James Smith (see above, p. 403) and William Smith in Dilspro. The latter was the father of :
   1. John Smith (see below).
   2. Adam Smith, burgess in Aberdeen m. (1) in 1664 Marjory Robertson : James (b. 1665), Christian (1667), John (1668), Alexander (1672), William (1672). m. (2) in 1674 Elspeth Moir, by whom he had a son, Patrick (b. 1675).

III. John Smith in Seaton, who had the following family :
   Isobel, b. 1652.
   Jean, b. 1658. } One of these was the mother of William Walker.
   Alexander, b. 1662, writer in Edinburgh, General Collector of Taxation in Scotland, Postmaster General of Scotland, m. in 1696 Margaret d. of Patrick Crichton, d.s.p. 1701-2.
   William, b. 1665, probably father of William who succeeded his uncle Adam, W.S., as Secretary to Hugh, Earl of Loudoun, and who held several other appointments (p. 396).

[1] Bannerman Papers, Univ. Libry. Glasg., under above dates.
[2] *Ibid.*, William Smith, Old Aberdeen, to William Smith, writer, 8th April, 1712.

James, b. 1668.
Barbara, b. 1671.
John, b. 1674.
Adam (see below).
John Smith, died 4th April, 1712.

IV. Adam Smith, b. May 6, 1679, W.S. 1707, Secretary to Hugh, Earl of Loudoun, Clerk of the Courts Martial and Councils of War in Scotland 1707, Comptroller of Customs at Kirkcaldy 1714.

    m. (1) Lilias Drummond, e.d. of Sir George Drummond[1] of Milnab, Provost of Edinburgh, 1684, M.P., and had a son: Hugh, b. 1709, d. in 1750.

    m. (2) in 1720, Margaret, d. of Robert Douglas, M.P., of Strathenry (see below, p. 414), and had a son,

V. Adam, who was baptised 5th June, 1723, died 17th July, 1790, author of *The Wealth of Nations*.

Adam Smith, W.S., died 25th January, 1723.

APPENDIX II

PROPRIETORS OF PROPERTIES AT THE CASTLEGATE, ABERDEEN

Towards the end of the seventeenth century the land near the West Gate of the Castle (the modern Castlegate, opposite the Town House) was owned by four families which were connected. On the north the inland and back land had been owned by James Smith, a burgess of Aberdeen who was succeeded by his only son, William Smith, on 7th March, 1688, and on 14th March, 1713, Patrick Smith, younger, of Inveramsay, had sasine of this or other land on the north side.[2] The proprietor of the foreland on the south was Gilbert Walker of Orchardstone who on 27th January, 1686, disponed this property to William More, a Clerk of the Lords of Council and Session. The foreland on the east side belonged to William Walker, Clothier, a burgess of Aberdeen, who had sasine on 6th July, 1682.[3] The Smiths were connected by marriage with the Mores or Moirs and the Walkers.[4] The remaining foreland—that on the west side, on which there had once been a timber shop, was purchased on 8th July, 1675, from Jacob Robertson by Adam Smith (the uncle of Adam Smith, W.S.) and his wife Elspeth Moir for £1000

---

[1] Fountainhall notes that Sir G. Drummond was the first Provost of Edinburgh who, during his term of office, was compelled to take refuge from his creditors in the Liberties of Holyroodhouse —the Edinburgh Alsatia—*Hist. Notices of Scottish Affairs*, p. 144. In the first half of the next century there was a more famous George Drummond, who was six times provost—*Book of Old Edinburgh Club*, iv, pp. 11-33; Sir T. B. Whitson, *Lord Provosts of Edinburgh*, p. 52.

[2] Sasines at the General Register House, Edinburgh.

[3] Sasine, at the General Register House, Edinburgh.   [4] See above, p. 130.

SCOTTISH POSTMASTERS GENERAL, 1688–1701

Scots.[1] Adam Smith, burgess, was succeeded by his eldest son James Smith. The latter had been some time in possession, and his sasine was recorded on 7th June, 1697, on which date he sold to Alexander Smith, writer in Edinburgh —the elder brother of Adam Smith, W.S.[2] Alexander Smith executed a marriage contract, dated 14th February, 1696, by which his wife, Margaret Creightoune, was to receive an income charged on this and other property. He died during the winter 1701-2, and was succeeded as heir by his brother, William Smith of Aberdeen. The latter failed to pay the income reserved to Margaret Smith or Creightoune, and by 21st July, 1709, the arrears were proved to amount to £1500 Scots.[3] William Smith renounced his heirship and Adam Smith, W.S., undertook to pay this sum and received sasine on 21st January, 1713, on behalf of himself and his wife Lilias Drummond in liferent and their issue, whom failing the nearest heirs.[4] Under this instrument and the will of Adam Smith his eldest son, Hugh, succeeded. In 1750, on the death of Hugh, his half brother, Adam, became the proprietor. He did not hold the property long, for on 14th May, 1757, he sold it for £115 sterling, which was less than his father had paid for it.[5] In view of the present value of the property—the Athenæum Hotel (which stands on a part of the site) was sold recently for about £34,000—one might be disposed to wonder whether Adam Smith was careful to dispossess himself of a future unearned increment or whether he was a poor man of business. The reason was quite different, being a transaction within the family. The purchaser was Hugh Gordon who had married a daughter of Patrick Smith of Inveramsay and who was, later, one of the co-heiresses of the estate of Drimmies. Hugh Gordon[6] and his wife, Clementina, had an only daughter, Jean, who married John Craig of Mugiemoss, Sheriff Clerk Depute of Aberdeenshire, and their son, Thomas, sold the Castlegate foreland to the New Street Trustees of Aberdeen Burgh, through whom it came into the possession of the Corporation.

APPENDIX III

SCOTTISH POSTS AT THE END OF THE SEVENTEENTH CENTURY IN RELATION TO ALEXANDER SMITH, POSTMASTER GENERAL FOR SCOTLAND

The development of a postal system in Scotland was slow. Though the city of Aberdeen had established a service for the delivery of letters within a convenient radius as far back as the end of the sixteenth century, elsewhere posts

---

[1] Sasine at the Town House, Aberdeen, also the will of Adam Smith, W.S., above, pp. 129-33.
[2] Sasines, General Register House, Edinburgh.
[3] Decreet of Adjudication—Crichton ag^t Smith—Mack Office, General Register House.
[4] Sasine, General Register House, Edinburgh.   [5] Sasine, Aberdeen Town House.
[6] In 1788 Hugh Gordon was one of the 178 freehold voters of Aberdeenshire—*Political State of Scotland in 1788, a Confidential Report*, ed. by Sir C. E. Adam, Edin., 1887, p. 2.

S.A.S.

were few, and such as existed were irregular. The disturbed state of the country and, particularly, the bad condition of the roads, made an efficient service difficult, if not impossible. As late as 1678 a scheme for a stage-coach between Edinburgh and Glasgow, which was to make the journey of 88 miles for the double distance in six days, proved a failure.[1] During the Civil War and after the Restoration an improved post was required for purposes of the conveyance of official intelligence. In 1660 Robert Muir was appointed Sole Keeper of the Letter Office in Edinburgh. A few years afterwards Patrick Graham of Inchbreck was made Postmaster General of Scotland at a salary of £500 Scots yearly ; by 1674 the salary had been increased to £1000 Scots. This service suffered seriously the time of the Revolution, when the posts were frequently stopped for political ends.

When the new Government had become established steps were taken to establish control of the posts and to improve them. By an Act of the Scots Parliament in 1695 the Postmaster General was to receive a salary of £300 sterling a year and the whole profit of the office. The first incumbent under this system surrendered his patent, finding it " unprofitable and irksome ".[2] By 1699 Alexander Smith was Postmaster General, receiving a salary of £1200 Scots per annum. He was unfortunate in assuming office at the time of the local crisis caused by the difficulties of the Darien Company. His accounts show that his chief returns came from the conveyance of the official correspondence between Edinburgh and Berwick. He claimed that receipts were so much reduced that it was necessary he should receive a grant of £300 sterling a year " for so much as the postage is lessened by the decay of trade, occasioned by a supervenient law discharging most part of the forraign trade from which postage did arise ".[3] The appointment was usually for two years, renewable, but Alexander Smith died before the end of his term. In the inventory of his goods the space for his death is blank, but it is clear that it occurred after Martinmas and probably before the end of the year 1701. Like several Postmasters General before and after him, the impression was produced that the expenses of his office had consumed his private fortune.[4] But this was followed by an amended statement which showed £10 sterling owing to the Estate by the Principal, Regents, Masters and other members of the University of Glasgow for the supply and delivery of newspapers.[5] It is a curious sidelight on the times that about fifty years later the University paid the post-boy five shillings sterling a year in order that he should blow his horn as he rode past the University—not " to arouse the dead ", but, presumably, to indicate the arrival of the mail and to collect letters.

[1] W. Lewins, *Her Majesty's Mails*, 1865, p. 79.
[2] T. B. Lang, *Hist. Summary of the Post Office in Scotland*, 1856, pp. 3-10.
[3] General Register House, Edinburgh—Box of Post Office Accounts, 1689-1707.
[4] Testament Dative and Inventory, 17th November, 1704, General Register House, Edinburgh.
[5] Testament Dative *ad omissa*, 25th April, 1705, General Register House.

APPENDIX IV

THE STRATHENRY-FORRESTER-DOUGLAS FAMILY OF STRATHENRY, FIFE

In the part of Scotland between the Firth of Tay and the Firth of Forth there stand the Ochil Hills, like a rampart of Titans; and before them, facing south-east, as a lesser outwork, the Lomonds. On the lower slope is Falkland with its Palace and, about seven miles south-west, Loch Leven. Between them, but a little advanced to the south-east, is Strathenry. This place was settled early in the history of Scotland. A stone coffin and copper spearheads have been found there. The name " Gallant Knowe " is supposed to commemorate a battle which has otherwise been forgotten.[1] It is believed that somewhere near was the seat of a Pictish kingdom which endured till the end of the ninth century. Strathenry is, in its origin, Strath-an-righ, the King's strath [2]—thus anticipating the Kingsbarns, Kingskettle, Kinghorn of a later dynasty.

At a very early period the place was owned by a family of note, the Strathenrys of Strathenry. In 1496 the male line failed and the heiress married a son of Forrester, laird of Gairden in Perthshire, one of the important landed families of the period.[3] It was probably this Thomas Forrester who was Sheriff Depute for Fife in 1516.[4] A descendant, with the same initials, built the present castle or tower which bears the Forrester arms with the letters T. F. over other arms, now weather-worn, apparently Lumsden, with the initials I. L. The castle is a good late sixteenth-century building, measuring, according to the survey of the Ancient Monuments Commission, 39 ft. by 26 ft. externally.[5] The eastern gable is surmounted by a bartizan. It has to be remembered, when looking at the views of it at p. 24, that the windows, as now existing, have been enlarged to replace the narrower originals.

In a little over a century and a half a male heir again failed, it being recorded that " Young Strendry (surnamed Foster) depairted out of this life at Strendry; he died of a purpie feaver. He was interred att Leslie, Sp. 30 1655 att night ".[6] Again the property devolved on an heiress, Helen Forrester, who, as will be

---

[1] *Old Statistical Account*, vi, p. 52.
[2] James Wilkie, *History of Fife*, 1924, p. 14.
[3] Sir R. Sibbald, *History of Fife*, 1803, p. 372.
[4] *Sheriff Court Book of Fife*, S.H.S., p. 40.
[5] *Royal Commission on Ancient and Historical Monuments of Scotland, Eleventh Report*, 1933, p. 187.
[6] *Diary of John Newton*, 1649-1671 (Maitland Club), p. 87.

seen below, was twice married. Her second husband, Robert Douglas of the Kirkness branch of the Loch Leven family of Douglas, descended from William, fourth Earl of Morton. Helen Forrester died without issue, and Robert Douglas married in 1688 Susan Balfour, the eighth daughter of John, Lord Burleigh.[1] Margaret Douglas, the mother of Adam Smith, was a child of this latter marriage.

It will be seen that Margaret Douglas (and through her, her son Adam Smith), continued the Strathenry-Forrester line, not through Helen Forrester but by the issue of an earlier marriage of Margaret Forrester with Sir George Douglas of Kirkness early in the seventeenth century[2]—his great-grandson being Robert Douglas, mentioned above, who became laird of Strathenry by marriage. These facts lend point to one of those transient and often tantalising glimpses which are sometimes caught of Adam Smith. Colonel Robert Douglas, who was proprietor of Strathenry in 1764, evidently wished to know of the Forresters whose arms were over his front door; indeed it seems from the reply that he was uncertain whether he had descended from them or not. No doubt it was due to Adam Smith's intervention, just before he left for France, that some one,[3] interested in genealogy and heraldry, replied from the Custom House, Edinburgh, on 19th January, 1764. As to the genealogy, the following account will show several errors into which he has fallen: as to his heraldry, one rather gathered from the present Lord Lyon's smile, that it is not beyond reproach.

"The son of Earl Morton who married the heiress of Strathenry had no issue, then he married one of the Burleigh family and his son Sir John Douglas remained in possession. This first family of Forrester carry the armorial bearings a chevron vert betwixt three hunting horns or bugles, sable, garnished gules—no crest nor motto (Crawford Old MSS.). The present family of Douglas is not matriculated. I am told they should carry Forrester quartered with Douglas to show the antiquity of the family which is very ancient."

There were in fact two Douglas-Forrester marriages. The first that of Sir G. Douglas to Margaret Forrester (who was not the heiress) had issue. In the second Douglas-Forrester marriage these conditions were exactly reversed. It appears, however, that Sir G. Douglas lived for a time at Strathenry until he succeeded to Kirkness. It seems that it is his monogram which is on the north side of the stair at Strathenry. It is curious, that, as in the case of the Forresters, the new name demanded a new house, and Robert Douglas built one, known as Strathenry House, about a quarter of a mile from the castle.

---

[1] Fife Sasines, XV, 427, General Register House, Edinburgh.

[2] See below, p. 413.

[3] MS. Note in possession of Mrs. Bannerman. The signature is not legible.

DOUGLAS OF STRATHENRY[1]

XII. Sir William Douglas of Loch Leven (*Scots Peerage*, ed. Sir J. B. Paul, vi, pp. 343-71), born 1539-40, served heir to his father 1555, the custodian of Mary Queen of Scots during her imprisonment at Loch Leven Castle, succeeded to the Earldom of Morton as fifth Earl under the entail of James, the third Earl, who was Regent of Scotland from 1572 to 1578.[2] Sir William Douglas had obtained the estate of Kirkness on the northern side of Loch Leven in 1544, and he established his

XIII. fourth son, Sir George Douglas, in it, who married Margaret Forrester, daughter of Thomas Forrester of Strathenry. He was dead by 1641, having had issue by her:

1. Archibald Douglas of Kirkness (see below).
2. Robert.
3. William.

Anna who married George Gordoune of Achannachie.

XIV. Archibald Douglas of Kirkness married in 1625 Elizabeth Broun (who, after his death, married William Keith of Annacroich).

XV. Their son, Sir William Douglas of Kirkness (who had sasine in 1639), married Dame Isobel Hay (who, after his death, married Patrick Oliphant of Newtoune. She was alive in 1687).

Sir William Douglas died in 1650 leaving the following issue of his marriage:

1. William Douglas of Kirkness served heir in 1666, had sasine in 1667, married in 1662 Elizabeth, daughter of Robert Kirkcaldie of Grange. They had a son, Robert Douglas of Kirkness, who was served heir in 1683. In 1687 he married Jean, daughter of John, third Lord Balfour of Burleigh.[3]

---

[1] Fife Sasines—1666 Dec. 3, 1667 Ap. 18, 1667 Ap. 25, 1676 Ap. 4, 1686 Nov. 5; Register of Deeds—Durie—5.736, Mack—18,891, Dal.—11.120, Dal.—37.352, Mack—26.549, Dal.—42.49, Dur.—35.274, Dal.—41.484; General Register of Sasines—1639 Jan. 12, 1639 Feb. 14, 1639 Mar. 18, 1641 June 14, 1643 Aug. 24, 1644 May 31, 1656 Ap. 30, 1664 Feb. 29, 1670 Ap. 9, 1672 Nov. 21, 1685 Sept. 9, 1717 Sept. 3; Parish of Leslie, Baptismal Registers—no entries relating to the Strathenry family 1673 till 1688 and thereafter as noted below; Parish of Portenoak Baptismal Register, 1701-5; Kinross Sasines 1689 May 2, 1692 Mar. 16; Retours and Services of Heirs—1666 May 8, 1683 Jan. 23, 1719 Dec. 29; St. Andrews Testaments—1652 July 23 (Sir W. Douglas of Kirkness); following above dates a MS. pedigree of Douglas of Strathenry compiled by General Bannerman and Miss Mary L. A. Bannerman (in possession of Mrs. Bannerman). The Roman figures indicate the successions as given by R. Douglas, *Peerage of Scotland*, Edin., 1764, under Douglas, Earl of Morton.

[2] G. Crawford, *Lives of Officers of Crown and State in Scotland*, i, 1726, pp. 99-116.

[3] It will be seen an uncle, Robert Douglas (son of Sir William Douglas of Kirkness), and a nephew, Robert Douglas of Kirkness (son of William Douglas of Kirkness), married sisters—the nephew in 1687 and the uncle a year later.

2. Robert (see below).
3. George.
   Elizabeth, married in 1666 John Haliday.

XVI. Robert Douglas, M.P., who became of Strathenry by his marriage in 1676 with Helen Forrester of Strathenry (sasine 1676, 1686), the widow of Sir Alexander Martine who was dead by 1672. There was no issue of this marriage, and Robert Douglas married in 1688, secondly, Susan, daughter of John Balfour, Lord Burleigh.[1] He represented Fifeshire in the Scottish Parliament from 1703 till his death 25th April, 1706,[2] having had the following children :
   Isobel, b. 1689.
   John, b. 1690 (see below).
   Charles, b. 1692.
   William, b. 1693.
   Margaret, baptised 17th September, 1694, married 1720 Adam Smith, W.S. (marriage contract dated 17th November).
   Robert, b. 1695.
   Jean, m. 1718 David Skene of Pitlour.

XVII. John Douglas of Strathenry, married Cecilia Ross. They had issue :
   Colonel Robert Douglas, b. 1716 (see below).
   Susannah, b. 1717, m. 1734 Patrick Ross of Innernethie.
   Janet, who kept house for Mrs. Margaret Smith and her son, Adam. She died in 1788.

XVIII. Colonel Robert Douglas of Strathenry, married Cecilia, daughter of Robert Craigie, Lord President of the Court of Session, and died in 1771. They had issue :
   William Ann, b. 1753 (see below).
   Barbara, b. 1755, and buried before her mother, who died in 1774.[3]
   John Robert, b. 1757, in Engineers.
   Margaret, b. 1758, d. 1779.
   Robert, b. 1760, Captain 58th Regt., died of wounds received in action at St. Vincent, 1796.
   Charles, b. 1762, in McLeod's regiment (cf. p. 303).
   David, Lord Reston, b. 1769, married Elizabeth, d. of John Craigie of Glendoich, where he died in 1819 while on circuit. He was survived by two daughters (see Bonar, *Library of Adam Smith*, 1932, p. xvii).

[1] See p. 413 note [3].   [2] J. Foster, *Members of Parliament, Scotland*, 1882, p. 102.
[3] Baptismal Register of the Parish of Leslie and the sexton's notes of the burials in the Strathenry vault—the latter kindly copied for me by the minister, the Rev. W. H. Drummond Page. Over half a century the sextons found six different spellings for the name " Douglas ".

XIX. Colonel William Ann Douglas, married Rebecca Dalziel. He died in 1803, leaving issue :
    Cecilia, b. 1791.
    Lindsay, b. 1792.
    Robert, b. 1794, who married the Hon. Mary Sydney, d. of Lord Douglas of the Douglas Cause.
    Charles, b. 1795.
    John, b. 1796.

APPENDIX V

THE HOUSES OCCUPIED BY ADAM SMITH IN THE PROFESSORS' COURT OF THE OLD COLLEGE, GLASGOW

There would be considerable interest in tracing out the houses which Adam Smith lived in while he was a Professor so that the surroundings in which he wrote his lecture of 1755, *The Theory of Moral Sentiments*, the notes of the " Glasgow Lectures " and the draft of *The Wealth of Nations*, printed in Part III, may be to some extent visualised and one aspect of his life at this period may be realised less inadequately. At first the quest seems hopeless, for the earliest volume dealing with College Chambers begins in 1773.[1] In any case this volume deals only with rooms in the Outer and the Inner Courts and does not include the Professors' Court. The minutes of the University meetings, however, record the changes of occupation in these houses, though in a manner which makes identification difficult, still it is possible to ascertain fairly closely Adam Smith's changes of houses and the reasons for them.

    In the pre-Reformation College there was provision for residence both of regents and students. When a new College was built in the seventeenth century, funds were obtained only with difficulty, and it was not possible to do more than provide houses for the Principal and the Professor of Divinity. The former was at the right end of the main front and the latter balanced it at the left end (Plate IV). When the Professorship of Oriental Languages was founded in 1709 by Queen Anne, another house was made for this Professor which was directly behind that of the Professor of Divinity. These houses were distinguished as the " back Divinity house " and the " fore Divinity House " respectively —the house of the Professor of Divinity being that with its main door on the High Street. The other, or the back house, formed part of the outer court with windows looking into this court and also on the other side into what was then a garden.

[1] University MSS., vol. XLV.

In the eighteenth century, when the University was beginning to emerge from some of its financial difficulties through the profit derived from the tack of the Archbishopric, which has been previously mentioned (p. 72), it was proposed to provide further houses. At the same time, there was no money actually available, but it was considered that, if the funds were borrowed, it would be to the advantage of the Professors who obtained the houses to pay interest on the debt, while the surplus on the profit of the Archbishopric would gradually extinguish it. Two of the Professors, A. Dunlop (Greek) and C. Morthland (Oriental Languages) undertook to find the money and were entrusted with the building of the houses. Their credit was backed by that of the University. There was another reason for the scheme being carried out by individuals rather than the University. The latter did not own all the ground required, and it was considered that it would be possible to acquire the area needed on more moderate terms by the two Professors.

A scheme was accepted in 1722 which provided for the building of eight houses. Including the existing Divinity houses, there would be two Professors who would be left without College houses. It was agreed that each of those who occupied the eight new houses would pay £2 sterling to the two [1] Professors who were without houses, so that the value of a house at this time was fixed at £8 sterling, which appears very low, considering the accommodation, but possibly a nearer equivalent to modern conditions may be found by taking the rent as £96 Scots, in which currency the accounts of the building scheme (as well as most of the College accounts) were kept.[2]

Actual building began with the houses numbered 1 and 2 on the annexed plan (p. 420). These were constructed with a certain amplitude of conception, and there was a danger of the borrowing powers of the undertakers being exhausted. It became necessary to confine the plan to four more houses instead of six, and these were not quite so desirable as the first two. At 28th January, 1729, the balance due was £37,159 7s. 7d. Scots.[3] Thus each house cost, on an average, £516 sterling, so that the estimated annual value of £8 was about one-third of the interest at the current rate.

Still the Professors who lived in the houses were far from satisfied. It was claimed that they were burdened with a much higher payment than would have sufficed to rent houses outside.[4] Accordingly in 1739 they made the following proposal:

" That whereas several of the present Masters have for a considerable Number of Years been burdened with a much higher yearly rent for the houses

[1] That is, there were at this time twelve Professors. The scheme provided for eight houses, to which are to be added the two " Divinity Houses ".

[2] University MSS., vol. 36, pp. 62-4.   [3] University MSS., vol. 23, p. 87.

[4] This is a somewhat specious statement, since at an equal annual payment they would have been unable to procure comparable accommodation.

they possess in the new buildings than they might have got houses for in the Town sufficient for their purpose; and that they undertook this Burden partly that they might be near at hand to wait on their proper business, a thing equally the College's interest and theirs, partly that the rents to be paid by them for a time might together with the profits of the Tack of the Archbishopricke then subsisting and others appropriated for that end, serve as a sinking fund for diminishing at least, if not paying off the debt the College came under by the new buildings reckoning still that long before this time they would have been freed of that burden; those debts being considerably lessened and will be found more so a good deal, when the profits of the late Tack for the years not yet cleared and counted for are all applied for that end: And whereas it cannot but appear to every person who thinks of it a very unreasonable thing that the present Masters should be burdened with the payment of high rents of houses to put their successors in office in a much better condition than themselves, by possessing the same houses either for a very small rent, or at long run for none at all.

"It is therefor humbly proposed to the faculty to take this matter under their serious consideration, and to fall on such measures as may put the present Masters possessors of the said houses on a level with their successors in office. This piece of Justice they have the greater reason to expect now that the College have got a new Tack of the rents of the Archbishopricke, the profits of which it is hoped will do more than extinguish the remaining debts contracted by the new buildings." [1]

A Committee was appointed which produced a new scheme, the construction of which is credited to Francis Hutcheson. The residents in the new houses were freed from any contribution to the remaining debt on the buildings, but they were still liable for compensatory payments to the Professor in occupation of the back Divinity house and to the four[2] Professors who were without houses. These were at a declining rate—the first year varying between £4 9s. 6d. sterling and £3 9s. 6d. sterling. When one Professor in occupation of a new house had died, the contribution fell to between £3 18s. 6d. and £2 18s. 6d. When a second died the contribution became £3 5s. to £2 5s. On the death of a third the amounts became £2 7s. to £1 7s. Finally, when a fourth died the payments were to be £1 3s. to 10s.[3]

Matters remained in this state for some time until Craigie, not long before his death, built himself a house opposite to that occupied by the Professor of

---

[1] University MSS., vol. 36, pp. 54, 55.

[2] This is not inconsistent with what is said above concerning there being two professors without houses under the scheme of 1722. The houses, under that scheme, were reduced by two, increasing the number of professors, without houses, by a like amount.

[3] University MSS., vol. 36, pp. 58, 59.

Divinity which was generally known, first as the " new house " and later as the " house on the street ". On his death the University purchased it at £400 sterling.[1]

The position as to the Divinity houses was anomalous. Morthland was entitled to the back house. It appears that, in recognition of the work and risk he shared, he was permitted to occupy one of the new houses and he and Dunlop were the first tenants of the houses No. 1 and No. 2. The Professor of Divinity remained limited to the house assigned to this Chair. By this time it was showing signs of wear and even dilapidation, but, on the other hand, this Professor had the advantage that he, alone, was entitled to a house when he entered on his office. In 1751 Leechman asked his colleagues that he might be allowed to choose a house when the time came, and the meeting eventually acceded to his request.

The position, when Adam Smith became a Professor, was that there were eight houses and twelve Professors. The situation of the four for whom there were no College houses was alleviated to some extent through one or two of their seniors not wishing to occupy the houses to which they were entitled. There was the case of Robert Simson who never married and who lived in rooms in the College tower. Or a physician in practice, who became a Professor, would find a move to his College house disadvantageous from a professional point of view. Again, Professors were frequently appointed at an early age, and they were entitled to rooms for themselves and their servants in the Outer or the Inner Court. In the Inner Court only male servants were allowed.[2]

The principle upon which houses were allocated was only gradually evolved. In 1730 it was arranged, after some difference of opinion, that the choice was to be on the basis of academic seniority. If a Professor did not desire to occupy the house he became entitled to, he was allowed to let it ; and, after some debate, it was laid down he must offer it to the senior Professor who had not yet a house. Failing any Professor who would rent the house, he could let it to a person who was not a member of the University subject to obtaining the consent of the Faculty and on condition that the tenancy should terminate upon a Professor choosing this particular house.[3] In 1751, in order to make an equitable arrangement when a Professor let his house, rents were fixed according to the comparative values of different grades of houses. The two houses next the garden, numbered 1 and 2, together with the new house on the street, were rented at £13 sterling each, the other four houses, built before 1730, numbered 3 to 6, at £11 each, the back Divinity house at £9.[4]

---

[1] University MSS., vol. 37, p. 131 ; vol. 28, pp. 107, 108.
[2] University MSS., vol. 37, p. 89.   [3] University MSS., vol. 37, p. 20.
[4] University MSS., vol. 28, p. 66. The reason only one Divinity house is mentioned is that at this time (1751) the Professor of Divinity (in the Fore house) had no choice.

This discrepancy in the estimation of houses produced an extraordinary lack of permanency. A Professor who had reached sufficient seniority would probably move three times, as Adam Smith did. Since, on a house becoming vacant, it was not uncommon for five or even six families to flit, the extra removals may be attributed to the desire of the women of the household for some variety or superiority in the internal fittings.

Adam Smith did not reach the seniority which entitled him to make choice of a house until 1756. During the first year he was at Glasgow he may have had rooms in one of the old Courts, or he may have had accommodation with some family. It was not uncommon for the widow of a Professor to take a fairly large house and do the housekeeping for several persons connected with the University. Thus Mrs. Lindesay, widow of Smith's colleague, Hercules Lindesay, had such an establishment, as appears from the papers of Lord Cardross (afterwards Earl of Buchan), who had rooms there while he was studying at Glasgow. He had as fellow boarders F. L. Tronchin (son of Theodor Tronchin of Geneva, Physician to the King of France), who came to Glasgow to study under Adam Smith and John Robison, afterwards Professor of Natural Philosophy at Edinburgh.[1] Whichever course Adam Smith adopted, it is probable that it did not extend much beyond a year. This appears in an interesting way. Houses were chosen in 1751, 1752 (twice) and 1754, yet there is no mention of Adam Smith until 1756, when he, for the first time, becomes entitled to a College house. Yet on 11th June, 1755, there appears the mysterious minute that " Dr. Dick and Mr Clow are appointed to inspect Mr. Smith's house, and to order any necessary reparations that ought to be made ".[2] The explanation must be that Adam Smith had availed himself of the arrangement detailed above and had become tenant of a colleague. This would be entirely natural owing to the deep love he had for his mother and the desire to make a home for her.[3] Further, it is possible to guess to whom he was indebted for his start as a householder. His friend, Cullen, had obtained the back Divinity house in May 1752, and, being in practice, it is unlikely he would wish to give up the house he had occupied for a number of years. Cullen's letters during the time he was in Glasgow are fairly numerous, but he either gives no address or simply " Glasgow ". Adam Smith was also an offender in this respect.[4] The fact that the phrase " Mr. Smith's house " is used suggests that in 1755 he had been in occupation for some time. The University accounts provide confirmation of this view. It will

---

[1] Buchan's Diaries, Letter Book, 1763, Murray Coll. Libry, Univ. Glasgow.

[2] University MSS., vol. 28, pp. 146.

[3] This is contrary to the tradition at Kirkcaldy that Mrs. Smith remained there till Adam Smith went to Edinburgh. Lord Buchan's record is decisive—Diaries and Letter Book, 1763, Murray Coll. Libry., Univ. Glasgow.

[4] J. Thomson, *Life of William Cullen*, i, pp. 537-606.

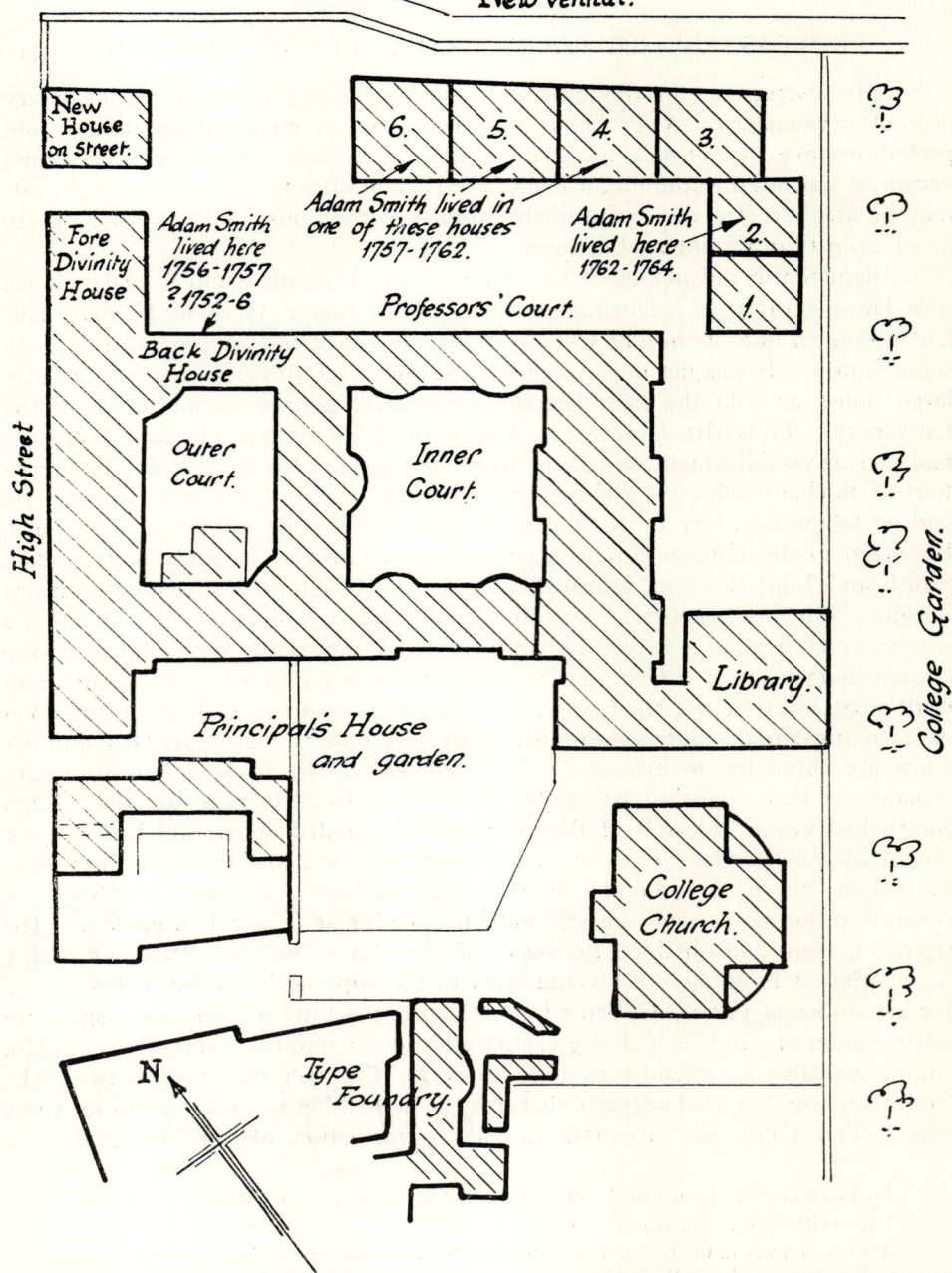

Based on McArthur's Map of Glasgow, *1778*, corrected by Map in *Report of University Commission of 1826* (Glasgow).

be remembered that, although Adam Smith was appointed in January 1751, he was not required to begin duty till October of that year. He paid chamber rents of £14 12s. 7d., which was four times as much as Moor paid and three times more than Clow. The date the amount was incurred is not quite certain. The account is dated 26th June, 1754, but with it is another relating to transactions of Craigie in 1751-2 which Adam Smith settled, so that the date the chamber rent accrued may be taken to have been the session 1751-2. On 6th May, 1752, Cullen obtained the " back Divinity house ". Thus it appears that Adam Smith may have been in College rooms for his first session. Then he may have occupied Cullen's house, as his tenant, as soon as it was made ready, succeeding to it in his own right in 1756.[1]

In 1752 Mrs. Smith was fifty-seven and her son Adam twenty-nine, and since he was fourteen they had been little together. Even if the house had defects, no doubt both mother and son found great compensations. Judging by the state of the Principal's house, which had involved Adam Smith in many meetings and much business (pp. 141-4), it was probably in a state of considerable dilapidation. It had some advantage over the fore Divinity house, which, like the other house facing on the High Street, had its windows broken, from time to time, by boys.[2] Otherwise, it was pleasantly situated with one part on the Outer Court facing south-east, while there was plenty of air and an open outlook from the other part. In that respect it was better situated than most of the other houses, since the Court was narrow and the view from the front restricted. In 1756 he succeeded by seniority to this house, or at all events to the back Divinity house.[3] Thus it is certain that the Lecture of 1755 was written in the Professors' Court and probable that the particular house Adam Smith occupied at that time was the one which has been described. It was here also that the greater part of *The Theory of Moral Sentiments* was written.

In 1757 Adam Smith succeeded Dick in one of the block of four houses, which were subsequently numbered 3 to 6. In the various minutes concerning succession to houses, these are not distinguished from each other, since when they were ready for occupation there is nothing to show definitely which of the first entrants chose a particular house. Until 1764 the usual type of record that B made choice of the house formerly in the possession of A. It is certain that Smith never lived in No. 3. This appears in the following way. In 1764, after the resignation of Adam Smith, no less than five Professors moved. It is noted that Anderson chose to remain in the house he had occupied previously, which was No. 3. He had gone there in 1762, the same year that Adam Smith made his final choice, but there had been two changes in that year—the one in January

---

[1] University MSS., Muniment Room, Drawer G.4, " Vouchers Chambers' Accounts," 26th June, 1754, and " Craigie's Account," 1752.

University MSS., vol. 30, p. 16. [3] University MSS., vol. 28, p. 193.

and the other in March. At the first of these Anderson followed Smith, at the second he changed to No. 3,[1] so it follows that Smith must have taken in 1757 one of the houses numbered 4 to 6. There he not only finished *The Theory of Moral Sentiments*, but, in addition, he was turning to the more detailed study of economic questions, being at this time interested in the historical development of Europe, both politically and economically, as is shown by a list of books he ordered for the Library.[2] The next year when Leechman, on his appointment as Principal, had gone to the Principal's residence, Adam Smith succeeded him in No. 2, where he remained until he resigned his Chair. It was during this period that the Glasgow Lectures, in the form in which they now exist, were delivered and the draft of *The Wealth of Nations* in Part III written.

Owing to the various complications in the identification of the occupants of the houses, the list of the changes made in 1764 may be added. Moor chose the new house on the street, Clow the second house counting from the gate into the garden (this being that vacated by Adam Smith), Anderson remained in the third house, Wilson chose the fourth, Hamilton the fifth and Black the sixth, and Millar the back house in the Divinity Court.[3]

These changes may be followed most easily on the plan on p. 420. It differs in a number of details from that made by David Murray, which represented the circumstances about a century later. There were then thirteen houses, against nine in Adam Smith's time. The position of one of these nine had been changed. In the mid-nineteenth century the back Divinity house had been merged in the teaching or administrative rooms of the College, and a new house had been made which was entered from the Lion and Unicorn staircase in the Outer Court. Reid, Adam Smith's successor, stated that he found a walk of about eight minutes from the house he had rented in the Drygate very burdensome in the winter. In 1768 he had found many rooms unoccupied and he stated that a number of these, in the position mentioned, could be made suitable for a family.[4] This was effected, and the dwelling which resulted remained a Professor's house till the demolition of the College.

APPENDIX VI

ADAM SMITH'S DIFFICULTIES IN THE INCORPORATION OF NEW MATERIAL IN HIS MANUSCRIPTS

The closely integrated summary of the argument in Chapters 3, 4 and 5 of the Draft of *The Wealth of Nations* (pp. 345-56) shows the logical development of Adam

---

[1] University MSS., vol. 30, pp. 118, 123. Anderson may not have been the most desirable of neighbours, as he kept a horse and hens in his back-yard, which was very small—Murray, *Old College*, p. 379.

[2] See above, p. 171.   [3] University MSS., vol. 31, p. 15.

[4] University MSS., vol. 31, p. 359.

Smith's thought: the specimens of his early work which have been recovered afford an example of how he incorporated additional information or new ideas as these were discovered. He was, in fact, the victim of his method of composition. If an argument is well knit together and the consecutive steps are stated in their mutual relations, an insertion can only be made in the existing text by going back and modifying the manuscript for a considerable distance prior to the proposed insertion. Alternatively, if the addition is of considerable size, it may be treated in a new chapter or an appendix to an existing chapter. The latter method, where it was applicable, was adopted by Adam Smith, which accounts for the " Digressions " which occur in *The Wealth of Nations*. Had he been prepared to re-write parts of his manuscript, the impression of a certain jerkiness in the treatment would have been avoided. The same reluctance to make changes in his manuscript for the purpose of incorporating smoothly the smaller additions explains why some of these appeared, even to himself, to be misplaced—notably in the case of the passage on the Atonement which has been described elsewhere.[1] To some extent the employment of an amanuensis may have contributed to this result.

The biographer of Adam Smith's colleague and friend, John Millar, has a passage which draws attention to the difficulty which many at this period found in incorporating new matter. It is to be premised that Millar lectured extemporarily from notes, and he is comparing this method, in respect to additions, with that of anyone who had a complete course of lectures, written in full. Thus, while what is said relates to University prelections, it has, also, an obvious reference to the problem with which Adam Smith found himself faced. " It is also a most important advantage attending extemporary lectures that the Professor can, with ease to himself, follow the general progress of science or insert the occasional results of his own private investigations. The trouble of making alterations on written lectures is apt, on the contrary, to deter from future enquiry and even to prevent the correction of acknowledged error. He who has with much labour transcribed a system of lectures sufficient for his regular course can neither omit or insert a topic without extending or condensing some other department of his subject ; he can change none of his principles without altering his inferences and expunging many allusions that may occur in other parts of his course ; he can neither adopt new opinions, nor admit new facts, without inserting new conclusions and new modifications of his other doctrines. Such a revision of written opinions will usually be found too great a task for human exertion."[2] That task was not too great for Adam Smith, but, for the reasons explained, he often failed to fuse the new matter with the old.

---

[1] See above, p. 58.
[2] John Craig, ed. *Millar's Distinction of Ranks*, Edin., 1806, p. xvii.

APPENDIX VII

ADAM SMITH AND HIS RUSSIAN ADMIRERS OF THE EIGHTEENTH CENTURY

By Michael P. Professor Alekseev, Leningrad

The once widely prevalent view advanced by Alexey Vesselovsky that the study of Adam Smith's teachings " had been delayed in Russia by a period of over 40 years "[1] may be regarded at present as having been finally renounced. Though the first Russian translation of the *Inquiry into the Nature and Causes of the Wealth of Nations*, made by N. Politkovsky,[2] was not published until 1802-1806 (in 4 parts) in Petersburg, a fairly large circle of Russian readers had been well acquainted with the ideas contained in this famous book for a long time past; moreover, the first signs of Russian " Smithianism " had even preceded by several years the publication of the English original of this work.

In the sixties of the eighteenth century the custom of sending young men abroad to get their university education became widely prevalent in Russia. At the time cases of Russians being sent to England or Scotland were not infrequent. For instance, in 1761 two Russian students, Simon Jefimovich Desnitsky and Ivan Andreevich Tretiakov, were sent to Glasgow University by order of the Curator of the Moscow University, Prince I. I. Shuvalov. Both of them, having taken their degree in philosophy and law at the Glasgow University, returned to Moscow and played a prominent part in the history of Russian legislative science.[3] Indeed, precisely these two people should be regarded as the first promoters of Adam Smith's teachings from the Russian University Chair. However, both these Russian students had enjoyed the benefit of Adam Smith's guidance but for a relatively short time, having arrived in Glasgow in 1761, while in January 1764 A. Smith left Glasgow on his way to France. And yet the lectures delivered by A. Smith and attended by them could not fail to leave an impress on them. The less gifted of the two students, Tretiakov, returned to Moscow, having completed his course of studies at Glasgow University and

---

[1] A. Vesselovsky, *Western Influences in Modern Russian Literature*, Moscow, 1916, pp. 174-5. It is of interest to note that the same writer in mentioning in this book the name of an original Russian philosopher of the early eighteenth century, *i.e.* Ivan Pososhkov (1670-1726), and his peculiar views on a people's welfare and economic reforms, states that the work of the latter writer, *A Book on Scantiness and Wealth*, even at that early date " foretold the theories of Adam Smith " (*ibid.*, p. 44).

[2] V. S. Sopikov, *An Essay on Russian Bibliography*, St. Petersburg, 1904, iii, N. 4511. The translator of this work received 5000 roubles from the Russian Government for its publication. See A. N. Pypin, " The Relations of Bentham with Russia," *Westnic Evropy*, February, 1869.

[3] Both matriculated under Anderson, Professor of Natural Philosophy, in 1761. Desnitsky graduated M.A. in 1765 and LL.D. (by examination) in 1767. Tretiakov obtained the same degrees in the same years; *cf.* above, p. 158 note [3].

taken his LL.D. degree on the presentation of his dissertation " Disputatio Juridica de in jus vocando ". (Glasgow, 1767). The very next year he was appointed professor at the Moscow University where he began delivering his course of lectures. However, his pedagogical career was short-lived, lasting only to 1776. In the year 1779 he died at a relatively early age.[1] His literary works were likewise small in number; the only literary inheritance he left us consists of three inaugurals delivered by him on Speech Days of the Moscow University. One of these is of particular interest to us, for it is clearly based on the lectures read by Adam Smith. The inaugural in question was delivered by Tretiakov on the Speech Day of the Moscow University held on 30th June, 1772, and bore the following title: " Discussion on the Causes of Abundance and the Slowly Progressing Enrichment of States, Both Among Ancient and Modern Peoples ".[2] It is of interest to note that *The Wealth of Nations* was first published four years later (1776) and yet in the above-mentioned speech Tretiakov had not merely laid down in brief the essential theses of Smith's treatise but in some cases had used the same illustrating examples as are given by Smith. Such were, for instance, the examples which served to confirm the theory of the division of labour.[3] This similarity should, of course, be attributed to the fact that Tretiakov had carefully followed the ideas advanced by Smith in the course of lecturing at Glasgow University and that his teacher had then been engaged in working out the separate parts of his future work. Indeed, Adam Smith is known to have expounded the essential theses of his economical teachings in his lectures on Jurisprudence read as early as in the fifties of the eighteenth century.[4] Unfortunately, Tretiakov has not left us any literary evidence of his sympathies with Adam Smith's ideas. In the year that *The Wealth of Nations* was first published Tretiakov resigned from his post at the Moscow University and never published anything during the last three years of his life, while all his papers have failed to reach us.

[1] For references to I. A. Tretiakov see *Biographical Dictionary of Professors and Teachers at the Imp. Moscow University*, Moscow, 1855, ii, pp. 505-507.

[2] See *Speeches Delivered at the Official Meetings of the Imperial Moscow University by the Russian Professors thereof, Containing Their Short Curricula Vitae*. Published by the Association of the Lovers of Russian Letters, Moscow, 1819.

[3] For instance, Tretiakov writes : " If a watchmaker or the manufacturer of the most trifling article, such as a needle, were to produce by himself everything necessary for the completion of these objects or the like of them, he would hardly be able to manufacture one watch a year or one needle a day—*cf*. above, p. 328."

[4] Zeyss, *Adam Smith und der Eigennutz*, 1889, S. 14-16. The student's notes on the " Lectures on Justice, Police, Revenue and Arms, delivered at the University of Glasgow by Adam Smith," published by Professor Cannan (Oxford, 1896), give us a clear idea of the extensiveness of the course which was likewise attended by the above-mentioned Russian students. Unfortunately, their own notes on these lectures are not available and are supposed to have been destroyed with their other papers in the Moscow conflagration of 1812—*cf. Economic Journal*, September 1935, pp. 427-38.

Tretiakov's friend and fellow student of the Glasgow University, S. J. Desnitsky, was a more important personality. The range of problems he was interested in was considerably wider ; he took up the study of problems connected with the origin of statecraft, the history of the development of marriage and of family relations, of property and, lastly, the problem of capital punishment from the point of view of criminal law. " All these are not the problems whose scientific study is indissolubly connected with the name of Adam Smith ", his biographer states. " In the choice of the subjects of his investigation Desnitsky was apparently entirely independent. But the lines along which he worked out these problems had been undoubtedly borrowed by him from Adam Smith ".[1] And indeed, it can be shown that Desnitsky was extremely susceptible to the new ideas which had been revealed to him by Adam Smith's lectures. Desnitsky's works constantly reveal obvious traces of the influence of his Scotch professor. However, there is no reason to believe that these were merely clever interpretations of the ideas he had heard advanced in the lecture room of Glasgow University, as was the case with his friend and companion, Tretiakov. In Desnitsky we have a mature and original thinker whose literary talent and vast knowledge made him one of the most influential professors of the Moscow University in the late eighteenth century and provided him a Chair in the Russian Academy (1783).[2]

On his return to Russia in 1767, after he had taken his degree at the University of Glasgow, Desnitsky was appointed in 1768 to the Chair of Roman Law and Russian Jurisprudence at the Moscow University, a post which he held for twenty years. In 1787 he retired, and in 1789 he died, thus preceding Adam Smith by a year.

In one of his inaugurals, delivered on a Speech Day of the Moscow University, Desnitsky developed the idea that the power of some people over others was based on (1) their superiority in bodily qualities (such as corpulency, plumpness), (2) their superiority in mental qualities (cunning, shrewdness, sagacity), (3) their superiority in riches and the abundance of all things. " But what mostly endows a man with honour, dignity and superiority ", states Desnitsky, " is his superior riches and abundance. This has been so extraordinarily well expounded by the judicious author of a new moral philosophy, Mr. Smith, that it no longer requires any description." [3] In yet another place Desnitsky mentions " Mr. Smith who has published his moral philosophy to the delight of the scientific world ". Generally speaking, Desnitsky repeatedly quotes Smith in his literary works, always mentioning him with the greatest respect. Desnitsky's paper,

---

[1] N. M. Korkunov, *The History of the Philosophy of Law*, St. Petersburg, 1898, p. 295.

[2] M. I. Sukhomlinov, *The History of the Russian Academy*, Issue V, St. Petersburg, 1880, pp. 3-8. See also *The Russian Biographical Dictionary*, St. Petersburg, 1905, pp. 331-5.

[3] He was also indebted to the lectures of John Millar, Professor of Law—cf. *Observations concerning Distinction of Ranks in Society*, 1771.

published in Moscow in 1781, under the heading "Legal Discussion on the Possession of Property under Various Conditions of Community" seems to coincide more closely than any of his other works with the outlook of Adam Smith and to be imbued with a spirit of Anglophilia so characteristic of Desnitsky. His knowledge of Smith's ideas can also be seen from the critical notes supplemented to his Russian translations of the works of Blackstone (*Commentaries on British Laws*, 3 volumes, Moscow, 1780-82) and of Thomas Bowden (*A Guidebook on Husbandry*, Moscow, 1780). Many of Desnitsky's other works also contain lyrical passages imbued with the spirit of his Anglophil tendencies. (For quotations, see M. Sukhomlinov, *op. cit.*, pp. 5-6.) Desnitsky is known to have once said that "the heroes of classical antiquity seem pale and petty if compared with the genius of the men who have been bred by England". His preface to the Russian translation of Bowden's works is truly a laudable discourse, written in blank verse in praise of Britain "which is great in her undertakings, successful in her achievements, formidable in her battles, glorious in her victories. . . ."

During the same years that the two Russian pupils of Adam Smith were propagating their teacher's ideas from the Chair of the Moscow University there were yet other people in Russia who had developed independently an interest in his teachings. Many of them were able even then to become familiar with the famous treatise in the original. In 1774 N. S. Mordvinov (1754-1845), a future admiral of the Russian Fleet and one of the most prominent personalities among the Russian high officials of the time, was sent to England with the view of completing his education in marine sciences. He spent three years in England and in the course of that time seemed to have developed a profound admiration for Britain's literature, science and government institutions. To quote his biographer: "Adam Smith's treatise *The Wealth of Nations* was published while Mordvinov was in England, impressing him for life, so that even in his later views he generally appears to have been an ardent adherent of Smith's teachings".[1] This statement seems fully confirmed by facts; beginning with the seventies of the eighteenth century Mordvinov always continued an ardent admirer of Adam Smith, as well as a tireless promoter of his ideas in Russia. His infatuation with Smith's teachings never weakened as he grew more advanced in years, and even seemed to increase. In his letter addressed to J. Bentham's brother and dating from 1806, Mordvinov calls Smith "one of the greatest geniuses" among those "who have done most towards benefiting mankind" and ranks him together with Bacon and Newton.[2] The influence of the treatise

[1] V. S. Iconnikov, *Count N. S. Mordvinov*, St. Petersburg, 1873, pp. 4-5. See also A. M. Gnjevushev, "The Political and Economic Ideas of Count N. S. Mordvinov," *The University Review*, Kiev, 1907, N 2, pp. 6-7, 13, 19, 50-52.

[2] *The Europe Herald* (Vestnik Evropy), February 1869, p. 816.

The Wealth of Nations is clearly seen in many of the pages of Mordvinov's *Discussion on the Benefits which may follow from the Institution of Private Banks in Governments* (St. Petersburg, 1811). Smith's name is also frequently quoted in the numerous notes, considerations and suggestions which Mordvinov used to hand in to the Russian Government in the course of his long-lasting and incessant activity.[1]

Another Russian traveller, Princess E. R. Dashkova (1744-1810) visited England and Scotland a few years later than Count N. S. Mordvinov. Princess Dashkova stayed in Edinburgh from 1776 to 1779, hardly ever leaving the city, for her son was studying at the University there. Later she always spoke of that period as the merriest time of her life—she frequented there among people she liked, and often entertained at her place the best teachers of Edinburgh University. In her *Mémoires*, Princess Dashkova casually mentions that " l'immortel Robertson, Blair, *Smith* et Ferguson venaient dîner et passer journée chez moi deux fois par semaine ".[2] Unfortunately, we lack any other information concerning these meetings. On the other hand, it is a well-known fact how keen an interest in Smith was felt by another family of Russian aristocrats, the Princes Vorontsov, who were famous in the late eighteenth century for their Anglophil sympathies. The eldest of the brothers, Alexander Romanovich Vorontsov (1741-1805) developed a strong attachment to everything English in spite of his having stayed in England but for a short time. Later, when living at his country seat in Russia, Alexander Vorontsov never lost his interest in Britain, keeping in close touch with English literature through the agency of his brother, Simon Vorontsov (1744-1832), who for twenty consecutive years (1785-1806) held the post of Russian Ambassador in London and supplied his brother's excellent library with the most important literary works published in England and France. Late in 1786 Simon Vorontsov enclosed among the other books he was sending to his brother the recent edition of *The Wealth of Nations*, begging him to make note of all the chapters and passages which might contain ideas contrary to his own views. The letter which Alexander Romanovich wrote in answer to his brother's request has never reached us, but it is reasonable to assume that he, too, was greatly impressed by Adam Smith's work ; at all events he is known to have sent several years later *The Wealth of Nations*—together with Condorcet's *Commentaries*—to Alexander Radistchev (1749-1802), a famous Russian publicist of the time, who was then in exile in Siberia.[3] With respect to Simon Romanovich

---

[1] See *The Archives of the Counts Mordvinov*, published in ten volumes by V. A. Bilbasov.

[2] Princesse Dashkova, *Mémoires*. Quotations have been taken from the best edition, reproducing the original manuscript (written in French)—*Archives des Princes Woronzow*, xxi (Moscow, 1881, p. 171).

[3] V. N. Alexandrenko, *Russian Diplomatic Agents in London in the XVIII Century*, Warsaw 1897, i, pp. 387-388.

Vorontsov it may be stated that his admiration of Adam Smith has been repeatedly proved. In his letters Simon Romanovich constantly mentioned Smith's " immortel ouvrage "; thus, in writing to Prince Chartoryisky, who was one of the high officials in the earlier years of Emperor Alexander the First's reign, Vorontsov said, " In the science of commerce Adam Smith has laid foundations which are as indisputable as those laid by Euclid in geometry "; [1] while in a letter to Emperor Alexander (1801) Vorontsov calls Smith " l'auteur le plus classique qui ait jamais existé sur le commerce, les manufactures, les finances des états ".[2] In the Scheme he drew up for the institution of a Diplomatic College which was to be under the auspices of the Russian Foreign Office (1802), Simon Romanovich wrote that in the seventh or the eighth year of studies " on leur ferait lire en original le traité d'Adam Smith sur la richesse des nations ".[3] Having learnt from the newspaper that a new tariff was being worked out in St. Petersburg, Vorontsov suggested that the Emperor should order those engaged in the working out of the new law " to read and re-read A. Smith's book on the wealth of nations so as to know it by heart ".[4] In one of his letters Simon Romanovich writes of " principes aussi sûrs que lumineux de l'immortel Adam Smith que le comte Roumanzew croit avoir été réfutés sans savoir et pouvoir nommer quand, par qui et comment ".[5] Lastly, from his letter to Prince A. B. Kurakin—which bears no date but apparently refers to 1798—we learn of Simon Romanovich having personally known and met Adam Smith. " This view was held in the last years of his life by the world-famous Adam Smith, whom I used to know ", says Vorontsov in some chance connection and then adds, " and the now famous Arthur Young is of the same opinion ".[6]

Such were the Russian admirers of Smith in the eighteenth century. For many reasons the teachings of the great Scotch philosopher failed to become known to larger circles at the time; most of his admirers were people who knew English, who felt an interest in England's intellectual life or had visited the country. However, before long *The Wealth of Nations* found its way to the writing desk of every government official and spread a strong influence over the wider circles of readers. The new interest in political sciences and national economy which became particularly keen within the first two decades of the nineteenth century was to a great extent due to the spreading of Adam Smith's teachings. Following the publication of the Russian translation of *The Wealth*

---

[1] V. Alexandrenko, *op. cit.*, pp. 391-92.

[2] *Archives de Pr. Woronzow*, x, p. 303. In another letter to the Emperor (dated 18th May, 1801), Vorontsov wrote: " Les gens instruits dans les matières de finances et de commerce, savaient depuis longtemps, mais Adam Smith l'a prouvé indisputablement dans son immortel ouvrage sur la richesse des nations que le commerce ne se fait qu'avec des capitaux, qu'il demande liberté et sûreté," etc. (*Arch.*, x, p. 360).

[3] *Arch.*, xv, p. 438.

[4] *Arch.*, x, p. 88.

[5] *Arch.*, x, p. 179.

[6] *Arch.*, xxx, p. 490.

of Nations the number of Russian " Smithianists " showed a rapid increase. Smith's teachings were propagated both from University Chairs and by the press.

After the death of S. Desnitsky the popularization of Smith's ideas was taken up at the Moscow University by Christian Schlözer (1774-1831), who, having completed his education in Göttingen, returned to Russia in 1796 and was first appointed professor at Dorpat and later to the newly instituted chair of political economy at the Moscow University, a post which he held for twenty-five years (1801-1826). Christian Schlözer was also the author of *The Elementary Foundations of State Economy* (1805, 2nd Ed., 1821), a book which was simultaneously published in Russian (Moscow) and in French and German (Riga), and was completely imbued with Adam Smith's ideas.[1]

At the same period (from 1789 on) the post of teacher at the cadet corps (military training school) in Petersburg was held by another Russian of German extraction, Heinrich Storch (1766-1835), who was elected as a member of the Petersburg Academy of Sciences in 1796 and soon after appointed teacher of political economy to the Grand Dukes Nicholas (the future Emperor Nicholas I) and Michael. As a philosopher and economist Storch at once declared himself to be an ardent adherent of Adam Smith. The lectures he delivered to the Grand Dukes were the foundation of his comprehensive work *Cours d'économie politique ou exposition des principes qui déterminent la prospérité des nations* (1819).[2] The book served to popularize the teachings of Adam Smith and gave rise to some polemics between the writer and J. B. Say.

The Russian translation of Storch's course could not be published at once for considerations of censorship, and therefore the work first appeared in French. However, extracts from Adam Smith's treatise, together with passages from the works of Ferguson and Bentham, were allowed to appear at the time in the official organ *The St. Petersburg Journal*, which was issued by the Foreign Office. Another Petersburg periodical, *The Journal of Statistics* (1808, v. ii, part 2) was also allowed to publish the work of yet another Russian " Smithianist ", G. Baludiansky, *On the Distribution and the Turnover of Wealth*, which actually repeated some of the ideas laid forth in *The Wealth of Nations*.[3] After the war of 1812 Adam Smith became extremely popular among the liberal youth of Russia who were organizing secret circles. In endowing the hero of his novel *Eugene Onegin* with a taste for economic problems and by making him read Adam Smith, Pushkin

---

[1] *Biographical Dictionary of Professors and Teachers at the Moscow University*, Moscow, 1855, ii, p. 628.

[2] In spite of the fact that many pages of Storch's course almost literally repeat certain passages of Adam Smith's treatise, the St. Petersburg economist should not be denied a certain originality in the working out of economical doctrines or in his independent criticism of some of the theses advanced by Smith, as, for instance, the definition of productive labour, the question of thriftiness, etc.

[3] To establish the connection between this work and the theories of Adam Smith and of his school, see V. M. Stein, *The Development of Economic Thought*, Leningrad, 1924, i, p. 126.

merely reproduced the actual feature of the time, the writer himself having had the same taste. In the Lyceum the great Russian poet studied political economy with Professor Kunitsin, who taught him the essential theses advanced by Adam Smith. The study of Smith's work greatly influenced the outlook of N. I. Turgenev and this influence made itself clearly felt in his book, *An Essay on the Theory of Taxes* (1818, 2nd Ed., 1819). Pushkin knew N. Turgenev personally, and, of course, must have read his book. The period from 1818 to 1825 being the time when Adam Smith's popularity in Russia was at its highest caused Pushkin to make Eugene Onegin " a profound economist ", arguing on the subject as to " why a state needs no gold when it has the natural product ".[1] In another decade, at the time of governmental reaction, Adam Smith's popularity in Russia was considerably shaken. In one of his uncompleted stories (*Extracts from a Novel in Letters*, 1831) Pushkin jestingly mentions that in 1818 everyone in the Petersburg high society tried to look thoughtful and to discuss gravely Adam Smith—" at the time the severity of regulations and political economy were in vogue ; we arrived at balls wearing our swords ; we thought it unfit to dance and had no time to spare on ladies. . . . All this has changed. French quadrille has now taken the place of Adam Smith ".

[1] N. L. Brodsky, *Commentary to Eugene Onegin*, Moscow, 1932, pp. 13-16.

INDEX

Abbot, Professor, 123 n.
Aberdeen, Adam Smith's property in, Sasine of sale, text of, 135, 397; proprietors of, 408-9
Academy of Arts, Foulis founds, 103, 104
Acceptance of report (Glasgow University), 94; its effect, 95
Accounts of Glasgow University, disputes over, 96, 155-60
Adam, Robert, 101
Adam Smith Club of Glasgow, 81
"Adam Smith's Seat," Kirkcaldy, 26
Adderbury, 232, 317, 396 n.
Addington, 302 n.
Administrative problems caused by Union, 11
Adscripti Glebæ, 353
"African king," 323 n.
Agriculture, 352 ff.
Alekseev, Professor Michael P., Russian admirers of Adam Smith by, 424-31
Alexander, Mr., 255
Anderson, James, *The Bee or Literary Intelligencer*, 52
Anderson, James, *Observations ... National Industry*, 282
Anderson, John, Professor of Oriental Languages and, later, of Natural Philosophy, and Boswell, 122, 123; character of, 87, 88; minutes regarding his translation, 188-90
Anderston Club, Glasgow, 82
Anker, Peter, Consul General of Denmark in Great Britain, letter to, from Adam Smith, economist, 280-1
Annandale, Marquis of, 6
debt collection, 9
Antiquities of Herculaneum presented to Glasgow University by the King of Sicily, 168
Appendices, 395-431
Arabs, 381
Arbuthnot, Robert, commissions, 9
Arcot, Nabob of, 277
Ardoyne, 400, 401
Argyle, Archibald, third Duke of, 66, 123

Argyle, John, second Duke, succeeds his father in 1703, 3; Lord High Commissioner to Scottish Parliament, 3; Commander-in-chief (Scotland) 1715, 14
Aristotle, 368
Art, foreign, in Scotland, 104
Astronomy Chair founded at Glasgow, 84
A Theory of Commerce and Maritime Affairs, 82
Attendants at Edinburgh lectures, 63

Baert, Baron de, 301
Balliol and Glasgow, tension between, over Snell Exhibitions, 43, 161-163
Smith enters, 37
Smith's teachers at, 37
state of learning at, described, 38
under Leigh's mastership, 43
Bank Notes, optional clause, 259
Bannerman, Mrs. H., of Edinburgh and Adam Smith's countenance, 77; explanation of loss of particulars of Adam Smith's ancestry, 397
owner of Douglas pedigree, 413
Bannerman, Mary A., letter of, 395, 396; pedigree compiled by, 413
Barbadoes 353
Bath Waters, 271
Bennochie, 400
Bentham, Edward, *An Introduction to Moral Philosophy* by, 40; interleaved and annotated copy found in Glasgow, 41 n.
Bentham's *Letter to a Young Gentleman of Oxford*, 44 ff.
Berkeley, *Querist*, 82
Billiards, students forbidden to play, 164
Bingham, Lydia M., 307 n.
Birkbeck, George, and higher education, 87, 88
"Birth brieves", 399
Black, Joseph, Professor of Medicine and Anatomy, 84, 99
letter to Adam Smith, Economist, 256
letter to, from Adam Smith, Economist, 301
Black, William, Regent, 7 n., 398, 403
Black Stone Chair, the, 33
Blair, Hugh, lectures on Rhetoric, 48, 52, 63

INDEX

Blavet, Abbé de, translation of *Theory of Moral Sentiments*, 279, 291 n.
Board, expenses of, in Glasgow University, 248-9
Bombelles, Marquis de, 292
Bonar, Dr., *The Library of Adam Smith*, 104 n., 171-2, 179 n., 266, 342 n.
Bonnet, 125
Boswell, James, and John Anderson, 122-3; his "facility of manners", 103
Bouffers, Mad. de, 110
Boulter, Hugh, foundation 74
Bounty on Corn, 346
Brougham, Lord, on Adam Smith, 100
Lives of Men of Letters, 395, 396
" Bristol, Baron of ", *i.e.* John, second Duke of Argyle, 3
Bruce, Professor John, 102; his *Elements of the Science of Ethics*, 299
letter to, from Adam Smith, Economist, 299-300
Buccleuch, Henry, third Duke of, 97
Adam Smith, tutor to, 97, 124, 283, 284, 317
and *The Wealth of Nations*, 124, 317
letter from, to Adam Smith, Economist, 311
Buchan, Earl of, *see* Lord Cardross
Buchanstoun, 400, 401, 402
Buildings, state of University, Glasgow, 69
Burke, Edmund, 278, 300
Burke, William, 268, 300
Burnet, James, 192 n., 194
Burns, Robert, on the earnings of a Supervisor, 360; poem on a relative of Adam Smith, 402
Busts, of Adam Smith, 105; by the Academy of Arts, 106; of David Hume, 106
Bute, John, third Earl of, and Professor Ruat's Case, 192, 192 n.
Buxton, Waters of, 272

Cadell, Thomas, letter from, to Adam Smith, Economist, 286
letters to, from Adam Smith, Economist, 291, 292, 299, 309, 374, 376
letter from, to Henry MacKenzie, 314
Calas case, 259 n.
Calcutta, dead treasure of, 277
Callander, John, of Craigforth, 20
and Smith's lectures on Jurisprudence, 54, 55
on Smith's Edinburgh lectures, 50
publications of, 63
Campbell, Captain Peter, 3
Campbell, Colin, (?) Chamberlain of Argyle, 3
Campbell, Miss Mally, daughter of the Principal, 36

Campbell, Mrs. Neil, 145
Campbell, Principal Neil, 90, 171; death of, 91
Cannan, Edwin, 124, 319, 321
Cantillon, *Essai*, 321, 345 n.
Canton, 383
Cardross, Lord, 51; and Adam Smith's lectures, 70
Carlyle, Alexander, of Inveresk, 36
and David Hume, 70
on Adam Smith, 100, 101
on student life at Glasgow, 36
Carmichael, Gershom, editor of Puffendorf, 112; on Natural Law, 113
Catalogue of Library of Adam Smith, MS., at Tokyo, 124, 125, 116 n., 172, 390, 391
Cato, 318, 356
Cattle, 354, 356
Cebes, *Tabula* of, marked by Adam Smith, 34
Chablot, Duchesse, 292
Chair, the Black Stone, 33
Challende, David, a courier, 264
Chalmers, George, letters to, from Adam Smith, Economist, 294-5, 296
Chesterfield, Earl of, 273
Child, Josiah, *On Trade*, 82
China, 383, 385
Civil Law, Adam Smith lectures on, in Edinburgh, 50
Civil List, Pensions on, 289
Clark, James, Collector of Excise at Kirkcaldy, terms of award, 134
Cleghorn, Professor Hugh, 102
Clerk of the Court Martial in Scotland, Adam Smith, W.S., and, 12
Clerk, Sir John, of Penicuik, 11, 62
Clermont-Tonnerre, Maréchal, 266
Clothing, inventory of, belonging to Adam Smith, Economist, in Paris, 261-2
Clow, Professor James, 67, 85
Clubs, demands on Adam Smith's time, 82, 83
in Edinburgh, 49
in Glasgow to which Adam Smith belonged, 81, 82
Cochrane, Provost Andrew, and the Commercial Club, 81
Cochrane's Club founded, 81
Cockburn, Lord, 85
Coke, Lord, 234
Colbert, Abbé de, 259
Collector of Customs, duties of, 16
Collieries at Kirkcaldy, 26
Colthurst, Sir John, 248
Colton, C., author of *Hypocrisy*, and Adam Smith, 61

INDEX

Commerce, aided by water carriage, 383
  growth of, in Glasgow, 80
  impeded by governments, 352
Comptroller of Customs, duties of, 16
Condillac, 125
Confusion with other Adam Smiths, 36
Cooper, Sir Grey, Bart., letter from, to Adam Smith, Economist, 275; mentioned, 287
Corn, bounty on, 282, 346
Cornwallis, Lord, 301
Courts Martial and outbreak of the Rebellion, 14, 15
Craigie, Robert, of Glendoick, 46, 48, 414
Craigie, Thomas, Professor of Moral Philosophy, Glasgow, death of, 66; 139
Cullen, Robert (afterwards a Lord of Session), 255
Cullen, William, Professor of Anatomy, 84
  letter to Adam Smith, Economist, from, 255
Cumberland, Richard, *Lex Naturæ*, 112
Cuming, Peter, 255
Curriculum for Arts degree at Glasgow, 33
Cursiter, Stanley, Director of Scottish National Portrait Gallery, 108

D'Alembert, 298
Dalkeith House, Townshend Papers at, 318
Dalrymple, John, Hydrographer, 102
Dalrymple, Sir John, 81 n., 82, 237
Dalrymple, William, Earl of Stair, 11
  Earl of Dumfries, 62
D'Anville, 125
D'Anville, Duchesse, 109, 292
Darien Company, conception and collapse, 4 ff.
Dashkova, Princess E. R., *Mémoires* by, 428
Davidson, John, W.S., 63, 288
  letters to, from Adam Smith, Economist, 267
Dawson, George, on Natural Law, 112, 113
Decreet Arbitral, clearing of Hercules Smith's accounts, 133-5
Demainbray, lectures on Experimental Philosophy, 1748-49, 48
Dempster, George, letter from, to Adam Smith, Economist, 287-8
Denis, Madame, of Ferney, depositions of, sent to Adam Smith, Economist, 1765, 260-1
Deputy Judge Advocate, 13; position, pay and duties of, 14
Deskford, Lord, 257
Desnitsky, Simon Jefinovich, 158 n.; Professor in Moscow, 424 ff.
  translates Blackstone and Bowden into Russian, 427
D'Espinasse, Mdlle., 298
Dewar, Duncan, itemised accounts, 30

Diderot, 279, 298
Dillon, Mr., trespasser on grounds of Ferney, 260
Disabilities of Scotland before the Union, 4 ff.
Dissertation " On the Origin of Languages ", 52
Disturbance by students at Mr. Seymour's dancing school, 164
Douglas Cause, the, Adam Smith, Economist, as Commissioner for taking evidence at Toulouse, 259-60
Douglas, Admiral Sir Charles, 307
Douglas, Colonel Robert, of Strathenry, 46, 304 n., 305, 414
Douglas, David, Lord Reston, 308-10, 397; letter to, from Adam Smith. Economist, 310
Douglas, " gentleman of name of ", author of *Letter . . . on National Defence*, 282
Douglas, George, and escape of Queen Mary, 18
Douglas, Janet, 65, 297, 306, 414
Douglas, John, Snell Exhibitioner, 38; Bishop of Carlisle and Salisbury, 39
Douglas, John, of Strathenry, 18, 132, 414
Douglas, Margaret, daughter of Robert Douglas, M.P., marries Adam Smith, W.S., 18, 130; death of, 290
Douglas, Sir William, of Lochleven, 18, 413
Douglases of Strathenry and Mary Queen of Scots, 18
Douglases of Strathenry, family of, 411-15
Dræby's Danish translation of *Wealth of Nations*, 280-281
Draft letter in Adam Smith's own hand to an unnamed correspondent, 288-90
Dreghorn, Allan, Architect, 141-4
Drummond, Lilias, or Lily, letter to, from Adam Smith, W.S., 15, 16; wife of Adam Smith, W.S., 15
Drummond, Sir George, of Milnab, father-in-law of Adam Smith, W.S., 15
Drysdale, George, 22
Drysdale, John, minister of Kirkcaldy, 22
Drygate, houses in, 31
Duhamel, du Monceau, 179, 330 n.
Dumfries, Lord, 235
Dundas, Henry, letter from, to Adam Smith, Economist, 302; letter to, from Adam Smith, 303
Dunfermline, Countess of, 402
  Earl of, 402
Dunlop & Wilson, Booksellers, Glasgow, 105-7
Dunlop, Professor Alexander, 31, 416
Dunmore, John, first Earl of, 240
Duties of tutors and curators in Scots Law, 21 n.

Economic interest, books of, printed in Glasgow, 82
Eden, William, 287
Edinburgh, Adam Smith honorary freeman of, 82 n.
 clubs, 49, 50
 culture in, 1748-51, 47
 lectures by Adam Smith used in Glasgow, 51
 legal studies in, 1748-51, 47
 Philosophical Society, 82
 Poker Club, 82
 political excitement in, 7
 public lectures in, 1748-51, 48
 Select Society, 82
 University lectures advertised in the Press, 49
 University lectures, ladies admitted to, 49
Edinburgh Review, contributions to, 116, 117
Edinburgh University, Adam Smith and a Chair there, 62
 Adam Smith's lectures not given there, 48
 better provided with Professors in 1784 than any other, 292
Education, cost of, in Glasgow, 28 ff.
Effect of kidnapping on Adam Smith's character, 26
Egypt, 384, 385
Elliott, Gilbert, of Minto, letter to Adam Smith, Economist, 239-40
Emoluments, professors', at Glasgow, 67
Encyclopédie, 53, 116, 124, 125, 171, 321, 329 n., 334 n., 347 n.
" Enquiry into the Laws which govern the Conduct of Individuals in Society ", 35— (?) essay by Adam Smith
Entails, 355
Ephémérides, 125
Epictetus, *Encheiridion* of, Adam Smith's copy, 33, 365
Erroll, fourteenth Earl of, Rector, 92
Errol, twelfth Earl of, 398
Erskine, Sir Henry, 237
Erskine, Professor John, advertises lectures on Roman Antiquities, etc., in Edinburgh, 49
Erskine, Sir James, 271
Essay on Military Law and the Practice of Courts Martial by A. Fraser Tytler, 13
" Essay on the Affinity between certain English and Italian Verses ", 59, 60, 370-373
" Essay on the Ancient Logic and Metaphysics ", 53
" Essay on the Imitative Arts ", 52 n., 59
" Eugene Onegin " quoted, 430, 431
Exchanging, power of, 379
 rule of, 345 ff.

Exchequer, Barons of the, University Accounts before the, 155-6
Extracts from Documents produced by parties in the Action for Declarator in the Court of Session relating to the Report on the Jurisdiction of the Rector in Glasgow University, 222 ff.

Faa (Faw), Patrick, 23
Faculty, Deans of, 91 ; and duties of, 91
Fate of Glasgow lecture of 1755, 120
Fees, University, cost of, 29
Fencing Academy in University, 149, 150
Ferguson, Adam, alleged plagiarism, 101
 letters from, to——, 236-7 ; to Adam Smith, Economist, 255, 273
Finding of the manuscript of draft of *Wealth of Nations*, 317
Findlater, Earl of, sale of cup, 9
Findlay, Robert, Professor of Divinity, controversy with Dr. Alex. Geddes, 29
 expenses for board, 30
Fingal, 110
Fire-engine, 344, 379
Fitzmaurice family, 239 n.
Fitzmaurice, Hon. Thomas, boarder with Adam Smith, 67, 69, 239-54
Fitzmaurice, Lord William, afterwards second Earl of Shelburne, letter to, from Adam Smith, Economist, 241
Foley and Thélluson, bankers at Paris, 264
Forrester of Strathenry, 411-14
Foulis, Robert and Andrew, and issue of books on trade, 82
 and their relations with Adam Smith, 103, 104 ; their work in Glasgow, 103, 104
Foulis, Robert, 148, 149, 149 n.
Foulis' *Homer* presented to the King of Sicily, 168
Fragments of lectures discovered in Bannerman MSS., now at Glasgow, 57; contents and importance discussed, 58, 59; reproduced, 379-85
France, 330, 346, 350
 King of, edict against new vineyards, 346
Free Masonry, students forbidden to enter, 164
French taught to children of better-class families, 40
French, T., Papermaker, 60
Friends of Adam Smith, 101-3

Gardiner, Richard, 378
Gee, *Trade and Navigation*, 82
Geddes, Dr. Alexander, and Professor Findlay, 29

INDEX

General Retour in favour of Adam Smith as heir to Hugh Smith, text of, 135
Germany, 353
Gillies, Alexander, amanuensis and transcriber of *The Wealth of Nations*; afterwards Officer of Excise, 360
Glasgow, Adam Smith's lectures in, 111-26
  Adam Smith made honorary burgess, 81
  Adam Smith's settlement in, 66-81
  as an academic centre, 28
  burgesses admitted gratis, 10
  clubs to which Adam Smith belonged, 81, 82
  commercial rise of, 79 ff.
  cost of education in, 28 ff.
  cost of living in, 68
  demand for books on trade, 82
  in seventeenth and eighteenth century, impression on travellers, 30
  Literary Society, 82
  minister of, 91
  Professor of Logic at, Adam Smith appointed, 66
  Robert and Andrew Foulis and their work in, 103-4
  social conditions in eighteenth century, 78 ff.
  student life in, 28 ff.
  tannery, accident to Adam Smith at, 324 n.
Glasgow Lectures, 80, 104, 171, 319, 388, 389
Glasgow University, accounts of the Tack of the Archbishopric, 155-6, 377
  accounts of the University Revenue, 1755-58, 156-7
  Adam Smith appointed Dean of Faculty, 75, 184-8
  and the City of Glasgow, relations between, 163-6
  appointments of, to professorships at, text of Minutes, 137-40
  elected Rector Magnificus, 228-30; re-appointed, 231
  Legality of Procedure as Vice-Rector questioned, 200; confirmed by Rector, 201
  report on the powers of Rector and Principal, 202-15
  resigns Professorship of Moral Philosophy, 220-1
  and Rev. William Thom, 75, 76
  a typical Faculty meeting, 150
  case of Professor James Moor, 195-9
  case of Professor William Ruat, 190-5
  conditions of matriculation, 136 n.
  constitutional question in, 1761-4, 84 ff.
  curriculum for an arts degree, 33, 243-5
  difficulties in government of, 89 ff.
  documents relating to Questions of Finance and Law arising out of the Administration of the University property, 150-60; *see also* Contents
  duties of professors, 73
  early history of, 71 ff.
  extracts from Documents produced by parties in the Action for Declarator in the Court of Session relating to the Report on the Jurisdiction of the Rector, 222 ff.
  feu duty of 12d. Scots, proposal to sell, 155
  general appearance of, 31
  government of, 73
  intellectual influences at, 31-32
  Library, Adam Smith's Quaestor Accounts, 1758-60, 178-84; catalogue printed by Andrew Foulis, 171; Barrowfield Fund, 169; extracts from Minutes, 1752-64, 173-8; gifts to,169; gowned students and library "stent", 175, 175 n.; its resources in the time of Adam Smith, 168-73; number of volumes in, 170; Principal Stirling Fund, 169; purchases for, by Adam Smith, 171; Quaestors, 1746-60, 173 n.; revenue from undergraduates, 169-70, from graduates, 170; state of buildings, 174-5; subjects of books in, 170
Munimenta, 89
"Oceana, Parliament of", a students' society, 85
opening of Session 1737-38 described, 32
position of, 30
professorial staff in, 84 ff., table at, 224
Professor James Moor's objections to Adam Smith's report, 215
regulations for Degrees in Arts, 187-8
respective powers of Rector and Principal, committee set up, 202
revenues of, 71 ff.
system of Keeping Accounts, 159, 159 n., 160
text of documents relating to the Administration by Adam Smith of the Property of the University, 140-50; *see also* Contents
text of minute of appointment as Professor of Logic, 138-9
text of Minute of appointment of Professor of Moral Philosophy, 139-40
text of minute of appointment as Snell Exhibitioner, 136-7
text of Minute of Resignation of Snell Exhibition, 137
text of resignation of Professorship of Moral Philosophy, 220-1

Glasgow University—*contd.*
  transactions relating to professors, 188-90
  translation of Professor John Anderson, 188-90
    Visitation of 1727, 90
    Visitors, Ordinary, 91
Glasnock, Ayrshire, charter issued to Adam Smith, W.S., by Loudoun, 8
Glassford, John, and the Commercial Club, 81
  letter from, to Adam Smith, Economist, 258-9
Godolphin and settlement of succession, 5
Gordon, Captain, 236
Gordon, Lord George, 305
Gordonsmilne, 400
Gray, J. M., on Adam Smith portraits, 108
Gray, W. Forbes, on Edinburgh clubs, 49, 50
Greeks, 353
Green, Captain, trial of, 6
Greenwich, Earl of, *see* John, second Duke of Argyle, 3
Grenville, 302
Grotius and Natural Law, 34, 112
Gypsies, their numbers and characteristics, danger to poor tenants, 23
Gypsy encampment at Kirkcaldy, 25

Hailes, Lord, letter to, from Adam Smith, Economist, 265-7
Haldane, Miss, 395 n.
Hamilton, Duke of, 259 n.
Hamilton, Thomas, Professor of Medicine, 86
Hamilton, William, of Bangour, poems collected by Adam Smith, 61
Harlaw, Battle of, 400
" Haunch-button ", 68 n
Hay, Lord Charles, 398
Heawood, Edward, on watermarks, 61
Helvetius, 298
Henry, Dr., 247
Herbert, Henry, *see* Lord Porchester
Hertford, Lord, 262
Hervey, Sir John, Baron of Bristol, 3 n.
High Borlace Club, 38
" High-broad " or " high-brow ", 109 n.
Highwayman stops Adam Smith, 274
History of the Reign of the Emperor Charles V., by William Robertson, 55 ; 236
Hogg, Robert, and Sir Walter Scott, 78
Holbach, Baron de, 298
Holland, 323, 333 n., 385
Holt, Andreas, Commissioner of the Danish Board of Trade and Economy, letter to, from Adam Smith, Economist, 281-4
Home, Earl of, 378
Home, John, 236, 238, 273, 312

Home, Henry, of Kames, *see* Lord Kames
Homer, edition of, edited by James Moor, 86, 88, 168 ; quoted 342
Hopeton, Lord, 257
Horses, regulation concerning keeping of, by students, 164
Hottentots, 381
Houses, professors', in Glasgow University, 68 ; 415-22
Howe, Viscount, 274
Hume's *Essays on Commerce*, 82
  Treatise of Human Nature, 34
Hume, David, and Adam Smith compared as speakers, 70
  and introduction to Adam Smith, 64
  and the Physiocrats, 125 n., 298 n.
  bust of, 106
  clamour against his Deism, 262
  letters to, from Adam Smith, Economist, 262, 263, 264, 271-2
  reception of Adam Smith's letter annexed to his *Autobiography*, 283
  urges Adam Smith to apply for Chair of Law at Edinburgh, 34, 42
Hutcheson, Francis, Professor of Moral Philosophy, 31, 57, 71, 112, 229, 320, 417
  medallion of, 106
Hutton, William, 129 n.
Hypocrisy, poem, 61

" Impartial Spectator ", 100
Indian corn, 353
" Indian prince ", 323 n.
Industries at Kirkcaldy, 26
Intellectual influences at Glasgow University, 31-2
Inveramsay, Smiths of, 395, 400, 403-4
Irwin, Dr., 378
Italian verses, 371 ff.

Jacobite plot (Baillie's plot), 11
  tendencies at Oxford, 44
Jake, by Naomi Royde-Smith, quoted, 78
Jerseys, the, 353
John Marshall's Loan, 25
Johnson, Dr. Samuel, and Adam Smith, disagreement between, 122, 123
  approves Adam Smith on verse, 53
  his *Dictionary*, 116 122
Johnstone, William (Sir William Pulteney), 63
  letter from Adam Smith, Economist, to, 236
Judge Advocate, origin of office, 13

Kames, Lord, 46 ff., 66
Keynes, J. M., 34

INDEX

Kidnapping by gypsies, reasons for, 24
Kidnapping of Robert Traill, 85
King George III., ceremonial address to, drawn up by Adam Smith, 166-8
Kippen, George, 258
Kirkcaldy and neighbourhood in 1732 : shipping, collieries, saltpans, nailery, 26
Kunitsin, Professor, 431

Lace, students forbidden to wear, 164
Ladies admitted to University lectures in Edinburgh, 49
Laissez faire, 111
Land tax, 281
Lannion, Countess, case of, 266
Law, Natural, George Dawson on, 112, 113 ; Gershom Carmichael on, 113
Law, *On Money and Trade*, 82
system of, 351
Lectures at Glasgow, Adam Smith's, 70
" Lecture of 1755 " read to the Commercial Club, 82, 117
Lee, General, 269
Leechman, William, Professor of Divinity and afterwards Principal of Glasgow University, 51, 86, 87
appointed Principal, 91
Legal studies in Edinburgh, 1748-51, 47
Legatsden, 400
Leigh, Dr., Master of Balliol, 38, 43, 137, 366
Leith, 383
Lindesay, Mrs., boarding house, 29
Literature, lectures on, by Adam Smith, topics of, 51
Living, cost of, in Glasgow, 68
Logan, John, letter from, to Henry Mackenzie, 285-6
letter from, to Adam Smith, Economist, 304-5
Logic, Professor of, at Glasgow, Adam Smith appointed, 66
Loudon (or Loudoun), John, Regent, Professor of Logic at Glasgow, 32, 138 n.
death of, 66
Loudoun, Hugh, Earl of, rapid advancement of, 6 ; appointed Secretary of State, 9
Loughborough, Lord, *see* Wedderburn, Alexander
letter from, to (?) David Douglas, 313

Mably, 125
MacFait, Dr. Ebenezer, lectures in Mathematics, 1748-9, 48, 49
Mackay, Professor Charles, advertises lectures on Scots Law, etc., in Edinburgh, 49

Mackenzie, Henry, author of the *Man of Feeling*, copy of his second letter to Mr. Carmichael in 1781, 284
letter from, to Adam Smith, Economist, 284-5
letter from John Logan to, 285-6
Maclaine, Dr. Archibald, and Adam Smith's favourite pursuits, 34
Macleod of Assynt, 401
Maconochie, Alexander, 259
Macpherson, John, M.P., letter from, to Adam Smith, Economist, 276-8
McRobert, A. T., 398
" Maid of Fife ", the, 65, 109
Malcolm II, Laws of, 266
Mar, Earl of, 6
Market, extent of, 380
Marshall, Alfred, 77
Martin, John, schoolmaster, Perth, 21
Matriculation, conditions of, at Glasgow, 136 n.
made compulsory on students, 164
Meal, Irish, price of, in 1711, 9
Medicine, Professors of, advertise lectures in Edinburgh, 49
Mediterranean, the, 384
Meikle, 401
Menteath, Sir Charles Stuart, 306-9
Menzies, Archibald, 274
Mercantilism, 114, 287
Metayers, 125, 354
Middleton, George, Comptroller at Aberdeen 17
Millar, Andrew, bookseller, letter to Adam Smith, Economist, with list of presentation copies of *Theory of Moral Sentiments*, 238
(?) letter to, from Adam Smith, Economist, 265
Millar, John, Professor of Civil Law, 63, 84, 85
account of Smith's lectures, 70, 115
his acknowledgment to Adam Smith, 56
letter from, to Adam Smith, Economist, 257
letter from, to David Douglas, 311-13
Ministers, change of, 6
Mirabeau, 125 n., 173 n.
Molendinar Burn, 145 n.
Money, 41, 346 ff.
Monied man, " his sordid sensuality ", 326
Monopoly, 353
Monteath (or Menteath), Rev. Dr. James Stewart, letter from, to Adam Smith, Economist, 308 ; letters to, from Adam Smith, Economist, 292-3, 306-7-9 ; Snell Exhibitioner, 39
Montesquieu, *Esprit des Lois* published, 112
Montrose, Marquis of, 401

INDEX

Moor, James, Professor of Greek, 67, 86, 88, 89, 90 ; case of, 195-9
Moral Philosophy, Chair of, at Glasgow, Adam Smith exchanges to, 67, 139-40 ; emoluments attached to, 67
Mordvinov, N. S., 427
Morellet, the Abbé, letter to, from Adam Smith, Economist, 298-9
Morthland, Matthew, University Factor, 96
Morthland, Professor C., 416
Mortifications by Countess of Forfar, 153, 153 n. ; Duchess of Hamilton, 153, 153 n., 154, 155 ; Lord Dundonald, 160, 160 n. ; parliamentary authority required for, 154
Morton, Charles, Secretary Royal Society, 265
Morton, Earl of, *see* Sir William Douglas
" Muir " portrait of Adam Smith, 108
Muirhead, George, Professor of Humanity, 86
Murdoch, Provost John, 163 n.
Musselburgh, Adam Smith, honorary freeman of, 82 n.

Naileries at and near Kirkcaldy, 26, 27
Nailmaking, customs of the craft, 27
Naturalism, 111
" Nature and causes of public opulence ", 317, 322 ff.
Natural Philosophy Class, equipment, 146, 147
Naval action between British and French frigates off Mull of Galloway, 173
Necker, 264, 270-1
Nelthorpe, Mr., 274
New England, 353
Nicol, Mdlle de, 110
Nile, the, 385
North American Colonies, 356, 384
  Indians, 381
North, Lord, 274, 277
Nova Erectio, the, charter of, 71, 89, 90

Octateuch, the Clementine (MS. Septuagint), acquired for University Library, 29
Office of Clerk of Court Martial and Councils of War in Scotland, duties of, 13 ff.
Official duties of private secretary of a Scottish Minister, 10
Ogle, Revd. Newton, 293
Opulence, 56, 114, 317 ff.
Orr, John, and the Barrowfield Fund of Glasgow University Library, 169
Oswald, Colonel St. Clair, 395
Oswald, James, of Dunnikier, 18, 21, 395, 396 ; appointed factor, 22 ; curator, 21 ; death of, 22 ; M.P. for Fifeshire, 46

Oswald, James, junior, 27, 47, 48 ; suggested to Adam Smith division of price into rent, wages and interest, 117, 320
Oswald, James Townsend, 395
Overseas trade of Scotland, 114, 115
Oxford, expenses for tuition and living at, 39 Jacobite tendencies at, and their effect on Adam Smith, 44

Paoli, General, 86
Parliament (Scottish), disorder in, 1704, 5
Paterson, George, lectures on Mathematics, 49
Pathead nailery, 27
Patronage difficulties caused by Union, 11, 12
Pennsylvania, 353
Pensions on Civil List, 289
Perquisites of Collectors and Comptrollers, 17
Petty family, the, 245 n. ; property in Ireland, 245
Petty, *Political Arithmetic*, 82
Petty Customs exacted from students at Glasgow, 163, 163 n.
Philip, John, 3
Philosophical Society of Edinburgh, 49, 50
Physiocrats, the, relation of Adam Smith to, discussed, 112, 124, 125, 126, 298 n., 319, 321 ; and to Hume, 125 n., 298 n.
Pigot, Lord, 300
Pitt, William, 302
Plagiarism, 55, 101
  charges of, discussed, 118
Poland, 353
Poolwals or Peelwalls, 400
Pope Nicholas V., 71
Porchester, Henry Herbert, Baron, boarder with Adam Smith, 68 ; letter from, to Adam Smith, 293-4 ; Wedderburn willing to work with him in Ministry, 270
Porteous Riots, 16
Portugal, 350
Portuguese Conspiracy, the, 241
Position of Glasgow University, 30
Postal system in Scotland, development of, 409
Postlethwayt, J., 124, 179
Postlethwayt, M., *Dictionary of Commerce*, 82, 126, 321, 345
Powers of Rector and Principal, report by Adam Smith on, 93, 94
Pownal, Governor, 282
Primo-geniture, 355
Professorial staff, changes in, at Glasgow, 68 business at Glasgow, 72
  staff in University of Glasgow, 84 ff. ; *see also* Glasgow, University of

INDEX

Professors' houses in Old College, Glasgow, 415-22 ; plan of, 420
Proposals for a Council of Trade in Scotland, 82
Prossor, James, and Professor John Anderson, 88
Provost Andrew Cochrane, 163 n.
Prussia, King of, 252, 304
Puffendorf, *De Officio Hominis et Civis*, ed. Carmichael, 112
Purveyance, 355
Pushkin, 430, 431

Quebec, 269
Queen Anne's Bounty, 157
Quesnay, F., *Essai Physique sur l'Oeconomie Animale*, 57 ; Essay on " Fermiers " in *Encyclopédie*, 125

Radistchev, Alexander, 428
Rae, John, 12, 13, 26, 36, 40, 48, 60, 61, 70, 72, 74, 82, 102, 105, 121, 122
Rankenian Club, the, Edinburgh, 49 n.
Rashivit, 400
Rebellion of 1715, 8 n., 14, 401, 404
Rebellion of 1745, 44, 85
Recommendation, letter of, from Adam Smith, Economist, on behalf of Colonel Francis Xavier Tyrry, Dr. John Andrew de Temes y Prado and Don Francis Codon, 305
Rector, duties of, 91 ; powers of, 93
Regents, meetings convened by, 90
Regulations concerning undergraduates' attendance at assemblies, etc., 164
Reid, Professor Thomas, emoluments, 67
Relation of the *Glasgow Lectures* to *The Wealth of Nations*, 319 ff.
Rents in kind and in money, 355
Rhetoric and the *Belles Lettres*, Adam Smith lectures on, in Edinburgh, 50
Ritchie, James, and the Commercial Club, 81
Robertson, Principal William, and Smith's lectures on Jurisprudence, 55-6, 63-4 ; *History of Charles V.*, 101 ; letter to Adam Smith, 238-9 ; recommended for D.D. Degree by Adam Smith, 76, 184-5
Robinson, John, Secretary of the Treasury, 278
Robison, Professor John, on Joseph Black, 99
Rochefoucauld, Le Duc de la, 292, 301 ; letter from, to Adam Smith, Economist, 278-9
Roebuck, Dr. John, letter from, to Adam Smith, Economist, 268-9
Romanes, J. H., W.S., owner of " Muir " portrait, 108, 109
Romans, the, 353
Ronald, Robert, Collector of Customs, Montrose, 399

Rose, Mr., of Kew, 238, 254
Ross, Lt.-Col. Alexander, letter to, from Adam Smith, Economist, 300-1
Ross, Lt.-Col. Patrick, 101, 300, 302
Rosse, Professor G., Glasgow, 68
Rosslyn, Earl of, *see* Wedderburn, Alexander
Rothiebirsben, 400, 401
Rothiebirsben, Smiths of, 395, 403
Row, Principal, 403
Ruat [Ruet, Rouet], Professor William, the case of, 190-5
Runnamede, 285
Russia, Adam Smith's teachings promoted in, 424 ff.
Russian students, loan to distressed, 158
Rustici, 353
" Rutherford, Dr.", *i.e.* John Logan, 304

Salary of Collector of Customs, 235 n.
Saltpans at Kirkcaldy, 26
Scarcity of money in Scotland, 5
Schlözer, Christian, 430
Scotland, overseas trade of, 114, 115
Scots Magazine, the, 360, 402
Scotsmen, unpopularity of, in England, 38
Scott, Hercules, of Brotherton, family of, 399
Scott, James, of Logie, family of, 399
Scott, Sir Walter, and his dictation, 78
Scottish Government before the Union, 4ff.
Scottish land tenure, 151 n.
Scottish Parliament, dissolution of, in 1703, 5
Scottish Postmasters General, 1688-1701, 409-10
Scruton's *Practical Counting House*, 106
Seafield, James, 1st Earl of, 3
Seasons, bad, 9
Seaton (or Seton), Smiths in, 395, 405 ; table of, 407
Secretaries of State in Scotland, importance of, 7
Security, Act of, 5
Select Society of Edinburgh, the, 50 n.
Session, University, opening of, described, 32
" Seven pearls of Loch Leven ", 18
Seymour's Dancing School, Mr., disturbance at, 164
Shankstown, Ayrshire, charter issued to Adam Smith, W.S., by Loudoun, 8
Sharp, Buccleuch, 296
Sharpe, Joshua, and Snell Exhibition, 161-2 and the University Accounts, 156
" Shaw Park Decree ", 97
Shelburne, first Earl of, letters from Adam Smith, Economist, to, 242, 243-5, 248-9, 249-50, 250-1, 251-2, 253-4 ; letter from, to Adam Smith, 245-6

Shelburne, second Earl of, afterwards Marquis of Lansdowne, 122, 123, 241, 298
Ship Bank, loan repaid to, 158
Shipping at Kirkcaldy, 26
Shuvalov, Prince I. I., 424
Sicily, King of, presentation of Foulis' Homer to, 168
Simson, John, Professor of Divinity, 32 ; heresy charge, 32
Simson, Professor Robert, mathematician, 68, 85, 85 n. ; and Loudoun, 10 ; Clerk of Senate, 32
Sinclair, Sir John, of Ulbster, letter to, from Adam Smith, Economist, 297
Sinclairtown nailery, 27
Sins of printer of *Theory of Moral Sentiments*, 254
Skene, David, of Pitlour, 22
Skene, David, General, 101
Skene's *Regiam Majestatem*, 266
Slaves, cultivation by, 353
Slezer, Captain, *Theatrum Scotiæ*, 31
Smith, Adam, at Aberdeen, grand-uncle of Lady Green, 297 n.
Smith, Adam, at Achath, 1689, 405
Smith, Adam, in Ardgrain, 1633, 405
Smith, Adam, burgess, Aberdeen, 1652, 405
Smith, Adam, burgess, Aberdeen (uncle of Adam Smith, W.S.), 1664, 130, 396, 397, 405, 406, 408, 409 ; family of, 407.
Smith, Adam, in Calsie Croft, 1607, 405
Smith, Adam, Collector of Customs at Alloa, 17, 37, 235, 397 ; letter from, to Adam Smith, Economist, 235
Smith, Adam, Collector of Customs at Kirkcaldy, 8, 22, 133-5, 397 ; Inspector General of the Outports, 134
Smith, Adam, at Dundee, 1535, 405
Smith, Adam, Economist—
  abbreviate of Retour as heir of his father, text of, 133
  absentmindedness of, 62, 77, 78
  accused of plagiarism, 101
  among his friends, 98-110
  and administration of the property of the University, documents relating to, 140-50
  and Glasgow University Library, 168-84
  annuity from Buccleuch Estate, proposal to surrender it, 284
  appointed Professor of Logic at Glasgow, text of Minute, 137
  appointed Professor of Moral Philosophy, text of Minutes, 139-40
  appointed tutor to Duke of Buccleuch, 97
  as administrator, 74 ff.
  as a student at Glasgow and Balliol, 28-45
  at Edinburgh, 46-65
  a very slow workman, 359
  awarded Warner Exhibition on nomination of Archbishop of Canterbury and Bishop of Rochester, 39
  baptism of, 20
  boyhood of, 20-7
  busts of, 105
  character of, 64, 65
  character of his mother, 20
  class room, 69
  Commissioner of Customs for Scotland, 275 ff.
  confirmed as Præses and Vice-Rector, 216-7
  copyrights sold, and prices realised, 314
  Dean of Faculty, Glasgow University, 184-8
  difficulties in adding new material to MSS., 422-3
  discipline, 69
  documents relative to, as student, 136-7
  Edinburgh lectures, subject-matter of, 50 ff.
  elected Rector Magnificus of Glasgow University, 228-30 ; reappointed, 231
  elected to Snell Exhibition, 37
  entry in Matriculation Album, 136, 364
  Essays on Philosophical Subjects (posthumous), 50, 314
  facsimiles of handwriting and signatures of, 362-92
  falls into a tan-pit at Glasgow, 324 n.
  freeman, Glasgow, Musselburgh and Edinburgh, 81, 82 n.
  goes to school at Kirkcaldy, 26
  graduates with distinction, 36
  handwriting of, and his amanuenses, 357
  hatred of act of writing, hence use of official and other copyists, 359
  held up by a highwayman, 274
  honorary burgess of Glasgow, 81
  houses occupied by, in Old College, Glasgow, 68, 415-22
  illnesses of, 123, 253
  influence of, in Glasgow, 104-5
  influence of London on, 100
  kidnapped by tinklers or gypsies, 23-5
  leaves Balliol, 43
  lectures, public, by, outlined, 48
  legality of procedure as Vice-Rector questioned, 200, but confirmed by Rector, 201
  love affairs of, 65, 109
  matriculates at Glasgow, 28, 136, 364
  matriculates at Oxford, 37
  on lowering of fees to Custom Officers, 17
  personal life in Edinburgh, 1748-51, 62
  place of birth, 20

INDEX

Smith, Adam, Economist—*contd.*
  portraits of, 107, 108
  Quaestor Accounts with Glasgow University Library, 1758-60, 178-84
  receives LL.D. Degree, 187
  recommendations by, 102, 103
  recommends Rev. William Robertson for D.D. Degree, 184-5
  relatives in Glasgow, 28
  report on the powers of Rector and Principal at Glasgow University, 202-15 ; and Professor James Moor's objections, 215
  rescue from the gypsies, 25
  resigns professorship of Moral Philosophy at Glasgow, 97, 220-1
  Russian admirers of, 424-31
  school buildings at Kirkcaldy, view of, 26
  smile, his characteristic, 76, 77
  Spartan in his mode of life, 325 n.
  studies of, in Glasgow, 32-7, 136-7
  studies of, in Oxford, 40
  studies, 1751-63, 111-26
  supporters of, for Chair of Logic, 66
  sympathy and power of judgement discussed, 100
  teaching, hours of, 69
  text of appointment to Snell Exhibition, 136, 137
  text of letter of resignation of Snell Exhibition, 137
  traces of, as undergraduate at Glasgow, 33
  tutors and curators of, 132, 133
  tutors at Oxford, 37, 38
  vote on the translation of Professor John Anderson, 188-90
  writing paper used by, in Glasgow University, 321
  see also Contents
Smith, Adam, in Hill of Beltie, 1625, 405
Smith, Adam, in Pervinnes, 1630, 405
Smith, Adam, in Scottistoun, 1631, 405
Smith, Adam, Postmaster, Aberdeen, 1700, 405
Smith, Adam, Servitor Earl of Sutherland, 1623, 405
Smith, Adam, student at Glasgow, 1709, 37
Smith, Adam, student at Glasgow, 1762, 37, 258 n., 368
Smith, Adam (father of the Economist), Writer to the Signet, private secretary to Earl of Loudoun, Secretary of State—
  admitted W.S., 12
  Commission to, as Clerk of the Court Martial of Scotland, text of, 129
  Comptroller of Customs at Kirkcaldy, 12, 16
  continues Secretary to Loudoun, 12
  death of, 19
  duties as Secretary to Loudoun, 3, 7, 9, 10
  Estate, Testamentary, of, 131, 395
  extra-secretarial commissions by, 9
  family of, 404-408
  library classification, 8 n.
  marries Lilias Drummond, 15
  marries Margaret Douglas, 18
  relatives mentioned in Wills of, 396 ff.
  studied under William Black at Aberdeen, 7 n.
  summary of family of, 406
  testamentary provisions of, 21
  total emoluments, 17 ; compared with earnings of important offices, 18
  two Wills of, 396
  Will of, text of, 129-33
  wrecked on coast of France, 7 n.
Smith, Agnes, " Mill of Tifty's Annie ", 402
Smith, Alexander, General Collector of Taxation and Postmaster General for Scotland, 8, 396, 402-7, 409-10
Smith, Alexander, in the Customs, 397
Smith, Alexander, son of William, Regent, 398
Smith, Elizabeth, wife of William, Regent, 398
Smith, Hercules, collector at Montrose, appointed to Kirkcaldy, 16, 133, 397-9, 403-4
Smith, Hercules, Junr., merchant in Kirkcaldy, 133
Smith, Hugh, son of Adam Smith, W.S., 15, 21, 408, 409 ; at boarding school at Perth, 21 ; illness of, 1724, 21 ; death of, 62 ; bequests to, by Adam Smith, W.S., 130 ; Tutors and Curators of, 131-2 ; Adam Smith, Economist, his heir, 135, 409
Smith, Isobel, married Principal Row, 403
Smith, James, at mill of Rothiebirsben, 400, 401, 403, 406
  in Logie, 399, 403, 405
  family of, 401-3
Smith, James, in Meikle, 401
Smith, James, son of Adam, burgess, 396
  burgess, Aberdeen, 408
Smith, John, in Inveramsay, 1633, 400
Smith, John, of Inveramsay (Treasurer of Aberdeen), died *c.* 1669, 399, 400
  family of, 404
Smith, John, of Inveramsay, died 1750, 399
  family of, 404
Smith, John, in Seaton, family of, 405, 406-7
Smith, John, Regent, 402
Smith, John, Snell Exhibitioner, 39 ; Savilian Professor of Geometry, 39, 162-3, 234 n.
Smith, Lily or Lilias, first wife of Adam Smith, W.S., 15, 16, 18, 396, 408

INDEX

Smith, Margaret, second wife of Adam Smith, W.S., marriage, 18, 397, 408, 414; portrait, 20, 107; character, 20-2, 29; *see* Douglas, Margaret
   letters to, from her son, Adam, 232, 233
Smith, Margaret, married Ninian Black, 403
Smith, Nathaniel, burgess, Aberdeen, 403-5
Smith, Patrick, at Ardoyne, 403-5
Smith, Patrick, of Inveramsay, family of, 404, 409
Smith, Robert, of Smiddieburn, family of, 403-5
Smith, William, nephew of Alexander and Adam, W.S., 8; becomes secretary to Earl of Loudoun, 8; letter to, 232, 233 n.; mentioned, 14 n., 40, 60, 258 n.; secretary to John, 2nd Duke of Argyle, 8; secretary of Office of Ordnance and Yeoman of King's Wine Cellar, 8; tutor and curator of Adam Smith, Economist, 130
Smith, William, Regent of Marischal College, Aberdeen, 8 n.; involved in the rebellion, dismissed as Regent, 8 n., 46, 66, 397-9, 404
   Author of *Oratio*, 1696, 398
Smith, William, Clerk of Chancery, 135
Smith, William, Mill of Tifty, 401
   family of, 402-3
Smith, William, of Dilspro, 398 n., 407
Smith, William, a smith, Aberdeen, 8, 12, 14 n., 21 n., 306, 396, 406, 409
Smithieburn, 401
Smiths of Rothiebirsben, Inveramsay and Seaton, 8, 395; summary of, 403
Smyth, William, at Mill of Rothiebirsben, 400, 403, 407
Smuggling, detection and prevention of, 16, 277, 287; affrays with smugglers at Prestonpans, Montrose, Nairn, 16
Snell Exhibition, Adam Smith's appointment, text of, 136-7
   conditions, Smith declines to take Orders, 42
   letter of resignation, text of, 137
Snell Exhibitioners, fellows of Adam Smith, 39
   unpopularity of, at Balliol, 38
Snell Exhibitions at Balliol College, Oxford, 1756-62, transactions relating to, 161-3
South Sea Scheme, 131 n., 351
Speirs, Alexander, and the Commercial Club, 81
Spottiswood, Mr., letter to, from Adam Smith, Economist, 275-6
St. Andrews, students' accounts at, 30
St. Jean, a valet, 264 n.
Stair, Countess of, material for granddaughter's gown, 9
Steelbow, 354

"Stent" payable to Glasgow University Library, 169-70, 174, 175
Stewart, Dugald, quoted from *Memoir* as to contents of papers destroyed, 58; early announcement of *laissez faire*, 111; on Adam Smith, opinions and character, 98, 99; states Adam Smith's indebtedness to James Oswald, 320
   the Glasgow lecture of 1755 discussed, 53, 117, 118, 395
Stewart, Professor John, advertises lectures on Natural Philosophy in Edinburgh, 49
Stewart, Professor Matthew, advertises lectures on Mathematics, etc., in Edinburgh, 49
Stirling, Principal John, 90
   bequest to Glasgow University Library, 169
Storch, Heinrich, 430
Strahan, William, letters to, from Adam Smith, Economist, 254-5, 276, 286-7, 290, 296
Stratheny Castle, 23, 325 n.; locality of kidnapping, 23
Street brawls in Edinburgh and London, 11
Stuart, Andrew, 259, 267, 278
Stuart, Gilbert, attack on Robertson, 64
Student life in Glasgow, 28 ff.
Student life in Oxford in 1740, 38, 39
Students, boarded by Professors at Glasgow, 67
   at Glasgow and Petty Customs, 163
Students' boarding-houses, 29
   accounts at St. Andrews, 30
Studium Generale, 71
Suard, Jean, 270
Sutherland, Countess of, case of, 266
Suttie, Charles, elected to Snell Exhibition, 37

Tallages, 355
Tartars, 381
Tassie, James, medallion of Adam Smith, 105-8
"Telamonian Shield" for Lord North, 278
Tenant Farmers, 355
Theatre, the, in Glasgow, 79
   erection of, in Glasgow, protests against, 163-6
Theatrum Scotiæ, by Captain Slezer, 31
Theory of Moral Sentiments, its place in history of British Philosophy, 121; list of presentation copies, 238; preparation of sixth edition, 309; writing of, 120, 121
Tifty or Tiftie, Mill of, 401; ballad of, 402
Tinklers, their numbers and characteristics, 23
Thom, Rev. William, minister of Govan, attacks Adam Smith, 75
Tobacco, importation of, 79, 80; cultivation of, 353

INDEX

Tokyo, " Catalogue of books belonging to Adam Smith in 1781 ", now at, 124, 125, 172, 321, 356, 390, 391
Townshend, Charles, Chancellor of the Exchequer, 317-18
Trade, books on, issued in Glasgow, 82
Trail, Robert, Professor of Oriental Languages and Divinity, 85, 86
Treaty of Union, Act for, agreed, ratified and becomes operative, 7
Tretiakov, Ivan Andreevich, 158 n. ; later Professor in Moscow, 424 ff.
Tucker, Dean of Gloucester, and economic investigation, 42 ; tracts by, in Adam Smith's library, 369
Tull, *Horse-hoeing Husbandry*, 172 n., 336 n.
Turgenev, N. I., *An Essay on the Theory of Taxes*, 431
Turgot, 125 n., 298
Tytler, A. Fraser, *Essay on Military Law and the Practice of Courts Martial*, 13
  Henry Home of Kames, 47

Union causes administrative problems, 11
University of Edinburgh, *see* Edinburgh, University of
University of Glasgow, *see* Glasgow, University of
University of Oxford, 44, 240-6
University lectures advertised in Press in Edinburgh, 49
University Library of Glasgow, books recommended by Adam Smith, 124 ; *see* Glasgow University, Library
  resources of, 116

Valladolid, University of, 305
Vanderlay, papermaker, 322
Virginia, 353
Visitation of 1690, rules for admission of Master or Regent, 138 n.
  of 1727, the meetings held under, 90
Visitors, ordinary, of the University, 91
Voltaire, 29, 261
Vorontsov, the Princes, 428

Walker, William (tutor and curator of Adam Smith), 21, 396, 406

Walpole, Sir Robert, 241
Warner Exhibition at Oxford awarded to Smith, 39
Water-carriage, 383
Watermark on writing-paper, 35-6
Watermarks on paper discussed, 60, 61
  on paper used by Adam Smith, 322
Watt, James, 149
" Wealth of Nations ", early use of the phrase, 323 n.
Wealth of Nations, additions to third edition, 284, 286, 287, 290, 296
  and Adam Smith's resignation, 97
  early draft of part of, Introduction, 317-22 ; and text of the manuscript, 322-56
  origin of, 124 ; growth of, 126
  presentation copies of, 280, 281, 291, 292, 367
  transcribed by Alexander Gillies, 360
Weaver's Vennel, the, 145
Webster, Alexander, 295
Wedderburn, Alexander, (Lord Chancellor of England), 63
  afterwards Lord Loughborough and Earl of Rosslyn, letters from, to Adam Smith, Economist, 233, 269-71, 274-5
Wedderburn, Peter, Lord Chesterhall, 234 n.
Wight, William, Professor of Church History, 86
Wilberforce, 302 n.
Williamson, Professor James, 85
Wilson, Alexander, Professor of Astronomy, 84
Window glass, as " protection of an effeminate and delicate race of mortals ", 325
Witchcraft, 401
Wodrow, Dr. James, 51, 86 ; and Adam Smith's lectures on Jurisprudence and Philosophy, 70 ; on Smith's lectures on Literature, 51, 52
Woodburn (student) and Professor Clow, 85
Woodhouselee, Lord, *see* Tytler, A. Fraser
Worcester, captain of, executed, 6
Writing-paper used by Adam Smith, 35 ; watermark as identification, 35-6, 321-2

York, Duke of, 305
Young, Dr., lectures on Practice of Medicine, 1748-9, 48
Young, Thomas, acted as substitute for Adam Smith in 1764, 97, 257